YOUR KITCHEN GARDEN

YOUR KITCHEN GARDEN

Gardening by George Seddon
Cookery by Helena Radecka

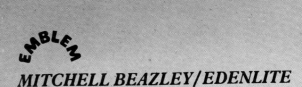

EMBLEM

MITCHELL BEAZLEY/EDENLITE

YOUR KITCHEN GARDEN was edited and
designed by Mitchell Beazley Publishers Limited,
Mill House, 87-89 Shaftesbury Avenue, London W1Y 7AD,
in association with Edenlite Limited,
Hawksworth, Swindon, Wiltshire, SN2 1EQ.

© Mitchell Beazley Publishers Limited 1975
Reprinted 1980

Editor
Rachel Grenfell

Art Editor
Barry Moscrop

Assistant Editors
Gillian Abrahams
Gail Howell-Jones

Designers
Len Roberts
Mike Rose

Editorial Assistant
Margaret Little

Executive Editor
Glorya Hale

Filmset by Tradespools Ltd, Frome, Somerset

Reproduction by Gilchrist Bros. Ltd., Leeds

Printed in Hong Kong by Mandarin Offset Ltd.

ISBN 0 85533 063 5   ISBN 0 85533 066 x
(Casebound edition)   (Limpbound edition)

Contents

The Garden of Eden was, first and foremost, a kitchen garden. It was not entirely typical, having arrived ready made and apparently needing no human to tend it. But in other ways it was the prototype of the epicurean kitchen garden, which has flourished in times of affluence throughout civilized history. Such a garden is designed more to gratify the tastes of its owner than to fill his stomach.

The Ancient Greeks had epicurean gardens and so had the Romans, who introduced them to much of Europe including Britain. The Normans revived them in England after the Dark Ages, and they thrived again under the late Tudors and Stuarts. The last flowering of the epicurean kitchen garden was in the nineteenth century in the châteaux of France and the stately homes of England.

Adam's other kitchen garden—that to which he was banished among thistles and thorns out-side Eden—was a different kind altogether. This was the garden of adversity, tilled at a time when man struggled to keep alive. It was the garden of the Dark Ages, of the Wars of the Roses, of the Civil War, of the dispossessed agricultural labourers of the nineteenth century and of the two world wars of the twentieth century.

The British kitchen garden of today, created out of the times in which we live, is developing a character of its own between these two extremes. In the last two decades, through more extensive travelling and trading abroad, we have become aware of a whole new range of fruit and vegetables. And science has provided us with varieties of many of these newly appreciated vegetables which will grow even in the northerly parts of Europe. In that sense we have become epicurean gardeners; our cabbage patch has become a calabrese patch.

In the past few years, on the other hand, we have, in our hundreds of thousands, become gardeners of necessity. We have grown tired of the tastelessness and tiredness of the fresh fruits and vegetables on sale. Increasingly, we have become worried about the use of poisons in the growing of our food. Many of us have felt that the only solution is to grow our own.

The final spur in what has now become a dramatic rush back to the kitchen garden has been the soaring cost of living. While the fruits of our own bit of earth may not be free, the cost is largely that of our own labour. And as Thomas Jefferson, the third president of the United States, wrote when he was sixty-eight years old, "No occupation is so delightful to me as the culture of the earth, and no culture is comparable to that of a garden. . . . Under a total want of demand except for our family table, I am still devoted to the garden."

An old north country gardener had a favourite saying: "There are two things you should always keep out of a garden—a woman and a scratching hen." But history is against him; women were the first vegetable gardeners, or so it would seem from the sparse evidence before recorded history. The historians' theory is that while the men spent their time and energies hunting, the women collected wild roots, leaves and fungi, and by slow degrees became not just collectors but cultivators. There is support for this theory in historical times, and contemporary attitudes in many societies make it credible. In Britain, even today, the majority of both arable and live-stock farmers regard the care of the kitchen garden as something beneath them, although, at times, they may be willing to help with the digging.

Whoever the first gardeners were, the first gardens arrived late in the world's history—not much more than a mere ten thousand years ago. Compare this with the half million years that man has known how to use fire—although not for cooking; that came much later.

When mankind finally did light on the idea of growing food instead of just foraging for it, the advance occurred independently in several parts of the world—the Near East, Central America and Southeast Asia—over a period of several thousand years. Between them the peoples of these areas were then cultivating what are still the world's major food crops.

It was from the Near East—the fertile valleys of the Euphrates and Tigris—that the knowledge of agriculture and horticulture spread southwards to Egypt, westwards along the Mediterranean, northwards into Europe and eventually to Britain. In about 2400 BC Mediterranean settlers, a short, dark people, arrived in England. They brought with them domesticated animals and seeds, which they cultivated on the chalk hills of southern England. The women tilled the soil as best they could with sticks and stone hoes. When these early people vanished so did this primitive

Adam and Eve in the Garden of Eden, as depicted in a sixteenth-century French woodcut.

horticulture. The Celts, pushing into Britain from France and Germany in the first century BC, revived it; they were skilled farmers, working first with bronze and later with iron hoes.

But their skill was rudimentary, whereas around the Mediterranean throughout this time agricultural methods were far more sophisticated. Although the staple diet of ordinary Egyptians was onions, washed down with beer, the rich lived in fine style on the varied produce of their large, slave-tended gardens and vineyards. The Ancient Egyptians were particularly attached to their vineyards. Wine had been made since at least 4000 BC and was first used for temple rituals and only later for drinking. The influence of Egyptian horti-culture on other civilizations was immense, as was their use of herbs and vegetables in medi-cine. Homer acknowledged their superiority when he wrote, "In Egypt the men are more skilled in medicine than any of the human kind." Almost all their remedies were of vegetable origin and their medical writings are a great storehouse of plant lore. For two thousand years and more this knowledge was passed on through classical and medieval writers and the compilers of the famous herbals of the fifteenth and sixteenth centuries.

Towards the end of the pre-Christian era, Greece was becoming an increasingly barren land. And, although their after-dinner conversation was excellent, the Greeks had no great reputation as gourmets. But at the beginning of the first century BC, in Homer's time, men of substance had elaborate gardens to supply the needs of their tables. The garden, however, was the responsibility of the mistress and not the master.

Homer described a large walled garden, in the town of Scheria, which belonged to Alcinous. It included a variety of vegetables set out in beds, and an orchard with apples, pears and figs. There were also olive trees and a vineyard. The Greeks knew the importance of maintaining the fertility of the soil and if there was a shortage of other manures they would resort to green manuring. Beans were one of the crops they grew for ploughing in—the leaves added humus to the light Grecian

soil and the bean roots provided nitrogen.

To the Romans, blessed with a good climate and a fertile soil, vegetables were of vital importance to both rich and poor. On their little patches of land the poor cultivated a wide range of vegetables. The rich not only ate well, but drew much of their wealth from the sale of fruit and vegetables raised by their slaves in market gardens on the outskirts of the city. They were gentlemen market gardeners. The kitchen garden of the Roman villa was the woman's responsibility and a woman was judged by how well it was run. Pliny wrote, "It was the sign of a woman being a bad and careless manager of her family when the kitchen garden was negligently cultivated; as in such case her only recourse was, of course, to the shambles or the herb market."

Salads—or what the Romans called "vine-gar diets"—were an important part of these gardens, and for the interesting reason, as given by Pliny, that they did not need cooking, so the family economized on fuel. They were also "found to be easy of digestion, by no means apt to overload the senses, and to create but little craving for bread as an accompaniment". The saving of bread must have been an im-portant consideration, for wheat had to be imported in vast quantities from North Africa and was expensive. To bring down the cost of living, bread was heavily subsidized, but at times these subsidies got completely out of hand, as when under the Emperor Augustus one-third of the population of Rome was re-ceiving free bread.

What were the vegetables on which the Romans so largely lived? Cato mentioned turnips, radishes, beans, basil, garlic, asparagus and cabbages. Later writers added carrots, parsnips, beets, onions, peas, lettuces, endive, chicory, parsley, sorrel, fennel, skirret, mus-tard, melons, gourds and fungi gathered in the fields and woods—a formidable list. People in many parts of Europe owed their first taste of some of these vegetables to the Romans, who came as conquerors.

Many vegetables were widely distributed throughout the world long before that, either cultivated or growing wild. The oldest un-

The History of the Kitchen Garden

cultivated vegetables in the world appear to have been such roots as turnips and radishes, members of the cabbage family and onions. (While many vegetables exist today in both wild and cultivated states, the onion is one of the exceptions; no wild form of the onion as we know it now survives.) Scarcely any place in the Old World can claim any vegetable as exclusively native to that area. The radish, for example, could have been found from earliest times in the mountains of central China and in central Asia. Onions were common to the Near East and to central Asia.

It took several thousand years for the cultivation of vegetables to develop, but by 3500 BC it was firmly established among the Sumerians in the Valley of the Euphrates. The Sumerians were largely vegetarians, and their staple foods were barley, onions and beans. But they also grew leeks and garlic, turnips, lettuces, cress and cucumbers. By 2000 BC the Egyptians were cultivating onions and garlic (the amounts they consumed of these were stupendous) as well as peas, cabbage, celery, lettuces, asparagus, chards, radishes (another great favourite) and such exotic fruits as melons, pomegranates, lemons, dates and figs. In Solomon's time the Jews were also growing onions and garlic, cucumbers and melons and herbs. Indeed, the vegetables grown in all countries around the eastern Mediterranean were much the same, for many of them were indigenous to the area. Different peoples, however, had different favourite vegetables. The Egyptians, for example, had an obsession with onions, while the Romans had a penchant for cabbage. Cato, the Roman poet and farmer, thought cabbage the best vegetable of all.

Such then were the culinary riches of the Mediterranean world which the Romans bestowed on Europe as they advanced northwards, finally to reach the unsuspecting Britons. After two abortive attempts by Julius Caesar, the tribes of Britain were first reduced by the Roman armies and then seduced by the Roman life-style. The change was dramatic, not least in the food they ate. The only thing the victors and vanquished had in common when the Romans invaded Britain in AD 43 was an attachment to cabbage. Over the next three centuries the Britons were to learn the pleasures of the good life—their first experience of *la dolce vita*.

The Romans set out to make inhospitable Britain a home away from Rome, for they had no intention either of leaving the island or of living like the Britons did. Even when they had subdued the tribes they still had the climate to contend with. And as bad luck would have it, two and a half of the four centuries they were in Britain were notably wet. In spite of this the Romans worked near miracles. Elegant cities were built, and as the forts and villas spread throughout the country the Romans established gardens of fruit, vegetables and the inevitable herbs, both medicinal and culinary. In the south of Britain they planted vineyards.

Among the native Britons, now citizens of the Roman Empire, the upper classes began to enjoy themselves in a thoroughly Roman way, while slaves and serfs looked after the pros-

perous farms of their masters. The Roman–British day, the eating and the social life, followed the Roman pattern. An early light breakfast would include fruit. Vegetables were served at the midday meal, which also was not substantial. The main meal of the day —"the elegant banquets" of which Tacitus wrote—began in the late afternoon, and with all the paraphernalia of silver dishes and goblets, finger bowls and dancing girls, continued in a leisurely way through several courses.

Suddenly the bottom fell out of this society. Late in the fourth century, the Picts and Scots and Saxon pirates started being troublesome. Nevertheless, the Romans hung on for another fifty years until the rottenness at the centre of the empire forced them to pull out of Britain and make for home. Invaded by the Angles and the Saxons, the Vikings and the Danes, Britain had to wait five centuries before

Norman invaders introduced a standard of living that at all approached that of the Roman occupation. On the other hand, for the better part of three centuries the weather improved.

These were the Dark Ages not only of Britain but of all Europe. Roman culture died out, and the agriculture and horticulture the Romans had brought with them all but vanished. The Roman influence and habits faded astonishingly quickly in Britain. The epicurean kitchen gardens disappeared and with them the "artificial dainties" of the table which Queen Boadicea had ranted against when first the Romans arrived. Many of the varieties of vegetables which the Romans introduced were no longer cultivated; it was several centuries before they were reintroduced. Until then the great stand-bys were leeks, cabbages and dried peas and beans.

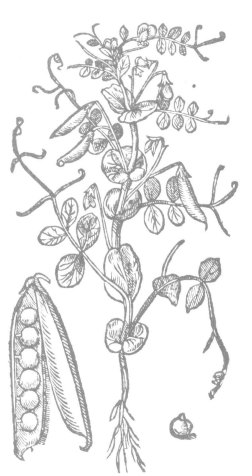

There is little information from the end of the Roman Empire until the Norman Conquest, six centuries later, about the state of gardening in Britain or in Europe generally. In Britain the leek was in the ascendancy; it could almost be regarded as the national emblem of the Saxons. It gave a new name to the kitchen garden—"leac tun"—and the names of several towns are derived from it. Basic gardening was, of course, continued by the peasantry, and a more refined form was developed by the church.

In the sixth century, St Benedict decreed that Benedictine monasteries must be self-supporting, a rule which almost makes him the patron saint of horticulture through those dead centuries. Not only were monasteries called on to create vegetable and herb gardens within their walls, but the Benedictine monks had to work in them, although there might

have been a professional gardener to help.

The most celebrated plan for a monastery garden, although it was never turned into reality, dates from the ninth century. It was drawn up for the abbot of St Gall in Switzerland and shows in great detail what the ideal garden should be. The cloister garden would have flower-beds. The physic garden was for herbs—sixteen raised rectangular beds, each labelled on the plan with the names of the herbs to be grown. The vegetable garden was planned as a large square containing eighteen raised beds. Fruit trees were to be planted between the rows of graves in the cemetery.

Plans also exist, from the early twelfth century, of the monastery gardens at Canterbury —a herbarium, orchards and vineyards, all to be watered by elaborate means of irrigation.

Roman traditions of gastronomy and garden-

ing probably remained stronger in the monasteries of Italy, Spain and France than in those of England. But all monks, by the nature of their monastic life, had an interest in the cultivation of vegetables. They were allowed to eat meat only on prescribed days, so fish, fruit and vegetables became of greater importance than they were outside the monastery walls. Inside the monastery walls, too, life was somewhat sheltered from the turbulent times outside and was more conducive to the cultivation of gardens.

Although war when waged at a distance is an incentive to grow food, gardening becomes impossible if the fighting is actually taking place on your land. The nobles learned this lesson during the next few centuries. They had managed to maintain a certain style of living in the post-Roman period. But later, to defend themselves, they were forced to build castles, which were mountain or moated fortresses and had no room for great gardens. It was then that women came into their own again, growing medicinal herbs and vegetables in their small plots. English history of that period can be best described as chaos punctuated by uneasy or unpleasant calm. One such calm period covers much of the tenth century, which was as settled politically as it was climatically—the first of two centuries of warm, dry weather during which wine production in England reached its peak.

The Norman Conquest ended another period of turmoil and brought in a spell of efficient despotism. The Norman nobles, who took over the estates of the English nobility, laid a Norman veneer on English society in much the same way as there had been a Roman veneer. Life at the top must have been both pleasant and well fed. But for the serfs, who had no choice but to grow food for their masters—and a little for themselves as a reward —life was both oppressive and squalid.

The Normans, by the rigidity of their feudal system, affected British agriculture for centuries after their rule ended. In this way, as in others, including their magnificent architecture, their influence was greater than that of the Romans. But the veneer of good living vanished after them as quickly as it had after the Roman departure eight centuries earlier.

In the twelfth century the Crusaders went warring against the Muslims in the Holy Land, and among the treasures with which they returned were shallots. The thirteenth century opened stormy, and throughout northern Europe the fourteenth century was cold and snowy. This may have been the reason, or it may have been coincidence, that the cultivation of vegetables was neglected. But whatever the climate, the warm wind of the Renaissance was beginning to blow, a prelude to one of the most dramatic changes in history that occurred in the sixteenth century, opening up vast new experiences, not least in our food. Nothing like it had been seen since the Roman invasion. This time Europe and Britain benefited not from invasion but from exploration, and the booty came not from the Old but from the New World.

The cultivation of food began in the New World several thousand years later than it did

The History of the Kitchen Garden

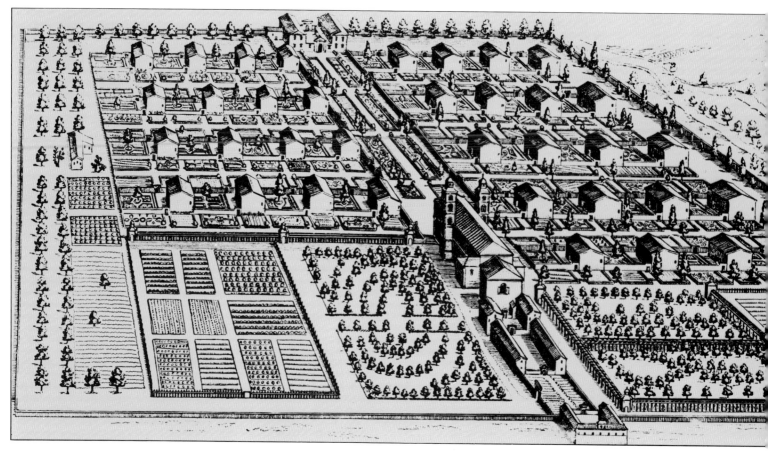

in the Old World, but in many ways it was more advanced by the time the Europeans, beginning with Cortes and Columbus, arrived. Caves in the Tehuacán Valley, south of Mexico City, have in the last two decades yielded up the secrets of man's development in the New World, which he may have reached more than thirty thousand years ago. The first nomads who used the caves merely collected wild plants to supplement their meat diet. But eight thousand years ago the cultivation of

Raised beds enclosed by boards were a feature of sixteenth-century gardens, as shown in this woodcut of 1542.

plants began, and slowly, over the next seven thousand years, a highly civilized society based on agriculture emerged. It was from such centres of established civilizations in America that European explorers—and pirates—of the sixteenth and seventeenth centuries brought home fruits, vegetables and grains they had never encountered before. Only a handful of plants out of the thousands growing in the New World already existed in the Old World.

The two American plants destined to become the most important in Europe were the potato (especially in the north) and maize (in the south). But the others include French and kidney beans, gourds, sweet peppers, Jerusalem artichokes, tomatoes (although it was a long time before they were accepted) and the cultivated strawberry. As William Harrison, Dean of Windsor in the late sixteenth century, wrote, "Strange herbs, plants and annual fruits are daily brought to us from the Indies, Americas . . . and all parts of the world."

As though this influx were not enough, Elizabethan England was finding in Europe a host of vegetables which were either new to Britain or had gone out of cultivation since Roman times. These included asparagus from France, globe artichokes and improved celery from Italy, cauliflowers from Spain, swedes from Bohemia and garden carrots brought by Flemish refugees. (They and other refugees brought many gardening skills with them.)

Paradoxically, one of the greatest periods of gardening, which lasted from the start of the

fifteenth century until the Civil War, coincided with the beginning of the "Little Ice Age", which continued for three centuries until the 1850s. There were upheavals at home and wars abroad, but gardening flourished. The day of the epicurean kitchen garden had returned. In fact, one major upheaval, the Dissolution of the Monasteries, helped to establish the grand gardens of Tudor times. The monasteries, which had done much to keep alive the growing of vegetables since Roman times, lost their lands. The nobles, into whose hands the land fell, created beautiful gardens on their ill-gotten estates. Such were Beaulieu, Audley End and Woburn. A list of the vegetables grown at Woburn includes asparagus, cucumbers, celery, peas, beans, onions, leeks, lettuces, endive and radishes, and among the fruits were strawberries, raspberries, peaches, nectarines, cherries and pears.

Even so, in many gardens the vegetable and herb gardens were beginning to take second place to the flower gardens. In 1629, Parkinson, in his *Earthly Paradise*, advocated putting the flower gardens at the front of the house "in sight and full prospect of all the chief and choicest rooms of the house, so contrariwise, your herb garden should be on the one or other side of the house for the many different scents that arise from the herbs, as cabbage, onions, etc., are scarce well pleasing to perfume the lodgings of any house". On the other hand, the gardens of the small manor houses and farms as well as the cottage gardens of the poor were still used strictly for practical purposes.

The revival of vegetable gardening was general throughout Europe. The Dutchman Erasmus, in *Convivium Religiosum*, described

plained in terms of astrology". One little volume published in 1603 is worth mentioning. Its title is *Profitable Instructions for the Manuring, Sowing and Planting of Kitchen Gardens*. It is said to be the first book dealing only with vegetables, and it was written by a linen-draper in Shrewsbury who also sold seeds and vegetables.

Pleasure gardens, which flourished under the late Tudors and early Stuarts, were not to the taste of Oliver Cromwell, who approved of only utilitarian kitchen and fruit gardens. But the lavish epicurean tradition had not had time to die out before it was given new life under the restored Charles II. It continued among the aristocracy, during the eighteenth and nineteenth centuries, but has diminished almost to the point of vanishing under the economic pressures of the mid-twentieth century. These families could no longer afford the upkeep of great flower and vegetable gardens and greenhouses for exotic plants with scores of ill-paid gardeners.

Two other trends developed as a large part of Britain changed from being a rural nation to an urban one. Market gardens had been a part of the London scene since the fourteenth century, and in the eighteenth century they began to spring up on the outskirts of towns throughout the country. And out of rural poverty, caused by the land enclosures of the late eighteenth and nineteenth centuries, rose the allotment movement. Although allotments were originally intended to help the agricultural labouring poor, they have now largely been taken over by land-starved townsmen.

From time to time during these later centuries new vegetables have arrived on the British scene. Brussels sprouts in the nineteenth century were the most important, but they had been growing in Belgium for eight hundred years before that. The cultivation of mushrooms was perfected. For the rest the British have had to be content with Chinese cabbage, Chinese artichokes, New Zealand spinach, Hamburg parsley and the American loganberry.

Now that there are probably no more new species in the world left to discover we can concentrate on improving the varieties of those we know. So far the results have been dramatic. The Netherlands, the United States and Japan have developed hybrids of vegetables which in their original form would never have survived the winters of northern Europe nor matured and ripened in its shorter summers. Britain has initiated great advances in the growing of fruit. But not all the changes have been for the good; improving the profit of a crop has often been a greater consideration than improving its taste. Unfortunately, too, many old, popular varieties have been lost. But on balance the kitchen garden, even the humblest, has never been better than it is now.

Monasteries were often self-supporting, as was the monastery near Turin, above, where hermit monks occupied separate buildings, each of which had its own garden attached. The engraving, right, shows the work for April in progress in a sixteenth-century castle garden.

a kitchen garden which consisted of the vegetable garden—"the women's kingdom"—a medicinal garden and orchard. In France, the great agricultural writer Olivier de Serres stressed the importance of the vegetable and herb gardens and the orchards and vineyards rather than of the flower gardens.

It was a great time not only for gardening, but for writing about it. Herbals started pouring off the newly invented presses in Germany, the Low Countries, Italy and England. They were largely concerned, in a scientific or pseudo-scientific way, with the medicinal qualities of plants, but are particularly enjoyable, even today, for anyone interested in the history of vegetables as well as for the often brilliant woodcuts and engravings which adorn them. John Gerard is undeservedly the best-known name among the English herbalists, for his *Herbal* of 1597 was merely a translation from a Belgian work to which Gerard's major contribution appears to have been the mistakes. Thirty-six years later, however, Thomas Johnson corrected, enlarged and improved the *Herbal*, and it is on this edition that Gerard's reputation rests. John Parkinson, apothecary to James I and botanist to Charles I, was much less concerned with the kitchen garden than he was with flowers. The last of the well-known English herbalists was Nicholas Culpeper (1616–54), whose obsession was botany "ex-

The History of the Greenhouse

Who loves a garden, loves a greenhouse too,
Unconscious of a less propitious clime
There blooms exotic beauty, warm and snug,
While the winds whistle and the snows descend.

It may seem odd to write even a bad poem in praise of a greenhouse, but many will agree with the sentiments of the eighteenth-century English poet William Cowper. Gardeners find it a great challenge to grow fruit, flowers and vegetables at times of the year and in places that Nature never intended.

The Greeks and Romans appear to have been the first to practise the art of forcing plants, and the Emperor Tiberius (42 BC–AD 37) gets most of the credit, or at least the publicity for it. He insisted on having his favourite cucumbers all the year round, and, Pliny records, "he had raised beds made in frames upon wheels, by means of which the cucumbers were moved and exposed to the full heat of the sun; while in winter they were withdrawn and placed under the protection of frames glazed with Lapis secularia". (The simple but unwieldy system of beds on wheels was also tried out in England in the early seventeenth century. The boxes of rich soil in which the plants were growing were hauled under cover every night.)

Although there is no supporting evidence,

the Romans may have brought their forcing methods with them when they invaded Britain. It was much later, in the thirteenth century, that the practice of forcing was developed in Europe. According to one story, the famous theologian and herbalist Albertus Magnus (1193–1280) was suspected of witchcraft because of his skill in growing fruit and flowers out of season. But the real pioneers were the Dutch and the French, and even when the use of hotbeds and frames spread to England the results were for a long time not as good as those in Holland and France.

At first, at the end of the sixteenth century, hotbeds were used only to raise the seedlings of cauliflowers, cucumbers and melons. But by the seventeenth century forced plants were spending all their growing lives on hotbeds. The beds were made with several feet of fresh horse manure, which generated great heat when the bacteria got to work on it. The manure was covered with 12 inches (30 cm) of earth in which the plants grew. As well as being pampered by the warmth from below, the vegetables were given protection against the cold from above. This was usually a covering of straw mats or painted cloth, supported by poles at the corners, or, as a refinement, an arch of poles over the bed. This somewhat rudimentary protection persisted in Britain

for a long time and was still being used fifty years after glass frames and cloches had been introduced from France, where they were used with great success at Versailles.

By the middle of the eighteenth century things were changing in London: the great enclaves of market gardens stretching westwards from Westminster to Chelsea and Fulham had caught up with continental ideas. In February 1748, a visiting Swedish horticulturist was greatly impressed. In one garden, in beds covered by glass frames, matting and straw, he saw cauliflowers 4 inches (10 cm) high and asparagus 1 inch (2 cm) high "and considerably thick". He also records the use of bell cloches with a few cauliflowers growing under each.

Lettuces, radishes, turnips and spinach, as well as the more exotic cucumbers and melons, were widely grown in systems of intensive intercropping, which made the operation exceedingly profitable. But in the middle of the nineteenth century, the expansion of London forced these market gardeners out into the country. Vegetable growing became less intensive, frames and cloches fell into disuse and France began supplying many of the early vegetables for the London market. Not until the 1930s, under the impetus of import duties, and with the help of Dutch lights, continuous cloches and a great increase in the number of heated greenhouses for commercial crops, was the trend reversed.

Historically, the heated greenhouse developed alongside the hotbed and the frame. The ruins of a kind of greenhouse were found at Pompeii, but it was not until the late sixteenth and early seventeenth centuries that greenhouses were built in Europe. Greenhouses were then orangeries. There was an extraordinary one at Heidelberg, where in autumn each year a large wooden and glass structure was erected to cover the Elector Palatine's four hundred orange trees. It was heated all winter and taken down in spring.

In England, many orangeries were in the grand style—substantial buildings of stone with large windows in the south wall and a stove or open fire to keep the plants warm. Others were more modest; indeed, some are described as little more than sheds.

When Cowper wrote his lines to a greenhouse it had already changed its character. The orangery had been adapted to accommodate the exotic plants which were all the rage at the end of the seventeenth century. It was not until late in the next century that vegetables—lettuces, cucumbers and French beans among them—were being forced in greenhouses.

During the period of greenhouse building which began after the Restoration, there was little understanding of the problems involved. Greenhouses were inadequately lit; there was little glass in the walls and none in the roofs until the early eighteenth century. Moreover, they were often sited so that they missed rather than caught the precious winter sun. The crudeness and inefficiency of early attempts at heating were almost laughable, but methods improved after the introduction of hot-water systems in 1816—forty years after the French first used them.

Sir Joseph Paxton's great conservatory at Chatsworth, above, which was followed by the Crystal Palace, marked the zenith of greenhouse construction in the nineteenth century. These greenhouses were preceded by many less successful endeavours such as the one, left.

There was a great technical leap forward in greenhouse construction in the 1830s with the production of sheet glass, which could be made in large sizes. Its use became general after the tax was taken off glass in 1845. Sir Joseph Paxton, a pioneer in the use of sheet glass, used it to build a large conservatory in 1837 at Chatsworth, when he was head gardener there. It covered more than 34,000 square feet (3,160 sq m)—although that was a mere nothing compared with the 19 acres (8 ha) covered by his vast glasshouse at the Great Exhibition of 1851—the greenhouse's greatest triumph and memorial.

But the day of the grand conservatory on private estates is over, for the costs of upkeep and heating are astronomical. In Britain, the twentieth century is the century of the small greenhouse in small gardens. Over the past few years more than a hundred thousand such greenhouses have been sold annually. "Who loves a garden, loves a greenhouse too." Cowper was right.

The History of the Allotment

to alleviate their poverty was overwhelming; the welfare state was a century over the horizon. Farmers, especially, were vehemently opposed to it, for to them it was obvious that men would spend all their time and energies on their allotments and be unwilling to work on the farmers' land. The farmers had their way. Even when allotments were provided, restrictions were often imposed. The most extreme conditions laid down that the labourers were not allowed to work on the allotments on Sunday, nor on weekdays between 6 am and 6 pm.

Finally, the Government came to the aid of the labouring poor. Under the General Enclosure Act of 1845 "field gardens", of no more than a quarter of an acre (1,000 sq m) could be provided, but it was too late, most of the land had already been enclosed. As for the Government's motives, they are described by the *Penny Magazine* in 1845: "The object in making such allotments is moral rather than economic: the cultivation of a few vegetables and flowers is a pleasing occupation and has a tendency to keep a man at home and from the ale house."

In spite of this background of sanctimoniousness, with a whiff of the Poor Law, the English allotments movement at last began to go ahead. It was especially strong in the towns and has been ever since. By the end of the nineteenth century there were nearly half a million allotments; just before the First World War six hundred thousand, and at the end of it

As a result of the Dig for Victory campaign during the Second World War, almost 1½ million allotments were under cultivation; even the Tower of London, left, gave up some of its land, for the cultivation of vegetables.

The seven hundred thousand Englishmen who grow their vegetables and fruit on allotments, fundamentally have the feudal system to thank. For under the feudal system, as consolidated by William the Conqueror in 1066, every man had his lord. At the bottom of the hierarchy was the peasant who slaved for the lord of the manor —slaved, indeed, for he was a villein, or serf. In return he was allowed to cultivate strips of land in the open fields of the manor, and was given meadow and grazing rights. These rights began to disappear in the sixteenth century with the closure of manorial commons. In far from adequate compensation, the peasant—no longer a villein—was given an "allotment" (not in the modern sense of the word), which was usually attached to his cottage.

In the next century some landowners allowed their labourers—no longer called peasants—to grow crops on "potato patches", but, of course, this privilege was usually re-

garded as part of their wage. The great upheaval came in the late eighteenth and early nineteenth centuries, with the virtual ending of the open-field system, which had for centuries been the basis of British agriculture. According to a 1969 British Government Committee of Inquiry into Allotments, some three thousand five hundred Acts of Parliament were passed between 1760 and 1818 enclosing five million acres of formerly open land. The results were devastating, far more so than they had been under the enclosures of Elizabeth I. They were on a more massive scale and only a fraction of the enclosure acts allocated any land to what had now come to be called the "labouring poor".

In the early nineteenth century a few great landowners did indeed voluntarily provide allotments, and by Act of Parliament parish wardens could rent out a little parish land. But the opposition to providing the poor with land one and a quarter million allotments. The Second World War started with seven hundred and forty thousand allotments and in a big "Dig for Victory" campaign rose to a million and four hundred thousand—a striking similarity.

Post-war developments were different, however. In 1919, vegetables were expensive and men back from the war with no prospects of jobs were applying for allotments at the rate of seven thousand a week. After 1945, food was short, but there was more money. In five years the number of allotments fell to something over a million—twice as rapid a fall as after the First World War. There was a curious reversal of the downward trend during the depression of the early 1930s. The Government took powers to requisition land for allotments for the unemployed—both to relieve poverty and to give the workless something to do; if you are digging at least you cannot be demonstrating. The project had a short life.

In England, in 1975, there were almost seven hundred thousand allotments—although they are officially called "leisure gardens" now. But the sixty thousand applicants on the waiting lists were not after leisure, one suspects, but anxious to grow their own vegetables.

In Holland, most allotments are near towns, and about two-thirds of them are devoted almost entirely to vegetables. But a quarter are chalet gardens, a concept little known in Britain although common in other parts of northern Europe. The chalet garden has the character of the garden of one's home, except that it is somewhere else, and the chalet is an attractive summerhouse, far removed from the shed of an English allotment. During the Second World War, however, even these attractive-looking gardens in Holland, Den-

During the Second World War, when it was difficult to import food into England, people began to grow their own fruit and vegetables. In London, many acres of park land, such as Kensington Gardens, above, and Clapham Common, left, were dug up and divided into allotments. In 1942, the produce from allotments amounted to approximately 10 per cent of England's total vegetable and garden production. After the war the demand for allotments dropped radically until the mid-1970s.

mark and Germany were ploughed up to grow vegetables and fruit.

Statistically, the allotment holder in England is a married man with two children who are no longer living at home. Gardening is his main hobby, and do-it-yourself another. But a more fascinating impression of him emerges from answers to questionnaires prepared by the 1969 British Committee of Enquiry into Allotments. They found that only 3·2 per cent of allotment holders were women, and only 1·8 per cent housewives. (It was assumed that the women were at home looking after the flowers in the garden there.) Although 80 per cent of allotment holders lived in towns, almost half of them had been brought up in the country. Half of them were sons of allotment holders. Twenty per cent were over sixty-five years of age and more than 62 per cent were between forty and sixty-five.

Away from their allotments 44·7 per cent were manual workers, or had been until retirement, and 30·6 per cent were professional workers—a proportion increasing among the young. The professionals included clerks, insurance agents, civil servants, architects, doctors, teachers and university lecturers. All gave as their reasons for having allotments, first a love of gardening and second a desire to grow better produce than can be bought.

Your Kitchen Garden

Everyone can have some kind of kitchen garden, even if it is only a few pots in the kitchen. The darkest basement kitchen could provide the perfect conditions for producing a constant supply of mushrooms and bean shoots, with herbs in a window box outside. In a well-lit kitchen, mustard and cress, chives and many herbs could be grown inside, and dwarf tomatoes outside in a window box.

On patios and balconies

A surprisingly large range of vegetables, fruit and herbs can be grown in containers on patios. Among them are such salad vegetables as lettuces, salad onions, and tomatoes and cucumbers grown in peat bags. Other vegetables and herbs include runner beans and marrows grown in tubs and trained up wigwams, French beans and courgettes in containers, and a bay tree in a tub and many other herbs in boxes and troughs. Strawberries can be grown in large strawberry pots and cordon gooseberries, red currants and vines can be grown against a sunny wall, by taking up some of the paving to provide pockets of soil.

The choice is somewhat more restricted for balconies, which tend to be windy and scorchingly hot in the sun. Also they might not bear the weight of soil in large containers.

There is no lack of choice of containers for growing vegetables and herbs. Those made of plastic and glass fibre are the lightest. Hardwood containers are expensive but beautiful, and those made in such heavy materials as concrete and asbestos cement come in bold, simple shapes. Whatever type of container you choose, always fill them with first-rate compost. Plants in containers are totally dependent on you for feeding and watering.

In the flower garden

There are vegetable plants which in beauty of form rival conventional flowering plants and can be happily planted with them. Indeed, runner beans, tomatoes and asparagus peas were first grown for their appearance and not for eating. The foliage of asparagus, globe artichokes and fennel looks elegant among taller flowers. The leaves of beetroot, Swiss chard, carrots and dwarf lettuce form varied, attractive ground cover. Chives, parsley, thyme and asparagus peas make striking edging plants.

In the vegetable garden

A vegetable garden is, of course, the only way to grow vegetables in any quantity. An area of 100 square yards (84 sq m) should provide a family of four with adequate lettuces, runner beans, peas, carrots and turnips in summer, and with leeks, cabbages and sprouts in winter. To be self-supporting in most vegetables, given a family with hearty appetites, four times as much ground, 400 square yards (335 sq m) would be needed. The average English allotment measures 300 square yards (250 sq m). Further land would be required for main crop potatoes—100 square yards (84 sq m) or more, depending on the family's fondness for them. To estimate how much land you would need to give over to potatoes, you can reckon to get 12 pounds (6 kg) of main crop potatoes for every 10 feet (300 cm) of row cultivated.

In the Kitchen

On the Patio

In the Flower Garden

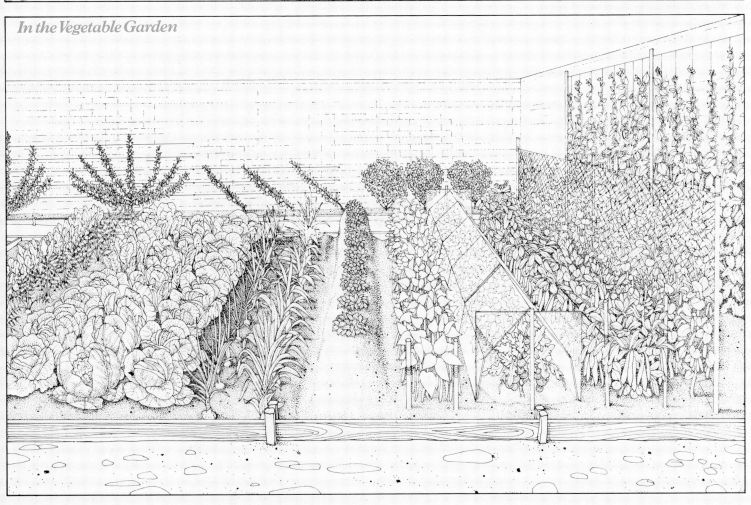

In the Vegetable Garden

The Layout of your Garden

The ideal kitchen garden does not exist; we have to compromise with reality. But, compared with the problems of weather and soil, the layout of a vegetable garden is a comparatively simple matter.

The gardens of most houses are rectangular. This is a good shape for the formal layout in which vegetables are most efficiently grown. Beds of regular shape are easier to dig, and it is more convenient to stake, and hoe between, plants in rows. A garden left as one large rectangle, however, looks intolerably dull. It is better split into several squares and rectangles, creating a pattern that gives character to the garden.

The most beautiful garden in which I have ever worked was surrounded by a twelve-foot-high wall, covered with trained fruit trees. Between gravel paths, there were square and rectangular beds edged with box. Pheasants laid eggs among the rhubarb, and if you were lucky, for this was wartime, abandoned them to you. This was not a typical modern garden, but if you scale down the essentials of it, as in the illustration opposite, the result is both practical and attractive.

The hypothetical garden on the opposite page is assumed to be a garden at the back of a house. It has three vegetable beds of roughly equal size, and the three main groups of vegetables—peas and beans, brassicas and roots—occupy each bed in turn over a period of three years. If the garden is large enough to grow main crop potatoes for the household, a fourth bed can be added, making a four-year rotation. (The rotation of crops is explained on pages 20 and 21.) Asparagus and rhubarb, raspberries, black currants and other soft fruits are given permanent beds.

Walls, fences and hedges are an important feature of the garden and must be considered carefully. A brick wall is ideal for the boundary on the north side of the garden, for it blocks the cold winds of winter. On the southern boundary an open fence is best. Chain-link fencing, for example, lets in the sun but tempers the wind. A garden entirely surrounded by walls tends to be a frost trap in winter, but if a fairly open hedge is grown at the lowest part of the garden, the cold air can escape.

Walls and fences are put to the fullest use if cordon apples, pears, gooseberries and red currants are trained against them. Sunny south-facing walls give larger and better-flavoured fruit, but by planting soft fruits against a north-facing wall the season can be extended.

Paths must be wide enough—36 to 48 inches (90 to 120 cm)—to provide easy access with a wheelbarrow to all parts of the garden. Because kitchen-garden paths get hard wear they must be laid on a solid foundation.

Space has been found in our hypothetical garden for frames and a greenhouse. The essential compost heaps are given a place at the bottom of the garden behind a screen of Oregon Thornless blackberries. If there is room, a shed can also be hidden away behind the blackberry bushes.

There is a lawn edged with runner beans or climbing roses. A few beds have been reserved for flowers; some have been strategically placed at points where the flowers will have most impact. Trees should not be planted in a vegetable garden, but think hard before cutting down any that are already there.

The garden in front of a house is often characterless. It can be turned into a beautiful and useful herb garden, conveniently close to the house. The illustrations below suggest one conversion—a rockery with herbs and scented flowers in pockets of soil among stepping stones, which give easy access for picking the herbs. A hedge of fierce Scotch thistle guards against acquisitive passers-by, although Scotch, or burnet, roses would be a more permanent and bristly alternative, as well as being attractive.

The illustration opposite shows a well-plan[ned] back garden designed to include all the ma[in] features of a typical kitchen garden, as well [as] flower beds and a lawn.

1. This is the first of the vegetable beds in [the] three-year rotation. Planted with peas, bea[ns] and lettuces as a catch crop, it is intercrop[ped] with onions, leeks, celery and spinach. The b[ed] has been given manure or compost. Herbs can [be] grown in the space nearest the house.

2. Cordon fruit trees (apples and pears) a[nd] fruit bushes (gooseberries and red currants) [are] growing against a south-facing wall.

3. Because it can be seen from the house, t[his] slightly raised flower bed is planted with spr[ing] bulbs, followed by summer bedding plants.

4. The second vegetable bed is currently occup[ied] by roots which have been given only fertilizer.

5. The greenhouse is sited in an open position.

6. Raspberries.

7. Black currant bushes.

8. A row of thornless blackberry canes.

9. Two compost heaps, one contains matur[e] compost while the other is being filled with fr[esh] garden and kitchen vegetable waste.

10. Rhubarb, horseradish and Jerusalem ar[ti] chokes.

11. A shapely, compact evergreen bush.

12. Globe artichokes.

13. Asparagus bed.

14. An open fence to admit as much sunshine [as] possible. It also provides some protection agai[nst] the wind.

15. Strawberries, cloched in spring.

16. Sweet corn.

17. Frames of Dutch lights for raising a[nd] hardening off plants in spring, growing cucu[m] bers in summer and overwintering lettuce.

18. The third vegetable bed, planted w[ith] brassicas which have been limed and fertiliz[ed.]

19. This slightly raised bed is filled w[ith] flowering perennials.

20. Lawn.

21. A trellis with runner beans growing against [it.]

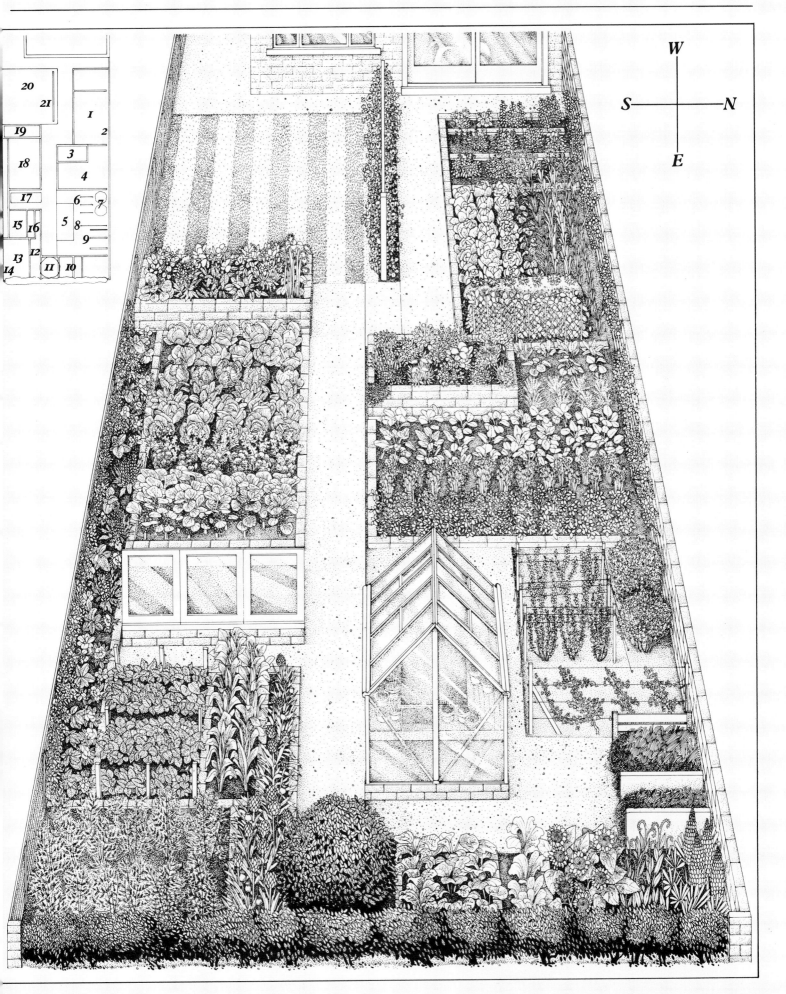

W

S ——— N

E

Cropping & Intensive Cropping

The vegetable garden is usually divided into three parts. Each part is devoted for one year to one of the three main groups of vegetables—peas and beans, brassicas and roots—in turn. After one year, the brassicas are moved to the ground where the peas and beans were growing, the peas and beans are moved to where the roots had been and the roots are moved to the bed previously occupied by the brassicas. Also, each of the three parts of the garden is manured according to the needs of the crop it carries that year. This process, known as the rotation of crops, is repeated year after year.

The reasons for not growing the same vegetables in the same part of the garden every year are twofold: to make the best use of the fertility of the garden, and to lessen the danger of disease.

Such vegetables as peas and beans, onions, leeks, celery, spinach and tomatoes need a rich soil and whatever manure the gardener can obtain. They also have first claim on the compost he makes.

Peas and beans, in league with micro-organisms in the soil, are able to fix nitrogen from the air and leave the soil richer in nitrogen through having grown in it. To supplement this nitrogen, a general fertilizer (nitrogen, phosphoric acid and potash) is given to the brassica crop which follows the peas and beans.

The general practice is to lime one-third of the garden each year, if a soil test shows that lime is needed. The lime is applied to that part of the garden where brassicas are growing because they appear to be more prone to club root, their most destructive disease, if the soil is short of lime.

Root vegetables often grow misshapen if they are given manure, so the ground they occupy in the rotation receives only a general fertilizer, there being adequate lime left from the previous brassica crop. Potatoes grown alongside the roots can be manured, but they must not have lime, because it may encourage scab.

If many potatoes are grown, the vegetable garden can well be divided into four, one part being given over entirely to potatoes. The vegetable cycle would then spread over four years instead of three, the peas and beans following the potatoes.

Besides being effective and economical in the use of manure and fertilizers, such a rotation helps to keep the plants healthy. Different vegetables attract different pests and diseases. The cabbages, for example, might suffer heavily one year from cabbage root fly, but the root crops which followed would not be affected. And the cabbages would not be attacked by the maggots of the pea moth. So the rotation, while it certainly does not guarantee a disease-free garden, does help towards it.

Not all vegetables are included in the three- or four-year rotation. More permanent beds must be found for the perennial vegetables—asparagus, for example—and for soft fruits. Even with these it is good practice to change the site of the beds when the useful life of the occupants is over and they have to be replaced.

Crop rotation is a concept to be adapted to each individual garden. What is grown in a garden will, in the first place, be decided by the likes and dislikes of the gardener within the limits imposed by space and weather.

More than eighty vegetables are described in this book; it is unlikely that anyone will want to grow all of them. Concentrate on those that you really enjoy eating—the rest are a waste of your time. So, too, are surplus vegetables. It is impossible to ensure that you will never suffer from gluts, but to have far more vegetables than you can eat fresh, freeze, preserve, or even give away, is bad planning. It is equally pointless to grow a crop which you know will be wasted because it will be ready when you are away on holiday. These points must be taken into consideration when you are turning the rotation plan into reality.

The smaller the garden the more impractical it becomes to follow a rotation plan rigidly, but the basic aims remain—to satisfy the manurial needs of each vegetable and to help it to resist pests and diseases.

Rotation of crops (opposite)

Bed A. *Peas, beans, onions, leeks, shallots, lettuces, endive, celery, radishes.*

Bed B. *Cabbages, Brussels sprouts, savoys, cauliflowers, broccoli, kale, spinach.*

Bed C. *Beetroot, carrots, turnips, swedes, parsnips, celeriac, salsify, scorzonera, potatoes.*

Bed D *(semi-permanent).* *Asparagus, rhubarb, herbs, raspberries, black, red and white currants, gooseberries.*

Intensive cropping

There are several ways of using a limited area to the full. You can, for example, sow and plant vegetables closer together in the rows, especially if you choose the smaller-growing, but still heavy-cropping, varieties. Conventional sowing and planting distances usually assume a fertile garden in a warm part of the country. In such a garden growth can be exceedingly lush, and cutting down on the spacing of vigorous growing varieties can lead to overcrowding, diminished crops and increased threat of disease. But where luxuriant growth is unlikely planting distances can be reduced without danger of overcrowding.

Reducing the space between rows, instead of between plants in the row, might rule out intercropping, which means sowing or planting smaller, quick-growing vegetables between the widely spaced rows of taller vegetables.

Different times of planting and rates of maturing are the basis of catch cropping, which involves sneaking in a quick-maturing crop before the ground is occupied by another crop.

Some quick-maturing vegetables which may be used for intercropping and catch cropping are: radish (ready from 6 weeks); kohlrabi and globe beetroot (8 weeks); lettuce and Chinese cabbage (9 weeks); carrots (10 weeks); spinach (11 weeks); endive and asparagus peas (12 weeks).

Crops which follow other crops are usually called succession crops. Some are, in fact, quick-maturing catch crops which will be harvested before winter begins. Others, for example cabbages, will stay in the ground over the winter. Succession crops are not to be confused with successional sowings—sowings of the same vegetables at intervals in order to avoid a glut.

Always be ready in spring, summer and early autumn to fill any ground which becomes vacant unexpectedly. This may happen if a crop has been harvested early, or if a sowing has failed. It is wise to jettison a row where germination has been very poor and to start again with the same vegetable or with another one.

In northerly parts of Britain only limited catch cropping is possible because of the shorter summer.

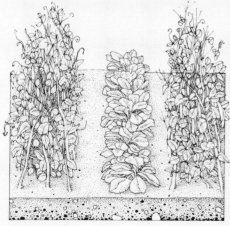
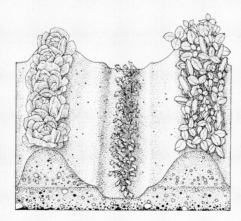
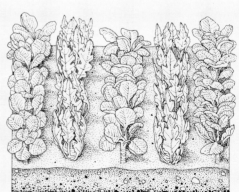

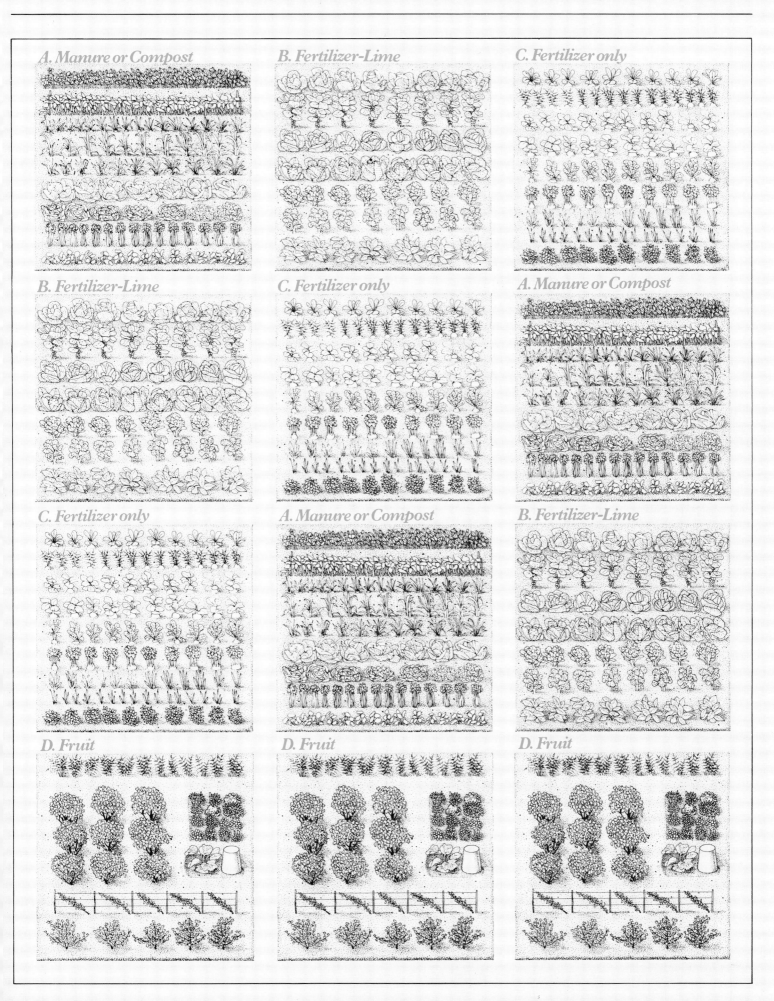

A. Manure or Compost

B. Fertilizer-Lime

C. Fertilizer only

B. Fertilizer-Lime

C. Fertilizer only

A. Manure or Compost

C. Fertilizer only

A. Manure or Compost

B. Fertilizer-Lime

D. Fruit

D. Fruit

D. Fruit

The Soil

Soil is formed over many millions of years by the gradual breaking up of the rocks of the Earth's crust. Different rocks produce soils with different characteristics, which are of vital importance to the gardener when he comes to cultivating them.

The texture of a soil depends on the size of the particles of which it is made. Sand particles vary from 2 millimetres to 0·02 millimetres; silt ranges from 0·02 to 0·002 millimetres and clay particles are less than 0·002 millimetres.

Sandy soil
Sandy soils are those in which more than 75 per cent of the soil is sand particles. They are fast draining because these comparatively large particles are irregular and there is plenty of space between them. Although sandy soils are easy to work and quick to warm up in spring, nutrients in the soil are soon washed out and deficiencies of calcium, nitrogen, phosphorus and potassium may develop. (For information about correcting these deficiencies, see pages 28 and 29.) Also, in sandy soils there is little reserve of moisture for plants in dry weather.

To overcome the drawbacks of sandy soil without destroying its virtues, add—and keep on adding—organic matter to the soil. This will be broken down by micro-organisms in the soil to form humus. Humus is the complicated substance that gives the soil its true fertility. It is present in the soil as minute, black, amorphous particles, or as a jelly-like coating of the sand, silt and clay particles.

In sandy soil the breakdown of organic matter into humus is fairly rapid, so even crude cow, pig or deep-litter poultry manure can be applied in quantity if it is dug in during the autumn or winter. Compost, spent mushroom compost and peat can be used as mulches to build up a fertile top-soil. Green manuring helps: sow lupins or mustard and, before they flower, dig them in to rot in the ground.

On a sandy soil thus improved, soft fruits, apples and pears, peas and beans, cauliflowers and potatoes will crop well.

Clay soil
Clay soils, which consist of at least 75 per cent clay and silt particles, are at the opposite extreme from sandy soils. The particles are minute and tightly packed together, so that even in hot weather the water is held in the soil instead of draining away. As a result the soil is cold and warms up only slowly in spring. When a clay soil is wet, it is sticky; when it is dry, it is like rock. Also, plant nutrients are not easily washed out of clay soils.

To make the most of its fertility, clay soil needs massive additions of humus in the form of farmyard manure, compost or peat. Combined with the clay particles, the humus will form a loamy texture, making the soil warmer, more aerated and less water-logged.

Soil conditioners can be used to create an open crumb structure in clay soil; calcium sulphate (horticultural gypsum) is widely used. Lime will also improve the soil's texture, and it makes the nutrients in the soil more available for the plants, as well as reducing its acidity. Improved in this way, clay soils will grow good crops of most fruit and vegetables, apart from roots.

Loamy soil
Loamy soils, consisting of more sand than clay particles and a lot of organic matter, are regarded as ideal for vegetables. They are reasonably warm and easy to work; they hold moisture well, and the plant nutrients are not rapidly washed out. The balance between sand and clay in a loamy soil is geological chance, but man can greatly change the other component parts, for better or worse.

Chalky soil
The level of calcium in the limestone and chalk areas of Britain creates two problems for the gardener. First the soil may be too alkaline for many vegetables that prefer a slightly acid soil. Secondly, chalk is made up mostly of calcium carbonate and calcium bicarbonate. These combine with such other soil elements as iron, boron, manganese and zinc, making them unavailable to plants. To counteract excess lime give heavy dressings of organic matter—farmyard manure, compost and peat. When adequately manured, chalky soils produce, in particular, good crops of fruit, brassicas and peas and beans. Do not, however, attempt to grow potatoes on chalky soil.

Peaty soil
Unlike other soils, peat is derived from plants. In the vast peat areas of Britain there are few gardens, because peaty soils are acid and badly drained. Liming and draining are the first steps in making a peat soil fertile. This will break down the raw peat, which is short of plant nutrients, into rich humus. Many vegetables—notably potatoes, celery, and the onion family—will flourish in a peaty soil which has been well cultivated. Fruit is less successful.

Elements in the soil
The elements which provide the plants with the nutrients they need to grow are present in all these soils in varying degrees. Some are present in large quantities, although not in their pure state, but as compounds. The three most important are nitrogen, phosphorus and potassium.

Nitrogen is made available to plants by the action of soil bacteria, which convert ammonia and nitrite into nitrate. It is particularly important for the growth of leaves and stems. A deficiency is indicated by yellowing leaves and stunted growth. An excess produces very dark green, sappy leaves, which look healthy but have little resistance to pests and diseases. The production of fruit and seeds also suffers.

Although phosphorus is present in considerable quantities in the soil, only a little of it is in a form available to plants. It is vital for the development of a good root system and for the plant's seed production. A deficiency is evident in stunted growth.

Potassium improves the quality and flavour of fruit, counteracts some of the effects of excess nitrogen and makes plants more resistant to disease. A deficiency is most likely to arise on sandy soils.

Other elements are vital for balanced plant growth, although they may be needed in smaller, or even minute, quantities. These include magnesium and sulphur and the "trace elements" iron, boron, copper, manganese, molybdenum and zinc.

Finally, it should be pointed out that much of "the soil" is not soil at all. As the great agricultural scientist Sir John Russell summed it up: "It seems incredible, but nevertheless it is true, that in an apparently solid clod of earth only about half is usually solid matter, the other half is simply empty except for the air and water it contains."

Life in the soil
Unceasing warfare is carried on in those air spaces between the solids in the soil. For, contrary to appearance and preconceptions, a garden is not a peaceful and idyllic place: it is a minute sector of a battlefield that covers most of the Earth and life on the Earth depends on the outcome of the battle. Before the gardener starts taking a hand in the fighting, it is as well for him to know who are his enemies and who are his allies.

His greatest allies are the bacteria in the soil. They are inconceivably small and are present in the soil in inconceivably large quantities. They multiply furiously; in theory, in a day one bacterium could turn into a colony of 1,300 square yards (1,000 sq m). In practice, however, long before that stage is reached, the bacteria would have starved themselves to death or been killed by the pollution of their own excreta.

The soil bacteria have two virtues. Some of them play a vital part in breaking down organic matter into humus, and a few of them are responsible for making nitrogen available to plants—perilously few, it seems at times, especially when you realize that without nitrogen the plant life we know, and therefore animal and human life, would not exist.

Some of these micro-organisms, for example Clostridium and Azotobacter, fix nitrogen from the air. Some groups fix nitrogen in the soil in association with such plants as peas, beans and clover. Even fewer bacteria can change the ammonia released from decomposing organic matter into nitrate, and fewer still can change nitrite into nitrate, without which not many of our crops would grow. These beneficial bacteria have their enemies in the soil. Fortunately, the beneficial bacteria normally have the upper hand.

Some soil fungi are good, others are bad. The good fungi live on dead plants or animal remains, build up humus and when dead provide plant food. The bad ones are the parasitic fungi, which destroy plant tissues. A particularly unpleasant one is the fungus which causes club root in brassicas.

Actinomycetes, which are a bit like fungi and a bit like bacteria, also attack beneficial bacteria. Some are parasites on plants; the best-known one causes scab on potatoes. (And the reason why you do not lime potato beds is because actinomycetes do not thrive in acid soil.)

The virus enemies of the bacteria are bacteriophages, the name simply means "bacteria

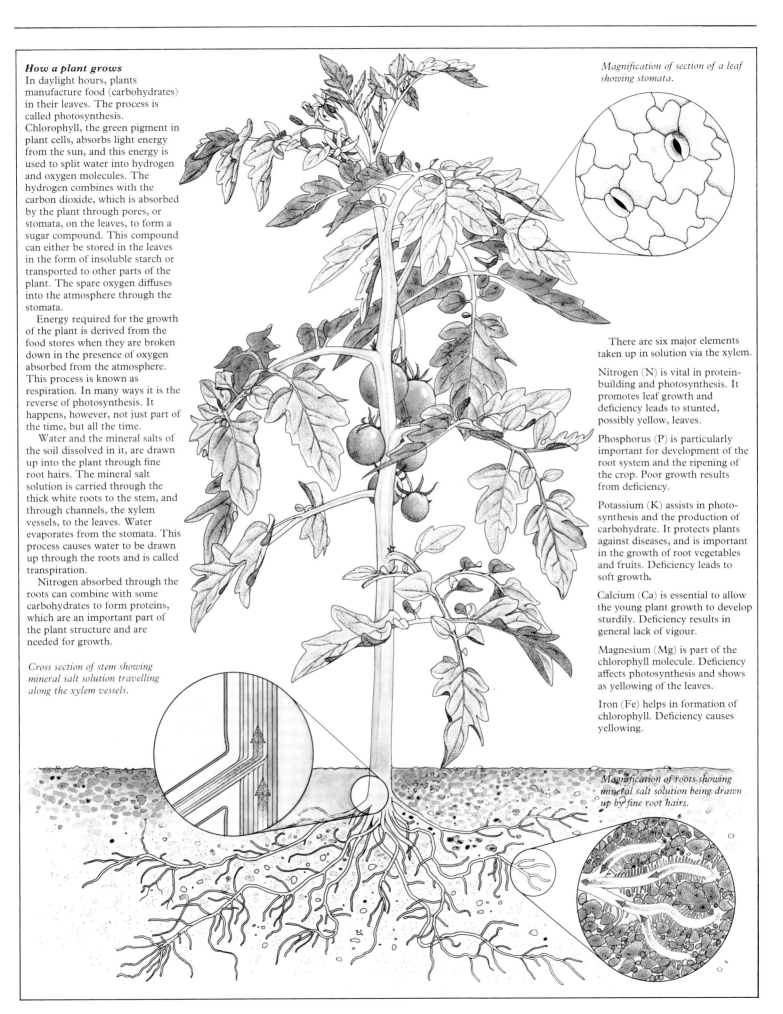

How a plant grows

In daylight hours, plants manufacture food (carbohydrates) in their leaves. The process is called photosynthesis. Chlorophyll, the green pigment in plant cells, absorbs light energy from the sun, and this energy is used to split water into hydrogen and oxygen molecules. The hydrogen combines with the carbon dioxide, which is absorbed by the plant through pores, or stomata, on the leaves, to form a sugar compound. This compound can either be stored in the leaves in the form of insoluble starch or transported to other parts of the plant. The spare oxygen diffuses into the atmosphere through the stomata.

Energy required for the growth of the plant is derived from the food stores when they are broken down in the presence of oxygen absorbed from the atmosphere. This process is known as respiration. In many ways it is the reverse of photosynthesis. It happens, however, not just part of the time, but all the time.

Water and the mineral salts of the soil dissolved in it, are drawn up into the plant through fine root hairs. The mineral salt solution is carried through the thick white roots to the stem, and through channels, the xylem vessels, to the leaves. Water evaporates from the stomata. This process causes water to be drawn up through the roots and is called transpiration.

Nitrogen absorbed through the roots can combine with some carbohydrates to form proteins, which are an important part of the plant structure and are needed for growth.

Cross section of stem showing mineral salt solution travelling along the xylem vessels.

Magnification of section of a leaf showing stomata.

There are six major elements taken up in solution via the xylem.

Nitrogen (N) is vital in protein-building and photosynthesis. It promotes leaf growth and deficiency leads to stunted, possibly yellow, leaves.

Phosphorus (P) is particularly important for development of the root system and the ripening of the crop. Poor growth results from deficiency.

Potassium (K) assists in photosynthesis and the production of carbohydrate. It protects plants against diseases, and is important in the growth of root vegetables and fruits. Deficiency leads to soft growth.

Calcium (Ca) is essential to allow the young plant growth to develop sturdily. Deficiency results in general lack of vigour.

Magnesium (Mg) is part of the chlorophyll molecule. Deficiency affects photosynthesis and shows as yellowing of the leaves.

Iron (Fe) helps in formation of chlorophyll. Deficiency causes yellowing.

Magnification of roots showing mineral salt solution being drawn up by fine root hairs.

23

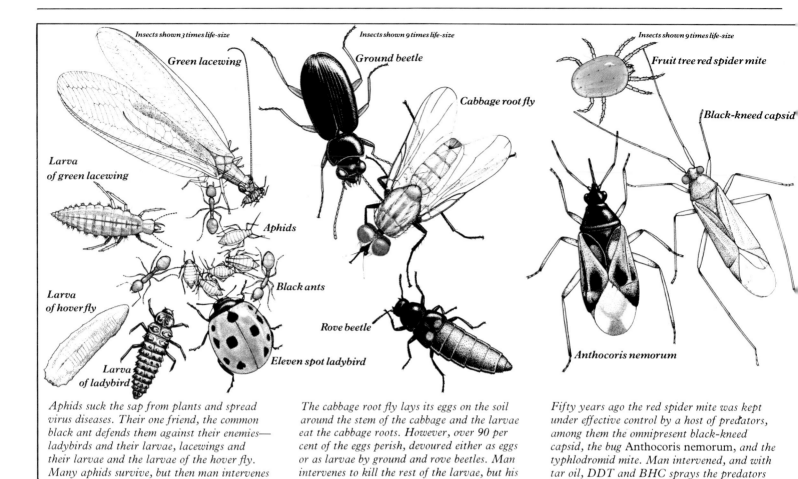

Insects shown 3 times life-size

Green lacewing

Larva of green lacewing

Larva of hover fly

Aphids

Black ants

Larva of ladybird

Eleven spot ladybird

Insects shown 9 times life-size

Ground beetle

Cabbage root fly

Rove beetle

Insects shown 9 times life-size

Fruit tree red spider mite

Black-kneed capsid

Anthocoris nemorum

Aphids suck the sap from plants and spread virus diseases. Their one friend, the common black ant defends them against their enemies— ladybirds and their larvae, lacewings and their larvae and the larvae of the hover fly. Many aphids survive, but then man intervenes with insecticides. These, however, also kill his allies—the ladybird, hover fly and lacewing.

The cabbage root fly lays its eggs on the soil around the stem of the cabbage and the larvae eat the cabbage roots. However, over 90 per cent of the eggs perish, devoured either as eggs or as larvae by ground and rove beetles. Man intervenes to kill the rest of the larvae, but his insecticides have proved more effective against the predatory beetles than against the pest.

Fifty years ago the red spider mite was kept under effective control by a host of predators, among them the omnipresent black-kneed capsid, the bug Anthocoris nemorum, *and the typhlodromid mite. Man intervened, and with tar oil, DDT and BHC sprays the predators have been effectively killed, while the red spider mite flourishes.*

devourers". Not all phages attack all bacteria, but for every group of bacteria there is a corresponding enemy phage. The mode of attack is curious. The phage forces the contents of its head through its own tail into the bacterium, and then completely disappears from view. Eventually, the cell of the bacterium dissolves and out of it emerges a host of phages.

Moving up in the size scale—although some can scarcely be seen—are innumerable small animals and insects inhabiting the air spaces in the soil. Mites are minute animals living on the remains of plants, or such other small soil animals as eelworms (nematodes) and small worms. One such mite, the harvest bug larva, has a fondness for human legs. Numerous in the soil are springtails, insects which feed on dead vegetable and animal matter, and are preyed on by mites, beetles and spiders. These can reasonably be classed as goodies.

Not so the eelworms, of which there may be up to two million in the soil beneath 1 square yard (1 sq m) of garden. Some feed on bacteria, other small soil animals and, occasionally, on the plant juices in the roots. But the evil ones are the parasitic eelworms which attack potatoes, tomatoes, beans, strawberries and black currants. Eelworms sometimes devour each other and are destroyed by some fungi, but there are not enough predators to prevent them from being a menace. The problem is that man has found no way of killing the egg-containing cysts, which can stay dormant but alive in the soil for many years.

Every gardener should feel the same affection for worms as did Gilbert White three hundred years ago when he wrote: "Worms seem to be the great promoters of vegetation, which would proceed but lamely without them, by boring, perforating and loosening the soil . . . and most of all by throwing up worm casts, which being their excrement is a fine manure. . . ." Charles Darwin, who was also an enthusiast for worms, pointed out in the book he devoted to them that all the soil in the country had passed through the bodies of worms many times and would continue to do so over and over again. There are more than two hundred species of worms in Europe, but only about one-tenth of that number in Britain. Only two of these species make casts, and because of this they are misguidedly poisoned. Man by his digging is also continually upsetting the good work worms do; far fewer worms are to be found in gardens than in undisturbed pasture land. Applying manure and compost helps to increase the worm population.

Of the thirteen hundred species of beetles whose main home is the soil, only one or two are the gardener's foes (one eats his strawberries). Indeed, many ground beetles and rove beetles are his firm allies. They have a great appetite for cabbage root fly, lettuce-root aphids and slugs.

Two beetles, however, must be classed as enemies because of their destructive offspring. Click beetles produce wireworms, which stay in the soil for several years, playing havoc with

potatoes, before turning into beetles. Cockchafers produce white grubs, which remain in the soil for two or three years getting fatter and lazier on the roots they eat. Fortunately, many birds find both these larvae very tasty.

Centipedes are good, whereas millepedes are bad, so it is important to distinguish between them. Their colouring is often similar, but the carnivorous centipedes have a faster turn of speed and wriggle more, and the vegetarian millepedes are fatter and slower.

At the surface of the soil, some damage may be done by earwigs, which eat tender leaves, and by woodlice in greenhouses and frames, but it is not usually excessive. Slugs and snails often become a plague. Some eat such plants as lettuces, which grow near the ground. Some climb up the plant for a feed. Some eat underground and especially enjoy the tubers of potatoes. Thus, although they are effective scavengers, on balance they are enemies. Bran and porridge oats are their undoing, for man panders to the slugs' weakness for them, but adds poison.

These are but some of the inhabitants of the soil, the devourers of dead plant life and of each other. All of them end up by providing food for a plant to grow. The seed that comes to life in the soil among this warfare emerges as a plant above ground to find itself in the middle of another battlefield. On it are engaged more bacteria and fungi, a whole new range of predatory animals, birds, rival plants—and man.

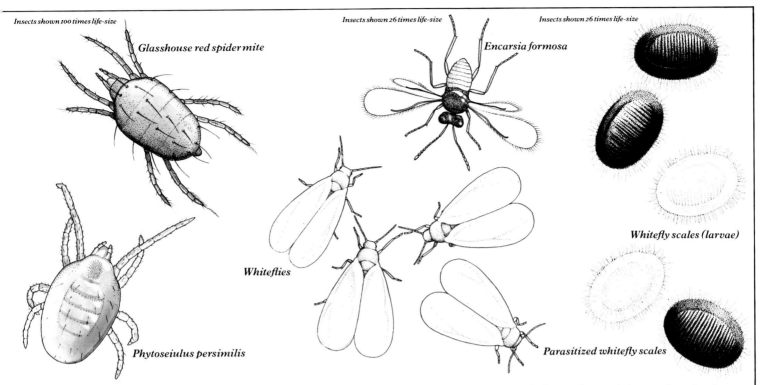

Insects shown 100 times life-size

Glasshouse red spider mite

Phytoseiulus persimilis

Insects shown 26 times life-size

Encarsia formosa

Whiteflies

Insects shown 26 times life-size

Whitefly scales (larvae)

Parasitized whitefly scales

Not all of man's interventions are harmful. Phytoseiulus persimilis (*available to amateur gardeners*), *for example, has been used to kill the glasshouse red spider mite, which is a menace to greenhouse crops. The predatory mite breeds faster than its prey, which it devours so voraciously that it can eventually starve itself to extinction.*

Glasshouse whiteflies are among the most persistent pests in the greenhouse. They resemble tiny white moths and are usually to be found clustering on the undersides of leaves, where they lay their eggs. The larvae which emerge are minute, flat and transparent and are hard to see with the naked eye. These immature whitefly are called scales. They are destructive,

feeding on the sap of plants and causing them to wilt. They also excrete a sticky substance on the leaves which encourages the growth of sooty moulds. The introduction of the parasitic wasp Encarsia formosa (*available to amateur gardeners*) *will efficiently eradicate this pest. The wasp lays an egg in a whitefly scale, the egg hatches and the scale turns black.*

Pest control

Although there may seem to be a formidable number of pests, fungi and viruses, the gardener is unlikely to come across all of them. Certainly through the years he can expect to encounter some pests and diseases among his plants, but not enough to justify indiscriminate chemical warfare.

There is no "safe" pesticide, fungicide or herbicide. If they were "safe" they could not do their job, which is to kill. The "safest" are the least effective. Each gardener must decide for himself which he is prepared to use.

Insecticides

The "safest" insecticides are derived from plants. Those which are more effective—and more harmful—are made from synthetic chemicals.

Derris is manufactured from the roots of Derris, and the killing ingredient in it is rotatone. It can be applied as a spray or powder. Derris is safe only because it is not persistent. If plants are sprayed in the evening, after the bees are back in the hive, the derris will have lost its toxicity by the time the bees are foraging again in the morning. It is not injurious to man or animals, but it is fatal to fish. It is harmful also in varying degrees to a number of beneficial insects.

When mixed with pyrethrum, derris can be used to kill aphids, caterpillars, red spider mites, flea beetles, sawflies and pea thrips.

For use against aphids, a safe alternative to derris is quassia, which is used as a spray. It is

harmless to bees and ladybirds.

Pyrethrum is made from the flower heads of several species of Pyrethrum and is also not persistent. Used as a dusting powder, pyrethrum kills aphids, white flies, beetles, sawflies and weevils. It is particularly useful against two mushroom pests, sciarid and phorid flies.

Gamma BHC (Lindane) is an organochlorine insecticide. It is persistent (but less so than DDT) and toxic to many beneficial insects, and should not be used haphazardly. It is effective against cabbage root fly, gall weevil, celery fly, onion fly and black carrot fly.

BHC (a mixture of other chemical isomers in addition to the gamma isomer) should not be used at all because it taints vegetables.

Carbaryl, a carbamate insecticide, is persistent and harmful to many beneficial insects. Sprayed on peas when they are in flower, it can prevent an invasion of pea moth maggots.

Molluscicides

Metaldehyde—or preferably methiocarb—mixed with bait in pelleted form is a chemical which kills slugs. Always prop a tile or slate over the bait so that animals and birds cannot eat it and be poisoned.

Fungicides

Thiram is an organic fungicide used on lettuce to prevent botrytis, and on lettuce and onions to prevent downy mildew.

Bordeaux mixture is a copper fungicide

which is widely used as a spray. It is harmless to most beneficial insects. Most often used to prevent blight on potatoes and outdoor tomatoes, it will also control mildew on peas, turnips and spinach; rust on asparagus foliage; artichoke, celery and broad bean leaf spot; and halo blight on beans.

A stronger copper-based fungicide, Burgundy mixture, must not be used within at least three weeks of harvesting.

A well-nourished soil does not prevent the appearance of pests and diseases, but it does make plants more able to resist them. Regrettably, the longer and more extensively that any vegetable has been growing in Britain the more firmly established are its particular pests and diseases.

Many of the newer and less popular vegetables, on the other hand, are fairly pest and disease free. Among them are globe artichokes, scorzonera, seakale beet and asparagus peas.

There is little reason why herbicides should be used to kill weeds in the vegetable garden. Mulches would be far better, they not only smother the weeds, but also improve the quality of the soil.

Alternatively, constant hoeing, although tedious, will keep annual weeds under control at no cost at all. The roots of perennial weeds should be pulled out of the soil during digging.

If total weedkillers are used on paths, take great care that they do not come into contact with any plants, or those will be totally killed as well.

Cultivation

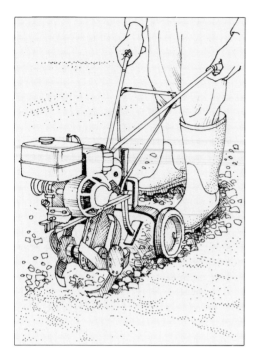

Always keep a straight spade. If you dig at an angle you will have to push the spade as far into the soil, but you will not dig as deep.

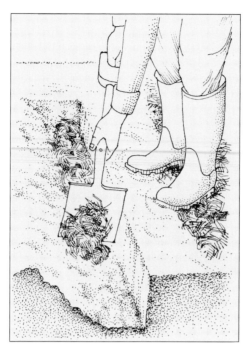

Spread manure or compost with a spade or a fork along the length of the trench. The soil from the next row of digging will cover it.

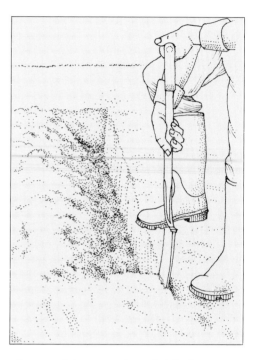

A motor cultivator speeds up the laborious process of digging a large garden or preparing new ground.

Left to its own devices the last thing that soil would do would be to grow bumper crops of vegetables in neat rows with the aim of feeding a family of four. To do that the soil has to be tamed.

Gardeners usually set about the taming by digging. First buy a really good spade. (For tools, see pages 36 and 37.) Then tackle the digging slowly, turning over small spadefuls at a time and stopping for the day before exhaustion sets in.

Generally speaking, there is no need to dig deeper than one spade's depth (a spit deep, as it is called). There are exceptions, for example when you need to enrich deeper pockets of soil for permanent plants or to improve the drainage of heavy soils.

Dig a shallow trench at one end of the plot, but instead of laboriously wheeling the soil to the other end of the plot, as is usually recommended, merely throw spadefuls of soil well behind you. Loosen the soil at the bottom of the trench with a fork (although you can omit this). If you are to dig in manure or compost, spread it along the shallow depression, which will now be all that is left of your original trench, and working back along the plot turn another row of soil on to the top of the manure. Loosen the soil in the trench thus made, and so on. The less soil you try to turn over at once, the deeper the trench will be.

Try to keep the trench straight, and if it goes askew, dig along only part of it until the whole length is straight again.

When you get to the end of the plot, you will have a shallow trench left. Next year, therefore, start digging at that end.

The reasons for digging are to bury the weeds, to incorporate manure or compost into the soil and to aerate the soil. Whenever possible, it is done in the autumn or early winter. The surface is left rough to expose as

much soil as possible to the frosts of winter: this lightens its texture. In spring, all that it should be necessary to do is to rake or lightly fork the soil, to prepare it for sowing or planting.

If the ground you are digging needs lime, whatever form of lime you use can be scattered over the soil and not dug in. The rains will wash it down. But never lime ground into which you have just dug manure—lime and manure interact chemically.

It is perfectly possible to grow good crops of vegetables without digging at all. No-diggers sow and plant in compost which is merely spread on the surface of the soil. Behind the practice is the theory of the "primeval forest floor", where year after year, layers of decaying vegetable and animal refuse are built up and converted into humus by bacteria. The no-diggers also point out that while digging does bury weeds, at the same time weed seeds which have been lying dormant in the soil are brought to the surface, where they spring to life. They contend, too, that worms are more efficient than man at taking organic matter down into the soil and aerating it.

The no-digging method certainly works; over the years great fertility builds up and vegetables grow exuberantly. But the labour saved by not digging must be set against the labour spent on making large quantities of compost. Sedge peat can be used instead of compost, but this can be expensive.

Digging is usually a once-a-year task, but weeding is a continuous chore. If the weeds are allowed to get out of hand, they may have to be skimmed off the surface with a spade. It is easier to tackle them with a hoe when they are small. If hoeing is done when the soil is dry, the weeds can be left to die on the surface.

Hoeing not only destroys weeds but also creates a layer of loose soil, which helps to conserve the moisture in the soil below.

Mulching has two advantages over hoeing. First, there is no danger of damaging the roots of plants near the surface of the soil and, secondly, when the mulch is eventually dug into the soil, or taken down by worms, it is converted into humus. Compost, peat and leaves all make excellent mulches. They need to be applied to a depth of at least 2 inches (5 cm) to be effective. A mulch should always be applied when the soil is moist; it will then keep the moisture in. Similarly, never lay a mulch down before the soil has warmed up in the spring, or it will hold the coldness in and block out the sun.

Straw is an effective mulch to keep down weeds in areas that are particularly difficult to get at, such as around black currant and gooseberry bushes. The straw should be about 6 inches (15 cm) deep, and is best put down in spring rather than autumn. Only a thin layer of lawn mowings should be put down at a time, or the mulch will turn into a steaming, slimy mess. Sawdust can also be used in moderation.

The modern mulch is strips of black polythene placed between rows of vegetables. It is certainly effective in holding in moisture and smothering weeds, but it adds nothing to the fertility of the garden.

Spades and hoes are for cutting into the soil; forks and rakes are for scratching it. A fork is usually used for surface cultivation. You would, for example, use it for forking in fertilizer that has been scattered over the surface. In sticky or very stony soil, however, a fork can be a very useful substitute for a spade.

The rake is used to break the soil down to a fine tilth after digging.

When the gardener has carried out all these steps of cultivation he has formed a thoroughly domesticated soil, eminently satisfactory for his needs.

A fork, rather than a spade, should be used to turn over heavy or stony soil, for shallow surface cultivation and for lifting root crops.

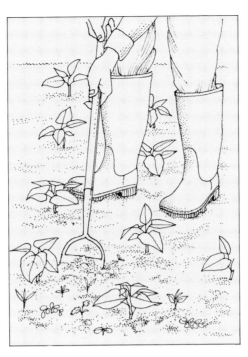

A Dutch hoe is used to kill young weeds by slicing them just below the surface of the soil and exposing the roots.

A rake, although not used as much as a hoe, is invaluable for breaking down the soil to the fineness needed for a seedbed.

Hydroponics

Although the gardener spends the major part of his time cultivating, feeding and watering the soil and fighting the pests and diseases that inhabit it, soil is not an essential part of a garden. It is perfectly possible and simple to grow vegetables while dispensing with the use of soil altogether.

The soilless culture of plants is called hydroponics. By this method the minerals which the plant normally obtains via the soil are fed directly to the roots in a solution of mineral salts in water.

The first experiments in soilless culture go back nearly two hundred years, but the breakthrough came about a century ago. It was not until the 1920s, when the Americans took it up, however, that hydroponics came to be exploited. During the Second World War it was used on a large scale to grow fresh vegetables for troops stationed in isolated places. Many of the carnations and roses sold by florists are grown hydroponically, and so are many tomato, cucumber and lettuce crops.

Hydroponic enthusiasts get as excited about their methods as dedicated organic gardeners or no-diggers do about theirs. They point out that soilless culture involves no digging or weeding. There is no manuring, and hence no smell. There is no soil and therefore no dirt. Germination is faster and the plants grow to maturity more quickly. They also insist that hydroponically grown plants taste better than plants grown in soil. What is certain is that the plants are less disease prone.

On a commercial scale, crops are often raised hydroponically in large tanks filled with a nutrient solution in which the roots of the plant are always immersed. This method (true hydroponics) is both tricky and expensive. The amateur can use the simple method of growing plants in containers filled with an inert aggregate which is kept moist with a mineral solution to provide the plants' essential needs of nitrogen, potassium, phosphorus, calcium, sulphur, magnesium and iron. Container cultivation makes it possible to grow at least some vegetables without a garden—either indoors, or on a patio, or on a flat roof (an excellent place).

All kinds of containers can be used—pots, window boxes, tubs, old kitchen sinks, wooden and plastic boxes (galvanized containers should be painted inside). Whatever the container it must have a drainage hole, or holes.

A box should be 6 to 8 inches (15 to 20 cm) deep and not too large to handle, say 24 to 30 inches (60 to 75 cm) long and 18 inches (45 cm) wide. Make a few drainage holes in the bottom. If it is a wooden box line it with polythene in which a few drainage holes have been cut. Place the box on a tray to catch the solution as it drains through. There is no need to empty the tray. The solution will be drawn up again.

Fill the box almost to the top with the aggregate which has been soaked in water. The aggregate can be coarse sand—fine sand becomes waterlogged; gravel or pebbles, perhaps mixed with some sand; broken bricks—the pieces $\frac{1}{2}$ inch (1 cm) or smaller; or possibly vermiculite. The box is then ready for sowing, which you do as though you were sowing in soil.

To feed the plants, the aggregate is watered with a solution made by mixing mineral preparations with water. These have been specially formulated to take the guesswork out of the process; just follow the instructions. Making up your own mineral mixtures is a little cheaper, although the saving is hardly worth the labour. One suitable formula would be 20 ounces (560 g) of ammonium sulphate, 10 ounces (280 g) superphosphate, 7 ounces (210 g) of potassium sulphate, 3 ounces (90 g) of magnesium sulphate, and the most minute pinch of iron sulphate. Mix them and crush them finely. Store the mixture so that it stays absolutely dry. Dissolve one-third of an ounce of the mixture in a gallon of water (10 g in $4\frac{1}{2}$ litres) as required.

In hot weather the aggregate must be watered daily, and every other day in cooler weather. Once a week, spray the plants with plain water.

After the crop has been picked, pour boiling water over the aggregate (to help keep it disease free) and make the next sowing. Among the plants which do well when grown hydroponically are lettuce and endive (take care that the lower leaves do not droop on to the wet aggregate and rot), French beans, tomatoes, strawberries and—although they would be an unlikely choice for a garden in the kitchen—towering Jerusalem artichokes.

Cross-section of a hydroponic bed.

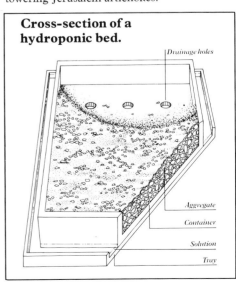

Drainage holes

Aggregate

Container

Solution

Tray

Feeding the Soil

Farmyard manure and compost are the two great, bulky, organic manures which both feed the soil and improve its texture. If you are able to obtain as much farmyard manure as you want you belong to a privileged minority. But any gardener can make compost, because the raw material of the compost heap is all the vegetable waste (if it is not diseased) from the garden and kitchen. If you do not recycle it in this way, you will be throwing away next year's food.

An enclosed compost heap works better than a heap in the open, which is liable to cool down and dry out before it has totally decomposed. In a properly made heap, spring rubbish should be compost by summer, summer rubbish compost by autumn, while autumn rubbish, taking longer to decompose through the winter, will be ready for use in spring. If the heap goes cold or dry before it has decomposed, turn it over with a fork so that the top of the heap ends up on the inside. Water the compost as you turn it.

Sedge peat, although not rich in plant food, is excellent for improving the texture of the soil. If applied as a mulch it gives double value. First it will suppress weeds, then later, when it is dug in, it will be broken down into humus. If it is forked in before sowing or planting, allow 3 pounds to the square yard ($1\frac{1}{2}$ kg to 1 sq m).

Testing for lime

Most vegetables grow best in a slightly acid soil, but if the soil becomes too acid other essential elements become unavailable to the plants. The acidity or alkalinity of the soil is expressed in what is called the pH value. This is reckoned from a base of pH 7; any higher pH number indicates the soil is alkaline and any lower pH number indicates the soil is acid. Because the scale is logarithmic, a change of one unit represents a tenfold increase or decrease in the soil's acidity, pH 5·5 soil, for example, is ten times more acid than pH 6·5 soil, which suits most vegetables.

There are cheap and simple soil-testing kits available to determine the pH value of the soil. It is then possible to work out how much lime, if any, should be added.

Testing for other deficiencies

There are other kits on the market for testing the levels in the soil of such important elements as nitrogen, phosphorus and potassium. Any deficiency can be made good by the use of organic or inorganic fertilizers.

Organic fertilizers

Organic fertilizers cost more than inorganic fertilizers. In general they act more slowly, but their effects last longer.

There are several types of organic fertilizers available. One made from ground hooves and horns of animals contains 12 per cent nitrogen and acts slowly over two years. Allow 2 ounces to every square yard (60 g to 1 sq m). Another made from ground, dried animal bones, acts slowly over three years. It contains at least 20

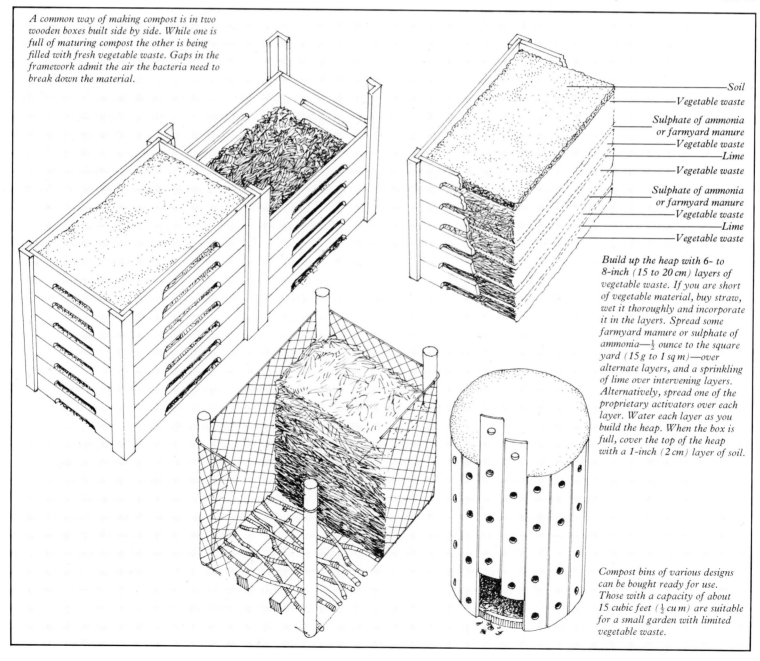

A common way of making compost is in two wooden boxes built side by side. While one is full of maturing compost the other is being filled with fresh vegetable waste. Gaps in the framework admit the air the bacteria need to break down the material.

Soil
Vegetable waste
Sulphate of ammonia or farmyard manure
Vegetable waste
Lime
Vegetable waste
Sulphate of ammonia or farmyard manure
Vegetable waste
Lime
Vegetable waste

Build up the heap with 6- to 8-inch (15 to 20 cm) layers of vegetable waste. If you are short of vegetable material, buy straw, wet it thoroughly and incorporate it in the layers. Spread some farmyard manure or sulphate of ammonia—$\frac{1}{2}$ ounce to the square yard (15 g to 1 sq m)—over alternate layers, and a sprinkling of lime over intervening layers. Alternatively, spread one of the proprietary activators over each layer. Water each layer as you build the heap. When the box is full, cover the top of the heap with a 1-inch (2 cm) layer of soil.

Compost bins of various designs can be bought ready for use. Those with a capacity of about 15 cubic feet ($\frac{1}{2}$ cu m) are suitable for a small garden with limited vegetable waste.

per cent phosphate and is low in nitrogen. Fish-meal fertilizer, made from dried, ground fish waste, acts slowly over two years. It contains about 10 per cent nitrogen and 12 per cent phosphate, although these percentages vary. Fertilizer made from powdered seaweed acts fairly quickly. It contains about 5 per cent potash and trace elements. Dried blood is a fast-acting fertilizer, especially when it is applied as a liquid feed—use 1 ounce to 1 gallon (30 g to 4½ litres) of water. It contains at least 10 per cent nitrogen.

Inorganic fertilizers

On the whole, inorganic fertilizers, which are made from chemicals, act quickly in providing the plant with vital elements, but they are soon washed out of the soil and leave no lasting improvement.

Compound fertilizers are widely used for vegetables. Growmore, one of the most economical, contains 7 per cent each of nitrogen, potash and phosphoric acid. Scatter up to 2 ounces to the square yard (60 g to 1 sq m) in spring or summer.

A straight fertilizer is used to remedy a marked deficiency of one element in the soil or to give a plant a boost. Nitrogen can be cheaply provided by using sulphate of ammonia, which is 20 per cent nitrogen and which acts within a few weeks. Use ½ ounce to the square yard (15 g to 1 sq m). Sodium nitrate, which is 16 per cent nitrogen, acts instantly. Use not more than 1 ounce to a square yard (30 g to 1 sq m).

Phosphorus is usually supplied by superphosphates, which are 20 per cent phosphoric acid. Use 2 ounces to the square yard (60 g to 1 sq m) in spring or summer. On acid soil, however, it is better to use basic slag, which acts much more slowly. It contains 17 per cent phosphoric acid. Apply ½ pound to the square yard (¼ kg to 1 sq m) in autumn or winter.

Potassium is generally provided by sulphate of potash, which is 50 per cent potash. Apply 1 ounce to the square yard (30 g to 1 sq m).

Watering the soil

However well fed a plant may be it will still not grow without plenty of water. Soils vary in how much water they can hold. The limit for sand is about 10 per cent; the limit for loam is up to 30 per cent, and the limit for clay is even higher. (When the soil can hold no more water it is at "field capacity".) As the soil dries out, the plant finds it harder to draw up water, even though there may be up to 20 per cent of water still left in clay. When the plant can no longer draw up any water, "wilting point" has been reached. The gardener should try to ensure that this never happens.

Absolutely no good is done by merely damping the surface of the soil. During a hot, rainless week in summer the gardener may have to provide the equivalent of 1 inch (2 cm) of rain, and that means 4½ gallons of water for every square yard (20 litres to 1 sq m). This is a formidable task for a man with only a watering can. Using a hose or sprinkler increases the chances that the plants will get enough water.

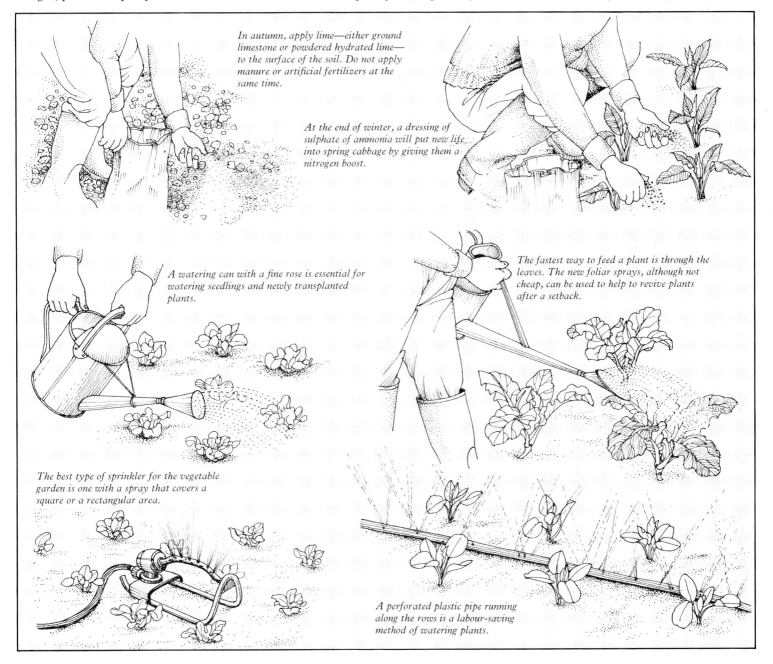

In autumn, apply lime—either ground limestone or powdered hydrated lime—to the surface of the soil. Do not apply manure or artificial fertilizers at the same time.

At the end of winter, a dressing of sulphate of ammonia will put new life into spring cabbage by giving them a nitrogen boost.

A watering can with a fine rose is essential for watering seedlings and newly transplanted plants.

The fastest way to feed a plant is through the leaves. The new foliar sprays, although not cheap, can be used to help to revive plants after a setback.

The best type of sprinkler for the vegetable garden is one with a spray that covers a square or a rectangular area.

A perforated plastic pipe running along the rows is a labour-saving method of watering plants.

Growing under Glass

Spring comes earlier and the onset of winter is later in a greenhouse, in frames and under cloches. All of them "trap" the sun. The short-wave rays from both direct sunlight and diffused light pass through the glass and warm up the soil. The soil in turn gives off this heat as long-wave heat rays, which will not pass through glass, so the heat builds up inside the greenhouse.

In the middle of winter, however, the temperature inside a greenhouse without artificial heating may be only a few degrees above the temperature outside. Even in a heated greenhouse you cannot create perpetual summer, for in winter lack of light inhibits plant growth. There are too few hours of daylight and the light is not strong enough to encourage growth.

Siting the greenhouse east to west makes the most of winter sunlight. The gain is even greater if the roof is angled to reflect the minimum of light, but this is costly, and if the house is sited north to south there is no advantage.

Greenhouses glazed to the ground obviously admit more light than those built on 2 to 3 feet (60 to 90 cm) of brick wall, which are warmer. The framework of an aluminium house obstructs less light than a wooden framework. These are two important facts to consider well when choosing a greenhouse.

A great deal of light is lost because of dirty greenhouse windows. Regular and thorough cleaning of the greenhouse will also help to combat plant diseases.

Obviously a greenhouse should be sited where it is not shaded by the house or by trees. But the farther it is from the house, the greater will be the cost of taking water, electricity or gas to it.

In summer the heat trapped in a closed greenhouse can raise the temperature so high that plants are damaged. Adequate ventilation is essential, therefore, and a system of automatic ventilation, although not cheap, avoids the necessity of having to visit the greenhouse several times a day.

Automatic watering devices also save a lot of time and work in the greenhouse. They include simple capillary trays or mats on which plants stand; trickle irrigation lines with drip nozzles at intervals; and full-scale combined trickle and mist watering systems, activated by the strength of the sunlight.

The most convenient—and now most expensive—way of heating the greenhouse is by electricity. Fan heaters and tubular heaters are widely used. If natural gas can be piped to the greenhouse the gardener is lucky, since it is relatively cheap. Whereas town gas gives off fumes which kill plants, the carbon dioxide given off by natural gas is beneficial to green plants, but it can be fatal to mushrooms.

The temperature of the greenhouse can be lowered, and the cost of heating cut, if a propagator is used for seed raising. A propagator is basically a miniature greenhouse which is heated cheaply, even to 70°F (21°C), by soil-warming cables. A large, thermostatically controlled propagator would make early seed raising feasible inside a cold greenhouse.

One piece of equipment that is vital in a greenhouse is a maximum–minimum thermometer; guesswork may kill your plants.

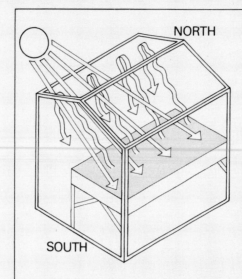

Short-wave rays from the sun pass through the glass of the greenhouse and warm the soil inside. Because long-wave rays given off by the soil do not pass out through the glass, the temperature rises inside the greenhouse.

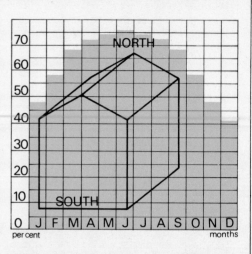

In winter, the glass of a north to south, even-span greenhouse admits less than half the available sunlight; it reflects the rest. When a greenhouse is situated east to west, about a quarter more sunlight penetrates in winter.

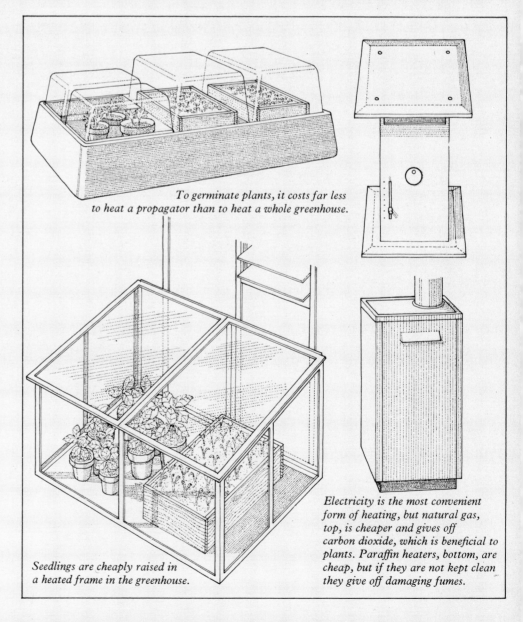

To germinate plants, it costs far less to heat a propagator than to heat a whole greenhouse.

Seedlings are cheaply raised in a heated frame in the greenhouse.

Electricity is the most convenient form of heating, but natural gas, top, is cheaper and gives off carbon dioxide, which is beneficial to plants. Paraffin heaters, bottom, are cheap, but if they are not kept clean they give off damaging fumes.

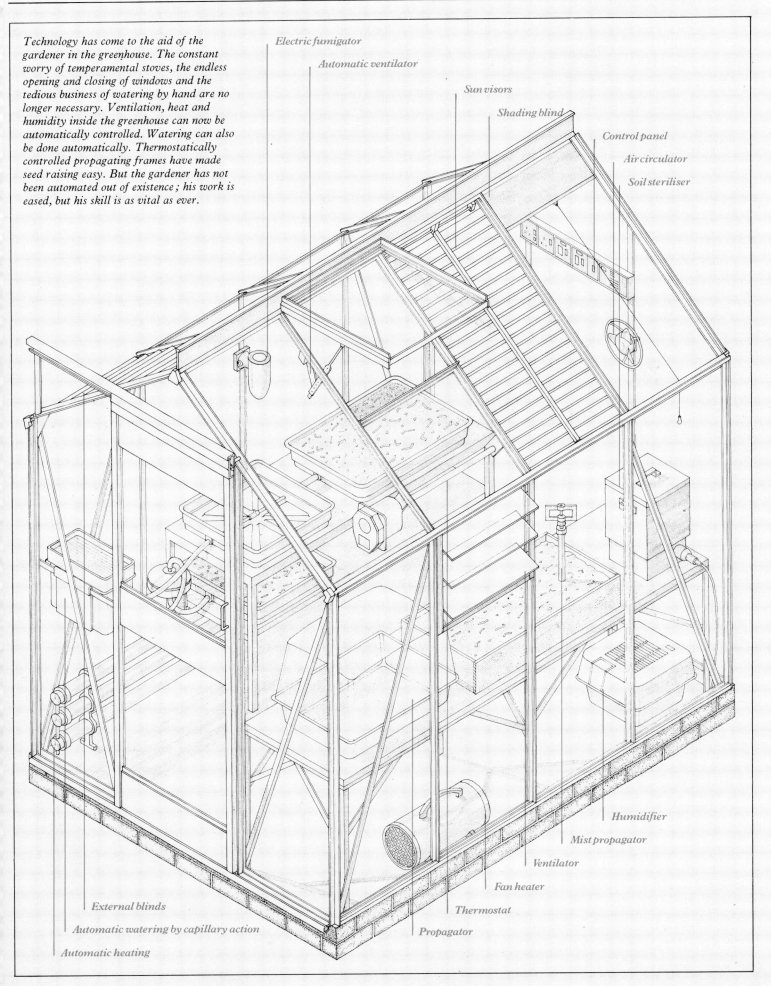

Technology has come to the aid of the gardener in the greenhouse. The constant worry of temperamental stoves, the endless opening and closing of windows and the tedious business of watering by hand are no longer necessary. Ventilation, heat and humidity inside the greenhouse can now be automatically controlled. Watering can also be done automatically. Thermostatically controlled propagating frames have made seed raising easy. But the gardener has not been automated out of existence; his work is eased, but his skill is as vital as ever.

Electric fumigator

Automatic ventilator

Sun visors

Shading blind

Control panel

Air circulator

Soil steriliser

Humidifier

Mist propagator

Ventilator

Fan heater

Thermostat

Propagator

External blinds

Automatic watering by capillary action

Automatic heating

Growing under Glass

A garden frame, especially one which is heated, can be used in conjunction with, or as an alternative to, the greenhouse. It is used for raising seeds or growing less-hardy vegetables. The drawback is that while a frame effectively protects the plants, unlike a snug greenhouse it offers no refuge to the gardener on a bleak winter's day.

The simplest frames are made of Dutch lights supported on a brick or wooden base. (Dutch lights consist of a grooved, wooden framework holding a piece of glass of a standard size—56 × 28¾ inches [140 × 72 cm].) Others, which have metal frameworks and glass sides, admit more light, but are colder at night. Frames can be heated by electric cables in the soil (like underfloor heating) or by air-warming cables fixed to the sides of the frame. Better still, the two methods can be combined. Fixing the cables is a job for a qualified electrician.

A cold frame is used for the toughening-up stage in the life of a greenhouse-raised plant, to prepare it for the rigours of the outside world.

Dutch lights are versatile. Greenhouses, as well as fixed frames, can be built from them, and they can be used to give portable protection to anything in the garden. For example, you may lean a row of lights against a wall to protect newly planted tomatoes. The lights must be firmly secured, otherwise, being large and fairly light, they are liable to be caught by gusts of wind and smashed.

Bell cloches have been used for centuries, although more by the French than the English. Continuous cloches are an English idea and their use, which dates from the beginning of the twentieth century, reached a peak in the 1950s. When interest in vegetable growing declined, cloches went out of fashion and many well-known designs went out of production. This is regrettable at a time when the kitchen garden is all-important again, but increasing demand may encourage manufacturers to fill the need.

Cloches are most useful to the gardener who lives in the colder areas of Britain. They enable him to sow crops earlier, especially if the cloches have been placed in position about a fortnight before sowing to warm up the soil. The less-hardy vegetables, which would fail in the open, can also be grown under them. Moving cloches can be wearying, but by careful forward planning of where vegetables are to be grown, the cloches can be lifted from one crop to another in an adjoining row.

Glass cloches are still the best, even though they are heavier, more liable to be broken, and more expensive than those made of plastic. Gardeners with small, football-playing children may prefer plastic for the safety of both cloches and offspring. Because they are so light and liable to be blown away, plastic cloches must be firmly anchored in the soil.

Tent and barn cloches (the names describe the shapes) are made of glass and plastic. There are also small tunnel cloches made of rigid plastic, and long tunnel cloches made of polythene stretched over hoops. Polythene cloches have a fairly short life, but are correspondingly inexpensive.

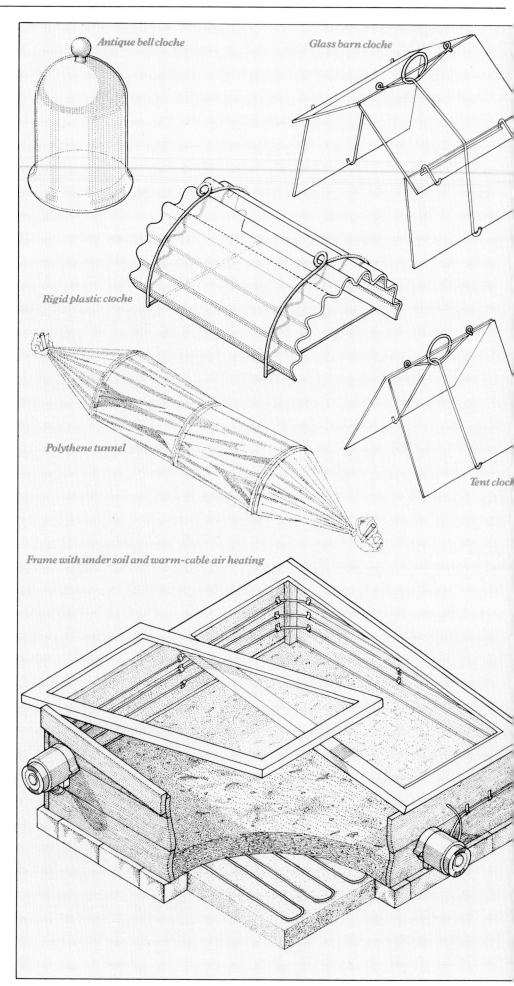

Antique bell cloche

Glass barn cloche

Rigid plastic cloche

Polythene tunnel

Tent cloche

Frame with under soil and warm-cable air heating

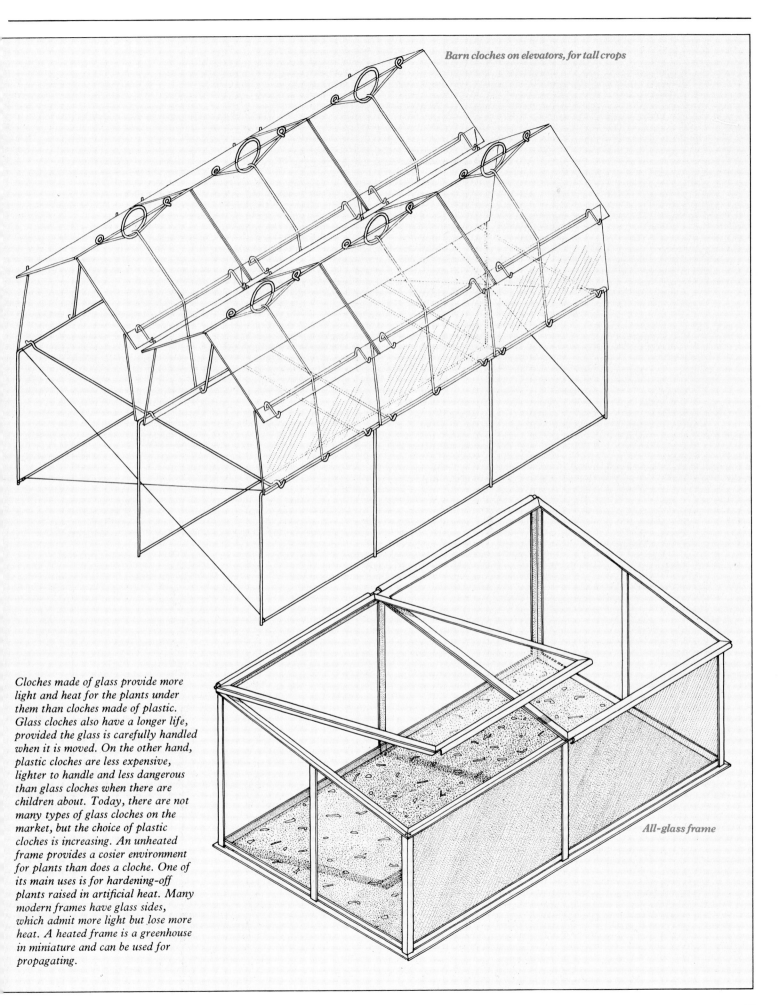

Barn cloches on elevators, for tall crops

Cloches made of glass provide more light and heat for the plants under them than cloches made of plastic. Glass cloches also have a longer life, provided the glass is carefully handled when it is moved. On the other hand, plastic cloches are less expensive, lighter to handle and less dangerous than glass cloches when there are children about. Today, there are not many types of glass cloches on the market, but the choice of plastic cloches is increasing. An unheated frame provides a cosier environment for plants than does a cloche. One of its main uses is for hardening-off plants raised in artificial heat. Many modern frames have glass sides, which admit more light but lose more heat. A heated frame is a greenhouse in miniature and can be used for propagating.

All-glass frame

Climate

Imagine a recipe which said "Cream together the butter and sugar when all danger of frost is past." Or, imagine if it were possible to make Yorkshire pudding only when there were more than fourteen hours of daylight. The cook has problems, but they are seldom climatic. The gardener, on the other hand, is the prisoner of the weather and can do nothing to change the overall pattern of the climate of his region.

The problems of the gardener in Britain and northern maritime Europe are made greater because, as depressions and anticyclones confront each other, the weather pattern is so unpredictable. Every year more than a hundred and fifty major depressions sweep in from the Atlantic. Comparatively small deviations in their usual tracks—north of Scotland, across Scotland, through the Midlands and northern England, or along the Channel and into northern France, the Low Countries and Germany—make what may seem disproportionate differences in rainfall and temperature. The build-up of anticyclones, bringing settled cold or warm weather according to their origin, is equally uncertain.

There are, however, averaged expectations of what the weather will be. Over northwestern Europe, January will be unsettled, with fewer than five days with temperatures below freezing. In February either high pressure over the Azores will bring mild weather, or high pressure over Russia will bring cold, dry weather (as it has done frequently in recent years). March is another anticyclonic month, with cold northerly and easterly winds, but the normally frequent anticyclones of April, May and early June bring warmer, settled weather until the Atlantic westerlies get the upper hand. From July until October depressions and anticyclones alternate, but November and December weather is again mainly affected by the Atlantic westerlies.

There are innumerable regional variations, but this has been the broad pattern over wide areas for many years. Now there are predictions of long-term changes. These, it is said, would bring colder, drier and shorter summers, but milder winters. If this is so, the gardener would be seriously affected. Colder, shorter growing seasons would make it more difficult to grow the less hardy vegetables—for example, sweet corn, French and runner beans, as well as early potatoes. It would become as hard for the southerner to carry out catch cropping as it now is for the northern gardener.

As well as suffering, or enjoying, the weather of its own region each garden has a microclimate of its own. Although some of the factors in creating this micro-climate may be beyond his control—the site of the garden, for example, or the shade or protection from wind of adjoining houses—the gardener can do much to make conditions more favourable for his plants.

Walls, fences and hedges temper the wind. But a solid wall may only divert the wind over the top, sometimes causing enough turbulence to damage the plants beyond the lee of the wall. More open fences or hedges are often preferable because they do not merely divert the wind but reduce its force. Plants growing against the sunny side of a wall, on the other hand, benefit from the heat which the wall reflects. Cold air flows downhill; if your garden is on a slope provide some way out at the bottom for the cold air to escape, or you will have made yourself a frost pocket. Late spring frosts are a particular menace if you are growing apples, pears, many soft fruits and potatoes.

Heavy clay soils are cold, but will warm up sooner in the spring if their texture is lightened with large quantities of organic matter. Dark, humus-rich soil absorbs more heat than lightcoloured soil. Mulches, too, help to keep heat in the soil.

The most obvious way of mitigating the cold is to grow crops under glass—greenhouses, frames or cloches. But even in heated greenhouses, the growth of plants in winter will still be inhibited by lack of light.

Nothing can be done about excessive rain, but drought can be overcome, laboriously with watering cans or effortlessly with sprinklers, provided no watering restrictions are in force in the part of the country where you live. In a drought large quantities of water will be needed (see page 29). Mulches help to prevent evaporation from the soil.

Too high a temperature can stop plants from growing, but in northern Europe it is only in greenhouses that this is likely to be a problem. Outdoors, plants which wilt during the day, because they give off more moisture through the leaves than they can take up through the roots, will revive at night. Tomatoes and potatoes, for example, prefer a cooler temperature at night than in the daytime and strawberries develop their best flavour in temperatures of about 50°F (10°C).

Phenology

Phenology is a study which relates climate to the development of plant life; for example, the times at which a plant starts to grow, or matures. As isotherms on maps connect places experiencing the same temperatures, so isophenes connect places where the same stage in plant development is taking place. The phenological map on the opposite page shows the dates on which grass begins to grow in various parts of Britain—which is, generally speaking, when the temperature reaches 42°F (6°C). The minimum temperature for growth (called the "zero temperature") of a plant varies from species to species. For peas, for example, the zero temperature is 40°F (4°C), for potatoes 45°F (7°C) and for sweet corn 50°F (10°C).

Superimposed on the map are the isotherms for July, 59°F (15°C), running east–west, and January, 41°F (5°C), running north–south. They indicate the basic regional differences in the British climate. The dry northeast has cool summers and cold winters. The rainy northwest has cool summers and mild winters. The dry southeast has warm summers and cool winters. The rainy southwest has warm summers and mild winters.

The map below extends the July and January isotherms from Britain over Europe to indicate the general weather pattern there.

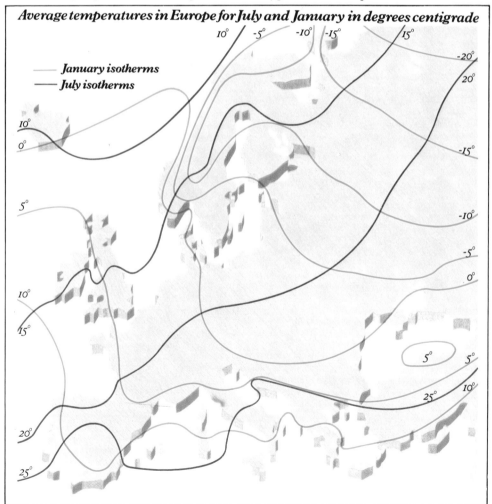

Average temperatures in Europe for July and January in degrees centigrade

January isotherms
July isotherms

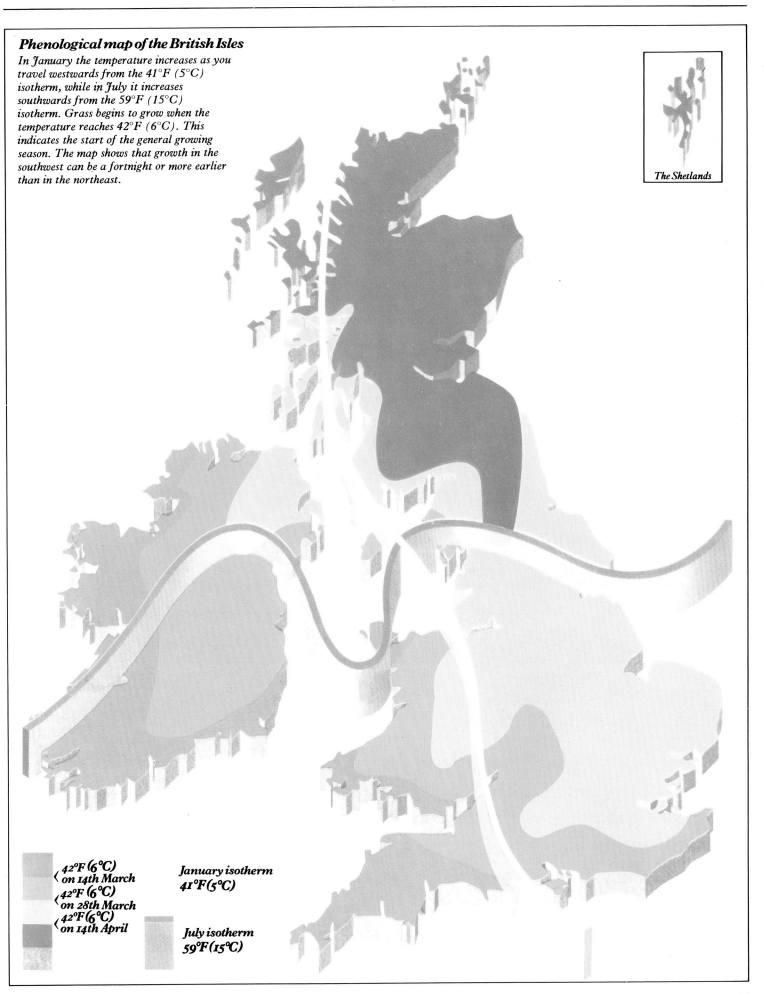

Phenological map of the British Isles

In January the temperature increases as you travel westwards from the 41°F (5°C) isotherm, while in July it increases southwards from the 59°F (15°C) isotherm. Grass begins to grow when the temperature reaches 42°F (6°C). This indicates the start of the general growing season. The map shows that growth in the southwest can be a fortnight or more earlier than in the northeast.

The Shetlands

42°F (6°C)
< on 14th March

42°F (6°C)
< on 28th March

42°F (6°C)
< on 14th April

January isotherm
41°F (5°C)

July isotherm
59°F (15°C)

Tools & Machinery

It is a false economy to buy cheap gardening tools, so be prepared to spend money on them. Begin with the five basic tools, and add to them only to get better results or to save labour. Avoid gadgets, invariably they are not used.

The five basic tools are spade, fork, hoe, rake and trowel. Add secateurs to this list if you are growing fruit. Next on the list of priorities are a watering can and a wheelbarrow. A dibber is useful for making holes to plant a vegetable such as cabbage. It can be made from the handle and about 8 inches (20 cm) of the shaft (sharpened at the end) from a broken spade. But that presupposes the existence of a broken spade; until then the trowel is a perfectly good alternative for planting out.

A garden line to mark out straight rows for planting is basically only a long piece of strong string tied to two sticks. Curiously, most gardeners either lose a home-made line or get the string in a hopeless tangle, whereas they take great care of the easily wound metal contraption they buy.

Spades
The standard size of blade is $11\frac{1}{2}$ inches (29 cm) long and $7\frac{1}{2}$ inches (19 cm) wide, but the small size, $10\frac{1}{2} \times 6\frac{1}{2}$ inches (26×16 cm) makes digging easier. Stainless steel blades go through the soil more easily, are easier to clean and do not rust. The price may be double that of an ordinary spade, but it is worth paying. Wooden shafts should be close grained and smooth. Polypropylene handles are lighter. Handles are either D or T shaped, the choice depends on which you find easier to handle.

Forks
The standard size of a digging fork is $12 \times 7\frac{1}{2}$ inches (30×19 cm) the small size is $10\frac{1}{2} \times 6\frac{1}{2}$ inches (26×16 cm). The tines may be of stainless or ordinary steel, and the handles of wood or polypropylene.

Hoes
The most important hoe is the Dutch hoe, used for weeding. The hoe for making drills for sowing is the draw hoe.

Rakes
Rakes are invaluable in creating the fine tilth needed for a seedbed. Widths range between 12 and 16 inches (30 and 40 cm) and shafts are about 60 inches (150 cm) long. Wooden shafts should be smooth and close grained, and, therefore, unlikely to splinter.

Hand tools
Stainless steel is worth investing in for a hand trowel, and probably for a hand fork, because both are frequently left out in the garden. Only the best secateurs are worth buying; blades which do not cut cleanly cause terrible damage.

Gloves
Many gardeners cannot bear to wear gloves. Others agree with the nineteenth century gardener Loudon, who wrote in his *Encyclopedia of Gardening*: "Never perform any operation without gloves on your hands that you can do with gloves on. Thus no gardener need have hands like bears' paws."

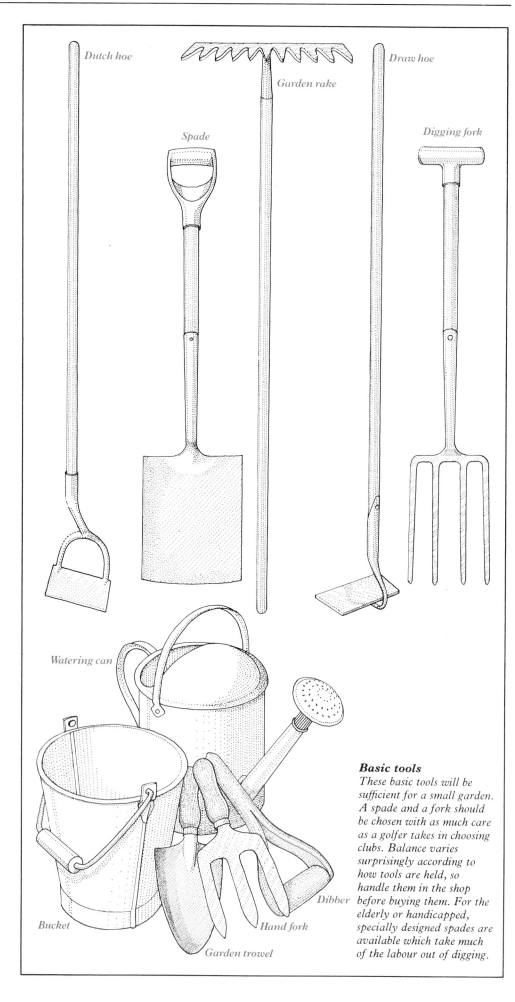

Dutch hoe

Garden rake

Draw hoe

Spade

Digging fork

Watering can

Bucket

Dibber

Hand fork

Garden trowel

Basic tools
These basic tools will be sufficient for a small garden. A spade and a fork should be chosen with as much care as a golfer takes in choosing clubs. Balance varies surprisingly according to how tools are held, so handle them in the shop before buying them. For the elderly or handicapped, specially designed spades are available which take much of the labour out of digging.

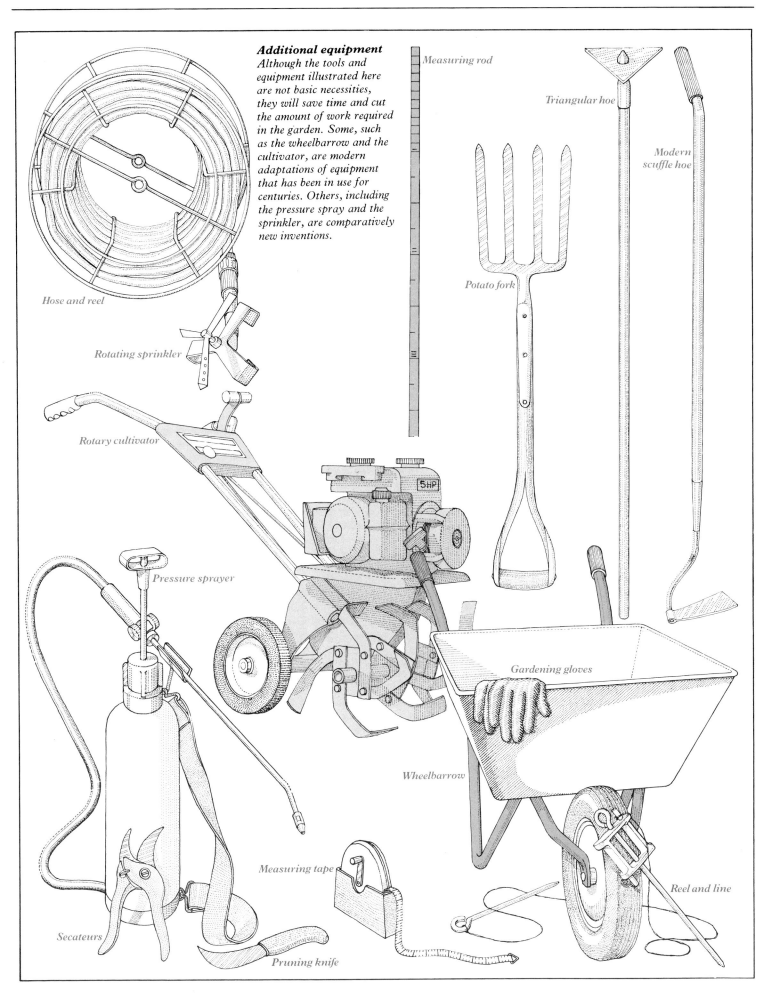

Additional equipment
Although the tools and equipment illustrated here are not basic necessities, they will save time and cut the amount of work required in the garden. Some, such as the wheelbarrow and the cultivator, are modern adaptations of equipment that has been in use for centuries. Others, including the pressure spray and the sprinkler, are comparatively new inventions.

Hose and reel

Rotating sprinkler

Rotary cultivator

Pressure sprayer

Secateurs

Pruning knife

Measuring rod

Measuring tape

Wheelbarrow

Potato fork

Triangular hoe

Modern scuffle hoe

Gardening gloves

Reel and line

Sowing

A seed is created to grow: that is its purpose. The gardener does not have to cajole it into growing, he merely has to give it the opportunity. For germination he provides a growing medium (not necessarily soil), moisture, warmth and, for healthy growth, adequate light and space.

Sowing under glass

Many vegetable seeds germinate best in a temperature of about 65°F (18°C). To avoid the heavy cost of heating the whole greenhouse to this temperature, a propagator can be used. If it is large and tall enough, the seedlings can be allowed to grow on in it, but at a lower temperature. This would, however, be a rather wasteful use of a propagator. If the seedlings are moved to the benches of a heated greenhouse, or to a heated frame within a cold greenhouse, the propagator can be used for raising a further batch of seeds.

The choice of a proper compost is the most important single factor in sowing. Any old soil will not do. There are specially formulated John Innes seed and potting composts, which consist of sterilized loam, peat and sand, plus fertilizers. Soilless composts are usually based on peat, or peat and sand, plus fertilizers. John Innes composts can be extremely variable in quality, but buying from a reputable source is some safeguard. The soilless composts are less variable, but need great care in watering. (Once peat has dried out it is hard to get it to absorb water again.)

Plastic seed trays can be kept cleaner than wooden boxes. Fill the tray, or box, level to the top with moist, but not sodden, compost and then firm it down with your hand. Scatter the seeds very thinly on the surface of the compost. By using your finger and thumb for sowing you will be able to space the seeds better than you will if you scatter them from the packet. (The larger pelleted seeds can be spaced as you wish.)

Sift a shallow covering of fine compost, not soil, over the seeds and firm gently. Label the tray with the name of the seeds and the date of sowing. Cover the tray with a sheet of glass to prevent the compost from drying out in the propagator. Wipe condensation off the glass every day. At the first sign of the seedlings coming through, remove the glass.

Pots are often used instead of trays for plants which will not tolerate the root disturbance involved in pricking-out from a seed-box. It also makes sense to use pots if only a few plants are being grown. Conventional round pots made of clay or plastic take up more room than trays, however. Space-saving alternatives are square, compressed peat pots (individual or in strips) filled with a seed compost, or peat blocks. These are made of a prepared peat compost, which is compressed into a block in a simple machine. If two seeds are planted in each block (pelleted seed can be used) and the weaker seedling removed, there is no root disturbance later.

If seeds are going to germinate they usually do it fairly quickly. Many germinate within a week, although the time will depend on the temperature. The bulk of seeds will germinate from a week to a fortnight. Celery takes up to three weeks and parsley is unpredictable.

Pricking-out

As soon after germination as possible, prick out the seedlings into another box or into pots. This is usually left too late. A seedling pricked out two days after germination suffers far less setback than one pricked out a week after germination. They may be fiddling little things to handle at two days, but the roots are less liable to be damaged then. Lift each seedling gently, hold it by one of the leaves—not by the stem—and replant it, using a plastic or wooden seed label as a dibber.

It is far better at this stage to prick out the seedlings into pots containing potting compost than into other boxes from which they may have to be moved again. Peat blocks made of potting compost can also be used. The old practice was first to prick out the seedlings, then to move the growing plant from a box to a pot (potting-off). When the pot became too small, the plant was moved to a larger pot (potting-on). Every such change is a major setback to the plant. It may, however, be necessary to compromise at the pricking-out stage because of the demand on space in the greenhouse at the height of the seed-raising season; pots do take up more space than boxes. When the pricked-out plants have been

watered from a watering-can with a fine rose, the pots or boxes can be put in a heated frame in a cold greenhouse or outside. Alternatively, they can be transferred to the benches of a heated greenhouse. The temperature is first reduced by about 5 degrees Fahrenheit (3 degrees Centigrade) from what it was in the propagator. Later, it can come down to 50°F (10°C). Do not force the plants; steady, sturdy growth is the aim.

Eventually, when the weather is suitable, the pots are transferred to a cold frame outdoors for hardening-off. To harden-off, raise the frame light a little at first, on mild days, but close the frame at night. The plants can be given a little more air each day until they are ready for planting out in the garden.

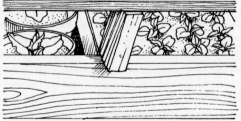

Outdoor seedbeds

Some vegetables, notably brassicas (see page 48), are sown out of doors in seedbeds. Level and rake a few square feet of the garden and, for brassicas, cover it with good compost from the compost heap. Make shallow drills with a stick 6 inches (15 cm) apart and sow the seeds thinly. Cover them with a scattering of sifted compost. Use the head of the rake to firm the bed. Do not let the bed dry out as the seedlings grow, but water gently from a watering-can with a fine rose.

Planting out

When the time finally comes for planting out, water the plants in the seedbeds or pots the day before the move. If possible, choose the evening of a cloudy day for planting out. However sturdy the plants may appear, treat them gently. Disturb the roots as little as you can by lifting them with as big a ball as possible of the soil or compost in which they have been

growing. Lower them into holes made with a trowel or dibber. Plants grown singly in pots or peat blocks suffer the least disturbance, and they will forge ahead faster than others. Avoid damage to leaves or stems which would make the plants vulnerable to diseases. Firm the soil around the transplanted plants and water.

Sowing outdoors in rows

Some vegetables, especially root crops, cannot be successfully transplanted. Instead, they are sown in rows in that part of the garden where they are to grow and mature. As a general but not rigid rule the rows run north to south, so that each side of the row gets its share of the sun.

Mark where the row is to be with a garden line, and alongside it make a drill in which the seeds will be sown. The phrases "½-inch (1 cm) drills" and "1-inch (2 cm) drills" should not be interpreted too literally; with even the finest tilth such precise measurements are impossible. Therefore regard a "½-inch (1 cm) drill" as shorthand for a very shallow depression in the soil along which very small seeds will be sown and very thinly covered. The simplest way of making such a shallow drill is by pressing the arm of the rake into the soil along the length of the row. The "1-inch (2 cm) drill" is somewhat deeper, but still shallow. This, and deeper drills, can be made with a draw hoe.

Sowing along the drill can be done in two ways—either thinly in a continuous row, if the seeds are small, or in groups of one, two or three seeds, placed at intervals along the row, if the seeds are large. The second is called station sowing, and the distances between the stations are given in the sowing instructions for individual vegetables. Pelleting of seeds makes it possible to sow even minute seeds in stations.

Seeds sown in stations of two or more will need thinning by the careful removal of the weaker seedlings in each station. (The risk involved in planting only one seed is that it may not germinate, or may turn out a weakling.)

Continuous sowing will involve thinning

along the row to leave adequate space for each plant to grow. Sowing thickly should be avoided; the plants will suffer all their lives from overcrowding at the seedling stage, and the thinning of crowded seedlings disturbs the roots of those which are left.

Times of Sowing

Times of sowing given on seed packets must be seasonally adjusted—to steal the statistician's phrase—to your own garden. "Early April" may mean tea on the lawn for some and battling through a blizzard for others.

The seed allows gardeners considerable latitude. Sir Alexander Fleming, of penicillin fame, was a gardener who was both unorthodox and successful. André Maurois wrote that Sir Alexander "liked sowing and planting out in those months of the year which were not advised by the experts, just to prove that the experts were wrong". His attitude was that plants "are responsive to kindness, but they can also withstand any amount of hard treatment. In other words, they are like human beings."

Making seed and potting composts with soil

John Innes seed and potting composts can be bought ready-made, but whether they will contain the top grade loam and the fertilizers of the original formulae is another matter. If a gardener can obtain a good loam he can make these composts himself. After mixing, the compost should not be stored for more than a few weeks.

The quantities given here may be scaled down or up according to how much is needed, as long as the proportions are the same. Many gardeners still think in terms of the now-discarded bushels rather than cubic yards. For practical purposes a bushel is one-twentieth of a cubic yard.

To make John Innes seed compost: mix 2 parts (by bulk not weight) of sterilized medium loam to 1 part of granulated peat and 1 part of sharp sand. To 1 cubic yard (1 cu m) add 1 pound (½ kg) of ground limestone and 2 pounds (1 kg) of superphosphate.

To make John Innes No 1 potting compost (for slow-growing seedlings): mix 7 parts of sterilized medium loam with 3 parts of granulated peat and 2 parts of sharp sand. To each cubic yard add 1 pound (½ kg) of ground chalk or limestone and 5 pounds (2½ kg) of John Innes base fertilizer. The base fertilizer is

made of 2 parts (by weight) of hoof and horn or dried blood to 2 parts of superphosphate and 1 part of potassium sulphate. To make John Innes No 2 potting compost (which is the one most generally used), add twice as much base fertilizer, and to make John Innes No 3 potting compost (used for tomatoes) add three times as much base fertilizer.

Composts without soil

To make soilless seed compost according to the formula developed at the University of California, mix equal parts (by bulk) of granulated peat and washed grit. To each cubic yard (1 cu m) add 5 pounds (2½ kg) of chalk or ground limestone, 1¼ pounds (600 g) of superphosphate, 15 ounces (450 g) of potassium sulphate and 10 ounces (300 g) of ammonium sulphate.

The University of California potting compost is made by mixing equal parts (by bulk) of granulated peat and washed grit. To each cubic yard (1 cu m) add 5 pounds (2½ kg) of chalk or ground limestone, 2½ pounds (1¼ kg) of magnesium limestone, 3¾ pounds (1¾ kg) of ammonium nitrate, 3¾ pounds (1¾ kg) of hoof and horn, 2½ pounds (1¼ kg) of superphosphate and 1¼ pounds (600 g) of potassium sulphate.

Many soilless composts are on sale under proprietary names. One such compost includes a substance which makes water more readily absorbed by the peat.

Pelleted seeds

Pelleted seeds are small seeds that have been given a coating of soil-clay to make them large enough to handle. They can thus be sown in stations, reducing or eliminating the need for thinning.

The soil in which pelleted seeds are planted must be moist enough to soften the coating or the seed will not be able to germinate. But if the soil is overwet, the clay coating will cling to the seed, preventing germination.

If the seeds are sown indoors, cover them with a layer of fine compost no deeper than the diameter of a pellet. If they are sown outdoors, the covering should be to a depth of twice the diameter of a pellet. Germination will take a day or two longer than for ordinary seed. The soil must never be allowed to become dry after sowing, overwatering will also be disastrous.

Pelleted seeds are more expensive than ordinary seeds because of the cost of coating them. They are, however, easier to handle and fewer are wasted.

The life of seeds

The seeds of such vegetables as turnips, swedes, parsnips and parsley have to be fresh to germinate properly. Others, including broad, French and runner bean seeds, pea seeds and spinach seeds will germinate reasonably well after two years. Seeds of such vegetables as leeks, carrots, kohlrabi, cabbages, cauliflowers, Brussels sprouts, broccoli, kale, lettuces and mustard and cress can be left for three years, while onion, radish, beetroot and spinach beet seeds can be planted when they are four years old.

Any seeds left over after the year's sowing is completed must be kept dry at normal room temperature or they will deteriorate. Remember to write the year of purchase on the packet.

A Gardening Guide

The novice gardener always asks for precise answers to questions to which there are no precise answers.

"How much of the garden will I have to dig up to grow enough vegetables for the family?"

"How many hours a week will I have to spend in the garden?"

"How much money will it save me?"

The answer to these questions—and to many others—is, "it depends", which is honest, but irritatingly unsatisfactory. The answers depend on the weather, the fertility of the soil, the absence or prevalence of pests and diseases, on how quickly the novice learns and on luck. It would, however, be cowardly not to attempt some answers to these questions.

Size of the garden. A garden measuring 400 square yards (335 sq m) can meet most of the vegetable requirements of a family of four. In Britain, in the warmer south, such a garden would provide a far greater variety of vegetables and a greater volume through intensive cropping than in the colder north, where the vegetables would be the more basic ones, roots and cabbages for winter for example.

The return from a garden in a novice's first year will be less than in later years. Even the second year will show a considerable increase. By the fourth year the garden will be reaching its peak, but only if you have invested in the fertility of the soil and not robbed it.

Time spent in the garden. The standard English allotment of 300 square yards (250 sq m) will take at least one hundred and fifty hours a year to cultivate. A 400 square yard (335 sq m) plot which included potatoes would add more than fifty hours, for potatoes take up a lot of time. But the work is not spread evenly throughout the year. March, April, May and June are laborious months, needing eight to ten hours a week in the garden. At the other extreme, you need hardly move out of doors in December and January.

There are ways of saving time. Cut out the tedious and lengthy earthing up of potatoes by growing them under black polythene sheeting. Grow self-blanching celery, which needs no trenching or earthing up. Avoid the earthing up of leeks by growing them on the flat. Reduce weeding by using weed-smothering mulches. A few years' experience will also make the work easier and faster, especially as you will learn when to cut corners.

On the other hand, an enthusiast can extend the time he spends in the garden to fill all the time he has to spare. And that is the reason many non-gardeners often get the discouraging impression that gardening is an endless task.

Saving money. Precisely how much money will be saved by growing your own vegetables is all but impossible to estimate. In the first year it could be nothing, especially if you are a beginner and have to buy all the tools you need. Any economy on tools should be made by buying only those which are essential. Gadgets are a luxury at any time, and most certainly at the start. But do not try to save money by buying shoddy basic tools—spade, fork, hoe and rake—if only because you will

suffer even more than the garden.

After tools, the first spending priority is to buy fertility, especially for an impoverished garden. But avoid throwing money away on highly publicized patent fertilizers, and still less on pesticides. The money is far better spent on peat, and on straw for making compost. Neither straw nor peat is cheap now, but building up the fertility of the garden is a long-term and profitable investment.

At first, therefore, do not imagine that you will be saving a fortune, although that may come later. Bear in mind, to avoid being discouraged at the start, that the gardening year is longer than twelve months. It would be that only if everything was sown in January and eaten by December. But vegetable sowing can go on over nearly nine months of the year, and harvesting over a period of eighteen months. That makes the first "year" short and not very profitable. Not until the second and third years will expenditure and returns from the garden establish a pattern by which profitability can be judged. In Britain, The National Society of Leisure Gardeners (the renamed National Allotments and Gardens Society) have published their estimate of what "an ordinary person with an elementary knowledge of gardening, should be able to grow on a 300 square yard (250 sq m) plot after a couple of seasons' experience".

Carrots	28 pounds (14 kg)
Parsnips	75 pounds (34 kg)
Beet	86 pounds (39 kg)
Lettuce	280 heads
Radishes	24 bunches
Broad beans	24 pounds (12 kg)
Peas	45 pounds (22½ kg)
Cabbage	66 heads
Spring cabbage	108 heads
Brussels sprouts	35 pounds (17½ kg)
Turnips	29 pounds (14½ kg)
Runner beans	61 pounds (28 kg)
Dwarf beans	19 pounds (9½ kg)
Savoys	66 heads
Marrows	24
Onions	192 pounds (87 kg)
Spring onions (thinnings)	20 bunches
Parsley	As required
Potatoes (early)	84 pounds (38 kg)
Potatoes (main crop)	410 pounds (186 kg)
Leeks	96
Broccoli	130 heads
Celery	48 heads
Swedes	44 pounds (22 kg)
Tomatoes	120 pounds (54 kg)
Gooseberries	18 pounds (9 kg)
Rhubarb	7 pounds (3½ kg)
Cucumbers (frame)	20

The society add that even "if you have never touched a spade before you can quickly save enough on the household budget to ensure a good holiday each year".

Sowing and harvesting. The alphabetical list of vegetables which follows is a rough guide to how long it will be after sowing before basic vegetables are ready for eating. Of course, the time it takes for a vegetable to reach maturity varies according to when it is sown and how favourable the weather is during the growing period.

The estimated sowing dates are, with a few exceptions, given for those vegetables sown out of doors in the south of England. They will be up to three weeks later as you garden northwards. By using cloches, dates of sowing can be advanced by about two weeks. Average sowing rates are given, but, annoyingly, few seedsmen indicate the average number of seeds in a packet.

The probable yields must be regarded as the roughest of guides. As well as all the imponderables of weather and disease, the choice of variety makes a great difference to the extent of a crop. In choosing a variety, quality should, sensibly, take precedence over quantity. It is no disgrace to get lower yields than other gardeners.

Beans, broad (See page 72.)
Sow February to April, July and November; ready from 3½ months; ½ pint (250 ml) of seed sows 30 feet (9 m). Yield: 25 pounds (11 kg) from 10 feet (3 m).

Beans, French (See page 70.)
Sow April to June; ready from 3 months; ¼ pint (125 ml) of seed sows 30 feet (9 m). Yield: 8 pounds (4 kg) from 10 feet (3 m).

Beans, runner (See page 71.)
Sow May, June; ready from 4 months; ¼ pint (125 ml) of seed sows 30 feet (9 m). Yield: 35 pounds (16 kg) from 10 feet (3 m).

Beetroot (See page 86.)
Sow March to June; ready in 2 months; 4 months for main crop; 1 ounce (30 g) of seed will sow 50 feet (15 m). Yield: 10 pounds (5 kg) from 10 feet (3 m) (main crop).

Broccoli, sprouting (See page 54.)
Sow April; plant May, June; ready from 4 months; 1 ounce (30 g) of seed produces more than 1,500 plants. Yield: 10 pounds (5 kg) from 10 feet (3 m).

Brussels sprouts (See pages 50 to 51.)
Sow March, April; plant May, June; ready from 6 months; 1 ounce (30 g) of seed produces more than 1,500 plants. Yield: 8 pounds (4 kg) from 10 feet (3 m).

Cabbages (See page 49.)
Sow March to July, planting out about two months after sowing; ready from 4½ months; 1 ounce (30 g) of seed produces up to 2,000 plants. Yield: 16 pounds (8 kg) from 10 feet (3 m); spring cabbage: 8 pounds (4 kg) from 10 feet (3 m).

Cabbages, Savoy (See page 49.)
Sow April, May; plant July; ready from 6 months; 1 ounce (30 g) of seed produces more than 1,500 plants. Yield: 16 pounds (8 kg) from 10 feet (3 m).

Carrots (See page 83.)
Sow March to July; ready from 5½ months (main crop); ½ ounce (15 g) of seed sows 50 feet (15 m). Yield: upwards of 3 pounds (1½ kg) from 10 feet (3 m), picked young; 8 pounds (4 kg) from 10 feet (3 m), main crop.

Cauliflowers (See page 52.)
Sow April; plant June, July; ready from 5 months; 1 ounce (30 g) of seed produces more than 1,500 plants. Yield: 12 pounds (6 kg) from 10 feet (3 m).

Cauliflowers, winter (See page 53.)
Sow April, May; plant June, July; ready from 5 months; 1 ounce (30 g) of seed produces more than 1,500 plants. Yield: 12 pounds (6 kg) from 10 feet (3 m).

Celery (See pages 62 to 63.)
Sow February to April in the greenhouse; plant June; ready from 7 months; there are 50,000 seeds in 1 ounce (30 g). Yield: 12 pounds (6 kg) from 10 feet (3 m).

Kale (See page 54.)
Sow April, May; plant June, July; ready from 5 months; 1 ounce (30 g) of seed produces 1,500 plants. Yield: 12 pounds (6 kg) from 10 feet (3 m).

Leeks (See page 75.)
Sow March, April; plant June; ready from 6 months; ½ ounce (15 g) of seed provides plants for a row of 60 feet (18 m). Yield: 10 pounds (5 kg) from 10 feet (3 m).

Lettuces (See page 43.)
Sow March to July; ready from 2 months; ½ ounce (15 g) of seed provides 2,000 plants. Yield: 12 lettuces from 10 feet (3 m).

Onions, from seed (See pages 76 to 77.)
Sow March, April; ready in 6½ months; ½ ounce (15 g) of seed sows 50 feet (15 m). Yield: 8 pounds (4 kg) from 10 feet (3 m).

Onions, from sets (See page 78.)
Plant March, April; ready in 5½ months; 1 pound (½ kg) of sets sows 50 feet (15 m). Yield: 9 pounds (4½ kg) from 10 feet (3 m).

Parsnips (See page 88.)
Sow February to April; ready from 7½ months; 1 ounce (30 g) of seed sows 50 feet (15 m). Yield: 10 pounds (5 kg) from 10 feet (3 m).

Peas (See page 68.)
Sow March to June; ready from 3½ months; 1 pint (500 ml) of seed sows 50 feet (15 m). Yield: 10 pounds (5 kg) from 10 feet (3 m).

Potatoes (See pages 91 to 92.)
Plant late February to May; ready from 3½ months; 7 pounds (3½ kg) of seed potatoes plant 60 feet (18 m). Yield: 10 pounds (5 kg) from 10 feet (3 m) (earlies); 15 pounds (7½ kg) from 10 feet (3 m) (main crop).

Radishes (See page 87.)
Sow March to August; ready in 1½ months; 1 ounce (30 g) of seed will sow 30 feet (9 m). Yield: 3 pounds (1½ kg) from 10 feet (3 m).

Shallots (See page 78.)
Plant February, March; ready from 6 months; 2 pounds (1 kg) of sets will plant 30 feet (15 m). Yield: 8 pounds (4 kg) from 10 feet (3 m).

Spinach (See page 56.)
Sow March to July; ready from 2½ months; 1 ounce (30 g) of seed sows 60 feet (18 m). Yield: 6 pounds (3 kg) from 10 feet (3 m).

Sweet corn (See page 67.)
Sow April, May in greenhouse; plant May, June; ready from 3 months; ½ ounce (15 g) of seed will sow 25 feet (7½ m). Yield: 12 cobs from 10 feet (3 m).

Swedes (See page 84.)
Sow May, June; ready from 5 months; ½ ounce (15 g) of seed sows 60 feet (18 m). Yield: 10 pounds (5 kg) from 10 feet (3 m).

Tomatoes, outdoors (See page 95.)
Sow February, March in greenhouse; plant May, June; ready from 5 months; ½ ounce (15 g) of seed could produce 1,000 plants. Yield: 4 pounds (2 kg) per plant.

Turnips (See page 84.)
Sow February to July; ready from 2½ months; ½ ounce (15 g) of seed sows 60 feet (18 m). Yield: 7 pounds (3½ kg) from 10 feet (3 m) (main crop).

By keeping a record of cultivation, manuring, sowing, planting, harvesting, weather and the incidence of pests and diseases, you will build up an invaluable reference work on how to cultivate your own garden to best advantage. It may also be a help to join the local allotment or horticultural society. There are model vegetable plots open to the public at The Royal Horticultural Society, Wisley, Surrey, and at The Northern Horticultural Society, Harrogate, Yorkshire. You can also join The National Society of Leisure Gardeners.

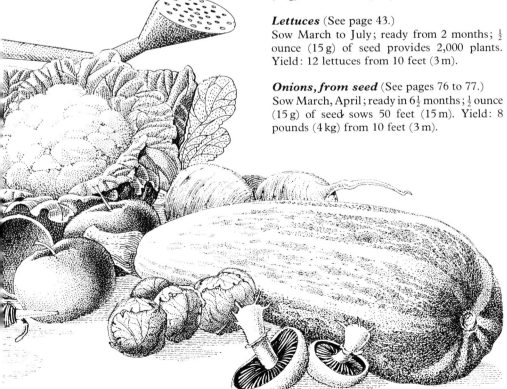

Salad Plants

*A*lmost all vegetables may be eaten raw, although most people prefer them cooked. With salad plants, however, the preference is reversed. Lettuce, endive and chicory may indeed be cooked, but they then lose their greatest appeal—their cool, refreshing crispness. To enjoy salad plants at their best they must be home-grown, for they cannot stand up to the disturbances and delays of marketing. When planning your salad beds do not only stick to the ubiquitous lettuce. Grow endive and chicory, too. American cress and corn salad are unusual and worthwhile salad plants, and the giant dandelion and celtuce (a lettuce on a celery-like stem) are easy to grow and very nutritious.

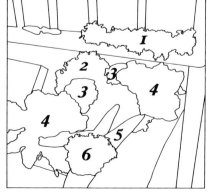

1 Watercress
2 Curly endive
3 Lettuce (crisp-hearted cabbage type)
4 Lettuce (soft, round cabbage type)
5 Chicory
6 Mustard

*L*ettuce

The Lettuce (*Lactuca sativa*) is firmly rooted in myth, even from the time of the immortals. Aphrodite laid Adonis, killed by the boar, on a bed of lettuce (not, of course, in the culinary sense). Some writers, from Pliny

in his *Natural History* to Beatrix Potter in *The Tale of the Flopsy Bunnies*, point to the soporific qualities of lettuce and others extol its health-giving properties. Even dragons, according to Aristotle, knew that its milky juice relieved the nausea that assailed them in the spring.

Suggestions about the origin of lettuce range from the Mediterranean to Siberia. It was being cultivated in England in the fourteenth century, but Catherine Parr, Henry VIII's sixth wife, preferred to send to Holland if she wanted a salad—as, in winter, the British still do. Today, it is feasible, however, to grow lettuce, outdoors or under glass, all year round.

Varieties

For summer. Soft, round, cabbage types: Tom Thumb, small, early maturing, for early sowing. Unrivalled, for sowing through spring and summer. Avondefiance, especially good for June and July sowing.

Crisp-hearted cabbage types: Webb's Wonderful, still the favourite, very large. Allow 18 inches (45 cm) between plants. Stands summer heat well. Avoncrisp, a crisp version of Avondefiance.

Cos types: Little Gem, early dwarf, excellent sweet flavour. Plant 5 inches (13 cm) apart. Lobjoit's Green Cos, large dark-green hearts.

Non-hearting types: Salad Bowl, a loose-leaved variety. Sow April to July and pick a few leaves from each plant as you want them. For winter. Cheshunt Early Giant and Kordaat.

For spring under glass. Unrivalled, Kloek, Knap and May King (cabbage types).

For spring in the open. Imperial Winter (cabbage) and Winter Density (Cos).

GROWING LETTUCE

Preparing the soil

Ideally, lettuce needs a rich, humus-laden soil that will hold moisture in summer. It also needs lime (pH 6·5), so test the soil. Lettuce, however, is often grown between rows of slower-growing vegetables or as a catch crop, using ground before or after another crop.

Sowing and transplanting

Lettuce can be sown in seed boxes or beds and the seedlings transplanted about a month later when they are not more than 1 inch (2 cm) high. Handle them with the utmost tenderness, for a damaged seedling is particularly menaced by grey mould. In spring and summer, you can sow lettuce in

½-inch (1 cm) drills in the open and thin the plants by stages until they are finally 10 to 12 inches (25 to 30 cm) apart, depending on the variety and the soil and weather you are blessed with. To ensure a steady supply of lettuce and to avoid a glut, sow little and often.

The year's work

Winter lettuce: sow Cheshunt Early Giant or Kordaat in a frame from early September. Transplant the seedlings to the greenhouse; the temperature must not fall below 50°F (10°C). Plant the seedlings in rows 6 inches (15 cm) apart, staggering them at 16-inch (40 cm) intervals. Keep the plants moist and well ventilated. The lettuces should be ready to harvest about three months after transplanting.

Early spring lettuce: begin sowing Unrivalled, Kloek, Knap or May King, which are all cabbage types, in a frame in early October. Transplant the seedlings to cloches or frames from mid-December. Plant the seedlings 12 inches (30 cm) apart each way. The lettuces will be ready to harvest in about April.

Spring lettuce: in late August or early September sow Imperial Winter, a cabbage type, and Winter Density, a Cos. The 1-inch (2 cm) drills should be 12 inches (30 cm) apart. Thin the plants a little in October

and again several times in the spring, until they are eventually 10 to 12 inches (25 to 30 cm) apart. Harvesting will begin in April/May.

Summer lettuce: in warmer areas begin sowing in March, elsewhere in April, and continue every fortnight or three weeks until July. Allow about 10 inches (25 cm) between the transplanted or thinned plants in the row. The rows must be 12 inches (30 cm) apart.

Early autumn and early winter lettuce: sow May King out of doors at the beginning of August. Transplant the seedlings under cloches or frames 12 inches (30 cm) apart each way.

Harvesting

Pull the lettuces out with the roots. Never let the plants go to seed in the rows. Remove them as soon as they begin to bolt.

Pests and diseases

Millipedes attack the roots of young plants, which then wilt. The best way to trap millipedes is to punch holes in the bottoms and sides of old tin cans and fit them with wire handles. Fill the cans with potato peelings and bury them upright alongside the lettuces, leaving the handles above the ground. Lift up the cans every few days and destroy the contents. Millipedes, which curl up when they are disturbed, are sluggish vegetarians and are not to be confused with the livelier carnivorous centipedes, which are good to have around.

Slugs are a menace. Use methiocarb or metaldehyde baits to destroy them.

To prevent grey mould on stems and leaves, which indicates an attack by the fungus botrytis, spray with thiram.

Whitish powder on the underside of the leaves is the downy mildew fungus. Spray with thiram.

Chicory

Chicory (*Cichorium Intybus*) is one of the simplest salad plants to grow, as well as one of the most desirable. It is neither the root nor the leaves which are eaten, but the blanched chicons, which are produced by forcing the roots in darkness and warmth.

Varieties

Witloof (Brussels chicory) is the one to grow for the chicons. There is another continental variety, Pain de Sucre (Sugar Loaf), which, like lettuce, does not require blanching. Sow Pain de Sucre from June to July. Thin the plants out to 15 inches (38 cm) apart.

Endive

The origin of endive (*Cichorium Endivia*) is highly disputed. Certainly the Greeks and Romans knew it. In Britain, in the seventeenth century, Culpeper said: "Endive is available for the faintings, swooning and passions of the heart. It cannot be used amiss."

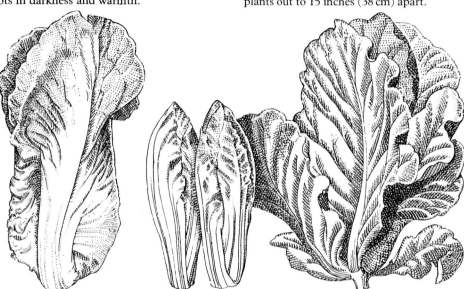

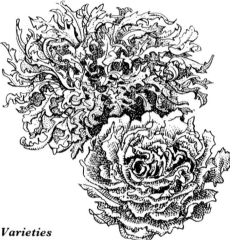

Varieties

Moss Curled, for late summer cropping. Batavian Broad-leaved, a type that looks more like a lettuce, for autumn and winter cropping.

GROWING CHICORY

Preparing the soil

Choose a part of the garden well manured and cultivated for a previous crop, such as leeks or celery, since newly manured land can cause forking of the roots.

Sowing

June. Sow the seeds early in June in the north and in the middle of June in the south. With earlier sowing the plants may run to seed in the warm weather. Sow in ½-inch (1 cm) drills 12 inches (30 cm) apart, and thin the seedlings out to 10 inches (25 cm) apart.

The year's work

Hoe to kill weeds, and water in dry weather. A peat mulch will help to keep the soil moist and to suppress weeds.

Harvesting

October/November. To begin, carefully dig up a few roots for forcing. Cut off the tops just above the crown. Plant the roots close together in a box of loamy soil with the

crowns of the roots at soil level. Water and cover with another box. The chicons must

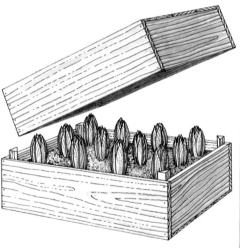

grow in total darkness if they are not to be bitter. Place the box in a greenhouse or even in a kitchen cupboard where the temperature is not less than 50°F (10°C). In four weeks or so the chicons will be about 6 to 8 inches (15 to 20 cm) long and ready for harvesting. If you break the chicons off carefully, instead of cutting them, a second crop of chicons will appear, smaller and looser, but just as tasty.

In November, when the foliage of the remaining plants has died back, dig up the roots and trim and store them in sand in a cool but frostproof room. Remove and force as many as you want every three or four weeks. Never pick the chicons until you need them. After even an hour in the light they will become limp.

Pests and diseases

Fairly trouble free.

GROWING ENDIVE

Preparing the soil

Like most salad vegetables, endive needs a soil rich in humus that will not dry out easily. In a hot summer, endive soon runs to seed, so plant it in a slightly shaded spot in the garden and do not sow too early.

Sowing

From late June. It is best not to transplant endive, so, having got the soil to a fine tilth, sow the seed of the curled varieties thinly in ½-inch (1 cm) drills 14 inches (35 cm) apart. Thin the plants out to 12 inches (30 cm) apart. Another sowing can be made three weeks later, and yet another sowing—of the hardier Batavian type—in August.

The year's work

Hoe between the rows and keep the soil moist, occasionally using weak liquid manure. In October, put the late-sown plants under cloches so that you will have endive until the end of the year.

Harvesting

October onwards. Curly endive is bitter if it is not blanched. Begin blanching three to four months after sowing. Put a large flowerpot (with the hole covered) over the plant, or replant the endive in moist soil in a pot or box and put it in a dark cellar or shed. In three weeks or more it will be creamy coloured and crisp, the bitterness gone. Whichever way you blanch, the leaves must be dry when you begin or they will rot. To blanch Batavian endive tie the leaves together lightly. This prevents the light reaching the inner leaves.

Pests and diseases

Fairly trouble free.

Mustard and cress

Man was eating mustard (*Sinapis alba* and *Brassica nigra*) seeds before 10000 BC. Cress (*Lepidium sativum*), the junior partner in the team, has the pepperwort as its ancestor and the Romans among its devotees.

American Cress

Similar in flavour but easier to grow than watercress, American cress (*Barbarea praecox*) also needs shade and tolerates considerable dampness—a welcome change from most garden plants.

Corn salad

Corn salad (*Valerianella Locusta*), also known as lamb's lettuce, grows wild in cornfields. The hardiness of the wild plant survives in the cultivated varieties, making it an ideal winter substitute for lettuce.

GROWING MUSTARD AND CRESS

In winter, sow cress indoors. Fill a small box with moist soil or bulb fibre and scatter the seeds over the soil. Press the seeds down with your hand. Cover the box with paper until the seeds germinate.

Mustard germinates faster than cress. Sow it in the same way four days later, either over the cress or in a separate box.

Sow about every fortnight and cut with scissors 15 to 20 days later.

From spring to September sow out of doors in exactly the same way.

GROWING AMERICAN CRESS

Fork plenty of organic material lightly into the soil. Firm the soil and rake it to a fine tilth. Sow the seeds every three weeks from April to August. Sow thinly in ½-inch (1 cm) drills, 10 inches (25 cm) apart. Germination takes about three weeks. When the plants are big enough to handle, thin them out to 6 inches (15 cm) apart.

Cut the cress eight to ten weeks after sowing. Cut only the young, tender shoots. To prolong the crop into winter, cover the late-sown rows with cloches.

GROWING CORN SALAD

Plant corn salad in a sunny, humus-rich plot which has been used for a previous crop. Fork the soil over lightly, firm it and rake it to a fine tilth.

Sow the seeds in mid-August and mid-September in drills 1 inch (2 cm) deep and 10 inches (25 cm) apart. Thin the seedlings at the three-leaf stage to 6 inches (15 cm) apart. Use cloches or straw to protect the plants in winter.

Harvest a leaf or two from each mature plant as you need them.

Dandelion

In Britain, the dandelion (*Taraxacum officinale*) is almost universally regarded as an intolerable weed. Not so on the Continent, where excellent strains of dandelion have been cultivated.

Watercress

Although watercress (*Nasturtium officinale*) is an aquatic plant, you can grow it without running water. It is a good way to make use of a dank, shady part of the garden.

Celtuce

Celtuce (*Lactuca sativa var. angustana*) is a lettuce on a stem. It came to Europe from the Far East by way of America. The leaves and the stem, or heart, may be eaten.

 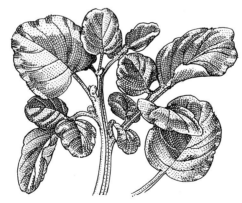 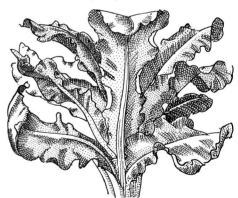

GROWING DANDELIONS

Dandelions will grow in any well-drained corner of the garden. For succulence, however, give them rich soil. Sow in April in shallow drills 12 inches (30 cm) apart. Thin the plants to 8 inches (20 cm) apart. Later, when the plants mature, be sure to cut off all the flower heads. Harvest in November. Carefully lift the roots, trim them and blanch a few of them as you would chicory. They will be ready in a fortnight if kept in a temperature of about 60°F (16°C). Store the remaining roots in sand until you are ready to blanch them.

GROWING WATERCRESS

Dig a trench 24 inches (60 cm) wide and 12 inches (30 cm) deep. At the bottom put 6 inches (15 cm) of decayed manure covered by 3 inches (8 cm) of soil. Make it firm and wet it well. Plant in early summer. Buy a bunch or two of healthy looking watercress and plant those cuttings which have small roots on them. Set them 4 inches (10 cm) apart each way. Water assiduously. As they grow, pinch out the leading shoots to make them bushy. Cut them right back if they start to flower. Watercress can also be raised from seed sown in spring.

GROWING CELTUCE

Celtuce requires a soil that has had plenty of organic manure forked in. Firm the soil and then rake it. Sow from spring to early July at fortnightly intervals in shallow drills 18 inches (45 cm) apart. Thin the seedlings, when they are 2 inches (5 cm) high, to 12 inches (30 cm) apart. Water the plants well. They will be tough if kept short of water. Hoe well between the rows to keep them free of weeds. Harvest the leaves as they form. The stems will be ready to eat in less than three months from sowing.

Brassicas

Brassicas are the backbone of many vegetable gardens. Three of them—Brussels sprouts, kale and cabbage—might indeed have been created for the climate of Britain and northern Europe, although in fact they are immigrants, not natives. These three need plenty of rain and they can brave northern winters.

Do not be alarmed by the seemingly fearsome pests and diseases which attack brassicas, for they are most likely to bring disaster to undernourished plants struggling to survive in poor soil. The remedy is in the gardener's hands. Economies should not be made where the fertility of the soil is at stake. All the brassicas, even kale, hardiest of them all, appreciate a rich, fertile soil which has been well manured for a previous crop.

Brussels sprouts are universally enjoyed in Britain. Their popularity is even more deserved since the introduction of many new varieties, including F_1 hybrids, which have almost ousted the old favourites. Kale, on the other hand, is grown only as an insurance against the worst winters, except in Scotland, where it is truly appreciated.

The cabbage, the chief of the brassica tribe, is still suffering unfairly from its past reputation. Older generations find it hard to forget the evil smell and unpleasant taste of the winter cabbages, savoys and tough spring greens of their childhoods. But the improvement in cabbage over the past two decades has been even more remarkable than in Brussels sprouts. Newer varieties are more subtle in flavour. It is a pleasant change to be able to turn what is usually a complaint into a compliment by saying that the taste is better because there is less of it. Nevertheless, those who still find cabbage overpowering should grow the milder Chinese cabbage.

The cauliflower did not always have its present appearance. When it was first cultivated in Britain over two centuries ago, its head, when full grown, was no bigger than a golf ball. The modern, improved cauliflower, the real favourite among brassicas, is the result of much painstaking work over the years. The cauliflower does not, however, take kindly to northern climates. The alternative is sprouting broccoli: the white and purple varieties are harvested in winter and spring, and the delectable green-sprouting calabrese is harvested in late summer and autumn. The real cauliflower enthusiast might like to grow star broccoli. Although perennial it is best to replace the plants every three years. Cultivated in the same way as other sprouting broccoli, each plant will produce six to twelve cauliflowers a year, if generously fed.

1 Purple sprouting broccoli
2 Chinese cabbage
3 Red cabbage
4 Curly kale
5 Cauliflowers
6 Winter cabbage
7 Brussels sprouts
8 Savoy

BRASSICAS
Preparing the soil

The normal three-year rotation of crops in the vegetable garden (see page 20) ensures that brassicas are planted where peas and beans grew the previous year. If, as the rotation plan provides, the bed was well manured for the peas and beans, no further manure or compost is needed for the brassicas. The peas and beans will, indeed, have left behind in their roots some of the nitrogen they themselves produced. However, a general fertilizer, 2 ounces to the square yard (60 g to 1 sq m), can be hoed in before transplanting.

If the cabbage patch was not manured for a previous crop, manure and compost will have to be provided. Brassicas must be fed well. Brussels sprouts need more feeding than cabbages, and cauliflowers are positively greedy. At the same time they must not be given too much nitrogen, which makes them flabby and unable to survive the winter.

Brassicas—especially Brussels sprouts and cauliflowers—need a firm soil, so the plot should be dug months in advance, giving the soil time to settle.

Lime is important. An acid soil discourages growth and encourages that scourge of brassicas, club root—aim at pH 6·5 to 6·8. It is also for the same reason—to keep club root at bay—that brassicas are not grown on the same piece of land more than one year in three. Land heavily infected by club root must not be planted with brassicas for seven years. (See page 55.)

Seedbeds for brassicas

Brassicas are usually raised in outdoor seedbeds and transplanted. The only exceptions are certain varieties of kale. A highly fertile soil is required to give the plants a good start in life. The ideal would be to cover the bed, after levelling and raking it, with thoroughly mature, sifted compost. Tread over this to make it firm and rake it lightly. Make shallow drills with a stick, 6 inches (15 cm) apart, and sow the

seeds thinly. Cover them with a scattering of compost and firm the bed with the head of the rake. This is a better method than

tramping over the bed and then having to rake lightly again. Always mark both ends

of the rows. Do not use empty seed packets on a piece of stick; they will probably disappear even before the seeds have germinated. Buy wooden labels or collect ice-lolly sticks and, with an indelible pencil,

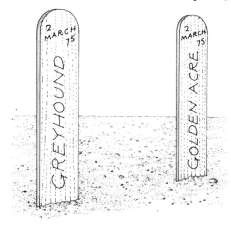

write on them the name of the variety and the date of sowing. Keep the seedbed moist, using a watering can with a fine rose.

The stage at which cabbage and Brussels sprouts should be transplanted is comparatively flexible. The sooner cauliflowers are in their permanent beds, however, the better. Water the seedbed well the day before you intend to transplant.

Transplanting

If practicable the rows should run north to south to get all possible sun. Mark out the rows with string for a straight line. With a dibber or trowel make holes ready to receive the plants, and if the soil is dry fill the holes with water. If you can arrange it, wait until late in the day to do the transplanting, especially on sunny days, to

minimize the plants' suffering; for them it is a major operation.

Lift the plants from the seedbed with as much soil as you can. Handle only a dozen plants at a time so as not to keep them out

of the ground too long. Lower each plant into its hole. With cabbages, the leaves at the base of the stem go down to soil level. Cauliflowers, however, must not be planted

any deeper than they were in the seedbed. Push the dibber or trowel into the soil alongside the plant—about 1 inch (2 cm) away—and press against it to make the soil firm. Or firm the soil around the plant with your hands, the dibber or the handle of the trowel. Brassicas must be planted firmly. Then water the row. Water gently or you will wash the plants away.

In a few days the plants should perk up.

Planting distances and the year's work are dealt with under each type of brassica.

Cabbage

In childhood, cabbage (*Brassica oleracea var. capitata*) was something that one was always being told to eat up. Nothing changes. The Emperor Tiberius reprimanded his son Drusus for not eating his greens.

The Greeks looked upon cabbage both as a means of preventing drunkenness and as a cure for a hangover. The Romans thought highly of it as a medicine, although they did not know that it is, indeed, rich in sulphur and nitrogen. Cabbage seems to go back in prehistory to the eastern Mediterranean and Asia Minor. The Romans brought it northwards, and in Britain in the Middle Ages monks were growing it in their kitchen gardens. The earliest cabbages were non-heading. Headed varieties turned up in the thirteenth century, hard, round-headed types in the sixteenth century and pointed heads in the eighteenth century. Although cabbage is too often badly cooked, it is an indispensable vegetable.

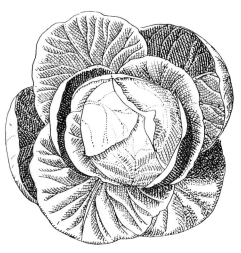
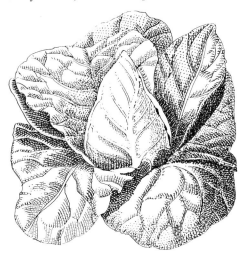

Summer varieties
For spring sowing: Golden Acre, early maturing, medium-sized solid heads. May Star (F$_1$), medium-sized ballhead. Greyhound, firm, pointed hearts with few outside leaves, or the newer Greyhound-type F$_1$ hybrid, Hispi.

The year's work
Sow the seed in early March under cloches or in late March/early April out of doors. Thin the seedlings carefully to 1 inch (2 cm) apart when they are large enough to handle. They are ready to leave the seedbed in May or early June, when the plants are about 4 inches (10 cm) in height. If necessary they could stay longer in the seedbed, but later transplanting sets them back. Plant 18 inches (45 cm) apart in rows also 18 inches (45 cm) apart.

Hoe, but carefully, since cabbages hate disturbance. When they have grown large enough the plants themselves will smother the weeds. Never let them get dry. And watch out for pests and diseases. (See page 55.)

Autumn and winter varieties
To sow in early summer: Winnigstadt, ready August onwards. Vienna Baby Head (Fillgap). Winter White, October/November. Autumn Supreme. Christmas Drumhead.

Savoys (*Brassica oleracea* var. *bullata sub-auda*): Best of All. Ormskirk Rearguard.

The year's work
Sow the seeds out of doors in shallow drills in late April or May for autumn and winter cabbages. Use a watering can with a fine rose and water the seedbed well. In July, plant out the seedlings 18 inches (45 cm) apart in rows 24 inches (60 cm) apart.

Firm the plants well with your hands or the dibber. Water them thoroughly but gently or, if the weather is very dry, fill the dibber holes with water before planting. Hoe lightly between the rows to keep down the weeds, being careful not to damage the young plants.

Savoys are sown in May and planted out in July or early August, 24 inches (60 cm) apart each way.

The autumn cabbages will be ready for harvesting from August and the winter varieties from late October or November.

Spring varieties
For late summer sowing: Harbinger, very early, small, pointed hearts. Flower of Spring, a little later, but a larger, delicious heart. Wheeler's Imperial, mild, tender, small heads. Early Durham (Unwin's Foremost), medium-sized, dark-green hearts, well flavoured.

The year's work
Because spring cabbages mature quickly after the worst of the winter weather is over, they never grow as large or as coarse as winter cabbages. Grow them in a sheltered part of the garden which had been well manured for a previous crop.

Sow the seeds thinly (in cold areas at the end of July, in warm areas early in August), in shallow drills 6 inches (15 cm) apart. Keep the seedbed moist.

Transplant the seedlings into moist soil in September or October, 12 to 16 inches (30 to 40 cm) apart in rows 18 inches (45 cm) apart.

For a month after planting out, hoe between the rows. From February on, when growth begins, hoe in 2 ounces to the square yard (60 g to 1 sq m) of nitro-chalk or sulphate of ammonia.

Chinese cabbage

Chinese cabbage (*Brassica pekinensis*) does not look like cabbage—it suggests rather an aristocratic Cos lettuce—and, praise be, it

does not smell like cabbage when it is cooking. Chinese cabbage has been known in China and parts of Asia since the fifth century. Europe had to wait until the middle of the nineteenth century for it to arrive and only now is it becoming appreciated for its delicate flavour, either cooked or raw in salads. Chinese cabbage is easy to grow as long as it is not sown too early (it will bolt) and is not transplanted.

Confusingly, there is another vegetable claiming the names of "cabbage" and "Chinese"—*Brassica chinensis*—but it is encountered more frequently in Chinese restaurants than in Western gardens. It does not heart, but grows like spinach, for which it can be regarded as a hardy substitute.

Varieties
Michihli, a large, tall head. Sampan (F_1), large and solid and less prone to bolting. Nagaoka (F_1), solid and cylindrical.

GROWING CHINESE CABBAGE
Preparing the soil
Unless it has a humus-laden, moisture-holding soil and a little bit of shade, Chinese cabbage is liable to bolt in high summer.

Sowing
July onwards. Because it quickly goes to seed after hearting up, sow a little and often, preferably not before July. The seeds are quite large and are planted 4 inches (10 cm) apart in ½-inch (1 cm) drills, with 12 to 18 inches (30 to 45 cm) between rows. Thin to 8 inches (20 cm) apart.

The year's work
Never let Chinese cabbage go short of water. When they begin hearting tie the leaves together with raffia.

Harvesting
Chinese cabbages grow quickly and may be ready only nine weeks after sowing. Pick

them, either as a salad vegetable or to cook, as soon as they are well hearted. Once they bolt they are useless except, of course, for compost.

Red cabbage

Of all the cabbages the red cabbage is the difficult one. To be at its best it needs a long growing season, which involves over-wintering.

Varieties
Niggerhead, dark red, dwarf, is delicious cooked. Blood Red, earlier and larger, good for pickling.

GROWING RED CABBAGE
The year's work
Sow the seeds in August or early September in a well-firmed and lightly raked seedbed in shallow drills 6 inches (15 cm) apart. Thin the seedlings in the seedbed.

A general fertilizer can be hoed in along the row before planting—2 ounces to the square yard (60 g to 1 sq m). In April, when the seedlings are about 4 inches (10 cm) high, plant them out 24 inches (60 cm) apart each way. Plant firmly or they will not grow large, solid heads.

In May, a handful of sulphate of ammonia can be scattered around each plant to encourage them for harvesting in the autumn.

Brussels sprouts

Belgium can lay greater claim to Brussels sprouts (*Brassica oleracea* var. *bullata gemmifera*) than any other country. The Belgians

seem to think they got them from the Romans, although the sprouts mentioned by Pliny may have been broccoli. It can, however, be reasonably assumed that Brussels sprouts have been growing in Belgium for eight centuries, but it was not until early in the nineteenth century that they came to Britain. It is a pity that the scorn the Belgians felt for all but the smallest sprouts did not come with them. It has taken the British two centuries even to begin to learn that lesson. But properly grown (solid), picked at the right moment (when small) and correctly cooked (not overcooked), Brussels sprouts are one of the great vegetables of autumn and winter.

Varieties
Many of the older favourites have been superseded by F_1 hybrids. Since more, and sometimes better, hybrids appear each year it is sensible to try new varieties from time to time.

Current F_1 hybrids include: Jade Cross, early, dark green, of excellent flavour. Peer Gynt, fairly dwarf, with medium-sized buttons. Prince Askold, semi-tall, late, bearing a heavy crop of very solid sprouts.

Among the non-hybrids worth trying are: Roodnerf Stiekema Early, small, solid buttons. Roodnerf Seven Hills, late, dark green, small to medium buttons. Red, a variety with smallish sprouts the colour of red cabbage and fine flavour. And, if you can find it, the excellent small French variety, Noisette.

GROWING BRUSSELS SPROUTS
Preparing the soil

While Brussels sprouts must have a fertile soil, it is better if the soil has been well manured for a previous crop. Above all, if

they are to produce the desired solid buttons, Brussels sprouts need a firm soil in which to anchor themselves. A fairly heavy soil works for the gardener here. A light, sandy soil will make it difficult to get the vital firmness.

Dig as far ahead as possible to let the soil settle.

Do not forget that Brussels sprouts have the brassicas' need for lime (pH 6·5 to 6·8).

Sowing

February, March/April. Brussels sprouts have a long growing season and need to be sown earlier than cabbage. Start in February in a frame, or out of doors mid-March to April in the kind of seedbed suggested for brassicas generally. (See page 47.) Sow in drills ½ inch (1 cm) deep and 10 inches (25 cm) apart.

Pea guards can be used to protect the growing seedlings, for which sparrows have an irritating weakness.

Planting

May/June. As early as the weather allows, in May or early June, get the plants into the well-firmed bed to settle down to the long growth to maturity.

Choose a wet day and, if possible, plant in the evening to help the seedlings make a quick recovery. Firm the soil around each plant with your hands or with a dibber. Firm planting helps to produce tight, firm sprouts.

Planting distances vary with the size and vigour of the variety—24 to 36 inches (60 to 90 cm) each way. Do not skimp on space —for their sakes and for yours when you come to pick among them on cold, wet winter days. The space is not wasted because, while the sprout plants are still small, quick-growing crops can be planted between the rows.

The year's work

Hoe and water if necessary. Brussels sprouts should not be pushed ahead with nitrogenous fertilizers; they have to grow hard to face the winter. In autumn, go along the

rows taking off yellowing leaves, firming the soil around the stem of each plant and drawing more soil around it to give support against the wind. Tall-growing varieties should be staked; it is disheartening to see a row flattened in a winter gale.

Even more infuriating is damage by birds in country gardens. They play havoc among much greenstuff in winter, but find Brussels sprouts particularly attractive. Wood-

pigeons do most damage and can devastate rows of sprouts in a few days. The remedy is fairly simple: a hood of wire or plastic netting will scare off the birds even though it does not cover the sprouts themselves, which can still be easily picked. The stakes to which the netting is fixed also act as support for the plants.

Harvesting

September to March. Pick the sprouts from the bottom of the stem as they get big enough. They can (lazily) be snapped off, but cutting causes less damage.

Cauliflower

To the gardener, cauliflowers (*Brassica oleracea var. botrytis cauliflora*) and heading broccoli are the same thing, but heading broccoli and sprouting broccoli are two different things altogether. The confusion is less if they are divided into summer cauliflowers, winter cauliflowers (which are heading broccoli) and sprouting broccoli (which is primarily grown for its sprouts and not for any head it may form). The sprouting broccoli is easy to

grow, summer cauliflowers less so, being not only greedy, but often temperamental, and winter cauliflowers are best forgotten in the colder parts of the country. On the other hand, producing a cauliflower with a flawless white curd is one of the really satisfying achievements of amateur vegetable growing.

The cauliflower is another brassica of antiquity, with a history going back thousands of years in Syria, Turkey and Egypt. It was introduced into Spain in the twelfth century, and appeared in England and France around the end of the sixteenth century.

It is an immensely popular vegetable—hence all the trouble taken to have it on sale all year round. There are, however, critics. Mark Twain dubbed it "a cabbage with a college education", and that most respected of English cookery writers, Elizabeth David, damns it for its "normal coarse flavour and soggy texture" and consigns it to soup.

Cauliflower devotees with a greenhouse and a warm garden can have summer cauliflowers from May to November, followed by winter cauliflowers from January to May. Gardeners labouring in a cold climate can gamble on an unusually mild winter, or grow sprouting broccoli instead.

Varieties

Summer cauliflowers to harvest in May/June/ July: All the Year Round. Snowball. Mechelse Classic.

GROWING CAULIFLOWER
The year's work

In September, sow the seeds thinly in a moist, firm seedbed. In October, as soon as the first leaves are formed, transplant the seedlings to a frame. Plant them 1 inch (2

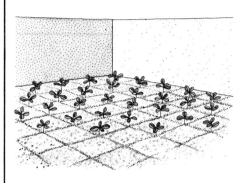

cm) apart. Harden off in spring in readiness for planting out in April.

Cauliflowers, if they are to produce large, compact heads, must be planted in humus-rich soil. Shortly before transplanting, hoe in a general fertilizer, 2 ounces to the square yard (60 g to 1 sq m). Cauliflowers, like all brassicas, require lime (pH 6·5 to 6·8). Lift the seedlings from the seedbed with as much soil as possible and plant them 24 inches (60 cm) apart, with the same distance between rows.

Reject all "blind" seedlings—those which have produced nothing more than the two seed leaves. It is pointless to plant them—they are barren.

Cauliflowers are fussy about being transplanted and if not handled with care produce small, premature buttons in lieu of heads. They should be replanted as quickly as possible and no deeper than they were in the frame. Their roots must be made firm if they are to make firm heads,

and they must be watered. As they grow they must never be short of moisture.

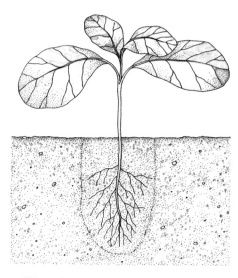

When the curds form, bend a few leaves over them to protect them from the sun. If

too many cauliflowers are ready for harvesting at the same time do not leave them in the garden to bolt. Lift them along with their roots, shake off the excess soil and hang them upside down indoors in a cool place and spray them regularly with water.

These varieties can also be sown in gentle heat, 55°F (13°C), in a greenhouse, in January and February. Prick out into frames and harden off for planting out in May and early June.

Autumn Cauliflower

Autumn cauliflowers to harvest from August to November: All the Year Round, living up to its name (August/September heading). Bondi (September heading). Kangaroo (September/October heading). South Pacific (October/November heading). The last three are among the increasingly popular Australian dwarf varieties.

The year's work

No sowings should be made out of doors until the pleasanter days of April. Sow the seeds in brassica-type seedbeds (see page 48) in shallow drills 6 inches (15 cm) apart. Cover them with a sifting of compost and firm the bed. If the weather is dry, keep the seedbed moist, using a watering can with a fine rose. Transplant the seedlings in late June to July—they must not be planted any deeper than they were in the seedbed—spacing the young plants 24 to 30 inches (60 to 75 cm) apart each way.

In late summer it is a sensible precaution to draw soil around the stems of the cauliflowers for support; like other brassicas they resent being rocked in the wind.

Winter Cauliflower

Winter cauliflowers (heading broccoli) to harvest from January to June: Superb Early White, for warm areas only (January/February heading). Both English Winter St George (March/April heading) and English Winter Late Queen (May/June heading) are reliable and extremely hardy varieties, which produce firm white heads.

The year's work

Sow seeds from mid-April to mid-May, depending on the variety. Transplant 24 inches (60 cm) apart each way. Water in dry weather and add a mulch of compost.

To help prevent winter cauliflowers from being killed by severe frost, heel them over before November so that they spend the winter facing north. (It is the sudden thawing of the frozen plant by direct sunlight which does the damage. If it faces north the plant thaws out gradually.)

To heel a plant over, move some soil away from the plant on its north side with a trowel. Push the plant over, carefully, and draw soil against its stem on the opposite side to hold it down, facing north. Firm the soil. As curds develop, break some leaves over them to protect them.

Soil deficiencies and how they affect cauliflowers

The importance of the elements in the soil to the proper growth of a plant cannot be overemphasized, and few vegetables demonstrate more vividly than cauliflowers when they are short of either major or trace elements.

A deficiency of the trace element molybdenum causes an extraordinary malformation of the leaves called whiptail. It is most likely to occur on acid soils in dry weather. The plant may go blind (that is, lose its growing points) and the curds may be non-existent or minute. Yet molybdenum makes up only 0·2 to 5 parts in a million in most soils in Britain. A couple of ounces of ammonium molybdate to the acre (60 g to ½ ha) would probably remedy the deficiency if such a small dressing were practicable. Instead, to make the molybdenum in the soil available to the plant, apply lime to bring the soil near to pH 7, which is approaching a neutral—neither acid nor alkaline—soil.

Boron is another vital trace element. Lacking it, cauliflowers grow small curds which are bitter, and both curd and flower stems turn brown. Boron deficiency can be corrected by watering the soil with a borax solution, using the finest of roses on the watering can. Use ½ ounce (15 g) of borax in ½ gallon (2 litres) of water to treat 30 square yards (25 sq m). Too much borax can make the soil toxic. There are other reasons for the browning of cauliflowers, especially winter cauliflowers; they are currently the subject of an extensive research study.

Starved of magnesium, the leaves of cauliflowers turn yellow, red or purple in patches (magnesium, one of the vital elements in the soil, is necessary to produce chlorophyll, the substance which makes plants green). Growth is poor and the plants become more liable to downy mildew. Signs of magnesium deficiency are frequently seen in highly cultivated gardens. It is not that magnesium is missing from the soil, but it has been made unavailable to the plant because other elements have been thrown out of balance. This may be the gardener's fault in applying inorganic fertilizers containing too much potash over a period of years. By using farmyard manure, or compost, or digging in green manure, that particular trouble can be avoided.

A potassium deficiency, causing yellowing of cauliflowers and poor curds, can follow heavy-handed nitrogenous manuring, throwing the nitrogen/potassium ratio in the soil out of balance.

These problems must not be regarded as diseases of cauliflowers, which are subject to enough already. They are mineral deficiencies which will affect many plants, although not always as spectacularly.

Calabrese

It would be an extravagance bordering on the criminal to buy frozen broccoli spears when calabrese (*Brassica oleracea* var. *Italica*) is so easy to grow. Unfortunately, it is not as hardy as purple or white sprouting broccoli; its

season will generally be over by October.

After the main cauliflower-like head has been cut, numerous side shoots sprout and grow smaller heads. These spears are superior in flavour to the first head.

Varieties

Express Corona (F_1) matures two months after planting and produces many side shoots over a period of weeks. Green Comet (F_1) matures even more quickly, but concentrates on a larger head and few side shoots. Italian Sprouting, cropping from September, is of particularly good flavour.

GROWING CALABRESE
Sowing
April. Calabrese needs the same kind of good, firm soil as other brassicas. Sow in the seedbed in early April, thinning the seedlings as soon as possible. Never allow them to get crowded before transplanting.

Planting
Late May. When the seedlings are 3 inches (8 cm) high they are ready for planting out, 20 inches (50 cm) apart in rows 24 inches (60 cm) apart. Plant firmly. Plant out on a showery day and, if necessary, continue watering until the plants have settled down.

The year's work
In the short growing season keep the plants moist and weed free.

Harvesting
July/September. Cut the centre head before it flowers. Afterwards spread a handful of general fertilizer around the plant. Side shoots begin to appear a couple of weeks later. Harvest the side shoots with 4 to 6 inches (10 to 15 cm) of stem.

White and Purple Sprouting Broccoli

The sprouting broccolis (*Brassica oleracea* var. *botrytis cymosa*) are among the most satisfying vegetables to grow, because the home-grown shoots are so much better in flavour than those grown commercially.

Calabrese is for autumn, but white sprouting broccoli and the even hardier purple sprouting

broccoli are for late winter through spring. Their flavour is not as fine as calabrese, but they are doubly welcome at that time of the year. The white sprouting varieties have a more marked cauliflower flavour.

Varieties
Early White Sprouting, very hardy, and Late White Sprouting.

Early Purple Sprouting and Late Purple Sprouting, very prolific and the best to grow if only one type is used. Between them they will crop from February to May.

GROWING BROCCOLI
Sowing
April. Sow thinly in April in the previously prepared seedbed. (See page 48.)

Planting
May/June. When the seedlings are 4 inches (10 cm) high they can be transplanted. Leave 24 inches (60 cm) between plants and 30 inches (75 cm) between rows. Plant firmly, and water well if the weather is dry at planting time.

The year's work
It saves a lot of weeding time if a mulch is put down between the rows in summer. Give a strawy mulch in winter. Stake firmly against winter winds.

Harvesting
February/May. Sprouting begins in February, or even in January with early varieties in favoured gardens. Cut the centre head first and keep cutting the side shoots young, or they will run to seed and exhaust the plant. Constant cutting produces more shoots. The plants will seed, in the course of nature, in May or June.

Kale

Kale (*Brassica oleracea* var. *acephala*) is a cabbage without a solid heart or head. It is either flat-leaved or curly leaved. Healthy, health-giving and hardy beyond belief, kale would be the ideal winter green if only its

flavour matched its other qualities. In the first millennium AD it was the staple of the peasants' diet in northern Europe. In Holland, its name is *boerenkool* (peasants' cabbage). In Scotland, *kail* soup is a traditional Highland dish.

Varieties
Hungry Gap and the even hardier Thousand-headed are the best of the plain-leaved varieties. The best of the curly types is Green-curled Dwarf. A new hardy cross, Pentland Brig, produces shoots and flower heads like sprouting broccoli.

GROWING KALE
The year's work
Kale, like all brassicas, requires a soil that has been well manured for a previous crop. It must not lack lime (pH 6·5 to 6·8).

Sow the curly leaved variety thinly in a seedbed in April or May, in 1-inch (2 cm) drills 10 inches (25 cm) apart. Plant out the seedlings in June or July, 18 inches (45 cm) apart each way. Choose a day when the soil is moist or water the ground before planting. Plant firmly. As the plants grow, firm the soil around them to prevent them from falling over in the wind. Hoe regularly to keep down weeds.

Sow the plain-leaved varieties thinly in early July, in the plot where they are to grow, in rows 18 inches (45 cm) apart. These varieties do not suffer transplanting well. Eventually thin the plants to 18 inches (45 cm) apart.

Harvesting
Kale is grown to fill the gap when other winter vegetables are scarce in January or February. Harvest when the leaves are young and tender.

Brassica pests and diseases

The brassicas, apart from some of the stalwart kales, are at risk from more unpleasant pests and diseases than any other common vegetable. It is comparatively easy to cope with birds and slugs, more tiresome to combat cabbage butterflies and moths and difficult to tackle cabbage root fly. But the real bogy is club root.

Confronted with a heavy infestation of club root, both cabbage and gardener are fairly helpless. The fungus is *Plasmodiophora brassicae*, and in an infected garden thousands of millions of its minute spores can inhabit one square yard. When a spore germinates, triggered off by the presence of a cabbage, it develops a tail which enables it to move towards the root of the plant. It enters the root, loses its tail and produces different spores, causing swelling in the root, which then degenerates into a slimy, stinking mess. From this, millions more spores go into the soil to infect other brassica roots. The spores may infect the soil for up to twenty years. So far not enough has been discovered about club root, although it has been around for centuries, to effect a certain cure. It often, but not always, greatly helps if the soil is adequately limed; over-liming, however, will lock up essential minerals in the soil, making them unavailable to plants. Growing brassicas in different parts of the garden also helps; but the dormant spores can survive far longer than the usual three-year rotation. Dipping seedlings in calomel (mercurous chloride) when they are transplanted is frequently recommended, but this fungicide is expensive and mercury is not lightly to be introduced into the soil.

In spite of these depressing facts, there are some useful things an amateur gardener can do:
(1) Raise your own plants from seed or buy them from nurseries, which by law must not grow seedlings on infected land.
(2) See that the brassica patch is not acid, is rich in humus and properly drained. A healthy plant has the best chance of defeating the fungus.
(3) Dig up the stumps as you cut cabbages and finish picking Brussels sprouts. Do not leave them in the ground all winter. Burn all infected roots.
(4) As a last resort you could try the methods some dedicated organic gardeners adopt. They put pieces of rhubarb or a bit of mothball down the dibber hole when planting to mask the cabbage smell and fool the fungus.

Of course, innumerable gardens never suffer club root. And a swollen root does not always mean the fungus has struck. Slice open the swelling. If there is a maggot inside, the gall weevil is the enemy and you can breathe again (after destroying it).

Protect the seedlings from birds with fine nylon netting supported on sticks. This does not harm the birds as cotton can, but it scares the wits out of them.

Large and Small Cabbage Butterflies. The caterpillars of these two white butterflies eat the leaves of the cabbage. Look under the leaves for the yellow eggs and destroy them by hand or spray the plants with derris.

Cabbage Moth. The caterpillar of this grey nocturnal moth is more difficult to control because it burrows deeply into the cabbage and eats the heart. As with cabbage butterflies destroy the eggs or spray with derris.

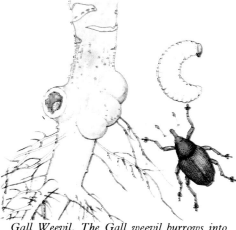

Gall Weevil. The Gall weevil burrows into the root causing it to swell. Control the weevil by dusting the soil when planting with gamma BHC (Lindane).

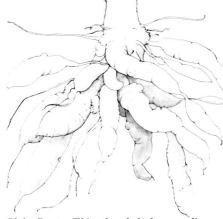

Club Root. This dreaded fungus disease attacks many plants of the brassica family. The roots swell and rot and the plants fail to grow properly.

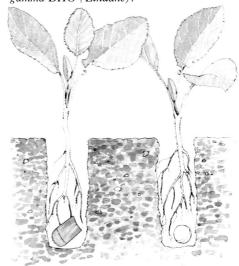

Club Root. To mask the smell of brassicas, which attracts the fungus, some gardeners drop small pieces of rhubarb or a bit of mothball into the dibber hole before planting.

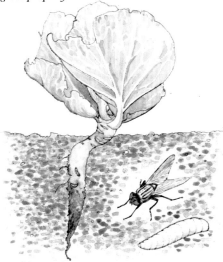

Cabbage Root Fly. The larvae—small, white grubs—appear from May onwards and eat the stem below soil level. Spray around the base of the seedlings with gamma BHC (Lindane).

Spinach

Spinach (*Spinacia oleracea*) can be tricky to grow. The summer varieties do not like hot and dry weather, and the winter ones do not like it when it is cold and wet. Nevertheless,

the satisfaction of eating spinach fresh from the garden, instead of wilted from the green-grocer, is worth some gamble in growing it, and proper cultivation of suitable soils will greatly lessen the odds against your success. If you fail, do not despair, you can always turn to the spinach substitutes.

Spinach has a long and respected history. Its origin is vague, like that of many ancient vegetables, but Persia has as strong a claim to being its birthplace as any country. Certainly the Greeks and Romans ate it. The Arabs valued it and in the fourteenth century took it to Spain, from where it quickly spread throughout Europe. Then it was part of a peasant diet. Today it is frequently the gourmet's choice.

Varieties

For growing in spring and summer: Long-standing Round (it is the seeds which are round) has dark-green leaves, grows quickly and is less prone to bolt than most varieties.

For growing in winter: Greenmarket and Long-standing Prickly (prickly seeds). Both are hardy.

GROWING SPINACH

Preparing the soil

For summer spinach choose a site in partial shade and manure it well. Winter spinach will need the same kind of rich soil, but in a sunny, sheltered part of the garden. Both need lime; the pH level should be 6·5 to 6·8. Although a loamy soil is best, it is possible to grow spinach on heavy soil. A light sandy soil, however, will encourage spinach to run to seed, in which case it is better to grow such spinach substitutes as spinach beet, New Zealand spinach and seakale beet.

Sowing

March to end July. Sow summer varieties every three weeks in 1-inch (2 cm) drills, 12 inches (30 cm) apart. Thin the seedlings as soon as they are big enough to handle to 6 inches (15 cm) apart. August to September. Make two sowings of the winter varieties, one in early August and the other in September. Sow in 1-inch (2 cm) drills, 12 inches (30 cm) apart, thinning the seedlings to 6 inches (15 cm) apart.

The year's work

Keep down weeds. Keep the soil moist by watering in dry weather or the plants will bolt and your labour will be wasted. In the middle of summer, spinach seeds can be sown between rows of such other vegetables

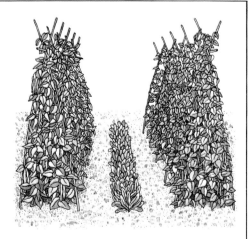

as peas, beans and carrots, which will provide shade for the growing plants. In most parts of the country the winter crop will need some protection—a covering of straw or, better still, cloches—from October or November.

Harvesting

Most of the year. Summer varieties will be ready 8 to 11 weeks after sowing. Pick young and tender leaves, but leave a few on the plant so that it can go on growing. Pick the winter varieties sparingly, particularly in bad weather. They, too, need some covering to keep warm.

Diseases

If there are yellow patches on the leaves and a grey mould on the under surfaces, downy mildew has struck. Crowding and bad drainage encourage it and a spraying with Bordeaux mixture may help to check it.

Yellowing of the younger leaves indicates spinach blight due to cucumber mosaic virus. The leaves roll up and gradually die.

Spinach Beet

Spinach beet (*Beta vulgaris* var. *Cicla*), also called perpetual spinach, has coarse, spinach-like leaves. Lacking the spinach tem-

perament, it will not bolt in summer nor freeze to death in winter. It does not even need as rich a soil as spinach, although it will be none the worse for getting it.

GROWING SPINACH BEET

Sowing

April and July. Sow in 1-inch (2 cm) drills, 18 inches (45 cm) apart. Thin the seedlings as soon as they are big enough to handle to 8 inches (20 cm) apart.

Harvesting

The year round. Keep picking the leaves to ensure a constant supply of young, tender ones. Take the leaves from the outside of the plant, but do not strip it bare.

The July sowing may be ready for autumn picking, but the real purpose of growing spinach beet is to provide leaves in winter and early spring. The plants can be kept for another year, but there is little point, since they crop less well and new plants are so easy to grow.

Pests and diseases

Fairly trouble free.

New Zealand Spinach

New Zealand spinach (*Tetragonia expansa*) is not a spinach at all, but it does come from New Zealand, where it was found during

Captain Cook's voyage in 1770. Sir Joseph Banks, the great horticulturist, brought it back to England. It never became popular in Britain, however, as it did in Europe and the United States. The virtue of New Zealand spinach is that it will thrive in a hot, dry summer, such as would make ordinary spinach not just run but gallop to seed. It takes up space, but it provides mild-flavoured leaves in abundance.

GROWING NEW ZEALAND SPINACH
Preparing the soil
Plenty of humus is needed, as for spinach.

Sowing
May. New Zealand spinach is not hardy. You either raise plants under glass—sowing in March and planting out when all risk of frost is gone—or wait until May to sow out of doors. The skin of the seeds is very hard; to help germination soak them overnight in water. The seeds are large, so it is simple to sow three together, ½ inch (1 cm) deep and at 36-inch (90 cm) intervals in the row. Allow the sturdiest seedling in each station to grow on and pull up the others.

The year's work
At first, hoe to keep down weeds, but later the thick growth of the plants will keep weeds under control. When the plants are well grown, pinch out the tips to produce branching and more young leaves. Water in dry weather.

Harvesting
Midsummer onwards. This is a cut-and-come-again vegetable, so pick regularly, a few leaves from each plant. Cut near to the base of the stalks, although it is only the leaves that will be cooked.

Pests and diseases
Fairly trouble free.

Seakale Beet

The leaves of seakale beet (*Beta vulgaris* var. *Cicla*), which is also called silver beet or Swiss chard, may be substituted in the

kitchen for spinach. The stems and midribs may be used instead of seakale. Seakale beet is easy to grow and handsome enough for the flower garden.

Varieties
Silver Beet is white and green. Ruby Chard is even prettier, but not as palatable.

GROWING SEAKALE BEET
Preparing the soil
Seakale beet is extremely tolerant about the kind of soil and position it is grown in. It will grow in a light sandy soil, which would be anathema to the true spinach, as well as in heavy clay. Similar to other beets—although this one is grown for its leaves—it needs lime, pH 6·5 to 6·8, and ground manured for a previous crop suits it well. Seakale beet can be sown in shade or sun, but any late sowing under cloches, to get a winter crop, should obviously be in a warm part of the garden.

Sowing
April and July. In April, sow three seeds together ½ inch (1 cm) deep, every 15 inches (38 cm) in rows 18 inches (45 cm) apart, thinning the seedlings to the strongest one in each station. Another sowing in July, to be covered by cloches through the winter, will provide greens in spring.

Harvesting
July onwards. Always take the stems from the outside of each plant to allow the central stems to develop. Pull them as you do rhubarb; cutting makes them bleed. Seakale that has wintered under cloches will provide leaves through the following spring and autumn.

Pests and diseases
Fairly trouble free.

Good King Henry

Good King Henry (*Chenopodium Bonus-Henricus*) is a native of Britain, and for centuries was grown in cottage gardens. It has,

however, disappeared altogether from modern gardens in England.

Good King Henry, also known as Mercury, wild spinach and Lincolnshire (or poor man's) asparagus, increases its output each year. It can be a substitute for spinach or asparagus according to taste.

GROWING GOOD KING HENRY
Preparing the soil
Although Good King Henry will tolerate poor soil, it deserves better. By maintaining the soil rich in humus both the quality and the quantity of the crop will be improved.

Sowing
May. Sow in ½-inch (1 cm) drills and thin to 10 inches (25 cm) apart. Allow 18 inches (45 cm) between rows.

The year's work
In the autumn cut down dying foliage and give the plants a mulch of compost. To produce more plants, lift and divide one or two in spring—even small pieces will grow. If you wish to treat the vegetable as asparagus you must blanch the shoots, from March onwards, by earthing them up as they come through the soil.

Harvesting
April onwards. The young shoots provide the first (asparagus substitute) crop. They are cut when they are about 6 inches (15 cm) long. Next come the flower buds, a delicacy in their own right. Finally, you can pick the leaves as a spinach substitute.

Pests and diseases
Good King Henry is not only now neglected by gardeners, but also by all pests and diseases.

Stalks & Shoots

Stalks and shoots are the undoubted aristocrats of the kitchen garden and asparagus is the noblest of them all, even among such competitors as globe artichokes, seakale, cardoons and Florence fennel. The great gardener Arthur Kidner said that asparagus "is somewhat of an acquired taste, and the short natural season does not allow customers time or opportunity to acquire it". Conversely the shortness of the season means that there is no time to get tired of these Epicurean vegetables. Rhubarb may seem to be an intruder in these high places, but this is not so. Like many other aristocrats it ages badly, but for its uncommonly beautiful pink youth much may be forgiven it.

1 Celery
2 Seakale
3 Forced rhubarb
4 Globe artichokes
5 Florence fennel
6 Asparagus

Asparagus

Asparagus (*Asparagus officinalis*) has outlived many civilizations. The Egyptians were eating it, or something like it, in the third millennium BC. The Greeks knew asparagus and, inevitably, invented a myth about it—that it grew from a ram's horn stuck in the

ground; the starting point, perhaps, of later ribaldry associating asparagus with cuckoldry. It advanced with the Roman armies, and when the empire fell the plant declined, but survived. Asparagus was one of the spoils of war for the Arabs in their North African and Spanish conquests. Then it found its way back into Europe: to France in the fifteenth century and England in the sixteenth century.

Asparagus is a member of the lily family. The edible parts are the immature shoots of the tuberous roots. Those which are not eaten develop into asparagus fern. To grow asparagus you need a fair amount of room, a lot of patience during the first three years, when you must not cut any, and, thereafter, enough will power to curb your greed, so that you do not eat the bed to death.

Varieties

Connover's Colossal, a very early American variety with thick, greenish white shoots. Argenteuil, a late French variety of superb flavour. For an extended cropping season grow both varieties.

Pests and diseases

Basically there are three pests and diseases to watch for. Asparagus beetles and grubs may devour, perhaps strip, foliage in summer. Spray with gamma BHC (Lindane), unless cutting is still going on, when derris should be used. To counter rust on foliage in midsummer, spray every two weeks until September with Bordeaux mixture. Slugs also appreciate asparagus; use baits with methiocarb and metaldehyde.

GROWING ASPARAGUS
Preparing the soil

Choose a sunny part of the garden. In autumn prepare a loamy, well-drained bed with plenty of such organic manure as farmyard manure, old mushroom compost or seaweed. Add lime to achieve pH 5·6 to 5·8. The success of the crops over the next decade will depend on how painstaking you are at this stage.

Planting

March/April. In the prepared bed dig trenches 10 inches (25 cm) deep, 12 inches (30 cm) wide and at least 36 inches (90 cm) apart, for the fleshy roots will spread enormously. Asparagus can be grown from

seed, but buying one- or two-year-old plants cuts time off waiting for crops. One-year-old plants are cheaper and transplant more readily. Plant them in the prepared bed as soon as they arrive so that the roots do not dry out and suffer as little exposure to the air as possible. The crowns should be 24 inches (60 cm) apart in the

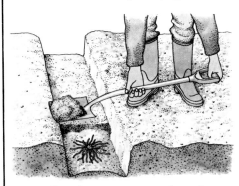

rows. Fan the roots out evenly and cover them at once with 3 inches (8 cm) of soil, leaving the rest of the soil to fill in the trench gradually during the first summer.

The year's work

The asparagus fern stalks will turn yellow in the autumn; cut them down near to the

ground. Each February or March give the bed a dressing of general fertilizer, 3 ounces to the square yard (90 g to 1 sq m). Then mound up the soil a few inches deep along

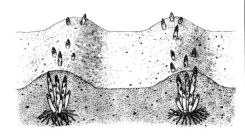

each row. In summer, give the plants a mulch of decayed farmyard manure or compost. Asparagus are male (more productive) and female (berry bearing). Pick off all berries before they ripen or you will be cursed with seedlings of unpredictable parentage.

In about the tenth year, start another bed or, preferably, add another row each year, so that as the original bed declines you do not have that agonizing three-year wait all over again.

Harvesting

May/June. Do not cut at all, not even the fern, for the first two years after planting. In the third year you can take no more than one or two sticks from each plant, stopping altogether in early June and allowing the remaining shoots to produce fern. The time to take a shoot is when it is about 4 inches (10 cm) above the ground and while the tip is still tightly closed. The base of the stick is tough; a special knife makes the job easier. In the fourth year all shoots can

be cut for five weeks after you begin. Then stop. Each year afterwards cut for only six weeks if you want the bed to survive. In the summer, especially if the weather is dry, remember to keep the asparagus bed moist. When they are five years old, a couple of flourishing plants should provide one person with one helping each week for the six weeks of cutting.

Globe Artichokes

The Mediterranean was the original home of the globe artichoke (*Cynara Scolymus*). Ancient Greek writings mention it often and the Romans may have introduced it to Britain. It was, however, not until the sixteenth century, again by way of Italy, that globe artichokes became established in Britain. Like many vegetables, the artichoke developed a reputation as an aphrodisiac, which may explain Catherine de Medici's passion for it.

The globe artichoke has always been considered an Epicurean vegetable. It is, however, quite simple to grow. Regard it as a thistle, which it is, rather than as something foreign and exotic. The globe artichoke has absolutely nothing to do with either Jerusalem or Chinese artichokes, the roots of which have a supposedly artichoke flavour.

The delicate bits of the globe artichoke are in the immature flower head, the fleshy scales and the fleshy base, or heart. The hairy centre, the choke, is not edible.

When the globes have been harvested, older plants about to be replaced can, in their last autumn, be made to produce another but different crop—the chards or stems. These spring up after the plant has been cut down.

Varieties

Green Globe and Purple Globe are the usual English varieties, but the gourmet's choice is the French Vert de Laon, with pale-green head and plenty of flesh in the scales.

Diseases

If the leaves turn brown and the plants begin to die back in warm, humid weather the cause is likely to be artichoke leaf spot. Before the heads form spray with Bordeaux mixture, half strength.

GROWING GLOBE ARTICHOKES

Preparing the soil

The globe artichoke does not have to be grown in the vegetable garden. With its attractive, fern-like, grey-green leaves it can more than hold its own in any flowerbed. However, it needs a well-drained, rich soil, in a sunny, sheltered spot. Test for lime (pH 6·5). The plants have a useful life of three years, so at the start dig in plenty of well-rotted manure or compost. Before planting, spread 3 ounces of general fertilizer to the square yard (90 g to 1 sq m).

Planting

April. It is unwise to grow artichokes from seed as they may not come true. To begin, buy plants (suckers from an established

plant) and thereafter you will be able to provide your own replacements. Plant them, firmly, at least 3 feet (90 cm) apart and water well.

The year's work

To produce tender heads artichokes need moisture in their roots; each summer apply

a mulch of manure or compost and, occasionally, liquid manure. Each autumn get rid of dying leaves and old stems. Except in the warmest parts of the country, cover the crowns with leaves or straw for winter protection.

Although plants will crop longer, they deteriorate after three years. Renew the bed by taking 6- to 9-inch (15 to 23 cm) suckers, with a few of the roots, from around the crowns of parent plants. And so the cycle starts again.

Harvesting

July to September. Cut the heads when they are plump but still young and tender, and the scales still tight. The terminal bud will

be ready first. If you want very large heads from the terminals remove the laterals when they are not much more than 1 inch (2 cm) in diameter. These are particularly delicious eaten whole.

Chards

In late September and October, plants which are to be discarded can be made to produce a second, different, crop of chards. After the globe heads are finished, cut down the main stems of these plants to within 1 foot (30 cm) of the ground. Mulch them and water frequently. When the new shoots are about

24 inches (60 cm) high, tie them together and earth them up like celery (see page 62) to blanch them. It is the stems which are eaten, cooked like cardoons, to which the globe artichoke is botanically related. After all the chards have been picked, the parent plant is of no further use, except for compost.

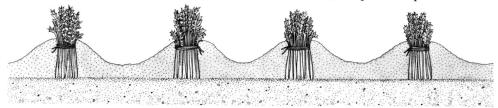

Seakale

Seakale (*Crambe maritima*), growing wild along the coasts of Britain (it is also a native of most of the coastal areas of western Europe), has provided spring greens for country dwellers for centuries. But the cultivation of the forced white shoots, which are sweet and succulent, goes back to the middle of the nineteenth century. Its old name was sea-colewort. It belongs to the *Cruciferae* family and is a relative of the cabbage.

Seakale is easy to grow and to force. It is

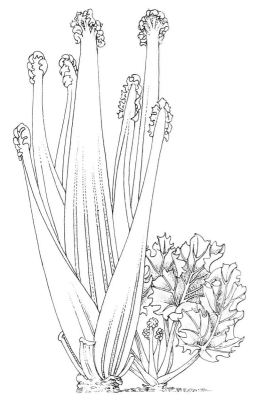

remarkably hardy, usually free of all pests and diseases and a fine, wholesome vegetable with a delicate, nutty flavour. Seakale may be forced indoors or in the garden. Although outdoor forcing may provide the better flavour (one of the most esoteric arguments among devotees), there is much to be said for having seakale in the middle of winter. For the outdoor crop you will have to wait until early spring. The curly green leaves of unforced seakale are delicious eaten raw in a salad. The stalks, too, can be eaten raw like celery.

Roots forced indoors are thrown away after all the stems have been used—but they will already have provided cuttings for the next season. Outdoor beds remain productive for four or five years, but do not start forcing them until eighteen months after planting.

For a worthwhile supply of shoots you will need at least fifteen plants. Cut the shoots young, before the leaves have fully developed, for a most excellent spring vegetable.

Variety

Lily White provides a good crop of very white, pleasantly sweet shoots.

Pests and diseases

Fairly trouble free.

GROWING SEAKALE

Preparing the soil

Seakale needs a well-drained soil, rich in humus, especially if you are establishing a five-year bed for outdoor forcing. A maritime plant, seakale appreciates seaweed as a manure. There must also be adequate lime (pH 6·5) in the soil.

Planting

March. Although seakale can be raised from seed it is more sensible to buy root cuttings, which are called thongs, and save waiting two years for the first crop. The thongs are planted in March. So that you know which

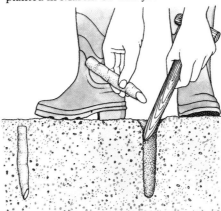

is the right way up to plant them it is the general custom for nurserymen to cut the tops straight and the other ends slanting. It is wise to get into the habit of doing this when you yourself take cuttings each autumn. Plant the thongs with the tops ½ inch (1 cm) below the surface of the soil in rows 18 inches (45 cm) apart, allowing 12 inches (30 cm) between the thongs.

The year's work

As the seakale grows, remove all shoots except the strongest one. Keep the weeds down, either by hoeing or, preferably, by giving a mulch of peat or compost. Water in dry weather. Remove any flower stems. In October, remove the foliage as it dies down.

Forcing indoors

November onwards. Carefully dig up the roots in November. First cut the thongs from the roots. These are the slim sideshoots of the root, about 6 inches (15 cm) long, which will be next year's plants. Cut the top of each one level and the other end slanting.

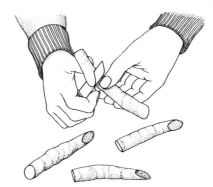

Tie them in bundles, store in sand and keep in a cool place ready for planting in March.

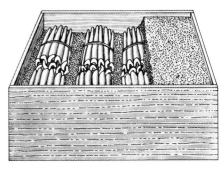

The roots themselves should also be stored in sand until ready for forcing. Force a few at a time at regular intervals. To

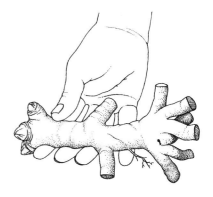

force, plant the roots in rich, loamy soil in boxes or flowerpots—about 3 roots to a 8-inch (20 cm) flowerpot—with the crowns just showing above the surface of the soil.

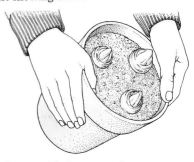

Cover with boxes or flowerpots—total darkness is vital—and put them in a place where the temperature is a constant 50°F (10°C). In a month to five weeks the shoots will be 6 inches (15 cm) or more long and ready for cutting. Do not cut the shoots, however, until immediately before you use them.

Forcing outdoors

January onwards. An outdoor bed should not be forced the first winter after planting. When the bed is established the following winter, either place boxes or flowerpots over the plants or pile up the soil from between the rows to a depth of 10 inches (25 cm) over the plants. Either method, carried out in January, will produce stems for cutting in April.

Celery

Celery (*Apium graveolens*) is such a popular vegetable that it can do without any testimonials from the Ancient Greeks, Romans,

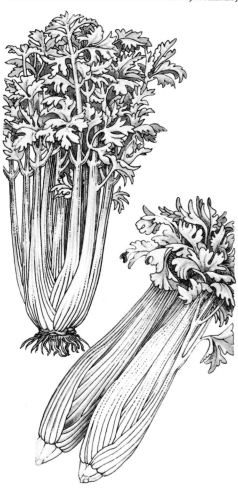

Egyptians and Chinese—all of whom held it in high regard as food, flavouring and medicine. The Romans even believed that a celery wreath worn around the head would ease a hangover.

Most probably native to the Mediterranean regions, celery was developed from a plant very similar to the common English weed smallage, which still flourishes in many parts of England, Europe and western Asia.

Celery as we know it today is the result of work done by sixteenth-century Italian gardeners, who developed the finely flavoured, succulent stalks from the bitter and foul-tasting weed.

It is regrettable that celery is not easy to grow—being demanding rather than difficult. Celery requires a heavy, peaty soil, plenty of moisture and a lot of space. The stalks must be blanched if they are to lose their inherent bitterness, and this takes time and patience. Busy gardeners could settle for the less-demanding self-blanching celery or the much more amenable celeriac, the turnip-like root with a celery flavour.

Varieties

Giant White, large. New Dwarf White, for late cropping. The whites have the better flavour, but the pinks and reds are hardier. Giant Pink, good flavour and strong. Giant Red, crisp and hardiest of all.

GROWING CELERY

Preparing the soil

If you were searching for somewhere to live, with the major aim of growing celery, you would choose an area with peaty soil and a high water table. Failing that the celery plot must be provided with much well-rotted manure or compost. Do not add too much lime (pH 5·8 to 6). In spring, well before they are needed, dig trenches 12 inches (30 cm) deep and 15 inches (38 cm) wide if the celery is to be planted in a single row, or 18 inches (45 cm) wide for a double row. Single rows are better for small quantities; double rows are space-saving and look handsome, but make earthing up more difficult. If there is more than one trench, dig them 3 or even 4 feet (90 or 120 cm) apart. The space in between can profitably be used for such fast-growing catch crops as lettuces and radishes.

When digging out the trenches put half the soil in a ridge on one side of the trench and half on the other. Fork the manure into the soil at the bottom of the trench, treading it

down to make it firm. Then fill the trench with some of the soil from the ridges to within 5 inches (13 cm) of the top. The trenches are now ready for later planting.

Sowing

February/April. Buy only seed which has be treated with formaldehyde against leaf sp These seeds must not be put to any culin or medical use. Conversely, do not plant a celery seeds bought for use in the kitchen. T seeds are small, fifty thousand to the oun and, since germination is slow, taking three four weeks, the first batch should be sown ear in February, in a greenhouse heated to 60 (16°C). Sow the seeds thinly in pots of Jo Innes seed compost and cover lightly. Wh the seedlings are big enough to handle, pri them off into boxes of John Innes No compost. After they have settled down fr this upheaval, transfer them to a cold fra and gradually harden them off. The seedlin should be ready for planting out at the beg ning of June. Depending on the weather, should be possible to prick off the seedlin of the March and early April sowings straig into frames. To avoid this labour, ma gardeners sensibly buy plants from a nurser although this limits the choice of varieties.

Planting

June. Plant celery 12 inches (30 cm) apart. C planting, water liberally unless it is raini heavily at the time.

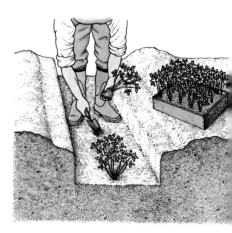

The year's work

If the summer is at all dry, prodigious wateri will be needed throughout. Dilute liqu manure will help, as will two or three dressin of a general fertilizer, 2 ounces a yard r

to 1 m), between July and September. ...ove side shoots (suckers) from the plants. ...arthing up is usually done in three stages. ... August, when the plants are 12 inches ...m) or more high, loosely tie pieces of ...spaper or black polythene around the ...ks. This is to prevent soil from getting ...ween the stalks (an abomination to the cook). ... that the soil is moist before you begin ...hing up. Earth up only a little the first ... The second and more generous earthing

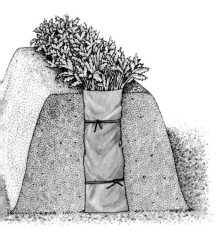

...must take place three weeks later. The final ...hing up after another three weeks should ...pletely cover the stalks. The leaves should ...er be covered with soil. Keep the sides of ...ridges steep so that the rain will run away ...n the celery and not into its heart to rot it. ... touch of frost improves the crispness and ...our of celery, but late crops often go rotten

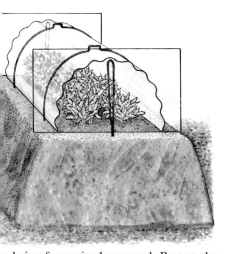

...r being frozen in the ground. Protect the ...nts with straw or, better still, by placing ...ches over the celery along the top of the ...ge.

...rvesting
...vember onwards. The celery should be ...quately blanched about nine weeks from ...start of earthing up. Dig up the plants as ...need them, working from the end of the ...and being careful to disturb adjoining ...nts as little as possible.

Self-blanching Celery

Until celery was developed by Italian

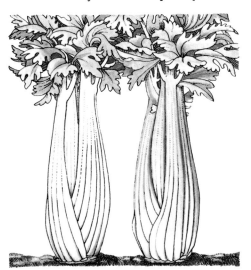

gardeners of the sixteenth century, it had an unpleasant smell and a bitter taste—a fact which supports the theory that it was celery, not parsley, that was the classical and Egyptian funerary plant. In spite of such morbid associations, celery is well worth growing. Gardeners who are not celery addicts, to the point of getting deep satisfaction just out of the labour of growing it, should stick to the yellow and American green self-blanching types, which do not have to be earthed up. Thus the gardener is saved the effort of digging trenches. Self-blanching celery, however, is less hardy than ordinary celery and has a milder flavour. It is ready earlier, and over earlier, than the white, pink and red varieties.

Varieties

Golden Self-blanching and Lathom Self-blanching are both yellow compact heads for use from August. Greensleeves is ready from October.

GROWING SELF-BLANCHING CELERY

Preparing the soil

Self-blanching celery needs a well-manured, well-dug soil but no trenches.

Sowing

Sow the seeds in a greenhouse towards the end of March. Prick off the seedlings into boxes and harden them off in cold frames.

Planting

June. Plant in blocks 9 inches (23 cm) apart each way. This is better than planting in rows, for the plants provide shade for each other. Although they are self-blanching, the yellow varieties will be more tender if a piece of black polythene is tied around each plant a few weeks before lifting.

Pests and diseases

Celery fly (*Philophylla heraclei*) attacks celery plants from May throughout the summer. It is the tiny fly that lays the eggs, but the resulting grub that does the damage—tunnelling its way through the leaf tissues and raising brown blisters. Dust the soil along the rows with old soot and spray the plants with gamma BHC

(Lindane). Destroy all affected leaves.

Brown patches on leaves and stems, which then wilt, indicate the fungus celery leaf spot. Buy only seed that has been treated against the fungus and at the first sign of the disease spray with Bordeaux mixture, continuing every fortnight through to October.

Finocchio or Florence Fennel

Although Florence fennel (*Foeniculum vulgare* var. *dulce*) is often difficult to grow in northern climates, it is still worth cultivating for its sweet aniseed flavour.

Cardoons

The British have less regard for the cardoon (*Cynara Cardunculus*) than other Europeans. Admittedly George III liked cardoons as avidly as did the gluttonous Romans

fourteen centuries before him, but he did not have to grow them himself. The cardoon is troublesome to grow, taking as much time and space as celery, and it is cultivated in much the same way. The cardoon, however, is a thistle, closely related to the globe artichoke. The name is derived from the French word *chardon*, meaning a thistle. In Australia, where the cardoon grows like a weed and is regarded as a nuisance, it is known as wild artichoke. It is certainly a tenacious plant—it was introduced into South America and promptly spread over large areas of the pampas.

If the cardoon is allowed to, it will produce similar but smaller heads than the artichoke, but it is for its blanched stems and not for its heads that the cardoon is grown. In the south of Europe it is grown also for its roots, which are thick and fleshy.

Varieties

The choice is between Spanish and French. The Spanish, Ivory White, is hardier and does not have spiny leaves, but is liable to run to seed. The French, Tours, is the usual choice, tastes better and has longer stems, but the prickly leaves are nasty to handle when earthing up.

GROWING FLORENCE FENNEL
Preparing the soil
Florence fennel needs a much richer soil than the herb. Soil rich in humus and decayed manure will keep moist better in summer and encourage the stem base to swell.

Sowing
April to August. Florence fennel needs as much sun as possible to produce a good crop. So sow it in as sunny a position as the garden has to offer. Sow the seeds in ½-inch (1 cm) drills 18 inches (45 cm) apart. Sow a little each month to ensure a continuous supply. As the plant is not large, growing to approximately 24 inches (60 cm) high, thin out the seedlings to only 7 to 8 inches (18 to 20 cm) apart.

The year's work
Florence fennel demands a lot of water, and if it is not watered in dry weather it will certainly not produce bulbous stems. When the swelling is about the size of a golf ball, draw some soil around it, partly covering it. As the bulbs are so small this may be simpler than the alternative method of wrapping paper or black polythene around the bulb, tightly secured with string.

Harvesting
After two or three weeks the bulb will have blanched and grown in size. Pull the bulbs as you need them when they are the size of a tennis ball.

Pests and diseases
Fairly trouble free.

GROWING CARDOONS
Preparing the soil
Dig a trench 18 inches (45 cm) deep, as for celery. Put plenty of manure or compost in the bottom of the trench. After forking in the manure, the trench should be 12 inches (30 cm) deep. If there is more than one trench, dig them 48 inches (120 cm) apart.

Sowing
April. Although perennial, cardoons are always raised from seed each year, not from suckers, as are globe artichokes. Sow in pots, one seed to a pot, under glass, unheated, in April. Harden off ready for planting out at the end of May.

Planting
End May. Disturbing the roots as little as possible, plant firmly 15 to 18 inches (38 to 45 cm) apart. Water the seedlings well after planting.

The year's work
Little needs to be done during the summer except weeding and watering and more watering. If cardoons are not kept moist they will start to produce flower-heads—unwanted, although edible, if, like globe artichokes, they are cut before the scales are too open.

Start blanching in September. By then the plants will be fully grown, up to 36 inches (90 cm) or more in height. Remove dead and yellow leaves. Then, either tie the stems together with raffia in two or three places, depending on their height, or tie corrugated paper around the stems. It is best to wear gloves for this job—cardoon leaves are extremely prickly.

Earth up as for celery (see page 63), using the soil from each side of the trench. Cardoons are not hardy and will need a plentiful covering of straw or bracken as protection against frost. Place the straw around the earthed-up cardoons and cover with more soil to keep the straw in place.

Harvesting
After five or six weeks the cardoons will be fit to use; at least the crisp hearts will be, the tough outside stems are fit only for the compost heap. By earthing up a number of plants at intervals, a succession of stalks will be ready for cropping.

Pests and diseases
Fairly trouble free.

Rhubarb

Although to many people rhubarb (*Rheum Rhaponticum*) may seem a curiously English fruit, it is in fact a vegetable, native to China and Tibet, with a name derived from Latin. As far back as 3000 BC, the root of the plant was being used medicinally in its countries of

origin. It was put to the same use when it arrived in Britain via the Volga region of Russia. After a period of near oblivion it turned up again in the early 1800s, this time as stalks, forced and blanched, and used as a fruit. Rhubarb has not gathered a literature around it in the way that other ancient vegetables have, but Kingsley Amis's Lucky Jim confessed to a love–hate relationship with it. For most people, however, it is either love or hate. In its favour, it is easy to grow, very productive and most attractively pink when forced in winter.

Varieties

Varieties are legion, and if you grow from seed you will produce more, although whether they will be good is a gamble. Timperley Early and Hawke's Champagne are of excellent flavour for forcing. Sutton is hard to beat for the main crop.

Pests and diseases

Occasionally crown rot causes rotting of leaves and stalks. Dig up and burn the affected plants. Any other disasters are unlikely.

GROWING RHUBARB

Preparing the soil

Rhubarb thrives best in fairly heavy soil, given massive organic manuring to produce succulent stalks (pH around 5·8).

Sowing

April. Raising from seed is easy, but you must then wait an extra 18 months for the first crop. Sow 1 inch (2 cm) deep out of doors in April and thin to 6 inches (15 cm) apart. Move the plants to the permanent bed in the autumn.

Planting

It is more reliable to buy roots than to raise from seed. They are planted when buds are dormant, either in October/November or February/March. Allow 3 feet (90 cm) between plants and between rows, and plant to a depth that will leave the buds not more than 2 inches (5 cm) below the surface of the soil. Plant firmly.

The year's work

In the first year the plants will be establishing themselves and no stalks are picked. Pick only a few in the second year and none at all from plants which you intend to force in the winter. After that the bed has five years or more of useful life ahead of it. A rhubarb bed can be forgotten for most of the year. The plants are almost always healthy and their large leaves smother the weeds. However, watch out for and remove all flower heads. Flowering rhubarb is as unproductive as a broody hen. Rhubarb needs feeding—a handful of general fertilizer should be scattered around each plant after pulling finishes each year. A good dressing of compost or manure should be forked into the bed in February. But fork carefully so that the crowns are not damaged.

To keep up a constant supply of three-year-old roots for forcing, divide some of the established clumps each year in October/November or February/March. This is done by digging up the clumps and cutting them into pieces. The pieces can be small, but each must have an undamaged bud. Plant them in the gaps left by the roots removed for forcing, having seized the chance to refresh the soil with more manure.

Harvesting

Mid-April to July. Pull—do not cut—a stick or two from each crown as you need them, balancing your needs with what the plant is capable of producing. If you over-pull you will suffer for your greed the following year with a smaller crop from weakened plants. Stop pulling in July.

Forcing outdoors

With a bucket and some straw, outdoor rhubarb can be hurried on for pulling a few weeks earlier. In mid-January or February invert a bucket or box over each of the few crowns you want to force. Over

and around them put plenty of straw (or, ideally, strawy manure for greater warmth). You could gain three weeks this way, but

do not overdo it, because the debilitated roots will need time to recuperate. The sensible thing is to force only those plants due to be retired.

Forcing indoors

Pre-retirement plants—strong clumps at least three years old—are also those you choose for forcing indoors. Dig them up when the leaves die back in late October and November. If you leave the roots exposed to the cold for a couple of weeks they will grow faster when brought into warmth and darkness. Lay the clumps close together in a box, barely cover them with soil and give them a good watering. Put another box on top and cover with black polythene to keep out all light. Keep the covered box in the greenhouse or kitchen

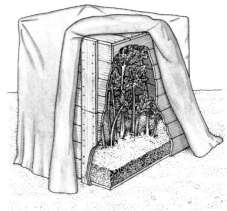

at a temperature of about 50° to 55°F (10° to 13°C). Below 45°F (7°C) growth is very slow; above 60°F (16°C) the stalks will be spindly, anaemic and tasteless. Water occasionally to keep the roots moist (not wringing wet), using a watering can with a fine rose. Stalks should be ready for pulling in five to six weeks. By staggering the times when the roots are boxed for forcing, a succession can be obtained. When all the stalks have been pulled, throw the roots away. They will be worn out.

Pods & Seeds

*O*nce, that dreary period which is neither winter nor spring could be borne by looking ahead to the first broad beans, the first garden peas, the first French and runner beans. Now, all through the winter you can buy these vegetables—either frozen or "fresh"—brought by air from all over the world. We tend to forget that they taste entirely different when they are picked young from the garden. Surely this is reason enough for growing all kinds of peas and beans. Sweet corn is not easy to grow in many parts of the country, but you will never know the true flavour of sweet corn until you have picked it in its prime and cooked it immediately.

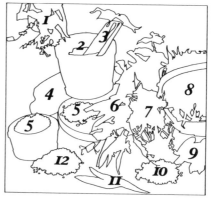

1 Petit pois
2 Dried haricot beans
3 Haricot verts
4 Sweet corn
5 Red and green
   dried kidney beans
6 Garden peas
7 Bean shoots
8 French beans
9 Sugar peas (or
   Mangetout peas)
10 Soya beans
11 Runner beans
12 Mung beans

Sweet Corn

The forebears of sweet corn (*Zea Mays* var. *saccharata*) may have been growing in Mexico earlier than 5000 BC. Columbus brought seeds of Indian maize back from Cuba to Spain, from where it spread throughout

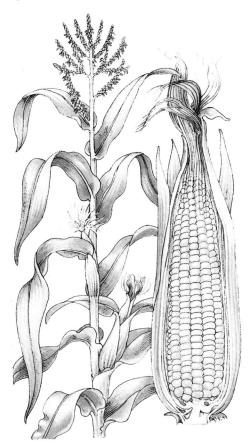

the Mediterranean and beyond. The English herbalist Gerard had this to say about it in 1597: "The barbarous Indians, which know no better, thinke it a good food; whereas we may easily judge, that it nourisheth but little, and it is of hard and evill digestion, a more convenient food for swine than for man." In one respect he was right: in many parts of the world it is the food of animals rather than of men. But in defence of the sweet corn of today, it cannot be judged on the weary cobs on sale in greengrocers, for sweet corn goes downhill rapidly, even within the hour of being picked. The only way to know its true character is to grow it. With the new, quick-maturing hybrids it is not hard to grow sweet corn in warmer parts of the country.

Varieties

The most reliable, quick-maturing varieties (all F_1 hybrids) are John Innes Hybrid, Earliking, Kelvedon Glory and, especially for cold areas, North Star. Another new F_1 hybrid, Early Xtra Sweet, has the advantage of keeping its sweetness for a day or two after picking. This hybrid should be grown on its own, because if it is pollinated by other varieties of sweet corn its flavour is diminished.

Pests and diseases

Sweet corn is, so far, remarkably free of pests and diseases.

GROWING SWEET CORN

Preparing the soil

Choose an open site for the greatest possible amount of sun. The soil must be well manured. Sweet corn also requires lime (pH 6·5 to 6·8).

Sowing

April/May. A balance has to be struck between giving the sweet corn as long a season as possible in which to grow and not exposing it to any danger of frost. Therefore, sow in a greenhouse at a temperature of 55°F (13°C) in April or in cold frames in late April or early May (depending on which part of the country the garden is in), and harden off the young shoots ready for planting out in late May or early June.

Unfortunately, sweet corn hates to be disturbed by transplanting. To get round this use small pots. Sow two seeds in each pot, 1 inch (2 cm) deep. If both seeds grow, reject the weaker. Alternatively, seeds can be sown out of doors in late May. Sow two seeds together at 16-inch (40 cm) intervals in rows 24 inches (60 cm) apart, later thinning out the weakest of the pair.

Planting

Late May/June. Plant the sweet corn in blocks in a number of short rows 24 inches

(60 cm) apart. This increases the chances of pollination: the male flowers are at the top of the plant and the pollen has to fall or be carried by the wind on to the silks of the female cobs lower down the stem.

The year's work

Weed, hoeing carefully to avoid the roots of the plants. Give the sweet corn a good soaking in dry weather. A mulch will help to keep the soil moist and occasional liquid manure will encourage growth. As the stems grow, support them with stakes.

Harvesting

From end August. When the silks wither, press one of the sweet corn seeds to test for

ripeness. If the juice that comes out is clear you are too early; if it is milky, on time; if dried out, alas, too late. Pull the cobs by giving them a sharp twist and lose no time in delivering them to the kitchen.

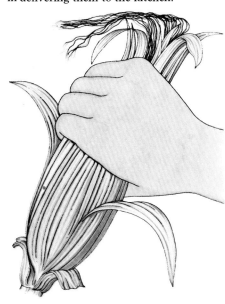

Garden Peas

Recently, an archaeological expedition reported finding peas (*Pisum sativum* var. *hortense*) near the Burma–Thailand border and carbon dated them at approximately 9750 BC. This is a much earlier finding than the peas found in Bronze Age (approximately 3000 BC) lake dwellings in Switzerland and

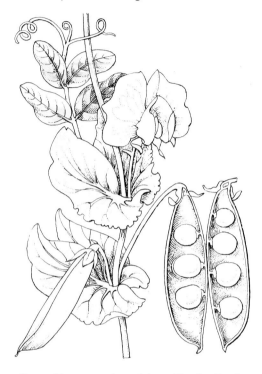

Savoy. Peas were also cultivated by the Greeks, and they were brought to Britain by the invading Romans, who back home ate them by the plateful at the circus. But to the poor of medieval Britain these dried peas soon became staple fare—unlike the Romans they had to be satisfied with the "bread" but do without the circuses. Not until the sixteenth century did fresh garden peas spread from Italy through northern Europe. A century later they became the fashion in England. Peas have the dubious honour of being the first vegetable to be canned and, later, deep-frozen.

Varieties

Garden peas are either round-seeded or wrinkled, (marrowfats). For flavour the round-seeded are not half as delicious as the wrinkled, but they are hardier, and these are the varieties to sow in November to provide peas in May or June. The sweeter marrowfats are sown from the beginning of March; they are ready in twelve to sixteen weeks.

For autumn sowing: Meteor (round-seeded) is probably the hardiest, with Feltham First an alternative. Both are dwarf varieties, growing to 18 inches (45 cm) in height, and do well under cloches.

For spring sowing: Feltham First, followed by the wrinkled Little Marvel, 18 inches (45 cm). Early Onward, 24 inches (60 cm). Kelvedon Wonder, 24 inches (60 cm) and Onward, 24 inches (60 cm), are two of the most popular. The more recent Hurst Green Shaft, 24 to 30 inches (60 to 75 cm), has long, well-filled pods and is very disease resistant.

GROWING GARDEN PEAS

Preparing the soil

Peas need a rich, loamy soil that has been well manured in the autumn or early winter. If fresh manure is dug in during the spring, too much greenery and too few peas will be produced. Peas also require lime (pH 6·5).

Sowing

October/November. Successful outdoor sowing at the end of the year depends on a mild winter, but the reward is peas from the end of May. Cloches will be needed in

cold, exposed gardens. Take out a trench (not a drill) a spade's-width across and 2 inches (5 cm) deep. Dip the seeds in paraffin, to discourage mice, and sow them along the bottom of the trench 2 inches (5 cm) apart in two rows 4 inches (10 cm) apart. Cover the seeds with the soil taken out of the trench.

March to June. By choosing varieties that mature at different times, spring and early summer sowings will provide peas from the end of June to September. Spring sowings can begin early in March in the south. If you live in the north, be in no hurry—the end of March to mid-April will do if the weather is cold. Sow at fortnightly intervals. The last sowing, in early June,

should be of the quick-maturing Kelvedon Wonder.

Alternatively, sow seeds in a cold frame in February, in small pots of John Innes No 1 compost, one seed to a pot. Harden off the plants so that they are ready to go outside in late March or in April. Plant the seedlings 3 inches (8 cm) apart, disturbing the roots as little as possible.

Distances between rows of peas should be roughly equal to the height the plants are likely to grow. What may seem to be wide open spaces between the taller varieties at the start should not be wasted but used for inter-cropping.

The year's work

When the plants, dwarf varieties included, are about 3 inches (8 cm) high, give them a little support with small twigs or pieces of cane. The taller varieties will soon need much more; use posts and wire or plastic

netting for them to cling to since pea sticks are now scarce. Hoe to keep down weeds. Water in dry weather. Give a 1-inch (2 cm) mulch of peat or grass mowings between the rows.

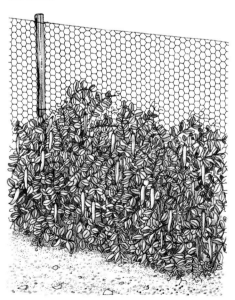

Harvesting

June to September. Pick the pods regularly from the bottom of the plants as they fill. When all the peas have been picked do not pull up the haulm, but sever it with a hoe at soil level, leaving the roots with their nitrogen-rich nodules in the soil.

Petit Pois

The sweetness of *petit pois* was almost the undoing of Louis XIV—he very nearly stuffed himself to death on them—and it is easy to understand why. They are the most aristocratic of all the peas.

Sugar Peas

The sugar pea (*Pisum sativum* var. *saccharatum*), also called *mangetout* and snow pea, was praised by Gerard as an "exceeding delicate meate" because it could be eaten "cods and all the rest".

Asparagus Peas

The asparagus pea (*Lotus tetragonolobus*), also known as the winged pea, is not only not a true pea but tastes delicately of asparagus. In common with the sugar pea it is eaten pod and all.

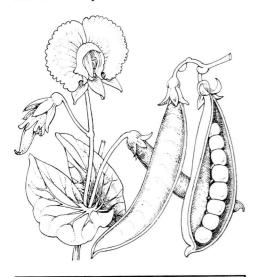

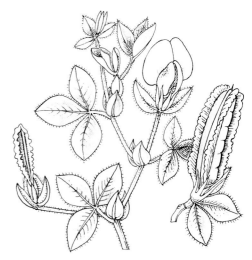

GROWING PETIT POIS

Like other peas, *petit pois* require a rich, well-drained soil that has been manured for a previous crop. They also prefer a soil with a fair amount of lime (pH 6·5).

Sow from April to June for a succession of crops. Take out a shallow trench 1 inch (2 cm) deep. Sow the seeds in two rows 6 inches (15 cm) apart each way. The trenches should be 40 inches (100 cm) apart.

Petit pois grow about 40 inches (100 cm) high, so as the plants grow give them some support. Keep the soil moist, especially in dry weather. A 1-inch (2 cm) mulch of grass mowings or leaf-mould between the rows will help retain the moisture. Harvest the pods as they fill.

GROWING SUGAR PEAS

Carouby de Maussane, an old favourite, has the disadvantage of growing 60 inches (150 cm) high. A preferable variety, satisfied with about 36 inches (90 cm), is Dwarf Sweet Gem. Sow the seeds in double rows in spade-wide trenches 2 inches (5 cm) deep and 2 to 3 inches (5 to 8 cm) apart each way. The trenches must be as wide apart as the height of the fully grown plant. Follow the first sowing in April, which produces pods two months later, by sowings in May and June. From early on support the plants. Water well in dry weather, and apply a 1-inch (2 cm) mulch of grass mowings. Occasionally give a dressing of liquid manure. Hoe to keep down weeds.

GROWING ASPARAGUS PEAS

Given a rich, light soil, a sunny position and a good summer, asparagus peas crop well.

Sow under glass in early April, barely covering the seed. Plant out about six weeks later, 12 inches (30 cm) apart. Or sow out of doors in early May and thin to 12 inches (30 cm) when the plants are big enough to handle. The plants grow about 18 inches (45 cm) high and need support.

The asparagus pea, with its brownish-red flowers, is attractive enough for the flower garden, which two hundred years ago was its usual home. The pods are too good not to be eaten, as long as they are picked when they are about 1 inch (2 cm) long and are not overcooked. By good fortune, pests and diseases find them less attractive.

Pea Pests

In June and July, Pea moths lay the eggs which produce those familiar maggots inside the pods. No spray can reach them there, so the attack must be made before

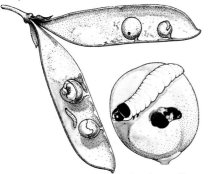

that stage, when the peas begin to flower. A carbamate insecticide, used seven to ten days after flowering starts, is generally recommended. Carbaryl is a persistent insecticide, but it is probably more acceptable than pirimicarb. Or you can take

action in the winter to lessen the menace for the following year. The pupae hibernate a few inches below the soil. If you dig the ground shallowly in winter, birds will help to dispose of the chrysalids.

Thrips, small black insects, lay eggs on flowers and foliage in May and June, and the eggs hatch into orange nymphs. Spray with a derris and pyrethrum mixture if the peas are at the picking stage.

Mice and pigeons eat newly sown peas.

To stop them, dip the seeds in paraffin just before sowing. Sparrows peck the seedlings. Cover them with small-mesh chicken wire, or fine nylon netting draped over sticks. (See page 55.)

Pea Diseases

White powdery patches on leaves indicate mildew, which is rampant in August and September. Watering will help to prevent it and spraying with Bordeaux mixture will help to control it.

French Beans

The French bean (*Phaseolus vulgaris*), also known as the kidney bean, haricot bean or, as in the United States, the string bean, is the ancient bean of the New World, just as the broad bean is that of the Old World. There is no doubt that the home of the French bean was Central and South America. Thousands of years later, early in the sixteenth century, it made the journey to Europe. Some authorities consider that it was brought to Britain by way of Holland. Others say it was the French Huguenot refugees, who started to cultivate it this side of the Channel when they fled to England during the reign of Elizabeth I. This,

they say, is why it became known as the French bean. Popular though it became in Britain, it was the French cooks who first took the bean to their culinary hearts. They called the dried seeds of the beans haricots, because they put them in *ragoûts* or *haricots* of mutton. The young pods, eaten whole, were called *haricot verts* and the shelled beans, eaten extravagantly young, became known as flageolet beans—the name is a corruption of the Latin *phaseolus*, and also relates to the fact that the French imagined the bean resembled a flute known as a flageolet. The dried, mature bean was called *haricot jaune*. In the nineteenth century, according to *Robinson's Family Herbal*, dried and powdered French beans were thought to strengthen the kidneys. They were also used to relieve shortness of breath—brought on, perhaps, by copying Charles Darwin's habit of playing the trombone to his beans to encourage their growth. Today the French bean is known to be valuable for its vitamin and mineral salt content.

Varieties

Dwarf: The Prince and Masterpiece, two old favourites, both early and stringless if picked young. Masterpiece is good for forcing. Dwarf, stringless: Phoenix Claudia, Tendergreen and the newer Cordon.

Climbing: Blue White, white seeded, stringless and of excellent flavour. (It is grown in the same way as runner beans.)

GROWING FRENCH BEANS

Preparing the soil

A light but rich soil is best for French beans—cold wet clay is deadly to them. Choose an open, sunny part of the garden and, in the autumn, dig in compost or manure. Like all peas and beans they need lime (pH 6·5).

Sowing

French beans like getting into a warm bed, indeed, in cold soil the seeds tend to rot. This means that French beans cannot be sown unprotected out of doors until mid-April or early May, depending on where the garden is and whether spring has come early. Err on the safe side. Rake the bed to a fine tilth some days before you sow. Take out a drill 2 inches (5 cm) deep and plant the beans 10 inches (25 cm) apart. Rows are

18 inches (45 cm) apart, or make them 24 inches (60 cm) apart to give more space for picking later. At the end of the row, sow a few extra beans to fill any gaps in the rows where the beans fail to germinate. A second sowing can follow three weeks later. Another in late June will give a crop in September and October, although cloche protection may then be needed.

To sow French beans early—late March in warm areas and mid-April in cold areas —warm up the soil by putting cloches over the rows three weeks before sowing. Or sow indoors in February in pots filled with John Innes No 1 compost and leave to germinate in gentle heat, 55°F (13°C). Harden off the plants. Plant out in June.

French beans can also be grown successfully in pots in a heated greenhouse. Sow them in peat blocks in the greenhouse or in a propagator in January. Transplant each seedling to a 6-inch (15 cm) pot filled with John Innes No 3 compost. The roots should always be kept moist, and if the heat in the greenhouse rises above about 65°F (18°C) open the windows until the sun has moved off the plants. These will produce a crop of the tenderest beans in April.

The year's work

Hoe to keep down weeds, and water in dry weather. A mulch of straw or strips of

black polythene in late June will help to smother weeds, keep the ground moist and protect the beans from getting soiled. Dwarf French beans can be beaten down by heavy rain, so support them with sticks or lines of string. Spraying the plants with water on dry days, when the flowers begin to appear, will help them to set. This is a tedious chore, but one which pays dividends in the resulting crop.

Harvesting

July onwards (outdoors). Always pick the beans when the pods are young, about 3 inches (8 cm) long. They taste better then and the plants will be induced to go on producing more beans. When they are picked, French beans snap off the plant, which is why they are sometimes called snap beans. Take care when harvesting the beans not to loosen the roots of the plants.

Runner Beans

Runner beans (*Phaseolus multiflorus*) followed French beans from South America within a hundred years. At first they were grown for their beauty and not for their beans. Now we can enjoy both. Nor is there just the scarlet runner—Blue Coco has purple flowers and violet pods, Blue Lake has white flowers and the old Painted Lady's flowers are scarlet and white.

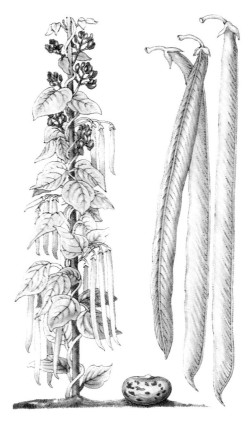

Varieties

Tall: Achievement, Prizewinner, Streamline and the stringless Fry. To treat as non-climber: Kelvedon Marvel. Dwarf: Hammond's Dwarf Scarlet and Hammond's Dwarf White.

Staking

Some varieties of runner beans grow to 12 feet (360 cm) high and they must be sturdily staked. There are several possible methods.

A batten may be fixed near soil level on the wall of the house and another at 10 or 12 feet (300 or 360 cm). Screw hooks into them at 10-inch (25 cm) intervals and tie tomato string between the hooks for the beans to climb up.

Another method is to make a tent of four canes tied together near the apex.

An inverted "V" frame can be made along the row with bamboo canes or bean poles, if you can get them, one to each plant, reinforced with canes tied horizontally along the top.

To stake runners in flower beds or in large, deep tubs, tie ten poles together at the top. Fan out the poles to make a wigwam and push the ends into the ground. Circle the bottom end with a wire hoop. Run strings from the hoop to the top of the poles for the beans to swarm up.

The dwarf varieties need no staking.

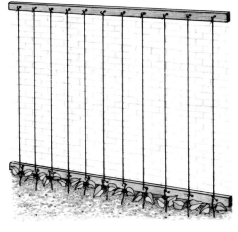

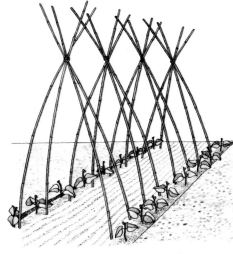

GROWING RUNNER BEANS

Preparing the soil

Runner beans must have a rich, deeply dug soil (pH 6·5) in a sheltered part of the garden. If they are to be grown in a row, take out a trench in February or March 18 inches (45 cm) wide to a spade's depth. Dig plenty of compost or well-rotted manure into the soil at the bottom of the trench. If the beans are to be grown in a group, manure a large circle of ground over which the wigwam will be put.

Sowing

Runner beans are easily damaged by frost. To prevent this, sow in peat pots, one bean to a pot, in the greenhouse at a temperature of 55°F (13°C), in April, and harden off for planting out in late May or June. Alternatively, sow the beans out of doors where they are to grow, but not before the start of May. In warmer areas sow again in June for a late crop. Sow the seeds 2 inches (5 cm) deep and 10 inches (25 cm) apart in double rows 12 inches (30 cm) apart. If there is to be more than one double row of beans and they are to be permitted to grow tall, allow 60 inches (150 cm) between the double rows. If all the plants are to be dwarfed, the double rows need be only 24 inches (60 cm) apart.

The year's work

Put in the stakes for the tall varieties when two leaves have opened out. Hoe to kill weeds and give a mulch of peat. Keep the beans well watered in dry weather, especially if they are being grown against the house, where soil always tends to dry out. A crucial time for watering is when the flowers begin to open. Spray, preferably with rain-water, in the evenings. When the beans reach the top of their supports nip out the growing tips.

To avoid staking, plants can be dwarfed as they grow. As soon as they start running, at about 12 inches (30 cm) high, pinch out the main growing shoot. Side shoots will then form. Pinch these out from time to time and the plants will grow bushy and stay low. Kelvedon Marvel is one of the best to treat this way. Dwarfing of tall varieties has the disadvantage of often producing curved pods, but they taste the same. In windy areas dwarfing is the sensible way to grow runner beans. The true dwarf runner bean, Hammond's Dwarf Scarlet (or White), will bush of its own accord without pinching. Like French beans, however, they benefit by being supported off the ground, if only to be slightly less accessible to slugs.

Harvesting

July to October. The aim is to grow beans fit to eat, not monsters to boast of with strings in them like old rope. Pick regularly when the beans are young and tender. Young beans are delicious to eat and picking encourages the plants to go on producing.

Broad Beans

Beans are as venerable as peas, and in the Old World the broad bean (*Vicia Faba*) is the doyen of all. Its prehistoric origin is doubtful. It probably came from the Near East, but it turns up in history, myth and archaeological sites in Europe (especially around the Mediterranean), North Africa and China. Curiously, the broad bean has had less

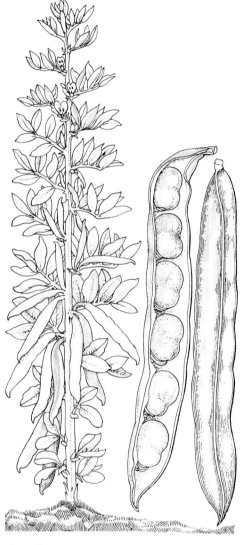

than its proper share of veneration. The Romans offered it to some of their gods, but for others it was taboo. According to Herodotus (484 BC), Egyptian priests regarded the broad bean as unclean, and Pythagoras blamed it for insomnia and bad dreams.

Yet in times of hardship the dried broad bean has been an invaluable source of protein. Bean meal was one ingredient in the hard-tack recipe given by God to Ezekiel in the vision of the disasters awaiting Jerusalem. And in medieval England many a peasant owed his survival to the broad bean.

Varieties

The long-pod Aquadulce for autumn sowing. The Sutton, growing only 12 to 18 inches (30 to 45 cm) high, sown autumn, spring and summer. Imperial Green Windsor and Green Windsor, heavy-bearing main crops and good for freezing.

GROWING BROAD BEANS

Preparing the soil

A well-dug, well-manured, fairly heavy soil suits broad beans. November-sown seeds, for early cropping in spring, do better in a somewhat lighter soil and demand warm, sheltered gardens. Rake the bed to get a fine tilth when you are ready to sow.

Sowing

Early November, February to April and July. Sow in double rows 10 inches (25 cm) apart and 2 inches (5 cm) deep. The easiest way is to make a hole with a trowel for each bean. Allow 24 to 36 inches (60 to 90 cm) between each double row, depending on the height and vigour of the variety.

The November and February/early March sowing will be of the hardier Longpods or the dwarf Sutton. The Windsors, better-tasting beans, will be sown out of doors from late March. The Sutton, sown again in July as a catch crop (possibly after a row of early potatoes), will crop again in September.

Alternatively, broad beans can be sown at the end of February or the beginning of March in a greenhouse or frame. Plant out, properly hardened, in April. If the weather is not warm enough, plant out under cloches.

The year's work

Autumn-sown beans will be helped to survive the winter if 3 to 4 inches (8 to 10 cm) of soil are drawn up around the base of the stems before the severe weather begins. Even so, casualties are often heavy if the winter is cold and wet.

Hoe between rows of spring-sown beans as they begin to grow, and never let the soil dry out.

Tall varieties, whether sown in autumn or spring, will have to be supported. This can be done by placing poles at intervals along both sides of each row, close to the plants. Tie twine to the poles about 12 inches (30 cm) above ground level, so that the beans can have something to lean against. When the plants are about 24

inches (60 cm) high, tie more twine farther up the poles to hold up the beans.

Broad beans under cloches can be de-cloched in late March or early April. By that time they are likely to have reached the tops of the cloches. (Only a dwarf variety such as Sutton is small enough to stay under cloches until cropping time.)

When the flowers are setting well—the taller varieties will then be about 36 inches (90 cm) high—take out the growing points, along with 6 inches (15 cm) of stem. This helps to thwart blackfly, the curse of broad beans. Blackfly attack the juicy growing points of spring-sown broad beans in force, although they are seldom found on autumn-sown beans. (For a spraying programme against blackfly, see bean pests.)

Harvesting

June to September. Like all peas and beans, broad beans should be picked when they are young, long before they have grown a thick, indigestible skin. Moreover, picking encourages production. The plant is determined to produce mature beans to perpetuate the species; the gardener is determined that it shall not. When the crop is over, the plants may be dealt with in two ways. Either cut the tops right down and dig the roots into the soil, or pull the plants up and put everything on your compost heap, which will benefit from the nitrogen the beans have manufactured.

Soya Beans

The soya bean (*Glycine hispida*) is, economically, the most important bean in the world. It has been cultivated in China for centuries, but was not known at all in Europe until the seventeenth century. It is still little known in Britain.

Bean Sprouts

The mung bean (*Phaseolus mungo*), the bean most commonly used for producing bean sprouts, is native to India, where the beans are cooked, puréed and eaten as part of the daily diet. In China, however, the beans are cultivated for their crisp, refreshing, delicately flavoured young shoots.

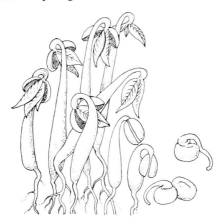

Haricot Beans

Haricot beans are the ripe seeds of French beans. Napoleon was so fond of them that when he was imprisoned he ate haricot-bean salad every alternate day. Both the French and Italians so enjoy haricots that they have invented many bean dishes.

GROWING SOYA BEANS

Some hardy strains of soya bean have been bred, notably a Swedish variety, Fiskeby V. Mice can be a nuisance, devouring the newly sown beans, but the most likely reason for failure with this vegetable is too-early sowing. Sowing out of doors from early May is soon enough. Sow the beans 1½ inches (4 cm) deep, and 3 inches (8 cm) apart, in rows 12 inches (30 cm) apart. The plants, which are attractive enough to be grown in the flower garden, grow to only 12 inches (30 cm) or so in height. The pods, picked young, can be eaten whole or, picked later, can be shelled for the beans. Each pod contains three or four oval beans.

GROWING BEAN SPROUTS

All you need is somewhere warm, about 70°F (21°C), mung beans and total darkness. Rinse the beans and soak them in a bowl of water for a day or two. When the skins begin to burst, spread the beans on a piece of damp towelling or blanket and put them in a warm, dark cupboard. They will have to be watered several times a day to keep them constantly damp. You will quickly learn how much water they need, for if they are too wet and too warm they will get mouldy. All being well, however, in a week to nine days the fat shoots will be about 2 inches (5 cm) long and ready to pull or cut with scissors.

GROWING HARICOT BEANS

Haricot beans need a warm, sheltered garden to mature in and a lot of space to produce a sizeable crop. Leave all the pods on the plants until early autumn, when they turn yellow. Then pull up the plants on a day when there is no rain on them. Hang the plants up in a well-ventilated shed to dry thoroughly. Shell, and store the beans in perforated cardboard boxes. If stored in tins or sealed jars the beans will perspire and will deteriorate in quality. Comtesse de Chambord is a good variety to grow for drying. It produces thin-skinned beans, which will need less soaking than other varieties before cooking.

BEAN PESTS

Blackfly, the aphis that adores broad beans, attacks in April (if the weather is good), May and June. Spray with derris, not waiting for the infestation to build up and weaken the plant. When using derris and pyrethrum always spray in the evening

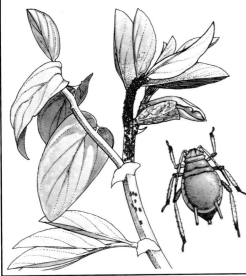

when the bees are back in the hive. By the next morning, when they are out and busy pollinating again, the bees will no longer be poisoned by the sprays. Repeat the spraying each week, if necessary, during the dangerous months. Blackfly usually choose the succulent growing tips of the spring-grown plant. Remove this temptation by cutting off about 6 inches (15 cm) of stem with the growing shoots as soon as a good number of flowers have set and pods are forming. (By the time the fly arrives, the leaves of autumn-sown beans are generally too tough to be attractive.) If French beans are attacked by blackfly, as sometimes they are, unfortunately, spray them similarly with derris.

Bean Diseases

Brown spots and marks on broad bean leaves and stems mean an attack of chocolate leaf spot, a form of botrytis. Attacks in early summer, especially in damp weather, are more likely to be serious and may kill the plant. Spray with Bordeaux mixture.

Semi-transparent spots surrounded by a yellow ring on the leaves and pods of French

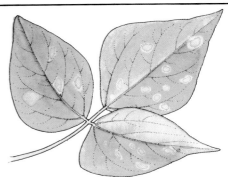

(and sometimes runner) beans is halo blight, a bacterial seed-borne disease which can kill the plant. The practice of soaking beans in water before sowing to help them to germinate, spreads the disease from infected to healthy seeds. Spray with weak Bordeaux mixture.

Stunted growth, yellowing leaves and a quickly dying plant may be caused by the fusarium wilt fungus attacking the root. It is less evident on well-cultivated land, but if it does appear, grow only such wilt-resistant varieties as Hurst Green Shaft, Vitalis and Recette in following years.

Onions

The onion is one of 450 species of allium. Regrettably, most of the rest, although highly ornamental in the garden, are not for eating. None the less, there is a whole range of onion flavours which are worth cultivating, from the gentle chive to the strong-flavoured garlic. Home-grown salad onions are cheaper than those bought in the shops. Home-grown garlic is absurdly cheap and much juicier. Leeks taste much better when just taken out of the ground, and since they are incredibly hardy there is no excuse for not growing them. Some of the other onions included in this section are unusual, but interesting. Sadly, the useful potato onion is now virtually unobtainable.

1 Strings of onions
2 Salad onions
3 Onions
4 Garlic
5 Shallots
6 Pickling onions
7 Leeks

Leeks

The Emperor Nero believed that leeks (*Allium Porrum*) were good for his singing voice. Romany Leon Petulengro believes that they are good for his hair. Most of us are content that they are just good to eat. Juvenal, a contemporary of Pliny's, must have been of the same opinion, since he complained so bitterly at their being adopted as divine: "... to injure the leek and onion is wicked, and to crush them with the teeth—O Holy race! Whose gods are born in the kitchen garden!" Never are leeks better to eat than in the grim days of February, although it means going out into the garden to dig them up.

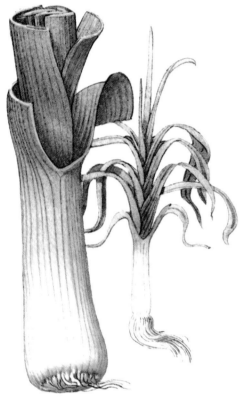

Growing leeks is a good introduction to other members of the onion family. You are hardly ever likely to fail, even in the coldest parts of the country. Disaster with main crop onions is far more likely, and can sour a novice for years.

There are two common ways of growing leeks. One, for the ordinary gardener, is simple. The other, for the gardener whose principal aim is to win medals and cups, is tedious and arduous. But the gardener who is as concerned with eating leeks as with cultivating them, can adopt something of both approaches.

Varieties

Marble Pillar, long, slender stems, mild and sweet when blanched. Musselburgh, long, thick stems, very hardy, resistant to frost, with excellent flavour.

Pests and diseases

Although leeks can suffer the pests and diseases to which the onion family is prone (see page 79), they seldom do. This is a worthy plant.

GROWING LEEKS

Preparing the soil

Although leeks are not as greedy as onions, no harm is done by giving them the same treatment—digging in compost or rotted manure the previous autumn—and the same place in the rotation, although they are planted later in the year. Add lime to achieve pH 6 to 6·5.

Sowing

Late January. Leeks can be sown in boxes of John Innes seed compost, 1 inch (2 cm) apart each way. Keep in a greenhouse at 55°F (13°C). Prick out to 2 inches (5 cm) apart each way when the seedlings are 1 inch (2 cm) high and then harden off for planting out in April or early May by moving them into frames in late March.

March/April. Leeks meant only for the kitchen and not for show are sown out of doors in 1-inch (2 cm) drills in a brassica-type seedbed. (See page 48.) The earlier the sowing the better, between late February and mid-April, depending upon where the garden is and the earliness of spring. On the day before transplanting, water the bed well.

Planting

Late June. Lightly fork over the rows where the leeks are to go and then rake them. Using a garden line to get the row straight, make holes with a large dibber 6 inches (15 cm) deep and 8 inches (20 cm) apart. Leave 12 inches (30 cm) between the rows. Lift the leek seedlings carefully from the seedbed. A handfork is the least

likely to damage them. By this time they will be 6 to 8 inches (15 to 20 cm) high. Reject the weaklings. Lower a leek seedling into each hole, but do not fill the hole up with soil. Instead, pour water into it gently, for the purpose is to anchor the roots without drowning or floating the seedling.

Another method is to take out two drills 4 inches (10 cm) deep and 6 inches (15 cm) apart, using a trowel for making a hole for the roots. Stagger the seedlings 10 inches (25 cm) apart along the two drills. Do not plant too deeply; only the roots and the base of the bulblet should be below the

surface. Allow 24 inches (60 cm) between these double rows. This will give room for earthing up later, to produce longer, whiter leeks.

The year's work

Hoe occasionally to keep down weeds. In dry weather in July and August water may be needed. Afterwards, all that remains to be done with those leeks which were merely dropped into holes in the ground is to dig them up through the winter as you want them.

Earthing up and blanching of leeks sown in double rows begins in September or October. The tedious part of this operation is to ensure that soil does not get into the leek. Tie paper or polythene around the stems to the base of the leaves before drawing up the soil (with a draw hoe) from between the rows. Further earthings up until the plants stop growing around November may make it necessary to add another collar.

Harvesting

November/April. Dig up the plants with a fork as you want them. They are very hardy. Any plants left in the ground when it is needed for the new season's crop can be heeled in in a small trench until needed.

O*nion*

The onion (*Allium Cepa*) goes further back in time than historians can. A Turkish fable, attributing the onion's creation to the devil, dates it from the time when he was thrown out of paradise and landed on Earth.

Other more reliable authorities have surmised that it originated in Central Asia and record it as being invested with divinity, not devilry.

Fortunately, however highly the onion has since been honoured, no one has regarded it as too sacred to eat, as the Egyptians came to do two thousand years ago. There was no hesitation about eating it among the Greeks or the Romans, who brought it to Britain.

In Britain the history of the onion has been occupied more with its medicinal than its magical properties. Among the more notable observations is the notion in Gerard's *Herbal* that the juice of the onion "anointed upon a bald head in the sun bringeth the haire again very speedily". Gerard was less enthusiastic about the onion's culinary qualities: "The onion being eaten, yea though it be boiled, causeth head ache, hurteth the eyes, and maketh a man dim sighted, dulleth the senses, and provoketh overmuch sleep, especially being eaten raw." In spite of Gerard's damnation of the onion, its culinary reputation increased as surely as the faith in its magical properties declined.

Varieties

For sowing in August: Reliance, large, flat, mild. Solidity, large, flat and unlikely to bolt. Express Yellow F_1, dark yellow globe, one of the new Japanese varieties.
For sowing in January under glass: Ailsa Craig, the old faithful, large golden globe.
For sowing in spring: Bedfordshire Champion, large, well-flavoured globe and a good keeper. Giant Zittau, medium-sized, semi-flat bulbs and an exceptional keeper. Rijnsburger Wijbo, large, solid globe that keeps well.

GROWING ONIONS
Preparing the soil

Once upon a time everyone was advised to make a permanent onion bed and, by heavy manuring every year, build up a soil of incredible fertility, which would produce monster onions. For the gardener who grows onions to eat it is both unnecessary (because an ordinary sized and tasty onion does not need force feeding like an Alsace goose) and dangerous (because the plot is as likely to build up disease as fertility). So let the onion bed rotate with the rest of the vegetable garden. It usually goes along in the cycle with the peas and beans.

Add lime to achieve pH 6 to 6·3. Dig in compost or well-rotted manure in the autumn, to give the soil time to settle, and let the winter break down the soil to a fine tilth. Rake in the spring. Onions prefer a medium soil, but it must be firm—hence the ritual of treading up and down the bed before sowing or transplanting. But wait until the soil is dry and friable enough not to stick in great clods on your boots.

Sowing

August. Sowings in shallow drills 12 inches (30 cm) apart can be made where the onions are to grow the following year (in ground, for example, that was cleared of the crop of early potatoes). It is better, however, to prepare a

seedbed in a very sheltered part of the gard leaving the seedlings unthinned over the win and transplanting them in March or ea April. Autumn sowings are worth while o in warm gardens, and even then losses will heavy, although covering the seedlings w cloches by the end of October will help reduce them. Only certain varieties are suita for autumn sowing; Ailsa Craig is the m popular.

January, under glass. Sow in January in se trays in a heated greenhouse—60°F (16°C) ensure adequate germination, thereafter dro ping the temperature to around 50°F (10° by daytime and 45°F (7°C) at night. Or sow peat pots, 3 or 4 seeds to the pot, removing but the strongest seedling. Harden off in a c frame towards the end of March, ready f transplanting in early April. Seeds can also sown in frames or under cloches, but obvious germinate more slowly.

March/April, out of doors. In the bed that all ready and waiting, take out shallow dril 12 inches (30 cm) apart. If you have large clumsy feet allow more space between rows that you can later weed in comfort. Sow thin and just cover the seeds with soil or sift compost, firming the rows with the back of rake. Since the seeds are black and not ve

rge it is a good idea to give them a pre-sowing
usting of flour. This makes it easy for you to
e whether you are sowing them as thinly
you should be. The less thinning that has to
: done later the better, for the disturbance of
e roots and the soil during thinning is an
lorous invitation to the onion fly to get to
ork. (See pests, page 79.) Thinning is usually
one in two stages, the first to 2 inches (5 cm)
art and the second to 4 to 6 inches (10 to
cm) apart.

lanting

larch/April. Autumn-sown seedlings will be
ansplanted in March or April, according to
e state of the soil and the weather. Allow 12
ches (30 cm), or more for those large feet,
tween rows and 6 inches (15 cm) between
ants. Planting must be done with care.

Do not plant too deeply. Make a hole with
trowel deep enough for the roots of the seed-
ng to go their full depth in the soil, but the
ottom of the bulblet should be not more than
inch (1 cm) below the surface of the soil. And
lant firmly.

Try not to damage the leaves of the seed-
ngs. Even if you do not notice the smell of a
ruised leaf the female onion fly may, and will
ome homing in to lay her eggs.

Seedlings raised under glass will be ready for
ransplanting from the middle of April.

he year's work

Veed, preferably by hand, because onions
esent you digging around their roots with a
oe. In dry weather water may be needed. A
eat sedge mulch will inhibit weeds and con-
erve moisture, but it should not bury any
art of the swelling bulb, which needs the
un. Stop watering as soon as the bulbs begin to
pen, from late July to August. In a dry sum-
er the leaves will topple over on their own. In
n a wet summer you may have to help by
ending the leaves over. (In a very wet summer
ne onion may go on producing foliage when
should be swelling into a bulb, and bull-
ecked onions which will not ripen or keep
ill be the result.) When, after two or three
eeks, the leaves have turned yellow and
hrivelled, the onions are ready for harvesting.

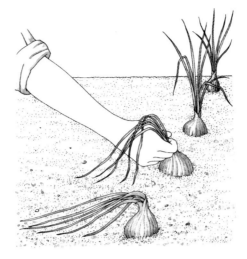

Harvesting

August/September. Choose a dry day. If
the bulbs are ripe they can be pulled by hand
or eased up with a fork. If the weather is thoroughly settled they can be laid on sacking or,
better still, on a raised wire netting frame, and

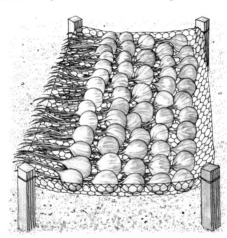

left in the garden with their roots facing south
to the sun. If the weather is uncertain, spread
the bulbs out in a greenhouse or in a well-
ventilated, covered frame.

When the leaves are brittle the onions are
ready for storing. Store them where they will
be dry and cool, but safe from hard frost. Dutch
trays can probably be acquired from greengrocers. Fill each tray with one layer of onions,
and stack. Ropes of onions take up less room,
and there is a certain satisfaction in being able
to rope at all, and much pride in being able to
do it well.

Store only sound, firm bulbs, and inspect
them frequently during the winter, removing
any which have gone soft. By May even the
longest keeping varieties will have abandoned the effort to live up to their name.

Stringing onions

When the onions are properly dry they can be
strung as a rope, which is the most convenient
way to store them. This method has the advantages of taking up less room than stacking
in trays and of allowing a flow of air around the
onions.

To string onions, take a length of stout string
or twine and tie it to form a loop. Hang the
loop over a hook at a convenient height for
working and proceed as shown below.

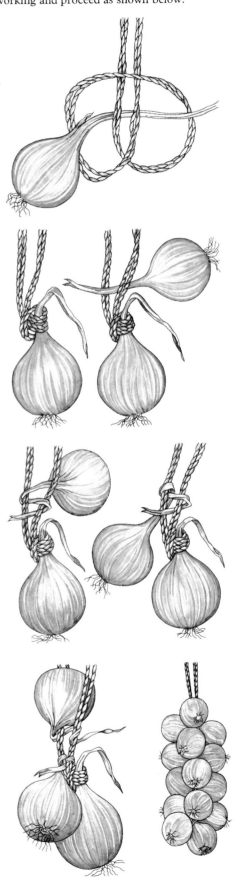

Onion sets

Some gardeners, especially those who live where the summers are short and wet, will never be able to grow satisfactory main crop onions from seed. Their alternative is to grow onions from sets. These are small immature onions raised from seed one year (usually by

specialist growers) and planted by gardeners the following spring to grow into full-sized onions. The young onion having, as it were, borrowed time from the previous year has a chance to grow to maturity and ripeness before the onset of autumn. This method was once frowned on as near-cheating, but is now plain common sense. Years ago, the varieties available as sets were, alas, limited, sources of supply dubious and sets were given to bolting after replanting. Dutch strains and Dutch growers, however, have altered all that, and no gardener now needs to sow another onion seed in his life unless he wants to. The onion set has a further advantage; it is generally regarded by the onion fly as too tough and unattractive a target. The only drawback is that sets are more expensive than seed, but not prohibitively so, considering that one pound of sets should produce fifty times that weight of onions.

Varieties

Sturon, mild, round and a good keeper. Stuttgarter Giant, semi-flat, will keep until February or later. Rijnsburger Wijbo, heavy cropper and good keeper. Many growers now heat treat onion sets to kill the dormant flower stem in the bulb and so prevent bolting. If the bulbs arrive before planting time, unpack them and spread them out in a cool place and in full light so that they do not sprout.

GROWING ONIONS FROM SETS

Preparing the soil

Sets are not as demanding as onions grown from seed. Do not manure the ground for this crop, but apply a dressing of general fertilizer, 4 ounces to the square yard (120 g to 1 sq m), ten to fourteen days before planting. Onions need a firm soil.

Planting

March/April. The bulbs should be of a fairly uniform size about ½ inch (1 cm) in diameter. Any much smaller are not worth planting because they will not grow into decent-sized bulbs. Before planting trim

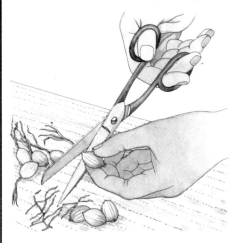

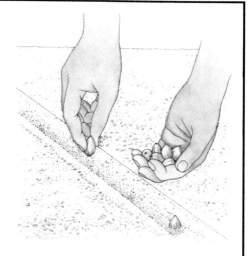

the old dry stems of the bulbs, but do not cut back into the flesh of the onion or it may rot. The purpose of this trimming is to leave less purchase for birds trying to tug them out of the ground, as they will. (Trimming is even more advisable for shallots, which tend to have more stem on

them.) Plant the sets just deep enough for the tips to show. Do not plant more deeply, even to cheat the birds. The bulbs should be 6 inches (15 cm) apart, in rows 12 inches (30 cm) or more apart. Make the soil firm around them.

The year's work

Except for the difference in planting, onions grown from sets need the same treatment as those grown from seed. It is unlikely, however, that there will be any trouble from onion fly.

Harvesting

Harvesting and storing are the same as for seed-grown onions. The problem is to provide enough sun to dry the onions out for storing, and this is not altogether in your hands. Northern gardeners, however, will find that onions from sets ripen more readily.

Shallots

Shallots (*Allium ascalonicum*), reputedly brought to England by the returning Crusaders, may be grown as a milder alternative, or as an addition, to onions. They are planted as off-sets, but instead of growing bigger—for they

are already mature—they produce a new generation of clusters of bulbs, anything from six to a dozen.

Varieties

Giant Yellow Long Keeping. Giant Red Long Keeping, which has smaller bulbs. Hative de Niort has round bulbs, but they do not keep well.

GROWING SHALLOTS

Preparing the soil

Grow shallots in a bed prepared as for onions. Shallots prefer a soil which has been manured the previous autumn and which has had time to settle. The soil must be firm, but do not tread it down until it is dry enough not to stick to your boots.

Planting

February/March. Planting should be done as early in the year as possible. Trim back any dead, long leaves which birds might fancy for their nests or worms for their burrows. Push the bulbs into the soil leaving the tips just showing. Since shallots have a way of pushing themselves out of the soil, or being pushed out by frost, watch out for any which may need replanting.

The year's work

Weed, with care. In June, draw the soil slightly away from the clusters of bulbs which will have developed, to help them to ripen.

Harvesting

June/July. When the leaves turn yellow dig up the shallots and leave them in the sun to dry. When dried rub them with your hands to remove brittle foliage and loose skin. Put on one side enough healthy looking small bulbs for next year's planting. Hang the rest in a cool place in string bags for use in the winter. Look at the bulbs occasionally. Remove any going bad.

Pests and diseases

The onion fly is the curse of the onion family, especially in May and June, although the plants may be attacked by later generations of onion fly right up until September. Main crop onions from spring sowings are those most likely to be attacked. Onions planted in light soil are also in danger of

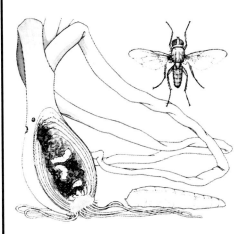

attack. Onion sets, shallots and leeks are less vulnerable. The onion fly, which resembles the house fly, lays eggs in the soil. When the destructive off-white maggots emerge, they burrow into the bulbs and eat them away. The first sign above ground of their presence below—yellowing and dying of leaves—comes too late for action. Dusting the soil with gamma BHC (Lindane), immediately after planting and again a fortnight later, discourages the flies. Above all, take great care when you are thinning out your onion bed. Disturbed roots, damaged leaves and thinnings left lying about put the onion fly on the scent of your crop.

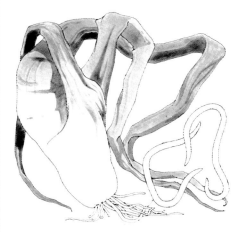

Eelworms, as their name implies, look like minute, transparent eels. However, they are invisible to the naked eye. Their rate of propagation is phenomenal—an infected bulb could contain literally millions of these pests. Of the thousands of species of eelworm there is one parasitic form which is attracted to onions. Secretions from the roots make the dormant

cysts burst into life and the microscopic eelworms (nematodes, see page 24) burrow into the bulbs and then into the stems, which swell and go soft. Burn all affected plants. After an outbreak you must abandon growing any of the onion family on that ground for at least five years. Chickweed is a host to the same eelworm, hence the importance of keeping a weed-free onion bed.

Cool, wet autumns may produce ideal conditions for downy mildew. This fungus grows deep into the onion plant. The leaves become velvety, die back from the tips, then finally collapse. If there has been a fair amount of rain, the leaves may also turn purple.

Warm summers may encourage white rot in onions, particularly in White Lisbon. The leaves turn yellow, the bulbs rot and are covered with a growth of white-grey fungus. Burn affected plants, and do not use that ground again for onions for at least eight years. There is less danger of an attack

on fertile, organically manured soil. Leeks and some varieties of onion, especially Bedfordshire Champion, are less likely to be attacked by white rot; however, Bedfordshire Champion is very susceptible to downy mildew.

Neck rot and bulb rot are caused by one

of the botrytis fungi, producing masses of white and grey mould or brown rot on onions in store. The fungus is most likely to develop if the bulbs have been damaged, for example by hoeing, or have not been dried thoroughly when harvested and are stored in a damp and ill-ventilated place. Do not try to store onions with green, fleshy necks.

Shallot virus yellows produces yellow streaks on the leaves of shallots and causes dwarfing of the plants. Onions are only occasionally affected. Burn the diseased plants as soon as you notice the signs. The virus is spread by greenfly, so control begins there with sprayings of derris or pyrethrum.

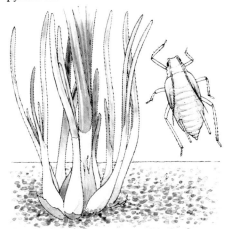

Onion smut is easily recognizable: the diseased young onion leaves are covered with blisters, which contain black, powdery spores. The blisters also appear on the bulbs. To avoid onion smut, mix a quarter of a pint of formalin in four gallons (125 ml in 18 litres) of water, and water the drills with this mixture when sowing.

These are the main pests and diseases, and there are more than a dozen others that could be mentioned. But by maintaining a fertile soil and not making life too easy for the onion fly, you have a good chance of avoiding all of them. It is important that you should recognize the symptoms, so that you may always be on your guard.

Chives

The chive (*Allium Schoenoprasum*) fills a spring gap in the onion year. It has been grown in Britain and throughout Europe for centuries, and in China for thousands of years.

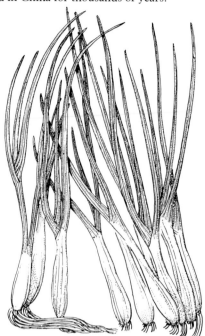

GROWING CHIVES

Preparing the soil

In the garden, chives are fairly tolerant about soil and position, but produce far more succulent grass in humus-rich, moisture-holding soil. In poor soil the leaves quickly yellow at the tips.

Sowing and planting

Chives can easily be grown from April-sown seed, but germination is slow and the first year is fairly unproductive. Buying clumps in spring is better, for cutting can begin less than two months later when the shoots are about 3 inches (8 cm) high. Divide them into clumps of up to half a dozen bulbs and plant them 8 inches (20 cm) apart in a row. They can be planted as an edging in the vegetable, flower or herb garden. Every third year divide the clumps and replant them in another part of the garden. Given good soil and not allowed to get dry, chives are also excellent for window-sill pots or window-boxes.

The year's work

Although a hardy perennial like the Welsh onion, chives are not evergreen. If you want early chives, however, they can be grown indoors. Dig up a few clumps in late autumn, divide them up, plant in pots and then cut the foliage to within a couple of inches of the soil. Keep them moist and cut and use the new shoots before they get too tall and tough. Constant cutting, both indoors and out, is essential if you are to keep up a supply of leaves. They should certainly be cut back when they flower—if you can bear to do so, for the flowers are particularly attractive.

Salad onions

Not satisfied with thinnings from main crop onions, the true onion lover demands "spring" onions all year round, and with a little bit of care he can almost get them. White Lisbon is the variety usually chosen.

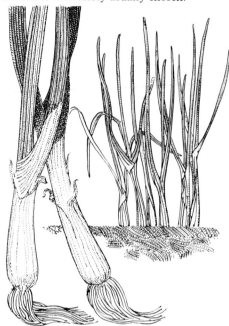

GROWING SALAD ONIONS

Preparing the soil

Prepare the ground as for other onions—raking to a fine tilth soil that has been manured for a previous crop.

Sowing

For the earliest spring crop sow under cloches in August or early September in ½-inch (1 cm) drills, 10 inches (25 cm) apart. Sow fairly thickly.

For a later crop (June onwards) sow under cloches in February or in the open in March/April. Sow again in May/June for pulling in the autumn.

The year's work

Weed carefully by hand in the early growing period and regularly thereafter—the young plants are delicate and can be easily enveloped by weeds.

Harvesting

Pull the onions as they get big enough to use.

Japanese bunching onions

The Japanese bunching onion is very similar in habit and hardiness to the Welsh onion (which in Japan is called the Japanese leek). It is untroubled by pests and diseases. If growing Japanese bunching onions from seed, sow in April and thin to 10 inches (25 cm) apart. By the following year each bulb will have produced a considerable number of scallions, with crisp, tender leaves and stems for use in salads. Like the Welsh onion it can be divided to provide further clumps. After several years it benefits from division, only the younger bulbs being planted and the rest eaten.

Welsh onions

The perennial Welsh onion (*Allium fistulosum*) is a native of Siberia, being correctly not "Welsh", but *walsch*, meaning foreign. Its hardiness makes the scallions it produces a substitute for spring onions in winter and early spring.

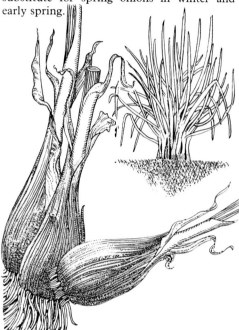

GROWING WELSH ONIONS

Preparing the soil

There is no need for any special preparation as these hardy, non-bulbous onions thrive in any convenient part of the garden, as long as it is fertile and well drained.

Planting

Although Welsh onions can be raised from seed by sowing in April in a shallow drill, it is preferable to buy a few plants. Plant 10 inches (25 cm) apart as an edging in the vegetable garden or in the herb garden. They do not need pampering, but give them a sheltered spot if you plan to dig them up in the depth of winter.

The year's work

Welsh onions require little attention. After harvesting, leave some of the scallions in each clump to multiply again. The next year, each plant will have produced a couple of dozen more. After three years, divide the clumps, giving them a change of ground.

Harvesting

From June onwards. Cut whole clumps—both the leaves and shoots are good to eat.

Potato onion

It is a pity that this mildest, sweetest and most disease-free of onions is almost impossible to buy, and yet it was once grown in most cottage gardens in southern England and Ireland. Potato onions are grown like shallots from offsets and need much the same cultivation, but the new bulbs form below the soil like potatoes. Planted in January in warm gardens, they are ready for harvesting in July/August. The best bulbs are saved for replanting and the rest stored like shallots.

Tree onion

The tree onion (*Allium Cepa* var. *aggregatum*) is the eccentric of the onion family, making it something of a conversation piece in the garden. Its oddity is that it grows bulbs underground and bulbs in the air, at the end of its hollow stems. In fact it grows bulbs in place of flowers.

Egyptian onion is another of its names. It is, however, the Canadian branch of the alliums, and arrived in Britain about a hundred and fifty years ago. It is perennial, hardy, easy to grow and the bulbs, although small, are extremely pungent. It can be pickled, or chopped raw in salads (in moderation) or cooked in stews. It makes an ideal substitute for any other onions if garden space is limited.

GROWING TREE ONIONS
Preparing the soil
Because the plants are going to stay in one spot for several years, start them off well by digging in compost or rotted manure.

Planting
Plant the bulbs in a sunny well-drained position, as for shallots. Both the airborne and the subterranean bulbs can be planted in autumn or spring, 12 to 18 inches (30 to 45 cm) apart. Although the clusters of bulbs can be split, you get better results if you plant the whole clump of bulbs.

The year's work
The first year's growth will not produce much, but a mulch of compost in summer will encourage it. In the next two years the plant shows what it is capable of, growing perhaps to 3, 4 or 5 feet (90, 120 or 152 cm). Left to themselves the stems will bend over and deposit the ripe bulblets on the soil to grow all around. To thwart them in this, give the plants adequate support by tying them to a trellis or plastic netting.

Harvesting
The onions can be picked off the stems as you need them for eating or storing.

Garlic

Garlic (*Allium sativum*) is one of the oldest and certainly the strongest of the edible alliums. The Romans, believing that it gave strength, fed it to their soldiers to fight the better and to their labourers to work the harder,

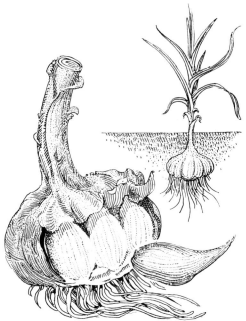

as the Egyptians did to the slaves building the pyramids. Today, the widely held theory is that garlic originated in the Kirghiz region of central Asia. In spite of its long history there is still much prejudice against garlic, but nowhere is it so evident as in parts of India, where it is associated with the devil. There is no need to buy garlic, because it is extraordinarily easy to grow.

GROWING GARLIC
Preparing the soil
A row or part of a row in full sun in the ground prepared for the onions would suit garlic, but it does not need the same firmness. The sun, however, is vital.

Planting
November to March. Plant the cloves, pointed end up, in holes 1 inch (2 cm) deep and 6 inches (15 cm) apart.

The year's work
Weed well, preferably by hand to avoid hoe damage. If there is a lot of top growth, support the stems with lengths of string between stakes.

Harvesting
July/August. When the stems and leaves lose their greenness and topple over, it is time to take up the bulbs. Do not tug them up; you may damage the stems and make them rot. Ease them out of the ground with a fork. Let the bulbs dry outside in the sun if possible, but dry them indoors if there is any danger of their getting wet. After a few days drying, hang them up in a string bag. Save as many as you need of the sturdy, outside cloves for planting the next year.

Pickling onions

Although tree onions can be pickled, the onions specially grown for pickling are the mild-flavoured varieties, which are lifted before they are fully grown. The best of these are Paris Silverskin, Cocktail, The Queen and Barletta Barla.

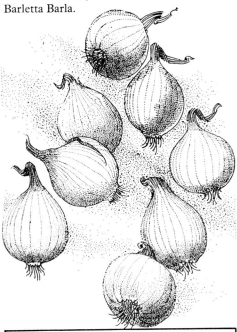

GROWING PICKLING ONIONS
Preparing the soil
Pickling onions are modest and convenient vegetables to cultivate: they actually prefer to grow in poor soil, so they can be planted in any corner of the garden that has been rejected by other fussier vegetables. All that it is necessary for the gardener to do is to rake the ground to a fine tilth before sowing the seeds. Pickling onions can also be grown in soil that had been manured for a previous crop.

Sowing
April. Broadcast the seeds fairly thickly or sow them in shallow drills 10 inches (25 cm) apart. Seeds sown shallowly produce round onion bulbs. Those which are planted about an inch (2 cm) deep produce oval-shaped onions.

The year's work
All that is required is to keep the plot free of weeds, which, if allowed to thrive, will dominate the pickling onions. Remove the weeds by hand. Pickling onions do not require thinning. Allow them to grow without interference until the tops have begun to die down. They will then be ready for lifting.

Harvesting
Because the onions have not been heavily manured and have grown in crowded conditions they mature early and should be ready for lifting by about the end of August. Fork up the onions and if the weather is good, leave them on the ground for a week to ten days, turning them over occasionally so that they can ripen and dry.

Roots

"**T**he roots have a peculiar flavour", was the catalogue recommendation, many years ago, for some obscure Chinese vegetable. The same can be said of any of the roots in this section. Which roots you grow depends on which peculiar flavours appeal to you. My own prejudices are against all of them except swedes, celeriac and cold beetroot. The common objection is that roots are too sweet. Only the radish escapes being condemned for that; instead it is blamed for being indigestible. It is a pity about the prejudices, for, in the barren winter months, roots are invaluable as vegetables in their own right, and as ingredients in other dishes they are indispensable.

1 Carrots
2 Swedes
3 Turnips
4 Beetroot
5 Parsnips
6 Celeriac
7 French radishes
8 Kohlrabi

Carrots

The carrot (*Daucus Carota*), a native of Afghanistan and neighbouring regions, grows wild in Europe and in the United States. As a cultivated vegetable it was well established in the Mediterranean region more than two thousand years ago, and spread east to China and northwards in Europe six hundred years ago. The Flemings brought garden carrots to England in the reign of Elizabeth I, and to this

day Dutch varieties are among the best.

Unlike that of many vegetables, the foliage of carrots is most attractive. At the court of Charles I, ladies wore the leaves for adornment. On a more mundane level the carrot has long had a reputation as a breaker of wind. Athenaeus, in *The Sophists at Dinner*, included this tribute to the carrot from Diphilus, one of the diners: "This is pungent, very nourishing and fairly wholesome, with a tendency to loosening and windiness; not easy·to digest, very diuretic, calculated to rouse sexual desire, hence by some it is called 'love philtre'."

Varieties

For sowing under cloches and early out of doors: Amstel (Amsterdam Forcing), the very stumpy Early Gem and Early Nantes.

Pests and diseases

The black carrot fly is the real menace, especially in late May and early June, and again in August and September. Dusting the very

small seedlings with gamma BHC (Lindane) gives control, but remember that BHC is persistent and toxic in the soil. Care in thinning reduces the danger of attack.

GROWING CARROTS

Preparing the soil

The ideal soil is sandy loam and it will also have to be deep for the long-rooted varieties. In heavier soils the stumpier and intermediate varieties are better. Heavier soil should be dug before winter so that frost can make it friable. The ground must not be manured for carrots; freshly manured land encourages the roots to fork. Apply lime to get a pH of 6·3 to 6·4. Just before sowing spread a general fertilizer, 4 ounces to the square yard (120 g to 1 sq m), and rake the soil to a fine tilth.

Sowing

March to July. The most desired carrots— the early ones—are the most trouble to grow. The earliest to be harvested would be those sown in February in a frame over a hotbed, but manure is too scarce for old-fashioned hotbeds and electricity too expensive to pamper carrots with soil-warming cables. With a little patience, however, a start can be made in March under cloches. Sow in ½-inch (1 cm) drills in rows 10 inches (25 cm) apart. As with all early sowings the cloches are put in position some weeks—at least two—before sowing, to warm up the soil.

The first main crop sowing can be made in April, and again in May, June and early July. Because the seeds are small, it is better to use pelleted seeds, if you can get them in the varieties you want. This allows you to space out the seeds and eliminates thinning.

The year's work

Once the seedlings are well through, water if the soil is dry. When they are 1 inch (2 cm) or so high, start thinning. This is a

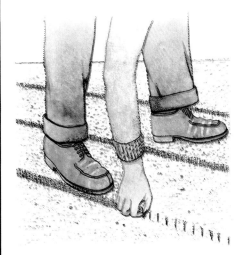

perilous time for carrots, for once you set about thinning them carrot flies for miles around, attracted by the smell, are likely to come and join in. Their eggs produce maggots, which eat away the root. To lessen the danger, thin on the evening of an overcast day and water the rows well after thinning. Do not leave the thinnings lying around on

the soil. Bury them in the compost heap instead of just leaving them on the top.

The first thinning should be to 2 inches (5 cm) apart and the second, two weeks or so later, 4 to 6 inches (10 to 15 cm)—the long-rooted varieties need more room to spread than the others. Hoe to keep weeds under control.

Harvesting

Summer and October. Pull the early carrots when they are young and tender, as wanted

during the summer. Those for storing are lifted, eased out of the ground with a fork, in October before the first frosts occur. If they are left in the ground too long in wet weather the roots will start to split. Store only the healthy undamaged carrots. Twist off the leaves and store the roots (not touching each other) between layers of sand or peat in boxes or plastic bins in a cool frostproof place.

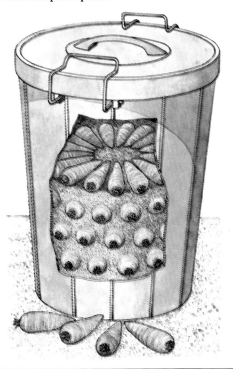

Turnips

Turnips (*Brassica campestris* var. *rapa*) were a staple food of the poor of northern Europe until they were ousted by potatoes. Viscount "Turnip" Townshend, advocate of

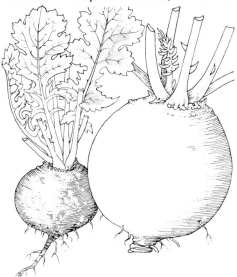

the concept of the rotation of crops in Britain in the eighteenth century, made them the food of sheep. But, in the first century AD, they were not beneath the notice of Gavius Apicius, Roman man-about-town and ostentatious bon viveur, who preserved them with myrtle berries, honey and vinegar. Sir Thomas Elyot, in 1539, in his *Castel of Helth*, wrote that not only were boiled turnips nourishing, but they "augmenteth the sede of man, provoketh carnall lust", a considerable claim for a vegetable which is over 90 per cent water. Those who wish to can have turnips for a large part of the year, but the turnips picked in their infancy in early summer are the most delicious.

Varieties

Early: Snowball, a quick-growing, round, white root. Red Top Milan and White Milan have flattish roots.
For winter use: Golden Ball, yellow fleshed and hardy. Manchester Market (Green Top Stone), good keeper and mild flavour.

Pests and diseases

The flea beetle is a menace. It is small and black and noted for its jumping ability and voracious appetite. The young leaves are particularly vulnerable to attack in dry weather and are quickly reduced to lacework if the pest is not checked. Do this with dustings of derris.

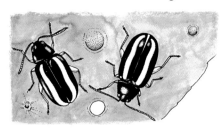

Club root is the commonest disease, as with cabbages. (See page 51.) In autumn, watch for mildew on the leaves, and if it appears spray the plants with Bordeaux mixture.

GROWING TURNIPS
Preparing the soil

Early turnips to be at their best must be grown quickly. This means a fertile, moisture-holding soil manured the year before. Winter turnips can be grown on ground vacated by other early crops. Both early and winter turnips require a dressing of general fertilizer, 2 to 3 ounces to the square yard (60 to 90 g to 1 sq m). Turnips need a firm brassica-like seedbed, or they may bolt. The soil must be adequately limed (pH 6·5 to 6·8).

Sowing

Late February to late July. The early sowings will have to be made under cloches or in frames. In early April, sowing can begin in the open and continue every three weeks until the beginning of July. In late July, sow seed of late variety turnips, to be stored for use in winter. All varieties are sown in ½-inch (1 cm) drills. Space the rows 12 to 16 inches (30 to 40 cm) apart.

The year's work

The first thinning, to 3 inches (8 cm) apart, is done when the seedlings have grown their first rough leaves. The second, a couple of weeks later, reduces them to 6 inches (15 cm) apart. Hoe constantly and water well if the weather is at all dry. Never, at any stage, must they go short of moisture.

Harvesting

Pull the early varieties as you need them. The turnips should be no smaller than a golf ball and no larger than a tennis ball. In October, the late varieties will be ready for lifting—use a fork. Twist off the tops,

and store the roots in sand-filled or peat-filled boxes in a cool, frostproof place. Do not try to store any which are damaged or diseased.

Swedes

Swedes (*Brassica campestris* var. *rutabaga*), or Swedish turnips, were once confused with turnips, but they are in fact larger and sweeter.

In Britain, they are most fully appreciated in the north, in part because they are so much hardier than turnips. Swedes are particularly good for storing.

Varieties

Purple Top, either to store or eat young, is the usual garden variety. Chignecto has been bred for its resistance to club root, but none the less has a good flavour.

GROWING SWEDES
Preparing the soil

The swede, like the turnip, needs a fertile, adequately limed soil (pH 6·5 to 6·8) that does not dry out quickly in summer.

Sowing

May/June. Swedes, slower maturing than turnips, are sown early in May in the north. In the south, sowing is delayed until mid-June; there is then less chance that the leaves will be attacked by mildew. Sow in ½-inch (1 cm) drills, 18 inches (45 cm) apart.

The year's work

Thin the seedlings to 12 inches (30 cm) apart as soon as they are big enough to handle. Keep the rows free of weeds. In dry weather give the plants a thorough watering.

Harvesting

October. Immature swedes can be pulled in late summer, and excellent they are, too. But the main virtue of swedes is as a winter vegetable. They will be mature in October and can be lifted and stored like turnips. In milder areas they can be left in the ground and dug up as required.

Pests and diseases

Dust with derris, especially when the seedlings start coming through the soil, to deal with the flea beetle. Swedes are affected by brassica diseases generally, but more particularly by brown heart—the heart turns brown and glassy-looking—which is usually recognized only when the root is cut open. The cause is a deficiency of boron. Water lightly with a borax solution—½ ounce to a gallon of water (15 g to 4½ litres).

Kohlrabi

Kohlrabi (*Brassica oleracea Caulorapa* var. *gougyloides*) is a cabbage with a swollen stem. It looks like the root of a turnip growing out of the ground. Kohlrabi can be grown in

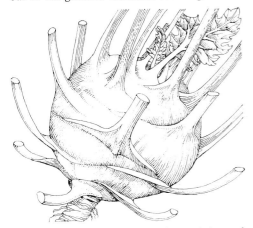

places where the summers are hot and dry and turnips are, therefore, likely to fail. It can stand drought and heat without losing its flavour.

Varieties

Early White Vienna and the slightly later maturing Early Purple Vienna.

GROWING KOHLRABI

Preparing the soil

Kohlrabi prefers a light soil, but to achieve the fast growth necessary for tender roots, well-rotted compost or manure should be dug in well before sowing. Because kohlrabi is actually a brassica, make sure the soil is adequately limed (pH 6·5 to 6·8).

Sowing

April to July. Make small successional sowings every three weeks from April to July. Sow in drills 1 inch (2 cm) deep and 16 inches (40 cm) apart. Sow three seeds every 8 inches (20 cm) along a row and leave one seedling at each station when thinning. Late sowings should be of the purple variety if you want to have some for winter. They will produce large and coarser stems, and they will not have the quality of the summer variety.

The year's work

It is important to thin the seedlings as soon as they are large enough to handle. When hoeing take great care not to hit and damage the roots.

Harvesting

June onwards. In summer, kohlrabi is pulled as needed when the roots are about 2 inches (5 cm) in diameter. Although the remaining produce of the late sowings can be lifted in October and stored in peat, they shrivel more than other stored roots.

Pests and diseases

For a brassica, kohlrabi is remarkably free of pests and diseases.

Celeriac

Celeriac (*Apium graveolens*), often called turnip-rooted celery, is, in spite of its shape, a true celery and has, both raw and cooked, the authentic celery taste. The texture is different, however, for it is the swollen base, not the stalks, for which celeriac is grown. In fact, the celery-like tops can be eaten—the leaves themselves as celery-flavoured spinach and the leaf stalks as celery-flavoured seakale. Unlike kohlrabi, the celeriac root should be allowed to swell to a decent size. This calls for a long growing season, but otherwise the plant has much to commend it. It is as hardy as celery, but less tiresome to grow because it requires no earthing up. It is surprising that this versatile vegetable has not gained more popularity in Britain.

Varieties

Globus has a good flavour. Marble Ball has large roots and produces few side roots. Iram remains white after cooking.

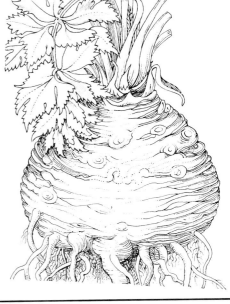

GROWING CELERIAC

Preparing the soil

Celeriac is a Mediterranean plant and should have as much sun as possible. Dig in as much rotted manure or compost as you can spare. Do not overlime, a pH of 5·8 to 6 is quite adequate.

Sowing

March. Since celeriac plants, unlike celery, can seldom be bought from nurserymen, you will have to raise them from seed. For this, if the growing season is to be long enough, heat will be needed. If you do not have a heated greenhouse use an electric seed propagator. Sow early in March at a temperature of 65°F (18°C). Failing that, try raising the plants in good light indoors, sowing the seeds in pots in John Innes seed compost at the end of March. Press down the soil firmly and sprinkle the seed thinly over the top. Cover with a fine

sifting of compost and water lightly. Seedlings should begin to show through from a fortnight to three weeks. When they are large enough, transplant to a frame and gradually harden off.

Planting

End May to early June. Plant the seedlings 12 inches (30 cm) apart in rows 16 inches (40 cm) apart. Make sure that the little bulbous swelling at the base of the plant is not buried in the process, but stays at soil level. Then water gently.

The year's work

Keep the ground reasonably moist, although celeriac does not need such prodigious watering in dry weather as does celery. Celeriac responds well to liquid manure applied fortnightly from July, or to a mulch of well-rotted manure. If the plants

put out any side shoots cut them off. In late September, draw some soil round the swollen roots to keep them white.

Harvesting

From October. Dig the celeriac as needed. Cover the roots with straw for protection. In November, however, especially in cold areas, it is safer to lift them for storing. Left in the ground they are vulnerable to frost. They store well. Remove the foliage and keep the roots packed in boxes with sand or peat in a cool, frostproof room.

Pests and diseases

Both pests and diseases usually avoid celeriac.

Beetroot

Beetroot (*Beta vulgaris*) is a very ancient vegetable, but the Greeks and Romans grew it for its leaves and not for its roots. Pliny credited beet leaves with the virtue of restoring

to its original flavour wine which had deteriorated in the vat. The gourmandizing Apicius recommended beetroot as a laxative. In Britain, Robinson's nineteenth-century *Family Herbal* prescribed snuffing beetroot juice up the nose to promote sneezing as a cure for toothache. Three hundred years earlier, Gerard also recommended inhaling the juice up into the nostrils to draw forth phlegm and purge the head. He did not, however, think much of the leaves, which "nourisheth little or nothing, and is not as wholesome as Lettuce". But of the red and beautiful root it "is to be preferred before the leaves, as well as in beautie as in goodness".

The long-rooted varieties of beetroot have been cultivated in Britain since the sixteenth century. The globe varieties, now the most popular both to grow and to eat, are a late development. Although the leaves are now generally thrown away, they are perfectly wholesome to eat as a substitute for spinach.

Varieties

Early globe: Boltardy, good colour and flavour, and not given to running to seed.
Maincrop globe: Crimson Globe, dark flesh without the unattractive pale rings. Detroit Red, of excellent flavour.
Late globe: Little Ball, deep blood red. There are also a yellow-fleshed beetroot, Golden, which is sweet and mild, and a white one, Snowhite.
Long rooted: Cheltenham Green Top, a conventional tapering good keeper, and the cylindrical Housewives' Choice (Spangsbjerg Cyclinder), 6 inches (15 cm) long and 2 inches (5 cm) in diameter, with the qualities of the globe varieties.

Pests and diseases

Beetroot are usually remarkably free from pests and diseases, but keep half an eye open for mildew.

GROWING BEETROOT

Preparing the soil

Like the other root vegetables, beetroot should not be grown on recently manured ground. Yet it needs a soil which is fertile and friable—one, therefore, which has been well manured and cultivated for a previous crop. If you dig the soil in the autumn and let winter work on it, you will have to labour less in the spring to get it to a fine tilth. Add lime to achieve pH 6 to 6·4.

Sowing

March to June. To have small and tender beetroot in June, seed will have to be sown under cloches. Using a globe variety, Boltardy for choice, a start can be made in March in the south and at the end of the month in the north. Beet seed is large, in fact in all varieties except one it is a little cluster of seeds, so station sowing is possible. This cuts down on thinning, an especially tiresome operation when crops are under cloches. Make two drills 1 inch (2 cm) deep and 8 inches (20 cm) apart, and place two clusters of seeds (or three for extra insurance against failure) every 6 inches (15 cm) along each row. Germination is helped

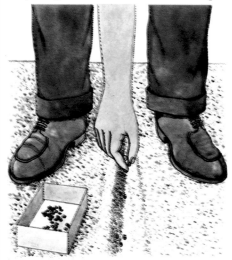

if the seed is soaked overnight before sowing. To thin, just remove all but the strongest seedling when the first rough leaves appear. Because they grow from clusters make sure that only one seedling is left. The one variety that produces a single seed and not a cluster is Mono King Explorer. Sow these seeds 2 inches (5 cm) apart, thinning to 6 inches (15 cm). Globe varieties are also used for early sowings in open ground in April or early May. These will produce large beets, so the spacing should be 12 inches (30 cm) between rows and 8 inches (20 cm) between the stations of seeds.

The long-rooting varieties, which are used only as a main crop, are not sown until late May or early June. Many gardeners stick to globe varieties as the main crop for winter storage as well as for early summer use. A final sowing of the globe variety Detroit Little Ball in July will provide salad-size beetroot in late autumn.

The year's work

Hoeing will be needed while the seedlings are young, but the fully grown beet leaves will themselves suppress most weeds. This

is as well, for careless hoeing can damage the beets and make them bleed. If the leaves do not succeed in keeping down the weeds, apply a peat mulch, which will also stop the roots from going hard. But—to repeat an earlier warning—never put a mulch down when the soil is dry. Keep the soil moist. Denied water in warm weather the plants tend to run to seed prematurely. Pull the beets you need for current use as soon as they are big enough—the smaller they are the sweeter they taste.

Harvesting

October. The main crop is lifted for storing on dry days at the end of September and early October. After working hard to grow the beets it pays to take extra care at this stage to ensure that they will be successfully stored through winter and spring. The roots are best pulled up by hand, since there is always the risk of damaging them

if a fork is used. Twist off the tops, not too near the crown; if they are cut they will bleed. Reject any roots which have been attacked by pests. Damaged roots will rot in store; do not bruise them by careless handling. Tea chests, if you can get them, are ideal for storing beets, but any large box or plastic bin will do. Starting with peat, layer the beets (not touching each other) and peat until the box is filled. Store in a cool, frostproof room.

Radish

The radish (*Raphanus sativus*) is by any standards an ancient vegetable. It was being cultivated in China, where it may have originated, in the seventh century BC. The pyramids of Egypt are, in a sense, built on a foundation of radishes, onions and garlic for, according to Herodotus, this was the staple diet of the slaves working there. The Greeks were fond

of radishes. Pliny slightingly commented, "Such is the frivolity of the Greeks that in the temple of Apollo at Delphi, it is said, the radish is so greatly preferred to all other articles of diet as to be represented there in gold, the beet in silver and the rape in lead." The Romans, however, were more down to earth; they used to hurl radishes at politicians. Culpeper, the seventeenth-century English herbalist, was not enamoured of them. "Garden radishes", he wrote, "are in wantoness eaten as a sallad, but they breed scurvy humours in the stomach, and corrupt the blood."

The modern Japanese would certainly not agree. They are extremely fond of radishes, especially pickled, and grow quantities of them, some to monstrous sizes. Japanese, Chinese and Spanish radishes, the winter radishes, are usually eaten cooked. The summer radish, however, is essentially a raw salad plant.

Varieties

Salad radishes. Round: Cherry Belle remains crisp longer than most varieties. Sparkler, scarlet tipped with white, sweet.
Cylindrical: French Breakfast, fast growing and mild. There is also a totally white tapering variety, Icicle, and a yellow-skinned one with white flesh, Yellow Gold.
Winter radishes. Japanese: Mino Early produces a mild-flavoured parsnip-shaped root 2 inches (5 cm) in diameter and 12 inches (30 cm) long.
Chinese: Chinese Rose, red and white radish-looking roots, but about 6 inches (15 cm) long.
Spanish: Black Spanish Round (turnip shaped) and Black Spanish Long (stumpy carrot shaped) have black skins, which must be peeled, and white flesh.

GROWING SUMMER RADISHES
Preparing the soil

Unless salad radishes are grown quickly they are not worth growing. A slow-grown radish will be hot on the tongue and as unpleasant to chew as cotton wool. For rapid growth, a rich, moisture-holding soil, adequately limed (pH 6·5), is essential. Radishes, however, seldom have a patch of ground specially cultivated for them. They are the catch crop above all catch crops, taking only three to four weeks from sowing to eating. Their needs, therefore, come second to those of the crops alongside them. But at least the soil must be fertile, and before sowing the radishes 2 ounces of general fertilizer should be applied along each yard (60 g to 1 m) of row. The soil should also be broken down to a fine tilth. In high summer, radishes must be given a moist, shady place in which to grow.

Sowing

February to August. The earliest sowings are in frames or cloches in February and early March. Sow the seed thinly in the shallowest of drills, with a fine covering of soil, allowing 6 inches (15 cm) between rows.

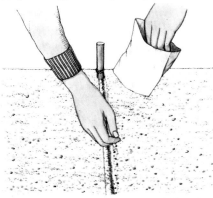

First sowings out of doors can follow from early March in similar shallow drills. Always sow thinly; thick sowing produces a lot of leaves and miserably small roots. If you choose the cylindrical French Breakfast or the round Scarlet Globe or Sparkler, intervals between sowings should be as little as ten days or a fortnight. This is because they not only grow quickly, but are soon past their best. Cherry Belle stays crisper longer, so the intervals between sowings can be stretched to three weeks or more. Times of sowings will also be dictated by the time at which space becomes available after other crops—for example, after clearing a row, or part of a row, of lettuce. Slip in a short row of radish whenever and wherever you can.

The year's work

Radishes are scarcely in the ground long enough for them to need, or to be given,

Pests and diseases

The flea beetle eats the leaves of seedling radishes. Dust along the rows with derris.

Radishes are liable to get all the diseases that attack turnips and brassicas generally,

any attention. Birds, however, enjoy the young leaves and may have to be kept off with nylon netting. In a hot, dry spell the radishes should be watered or given up as lost.

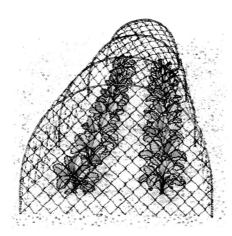

Harvesting

Pull radishes young, when they are about the size of a new penny piece.

GROWING WINTER RADISHES
Preparing the soil

Winter radishes should not be sown in freshly manured ground, but, like other roots, should follow a crop which had manure or compost. They also need lime—pH 6·5. Before sowing make the seedbed firm and rake to a fine tilth.

Sowing

Japanese varieties are sown in March for use in summer, and again at the end of July for roots to store for winter. The seeds are large enough to be sown in twos or threes in stations 6 inches (15 cm) apart and ½ inch (1 cm) deep, in rows 12 inches (30 cm) apart. Leave only the strongest seedling to grow on. Chinese and Spanish varieties run to seed if sown early. The best time to sow them is from the middle of July in the north to late August in the south. Sow in ½-inch (1 cm) drills in stations 8 inches (20 cm) apart.

The year's work

The soil must be kept moist and free of weeds.

Harvesting

Winter radishes will be ready to eat two or three months after sowing. The late-sown Japanese radishes can be lifted and stored in peat at the end of October. The Chinese and Spanish radishes are sometimes left in the ground and dug up as needed during the winter. But they, too, are better stored in peat.

but they seldom do and even more seldom suffer seriously. Because winter radish is in the ground longer than the summer varieties, it is somewhat more at risk from club root, but generally escapes.

Parsnips

Parsnips (*Peucedanum sativum*) have been eaten in Britain for some two thousand years, and may even be native. Their distinctive

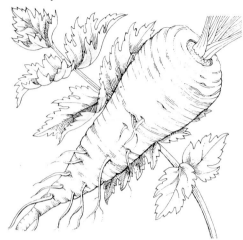

sweetness is an acquired taste, and in the last few decades fewer people have been acquiring it. Although parsnips are outstandingly hardy and could, therefore, be grown in any part of the country, they do need a depth of soil, especially for the long-rooted varieties, which many gardens lack. Other gardens may be too stony to grow straight roots, and forked roots are infuriating to lift. Devotees of the parsnip, however, can overcome these obstacles. Gerard, the sixteenth-century herbalist, was evidently not an addict. He reported that his friend Mr Plat had made a pleasant bread from parsnip roots, but Gerard tartly added "which I have made no tryall of, nor meane to do". People who do not enjoy eating the roots often relish them in the form of parsnip wine, however.

Varieties
Choose a variety of parsnip not only for its flavour but also for its resistance to canker. The depth of soil is also a consideration which will determine the type of root you grow. Tender and True has longish roots, good flavour and is fairly resistant to canker, as is the excellently flavoured Student, which is medium sized. Avonresister is most resistant to canker, has small roots and can be grown just 3 inches (8 cm) apart.

Pests and diseases
The main trouble is canker. Some cankers are caused by a fungus, but the more common orange-brown canker occurs when there is cracking of the roots. The cause may be lack of lime or excess nitrogen, therefore make good the shortage of lime and avoid digging in fresh manure. A wet autumn after a dry spell encourages canker. Late-grown crops are less liable to suffer from canker.

GROWING PARSNIPS
Preparing the soil
A parsnip is capable of thrusting 3 feet (90 cm) or more into the soil. Although this is not to be encouraged, deep, well-cultivated soil is vital. Like other roots, parsnips are also liable to fork in newly manured ground. Grow them where manure was given to the previous crop. Canker is encouraged by soil which is too rich in nitrogen or deficient in lime. Aim at pH 6·3. Before sowing, spread 4 ounces of general fertilizer to the square yard (120 g to 1 sq m).

If the ground is stony the roots will fork. To provide a stone-free environment for each root, push a crowbar 18 inches (45 cm) or more into the soil and rotate it to make a hole about 3 inches (8 cm) in diameter at the top. Fill this with sifted soil mixed with a little sedge peat and mark with sticks.

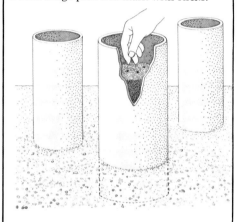

Alternatively, stand 4-inch diameter (10 cm) land drains on end, about 8 inches (20 cm) apart and sunk 2 inches (5 cm) or so into the soil, make firm and fill in the same way.

Sowing
Parsnips take a long time to grow. If the weather allows, begin sowing in February, otherwise leave it until March. Sowings in April are less susceptible to canker. Take out 1-inch (2 cm) drills, 18 inches (45 cm) apart. Sow three seeds in stations 8 inches (20 cm) apart or sow in bore holes or land drains. Parsnip seeds are painfully slow to germinate. To mark the rows before the seedlings appear—so that you do not hoe through them—sow quick-germinating radishes between each station. Buy fresh parsnip seed each year.

The year's work
There is little to do except harvest the radishes and thin the parsnips to the strongest in each group. Hoe carefully or give them a mulch. The roots in the land drains, if they are used, will need frequent watering.

Harvesting
October onwards. Dig the parsnips as needed, but in cold areas lift the roots in November.

Salsify

The true salsify (*Tragopogon porrifolius*), like black salsify (scorzonera) and Spanish salsify (scolymus), belongs to the daisy (*Com-

positae*) family and so escapes the diseases of the brassica roots. Salsify is grown not only for its long white roots but also for its chards.

Varieties
Mammoth Sandwich Island and Giant.

GROWING SALSIFY
Preparing the soil
Salsify prefers a light soil that is deeply cultivated and free from stones. It must not be grown in freshly manured ground. Adequate lime (pH 6·5) is essential.

Sowing
Early April. Sow in ½-inch (1 cm) drills, in rows 12 inches (30 cm) apart. The seeds are quite large, so they can be easily sown in stations, three to a station, 8 inches (20 cm) apart, the distance to which they will be thinned if you sow continuously along the drill.

The year's work
The plants need little attention beyond being kept moist and weed free. A mulch of sedge peat or compost is better than hoeing, because a hoe can easily and fatally damage the roots, which readily bleed.

Harvesting
Mid-October onwards. The roots are deep in the ground and must be lifted with great care. They are hardy and in many parts of Britain can be left in the ground all winter and taken up as needed.

April to June. Salsify is biennial and roots left in the ground will begin to put up shoots in April. In January or February, remove dead foliage and ridge up the soil 6 to 8 inches (15 to 20 cm) over the roots, and the shoots will be blanched as they grow. Cut them just above root level to use raw in salads.

Alternatively, do not cover the roots with soil, but cut the shoots (chards) when they are about 5 inches (13 cm) long and cook them as spinach. By frequent cutting the root can be induced to send up shoots still fit to eat until late May.

Pests and diseases
Fairly trouble free.

Scorzonera

Scorzonera (*Scorzonera hispanica*) looks like a black-skinned version of salsify, hence one of its names—black salsify. Although the

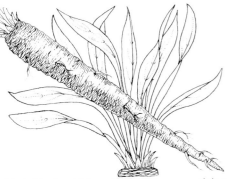

skin is black, which makes it look unappetizing, the flesh is white and of a better, more pronounced flavour than salsify. In spite of this, little scorzonera is grown in Britain.

GROWING SCORZONERA
Scorzonera needs rich, moist soil which has been deeply cultivated, for the roots often go down 18 inches (45 cm). Sow the seeds in shallow drills in late April. Thin the seedlings to 4 inches (10 cm) apart. In November, lift the roots—take care because they snap easily. In warm areas leave them in the ground, because freshly dug roots have a better flavour. Scorzonera left in the ground will provide spring shoots.

Chervil

The biennial turnip-rooted chervil (*Chaerophyllum bulbosum*) must not be confused with the annual chervil, the aniseed-flavoured herb. Chervil is fairly common in

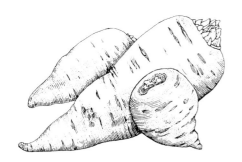

France and Italy, but is seldom grown in Britain. The slightly yellow roots are sweet and nutty, and rather floury when cooked.

GROWING CHERVIL
Once the seed has germinated, growing the plant is not difficult. Seed sown in shallow drills in October does not germinate until the following spring, and if it is sown in April it takes a year to germinate. The seedlings should be thinned to 6 inches (15 cm) apart. Growth thereafter is rapid, if the plants are kept moist. By July the leaves will begin to die and then dry. The roots are then ready for lifting and storing in peat. They store well.

Hamburg parsley

Hamburg parsley (*Petroselinum crispum*) has parsley-flavoured leaves and a parsnip-like root up to 6 inches (15 cm) long, with a

hint of a taste of celeriac. It arrived in Britain from Holland at the beginning of the eighteenth century. Hamburg parsley is hardy and needs a long growing season.

GROWING HAMBURG PARSLEY
Sow in shallow drills from mid-March to April, in soil manured for a previous crop. Thin the seedlings to 8 inches (20 cm) apart. Water well in summer. Harvest late because the rate of root growth is greatest in the autumn and, unlike most vegetables, the largest roots taste best. Leave them in the ground all winter, but it is safer to lift them in late October or November and store them in the same way as beetroot.

Rampion

Rampion (*Campanula Rapunculus*) survives vigorously in the wild and also in fairy tales. The brothers Grimm wrote about the theft of rampions from a magician's garden

and the heroine herself was called Rapunzel (rampion). The roots are like those of a very small turnip, sweet and milky.

GROWING RAMPION
Give the plant good soil and some shade for summer. The seed is minute and should be mixed with fine sand so that it can be spread thinly enough along the row. Sow in shallow drills in May and thin as soon as possible to 4 inches (10 cm) apart. The leaves may be picked sparingly when young for use in salads, and the roots will be ready by November. They can be pulled as needed during the winter and eaten cooked or raw in salads.

Skirret

Skirret (*Sium sisarum*) is an ancient root, probably a native of China, which four hundred years ago was greatly valued in Britain. In

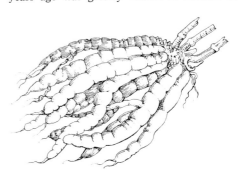

Tudor times its parsnip-like and carrot-flavoured root was universally popular. Today it is still eaten in China and Japan, although it is sadly neglected in Britain.

GROWING SKIRRET
Divide a cluster of skirret roots and in April plant each root 3 inches (8 cm) deep and 10 inches (25 cm) apart in soil manured for a previous crop. Otherwise, sow seeds either in late March for an October crop or in early September for a crop in late spring. Drills should be 1 inch (2 cm) deep and the seedlings thinned to 10 inches (25 cm) apart. Harvest when the roots are about 4 inches (10 cm) long.

Scolymus

Scolymus (*Scolymus hispanica*) completes the trio of plants which are dubbed salsify. This one is Spanish salsify, the stalks of which can be eaten. Scolymus is, however,

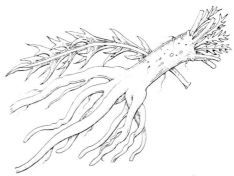

cultivated largely for its roots, but their taste is less satisfying than that of the true salsify or of scorzonera.

GROWING SCOLYMUS
Sow in shallow drills in early April on land manured for a previous crop. Thin the seedlings to 12 inches (30 cm) apart. The roots must never go short of water and occasional doses of diluted liquid manure will help them to put on weight and improve their flavour. They will be ready to eat from November. Scolymus roots can be lifted and stored, but if they are left in the ground they will retain their flavour better.

Tubers

The potato is the most versatile vegetable of the Western World and the most widely eaten.

Many varieties with superior texture and flavour, however, have gone out of commercial cultivation altogether because they crop less profitably. If you want first-rate potatoes you will probably have to grow them yourself. If you have no room in your garden that is the end of the matter, but consider carefully whether there are other vegetables that it might be better to abandon.

The other tubers of note—light years behind the potato in popularity—are Jerusalem and Chinese artichokes. They make a welcome addition to winter diets.

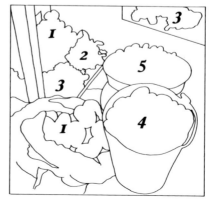

1 Main crop potatoes
2 Chinese artichokes
3 Jerusalem artichokes
4 Seed potatoes
5 New potatoes

Potatoes

The potato (*Solanum tuberosum*) came to Europe as recently as the sixteenth century, brought back by Spanish explorers from South America. There it had been cultivated since the beginning of the Christian era. The sweet

potato came first, and the common potato followed it to Europe. For a long time the potato was eaten only by the wealthy, and then as a delicacy. Not until the nineteenth century did it become the staple diet of the poor. In Scotland and Ireland the potato had to battle against the prejudice that it was not mentioned in the Bible. In Burgundy it was held to cause leprosy. The Swiss blamed it for tuberculosis. The English thought it induced lust. Now they blame it for inducing overweight. But the potato survives. It is hard to imagine a world without it.

Varieties

In Britain there are about ninety varieties of potato which can be sold for planting, but a gardener will be lucky to find a seedsman with more than a handful of them. The flavour of a variety can vary greatly depending on the nature of the soil in which it is grown (chalk, clay or loam) and the manurial treatment which the soil has had. It is, therefore, wise to experiment each year with a few plants of a variety not previously grown. The following varieties are suggested for their above-average flavour, but some have drawbacks.

Waxy: the pale yellow-fleshed Duke of York crops well, but is most safely grown as a first early (ready June/July) in order to avoid blight, to which it is susceptible. Sharpe's Express is an excellent early variety for growing in the north. Neither of these varieties is immune from wart disease. Follow with Record, a good main crop potato, although it is past its best by the end of winter.

Floury: Home Guard (immune) crops and cooks reasonably well. It can be followed by Maris Peer, an immune and blight-resistant second early (August/September). Outstanding for flavour among the main crops is King Edward VII. It cooks well and stores well, but it is a very unreliable cropper, especially in garden conditions, susceptible to blight and not immune from wart disease. Both Kerr's Pink and Golden Wonder are immune; they crop better and are more popular in the north.

GROWING POTATOES

Preparing the soil

In the autumn, dig in plenty of well-rotted manure or compost. Add peat to lighten heavy soil and to give body to light soil. Do not lime. Potatoes prefer a slightly acid soil (pH 5·6).

Sprouting the tubers

Encouraging the tubers (usually called seed potatoes) to sprout before planting (a process called chitting) has the same effect as adding a few weeks to the growing season. If, however, you tried to gain the same time by planting them earlier, they would be damaged by frost. Order the seed potatoes early so that sprouting can be started some six weeks before planting. Use Dutch wooden trays or fibre egg trays and place the tubers in them, "rose end" up—the rose end is the end which has the most

eyes and is usually the widest. Place the boxes in the light, but not in the sun, in a room which is frostproof but not warm. Warmth will produce weak, spindly growth, whereas the aim is sturdy shoots $\frac{3}{4}$ to 1 inch (1 to 2 cm) long.

Planting under glass

January/February. If you cannot bear to wait for the first outdoor new potatoes a few can be raised under glass. In a greenhouse which has a little heat, plant sprouted tubers in January, three to an 8-inch (20 cm) pot, in John Innes No 3 potting compost. By the middle of April the young potatoes should be ready for eating. In an unheated greenhouse, plant late in February and expect to eat the potatoes during May.

Planting outdoors

February to May. Because the young shoots of potatoes are easily damaged by frost as they appear above the soil, the time of planting depends on when your garden usually gets its last spring frosts.

The usual method of planting is to take out flat or V-shaped drills at least 5 inches (13 cm) deep and 24 inches (60 cm) apart for the first early varieties, and 30 inches (75 cm) apart for the later varieties, which

make more top and root growth. The first earlies are planted not more than 12 inches (30 cm) apart, but the others need 15 inches (38 cm). Plant the tubers with care, rose end up, rejecting and burning any which are weaklings or diseased. After setting out the potatoes along the drill,

cover each with a handful of peat or soil to protect the tender shoots from damage as you draw the soil back into the drill. The tubers should finish with a covering of 3 inches (8 cm) of soil, perhaps leaving a slight ridge the length of the row. Alternatively, if the soil is reasonably light, it saves time to make holes with a dibber and drop the tubers in.

After planting, scatter general fertilizer over the rows, 2 ounces to the square yard (60 g to 1 sq m).

The year's work

If the shoots emerge into late frosts, draw a little soil over them or cover them with straw. If you intend to earth up, loosen the surface soil between the rows with a fork when the plants are 6 to 8 inches (15 to 20 cm) high. Then, with a hoe, draw the soil towards the plants from each side of the

row. If after three weeks the potato haulm (foliage) has not grown dense enough to smother any weeds, a second minor earthing up can be done. In dry weather potatoes need water. Give it to them by flooding the trenches formed by earthing up. Spray against blight with Bordeaux mixture early in July and once every fortnight until September.

Harvesting

June to October. The first early varieties will be ready 10 to 12 weeks from planting. Once the flowers are fully open, dig up a root to see whether the potatoes are large enough to eat. If they are not, wait another week. Never dig up more potatoes than you need for one or two meals. The longer they are out of the ground the harder they will be to scrape. And while they are still in the ground they are still growing.

Potatoes for storing, whether second earlies or main crop, are left in the ground until the haulm has died down. Choose a dry day for harvesting. Use a fork to lever the potatoes out of the ground not to spear them. Damaged potatoes cannot be stored. Work along the sides of the ridges, not head-on along the rows. Root systems vary, but when you have carefully forked up a few roots you will have found how that particular variety grows and where most of the tubers lie. Pick up all tubers, however small. Any left in the ground will be a nuisance when they grow next year, and will help perpetuate eelworms and the fungus that causes blight. After lifting, dry the potatoes on sacks or Dutch trays in the sun. Sort out diseased tubers and burn them. Pick out the damaged and small potatoes for using first. The rest of the crop is then ready for storing.

Storing

Do not try to keep potatoes in clamps; on a garden scale they do not work. Avoid sacks; one potato rotting away unseen can infect dozens. Use Dutch trays, for they make inspection easy. It is vital, however, to cover the trays—preferably with sheets of black polythene—to exclude all light or the potatoes will become green and dangerous to eat. Alternatively, apple boxes or tea chests can be used. These also must be covered.

Stored potatoes will be ruined by frost. They must not be warm or they will sprout, or sweat and rot. Inspect them from time to time and remove any which are diseased. From January, when going through the potatoes each month, remove all the small shoots that they will have started producing.

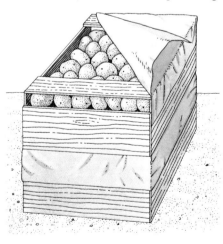

Growing potatoes under plastic sheeting

Another simple way to grow potatoes, which involves no weeding and no earthing up, is to grow them through holes in black polythene sheeting. This method, however, adds to the cost and possibly encourages slugs.

Prepare the ground as for conventionally grown potatoes and plant the tubers in the same way. Then, 12 inches (30 cm) on each side of the planted row, mark parallel lines with string and with a spade make a slit in the ground along the length of each

line. Similarly make slits at each end of the row to join the lengthwise slits. Take a roll of 150-gauge polythene sheeting, 36 inches (90 cm) wide and tuck the short edge of the sheeting into the slit at one end of the row and make it firm in the soil. Unroll the sheeting to the other end of the row and cut it to length, leaving 6 inches (15 cm) over, which you tuck into the soil at that end. Then tuck the sheeting into the ground along both lengths of the row, weighting the edges down with some soil. If there is more than one row, leave 6 inches (15 cm) space between the polythene strips to give you access. To avoid having to weed that bit of bare soil, cover it with a peat mulch up to 2 inches (5 cm) deep.

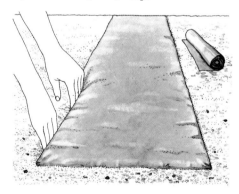

In May, bumps will be seen along the polythene strips. These are the potato shoots demanding to be let out. Cut holes in the sheeting just large enough to pull them through, taking care not to damage the shoots. For harvesting, fold back the sheeting. Unlike earthed-up potatoes, most of the tubers underneath will be near the surface of the soil.

Jerusalem artichokes

The Jerusalem artichoke (*Helianthus tuberosus*) is confusingly named. The tubers for which it is grown have something of the flavour of a globe artichoke, but the plant is a relative of the sunflower. It certainly has

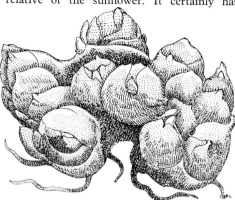

nothing to do with Jerusalem, for it is a native of North America. Jerusalem, the theories go, is either a corruption of *girasole*, the Italian name for sunflower, or of Ter Heusen, the Dutch village from where the vegetable was brought to England. The Jerusalem artichoke is easy to grow—indeed it is often more difficult to get rid of than to establish.

Varieties

White-skinned varieties are superior to the purple-skinned varieties.

GROWING JERUSALEM ARTICHOKES

Preparing the soil

Although the Jerusalem artichoke will tolerate poor conditions, it will then produce miserably small tubers. Therefore, dig in as much compost or manure as can be spared. Add lime if the pH is below 5·8. Lift all the tubers each year, replanting in new ground, for even the smallest tuber left in the soil will shoot up the following year.

Planting

February/March. Jerusalem artichokes should be planted as early as possible—according to local weather. Plant the tubers 6 inches (15 cm) deep and 12 inches (30 cm) apart, using either a trowel or a dibber, or spacing them along a drill. Leave up to 36 inches (90 cm) between the rows.

The year's work

Hoe if necessary and give liquid manure occasionally. In May, earth up the plants a little. Staking will be needed, for if the stems break the crop will suffer. Cut off just the top of each plant in August to limit further growth.

Harvesting

October/November. The tubers will be ready for lifting from the end of October, but they taste better if they are left in the ground and lifted as needed through the winter. Save and store some of the smaller (1½ inch, 3 cm), smoother, healthy tubers for replanting next season.

Chinese artichokes

The Chinese—or Japanese—artichoke (*Stachys affinis*) is not an artichoke, but it is a native—and a venerable one—of the Far East. It arrived in Europe in 1882, when Dr Bretschneider, doctor to the Russian am-

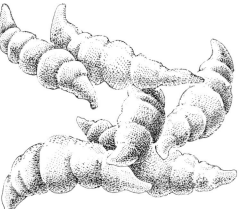

bassador in Peking, sent tubers to M Pailleuz, of Crosnes—and *crosnes* is the name the vegetable goes by in France. Dr M. T. Masters, FRS, is credited with having introduced it into Britain in 1888. Such precision in the history of a vegetable is worth recording if only because it is so rare. Chinese artichokes are grown for their ivory-white tubers, which are produced in abundance.

Although easy to grow and delicate of taste they are not popular in Britain because they appear to be fiddly to prepare. Chinese artichokes are great colonizers, so be sure to clear the ground of tubers at the end of the year.

GROWING CHINESE ARTICHOKES

Preparing the soil

Even more than the Jerusalem artichoke, the Chinese artichoke needs a humus-rich but lightish soil if it is to produce tubers of any reasonable size. Add peat to heavy soil. Choose a warm, sunny position.

Planting

March. Plant the tubers 4 inches (10 cm) deep, 10 inches (25 cm) apart, in rows 18 inches (45 cm) apart.

The year's work

Chinese artichokes quickly shrivel if dry, both in the ground or in store, so watering is essential in dry weather. From August onwards weak liquid manure, given every ten days or so, will add much-needed flesh to the tiny tubers. No staking will be necessary—the plant is bushy and only about 18 inches (45 cm) tall.

Harvesting

October onwards. The leaves begin to die down during October and the tubers can then be lifted as needed. They dry out quickly if stored. On the other hand, they are damaged by frost and in colder parts of the country will need protecting against it. Remember to keep enough tubers for planting the following year.

Pests and diseases of tubers

Jerusalem artichokes and Chinese artichokes are troubled by scarcely a pest or disease, but potatoes are beseiged on all sides, at least by the threat of them. However, with constant care and occasional luck it is possible to escape disaster for years or even for a lifetime. There are two evil pests—the Colorado beetle, which is very rare, and eelworm, which is not. These are matched by two evil diseases—wart disease, which is now not common, and blight, which is.

The Colorado beetle is ½ inch (1 cm) long, has orange-and-black-striped wings and lays orange eggs, which turn into destructive orange grubs. It is unlikely you will ever see one, but if you do see one in

England you must inform the Ministry of Agriculture—the simplest way being to tell a policeman.

The home of the potato root eelworm (*Heterodera rostochiensis*) is Peru, but mysteriously, and unfortunately, the pest turned up in Europe early this century. Cysts containing hundreds of eggs can stay dormant in the soil for ten years or so. Excretions from a growing potato activate the eggs and the minute larvae burrow into the root. Healthy potatoes can withstand the attacks of thousands of eelworms, but there comes a point when enough is too much, and the foliage dies and the crop is poor. No way has been found to destroy the cysts, and if the land is heavily infested the gardener has to give up growing potatoes for years. To help to avoid a build-up, do not grow potatoes on the same ground two years running. Fertile soil is the greatest ally against this enemy.

Wireworms are the yellow, tough-skinned larvae of the click beetle which bore into the tubers. They are encountered most in new gardens which were previously grassland, and there may be trouble for a couple of years if you dig up a lawn to make a vegetable garden. Trap them with the millipede trap described on page 43. Slugs usually damage only main crops. Use methiocarb or metaldehyde baits.

Some of the newer varieties of potatoes have been bred for their greater resistance to attacks of blight. Blight is caused by the fungus *Phytophthora infestans*, the

culprit of the Irish potato famine in the mid-1840s. The fungus is carried forward from one year to the next in infected tubers, and the build-up starts in the spring. Given certain well-defined warm and moist weather conditions, usually occurring in July and August, it can spread like wildfire. If over wide areas there are two days when the temperature has not fallen below 50°F (10°C) and relative humidity stays above 75 per cent, watch out for blight in the next week or fortnight. The danger is greater in the wetter western side of the country. The first outward signs are dark-brown marks on the leaves and stems. The haulm dies, and affected tubers later rot. There is no cure, so take precautions. Always, as a matter of course, burn affected tubers—they are the source of next year's infection. As an insurance, spray with Bordeaux mixture early in July and thereafter fortnightly until the middle of September. After an attack burn all haulm. And to repeat, never grow potatoes on the same ground two years running.

Wart disease, for which the fungus *Synchytrium endobioticum* is to blame, is far less of a menace than it was, because many of the varieties now grown are immune to it. Sadly, some of the favourites, such as Duke of York, King Edward, Sharpe's Express, are not. Only immune varieties can be grown on infected land. Wart disease, like the Colorado beetle pest, is notifiable.

Common scab looks nasty, but the damage is only skin deep. The fungus which causes it, *Actinomyces scabies*, is encouraged by liming (never lime land which is to be cropped with potatoes that season) and is discouraged by the presence of humus.

Aphids spread viruses. The five species of aphids which descend on potatoes can be destroyed by derris or pyrethrum.

Vegetable Fruits

V egetable fruits are the exotics of the kitchen garden. Many of them come from the tropics and that they grow in Britain as successfully as they do is largely because of the immense work that has gone into raising new varieties. For the amateur gardener who wants to grow these vegetable fruits, a greenhouse, frames and cloches are a worthwhile investment. But he will make his task harder and failure almost certain by trying to grow them out of season. He must accept that the British winter is too long, too cold and, above all, too dark for these tropical plants. In summer, however, they can be raised outdoors in many parts of the country.

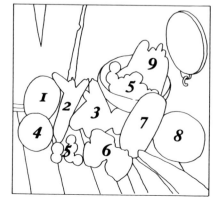

1 Winter melon
2 Cucumbers
3 Aubergines
4 Cantaloup melon
5 Tomatoes
6 Red and green capsicums
7 Vegetable marrow
8 Golden squash
9 Courgettes

*T*omatoes

The tomato (*Lycopersicon esculentum*) arrived in Europe from South America less than four centuries ago. It was then regarded as decorative but dangerous, for it is a relative of poisonous and narcotic plants of the *Solanaceae* family, one of which is deadly nightshade. The tomato's bright colour did nothing to allay people's suspicions.

After two centuries, the fear of eating tomatoes had been largely overcome, but it is only in the last fifty years that tomatoes have become universally popular. But while the tomato has risen in popularity it has declined in quality. The reasons for the decline in flavour and texture are commercial. If the professional grower is not to go bankrupt he must plant varieties which crop heavily and which travel well to market.

The amateur gardener, however, can still grow tomatoes for flavour. He can follow long-established practices or adapt some of the newer methods used by the professionals. (See page 97.) Anyone who can provide a reasonable amount of sun can grow tomatoes, with or without a garden. In the north, an outdoor crop is often a gamble, but the use of cloches makes it less so.

Varieties

Gardener's Delight, with small, sweet fruit, and Outdoor Girl, well flavoured and heavy cropping, are two old, tasty favourites. Other choices could be Ailsa Craig and Harbinger, and Yellow Perfection, which is a good yellow-fruited variety for outdoors. (The yellow varieties are sadly neglected, although they taste better than many of the reds.)
Bush tomatoes: Amateur is widely grown, but the flavour is not outstanding. Sigmabush and Sleaford Abundance are two excellent F_1 hybrids. Tiny Tim, with small, good-tasting fruits, is best for window boxes and pots.

GROWING TOMATOES OUTDOORS
Preparing the soil
The most important thing is the choice of a site for the outdoor tomato bed, especially in colder areas. More of the crop is likely to ripen if the plants are grown along a sheltered south-facing wall. Failing that,

build a protective south-facing wall of bales of straw. (Slugs may find a home there; put down bait. The straw can be composted at the end of the season.) The soil must be rich in humus. Early in the year dig in well-rotted manure or compost at the rate of 1 cwt to 10 square yards (50 kg to 10 sq m), plus plenty of peat. The pH to aim at is 6·5, but if lime is needed to bring it to this it must not be applied with the manure. A fortnight before planting out apply a general fertilizer at 4 ounces to the square yard (120 g to 1 sq m).

Sowing
As described for indoor tomatoes. (See page 96.)

Planting
Late May/June. If cloches are used to warm up the soil and to give early protection, planting will be possible about a fortnight earlier than without them. The plants, raised in pots under glass or bought from a nurseryman, will be about 8 inches (20 cm) high and the first flower truss will be forming. Water the plants the day before

they are to go out. Mark out a row and, at 18-inch (45 cm) intervals, make holes with a trowel as big as the size of the pot. To get the plant out of the pot, spread your fingers over the surface of the soil, turn the pot upside down and hit the base sharply with the back of the trowel. Without disturbing the roots put the plant in the hole and fill any gap with sifted soil, firming it with your hand. If cloches are being used, put them back in place until the plants are well established. All tomatoes need adequate support, especially those out of doors. (See page 97 for methods of staking.)

The year's work
Ensuring that the plants are adequately supported as they grow is a job not to be neglected. Cut out or snap off cleanly side shoots when they are about 2 inches (5 cm)

long. The main stem itself has to be cut (this is known as pinching out), so that the plant's energies can be concentrated on fruiting, not growing, one leaf beyond a flower truss. This will be the third truss in cooler areas or in cool summers elsewhere. Otherwise it should be possible to ripen four or, exceptionally, five trusses. Do not let the plants go short of water; a peat mulch helps.

Harvesting
Pick tomatoes when they are red and ripe. At the end of the summer spread straw along the row, cut the string supporting the plants and lay the plants along the row. Cover with cloches and many of the still green tomatoes will ripen.

Tomatoes under glass

Tomatoes in greenhouses are grown either in the border, if it is well lit, or in containers on a staging. Unfortunately, not only tomatoes but the diseases to which they are prone flourish in greenhouse conditions. To get rid of infection in the soil of the border it should be sterilized each winter, a job difficult for the amateur to do efficiently. Removing the old soil and replacing it with new is effective but laborious. Many greenhouse growers are turning to ring culture (see below) as soon as the crops in the border show signs of diminishing through a build-up of disease. Ring culture is also suitable for use on a staging.

Tomatoes can be grown successfully in greenhouses without heat. The crop will be less and later than with heat, but better and earlier than an outdoor crop. Cloches can also be used, and in the north keeping the crop under them all the summer will get better results than by growing them outdoors. Adaptors will be needed to give the large barn cloches an extra 12 inches (30 cm) height. Bush varieties under cloches all through the summer can be given enough extra space without the use of adaptors by planting them in a 6-inch-deep (15 cm) trench. Put straw under the trusses to keep them off the soil.

Varieties

Ailsa Craig, Harbinger and Alicante are the most popular of the reds. Big Boy (F_1) produces tomatoes which weigh one pound each and more; allow three trusses only. Golden Queen is a good sweet yellow. Tangella is a bright tangerine colour and has superb flavour. And, for an oddity, Tigerella is red with yellow stripes.

Bush varieties for cloches are those recommended for outdoors, but Amateur is less successful under glass than in the open ground.

GROWING TOMATOES UNDER GLASS

Preparing the soil

Dig into the border of the greenhouse well-rotted manure or mature compost—1 cwt to 10 square yards (50 kg to 10 sq m). The pH of the soil should ideally be 6·5. Hoe in fish manure just before planting, 5 ounces to the square yard (150 g to 1 sq m).

Sowing

From mid-February. The tomato needs warmth and light. Both can be provided artificially—at a cost. The amateur gardener will do better to wait and let Nature provide all the light, from April, and as much of the heat as possible for them to grow in. Allow nine weeks from a mid-February sowing to planting time and eight weeks from a mid-March sowing.

Tomato plants can be raised inexpensively by using an electric propagating frame inside the greenhouse. A day and night temperature of 65°F (18°C) is suitable until the seeds germinate, when it is reduced to 60°F (16°C). Sow the seeds in soil blocks, one to each block, or thinly in a seed tray, in John Innes seed compost. Cover very lightly with sifted compost and press it down with your hands. Water a little using a watering can with a fine rose, and put the plants in the propagator. The seeds germinate better in the dark, but remove any covering as soon as the seedlings come through —in about eight days. During this time the compost must be kept moist.

Prick out the seedlings, within a few days of the seed leaves appearing, into 4-inch (10 cm) pots of John Innes No 1 potting compost. Hold the seedling by a seed leaf, never by the easily damaged stem. Do not plant the seedlings into cold compost; keep the compost in the greenhouse for a couple of weeks in readiness for pricking out. The temperature in the greenhouse at this point should be around 60°F (16°C), possibly a few degrees more in the day, but not less than 55°F (13°C) at night. Put the pots on a greenhouse bench where there is plenty of light. Do not crowd them.

Planting

From end of March. When planting out allow 18 inches (45 cm) between plants and 30 inches (75 cm) between rows. The soil in the border at planting time should be 55°F (13°C), or very near it, and the greenhouse air temperature 60°F (16°C). Amateurs in many areas will be able to achieve this in late March and April without exorbitant expense. But it is the levels of light as much as of heat which are the determining factor in the growth of the plants.

The year's work

For several days after planting a humid atmosphere helps the plants to settle down. After that they need a warm but adequately ventilated atmosphere. It must not be like a Turkish bath. Give the plants support as soon as possible. (See page 97.) Take out side shoots when they are about 2 inches (5 cm) long. To help pollination, spray the plants with water in the mornings, but only on bright days. After the second or third truss of flowers has set, give a weekly proprietary liquid feed, following the instructions absolutely. In the height of summer the tomatoes may need to be lightly shaded from direct sunlight.

Greenhouse plants are allowed to develop twice as many trusses as those outdoors, say

eight or ten, but in any case cut the main stem when it is about to hit the roof. Some of the leaves may be removed below trusses of fruit as each truss ripens, but do not overdo defoliation; the leaves are there to manufacture food for the plant.

Harvesting

Pick the tomatoes as they ripen by snapping the stalk from the main stem and not by pulling it away from the calyx. Apart from the fact that the tomatoes will stay fresh longer if the calyx is removed with the fruit, if the calyx is left on the plant it may be a starting point for botrytis. Moreover, one of the joys of eating a home-grown tomato is to savour the beautiful smell of the calyx as you wrench it from the fruit.

The point in the autumn at which you decide to pick all the remaining fruits and dig up the plants depends on what other uses you have for the greenhouse—whether, for example, it is needed for chrysanthemums.

Growing tomatoes by other methods

There are other methods of growing tomatoes, and two of them, by ring culture or in bags of specially prepared peat, do not involve too much labour for the amateur gardener. In growing by ring culture the plants draw their food from a bottomless container of rich compost, and their water from a base of aggregate (usually gravel) into which their roots penetrate. The advantage is that the plants are not exposed to infection from soil diseases as they are when grown in the border of the greenhouse. The system of growing tomatoes in bags of specially prepared peat is good for such confined spaces as patios, balconies and verandas.

Ring culture

This method is most used in greenhouses where diseases have taken hold, but it may be employed out of doors. The rings are bottomless containers 9 inches (23 cm) in diameter and 9 inches (23 cm) deep. They can be of whale-hide, for one year's use, or of plastic, which lasts longer. Place them in rows 18 inches (45 cm) apart from centre to centre on a bed of aggregate 6 inches (15 cm) deep. One satisfactory material is gravel, not more than $\frac{1}{4}$ inch ($\frac{1}{2}$ cm) in size, which has been washed to get rid of dust. Two weeks before planting fill the rings with John Innes No 3 compost; a 56-pound (25 kg) bag will be enough for five of the 9-inch (23 cm) rings, filled to within ½ inch (1 cm) of the rim. By filling the rings in advance the compost will have time to warm up in the greenhouse. Two days before planting, water both the compost and the aggregate. The times of planting are the same as those for orthodox greenhouse growing. When the plants have been moved to their containers give each one about 2 pints (1 litre) of water. Any further watering for the next ten days should be done through the rings, but not after that period, when the roots will have reached the aggregate.

Feeding the plants
This is always done through the rings and not through the aggregate. Start the weekly feed of a high potash proprietary liquid fertilizer—about 2 pints (1 litre) per plant—when the petals have fallen and the fruit is forming on the first flower truss. Try not to spill fertilizer on the aggregate.

Watering
In hot, dry weather reckon to apply at least ½ gallon (2 litres) of water to the aggregate around each ring each day. In cooler, duller weather every other day will be enough.

Tomatoes grown in this way may be carrying up to a dozen trusses and, therefore, will need adequate support.

Peat bags
The bags are bought already filled with a specially prepared peat compost. Indoors, three plants can be grown in each bag, and four in each bag outdoors. The compost contains all the requirements the plants need for the first few weeks. Afterwards they will need liquid feeding according to the instructions. Because there is no drainage from the bag—an advantage allowing it to be sited anywhere—a watering problem is created. The peat must not become waterlogged, nor must

it dry out, and avoiding this may involve watering twice a day in hot weather. There is no doubt, however, that this method produces excellent crops of tomatoes.

Staking tomatoes
Tomatoes by nature trail along the ground. Because we insist on growing them vertically instead of horizontally we must give them adequate support. Outdoors the support must be strong enough to enable the plants to withstand winds, particularly if the crop is being raised in very flat or coastal areas or if there is no protective wall near the tomato bed. In the greenhouse the support must be strong enough to carry a heavy crop—each plant may be bearing ten pounds of tomatoes at peak times. Bush tomatoes need little or no support. Numerous and often complicated means of providing support have been devised for the tall varieties, indoors and outdoors. For the amateur gardener, the simpler the support the better.

Out of doors
Drive 8-foot (2½ m) wooden stakes 18 inches (45 cm) into the ground at each end of the row, and at 6-foot (1¾ m) intervals if the row is a long one. Join the tops of the stakes with wire, extending it to straining posts at both ends of the row. After planting out the tomatoes push a cane into the soil behind each plant—not into the roots—and fasten the top of it to the wire. As the plants grow they are tied

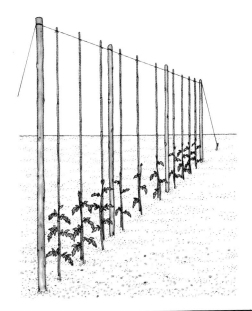

loosely to the canes with twine every 10 or 12 inches (25 to 30 cm).

Under cloches
Tomatoes spending the whole summer under tall cloches can be allowed to develop one shoot in addition to the main stem. From stakes at each end run a wire the length of the row, a

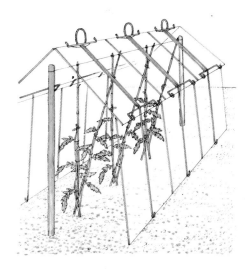

few inches below the top of the cloche. Each plant has two canes, tied to the top wire, to support it—one vertical and the other diagonal. The two shoots are tied loosely to the canes as they grow.

In the greenhouse
The simplest method is to use tomato fillis (strong, soft twine), tied between two stout wires. The top wire is run near the roof of the greenhouse and the bottom wire a few inches above the soil or the containers in which the plants are growing. The wires can be

fastened to stakes, or to the end framework of the greenhouse if that is strong enough. It is unwise to fix the wire to roof spars because of the strain the weight of the crop will impose upon them. As the plants grow they are gently twisted round the fillis. Do this each time the plant grows 6 inches (15 cm). This method can also be used for outdoor plants.

Cucumbers

Cucumbers, Pliny records, were "a wonderful favourite" with the Emperor Tiberius, who ate them every day, thanks to the skill of his gardeners, who "forced" cucumbers in winter. Tiberius' devotion to the cucumber

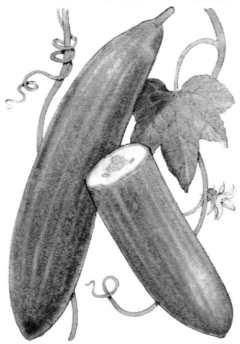

was not shared by the egregious Dr Samuel Johnson, who wrote, "A cucumber should be well sliced, and dressed with pepper and vinegar, and then thrown out, as good for nothing." The verdict of history is against him. The cucumber (*Cucumis sativus*) has been grown for thousands of years. It is probably a native of northwest India, but it travelled west long before the Christian era.

The Roman Apicius had a recipe for boiling cucumber with brains, honey, cumin, celery seed, oil and eggs. The English herbalist Gerard advocated boiling it with mutton and mixing it with oatmeal. This concoction, he said, "doth perfectly cure all manner of sauce flegme and copper faces, red and shining fierie noses".

There are two types of cucumber. Ridge cucumbers, with rather knobbly skins, can be grown out of doors. The greenhouse or frame cucumbers need the protection of glass. Unfortunately, tomatoes and cucumbers, although indissolubly associated as ingredients of salad, are bad companions in the greenhouse. Both like warmth, but the cucumber likes steamy heat, which would be disastrous for tomatoes. The amateur gardener would probably do better to leave the greenhouse to tomatoes and grow cucumbers under frames, heated or cold, and cloches.

Varieties

Butcher's Disease Resisting as well as living up to its name, crops well, even in the north. Telegraph Improved is an ever-popular variety for frame culture. Sigmadew, which is almost white-skinned, is of excellent flavour. New all-female-flowered varieties and hence no danger of bitter fruits (see the year's work), include Femspot, Femina and Fertila.

GROWING CUCUMBERS

Preparing the soil

In the centre of each frame dig a hole 12 inches (30 cm) square and 12 inches (30 cm) deep and fill it in with a mixture of well-rotted manure or compost and peat. (This method—digging a hole in preference to a trench—economizes on precious manure and compost.) For cucumbers under cloches the enriched holes should be 36 inches (90 cm) apart down the centre of a row.

Sowing

The time of sowing will depend on whether your garden is situated in a warm or cold area. It also depends on whether you are planting out to a frame with some heat, or to a cold frame, cold greenhouse or cloche. Allow about five weeks from sowing to planting out. If you are using a heated frame in a southern area, sow in mid-March. The seedlings will be ready for planting out in late April. For an unheated frame in the south, sow towards the end of April to plant out in May or early June. In the north, sowing and planting dates are at least a fortnight later.

Cucumbers thoroughly dislike root disturbance, therefore they should be sown in individual 3-inch (8 cm) pots, or soil blocks, in John Innes seed compost. Push two seeds, on their edges, $\frac{3}{4}$ inch (2 cm) into the compost, which must not be pressed down; the cucumber is an exception to the general rule of firm planting. Water the

pots or blocks, using a watering can with a fine rose, and put the pots or soil blocks in the propagator. For quick germination the temperature should be 65°F to 70°F (18°C to 21°C). When the seedlings show through in two or three days make sure they have plenty of light, but not direct sunlight, and keep them moist. Temperatures should be about 65°F (18°C) by day and not less than 60°F (16°C) at night. They will be ready for planting out when the third or fourth true leaves have appeared.

Sowing without heat

In the south, sow seeds in an unheated greenhouse or frame at the end of April or early May. In the north it is better to buy plants from a nursery in May or early June.

Planting

Set one plant in a slight mound of John Innes No 3 compost in the centre of each frame. (The mound is to help to prevent water from collecting at the base of the plant's stem and causing stem rot.) Under cloches the cucumber plants should be 36 inches (90 cm) apart.

The year's work

Cucumbers need a lot of attention. The soil must be kept moist, but not sodden, and the atmosphere in the frame must be humid. Shading may be needed against scorching sun to ensure that the temperature in the frame does not soar above 85°F (29°C). Training and pinching back of the shoots is essential for a decent crop. The male flowers must be removed so that they do not pollinate the fruiting females. Fortunately, it is easy to spot the difference: the incipient cucumber can be seen behind the flower of the female. If the male flower is not removed the result will be bitter cucumbers full of large seeds. This chore can be avoided, however, by choosing only the female-flowering varieties.

Training

In frames. When the plant has six leaves, pinch out the growing point. When laterals appear, select the best four and lightly peg them down, one towards each corner of the frame. Pinch out the growing shoot of these laterals when they near the corners.

Under cloches, pinching back is done to just above the fourth leaf. Keep two laterals to train in opposite directions along the cloche row. Thereafter, in frames and cloches non-fruit-bearing shoots are stopped at the fourth leaf. Fruit-bearing shoots are stopped two leaves beyond the developing cucumber. Male flowers must be picked off to prevent pollination. Liquid manure feeds should be given every week when the fruits begin to develop. As a cucumber develops, place a slate or piece of wood under it to keep it off the soil.

Harvesting

July onwards. Pick the cucumbers before they get old and large. The young ones taste better, and removing them induces the plant to go on producing more.

Ridge cucumbers

For a long time the smaller ridge cucumbers were regarded as the poor relation of the frame cucumber, but not any longer. There has been a vast improvement in quality among new varieties, and there is a far wider choice. Ridge cucumbers are, above all, so much

easier to grow than frame cucumbers; they can be sown and grown out of doors in most parts of the country with only a minimum of protection at the start. They are also wildly prolific if they are planted in very rich soil. Even people without gardens could well grow them in boxes or tubs on patios or balconies, as long as the soil is rich to begin with and kept moist all along. Peat bags can be used instead of boxes, in the same way as they are for tomatoes, with a compost specially prepared for the needs of cucumbers.

It is not necessary to be content with only the green varieties of ridge cucumbers. The white cucumber, a great favourite on the Continent, has a delicately flavoured, juicy flesh, which is not indigestible as is the case with most cucumbers. And because the plant does not trail as vigorously as most ridge cucumbers it takes up far less room in the garden. The prejudice against it must be because its skin is creamy-white and not the regulation green—the kind of prejudice felt against yellow tomatoes and raspberries for not being red.

Another delicious-tasting cucumber is conventionally wrong both in shape (slightly oval) and colour (yellow). This is the apple cucumber which, if it is picked when it is the size of a small apple, is the juiciest and crispest of all.

The Japanese climbing cucumber can be grown up a trellis or netting against a sunny wall in the south of England. It really does better, however, in an unheated greenhouse which, unlike most cucumbers, it will share amicably with tomatoes.

Varieties

Burpless (F₁) has had the indigestibility of cucumber bred out of it by the Japanese. Burpee Hybrid (F₁) produces a heavy crop of fine-flavoured, white-fleshed fruits. Baton Vert (F₁) is longer and more slender than most outdoor varieties, and the taste is outstanding. Apple-shaped is the undeservedly neglected yellow cucumber. To grow gherkins suitable for pickling choose Venlo Pickling or Prolific.

GROWING RIDGE CUCUMBERS

Preparing the soil

The simplest way to grow ridge cucumbers is to sow them where they are to grow. This labour-saving method also suits them, for they dislike having their roots disturbed. Forget that they are called ridge cucumbers. The practice of growing ridge cucumbers on ridges was intended to prevent them from becoming waterlogged, with resulting rotting of the stems. But ridging often leads to the equally fatal result that the roots dry out. So grow them on the flat, but give them a warm, sunny and well-drained position and exceptionally humus-rich soil. This is most economically done by making holes 12 inches (30 cm) deep and 12 inches (30 cm) square at 36-inch (90 cm) intervals along a row. Almost completely fill the holes with a mixture of compost or manure and peat and cover it with soil. Mark the centres of the holes to show where the seeds have later to be sown. If cloches are available put them in position along the row a fortnight before sowing to give the soil a chance to warm up.

Sowing

Sow in early May in the south, but later as you go north—up to the end of May or early June—so that there will be no danger of the young plants being damaged by late frosts. Plant two seeds, edgewise and 1 inch (2 cm) deep, at the centre of the prepared holes, the weaker seedling to be discarded later. Cover with cloches. If cloches are not available some other cover must be devised—a small polythene bag over wires, or a sheet of glass on top of a square formed by four bricks. Remove these when the two seed leaves have opened. Cloches would remain longer.

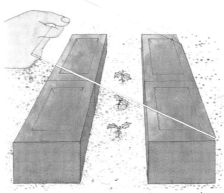

Alternatively, seeds can be sown in a greenhouse or propagator from the end of April for planting out at the end of May or early June. Sow seeds singly in soil blocks—to avoid root disturbance—and raise them in the same way as frame cucumbers. The plants must be thoroughly hardened off before they are put out of doors.

Gherkin varieties should always be sown where they are to grow and treated as ridge cucumbers. However, the distance between the plants need be only 24 inches (60 cm).

Planting

June. Plants grown in pots should be set out in the garden 36 inches (90 cm) apart in early June, or earlier if cloches are being used.

The year's work

Cloches can be removed as soon as the plants are established and when the weather is good. When the plant has seven leaves, pinch out the growing tip to encourage

side shoots. That is all that is needed in the way of training. Unlike frame cucumbers, which grow bitter if they are pollinated, ridge cucumbers have to be pollinated if they are to fruit at all. This task can safely be left to the bees. Keep the soil moist; a mulch, that is not too deep, of peat or lawn mowings will help. Water, when needed, should be given around the plants and not

over them. As the fruits appear lay a slate or a piece of wood under them to keep them off the soil.

Harvesting

July onwards. Ridge cucumbers are prolific if well fed, some plants producing up to forty cucumbers. But if the plants are to provide anything like this number of cucumbers it is essential to keep picking and not to let the cucumbers grow big. Gherkins especially should be picked young, when they are 2 to 3 inches (5 to 8 cm) long. When the first frosts of autumn are imminent pick the rest of the cucumbers before they are ruined.

Marrows and squashes

Marrows, squashes, pumpkins and gourds are all cucurbits, but there is not much precision about which name should be attached to which species. They are one of the very ancient vegetables of the world—dating from 7000 BC in Central and South America, and from 1000 BC in North America. A further two and a half thousand years went by before they arrived in Britain, where, of all the cucurbits, the marrow was most readily accepted.

Squashes and pumpkins are regarded as American. Squashes have a more solid texture than marrows. The name pumpkin only dates to the seventeenth century and comes from the Greek—*sikuos pepon*. The sun is certainly an important factor in growing all cucurbits, and in Britain it would never be possible to produce pumpkins weighing seventy-five pounds as in America—thank goodness.

As the taste for growing large marrows is at last waning in Britain, so the popularity of the young, small fruits increases. A large marrow is particularly tasteless, not surprisingly, since up to 99 per cent of it may be water. The Romans made marrow palatable by smothering it with pungent sauces—one recipe by Apicius contains thirteen ingredients, including pepper, cumin, coriander, mint, honey, vinegar and oil—and it was again sprinkled with pepper when served.

Marrows are *Cucurbita Pepo* var. *ovifera*, *Pepo* indicating that the plants bear a fleshy berry, and summer squashes are *Cucurbita moschata*. Courgettes are small marrows, but special varieties have been raised to produce as many of them as possible from one plant. The winter squash (pumpkin) is *Cucurbita maxima*, *maxima* giving some idea of the size to which they grow. They are less watery and contain more nourishment than marrows and summer squashes, but they are less widely grown in Britain than in America because British summers are hardly long enough to give them the four months they need to mature.

For the greatest nourishment you have to turn to the sprouts of pumpkin seeds, which are particularly rich in protein and fats. They can be grown like bean sprouts and will be ready for eating in three days.

Varieties

Bush: Tender and True is an early, round, mottled green marrow. Green Bush Improved has dark-green fruits with pale-green stripes. Avocadella is a summer squash bearing dark-green round fruits about 6 inches (15 cm) in diameter, with firm yellow flesh. The softer-fleshed Casserta is at its best when 8 to 10 inches (20 to 25 cm) long, about half its full-grown size. Gold Nugget is a golden, round American variety which stores well. The curiously shaped Custard Yellow has attractive yellow fruits and a firm flesh. Another oddly shaped, bright-yellow summer squash is Baby Crookneck (F_1).

Trailing: Table Dainty matures early and has striped, dark-green fruit up to 10 inches (25 cm) long. Little Gem, a South African variety, has small, round and succulent green fruits. Hubbard Golden bears large fruits when mature, as they must be if they are to keep well and taste good. It is one of the best winter squashes for storing. Vegetable Spaghetti is a curious, easy-to-grow marrow. It has bright-yellow fruits, about 8 inches (20 cm) long, and the flesh when boiled looks like spaghetti, with the advantage that it is non-fattening.

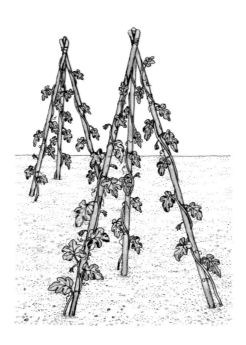

Trailing varieties grown on the ground take up a lot of room, for the shoots can be several yards long. But they can successfully be grown up fences or trained up tripods made of 7- to 8-foot (2 to 2½ m) poles tied together at the top. One marrow plant is grown up each pole. A tripod is a good way of planting marrows in a flower border.

GROWING MARROWS AND SQUASHES

Preparing the soil

Rich soil and sun are essential. To make precious compost or manure go further, concentrate it at the points where each marrow is to be planted. Dig holes 12 inches square (30 cm sq), 36 inches (90 cm) apart for bush marrows and 48 inches (120 cm) apart for

trailers, and fill them with a mixture of well-rotted manure or compost, peat and soil. Marrow roots do not go very deep, so do not bury this richness out of reach. The pH should be close to 6.

Sowing

April/May. Sow seeds in small pots or soil blocks, because marrows hate having their roots disturbed in transplanting. Sow two

seeds to a pot, the weaker seedling to be discarded later. In a heated greenhouse, sowing can be done early in April in a temperature of 65°F (18°C). In an unheated greenhouse or frame wait to sow until the end of April or early May. Outdoor seed can be sown

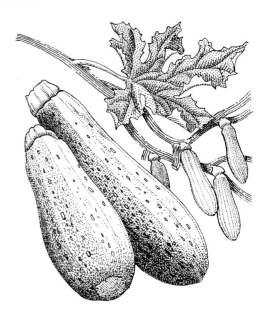

from mid-May in the prepared positions where the plants are to grow. It will help outdoor sowings, of course, if the soil has been warmed under cloches for a few weeks.

Planting

Early June. Plants raised indoors can be put out, properly hardened off, from early June. Water them before transplanting and disturb the roots as little as possible.

The year's work

Slugs are greatly attracted to young marrow plants, so if your garden is a haunt of slugs lay down bait. Be ready always to water the plants when needed—they are very thirsty. Give liquid manure weekly after the first fruits begin to form, during July. When the shoots of the trailing varieties are about 36 inches (90 cm) long the growing points can be pinched out to encourage fruit-bearing side shoots. Marrows trained up fences or tripods should have their growing points pinched out when the vines are about 60 inches (152 cm) high. Bush varieties will need no stopping.

Insects pollinate the flowers, but human help may be needed, especially when the weather is too inclement for insects. The female has a recognizably marrow-like swelling behind the flower, the male flower has not. Dust a little ripe pollen from the male flower into

the fully open female flower. This can be done with a stick tipped with cotton wool. Or pick one of the male flowers, turn back the petals, and gently press it into the centre of the female flower.

Harvesting

July onwards. If the marrows are cut when young the plant will go on producing more fruit. If you want to store any for use in winter leave a few to grow large and mature. Marrows are easily damaged by autumn frost so they must be harvested before there is any danger of that. Hang the marrows for storing in string bags in a frostproof place.

Courgettes

Courgettes, which are only marrows picked when they are very young, have a delicate taste. They have become increasingly popular in Britain in the last decade, perhaps as a result of the increase in the numbers of people who go abroad for their holidays. Courgettes have long been favourites in France, and are even more popular in Italy, where they are called *zucchini*. The Italian name is also used in the United States.

Varieties

Although courgettes are basically small marrows, special varieties have been bred to bear numerous small fruits instead of the one-time monsters.

Green Bush (F_1) Courgette is very bushy, prolific and early. Its fruits are dark green with pale-green stripes. Zucchini (F_1), another early variety, has slender, dark-green fruit. Golden Zucchini is similar, but the fruits are a rich yellow.

GROWING COURGETTES
Preparing the soil

The courgette needs the same kind of soil as the other varieties of marrow.

Sowing and planting

The methods are the same as for other marrows, but the courgette varieties need to be planted only 20 inches (50 cm) or so apart. They grow and fruit particularly well if started under cloches.

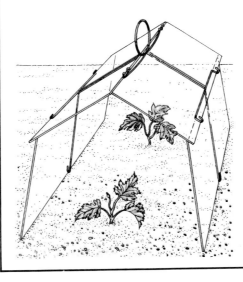

The year's work

The aim is to grow courgettes quickly; this means keeping them moist but not sodden. Water the soil around the plants regularly, particularly during dry weather. If you water over the plants the fruit may rot. Regular watering helps prevent mildew. Give courgettes a weekly feed of liquid manure as soon as the first fruits form. Lay down bait against slugs, which unfortunately have an inordinate fondness for both the leaves and the young fruit. Using a hoe, weed between the rows of plants as often as is necessary. Taking great care not

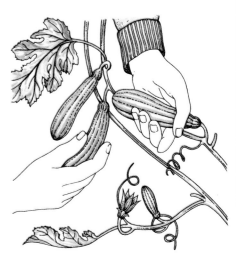

to bruise the fruits or damage the plants, pick the courgettes when they are not more than 4 inches (10 cm) long if they are to be used whole in cooking. They could be allowed to grow up to 8 inches (20 cm) if they are to be sliced, as for ratatouille, the French vegetable casserole. But the longer the fruits are left on the plant the fewer female flowers will grow, and the more the later crop will be reduced. If they are left to mature they will turn into ordinary British marrows, and the whole point of growing them will be lost.

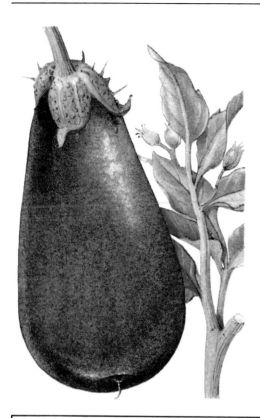

Aubergines

The aubergine, or eggplant (*Solanum Melongena* var. *esculentum*), is another tropical vegetable fruit, a native of southern Asia, which was regarded with deep suspicion when it was first imported to Europe in the thirteenth century. It was grown only for its ornamental value until the late fourteenth century, when doubts were overcome and people began to eat it. Outside Europe, however, it was the Arabs who first dared to eat it as long ago as the fourth century. The aubergine, which has become increasingly popular in Britain, also belongs to the potato family and, therefore, is related to the sweet pepper. Aubergines, however, are somewhat harder to grow than peppers and are best raised in greenhouses or under tall cloches. In very favourable parts of Britain the plants will succeed out of doors, especially if grown against a south-facing wall. On a sunny patio aubergines can be raised in pots, as they are in the greenhouse.

Varieties

Burpee Hybrid (F_1), which is disease resistant, and Early Long Purple are the most reliable varieties and they both have very good flavour.

Capsicums (sweet peppers)

The sweet pepper (*Capsicum annuum*) is a relative of the potato and the tomato, and cultivation is much the same as for the tomato. The green peppers are the unripened fruit, and are usually picked at that stage in Britain. They are slow to turn red and taste none the better for it.

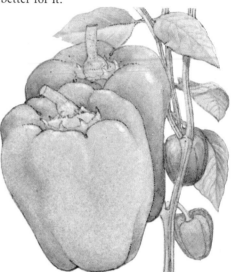

Varieties

New Ace (F_1) is both early and prolific. Canape (F_1) is sweet and quick maturing.

GROWING AUBERGINES

Preparing the soil
If the plants are to be grown under cloches dig in plenty of mature compost.

Sowing
February. For greenhouse plants sow seeds in early February in pots or soil blocks, using a seed compost. Keep in a temperature of 60°F (16°C). The seeds may take two weeks or more to germinate. Move the seedlings to larger pots of John Innes No 1

compost and later to 8-inch (20 cm) pots of John Innes No 3 compost. Plants destined to go outside should be sown in late March, similarly repotted, and later hardened off for planting out in late May or early June.

Planting
May/June. Plant the seedlings 24 inches (60 cm) apart in a single row under large barn cloches, which will later have to be raised.

The year's work
When the plant is 6 inches (15 cm) high, pinch out the growing tip. After four fruits have set, remove the rest of the flowers and pinch out all the side shoots. Water well and give two or three liquid manure feeds at intervals in July.

Harvesting
August onwards. Take care to pick the aubergines while the bloom is still on them. As the shine goes, bitterness creeps in.

GROWING CAPSICUMS

Preparing the soil
Add well-rotted compost. Too rich a soil, however, encourages leaf, not fruit, growth.

Sowing
March. Plant individual seeds in soil blocks. Sow in March in a propagating frame in a temperature of 60°F (16°C). When the first true leaves appear, transplant the seedlings into 4-inch (10 cm) pots and harden them off for planting outside.

Greenhouse plants will not need artificial heat in southern areas after mid-May. Pot them on in late May to 8-inch (20 cm) pots, using John Innes No 3 compost.

Planting
Late May/June. Set the young plants 18 inches (45 cm) apart in a single row under large barn cloches. The cloches will have to be raised later, for the plants reach 24 inches (60 cm) or more in height.

The year's work
Pinch out the growing point when the plant is 6 inches (15 cm) high and pick off the first few flowers. Support the plants. In the greenhouse spray daily to keep the atmosphere moist, and discourage red spider. Indoors and out, keep the plants well watered, and when the fruits start swelling give a weekly feed of liquid manure.

Harvesting
August onwards. Begin picking the fruits in August while they are still green.

PESTS AND DISEASES OF TOMATOES, AUBERGINES AND CAPSICUMS

Tomatoes are liable to more than their fair share of pests and diseases, but fertile soil and thoroughly clean greenhouses will help in escaping them. Aubergines and capsicums, of the same family as tomatoes, are liable to suffer tomato pests and diseases, but in fact do so less frequently. Aphids spread virus diseases. Spray with derris.

Red spiders (shown below 55 times life size) are especially the bane of capsicums.

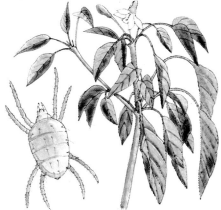

The mites suck the sap of the plants, particularly in hot, dry weather. It is important, therefore, to keep the atmosphere of the greenhouse humid. It may involve spraying once or twice a day. Do not, however, let too much water fall on the leaves of the plants.

The nymphs of whitefly suck the sap and excrete unpleasant honeydew. The nymphs are very resistant to chemicals, but thorough cleaning of the greenhouse will get rid of the over-wintering fly. Or control them with the parasitic wasp *Encarsia formosa*. (See page 25.)

Potato blight can also affect tomatoes, mainly those which are grown outdoors. The control measures are the same as for potatoes. (See page 93.)

Verticillium wilt is caused by a fungus which cuts down the flow of sap to mature plants when they are laden with fruit. The disease is often associated with low temperatures, but the wilting itself occurs on hot days, and the plant may appear to recover in the cooler evenings. Badly affected plants should be burned. For the less badly affected plants heat the greenhouse to 77°F (25°C) for a fortnight. This will kill

the fungus and may enable plants to survive.

Leaf mould, marked by yellow patches on the upper surfaces of the leaves and brown patches underneath, was once a serious disease of greenhouse crops. Many varieties are now resistant to at least some strains of the fungus, which, in any case, tends to leave amateurs' plants alone.

Botrytis stem rot usually affects plants in the greenhouse, in humid surroundings. Avoid crowding. Keep the greenhouse ventilated. Above all take care not to damage the plants—for instance, when removing side shoots cut cleanly with a sharp knife, and when picking the fruit do not leave the calyx on the stem. These are the danger points at which the spores enter. Do not let the lower leaves rot on the plant or leave any lying around on the soil.

Virus diseases are legion; the most common serious one is tomato mosaic

(yellow mottling of the leaves and stunted growth). There is no cure. Handle the diseased plants only after dealing with other plants, or you will pass the infection on. Some viruses are common to tomatoes and tobacco, so smokers would be advised not to handle the plants after smoking.

PESTS AND DISEASES OF CUCUMBERS AND MARROWS

Cucumbers and marrows share a number of pests and diseases. The pests are slugs (use methiocarb baits) and aphids (spray with derris).

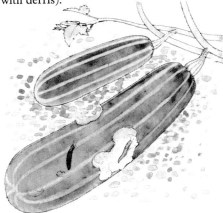

Cucumbers, and marrows even more, are very susceptible to cucumber mosaic virus.

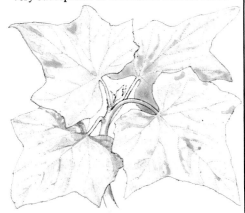

There is no cure, but greenfly are the main carriers of the disease and should be destroyed. The symptoms of the disease are yellow mottling and shrivelling of the leaves, stunted growth and fruit which die before they develop. Burn infected plants.

Mildew often attacks marrows in the

autumn, showing as white powdery patches on the leaves and stems. It is encouraged by a combination of humid air and dry soil. Marrow beds should never be allowed to get dry. Reduce the risk of mildew in greenhouses by being careful to prevent draughts or sharp changes in humidity.

Mushrooms

Mushrooms have been growing and have been eaten for thousands of years, but it was less than three centuries ago that man discovered how to cultivate them as we do today. We have the French to thank for that advance, while the Americans are responsible for many of the scientific developments in mushroom growing in the twentieth century. But there are still enormous gaps in our knowledge of this mysterious, lowly form of

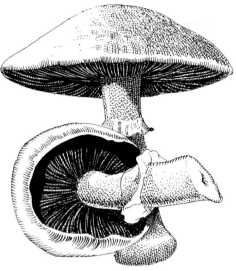

plant life (*Psalliotra campestris*), and a vast amount of research continues in Europe and the United States to fill them.

The mushroom is a fungus and, therefore, obtains its food in an entirely different way from any other vegetable in the kitchen garden.

A fungus has no leaves and no chlorophyll and cannot absorb and use carbon dioxide from the air. Some fungi are parasitic, feeding on living matter, but the mushroom is a saprophytic fungus, that is it lives on dead matter. It starts life as a spore from the parent mushroom. On germination the spore puts out minute threads called hyphae, which branch out in all directions and form the mycelium. (An example of mycelium that can be seen in the kitchen is the white fluff on mouldy bread.) The mushroom's mycelium produces enzymes, which break down the organic matter in which they are growing to provide food for the mushroom itself, the fruiting head, to grow.

The amateur gardener starts his cultivation of mushrooms by buying mycelium as spawn—either composted manure or grains inoculated with mycelium. As the spawn grows the fruiting head develops—the mushroom to be. It emerges above the surface of the soil as a small white ball, then a stalk appears, and lastly a cap develops. When the cap opens, pink gills can be seen inside it. These turn brown as the spores growing on them mature. (The black spots on that mouldy bread in the kitchen are spores.) Before the mushroom dies it will have produced and shed five to six thousand million minute spores. Fortunately for the future of mankind few of the spores even get a chance to grow—if they did the whole world would soon be taken over by mushrooms. But mushrooms have many enemies to keep them firmly in check—far too many for the good of his crop, the gardener may think.

Mushrooms are curiously exciting things to grow, but they are unpredictable. Although

you will have no difficulty in finding a place for them to grow—you could even have a box of them under the bed—do not be too surprised, or too bitterly disappointed, if sometimes they do not come up.

Reduced to deceptive simplicity, mushrooms grow in compost which has a covering of soil (called a casing in mushroom jargon). They will grow in the dark or in light, but avoid direct sunlight. The optimum temperatures for growth are between 50 and 55°F (10 and 13°C); and none will grow if the temperature is below 40°F (4°C). Ventilation must be good, for an excess of carbon dioxide in the air will stop growth.

A programme for mushroom growing indoors without heat might be: Composting, March. Spawning, April. Cropping, May to August. Then disinfect boxes. Composting, August. Spawning, September. Cropping, October to November. After a break, when it is too cold for growing, it starts up again from March to April with the return of the warmer weather. Then disinfect boxes.

Varieties and spawns

Brown mushrooms grow more vigorously, are more disease resistant and taste better than white mushrooms. But the white are more popular merely because they look more attractive—before they are cooked. A cream variety is halfway between the white and the brown in its qualities.

Manure spawn is made from composted manure, grain spawn from crushed rye, wheat or barley grains. Grain spawn is growing in popularity, but, on balance, manure spawn is probably the safest for the beginner.

Pests and diseases

The larvae of the prolific sciarid flies eat both the compost and the spawn and burrow into the stems and caps of the mushrooms, ruining

them. Dust the boxes or beds with pyrethrum every 10 to 14 days after the spawn has been put in the compost, but do it between flushes in the crop.

The phorid, or manure fly, is an equal menace—its shiny yellow larvae devouring the

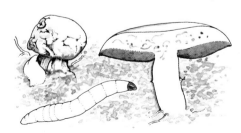

growing spawn. Dust the boxes or beds every 10 to 14 days with pyrethrum.

Mushroom mites, too small to be seen, breed at a fantastic rate. They feed on the mycelium

and damage the mushroom caps. To try to prevent a build-up, dust the compost once with Lindane while turning it. Do not use Lindane on growing mushrooms.

Eelworm also feed on the mycelium, but

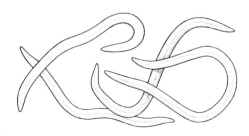

the danger from them is less if the compost has been well made and is not soggy.

Bubbles is the innocent-sounding name of the worst fungus disease to attack mushrooms; the Latin name, *Mycogone perniciosa*, is far more suggestive of its evil effects. These are distorted, mouldy mushrooms from which oozes a brown, foul-smelling substance. Burn them and disinfect your hands. The casing is probably the source of the disease, so amateurs growing mushrooms on a small scale would do well to buy sterilized soil for the casing.

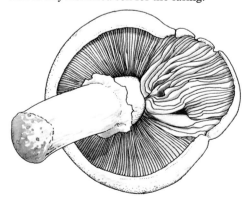

Two moulds, well described by their names —White Plaster Mould and Brown Plaster Mould—are diseases usually associated with improperly made or wet compost.

GROWING MUSHROOMS

Some simple ways to grow mushrooms:

Anyone who is keen to cultivate mushrooms will almost certainly be able to find a suitable place to put them while they are growing. Mushrooms do not require daylight and can be grown indoors in a kitchen cupboard or in a cupboard under the stairs. Buy buckets or sacks of prepared compost, complete with spawn. Water, cover with the casing provided and wait. Or fill 9-inch (23 cm) pots with compost, plant with spawn and cover. (For methods of composting, spawning and casing, see below.)

Growing mushrooms in sheds, garages or cellars: The spawn is planted in 9-inch-deep (23 cm) compost in boxes which are stacked to give good ventilation and room for picking.

Growing mushrooms outdoors in boxes fixed to walls: Choose a sunless wall. The boxes must be at least deep enough to hold 9 inches (23 cm) of compost and 1½ to 2 inches (3 to 5 cm) of soil covering.

Growing on beds in sheds or cellars: The compost in the bed should be 18 inches (45 cm) deep.

Preparing the compost

The one tedious operation in mushroom growing is making the compost in which the mushroom spawn is planted. It can be avoided by buying prepared compost, but if you have time, energy and room it is worth doing, because after the mushroom crop is finished you are left with a supply of good humus which can be used in the garden. Experience makes it easier than it sounds.

The ideal compost is made from the wheat straw of hard-working (and presumably well-fed) horses. But these days not only will you not be able to be choosy about your horses, you may well have to do without any horse manure at all. The alternative is to use a proprietary activator, such as Adco M or Boost. Try, however, to get wheat straw, because it composts best. 2 cwt (100 kg) of straw treated with activator will produce enough compost for about 60 square feet (6 sq m) to a depth of 9 inches (23 cm).

The straw must first be thoroughly saturated with water; it takes a lot. Make the heap as compact and tall as possible or you will lose a lot of heat. Start with a layer of shaken-out straw 6 inches (15 cm) or more deep. Sprinkle the activator, according to the instructions, on top of it. Then add another layer of straw and activator, and so on. The addition of even a little manure—horse, pig or dry poultry manure—makes a better compost, which produces a bigger crop.

In a few days the heap will get hot, and after a week turn it so that the colder outside is put to the centre of the heap to heat up. Shake the straw in turning, and water if it has dried out. At this stage gypsum should be added, at least 1 pound to each cwt (½ kg to 50 kg) of straw, to prevent the compost from becoming sticky. Turn the heap again after a week, and again after another week. By then the compost should be a rich brown with a pleasantly earthy smell, not black and greasy, and moist but not wet. The pH of the compost, which varies greatly while it is being made, should now be 7.6 (slightly alkaline). If the pH and the texture are correct and the temperature of the compost in the heap, taken with a soil thermometer, has fallen below 80°F (27°C), the compost is now ready for transferring to the boxes or beds in which the mushrooms are to be grown.

Spawning and casing

Put the compost into the boxes, pressing it down hard with a brick to an even depth of 9 inches (23 cm). When the temperature of the

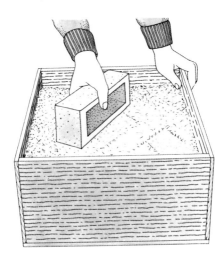

compost has fallen to 70 to 75°F (21 to 24°C) plant the spawn. Manure spawn is broken into ¾-inch (2 cm) lumps and pushed 2 inches (5 cm) into the compost. Use staggered formation planting, 10 inches (25 cm) apart each way. Grain spawn is usually scattered on the

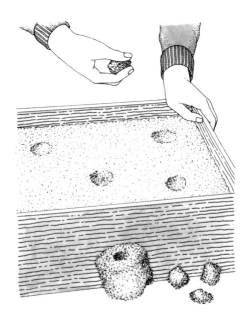

surface. Do not water the compost, but cover the boxes with black polythene sheeting to keep the surface moist. If all goes well the mycelium will be spreading through the com-

post by the end of one week.

After 10 to 14 days the bed is cased. This means covering the compost evenly with a 1½- to 2-inch (3 to 5 cm) layer of moist, sterilized soil (pH 7)—other materials are often used commercially. Do not use soil from the garden, which may be seething with enemies of the mushroom. Do not firm the covering. It must be kept moist, but never given so much water that any soaks into the compost below; that will kill the spawn. Water evenly, using a watering can with a fine rose. If the air temperature is about 65°F (18°C), which is hot for mushrooms, watering may have to be done every other day; with temperatures about 50°F (10°C), perhaps once a week. You will quickly learn to judge when the casing appears to be drying out.

The first pinhead mushrooms may begin to appear three weeks after casing. A week or ten days later they will reach maturity. Most people pick them too soon—before they are open. Big open mushrooms have a far better taste than the buttons. When picking, never pull the mushrooms out of the soil, but give a twisting upwards movement. Fill the holes

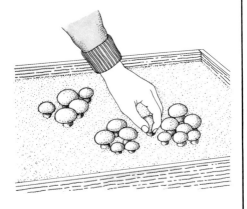

left with some casing. Mushrooms, if thriving, tend to crop in flushes, at intervals of ten days or so, and may continue for two months. Then the beds have to be renewed. The exhausted compost provides valuable humus for the garden.

Fruit

Galen, the Graeco-Roman "prince of physicians" who died in AD 200 a stripling of only seventy years, was of the opinion that his father had lived to be a hundred because he never ate fruit. Even if we accepted the young Galen's theory, we could still wonder whether those extra years were worth his father's sacrifice. It is hard to imagine a life deprived of such experiences as the heady aroma of strawberries, the hint of earthiness in ripe blackberries, or the sensuous juiciness of pears. Since we now believe that fruit is good for us, there is no reason why we should not grow our own, because many fruits are not difficult to cultivate.

The kitchen garden is not an orchard, but there is often room for soft fruit. Strawberries give the quickest return—they will bear fruit in less than a year. Raspberries can be picked within eighteen months and give bigger crops over the years for the space they occupy than any other soft fruits. Currants and gooseberries take longer to come to full cropping, but they then have a longer fruiting life.

Apples and pears take up little room if grown as cordons against a wall facing south, and they give a reasonable return. Almost double the crops could be expected if they were grown as dwarf pyramids, but then they would take up more space.

Vines have been growing in Britain since Roman times, through both warm and bitterly cold centuries, and are much hardier than many people imagine. There are now varieties of grapes which will ripen farther north than was once thought possible.

Only the easiest and the hardiest fruits have been included in this section, but after gaining a little experience and more confidence you could turn to the intricacies of espalier-trained apples and pears and to fan-trained plums, peaches and Morello cherries. Figs are undemanding, except for sun.

Melons are an exciting fruit for the amateur gardener. If you wish to live to be a centenarian, however, it might be as well to avoid an excess of melons, for a surfeit of them is reported to have been responsible for the deaths of Pope Paul II in 1417, of the German King Frederick the Peaceful in 1493 and of his son Maximilian I in 1519. On the other hand, Catherine de Medici, immoderate in so many things, was inordinately fond of melons without apparent harm.

Although many varieties of melons have to be greenhouse grown, new cantaloup hybrids will crop well in frames and under cloches, although the seeds have to be sown in heat.

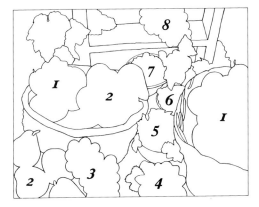

1 Dessert apples
2 Pears
3 Black grapes
4 Strawberries
5 Black currants
6 Blackberries
7 Raspberries
8 White grapes

Raspberries

After strawberries, the soft fruits which show the quickest return are raspberries (*Rubus idaeus*), blackberries (*Rubus fruticosus*) and loganberries (*Rubus × loganobaccus*). A year and a half after planting the canes you will be eating the fruit.

The most popular is the raspberry. Eastern Asia is probably its original home. Pliny describes it growing wild on Mount Ida, and it still grows wild in much of the northern hemisphere. In Britain, the raspberry has been cultivated in gardens since the middle of the sixteenth century, although few varieties of raspberry grown today go back more than twenty-five years.

Varieties

Summer fruiting: The latest, much publicized, variety is the Glen Cova, prolific and of good flavour. A good mid-season variety is Malling Jewel and a late one, Malling Admiral. The one old variety, Lloyd George, best flavoured of all, is so virus prone that it is grown less and less.

Autumn fruiting: September, a compact American variety, fruits in September, October and even into November in the south. Zeva, a Swiss variety with big, sweet berries, is an excellent alternative.

Pests and diseases

Where there are raspberries there are usually the little white maggots that lurk in the plug of the fruit. Attack the beetle, not the maggot. Spray the flowers with derris about a week after flowering begins and again a fortnight later. This will be approximately from the middle to the end of June.

Raspberries are prone to virus diseases, which eventually kill them. There is no cure. Buy healthy stock, Ministry certified, if possible.

GROWING RASPBERRIES

Preparing the soil

The ideal soil for raspberries is loam, well drained but moisture holding and rich in humus. It should also be slightly acid with a pH around 6. Many gardens will fall short of the ideal yet still grow raspberries well. But you will inevitably be disappointed if you expect raspberries to thrive in poor or waterlogged soil. In August or early September, dig a trench 12 inches (30 cm) deep and 30 inches (75 cm) wide and put in the bottom as much manure or compost as you can find, or spare, remembering that the raspberries (viruses permitting) will be there for eight to ten years. Raspberries have a mass of surface roots as well as their deeper roots, so you cannot hope to dig in manure in later years to make up for a bad start. If you cannot be extravagant with manuring, $\frac{1}{4}$ pound of bone meal to the square yard (120 g to 1 sq m) should be raked in a few weeks before planting.

Raspberries (and blackberries and loganberries) are less liable to be damaged by frosts than gooseberries or currants. However, they need protection from winds, which all too easily snap off shoots laden with fruits. Raspberries will tolerate some shade, but for the finest flavour give them sun. If rows run north to south all the canes get an equal share of sunshine.

Planting

Raspberries, like most soft fruits, are plagued by debilitating virus diseases. It is essential, therefore, that the raspberry canes you buy should be certified; then, at least, they will be healthy when you get them.

Try to plant them as soon as canes are available, which will be from late October. Plant the canes 18 inches (45 cm) apart in rows 60 inches (150 cm) or more apart. They should go about 3 inches (8 cm) deep in the soil. Firm the soil around each cane. A week or two after planting, cut back the canes to 8 to 10 inches (20 to 25 cm) above the ground, for they are not allowed to fruit in the summer after planting. That first

year has to be spent in building up a strong root system and healthy canes for the following year.

The year's work

Give a dressing of $\frac{1}{2}$ ounce to the square yard (15 g to 1 sq m) of sulphate of potash in March and a thin mulch of lawn mowings in May, when the bed is moist. Support must be provided for the growing canes. Fasten three rows of wire to strong, supporting posts at each end of the row, at

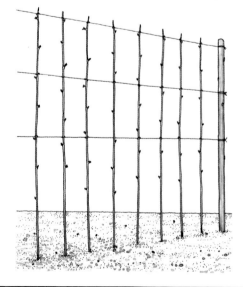

24 inches (60 cm), 40 inches (100 cm) and 60 inches (150 cm) from the ground. Tie the canes to this as they grow to keep them straight and to help to protect them from damage by the wind. Water when necessary with a perforated hose on the ground along the row. At the end of the summer cut away the stumps of the original canes, remove any weak new canes, and tie the rest, spaced out, to the wires, to withstand the autumn gales.

The following year's work

Cut 6 inches (15 cm) from the top of the strongest canes and 3 inches (8 cm) from the smaller, in February, to encourage fruiting. Dress the soil with potash in March and mulch in May as in the first year. Temporarily tie the canes as they grow. Prune as soon as the crop is finished. First cut down the canes which have fruited to just above the soil. Then cut away all but the five or six stronger new canes, spacing them out to 3 to 4 inches (8 to 10 cm) along the wires—retying where necessary.

Autumn-fruiting raspberries are grown in the same way, but the system of pruning is different. They fruit on canes which have grown the same year. After fruiting they are left unpruned until the end of February, when all the canes are cut to ground level. New canes then grow.

Harvesting

Summer fruiting, July to August. Autumn fruiting, September to October. Try not to pick when the fruit is wet—they go mouldy rapidly. Pick the berries and leave the cores.

Propagation

Raspberries are easily propagated, but it would be folly to reproduce any but the healthiest stock. October is the best time but it can also be done in spring. Simply lift some of the strongest suckers that have come up some distance from the row, along with some root, and replant them in new beds. (If suckers that stray from the rows are not wanted for propagation, dig them up and throw them away.)

*B*lackberries

The wild blackberry grows widely, and often rampantly, in the temperate regions of both the Old and New World. The cultivated blackberry scores over its bramble forebears in size, sweetness and juiciness, if not in flavour. Now it has been grown without thorns, and is tame enough for even small gardens, especially when well trained against a tall fence or wall.

Varieties

For the small garden there is only one first-rate variety, Oregon Thornless. It has a good blackberry flavour, and its parsley-shaped leaves look attractive even in winter. To succeed it must have good soil. For the original blackberry flavour you can, of course, track down an outstanding wild bramble and remove it to your garden, where it will undoubtedly respond to your kindness and care.

*L*oganberries

The loganberry, which has a rather more acid taste than the blackberry, began its life in California in 1881. The man who raised and gave his name to it was an amateur gardener, Judge Logan, of Santa Cruz. The loganberry arrived in Britain at the end of the century and within twenty years had become very popular. Then virus struck, and over the next thirty years the loganberry got itself a bad reputation. With the raising of a virus-free variety and the arrival of American thornless loganberries it has now started the climb back into favour.

Varieties

LY59 is an English variety of which virus-free certified canes are available. It crops heavily—10 to 12 pounds (5 to 6 kg) a plant—but it has thorns. L654, raised in California, is equally heavy cropping and is thornless.

GROWING BLACKBERRIES AND LOGANBERRIES

Preparing the soil

Blackberries and loganberries are less demanding than raspberries. A reasonably good soil will do for most varieties, and a certain amount of shade will be accepted. The soil should be slightly acid (pH 6). But the better the treatment they get the better they will crop over the twelve or more fruitful years you can expect of them. Blackberries flower later than raspberries, and loganberries even later, so they usually escape spring frosts. But loganberry canes can be damaged or even killed by severe winter frosts, so choose a sheltered site.

Planting

October through winter. Plant the canes from late October, spreading the roots out well and firming the soil. They should go

as deep in the soil as they were in the nursery. Even the less vigorous varieties need a lot of room: each blackberry plant should have at least 96 inches (240 cm) of space to spread in, and a loganberry at least 120 inches (300 cm). Cut back the canes to not more than 12 inches (30 cm) above the ground.

Support and training

Blackberries and loganberries grow long, trailing canes, which need supporting and training. Galvanized or plastic netting, 72

inches (180 cm) high, can be fixed against walls, or lines of galvanized wire, 12 inches (30 cm) apart, can be strung between sturdy, long-lasting posts of galvanized iron or concrete. Fan training on the wires is probably the most straightforward for the amateur gardener, although it does involve a lot of tying. Fruiting canes are trained left and right along the wire, leaving the centre open for new canes, which are loosely bunched together and tied to the wires with fillis string as they grow. (As shown below

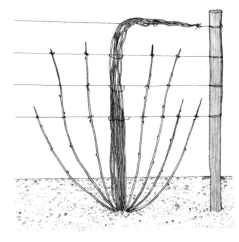

without leaves.) When the old canes have fruited and been cut down to the ground the new canes are securely tied fanwise to the wires, as the old canes were. The centre is left empty for the next year's growth of cane. Or the new canes can be left bunched together during the winter and fanned out later, in February or early in March.

The year's work

Give a dressing of rotted manure or compost around the roots each spring. This will produce better fruit that year and healthier canes to fruit the following year. For the same reason, water well if the soil is at all dry, as it may well be if the plants are being grown against a wall. In the first summer few canes will be produced, but the sooner

the planting has been done after October the more canes will grow. Tie them carefully, fanwise, to the wires. The beetles which put the maggots into raspberries may also be attracted to loganberries. Spray the flowers with derris a week or so after flowering begins and repeat the spraying in two weeks.

Birds prefer raspberries to blackberries and loganberries, so while raspberries must be protected if you are to have any, blackberries and loganberries need not be netted if you are willing to lose a few to the birds. But be prepared with nets in case they are needed.

Harvesting

August/September. Pick carefully or really ripe berries will go to mush between your fingers, and pick the berries, if possible, when they are dry. The core usually comes away with the fruit. Loganberries fruit for only two or three weeks, but blackberries go on bearing and ripening much longer.

Pruning

The time to prune is when all fruit has been picked. The principle of the operation is simple—remove all the old canes (those which have fruited). Carrying out the operation can be appalling unless you have, wisely, chosen a thornless variety. If you have inherited one with thorns, wear leather gloves and try to persuade someone to help you. Cut back all the old canes to ground level. (Burn them. You will bitterly regret it if you try to compost them.) Only when the old canes have been removed and cleared away, make a start on tying the new canes to the wire. Cut out the weaklings and the damaged canes, but keep as many healthy canes as you can, even if they seem crowded. The unripe canes, especially of loganberries, are liable to be killed by frost or damaged by wind, so it is sensible to have a reserve of canes against such losses.

If there are no losses, surplus canes can be removed at the end of the winter. In late February or March, cut back any dead tips of canes to the first live bud.

Strawberries

"Doubtless God could have made a better berry, but doubtless God never did." This tribute by Dr Butler, the sixteenth-century physician, first quoted by Izaak Walton in *The Compleat Angler* and requoted endlessly since, was in praise of the wild strawberry, which still grows all over the northern hemisphere. The fruits are minute, but the flavour is outstanding. The fat, juicy and less tasty commercially grown strawberries (*Fragaria × Ananassa*) of today have as their ancestors two species from the New World. The first to arrive, in the seventeenth century, was from

the eastern states of America. A century later, the larger West Coast Pine strawberry arrived in Europe and the two varieties were interbred for the first time. Large numbers of hybrids were produced and cultivated throughout Europe during the nineteenth century. In England, the most notable hybrid was raised by Thomas Laxton in 1892. It is still one of the most truly strawberry-flavoured varieties, but is susceptible to debilitating virus disease.

In the last fifty years breeders have concentrated on heavy-cropping, disease-resistant varieties, often at the expense of flavour. The discerning amateur gardener, however, will be concerned more with quality than quantity, and it is still available.

Pests and diseases

Birds and slugs are two of the most obvious threats to strawberries. Net the plants against the birds, and put down poison bait against the slugs.

Aphids are less obvious but dangerous, because they are carriers of virus diseases. Kill them relentlessly, using derris to avoid destroying too many beneficial insects.

Red spider mite may be a nuisance under cloches. Spray with derris from time to time.

Botrytis (grey mould) may cause great damage to fruit in warm, humid weather. Do not crowd the plants, keep the bed weed-free and remove rotting fruit.

Strawberry mildew may occur in dry weather and mainly affects the leaves. There are sprays to combat both these diseases;

By using cloches for an early crop and again for the autumn fruiting varieties the normal, all too short, strawberry season can be extended.

Remontant, or perpetual, strawberries are more popular on the Continent and in the United States, where they are called everbearers, than they are in Britain. The essential character of remontants is their capacity to send up flower trusses from late spring to late autumn.

Alpine strawberries (*Fragaria vesca* var. *semperflorens*) are small, fragrant and bright red in colour. They make the best jam because they have a higher pectin content than other strawberries.

Alpines are raised from seed, as the plant does not produce runners. Although they are perennials, alpines fruit profusely for only one year and are, therefore, best treated as annuals.

Sow the seeds in John Innes seed compost in a greenhouse at a temperature of 50° to 60°F (10° to 16°C) in January or February. Prick out the seedlings into boxes, and transplant them in late May or June. Plants from later sowings without heat will produce a little fruit the same year, but will have a long fruiting season the following year.

Varieties

Summer fruiting, early: Cambridge Rival is a very dark red, sweet berry. Royal Sovereign, a paler red, is also sweet and is one of the most popular in spite of its vulnerability to grey mould, mildew and virus diseases.
Summer fruiting, late: Templar is a good-flavoured, sharper variety and very vigorous. Cambridge Late Pine, another sweet berry, is one of the latest.
Remontant strawberries: Triomphe bears large, juicy, melting berries late into the autumn. The glossy red fruit of St Claude looks almost too good to be true, but its sweet taste is not equal to that of Triomphe. Hampshire Maid is comparable to St Claude, but better. Sans Rivale produces endless fruits, but their rather too sweet flavour is not outstanding. The American variety Red Rich has the tartness which is popular in the United States.
Alpine strawberries: Baron Solemacher is the most widely grown, but Alexandria has larger fruits. Yellow Alpine is a good yellow variety.

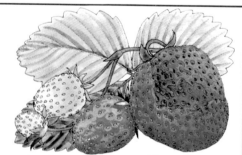

some, however, create problems of taint or cannot be used under cloches.

Virus diseases are the curse of strawberries, and of some varieties more than others. All you can do is to buy healthy, certified runners and wage constant war on aphids.

GROWING SUMMER STRAWBERRIES
Preparing the soil

Strawberries prefer loamy and slightly acid soil, but will prosper in other soils—even chalky soils if well manured. A barrow-load of manure to every 8 square yards (7 sq m) would not be overgenerous for non-chalky soils, but would be inadequate for chalky soils, which would need half as much again. Choose a sunny, sheltered position in the garden.

Planting

In the open. August/September or April/May. Buy only runners which have been officially certified as virus tested. Plant in August or early September for a good crop the following summer. Runners planted in late autumn and in spring should not be allowed to crop in their first season, and must be deblossomed to ensure that there is a heavy crop the following year.

Plants should be about 15 to 18 inches (38 to 45 cm) apart and the rows 30 inches (75 cm) apart. To ensure that the crown is not buried,

make two adjacent holes with a trowel. Put the plant on the ridge between the holes, with half the roots in one hole and half in the other. Firm the soil; the crown should now be level with the surface. Water well.

Alternatively, grow the strawberries through holes in black polythene sheeting. Make the surface of the soil convex so that rain will not collect on the sheeting, making the plants rot. Roll out a length of 150-gauge black polythene

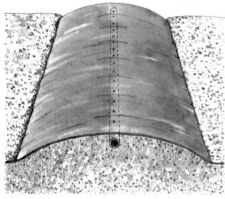

sheeting and bury the edges firmly in the soil.

Make a row of slits, 15 to 18 inches (38 to

5 cm) apart, in the polythene through which the runners will be planted. The soil must be moist before the polythene is put down. Plastic tubing can be laid under the sheeting to give trickle irrigation for summer watering.

The year's work

If the autumn-planted runners are pushed out of the soil by frost, make the roots firm again. Towards the end of winter a light dressing of sulphate of potash, up to 1 ounce to the square yard (30 g to 1 sq m), can be given. Do not give the plants nitrogen (sulphate of ammonia); it will produce leaves at the expense of fruit. Spring frosts are a problem, since the flowers are easily killed. If frost is forecast, cover the rows lightly with straw or strips of black polythene, but remove the covering during the day. Never put down a straw mulch at this early stage because, on frosty nights, it insulates the plant from the comparative warmth of the soil. (The purpose of a straw mulch is to prevent the strawberries from being splashed by soil, so it need not be put down until fruiting is well under way.)

Remove new runners as they appear. Water when the weather is hot, especially when fruiting begins. Early watering produces more foliage, but late watering swells the fruit, which is largely water. Stop watering when the fruit is ripening fast.

Birds like strawberries, so cover the rows with nets to keep them off. The nets are far more effective slung over 48-inch (120 cm) poles than draped over the plants themselves. A jam jar over the top of each pole prevents snagging the net when you lift it to pick the crop.

After the harvesting is over, cut back the dying foliage and generally clean up the bed. The plants can be cut back quite drastically as long as the crowns are not touched. New growth will then start.

For an earlier crop use cloches—either barn cloches or polythene tunnels. The cloches are put over the rows in February or early March (earlier in the north). The strawberries remain under the cloches until fruiting is over. When the plants start flowering, give them some ventilation on warm days, and more during the hot, fruiting days. Move the barn cloches a little apart, but not far enough to let the birds

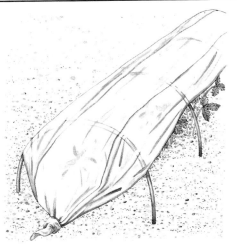

in. Do not take away the end glasses of the row. Lift up the sides of the polythene tunnels.

Strawberries grown in black polythene beds do well under cloches. The cloches are placed over the polythene. Trickle irrigation is then a great advantage.

Production tails off in the third year, and the bed should then be renewed. Some gardeners, especially if they are growing strawberries under cloches to get early fruit, prefer to treat the plant as an annual. The runners are planted as early as possible, in August, and they fruit the next year. Some plants, preferably grown in a separate part of the garden, may be used solely to produce replacement runners. These plants must not be

allowed to flower, and the runners they produce are pegged down in the soil or pots. By August the stalks from the parent plants can be cut and the young runner plants put in a new bed. Save some to provide the next year's runners. After three years it is wise to buy new certified plants so that disease does not built up.

Harvesting

June/July. The fruiting season of the summer varieties is short—as little as two weeks in a hot spell and three or more if the weather is dull. Pick the fruit when it is dry, pick frequently and carefully. Less damage to both berries and plants will be done by picking fruit with calyx and some stalk.

GROWING REMONTANT STRAWBERRIES
Preparing the soil

Many remontants crop more heavily than summer strawberries and correspondingly need even more generous manuring.

Planting

March/May. Plant from late March, in the south, to May, in the extreme north. Remontants need room—plant them 18 to 24 inches (45 to 60 cm) apart in rows 36 inches (90 cm) apart. Water copiously until they are well established, and afterwards whenever the weather is dry.

The year's work

All blossom must be removed until the end, or almost the end, of May. The first fruit will

come some six weeks after deblossoming ends and may be poor. This does not matter, as a later crop occurs, which is the important one. In the second year, cropping is not as heavy as in the first year, so the best results will be achieved by treating remontants as annuals. Remontants are propagated by runners, or by splitting up the original roots, or both. The best runners will come from plants that have not been allowed to fruit.

Runners taken in October can be planted for the winter in loose bunches of six or so, 6 inches (15 cm) apart. Mark them with small sticks in order not to lose track of them, for they die back completely. In colder districts, cloches help to get the runners established, but they must not be encouraged to grow. They are hardy, and although they may look unbelievably dead they will start some growth in March. Thereafter, when the weather permits, they can be set out in their fruiting bed. Runners produced very late in the year should be left attached to the parent plant during the winter and planted out direct in the spring.

Harvesting

August/mid-October, or November if the crop is grown under cloches or in mild parts of the country. Only a small amount of fruit will be available at any one time, but over a long period. Stop picking the fruit in November or the plant will be too weak to survive the winter.

Currants and Gooseberries

Currants and gooseberries are closely related in what, in botanical terms, is a very small family, the Grossulariaceae. It is a talented family, indeed, which can produce such beautiful fruits as the black currant (*Ribes nigrum*), native of all Europe and northern Asia, the red currant (*Ribes sativum*), whose

ancestors came from western Europe, Scandinavia and Russia, its variant the white currant and the gooseberry (*Ribes grossularia* var. *uva-crispa*), another native of all Europe. Yet all too seldom are these berries found in gardens. A mature black currant bush takes up a lot of room, but red currants and gooseberries can be trained as cordons. It is, therefore, possible to grow them even in small gardens.

Protecting soft fruit from the onslaught of birds can be a major problem. A temporary covering of netting can be devised for a few cordons or bushes, but if a great deal of fruit is to be grown it is best grouped within a permanent fruit cage. Ready-made cages are sold in sections. Alternatively, a cage can be built with a framework of strong wooden posts 7 feet (210 cm) high. The sides are permanently covered with $\frac{3}{4}$-inch (2 cm) mesh wire netting. The cotton or plastic netting on the top of the cage should be removable so that pollinating insects are not discouraged from entering the cage during blossom time.

Varieties

Black currants: Boskoop Giant, earliest, but cropping is poor in a cold spring; Wellington XXX, mid-season, very popular; Baldwin, a late variety with lots of Vitamin C; Amos Black, very late, a light cropper, but because it flowers late is good for frost-prone gardens.

Red currants: Laxtons No 1, early; Red Lake, a prolific American variety not immensely popular in Britain; Wilson's Long Bunch, very late.

White currants: White Grape, a heavy cropper, and the very sweet White Versailles are both mid-season varieties.

Gooseberries: The most widely grown are Careless (green) and Lancashire Lad (red). But there are tastier gooseberries—Langley Gage (whitish green), Whitesmith (yellowish white) and the large dessert Leveller (yellow).

GROWING CURRANTS AND GOOSEBERRIES

Preparing the soil

Currants and gooseberries must be fed generously. Black currants are the most gluttonous; red currants and gooseberries are less demanding. But the more manure and compost you dig into the soil the more you will be repaid over many years. If cordons are being grown against a house wall, the soil there is often very poor and needs particularly heavy manuring. The soil should be slightly acid; aim for a pH of about 6.

Currants and gooseberries must be planted where they are sheltered from winds and can be protected from spring frosts. They flower early (March/April) and the flowers are easily damaged by frost. Cold northerly or easterly winds in spring discourage pollinating insects and also damage the flowers. Currants and gooseberries will tolerate a certain amount of shade, but the fruits of all will taste better if grown in full sun.

Planting

Always buy bushes, preferably two-year-olds, from reliable sources. Black currants should be certified stock to avoid bringing virus-infected bushes into the garden.

Black currants: As soon as possible after the end of October, plant the bushes 60 inches (150 cm) apart with 72 inches (180 cm) between them. Unlike usual planting practice they should be planted about 1 inch (2 cm) deeper than they were in the nursery —it is easy to see the soil mark. This is to encourage more shoots to grow from below ground.

Red and white currants: From the end of October—the sooner the better—plant bushes 60 inches (150 cm) apart with 72 inches (180 cm) between rows. Unlike black currants, red currant bushes are grown on a stem. Plant at the depth of the nursery soil mark. Single cordons are planted 16 inches (40 cm) apart and double cordons not less than 24 inches (60 cm).

Gooseberries: As soon as possible from October onwards, plant the bushes at least 60 inches (150 cm) apart, with at least 90 inches (230 cm) between rows, partly for your own comfort. Gooseberry bushes should be planted at nursery soil level, or even slightly above. Single cordon gooseberries are planted 16 inches (40 cm) apart and double cordons at 24 inches (60 cm).

The year's work

Pruning, however tedious, must be attended to regularly every year, summer and winter. (See opposite page.)

Weeding must be done with the greatest care. All these soft fruits have shallow roots and a hoe can cause havoc. Strawy manure mulches in late spring each year are both a weed-deterrent and the food the bushes need. Red currants and gooseberries particularly need potash: give a dressing in February each year of sulphate of potash (not muriate), $\frac{1}{2}$ ounce to the square yard (15 g to 1 sq m). Water liberally, black currants especially. Net the fruit, particularly red currants, and also gooseberries, if they are allowed to ripen, against birds. Watch for the big bud mite on the black currant bushes. (See pests and diseases.)

Pests and diseases

Spray against aphids in late spring or early summer.

The green and black caterpillars of the black currant and the gooseberry sawfly, if allowed to

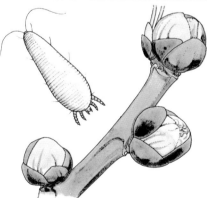

get a hold, can defoliate currant as well as gooseberry bushes in a few days. Spray with derris at the first sign of the caterpillars and repeat two weeks later.

The most dreaded pest of the black currant is the gall mite, or big bud mite. (Red currants are less affected.) The mites both destroy the buds (thousands of them will be found in one bud) and spread the incurable reversion virus disease, which spells the end of the bush's productive life. Every spring, as a routine measure, a 1 per cent lime sulphur spray should be used, first as the flowers begin to open and again three weeks later. This may help to keep the mite away. Bushes affected by reversion must be dug up and burned.

American Gooseberry mildew is the worst of the gooseberry diseases, causing powdery areas on young leaves and berries. Spraying regularly from March with a solution of washing soda—$\frac{1}{4}$ pound to a gallon (120 g to $4\frac{1}{2}$ litres) of water—will help to prevent attacks.

Pruning currant and gooseberry bushes

Red currant, white currant and gooseberry bushes are pruned in much the same way in winter and summer. In the first few years the aim must be to establish the framework of the bushes—sturdy main branches round an open centre. As the bushes grow older there will be more and more side shoots and these will have to be pruned back hard, while the leaders (the new growth of the branch) will need cutting back only a little. A two-year-old bush will have six or more strong shoots. In November, cut these back by half or more to an outward-pointing bud. Gooseberries which have drooping habits should be pruned back to an upward-pointing bud. Summer pruning consists of cutting the side shoots back to five leaves. But do not summer prune bushes which are not growing vigorously; summer pruning is to inhibit growth and to encourage fruit-forming buds.

This three-year-old bush is now establishing its shape. Cut back the eight or so leading shoots to half their length to an outward-pointing bud. Cut back the side shoots to leave two buds. In summer, cut back the side shoots to five leaves.

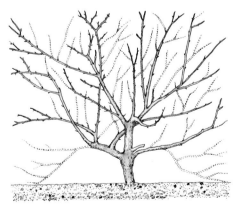

In later years the increasingly numerous side shoots should be cut back to a bud within 1 inch (2 cm) of the main branch. Later still, strong new growths from the base of the bush should be allowed to grow to replace the ageing branches, which can be cut away.

Pruning currant and gooseberry cordons

Gooseberries and red currants grown as cordons are pruned in similar ways. In winter pruning, however, the laterals of red currants are shortened more drastically than those of gooseberries. Pruning must be done regularly each year, summer and winter, or the cordon will get out of hand and be very difficult to retrain.

Summer pruning

From mid to late June cut back all side shoots to five leaves. Do this each year. The leader, which is the new growth on the main stem, is not cut in summer until it is as tall as you want it to be.

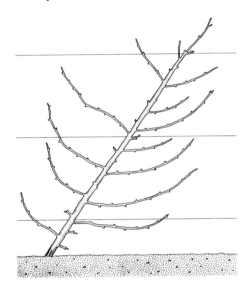

A gooseberry cordon shown without leaves, before summer pruning, above. Below, the side shoots have been pruned to only 5 leaves.

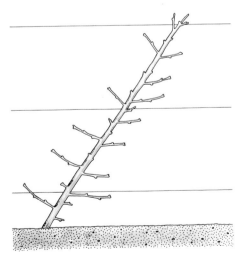

Winter pruning

Shorten the side shoots of the gooseberry cordons to three buds. The side shoots of red currants are shortened to one or two buds. The new growth on the leading shoot should be reduced by a third, or more if it has been racing ahead.

Pruning Black Currant Bushes

Plant two-year-old bushes from late October when conditions allow; the earlier the better. Plant about 1 inch (2 cm) below the depth they were planted in the nursery (to encourage new shoots from below the ground). Cut back all shoots to within 1 inch (2 cm) or so of the ground—down to one outward-facing shoot.

Perhaps six sturdy shoots will have grown in the first year after planting. These will fruit the next year. In the autumn cut back only the weak shoots.

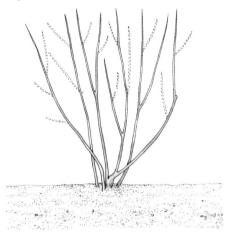

Black currants fruit best on one-year-old wood—that is, the previous year's new shoots. Some will have grown from the ground. Leave these shoots, unless they are weaklings. Other shoots will have grown from older wood which has fruited. A third of the old wood must go from the whole bush. First remove damaged or crowded shoots. Then cut down to the ground old branches with no new shoots, and finally old branches as far back as a new shoot.

The method is the same when the black currant bush is established. Take away a quarter or a third of the old wood so that both sun (to ripen the fruit) and you (to pick it) can get into the bush. But do not denude the bush. If both a main or all the side shoots of a stem have fruited, those are the first to be cut back.

Grapes

The vine has provided man with food and drink from time immemorial. Once the flood was safely behind him, Noah planted a vineyard, and in tending it, in spite of an occasional drunken bout, lived to the ripe old age of 950. The Romans brought vines to Britain, but it was the monks who most assiduously cultivated them. The tenth and eleventh centuries were unusually warm, and the growing of grapes

(*Vitis vinifera*) then reached its peak in Britain. Viticulture declined in succeeding, colder, centuries, but the comparative warmth of the twentieth century, after a particularly cold nineteenth century, has brought about a revival. While the kitchen garden is hardly the place for a vineyard, gardeners in the warmer, southern half of England could grow dessert grapes out of doors with a fair proportion of success over the 20 to 40 years of the vine's life.

Varieties

Muscat Hamburg is a rich black grape, for the most favoured parts of the country only. Brant crops vigorously, with small black grapes and brilliant autumn leaves (southern half of the country). Noir Hâtif de Marseille has small, black, muscat-flavoured grapes (Midlands). Siegerrebe, dark brown, is the one most likely to succeed in sheltered places in the north.

Pests and diseases

Vines grown out of doors are remarkably free from pests, but they may be affected by two unpleasant and destructive mildews, caused by fungi.

Powdery mildew, or oidium, shows as grey powdery patches on leaves, young canes and grapes, any time from spring to autumn. Dust with sulphur early in June and again during flowering.

Downy mildew—a thick white down on the underside of the leaves—spreads at a great rate once the vine is infected. It cannot be cured, but it can be avoided by regular preventive spraying with Bordeaux mixture. Begin spraying when flowering has finished and continue every two weeks or so until early September.

GROWING GRAPES
Preparing the soil

You have to worry more about where the vine is to grow than about the soil it is to grow in. Grapes need a sheltered place in the sun if they are to ripen properly: against a south-facing wall is best. The soil should not be too rich or the vine will produce too much leaf. Often, however, soil alongside walls will be too poor. A simple way to provide adequate soil and the good drainage that is vital for the vine is to dig a hole by the wall 12 inches (30 cm) deep and 36 inches (90 cm) square. At the bottom of the hole put a layer of stones or broken bricks to

drain away surplus water. On top of the rubble put a layer of compost or rotted manure and a covering of soil. Leave the rest of the soil to go back into the hole at planting time. The soil must not be acid, with a pH not lower than 6·5.

If several vines are to be planted, the distances apart will depend on the vigour of the variety and the method of pruning. For the single Guyot system illustrated on the opposite page allow at least 30 inches (75 cm) between the vines.

Planting

October onwards. Buy a vine cane from a nursery and plant it as soon as possible after the end of October. Before planting, water the vine in the pot in which it has been grown. Gently spread the roots, 5 inches (13 cm) deep, in the prepared hole so that the vine itself is about 10 inches (25 cm) from the wall. Cover the roots with sifted soil. Then fill up the hole, making the soil firm.

The year's work

The yearly winter pruning is best done in late December or January when the vine is dormant—otherwise there may be bleeding from the cuts, and the loss of sap will weaken the vine.

Give a mulch of compost each spring, unless the vine is producing vast quantities of leaf.

Water well in dry spells, in late spring and summer, particularly if the vines are growing against walls, where the soil dries out rapidly. Stop watering as the grapes swell.

Soon after the grapes have set begin the thinning of the bunches. An overcrowded bunch can produce only undersized grapes.

Using special vine scissors, start thinning the moment the larger grapes on the bunch are the size of peas. The first to be cut are those grapes which are seedless (they have not been fertilized), followed by those growing awkwardly into the bunch. After that, aim for a well balanced shape: reckon to remove two weaklings for every larger one you leave to grow. The more grapes that form the more severe the thinning must be.

As the grapes ripen, net the vines to keep off marauding birds.

Wasps can do immense damage to early ripening grapes. To tempt and drown them, sink jam jars, partly filled with sweetened water, in the ground around the vines.

Harvesting

When the grapes are ripe use secateurs to cut the lateral bearing the bunch of grapes about 2 inches (5 cm) on each side of the bunch. Hold them by this "handle"; do not touch the grapes themselves or you will rub off the bloom (that soft, dusty covering) and they will look less attractive. They can be eaten immediately but will keep for a week or two in a cool, dark place.

Training and pruning the vines

There are many rival methods of pruning vines. The one considered best for the amateur gardener, however, is called the single Guyot system, in which the vines are pruned to produce one fruiting cane each year and replacement canes for the following year. The single Guyot system can be used for vines grown on walls or under cloches and is suitable for colder parts of the country.

A wire support to which the vines can be tied must be provided. Fix three horizontal wires to "vine eyes" (long nails with eyes) driven into the wall. The lowest wire will be 18 inches (45 cm) from the ground, the middle one 30 inches (75 cm) and the third 48 inches (120 cm).

Alongside the vine, a 60-inch (150 cm) bamboo cane tied vertically to the wires will provide extra support.

If vines are to be grown under tall cloches, run wires between posts firmly driven into the ground at the ends of the row of cloches. Fix the lowest wire 3 inches (8 cm) above the soil, the second wire just below the top of the cloches, and the third wire outside the cloches at a height of 48 inches (120 cm).

After planting, cut back the cane to leave no more than three buds.

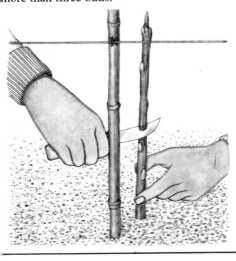

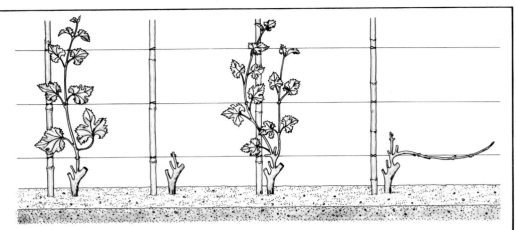

The first year's growth
When the three buds begin to grow in the following spring (April or May), remove the weakest shoot and let the other two grow. A few weeks later, when it is obvious which is the stronger of the two canes, the weaker of the pair may be cut back to a few inches. Many gardeners, however, let both canes grow throughout the summer. In any event, nip off all lateral shoots as they appear about 1 inch (2 cm) from the main stem.

In January, cut back both canes to three buds.

Single Guyot System

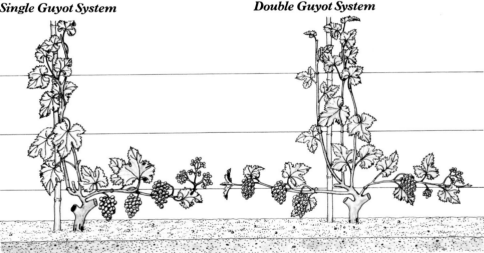

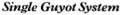

The third year's growth
Let two replacement canes grow. Pinch out the laterals on these two canes. On the fruiting cane wait to thin the laterals until the flower trusses show. Keep only the strongest-looking laterals, only two or three in the first year of fruiting, four the next, and in later years six or more. Never overcrop or you will suffer poor crops in later years.

Having chosen which laterals are to be allowed to fruit, pinch out all the others.

In January, cut away the cane which fruited during the previous summer. Choose the stronger of the two replacement canes to take its place, bending it over gently and tying it down along the bottom wire. Cut the other replacement cane back to two or three buds. This is the pattern for winter pruning in all succeeding years. As the vine matures and flourishes, the fruiting cane need not be cut back as far.

The second year's growth
In the spring of the second year remove all but two of the strongest shoots. The most vigorous one will be that chosen to fruit in the third year; the other will produce replacement canes. Pinch out lateral shoots as they appear and any flower clusters which develop. (The vine must establish a strong root system before it is allowed to fruit.)

In January, gently tie down the stronger cane along the bottom wire and cut it back to about eight buds. The lesser cane is cut back to two or three buds.

Double Guyot System

Double Guyot system
This system produces two shorter fruiting canes instead of one longer one (but do not expect a heavier crop). One bearing stem is trained to the right of the vine and one to the left along the bottom wire. Therefore, three replacement canes instead of two have to be grown each year, tied to the middle support. They need not be allowed to grow so tall as under the single Guyot system—36 inches (90 cm) is enough, or 30 inches (75 cm) if the vines are being grown under cloches.

When cloches are used, the fruiting canes grow under the glass, and thus have a better chance of ripening. The replacement canes, however, are trained up the supporting stakes through gaps between the cloches; in order to conserve the warmth inside the cloches, the gaps should be no wider than is necessary.

Apples

According to Genesis the apple (*Malus pumila*) was created three days before man, but, unlike man, it has never fallen from grace —it is the world's most cultivated tree fruit.

For a kitchen garden, choose rigorously trained trees grafted on dwarf rootstock. The cordon has a single stem with short side shoots and a mass of fruit spurs. The dwarf pyramid takes up more room, but needs no support and crops more heavily.

Varieties

Choose at least two varieties which blossom at the same time so they will pollinate each other. If your garden is liable to spring frosts choose varieties which flower late or whose blossom can tolerate some frost.

Varieties suitable for a small garden. Mid-season flowering: Fortune (September/October), dessert. Cox's Orange Pippin (November/January), dessert. Sunset (November/December), dessert. Peasgood's Nonsuch (October/November), a frothy cooker.

Late flowering: Ashmead's Kernel (December/February), dessert. Tydeman's Late Orange (December/April), dessert. Golden Noble (September/January) and Encore (December/April) are both cookers.

Very late flowering: Court Pendu Plat (December/May), probably the oldest dessert variety. Edward VII (December/April), cooker.

The Malling 9 (dwarfing) rootstock is suitable for most varieties grown as cordons. Use semi-dwarfing Malling 7 and Malling-Merton 106 for most varieties grown as dwarf pyramids.

Pests and diseases

Apples and pears have a frightening number of pests and diseases, but in a small garden with a few trees, lovingly cultivated and constantly watched, there is little danger of them getting out of hand. You should, however, be aware of some of the signs and take certain counter-measures.

Net pear cordons or bushes against birds or cover each fruit with a paper bag.

To prevent Codling moth caterpillars boring into apples, tie bands of sacking around the trunks near the ground early in July. Burn the bands and the caterpillars lurking in them in October.

Pears

Until a hundred years ago it would have been unwise to grow pears (*Pyrus communis*) in a small garden. Up to that time most pears were grown on pear-stock, which produced

huge trees. Today, pears are grown on quince-stock and can be trained as cordons or dwarf pyramids.

Pears are vulnerable to spring frosts, so in the north grow them as cordons against a south-facing wall. In warmer areas, dwarf pyramids will thrive and provide more fruit.

Varieties

The pollination needs of pears are vital and complicated. Most varieties are diploid and need to be cross-pollinated by another variety, some are triploid and should have two pollinators which will also pollinate each other.

The following varieties can be pollinated by one other variety in that group:

GROUP A. Easter Beurré (March/April) stores well, tastes similar to a William's. Louise Bonne of Jersey (October), deliciously sweet.

GROUP B. William's Bon Chrétien (September), the most popular pear but susceptible to scab. Thompson's (October/November). Beurré Hardy (October). Conference (October/November). (William's and Conference often successfully pollinate Doyenné du Comice in Group C.)

GROUP C. Glou Morceau (December/January) is one of the most reliable pollinators of Doyenné du Comice (November), which is the most flavoursome pear. Winter Nelis (November/January).

The apple sandfly lays eggs in apple blossom. Destroy the caterpillar-ridden fruit in June. Hoe around the trees in winter.

Grease bands put around the trunks 12 inches (30 cm) above ground from October to June stop moths climbing the trees to lay eggs.

Aphids can be sprayed with oil in winter. But this is a classic example of how one remedy creates another evil. (See page 24.)

Scab begins as blisters on apple or pear tree shoots and spreads to leaves and fruits. Remove the shoots at once. The fungus which causes brown rot in apples and pears enters through wounds on the fruits both on the tree and in store. Burn the affected fruits.

GROWING APPLES AND PEARS

Preparing the soil

Avoid choosing a site in the garden whe frost collects, for spring frosts damage blo soms. Pears are even more susceptible to fro than apples. The soil should be well drain but not rich, or too much foliage will be pr duced at the expense of fruit.

Planting

Plant cordon apples and pears 30 to 36 inch (75 to 90 cm) apart, and dwarf pyramids inches (100 cm) apart. Planting time is fro November to March, but better early in wint than late. If the trees arrive from the nurse in frosty weather, put them, unpacked, in frostproof place until the frost has gone. Whe planting, it is vital to leave the join betwee rootstock and scion 5 to 6 inches (13 to 15 cr above soil level. It the scion is covered roo will grow from it. Plant firmly.

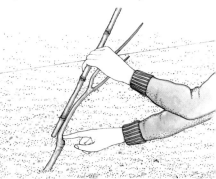

The year's work

Each spring the trees can be given a mulch compost or rotted manure—apples sparingl pears less so. On no account must the mulc touch the trunk, or rooting from the scion w be encouraged. The rest of the year's work pruning, thinning if needed, protecting ripe ing fruit from birds and watching for pests an diseases.

Thinning

No heavy thinning of apples will be needed o cordons or dwarf pyramids. If the crop light, leave doubles to develop. If the crop heavy, thin to singles. Pears usually need eve less thinning.

Harvesting

An apple is ready to pick when, if held gentl and given the slightest twist, it leaves the fru spur. Early varieties must be eaten soon aft picking. Late varieties can be stored for week or even months, according to the variety Handle each apple gently and wrap it in news paper. Store the apples in slatted wooden boxe or trays. A moist, cool room is best for storage 40°F (4°C) is the ideal. Look the apples ove from time to time and remove any that ar starting to rot.

A pear is ready to pull when it comes awa easily when lifted and twisted slightly. Earl varieties are best picked when unripe. Late ones stay on the tree longer. Do not wrap pear for storage. The temperature for storing ca be a little lower than for apples.

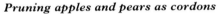

Cordons are tied to bamboo canes fixed at an angle of 45 degrees to wires tightly stretched between strong posts. The posts should be at least 72 inches (180 cm) above soil level.

The pruning of a maiden cordon in the summer after planting. The cordon is shown before pruning, above, and after pruning, right. Pruning continues in the same way in subsequent summers.

It is usual to train cordons, grown against wires, at a 45 degree angle. This will only save space if a large number of trees are to be grown. One or two trees are best grown upright against a wall.

Pruning apples and pears as cordons

Apples and pears grown as cordons are pruned in the same way. Cordons are pruned in summer every year, but are left alone in winter.

Prune apples in late July in the south and later in the north. Prune pears from mid-July. Cut back the laterals growing from the main stem to four leaves (not counting the cluster of leaves growing at the stem itself). Laterals growing from side shoots or spurs are cut back to one leaf beyond that basal cluster. Any secondary shoots which grow from shoots pruned in July should be cut back in late September or October to one bud.

Prune in the same way in succeeding summers. When the leader has grown as long as the supports will take, cut it back in May. If spurs become crowded, thin them out during winter.

Pruning apples and pears as dwarf pyramids

Cordons are pruned to produce fruit spurs on very short shoots: dwarf pyramids are pruned to allow fruit spurs to grow on much longer shoots.

A maiden tree is a single vertical stem. In the spring after planting, when the buds begin to grow, cut the stem back to about 20 inches (50 cm) above the ground, to an upward- and outward-pointing bud. Cut back to four buds any side shoots more than 6 inches (15 cm) long.

During the second winter, cut about 8 inches (20 cm) off the leader. Cut to immediately above a bud, which will grow in the opposite direction to the topmost bud you chose the year before. Cut the laterals back to about 8 inches (20 cm) to an outward-facing bud.

In summer, leave pear trees alone. In late July or August, cut back apple tree side shoots to four leaves from the basal cluster.

In the third and later winters, cut back the central leader by one-third of its new growth, always cutting back to a bud facing in the opposite direction to the one chosen the year before. Also cut back the main branches by one-third of their new growth.

When the pyramid approaches 7 feet (2 m) cut back by half the central leader and long

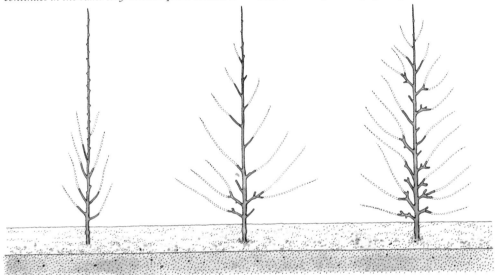

Skeleton drawing of apple or pear trees grown as cordons, above, and dwarf pyramids, below. The illustrations show the main stem and laterals of the trees without leaves and what has been cut away during the first, second and third summers.

Cordons are pruned only in summer and their leaders are left to grow until they are the required height. The pruning of dwarf pyramids is more complicated and the leader is first trimmed in its second winter.

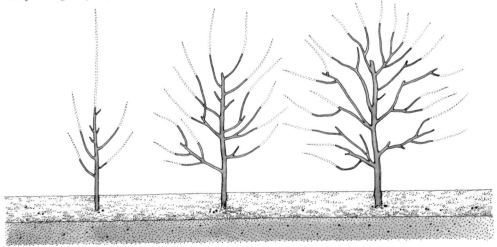

branches at the top of the tree, in May. Each May thereafter cut back the new growth on these branches to ½ inch (1 cm).

Many gardeners use a pruning knife on apples and pears, but prefer secateurs for soft fruits. Whichever you choose, the blades must be kept sharp. If you have to hack away at a branch you are inviting disease.

Herbs

There is room in every garden for herbs. If there is no garden, there is room for some herbs on a patio, in window boxes or indoors in pots in the kitchen. On the whole herbs are easy to grow. Most of them need sun for at least half the day. Mint, parsley, chervil, sorrel and horse-radish will grow in shade. The annual herbs can often be grown in the vegetable garden, either between rows of vegetables or after early crops have been cleared. Many a neglected front garden could be dug up and converted into a perfumed herb garden by planting herbs and such flowers as lavender, mignonette, alyssum, candytuft and sweet william, stocks and nicotiana (to smell, not to smoke).

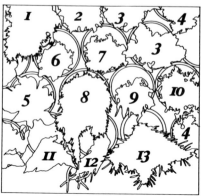

1 Dill
2 Chervil
3 Mint
4 Parsley
5 Sage
6 Marjoram
7 Thyme
8 Fennel
9 Tarragon
10 Summer savory
11 Bay leaves
12 Chives
13 Rosemary

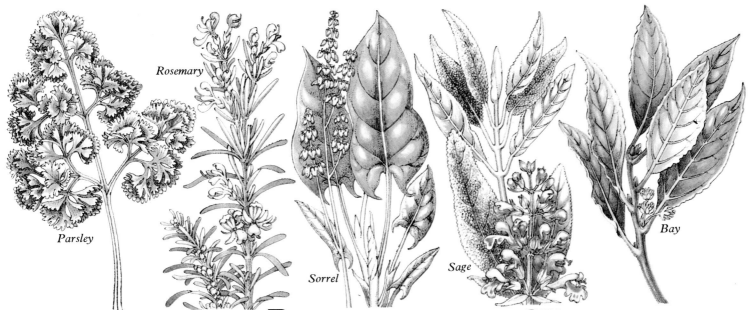

Rosemary

Parsley

Sorrel

Sage

Bay

Parsley

Parsley (*Petroselinum crispum*) in its long existence has been credited with many virtues. The Ancient Greeks thought parsley worthy of being fed to chariot horses; now it is used as a tonic for pet dogs. Victors at Greek games were garlanded with parsley; now it is the universal garnish in cookery. It is reputed to drive away the onion fly from onions grown near it and to protect humans from fleas. In addition to all that, parsley is the most widely accepted culinary herb.

Treat parsley as an annual or biennial. The moss curled varieties are the most attractive, but French parsley, with plain leaves, has a superior flavour and survives the winter better. The leaves of Hamburg parsley (see page 89) can also be used.

GROWING PARSLEY

Parsley should be given a rich soil with rotted manure or compost dug in. It needs moisture, so a shady position should be chosen for spring sowing. For a late summer sowing, to crop in winter, choose a sunnier part of the garden. Sow at intervals from April, in drills ½ inch (1 cm) deep, and cover only lightly with soil. Germination is painfully slow—it may take one month or two. Throughout, the soil must be kept moist or the seed will not germinate at all. In order not to lose track of the row, sow fast-growing radish seed with the parsley seed. The appearance of something green will at least curb your impatience.

Thin the seedlings, when at last they appear, to 3 inches (8 cm) apart. Keep picking the parsley during summer to maintain a constant supply of young leaves.

A late sowing can be made in August. Cover at least some of the plants with cloches for winter picking or carefully uproot some of the smaller plants (the tap roots of larger plants are long and easily damaged) and transplant them into pots to take indoors.

Parsley is an excellent herb for growing indoors (special parsley pots are available from gardening shops and centres) or in containers in yards and on patios.

Rosemary

Rosemary (*Rosmarinus officinalis*) is one of the most beautiful herbs to grow. Although it has been grown in Britain since the Middle Ages it is not one of the most popular in the kitchen. Rosemary is rampant around the Mediterranean ("dew of the sea" is the meaning of its Latin name), but the cold, wet and windy winters of northern Europe are often more than it can take. Its uses have been ritual, at solemn occasions in Ancient Greece, and medicinal, a brain strengthener and a disinfectant, as well as culinary.

GROWING ROSEMARY

Rosemary, a perennial shrub growing 24 to 48 inches (60 to 120 cm) high, must have sun and shelter, and a soil that is well drained and well limed. Growing rosemary from seed is slow; it is better to buy young plants for putting out in May, 36 inches (90 cm) apart. Protection will be needed in winter. Alternatively, plants can be raised in pots to spend the summer outdoors and the winter indoors. Rosemary is easily grown from cuttings, either to grow more or to replace winter casualties. Take cuttings of new growth from the main stem in spring or early summer and plant in a frame or greenhouse, where they will spend the winter. Plant them out in May.

Sorrel

In the past, French, or buckler-leaved, sorrel (*Rumex Acetosa*) was cooked in the same way as spinach and eaten as a vegetable. Today, the leaves are usually made into soup or eaten raw in salads. Do not gorge on sorrel, especially if you have gout, because of the oxalic acid it contains.

GROWING SORREL

Sorrel is a sharp-tasting perennial that likes an acid soil and can accept partial shade. It can be raised from seed (sow in April) or planted, from division of roots, in spring or autumn. Allow 12 inches (30 cm) between plants. Remove all flowering stems to encourage new leaf growth.

Sage

There is nothing that sage (*Salvia officinalis*) cannot do for you, if you accept all the claims made for it over the last two thousand years. It was supposed to give long life, cure the palsy, strengthen the sinews, fortify the memory, stop hair falling out, turn grey hair dark and, when used in brewing ale, make you "dead, or foolish or madde drunke". It is also useful in the kitchen.

Sage is an evergreen perennial. There is a broad-leaved variety and a more tangy, hardier, narrow-leaved variety.

GROWING SAGE

A moderately rich, well-drained, well-limed soil and sun are the needs of sage. Sow at the end of April and seedlings will appear towards the end of May. Thin the seedlings to 16 inches (40 cm) apart. Although perennial, sage wears itself out in a few years and some of the plants should be replaced each year. Take cuttings (with a heel) in April or May, root them in a frame and then plant them out.

Sage can easily be grown in containers or pots, but is best renewed regularly.

Bay

Sweet bay (*Laurus nobilis*) is one of the more literary herbs. It is also one of the classic herbs of *bouquet garni*, which is found more often today in cookery books than in use in the kitchen.

The bay is a native of the Mediterranean, where, in Roman times, it was made into garlands and placed on the heads of poets and victorious soldiers and athletes.

The bay has also been reputed to ward off thunder and witches, encourage elves and fairies and ameliorate wasp stings.

GROWING BAY

Bay trees can be grown out of doors in full sun in the south of England. It is an excellent tub plant, spending the summer in the garden and the winter indoors—always handy for when you need a few aromatic leaves. Bay can easily be increased with cuttings of that year's shoots.

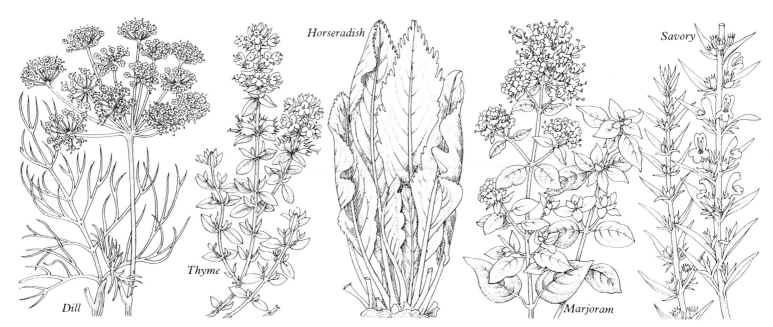

Horseradish

Thyme

Dill

Savory

Marjoram

Dill

Dill (*Peucedarium graveolens*) is a Mediterranean plant, but its name is Norse. It comes from *dilla*, to lull, so called because of its soporific effects. The Ancient Egyptians and Romans, who brought dill to Britain, used it as a cure for insomnia. Generations of mothers have given dill water to their fractious infants.

Dill is an annual, some 24 to 36 inches (60 to 90 cm) tall. Its graceful blue-green, feathery leaves are like those of fennel, but it grows more compactly. The flowers are yellow.

GROWING DILL

Dill needs sun, but is tolerant of almost any kind of soil as long as it does not dry out in summer. Sow shallowly out of doors from April to June to get a continuing supply of leaves for salads or fish dishes. Seedlings should be thinned to 8 inches (20 cm) apart. They cannot be successfully transplanted. Dill matures in less than two months, and the strongly flavoured seed for use in pickling will be ready in July from early sowings. Pick them when there are both flowers and seed heads on the plant.

Dill can easily be grown in window boxes or pots.

Thyme

The smell of thyme meant both grace and courage to the Greeks, for thyme was the herb of Venus as well as of Mars. Common thyme (*Thymus vulgaris*), which grows about 10 inches (25 cm) high, is hardier than the beautifully scented lemon thyme (*Thymus × citriodorus*).

GROWING THYME

The soil should be light, well drained and well limed. Plant 12 inches (30 cm) apart in April. Cut the shoots hard back in June to encourage new, young, bushy growth. Stock can be increased by dividing the roots or by taking cuttings of 2-inch (5 cm) new shoots with a heel from the old stem. Root them in sandy soil in a frame, and plant out in September.

Thyme grows well in containers.

Horseradish

Horseradish (*Cochlearia Armoracia*), which has its origins in eastern Europe, has been grown for centuries. The leaves and stems of the plant contain certain poisonous substances, but the root is safe in amounts that even the most confirmed horseradish sauce addict would be unlikely to exceed. For years horseradish was regarded only as a medicine, notably to prevent scurvy and alleviate rheumatism and chilblains. Now the roots are used mainly as a condiment. Horseradish is absolutely no trouble to grow; indeed, the greater trouble may be to stop it from taking over the garden in the same way that mint can.

GROWING HORSERADISH

Horseradish plants are usually consigned to some otherwise useless part of the garden and left to themselves to spread and spread. This is the totally wrong approach and quickly turns horseradish into a weed. Instead, give it a sunny spot, with deeply cultivated soil and plenty of manure or compost worked in. Such treatment will make all the difference to the flavour of the roots.

The best method of keeping a horseradish bed under control is to dig it up every autumn, instead of the usually recommended three or four years. This way the plants never get a chance to run amok, and the quality of the roots will be greatly improved.

To start a horseradish bed, early in the year buy root cuttings or "thongs" that are about 8 inches (20 cm) long and store them in sand. They will be sprouting by March. Make holes for them 12 inches (30 cm) apart by ramming the dibber into the soil at an angle of 45 degrees and far enough down to take the roots with the thicker end just showing. Make them firm. Keep the bed weed free while the horseradish leaves are still small.

Lift all the roots in October. The smaller, slimmer roots (thongs) are stored in sand during the winter for planting in a new bed in spring. The larger roots are stored for use as needed.

Marjoram

Marjoram is not one but three related herbs. There is wild marjoram (*Origanum vulgare*); pot marjoram (*Origanum Onites*), an easy-to-grow perennial, and the more subtly flavoured sweet majoram (*Origanum Majorana*), another perennial, which in Britain must be treated as a half-hardy annual.

GROWING MARJORAM

Sow sweet marjoram in a fairly rich, well-limed, finely sifted soil in a frame in March. Transplant in May, 6 inches (15 cm) apart. Or sow out of doors in late May. Germination may be slow; growth certainly is. Keep seedlings weed free and watered. If the leaves are to be dried, cut the plant, which grows about 8 inches (20 cm) tall, down to about 2 inches (5 cm) when flowers begin to appear, from July.

Pot marjoram, which is more reliable, needs sun and a light soil. It grows about 24 inches (60 cm) high and will produce for several years. Growing from seed is slow; plants can be put out in spring. In following years they are easy to increase by cuttings (early summer) or by dividing the roots (spring or autumn). Harvest for drying as for sweet marjoram.

Pot marjoram dies back in winter. If in late summer a plant is cut back hard, put in a pot and taken indoors, it will produce new leaves for flavouring winter dishes.

Savory

There is a choice of savories; summer savory (*Satureia hortensia*), a tender annual, and winter savory (*Satureia montana*), which has a stronger flavour and is a perennial.

GROWING WINTER SAVORY

Winter savory thrives best in rather poor, limy soil. Sow in August, but do not cover the seeds—they germinate in the light. Thin to 12 inches (30 cm) apart. Cutting can begin the following spring. In late autumn cut the plants back hard and give them some protection in cold areas. In early spring cut the plants back to 3 inches (8 cm) from the ground.

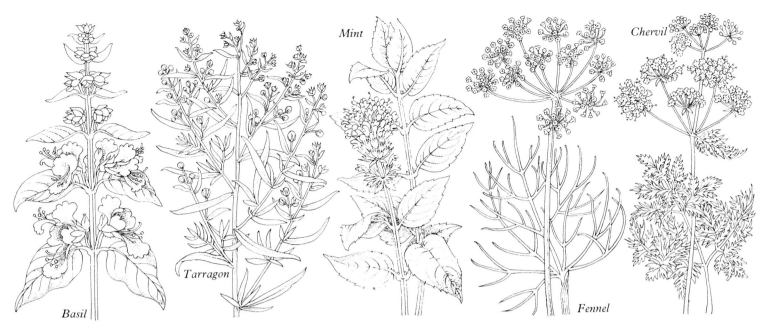

Mint

Chervil

Tarragon

Basil

Fennel

Basil

Basil (*Ocimum Basilicum*), a native of India, arrived in Britain over 500 years ago and is still not accustomed to the climate. Even the mention of the word frost appears to kill it. Planting it indoors in pots or containers will be easier than coaxing it outside. Basil has the added virtue of driving away flies.

GROWING BASIL

Sweet basil must be treated as an annual. Sow the seeds in soil blocks, at 55° to 60°F (13° to 16°C), in a greenhouse or propagator during March. Harden off for planting out. Plant out 8 inches (20 cm) apart at the end of May or early June. The soil must be rich, the position sunny and sheltered. Cut leaves for use as needed. At the beginning of September, pot a few plants to go indoors. Cut back hard and for a month or two you will have fresh green leaves to pick.

If basil is to be grown in containers throughout the year, choose the dwarf varieties—bush basil and Dark Opal basil. These grow about 6 inches (15 cm) high instead of the 24 inches (60 cm) of sweet basil, and can be planted more closely.

Tarragon

Tarragon (*Artemisia Dracunculus*) is a herb with a great reputation in *haute cuisine*. The French variety has an indubitably finer flavour than the Russian.

GROWING TARRAGON

Tarragon needs sun and a thoroughly well-drained but not rich soil. It is usually described as a hardy, evergreen perennial, but often sheds its leaves. In colder parts of the country it will benefit from protection in winter. Plant in early spring or September, 24 inches (60 cm) apart—tarragon grows 24 inches (60 cm) tall and as wide. Friends can be given underground runners in early spring or cuttings in late spring. It is customary to transplant tarragon to fresh ground after four or five years.

Mint

In mythology, the nymph Minthe, beloved by Pluto, was, out of jealousy, changed by Proserpine into mint. The Greeks associated the smell of the herb with strength and rubbed themselves with mint leaves—an early male deodorant that had the added virtue, it was thought, of frightening mice. The Romans brought the plant—and possibly the sauce—to Britain. Certainly the British have been consuming mint sauce since the third century.

In the sixteenth century, John Gerard wrote in his famous herbal: "Mint is marvellous wholesome for the stomacke. It is good against watering eies. It is poured into the eares with honied water."

Spearmint (*Mentha spicata*) is the variety most commonly grown, but the woolly leaved Bowles mint (*Mentha rotundifolia* var. *Bowles*) is better flavoured, taller—it grows from 24 to 48 inches (60 to 120 cm)—and resistant to the widespread virus that causes mint rust. Apple mint and pineapple mint are also popular.

GROWING MINT

Mint should be grown in a fertile, moist soil, in partial shade. In April and May take out 2-inch (5 cm) drills and lay the roots horizontally in them. Little can be pulled the first year. In the autumn, cut the stalks to the ground and cover the bed with a mixture of soil and manure. Mint spreads avidly. To keep it under control take up the bed every three years in March, divide the roots and replant them. This also improves the quality of the crop.

Mint can be forced for use in winter. Fork up some mint runners in November and put them 1 inch (2 cm) apart on a layer of soil in a box. Cover them with soil. If the boxes are put in the warmth, about 60°F (16°C), in greenhouse or kitchen and kept moist, shoots should be ready for cutting in three to four weeks. More roots can be forced as winter goes on.

Mint is easily grown in containers. Give it a container to itself, or you will find it overwhelming the other herbs.

Fennel

Fennel (*Foeniculum vulgare*) has been grown for thousands of years. During that time it has been variously credited with curing blindness in serpents, increasing courage and the flow of mother's milk and making the fat grow "gaunt and lank".

Fennel is a hardy perennial which grows 60 inches (150 cm) or more tall, with beautiful, feathery leaves of yellowy green. There is also a decorative bronze variety.

GROWING FENNEL

Fennel needs sun, but is otherwise not demanding; even a town garden suits it. However, the soil should be reasonably fertile because the plants have a useful life of up to five years. Sow the seeds in shallow drills in April or May and thin to 16 inches (40 cm) apart. When fully grown they will need support against wind. Remove all flower stems as they develop. Harvesting can be prolonged by transplanting a few plants into pots in late autumn and taking them indoors. In early spring, roots can be divided to replace those taken indoors.

Chervil

Chervil (*Anthriseus cerefolium*), one of the *fines herbes* which can be harvested fresh almost all the year round, has been grown in Britain since Roman times.

GROWING CHERVIL

A wet, heavy soil is the only one in which chervil will not flourish. Summer sowings should be in partial shade: sow at other times in a sunny part of the garden. Sow every few weeks in spring, in drills 12 inches (30 cm) apart, and thin to 8 inches (20 cm). Do not transplant. Always keep the soil moist. Pick off any flowers. Cutting can begin in six to eight weeks. Take the leaves from the outside of the plant. An August sowing will provide a crop in late autumn and again in spring in warmer parts of the country or if the plants have been cloched during the winter. Chervil can also be grown in containers.

Gardening Calendar

January

J. C. Loudon wrote in 1822 in his *Encyclopedia of Gardening*, "Perform every operation in the proper season." There is, unfortunately, no "proper season" which applies to all gardens; it can differ even in neighbouring gardens. In this gardening calendar, suggested dates for sowing apply in general to the south of England. Going northwards they will be up to three weeks or a month later in the spring. Conversely, late summer sowings will have to be done two or three weeks sooner because winter begins earlier. Common sense plus experience—yours and your neighbours'—must ultimately be your guide.

The calendar merely outlines what to do and when. How to do it will be found in the sections on individual vegetables.

Sowing
In a heated greenhouse you can sow cauliflowers (early varieties), onions, leeks and alpine strawberries, and plant a few potatoes and French beans for a very early crop.

Crops
In the garden there will be cabbages, savoys, Brussels sprouts, kale and possibly winter cauliflowers to gather, and celery, leeks, parsnips and Jerusalem artichokes to dig up. From store there will be roots, onions, potatoes, apples and pears. Seakale and chicory forced indoors will be ready.

Work
Start forcing rhubarb, salsify and seakale out of doors. Look over stored crops and throw away any going rotten. Prune outdoor vines. Net red currant and gooseberry bushes to prevent birds stripping the buds.

If you have not already done so order seeds; popular varieties are quickly sold out.

February

The year begins to stir a little, but do not be impatient. Even the hardiest seeds germinate only slowly in cold soil, and if it is also wet they will rot.

Sowing
Brussels sprouts, broad beans, peas and carrots may be sown in frames, and turnips and radishes in frames or under cloches. To warm up the soil always put cloches in place two weeks before sowing. In a heated greenhouse sow tomatoes, cauliflowers, celery, French beans and aubergines.

Planting
Out of doors plant Jerusalem artichokes, rhubarb, garlic and shallots.

Crops
In the garden there will be brassicas (including sprouting broccoli), leeks, parsnips and celery. In the heated greenhouse lettuce will be cropping. Variety can be added by chicory forced indoors and "kitchen crops" —mustard and cress, bean shoots and mushrooms. There are roots and onions from store.

Work
Seed potatoes intended for planting in April should be "chitted"—placed in trays in the light to sprout.

Towards the end of the winter it is most important to go through fruit and vegetables in store to pick out the rotten ones. Rub any sprouts off potatoes.

Dig. Lime those parts of the garden where soil tests show lime will be needed by the crop to be grown.

Dress the asparagus bed with a general fertilizer. Lightly fork in compost or manure on the rhubarb bed. Top dress gooseberries and currants with sulphate of potash.

Cut down to ground level the canes of autumn-fruiting raspberries.

March

In the south of England, March is the first of three busy months of sowing and planting. Farther north it will be April before a real start can be made.

Sowing
Out of doors, sow peas, leeks, onions, Brussels sprouts, round-seeded spinach (and every three weeks to the end of July), parsnips, Hamburg parsley, Japanese radishes, and more broad beans. For salads, sow lettuce and spring onions and, under cloches, globe beetroot for pulling in June. Also under cloches or in frames sow summer cabbages, radishes, carrots, turnips and French beans.

In the heated greenhouse, sow celery, self-blanching celery, celeriac, capsicums, cucumbers and tomatoes for planting in a cool greenhouse in May.

Planting
Plant Jerusalem artichokes, onion sets, autumn-sown onions, shallots and garlic (if not already done), seakale, Chinese artichokes, and horseradish; also potatoes at the end of the month in warm, sheltered gardens. Asparagus and remontant strawberries may be planted this month or next. In a heated greenhouse plant tomatoes.

Crops
Brussels sprouts will be past their best, but savoys, spring greens, sprouting broccoli and spinach beet should be in good shape. In store, roots, apart from swedes, will be deteriorating, but still usable. Corn salad can supplement lettuce in salads. A mushroom bed dormant in winter should be starting to crop again.

Work
Make compost for mushrooms.

Give a boost to spring cabbage with 1 ounce of sulphate of ammonia to each yard (30 g to 1 m) of row cultivated. Top dress raspberries with sulphate of potash.

As the gardener becomes more active so do his foes. Hoe weeds before they become large and put down bait for ravaging slugs.

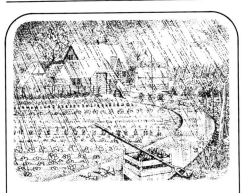

April

North or south, April is the most heartening month of the gardening year. In March, after a vicious winter, it can be hard to believe that anything will ever grow again. In April, we can see that it will.

Sowing
Continue the little-and-often sowings of lettuces, radishes and spring onions (and mustard and cress in the kitchen). Make a start with sowing calabrese, winter cauliflower, broccoli, salsify, scorzonera, scolymus, spinach beet, seakale beet, kohlrabi and Florence fennel. Sow more broad beans, peas (including sugar peas and *petit pois*), cabbages, Brussels sprouts, cauliflowers for autumn, curly leaved kale, globe beetroot, carrots, turnips, parsnips, leeks and onions. French beans can be sown under cloches; cardoons and asparagus peas in frames; and runner beans, sweet corn, marrows and courgettes in a heated greenhouse. Spawn mushrooms on compost made in March.

Planting
Plant potatoes, globe artichokes, asparagus and onion sets. Transplant red cabbage and cauliflowers sown in autumn, and onions, leeks and broad beans raised under glass.

Crops
There will be lettuces ready from autumn sowings, radishes, salad onions, perhaps a stick or two of asparagus, and the shoots of seakale forced outdoors, salsify and Good King Henry. Add to these the continuing cabbages, cauliflowers, sprouting broccoli, kale and the last leeks from the garden. There will be more forced rhubarb and some from outdoors. Dwindling stores may still include some usable roots and onions.

Work
Dig and manure the celery trench ready for planting in June. Spray black currant and gooseberry bushes with derris, because red spider mites, aphids and sawfly are at work.

May

In the south, May is the last of the big sowing months and transplanting has begun.

Sowing
A start can be made with sowing savoys, New Zealand spinach, Good King Henry, and—at the end of the month—swedes, French beans, runner beans, soya beans, long-rooted beetroot and sweet corn. Sow ridge cucumbers under cloches and frame cucumbers and marrows in a frame. (At the end of the month marrows can also be sown out of doors.) For follow-on crops continue to sow lettuce, spring onions, globe beetroot and radishes. Winter cauliflowers, calabrese, cabbages, carrots, peas, broad beans, spinach, turnips and kohlrabi can still be sown.

Planting
Plant out Brussels sprouts, sprouting broccoli, calabrese, cardoons, sweet corn (late in the month), asparagus peas, leeks and celeriac. Tomatoes, aubergines and peppers go out under cloches. Transplant alpine strawberries.

Crops
May, although a good month for growing, is a bleak one for harvesting. Established asparagus beds will be bearing well, but exercise great restraint with young beds. Lettuce, radishes and onions will provide salads. The vegetable stand-bys will be cabbage, sprouting broccoli and spinach. There may be mushrooms from April-spawned beds.

Work
Do not delay thinning early crops. Weed, or mulch where you can. Earth up early potatoes. Be ready to protect (with straw or another covering) any tender crops if late frosts are forecast.

Blackfly will descend on broad beans, and carrot fly, onion fly and the turnip flea beetle are other possible visitors. Be ready to spray.

June

June is a busy month—some sowing still to be done, and planting, thinning, weeding, watering, staking and waging war against pests and diseases. As a reward there will be broad beans, peas, early potatoes and soft fruits to eat.

Sowing
Sow chicory in the middle of the month (earlier in the north) and endive towards the end of the month. Further sowings may be made of French beans, runner beans, peas (an early variety), beetroot, carrots, turnips, swedes, kohlrabi, spinach, spinach beet, Florence fennel and, of course, lettuces and onions for salads.

Planting
The month's transplanting includes leeks, Brussels sprouts, cabbages, autumn cauliflowers, calabrese and other sprouting broccoli, celery and self-blanching celery, celeriac, ridge cucumbers, courgettes, marrows, runner beans sown under glass, aubergines and outdoor tomatoes.

Crops
Stop cutting asparagus by the middle of the month. To take its place there will be broad beans, peas, early potatoes and kohlrabi to supplement the cabbages, cauliflower, spinach and salad crops. Shallots may be ready for harvesting.

Work
Mulch where possible. Although mulching will cut down the amount of watering and weeding you will have to do, never let the vegetables go short of water in hot, dry weather, and hoe when necessary to keep down weeds. Stake peas and runner beans—indeed, stake anything that grows tall or climbs. Tomatoes, raspberry canes and vines will regularly need tying. Net soft fruit against birds. Prune currant and gooseberry cordons.

Gardening Calendar

July

July is a wonderful month in the vegetable garden, if all has gone well. Like a child at a Christmas or birthday party you can become bemused by the superabundance of things to eat. In the middle of this euphoria do not forget that pests and diseases may also be having a fine feast. And in this month's sowing programme there is a reminder of winter ahead. Such is gardening.

Sowing
For the winter, sow turnips and beet for storing, Hungry Gap kale, spinach beet and, in the north at the end of the month, cabbages for spring. For cropping this year, sow moss-curled endive, Chinese cabbage and Sutton broad beans. Further sowings can be made of fennel, purple kohlrabi, seakale beet, summer spinach, main crop carrots, summer and winter radishes and lettuces.

Crops
French beans and runner beans will be taking over from broad beans and peas. Other eagerly awaited crops are tomatoes, both frame and ridge cucumbers, courgettes and marrows, globe artichokes and potatoes. There will be soft fruit—strawberries, raspberries, black, red and white currants and gooseberries. There will also be beautiful calabrese, cauliflowers, as well as cabbages, New Zealand spinach, seakale beet, carrots and turnips. Dig up shallots and dry them for storing.

Work
Hoe. Water. Stake and tie tall plants.
Earth up main crop potatoes and start earthing up celery.
Cut down raspberry canes after they have fruited. Prune cordon pears (mid-month) and apples (late month). Thin grapes.
As a preventive measure, spray Bordeaux mixture on celery (against celery leaf spot) every two weeks from early July to October, and on potatoes (against potato blight) every two weeks until September.

August

This is often a holiday month and the garden is neglected. Try to find a friend who will at least keep crops picked—both to avoid waste and to induce the plants to go on producing until you return.

Sowing
Looking forward now to next year, sow cabbages for spring (around the middle of the month in the south), red cabbage, winter spinach, lettuces and onions (at the end of the month and in warm gardens only, and be prepared to cloche them in October).
Try sowing salad onions fairly thickly under cloches for an early spring crop.
For autumn and winter cropping sow Batavian endive and parsley.

Planting
Plant out rooted cuttings of strawberries. Rosemary, sage and mint can be propagated from cuttings.

Crops
Some vegetables will be past their peak, but new ones coming along are sweet corn, peppers, aubergines and onions. There will still be French beans, runner beans, even broad beans, peas, calabrese, cauliflowers, cabbages, globe artichokes, carrots, turnips, marrows and potatoes.
Remontant strawberries and autumn-fruiting raspberries take over from the summer varieties. Blackberries and loganberries help to fill the gap left by the finished currants.
Autumn-sown onions may be ripe enough for storing; garlic certainly will. Pickling onions will be ready by the end of the month. (August is certainly not the best time to be away.)

Work
If you have to go away get as far ahead as you can with the obvious work. For example, do not leave the garden already choking with weeds, and make sure that tall plants are securely staked and tied.
As the days shorten, remove the stakes from outdoor tomatoes and lay the plants on straw under cloches to help the fruit to ripen.
Make mushroom compost.
Prune dwarf pyramid apples.

September

There is nothing much to sow or plant, but plenty to harvest in September.

Sowing
Sow summer cauliflowers for transplanting to a frame next month and planting out next April. The last sowing of winter spinach can be made out of doors.
Spawn mushrooms on compost made last month.

Planting
Transplant seedlings of spring cabbage, and transplant the lettuces sown last month to frames or cloches.

Crops
For immediate use there will be the French beans, broad beans and peas sown in summer, runner beans, sweet corn, globe artichokes, carrots, marrows, ridge cucumbers, tomatoes, calabrese, cauliflowers, cabbages, the first Brussels sprouts and savoys, self-blanching celery and potatoes. All outdoor tomatoes, cucumbers and marrows should be picked before the frosts begin. Ripen the tomatoes indoors.
Onions should be lifted, dried off and stored for winter. Towards the end of the month potatoes may also be ready for lifting and storing.
Remontant strawberries are still fruiting, along with late raspberries and blackberries. The earlier apples and pears will be ready for picking.

Work
Start blanching cardoons. Earth up celery for the second time and leeks for the first. Draw soil around celeriac roots. Prune black currants. Cut off blackberry and loganberry canes after they have finished fruiting and tie in the new canes. Put greasebands on apple and pear trees to trap or deter various pests in winter and spring.

October

The gardener turns squirrel this month, wisely storing against the winter ahead. Roots are dug up and the healthy ones carefully packed in sand or peat to keep their plumpness. Potatoes also go into store. Apples and pears need particular care in handling and storing. These are tedious chores, but if you skimp on them your punishment will be shrivelled and rotten vegetables and fruit when you come to use them.

Sowing
Sow lettuce in frames, and peas either out of doors, or under cloches in cold gardens.

Planting
Vines and such soft fruits as gooseberries, black, red and white currants and blackberries and loganberries can be planted from the end of October. The earlier they are planted the better chance they will have in the following year. Divide and plant rhubarb.

Crops
This is the month for lifting many of the roots for storing for the winter: carrots, beetroot, turnips, swedes and winter radishes. Other roots can be left in the ground longer and pulled as required—celeriac, Chinese artichokes, Jerusalem artichokes, salsify, Hamburg parsley and horseradish. There will be cauliflowers and cabbages, and the Brussels sprouts will be improving in quality. There may also be mushrooms from last month's spawning.

Pick apples and pears for storing. Remontant strawberries may still be fruiting, especially if they have been cloched. Also the last of the raspberries and blackberries should be picked.

Work
Start forcing chicory and blanching moss-curled endive. Earth up celery and leeks again. Put cloches over winter spinach. Remove dead foliage from seakale. Cut down yellowing stems of asparagus and mulch the bed. Cut down Jerusalem artichoke stems to prevent the wind from blowing them over.

November

With scarcely anything to sow or plant, November is the time for digging and spring cleaning; do not wait until spring.

Sowing
Peas and long-pod broad beans can be sown in warm, sheltered gardens.

Planting
Soft fruits and rhubarb can still be planted if the ground is not wet and sticky or frozen.

Crops
There are still a lot of vegetables to be taken from the garden, as well as those in store. Blanched celery, leeks, parsnips, scorzonera and scolymus join Jerusalem artichokes, cauliflowers, Brussels sprouts and cabbages. Lift and store July-sown turnips and beetroots, Hamburg parsley, celeriac and, in very cold areas, parsnips.

The first forced chicory will be ready. Now lift all remaining chicory roots to store and force them as wanted. Use endive from last month's blanching.

There will be onions, potatoes, beet, carrots, swedes and turnips from store. Some apples and pears will be ready for use.

Work
Lift seakale roots for storing and forcing indoors as needed. Put mint roots in a box of soil for forcing in a warm kitchen.

Heel cauliflowers over to protect them from frost during the winter. Also, for protection against frost, put a layer of straw over earthed-up cardoons, Chinese artichokes and the crowns of globe artichokes.

Clean up the garden; a dirty garden can harbour disease. Take the yellowing leaves off Brussels sprouts. Fallen leaves of fruit trees may be diseased and are best burned.

Dig whenever you can if the soil is fit to work. Dig in farmyard manure or compost where next year's peas and beans, onions and leeks, celery and spinach are to grow.

December

This is the dead time of the year for doing, but you need to be thoroughly alive to your plans for next year. Write for seed catalogues and study and compare them well. Even the most reliable seedsmen tend to over-fertilize their catalogue prose. But while remaining suitably sceptical, do experiment each year with something new—perhaps a previously untried vegetable or a new variety of a favourite one. You may find it ideal both for your garden and your taste. Having decided, order quickly. Because of the vast increase in vegetable growing, only the early orders will catch the popular varieties.

Planting
Transplant to frames or cloches the lettuces sown in frames in October.

Crops
For this year you still have celery, leeks, parsnips, Jerusalem artichokes, cabbages, Brussels sprouts, spinach beet and broccoli in the garden. Blanched endive and forced chicory are available for salads, as well as the mustard and cress you grow indoors. Indoor chives and outdoor Welsh onions are there to add flavour. From store you can choose potatoes, onions, turnips, carrots, swedes, beetroot and salsify. There are still good-keeping apples and some pears.

Work
Protection against frost can include covering celery trenches with straw. Marjoram and rosemary may also need protecting.

Everything in store should be in a frost-proof, but not warm, place. Go through stored crops to make sure that nothing is rotting and corrupting the others.

In the Kitchen

There are few things more rewarding than gathering in the vegetables and fruits that you have grown in your own kitchen garden. The feeling of achievement is much the same as when you bake bread—a satisfying sense of fulfilment. Equally satisfying is the task of preparing and cooking the vegetables so that the taste is enhanced, the texture is preserved and the nutrients are not lost.

Vegetables are the richest and cheapest source of vitamins and mineral salts. To preserve the nutrients, as well as the flavour, it is best to pick vegetables when they are young and to put them in the pot as quickly as you can, pausing only to trim and wash them. Vegetables should be steamed, simmered in a little water or cooked in butter or oil, for the shortest possible time until they are just tender. They should then be served immediately.

Some people consider it more economical to allow vegetables to grow large before cropping them. They do not realize that the longer vegetables are left to mature, the coarser they will be and the more time it will take to cook them. Longer cooking not only destroys the flavour of vegetables but also their nutrients.

If vegetables require washing, wash them just before they are to be cooked or used. Never soak vegetables unless it is recommended in a particular recipe.

The less a vegetable is "prepared"—peeled and cut—the fewer nutrients it loses during cooking. In most vegetables the vitamins lie just under the skin, so if a vegetable must be peeled do it thinly.

The simplest methods of cooking vegetables are usually the best. Steaming is undoubtedly the most satisfactory way of cooking delicate young vegetables, which will lose goodness and flavour if boiled in water. You may need to buy either a steamer to fit one of your larger pans or a smaller, flower-shaped French steamer which will fit almost any pan. Be sure that the water is boiling before putting the vegetables in the steamer. For "tougher" vegetables, such as

beetroots and potatoes, it will be more economical of time and money to use a pressure cooker, but do not overcook the vegetables.

Steam-boiling is suitable for many vegetables, particularly asparagus, cauliflower and broccoli. The vegetable is put upright into a small amount of simmering water in a tightly covered pan. The more delicate heads cook in steam while the tougher stalks simmer in the water. Do not throw the water away after the vegetables are cooked. Use it to make soups or sauces.

If vegetables are cooked in water add a little lemon juice or vinegar—2 teaspoons to 1 pint (500 ml) of water—to preserve the colour.

The Chinese method of stir-frying is the quickest and tastiest way to cook vegetables. The time saved in cooking, however, is often spent instead in preparation as most vegetables must be cut into small, even-sized pieces.

When equipping the kitchen, good, stainless steel knives are one of the first priorities. They should be regarded as an investment and will probably last a lifetime, provided that they are looked after sensibly, are sharpened regularly on a steel, and are used in conjunction with a wooden chopping board. Only two knives are needed for vegetables: a 3-inch (8 cm) blade for peeling and paring, and a 9- to 12-inch (23 to 30 cm) blade for chopping and slicing.

Many recipes for both vegetables and fruit either start or end with a purée. To make a purée, you will need a fine nylon sieve and a wooden spoon. There is nothing, however, to match the versatility and convenience of an electric blender. It will not only blend, but will also grind breadcrumbs and nuts and chop herbs to a fineness that would take some time to achieve by hand.

The *mouli-legumes*, or vegetable mill, which does not have the wide application of an electric blender, but is considerably less expensive, is a fine compromise between a sieve and a blender. Choose a large model with three grinding plates ranging from coarse to very fine.

Growing your own vegetables and fruits gives you the opportunity to discover flavours and textures which many of us have either never experienced or have long since forgotten. Who could resist what the French call a *bouquet jardinière*, a platter of garden-fresh young vegetables, each one poached or steamed separately until just tender and served with either butter, coarse salt and freshly ground black pepper, with crisp buttered breadcrumbs, or with a meltingly smooth *hollandaise* sauce? Nothing could be simpler or more delightful in its simplicity, and this is precisely what growing your own vegetables is all about.

Salad Plants

Green salads have enjoyed a reputation as gastronomic delicacies for thousands of years. They were served at Roman banquets as part of the first course, and the guests' gustatory pleasure was doubtless heightened at the thought of the aphrodisiac—and medicinal—benefits they believed would result.

But aphrodisiac and medicinal considerations aside, a green salad makes a welcome accompaniment to practically any dish of meat, fish or fowl. After a rich main dish, a tossed green salad is particularly refreshing, or it can add the finishing touch to an informal meal of soup and bread and cheese.

Salad greens picked just before they are to be eaten have a fine, sweet crispness, as every gardening cook knows. Another advantage of growing your own vegetables is the diversity of salad plants available.

Besides the familiar lettuce, there is curly, mop-headed endive, which has an interesting, faintly bitter flavour. Pale whitish-green chicory adds interest to winter salads to which, for variety, bright, firm-textured corn salad leaves may be added. Celtuce is a cross between lettuce and celery and is rich in vitamin C. The leaves are used in salads or they may be cooked like spinach. The stems may be eaten raw, chopped or grated or cooked like celery.

Even young, cultivated dandelion leaves, peppery and tasty, make excellent salad greens. They should be washed quickly, trimmed and dressed with a light *vinaigrette*, or wilted in a hot bacon and vinegar dressing. Watercress, which is often thought of only as a garnish, also makes a fine salad, particularly when it is combined with thin slices of orange and tossed with a *vinaigrette* dressing to which has been added finely chopped shallots and a dash of cayenne pepper. Both American cress and mustard and cress can be used raw in salads, sandwiches and as a garnish.

Salad greens must be carefully washed and dried. The leaves should be torn into small pieces. Never use a knife as this will bruise the delicate leaves.

When preparing a salad, both the texture and the flavour of the ingredients should be considered. Add crunch with large pieces of chicory, chopped celery, cucumber or sweet pepper, slices of mild, sweet onion or shreds of crisp cabbage. Vary the colour with wedges of tomato, black olives or a few slices of anise-flavoured Florence fennel.

A salad is only as good as its dressing and a salad dressing is only as good as its ingredients. Experiment with various types of olive oil until you find the one that suits your taste. Dark, strong olive oil can be given a less heavy flavour if it is mixed with a light vegetable oil, such as corn or groundnut oil. Walnut oil, now rare and expensive, goes particularly well with chicory.

Good-quality red or matured white wine vinegar is essential for a good dressing. For a change try a herb vinegar, but never use malt vinegar, which is too strong and acid. Use lemon juice or a good cider vinegar for a milder dressing. Sea salt is preferable to ordinary table salt; its taste is somehow rounder and saltier. Pepper should always be freshly ground.

The classic proportions of a *vinaigrette*, or French dressing, are three parts oil to one part vinegar. If this seems too sharp try four or five parts oil to one part vinegar. Mix the vinegar with salt, a good grinding of black pepper and/or a little dry or French mustard. A pinch of sugar, anathema to purists, helps to tone down excess acidity. Add the oil, a tablespoon at a time, beating vigorously with a fork until the dressing is smooth and creamy.

Fresh herbs transform a salad dressing. Try coarsely chopped chervil, chives, tarragon, savory or parsley. For a light garlic flavour, rub the salad bowl with a cut garlic clove. If a stronger flavour is desired, chop the garlic finely, crush it in a garlic press or mash it well with a little salt, using the side of a knife blade. Then blend it thoroughly with the dressing. Another way to flavour a salad with garlic is to make a *chapon*. Rub a slice of stale French bread all over with a bruised garlic clove. Drop it in among the salad greens shortly before tossing them. Soaked with dressing, a *chapon* is a delicacy in its own right.

For a mustard dressing, dilute a heaped teaspoon of a coarse, mild French mustard, such as *Moutarde de Meaux*, with a tablespoon of cold water. Beat in 4 tablespoons of olive oil and season to taste with salt and a generous pinch of sugar. A mustard cream dressing, which is particularly good with endive, is made by beating 2 tablespoons of good-quality prepared mustard with 4 tablespoons of cream, seasoned to taste with lemon juice, salt and freshly ground pepper.

A soured-cream dressing, a central European classic, is traditionally used for salads served with baked or grilled poultry or pork. To make enough dressing for a large head of lettuce, beat $\frac{1}{4}$ pint (125 ml) of thick, commercial soured cream with 2 tablespoons of finely chopped chives, a good pinch of sugar, salt and freshly ground pepper to taste.

Do not toss a salad until just before serving. If the leaves are coated with the dressing for any length of time, the acid will wilt them.

Lettuce

"Lettuce maketh a pleasant sallad, being eaten with vinegar, oile, and a little salt: but if it be boiled it is sooner digested and nourisheth more." So said John Gerard, the sixteenth-century herbalist. Although the value of boiled lettuce may be disputed, most people will agree that lettuce makes a pleasant salad, particularly when it is gathered minutes before it is eaten. It is only when there are more lettuces in the garden than can possibly be eaten in salads that the cooked lettuce comes into its own—for soup, soufflé, casserole or purée.

To prepare a lettuce for salad, wash it carefully leaf by leaf. Shake the leaves free of moisture in a salad basket or gently pat them dry. If the lettuce is not required immediately, roll the leaves loosely in a cloth and refrigerate.

Corn salad, endive and dandelion leaves may be substituted for lettuce in salads or used in lettuce salads to add colour and flavour.

Green Salad
with Roquefort Dressing
An excellent accompaniment for steak. Chicory should be included in this salad because it adds flavour and crispness. Gorgonzola or Dolcelatte cheese can be substituted for Roquefort if desired.

SERVES EIGHT
3 tablespoons vinegar
10 tablespoons olive oil
Salt
Freshly ground black pepper
French mustard
Sugar
2 heads chicory
1 Cos lettuce
1 endive
12 dandelion leaves
3 oz (90 g) Roquefort cheese
Lemon juice, Tabasco sauce or
  cayenne pepper

Pour the vinegar into a small bowl and add the oil 1 tablespoon at a time, beating the mixture vigorously with a fork at each addition. Add salt, pepper, mustard and sugar to taste and beat again. Set aside.

Slice the chicory thinly crosswise and place in a salad bowl. Tear the lettuce, endive and dandelion leaves into bite-size pieces and add to the chicory. Set aside.

In a small bowl, mash the cheese to a paste with a fork. Add the prepared dressing and beat until blended. Flavour with a little lemon juice or a drop or two of Tabasco or a pinch of cayenne, and season to taste.

Pour the dressing over the greens and toss thoroughly. Serve immediately.

Caesar Salad
Caesar Salad is one of America's greatest culinary triumphs. A brilliant combination of flavour and texture, it has become a classic. Serve it as a first course or as a main luncheon dish.

SERVES SIX
Olive oil
3 garlic cloves
4 large, thick slices of bread, trimmed
  and cut into ½-inch (1 cm) cubes
2 Cos lettuces, washed, dried
  and chilled
1 egg
Juice of 1 lemon
16 anchovy fillets, cut into pieces
2 oz (60 g) Parmesan cheese, grated
Salt
Freshly ground black pepper

Heat 4 tablespoons of olive oil in a frying pan with 2 crushed garlic cloves. Fry the bread cubes until crisp and golden on all sides, adding more oil as needed. Drain the croûtons thoroughly on kitchen paper. Discard the garlic and oil. Crush the remaining garlic clove and rub it around a salad bowl.

Tear the lettuce into bite-size pieces and place in the salad bowl. Add 8 tablespoons of olive oil and toss until every leaf is thoroughly coated. Cook the egg in a pan of boiling water for 1 minute. Break the egg over the lettuce, add the lemon juice, anchovies, cheese, and salt and pepper to taste.

Toss gently until well mixed. Taste for seasoning and add salt if needed. Add the croûtons, toss again and serve immediately, while the croûtons are still crisp.

Wilted Salad
with Hot Bacon Dressing
A hot dressing is used to wilt the greens for this salad. Cos is the best lettuce to use for a wilted salad, although cabbage lettuce will stand up well to a hot dressing if it is fresh from the garden. This recipe is also good for curly endive or dandelion greens.

SERVES FOUR
1 garlic clove, halved
1 large Cos lettuce, washed and dried
1 teaspoon butter
4 thick slices streaky bacon, diced
1 tablespoon wine vinegar
1 hard-boiled egg, chopped
2 tablespoons finely chopped parsley
Salt
Freshly ground black pepper

Rub a warmed salad bowl with the garlic. Tear the lettuce into the bowl in bite-size pieces. Set aside.

Melt the butter in a small frying-pan. Add the bacon and cook gently, stirring, for 10 minutes, or until the fat runs. Pour the contents of the pan over the greens. Add the vinegar to the pan, swirl to heat it and sprinkle over the salad in the bowl.

Toss the salad thoroughly. Add the chopped egg, parsley and salt and pepper to taste. Toss again and serve.

Lettuce

An English Salad

This recipe comes from a famous English cookery book, *The Cook's Oracle* by Dr Kitchiner, which was published in 1817 and went through five editions in six years. In the words of Dr Kitchiner: "Boil a couple of Eggs for twelve minutes, and put them in a basin of cold water for a few minutes,—*the Yolks must be quite cold and hard, or they will not incorporate with the ingredients.* Rub them [the yolks] through a sieve with a wooden spoon, and mix them with a tablespoonful of water, or fine double cream, then add two tablespoonsful of Oil or melted Butter; when these are well mixed, add by degrees, a teaspoonful of Salt, or powdered lump Sugar, and the same of made Mustard; when these are smoothly united, add very gradually three tablespoonsful of Vinegar, rub it with the other ingredients till thoroughly incorporated with them; cut up the white of the egg, and garnish the top of the salad with it."

We can only guess at the size of Dr Kitchiner's teaspoons and tablespoons, but using standard measuring spoons the following quantities make a very good dressing indeed, enough for quite a large head of lettuce: 2 eggs, 2 tablespoons double cream, 2 tablespoons olive oil, $\frac{1}{4}$ teaspoon salt (more or less according to taste, but sugar is not a good idea in this case), $\frac{1}{2}$ teaspoon Dijon mustard and 2 tablespoons wine vinegar.

Lettuce Soup

This is an ideal dish to make in late summer when there is a glut of lettuce and the weather is chilly.

SERVES FOUR
4 cabbage lettuces, washed
1 oz (30 g) butter
1 small onion, finely chopped
2 tablespoons flour
1½ pints (750 ml) milk or chicken stock
Salt
Freshly grated nutmeg
2 tablespoons grated Parmesan cheese

Put the lettuce in a saucepan and cover it with water. Bring the water to the boil and cook for 5 minutes. Drain, rinse the lettuce in cold water, drain again and set aside.

Melt the butter in a large saucepan, add the chopped onion and cook, stirring frequently, for 3 minutes. Stir in the flour with a wooden spoon. Gradually add the milk or stock and, stirring constantly, bring to the boil. Add the lettuce to the soup. Reduce the heat and simmer for 3 minutes.

Liquidize the soup in a blender or put it through a mouli. Return the soup to the pan, season to taste with salt and nutmeg. Reheat the soup to just under boiling point. Serve sprinkled with Parmesan cheese.

Souffléed Lettuce

This is another delicious way of using up surplus lettuce. It makes an unusual accompaniment to grilled or roast lamb, or can be served as a supper or luncheon dish with poached eggs.

SERVES THREE TO FOUR
2 large or 3 small cabbage lettuces
1 oz (30 g) butter
2 tablespoons flour
3 spring onions, finely chopped
2 oz (60 g) ham, diced (optional)
1 lb (½ kg) floury potatoes, cooked and puréed
2 eggs, separated
Salt
Freshly ground black pepper
Lemon juice
2 tablespoons grated Parmesan or any good, hard, melting cheese

Preheat the oven to 375°F (190°C, Gas Mark 5). Wash the lettuces, keeping the heads whole. Shake off as much moisture as possible. Place them in a heavy pan and cover tightly. Cook over high heat for 5 minutes.

Drain and press out as much moisture as possible with the back of a wooden spoon. Chop the lettuce very finely or purée in a blender.

In another pan, melt the butter. Gradually blend in the flour and cook over low heat, stirring constantly, for 2 to 3 minutes to make a pale *roux*. Beat in the lettuce purée, the onions and diced ham, if used, and, stirring, cook over moderate heat for 1 minute longer.

Remove from the heat. Beat in the potato purée, then the egg yolks. Season to taste with salt, pepper and a few drops of lemon juice.

Whisk the egg whites until stiff but not dry. With a large metal spoon fold them gently but thoroughly into the lettuce and potato mixture.

Spoon the mixture into a deep, buttered baking dish or soufflé dish. Sprinkle with the grated cheese and bake for 30 minutes, or until puffed and golden. Serve immediately.

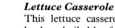

Lettuce Casserole

This lettuce casserole goes well with lamb or boiled beef. Serve each person with a whole head of lettuce.

SERVES FOUR
5 teaspoons butter
4 slices streaky bacon, diced
1 medium-sized Spanish onion, thinly sliced
2 carrots, quartered lengthwise and thinly sliced
4 tomatoes, blanched, peeled and chopped
Salt
Freshly ground black pepper
4 large cabbage lettuces
4 tablespoons water or stock

Melt 2 teaspoons of butter in a saucepan and simmer the bacon in it until the fat runs. Add the onion and carrots and fry until soft and lightly coloured, stirring frequently. Stir in the tomatoes and cook gently for 2 to 3 minutes, or until the tomatoes are slightly softened. Season with salt and pepper to taste. Set aside.

Wash the lettuces without separating the leaves. Trim the stems. Fill a large pan with salted water and bring to the boil. Blanch the lettuces, two at a time if necessary, by lowering them into the boiling water and, as they wilt, pressing them down gently with the back of a wooden spoon so that they are totally submerged. When the water returns to the boil, remove the lettuces and drop them into a large bowl of ice-cold water.

When the lettuces are cool enough to handle, squeeze them gently, extracting as much moisture as possible without spoiling their shape. Cut each lettuce in half vertically.

Melt the remaining butter in a heavy pan large enough to take the lettuces in one layer, swirling the butter around to coat the pan. Put the lettuce halves in the pan and sprinkle them with salt and pepper. Spoon the tomato mixture over them.

Moisten with 4 tablespoons of water or stock, bring to a simmer, cover, and cook gently for 20 minutes, or until the lettuces are tender.

To dry lettuce leaves without bruising them, use a salad basket. Twirl or shake thoroughly.

Chicory is a remarkably versatile member of the salad family. Some people shy away from it because of its bitterness. But so long as this is cleverly partnered by other flavours it can be turned into an advantage.

Equally good raw or cooked, chicory adds a juicy crunchiness to winter salads and also provides a subtly flavoured, bittersweet vegetable to serve as a separate course or as an accompaniment to meat dishes.

When serving chicory in a raw salad, you will need one large head per person; for a cooked dish two heads will be required.

The preparation of chicory is the same whether it is to be used raw or cooked. Pull off a layer of outer leaves. Trim the stem and carefully remove the core with the point of a sharp knife. Rinse under cold water or wipe with a damp cloth. Use the chicory immediately, as the cut surfaces soon discolour. Never leave the heads soaking in water, as this tends to make them more bitter.

Chicory and Orange Salad
A chicory and orange salad makes a wonderful accompaniment to roast duck or ham.

SERVES FOUR
1 tablespoon lemon juice
Salt
Freshly ground black pepper
French mustard
Cayenne pepper or Tabasco sauce
1 teaspoon honey
3 tablespoons olive oil
1 orange
4 heads chicory, prepared, washed and thinly sliced crosswise
12 black olives, to garnish

In a salad bowl, mix the lemon juice with a little salt, pepper, mustard, cayenne or Tabasco and the honey. Add the oil a tablespoon at a time, beating the mixture vigorously with a fork at each addition until it is smooth and creamy. Taste and add more lemon juice, seasoning or honey if necessary. Set aside.

Peel the orange and remove the pith. Slice the orange thinly on a plate and quarter each slice. Put the chicory, the orange slices and any orange juice left on the plate into the salad bowl. Toss gently but well. Serve immediately, garnished with black olives.

Braised Chicory
This dish may be garnished with chopped parsley, buttered breadcrumbs or finely chopped hard-boiled egg heated through in butter. Or serve with a *hollandaise* sauce, which sets off the bitter-sweet flavour well.

If the chicory is going to accompany a roast, substitute a few tablespoons of the juices from the roasting tin for some of the butter in the final braising.

SERVES FOUR
8 heads chicory, prepared and washed
Juice of 1 lemon
Salt
2 oz (60 g) butter
Freshly ground black pepper
Freshly grated nutmeg

Arrange the whole chicory heads in a large saucepan. Sprinkle each layer with a little lemon juice and salt. Pour over enough boiling water to cover the chicory. Partly cover the pan and simmer over low heat for 10 to 15 minutes.

Drain the chicory in a colander and squeeze out as much moisture as possible, using a clean cloth to protect your hands.

In a pan wide enough to hold the chicory in one layer, melt the butter without letting it colour. Add the chicory, turning each head to coat it well. Sprinkle with salt, pepper and nutmeg and a little more lemon juice to taste. Cover the pan and cook the chicory for 15 to 20 minutes longer, or until tender when pierced through the thickest part with a thin skewer. Turn the heads occasionally so that they colour evenly.

Chicory and Ham Mornay
Serve one head of chicory per portion as an *hors d'oeuvre*, two per person as a supper dish. Accompany with fresh crusty bread to mop up the delicious sauce.

SERVES FOUR
8 heads chicory, prepared and washed
Salt
Lemon juice
1 pint (500 ml) milk
1 chicken stock cube
1 small onion, coarsely chopped
4 black peppercorns
1 small bay leaf
8 slices ham, about 1 oz (30 g) each
Butter
4 tablespoons flour
¼ pint (125 ml) single cream
5 tablespoons freshly grated Parmesan cheese
5 tablespoons freshly grated Gruyère cheese
1 egg yolk
Freshly ground black pepper
Freshly grated nutmeg

Put the chicory heads in a pan of salted water. Add 2 tablespoons of lemon juice to each pint of water and bring to the boil. Cook for 15 minutes.

Meanwhile, pour the milk into a pan and add the stock cube, the onion, peppercorns and bay leaf. Heat, stirring until the stock cube has dissolved and the liquid comes to the boil. Remove the pan from the heat. Cover the pan and set aside for 15 minutes.

Drain the chicory. Squeeze each head between the folds of a cloth to extract as much moisture as possible, taking care not to spoil its shape. Wrap each head in a slice of ham. Pack them tightly head to tail in a buttered, oblong *gratin* dish just large enough to hold them.

Preheat the oven to 400°F (200°C, Gas Mark 6).

To prepare the sauce, melt 3 tablespoons of butter in a heavy pan without letting it colour. Blend in the flour smoothly with a wooden spoon and stir over low heat for 2 to 3 minutes to make a pale *roux*. Strain the infused milk into the *roux* gradually, stirring vigorously to prevent lumps forming. Stir in the cream. Bring the sauce to simmering point and cook gently, stirring frequently, for 15 minutes.

Remove the pan from the heat. Beat in 4 tablespoons each of the grated Parmesan and Gruyère, and the egg yolk. Season to taste with salt, pepper, a grating of nutmeg and a few drops of lemon juice.

Spoon the sauce over the chicory and ham rolls and sprinkle with the remaining cheese. Bake for 25 minutes, or until the sauce is bubbling and golden brown on top.

Let the dish rest for a few minutes before serving.

Brassicas

George Bernard Shaw had the right attitude to the brassica family. In *The Apple Cart*, King Magnus is being tempted by his rather tediously exalted mistress Orinthia to share her concept of the regal life. "Heaven", she complains, "is offering you a rose; and you cling to a cabbage." His answer is one which both the kitchen gardener and the cook would applaud: "But what wise man, if you force him to choose between doing without roses and doing without cabbages, would not secure the cabbages?"

There are more than forty species of the genus brassica, yet only one, *B. oleracea*, has found such favour in the kitchen. Even so, the variety of sub-species that are descended from it are without doubt one of the Old World's most valuable contributions to the kitchen garden—a rainbow of cabbages, green, white and red, smooth-leaved and curly, kale (borecole), to all appearances a cabbage that has not quite made it, and the Brussels sprout, which admirably succeeds in reproducing handfuls of tiny replicas of its cabbage cousins. Kale may be cooked like cabbage, but its stronger flavour and coarser texture make it unsuitable for any but the simplest dishes.

Cauliflowers, cultivated for their undeveloped flowers, were missing from the European culinary scene during the Dark Ages. When they reappeared in western Europe in the sixteenth century—seeds were brought from Cyprus via Italy to reach France in the seventeenth century—they were hailed as a great culinary novelty. The cooks of Louis XIV boiled them in stock flavoured with mace and presented them to the king topped with fresh butter.

Even today, cauliflowers are prized for their delicate flavour and are considered by many to be the aristocrats of the brassica family. They are particularly fine when gathered from the garden early in the day, with the dew still sparkling on the curds, the correct name for their knobbly white heads.

Like all the brassicas, broccoli, one of the many candidates for the title "poor man's asparagus", has been cultivated for thousands of years. One legacy of the Romans' love for both broccoli and cauliflower remains in the fact that even today you can never be quite sure which of the two is meant when an Italian recipe calls for "broccoli".

Most cooks could list the brassicas in order of preference, as likely as not influenced by their price at the greengrocer's. For kitchen gardeners, however, this is not a consideration, and they can concentrate on the goodness of the vegetables themselves.

One of the greatest crimes perpetrated on all the brassicas, but particularly on cabbage, is overcooking, which deprives these vegetables not only of most of their vitamins and mineral salts, but also of flavour and texture.

The nutritional value of brassicas also depends to some extent on the sulphur they contain, which, unfortunately, can cause them to give off a somewhat unpleasant odour during cooking.

Sauerkraut was considered one of the best ways to use white cabbage as long ago as 200 BC, when it was served to the labourers working on the Great Wall of China. Sauerkraut is an excellent way to preserve cabbage to last the whole year. To make it you need a large, glazed earthenware crock and a plate or board that just fits into the top of the crock. A 2-gallon (9 litre) crock holds about 15 pounds (7 kg) of sauerkraut.

Shred the cabbages finely, cores and all. A knife will do the job well, although the slicer/shredder attachment on a strong electric mixer is a great boon.

Layer the cabbage in the crock with salt; 3 ounces (90 g) is ample for 10 pounds (5 kg) of cabbage. Flavour it with two or three crumbled bay leaves, a little cumin seed and dill seed to taste. Chopped carrots and apples can be added if desired. Pack the cabbage down firmly until it is within 2 inches (5 cm) of the top of the crock. Cover the surface with a piece of scalded muslin. Lay the upturned plate or board on top of the muslin and weight it down with a scrubbed stone which is heavy enough to force the brine to come up and wet the muslin. Keep the crock in a warm place (65°F, 18°C) to start the fermentation, then store it in a cool place (about 50°F, 10°C) for at least a month until the fermentation process is complete. Skim the scum off daily and regularly scald the muslin and scrub the stone clean. Be sure that the surface is always covered with liquid, otherwise the sauerkraut may go bad. If you use canned sauerkraut, make sure that it is in brine not vinegar.

Cabbage

For economy and versatility, cabbages are difficult to surpass, although, all too often, they have suffered badly at the hands of incompetent or impatient cooks. Yet the peasant cuisines of Europe are a treasure house of imaginative dishes based on cabbage.

For most dishes either white or green cabbages may be used, although the looser green heads are easier to take apart for rolling and stuffing. Red cabbage is in a class of its own. It is most often used for salads, casseroles or pickles. When cooking red cabbage, always add a little vinegar or lemon juice. This will prevent it turning purple.

The best cabbage is heavy for its size. Strip off damaged or wilted outer leaves and trim the stem. Cut the head in half from tip to stem.

Then cut each half into thirds. Slice out the core and, if the cabbage is to be shredded, make a slit lengthwise down the middle of the thickest part of each piece, then shred it crosswise.

Cabbage may simply be cooked in a small amount of salted water—or chicken stock with a little chopped onion for extra flavour—until just tender, then thoroughly drained, seasoned and served with butter, or in a creamy white sauce. A good way to cook shredded cabbage is to wilt the shreds by pouring boiling water over them in a colander, then simmer the shreds in a little butter until soft and golden. Another way to cook shredded cabbage is to stir-fry it in a little oil with thinly sliced onion and slivered fresh root ginger. It takes only a few minutes to cook and it retains its colour and crispness.

Sauerkraut Salad

Sauerkraut salad goes well with pork dishes of all kinds. Try it, too, with fried fish. This recipe can be varied by substituting 1 tart dessert apple and 2 raw carrots, both coarsely grated, for the finely chopped onion.

Sauerkraut (pickled cabbage) can be bought in cans or from the barrel at delicatessens. To make your own sauerkraut see the recipe on page 132.

SERVES FOUR
¾ lb (360 g) sauerkraut in brine
1 medium-sized onion, finely chopped
3 tablespoons olive oil
Sugar
Freshly ground black pepper
Salt
GARNISH
Onion rings
Finely chopped parsley

Drain the sauerkraut and chop it coarsely. Put it in a bowl. Add the onion, olive oil and sugar to taste. Toss thoroughly with a fork to separate the shreds. Season with pepper and a little salt, if necessary.

Heap the sauerkraut in a serving dish. Garnish with paper-thin rings of sweet onion and a sprinkling of chopped parsley and serve.

Coleslaw

Originally a plain cabbage salad, coleslaw (the name is a corruption of the Dutch *koolsla*) now often includes such varied ingredients as pineapple, carrots and apples.

Celery seed, a traditional ingredient in American coleslaw, is not always easy to find in Britain. Celery salt makes an acceptable substitute, although it does not add the same interesting variety to the texture.

SERVES FOUR TO SIX
1 lb (½ kg) shredded cabbage
2 carrots, coarsely grated
1 crisp, tart apple, coarsely grated
2 shallots, finely chopped
3 tablespoons cider vinegar
½ pint (250 ml) thick home-made
    mayonnaise
¼ pint (125 ml) thick soured cream
1 tablespoon sugar
1 teaspoon celery seed or celery salt
6 drops Tabasco sauce
Salt
Freshly ground black pepper

Put the cabbage (weighed after shredding) in a large bowl. Add the carrots, apple, shallots and cider vinegar. Toss thoroughly.

In a small bowl mix the mayonnaise and soured cream together. Mix in the sugar, celery salt or seed, the Tabasco, salt and pepper, balancing flavours to suit your own taste. Pour the dressing over the salad and toss again until every shred of cabbage is coated.

Chill before serving.

Swedish Red Cabbage

This is an excellent dish served either as part of a vegetarian meal or with rich meats and such poultry as roast duck, as well as with all kinds of game. It also reheats and deep-freezes well.

SERVES EIGHT
1 head red cabbage, about 3 lb (1½ kg),
    finely shredded
2 oz (60 g) fat salt pork, diced, or
    rendered bacon fat
2 Spanish onions, thinly sliced
4 tablespoons brown sugar
½ lb (¼ kg) tart dessert apples, peeled,
    cored and chopped
¼ pint (125 ml) well-flavoured chicken
    stock
¼ pint (125 ml) red wine
3 tablespoons wine or cider vinegar
Salt
Freshly ground black pepper
1 small, raw beetroot, coarsely grated

Put the shredded cabbage in a large bowl. Pour over enough boiling water to cover the cabbage. Set aside.

In a large, heavy, enamelled pan or casserole, sauté the diced salt pork until the fat runs. If using bacon fat it need only be melted. Add the onions and fry, stirring frequently, over moderate heat until soft and transparent. Stir in the sugar and continue to fry gently until the onions are caramelized and a rich golden colour. Take great care not to let the sugar burn.

Drain the cabbage thoroughly. Add it to the casserole, together with the apples, stock, wine and vinegar. Mix well. Season generously with salt and pepper. Cover tightly and cook gently for 1½ hours, stirring occasionally.

Mix in the grated beetroot—this transforms the colour—and continue to cook, covered, for 30 minutes longer, or until the cabbage is soft. Correct seasoning and serve very hot.

Cabbage Quiche

This is an unusual and delicious quiche. The same cabbage mixture baked without the pastry in a *bain-marie* makes a delicate accompaniment for meat.

SERVES FOUR AS A MAIN DISH
Rich shortcrust pastry made with ½ lb
(¼ kg) flour
1 lb (½ kg) finely shredded cabbage
¼ lb (120 g) butter
3 eggs
½ pint (250 ml) single cream and milk,
mixed
4 tablespoons freshly grated
Gruyère cheese
3 tablespoons freshly grated
Parmesan cheese
Salt
Freshly ground black pepper
Freshly grated nutmeg

Preheat the oven to 425°F (220°C, Gas Mark 7). Roll out the pastry and line a 9-inch (22 cm) tart tin with a removable base. Line the pastry with greaseproof paper or foil, fill with dried beans and bake "blind" for 15 minutes. Remove the paper and beans, and let the base dry out for a further 5 minutes in the oven.

Reduce the oven temperature to 350°F (180°C, Gas Mark 4).

Meanwhile, put the cabbage in a colander and slowly pour a kettle of boiling water over it. Shake off excess moisture.

In a large, heavy saucepan melt the butter. Add the cabbage, cover tightly and cook over moderate heat until the

cabbage is soft and golden, shaking the pan to prevent the cabbage burning. The cooking time will depend on the type of cabbage used, but firm white cabbage takes about 30 minutes.

In a small bowl, beat the eggs with the cream and milk. Remove the pan from the heat. Let the cabbage cool slightly, then stir in the egg mixture and 2 tablespoons each of the Gruyère and Parmesan. Add salt, pepper and nutmeg to taste.

Carefully spoon the mixture into the baked pastry shell. Sprinkle the remaining cheese over the top. Bake for 30 minutes, or until the filling is set and a rich golden colour on top.

Cabbage Casserole

Like so many cabbage dishes, this one improves when cooked ahead of time and reheated. It also deep-freezes well.

SERVES SIX TO EIGHT
½ oz (15 g) dried mushrooms
1 head cabbage, about 3 lb (1½ kg),
shredded
Salt
2 oz (60 g) butter
4 rashers fat bacon, finely chopped
1 large onion, finely chopped
2 tablespoons flour
2 carrots, diced
1 small parsnip, diced
1 large cooking apple
2 tablespoons chopped parsley
3 allspice berries
1 small bay leaf
Freshly ground black pepper
3 ripe tomatoes, blanched,
peeled and sieved
¼ pint (125 ml) light stock

Put the dried mushrooms in a small bowl. Pour over ½ pint (250 ml) of boiling water and set aside to soak for 30 minutes.

Meanwhile, put the cabbage in a large pan. Sprinkle with salt. Pour over boiling water to cover. Cover the pan and bring the water to the boil again over high heat. Remove the lid for 1 to 2 seconds; replace it, lower the heat and simmer for 5 minutes. Drain the cabbage in a colander.

Pour the mushrooms and the soaking water into a small saucepan and boil them, uncovered, until they are very soft. Drain the mushrooms and reserve the remaining liquor. Chop the mushrooms finely and set aside.

Melt the butter in another large pan. Add the bacon and cook until the fat runs. Then add the onion and cook over low heat until it is soft and a rich golden colour. Blend in the flour and

stir over moderate heat to make a nutty brown *roux*.

Add the parboiled cabbage, the carrots and parsnip. Peel and core the apple, and grate it coarsely into the mixture. Add the mushrooms and their reserved liquor, the parsley, allspice berries and bay leaf. Season to taste with salt and pepper. Add the sieved tomatoes and stock and, stirring, bring to simmering point over moderate heat.

Cover the pan tightly and cook gently for 1½ hours, stirring occasionally, particularly at the beginning, to prevent the cabbage sticking to the bottom of the pan. Serve hot.

To shred cabbage, remove the stem and outer leaves. Cut the cabbage in half from tip to stem, then cut each half into three.

Make a slit along the thickest part of each piece, then cut out the core of the cabbage.

Finally, shred the cabbage thinly, cutting it crosswise.

Stuffed Cabbage Rolls

This classic dish requires very little meat, not more than 2 ounces (60 g) per portion, even less if the amount of rice is increased.

SERVES FOUR TO SIX
1 large head cabbage, white or green
¼ lb (120 g) short grain rice
1½ oz (45 g) butter
2 Spanish onions, finely chopped
¾ lb (360 g) lean lamb or pork, minced
2 tablespoons chopped parsley
4 tablespoons tomato concentrate
Salt
Freshly ground black pepper
Worcestershire sauce (optional)
About 1½ pints (750 ml) hot chicken or
beef stock

Trim the cabbage. Remove damaged outer leaves and carefully hollow out the stem end with a potato peeler. Plunge the cabbage into a large pan of boiling water. When the water comes to the boil again remove the pan from the heat. Cover the pan tightly and set aside.

Put the rice in a small bowl. Pour over enough boiling water to cover the rice

and let it soak for 5 minutes. Drain and rinse well.

Melt the butter in a large frying-pan. Add the onions and cook gently until they are soft and richly coloured. Scrape the onions and the butter into a large bowl. Mix in the minced meat, rice, parsley and half of the tomato concentrate diluted with ¼ pint (125 ml) of water. Season generously with salt, pepper and a few drops of Worcestershire sauce, if desired.

Drain the cabbage. As soon as it is cool enough to handle take the leaves apart, cutting them free at the stem end and carefully separating them from the head. If the inner leaves are still too crisp to handle, cover the head with more boiling water and let it stand for a few minutes longer. Stop taking the cabbage apart when the very small leaves that make up the heart are reached.

Use only the best and biggest leaves for making the cabbage rolls. Lay each leaf on a board and with a sharp knife pare down the thick central rib so that the leaf lies flat. Put a roll of filling at the stem end. Fold in the two sides over the

filling and roll the leaf up firmly to make a neat packet.

Line the bottom of a large, wide pan with some of the leftover cabbage leaves. Arrange the cabbage rolls in the pan side by side as tightly as possible so that they do not unwind—use pieces of cabbage heart to plug any spaces. Try to fit all the rolls in two, or at most three, layers. Cover with the remaining leaves.

Weight the cabbage rolls down with an upturned heatproof plate slightly smaller in diameter than the top of the pan. Blend the remaining tomato concentrate with the hot stock and pour it into the pan so that it just shows around the sides of the plate.

Over moderate heat bring the liquid to the boil. Cover the pan tightly and cook very gently for 1½ hours.

Serve the cabbage rolls with the pan juices or drain the pan juices and use them to make a light lemon or tomato sauce to spoon over the top.

Cabbage

Kulebiak

This Russian cabbage and mushroom pie is a party dish to serve on its own as part of a hot buffet or, with hot melted butter, as a first course. It may also be served as a main dish accompanied by a rich mushroom sauce.

Kulebiak may be time-consuming to prepare but it can be made in advance, baked and deep-frozen. Transfer it straight from the freezer to a fairly hot oven, 425°F (220°C, Gas Mark 7), for 35 to 40 minutes, covered with foil for the first 20 minutes to prevent the crust from becoming too brown.

If it is more convenient to prepare the *kulebiak* in two stages, start with the cabbage filling.

SERVES EIGHT TO TWELVE
CABBAGE FILLING
2 lb (1 kg) finely shredded cabbage
Salt
2 oz (60 g) butter
1 large Spanish onion, finely chopped
¼ lb (120 g) small button mushrooms, thinly sliced
1 large cooking apple, peeled, cored and coarsely grated
Freshly ground black pepper
2 large eggs, hard boiled and finely chopped
YEAST DOUGH
1 lb (½ kg) plain flour, preferably "strong"
1 teaspoon salt
1 oz (30 g) fresh yeast or 1 tablespoon dried yeast
½ pint (250 ml) lukewarm milk and water, mixed
2 teaspoons sugar
1 egg and 2 egg yolks, beaten
3 oz (90 g) butter, melted and cooled

Put the cabbage in a large pan. Sprinkle it with salt and pour over enough boiling water to cover. Put the pan on the heat and when the water returns to the boil reduce the heat and simmer the cabbage steadily for 5 minutes. Drain the cabbage in a colander, pressing out as much moisture as possible with the back of a spoon.

Rinse and dry the pan and return it to the heat. Add the butter. When it is hot stir in the onion and cook until soft and golden brown. Add the mushrooms and continue to cook gently until they have softened.

Stir in the parboiled cabbage and the apple. Mix well and season generously with salt and pepper. Cover the pan and cook over low heat, stirring occasionally. When the cabbage is very soft, remove the pan from the heat, adjust the seasoning and leave to cool.

Meanwhile, make the yeast dough. Sift the flour and salt into a large bowl, and warm it gently over the pilot light of a gas stove or in a 90°F (32°C) oven.

In a small bowl blend the fresh yeast smoothly with the milk and water and the sugar. Beat in enough of the flour to make a thick cream. Put the bowl in a warm place for 15 to 20 minutes until the mixture becomes spongy. (Dried yeast should be reconstituted according to the directions on the packet.)

Make a well in the centre of the flour. Pour in the yeast mixture and the eggs, reserving a tablespoon or two of the egg to glaze the top of the pie later. Using your hands, work the ingredients to a smooth dough. Depending on the flour, a little more milk and water or a handful of flour may have to be added. When the dough leaves the sides of the bowl, work in the melted butter.

When the dough is smooth again, turn it out on to a floured board and knead vigorously for about 10 minutes until it is silky soft and elastic. Rinse and dry the bowl and oil it lightly. Roll the dough into a ball and put it back in the bowl. Cover the bowl with a cloth and leave it in a warm place until the dough has doubled in bulk.

Deflate the dough, knead it lightly and divide it into two pieces, one double the size of the other. Roll out the larger piece and use it to line the base and sides of a deep, buttered baking tin 10 × 12 inches (25 × 30 cm). Spoon the cabbage filling into the baking tin and sprinkle the top evenly with the chopped hard-boiled eggs. Roll out the other piece of dough and cover the pie, sealing the edges. Make slits in the top to allow steam to escape. Put the pie in a warm place for about 30 minutes, or until the top is puffy.

Preheat the oven to 400°F (200°C, Gas Mark 6). Brush the top of the pie with the reserved egg and bake for 15 minutes. Reduce the heat to 350°F (180°C, Gas Mark 4) and continue to bake for 45 minutes longer, or until the pie is well risen and a rich golden brown on top. Serve hot.

To make cabbage rolls, place some of the stuffing at the root end of each blanched cabbage leaf.

Fold the sides of the leaf towards the centre and begin to roll up the leaf, starting at the root end.

Cabbage Dumplings

The excellent partnership of cabbage and pasta can be found in many culinary traditions from the Mediterranean to as far north as Poland. Cooked shredded cabbage simply tossed with buttered noodles makes a fine side dish for pork. Or try the same mixture dotted with butter, sprinkled with a little cheese and browned in the oven. Cabbage dumplings are a more elaborate variation on the same theme. The cabbage filling is made in the same way as in the recipe for *kulebiak*. Leftover dumplings are delicious fried in butter.

MAKES ABOUT FORTY-EIGHT DUMPLINGS,
SERVES FOUR TO SIX
½ recipe cabbage filling
6 oz (180 g) plain flour
½ teaspoon salt
1 egg
Dry breadcrumbs, fried in butter, to garnish

Chop the cabbage filling very finely or, if necessary, put it through the coarse blade of a mincer. Mix in the hard-boiled eggs.

The noodle dough should be prepared in advance to give it at least an hour to "relax" before it is rolled out. Sift the flour and salt into a bowl. Make a well in the centre and drop in the egg. Work the egg into the flour with your fingertips, together with enough lukewarm water—6 to 8 tablespoons—to make a firm dough. When the dough holds together, transfer it to a board dusted with flour and knead it vigorously until it is satin-smooth and elastic. When little blisters of air start forming just under the surface of the dough, stop kneading.

Roll the dough into a ball and put it into a plastic bag. Leave the dough for at least 1 hour to relax and soften.

Roll the dough out very thinly. Stamp out 2½-inch (6 cm) rounds with a plain pastry cutter. Taking one round at a time, put it in the palm of one hand and stretch it out slightly. Put a small heap of filling in the centre. Fold the circle in half and pinch the edges firmly to seal them. Arrange the plump little dumplings on a lightly floured board. Collect all the trimmings in the plastic bag as you work to prevent them drying out. Then roll them out to make more dumplings.

Bring a large pan of salted water to the boil. Drop in a batch of dumplings (about 20 at a time in a large pan). When the water comes back to the boil and the dumplings rise to the surface, stir once, cover the pan, reduce the heat and cook gently for 5 to 6 minutes. Using a slotted spoon, transfer the dumplings to a colander. Rinse the dumplings with boiling water and drain thoroughly.

Serve the dumplings very hot, with buttered breadcrumbs spooned over each portion.

The leaf should be rolled up tightly, right to the end.

The cabbage roll is now ready to be cooked. It may be held together with a cocktail stick if necessary.

Cauliflower

Although a much-loved vegetable, the cauliflower, in common with other brassicas, is often overcooked and unimaginatively served. With a little care, however, it can provide a satisfying main dish, as well as a tasty accompaniment to meat, fish and egg dishes.

To prepare cauliflower for cooking, first cut all around the base, removing all but the tiniest green leaves nestling around the head. Trim the stem so that the cauliflower will stand level. If there are any blemishes or bruised spots among the flowerets, cut them out. With an apple corer, hollow out about 2 inches (5 cm) of the stem. Wash the cauliflower carefully and leave it to soak for 10 to 15 minutes in a large bowl of cold water to which a handful of salt has been added. This will winkle out any grubs hiding in the interior.

Cooking a cauliflower calls for care. It must not be allowed to get even slightly mushy. The simplest way to avoid this is to cook it in a pan just large enough to hold the head comfortably. Pour in 1 inch (2 cm) of water, add salt and bring it to the boil. Put the cauliflower in the pan stem downwards. As soon as the water returns to the boil, cover with a tight-fitting lid. Cook over high heat for 15 minutes, a little longer if the head is very large. Using this method the flowerets cook in steam while the tougher stem end is boiled in water. Carefully transfer the cauliflower to a colander and drain it thoroughly. It may now be used whole or divided into flowerets.

A perfectly cooked head of cauliflower makes a marvellous dish with a sprinkling of coarse salt, a grinding of pepper and a few tablespoons of hot melted butter spooned over the top. Try sprinkling 3 or 4 tablespoons each of chopped parsley and chives over the dressed cauliflower just before serving. Or sauté a handful of slivered almonds in butter before pouring it all, sizzling hot, over the top. Or serve it *à la polonaise*, sprinkled with 3 tablespoons of fine, dry bread-crumbs that have been fried in butter until crisp and golden.

For special occasions, make a *hollandaise* sauce and pour it over the entire head just before serving. Mayonnaise is also extremely good spread over a chilled, cooked head of cauliflower and served as part of a cold buffet. For extra flavour, spoon a little *vinaigrette* over the cauliflower and let it soak in thoroughly before masking it with mayonnaise.

In Italy, tiny raw cauliflowerets are included in a basket of raw vegetables for dipping into *bagna cauda*, a hot oil and butter sauce flavoured with anchovies and garlic. Raw cauliflower also makes an unusual addition and provides a delicious crunchiness to a tossed green salad.

Cauliflower Appetizer Salad

As an alternative to this salad, serve the flowerets, raw or cooked, with an American-style, soured-cream cheese dip—soured cream blended with mild blue cheese, 1 teaspoon of finely chopped shallot or chives and a few drops of Tabasco sauce.

SERVES FOUR TO SIX
1 large cauliflower
Salt
8 tablespoons olive oil
3 tablespoons lemon juice
8 anchovy fillets, finely chopped
2 shallots, finely chopped or crushed in a garlic press
½ teaspoon French mustard
Freshly ground black pepper
1 canned red pepper, finely chopped
3 tablespoons finely chopped parsley
Pitted black olives, to garnish

Parboil the cauliflower in 1 inch (2 cm) of salted water for 8 minutes. It should remain distinctly crisp. Drain the cauliflower in a colander. As soon as it is cool enough to handle, divide it into flowerets and put them in a bowl.

In a small pan, combine the olive oil with the lemon juice, anchovy fillets, shallots, mustard and a grinding of pepper. Put the pan on the heat and slowly bring the dressing to the boil, stirring. Immediately pour it over the cauliflower. Add the chopped red pepper and parsley. Toss lightly and season to taste with salt. Chill and serve garnished with olives.

Cream of Cauliflower Soup

Cauliflower makes a satisfying soup, delicate in flavour and creamy in texture.

SERVES FOUR TO SIX
1 medium-sized cauliflower
1 pint (500 ml) milk
Salt
1½ pints (750 ml) chicken stock
1 oz (30 g) butter
2 tablespoons flour
Freshly ground black pepper
Sharp Cheddar cheese, grated

Cut off a handful of tiny flowerets no bigger than daisy heads from the cauliflower. Bring ¼ pint (125 ml) of the milk to the boil in a small pan with ¼ pint (125 ml) of water and a pinch of salt. Add the flowerets and poach them for 6 to 7 minutes, until they are cooked but still very firm. Drain them, reserving the liquor, and set aside.

Chop the remainder of the cauliflower into chunks. Put them in a pan with 1 pint (500 ml) of the chicken stock, the rest of the milk and the reserved cauliflower liquor. Bring to the boil and cook, covered, until the cauliflower is soft. Purée the contents of the pan in a blender or through the finest plate of a vegetable mouli.

In another pan melt the butter. Blend in the flour and stir over low heat for 1 minute to make a pale *roux*. Gradually add the remaining stock, beating vigorously to make a smooth sauce. Stir in the puréed cauliflower mixture and bring to the boil, stirring. Season to taste with salt and pepper and simmer for 5 minutes.

Taste the soup. If it seems too bland, stir in 2 or 3 tablespoons of cheese. Add the poached flowerets and heat them through. Serve the soup with a bowl of cheese for sprinkling over each portion.

"... In the midst of which Leaves, sometimes in the middle of autumn, and sometimes sooner, there rises up a great white Head of white hard Flowers closely thrust together, sometimes they are of a Milk, or Cream, or yellowish White color."

The English Herbal *by William Salmon, M.D., 1710*

Cauliflowers are considered by many to be the aristocrats of the brassica family. They are particularly fine when they are gathered from the garden early in the day, with the dew still sparkling on the curds.

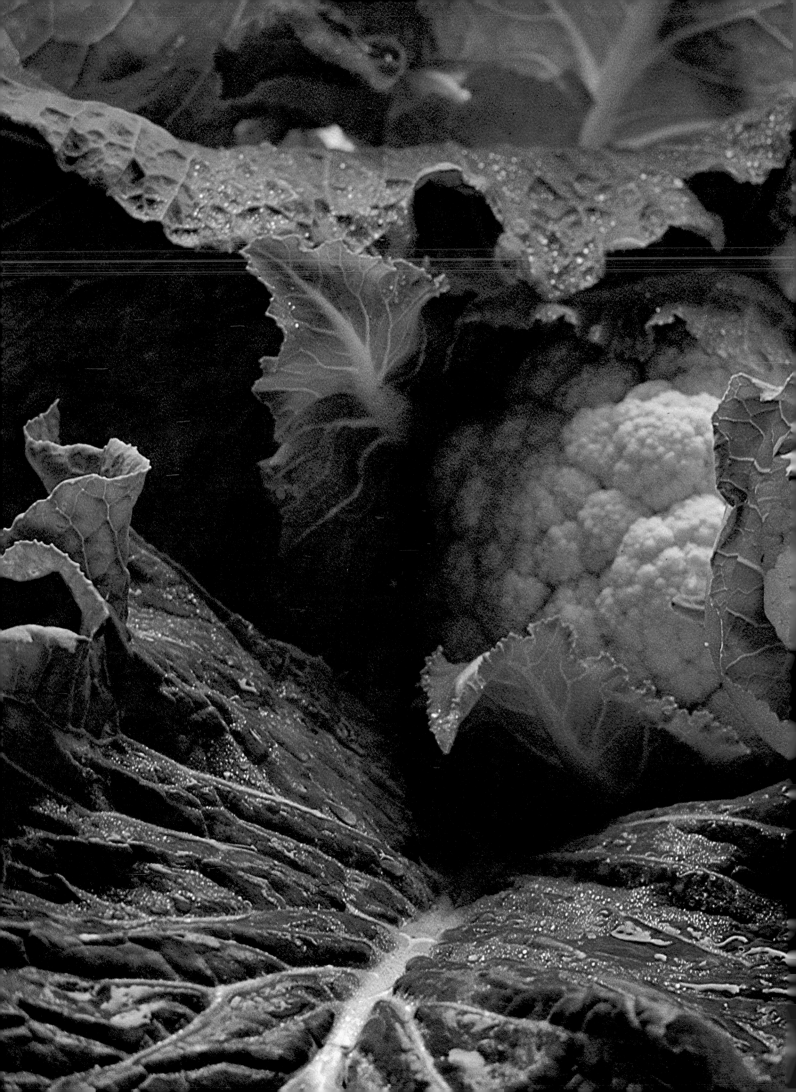

"*. . . Note also, That being boiled in Milk, and then eaten with Sweet fresh Butter and Salt, and Juice of Limons they have been found to restore admirably in Consumptions.*"

The English Herbal *by William Salmon, M.D., 1710*

Cauliflower

Cauliflower au Gratin

A family supper standby, this dish can be very good indeed, so long as the sauce is not too thick, the cheese flavour not too mild and the cauliflower underneath firm enough to stand upright. In spite of its French-sounding name this is a very English dish, so use a sharp Cheddar or crumbly Lancashire cheese for the sauce.

SERVES FOUR

1½ oz (45 g) butter
3 tablespoons flour
¾ pint (375 ml) hot milk
About 5 oz (150 g) grated cheese
1 egg yolk
Dry mustard or cayenne pepper
Salt
Freshly ground black pepper
Lemon juice (optional)
1 large cauliflower, steam boiled
3 tablespoons fresh white breadcrumbs

Preheat the oven to 375°F (190°C, Gas Mark 5). Melt the butter in a small saucepan. Blend in the flour and stir over low heat for 1 minute to make a pale *roux*. Gradually add the milk, stirring constantly, to make a smooth sauce. Simmer for 6 to 8 minutes, stirring occasionally, to cook out the raw flour taste. Remove the pan from the heat. Beat in ¼ pound (120 g) of the cheese, followed by the egg yolk. Season to taste with a pinch of dry mustard or cayenne, salt and pepper, and, if necessary, intensify the flavour of the cheese with a few drops of lemon juice.

Drain the cauliflower and put it in a buttered baking dish. Pour the sauce over the top and sprinkle with the remaining cheese lightly mixed with the breadcrumbs. Bake the cauliflower in the upper part of the oven for 10 to 15 minutes, or until the cheese on top has melted and the sauce is bubbling.

Serve immediately.

Cauliflower in Cider Sauce

Unusual and delicious, this sauce is ideal for cauliflower which is to be served with chicken or other delicate meats.

SERVES FOUR TO SIX

1 oz (30 g) butter
2 tablespoons flour
½ pint (250 ml) dry cider
¼ pint (125 ml) double cream
Salt
Sugar
Freshly ground black pepper
Freshly grated nutmeg
1 large cauliflower, steam boiled

Melt the butter in a heavy pan. Blend in the flour and cook over a low heat, stirring, for 1 to 2 minutes to make a pale *roux*. Gradually add the cider, beating vigorously to prevent lumps forming. Beat in the cream and bring to the boil, stirring constantly. Simmer the sauce for 5 minutes. Season to taste with salt, sugar, pepper and nutmeg. Simmer for 2 to 3 minutes longer.

Drain the cauliflower thoroughly and place it in a hot serving dish. Pour the creamy cider sauce over the cauliflower and serve immediately.

Cauliflower Cheese, Italian Style

This is another version of cauliflower *au gratin* that is even easier to make.

SERVES FOUR

1 medium-sized cauliflower, steam boiled
8 tablespoons freshly grated Gruyère or Emmenthal cheese
2 tablespoons freshly grated Parmesan cheese
2 tablespoons fine dry breadcrumbs
4 tablespoons melted butter

Preheat the oven to 400°F (200°C, Gas Mark 6).

Drain the cauliflower carefully in a colander and put it in a buttered baking dish.

In a bowl, toss the cheeses with the breadcrumbs and the melted butter. Sprinkle this mixture over the cauliflower and bake it for 10 to 15 minutes, or until the cheese has melted and the topping is sizzling and golden.

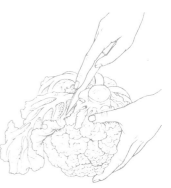

To prepare cauliflower, cut off the stalk and the leaves. Soak in cold, salted water for 10 minutes.

Cauliflower Fritters

Serve these crisp, light fritters with coarse salt, grated cheese or a sprinkling of soy sauce. Another way to make simple but delicious cauliflower fritters is this Turkish recipe: dip the cooked flowerets in seasoned beaten egg and then in flour. Deep-fry them in olive oil until crisp and golden. Serve the fritters very hot with a bowl of yoghourt or fresh tomato sauce.

SERVES FOUR

1 medium-sized cauliflower
Salt
Oil for deep-frying
FRITTER BATTER
¼ lb (120 g) plain flour
½ teaspoon salt
2 tablespoons olive oil
2 egg whites

Make the fritter batter at least 1 hour before it is to be used. Sift the flour and salt into a bowl, and make a well in the centre. Pour in ¼ pint (125 ml) of lukewarm water. Gradually beat the flour into the liquid until the mixture forms a smooth batter. Beat in the oil. Set aside.

Steam boil the cauliflower in 1 inch (2 cm) of salted water for 12 minutes. It should remain crisp. Drain the cauliflower well and divide it into bite-size flowerets. Leave to cool.

When ready to make the fritters, whisk the egg whites until stiff but not dry, and fold them into the batter. Heat a pan of oil for deep-frying to 350°F (180°C).

Dip the flowerets individually into the batter and deep-fry them, a few at a time, turning them over once, until they are crisply puffed and golden. Drain the fritters on crumpled kitchen paper and serve immediately.

Cauliflower may be cooked whole or broken into flowerets, which will cook in half the time.

Place the cauliflower in very little boiling, salted water. Cook, covered, until tender but not mushy.

Broccoli

The culinary confusion that arises over what qualifies as "broccoli" is not surprising, for there are many varieties. They are, however, all cooked and eaten in the same way.

Select tender, young broccoli. Do not break the stalks more than 4 or 5 inches (10 or 12 cm) long. Divide the heads into flowerets about 2 inches (5 cm) in diameter. If the stalks are thick, cut them in half lengthwise and peel them thinly.

Broccoli spears are fragile and 8 to 10 minutes' fast boiling in salted water should be ample to make them tender. They may also be steam boiled in the same way as cauliflower or asparagus, with the heads above the surface of the simmering water.

Eaten hot, broccoli is delicious with a sauce of melted butter, with brown butter mixed with capers or with butter in which flaked almonds have been sautéed. The hot spears may also be served with *hollandaise* or *mornay* sauce. Cold broccoli is excellent with a *vinaigrette* dressing or mayonnaise.

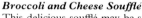

Broccoli and Cheese Soufflé

This delicious soufflé may be served as a main dish, a first course or as an accompaniment to any meat or fish dish.

SERVES THREE
Ground almonds or fine dry breadcrumbs
1 lb (½ kg) fresh broccoli
7 fl oz (175 ml) chicken stock, boiling
Milk
1 oz (30 g) butter
2 tablespoons flour
2 egg yolks (from large eggs)
1½ teaspoons lemon juice
1 small garlic clove, crushed
Salt
Freshly ground black pepper
Freshly grated nutmeg
2 oz (60 g) Gruyère or sharp
  Cheddar cheese, grated
4 egg whites (from large eggs)

Butter a 1½-pint (750 ml) soufflé dish and dust it with ground almonds or fine dry breadcrumbs. Pour 1½ inches (4 cm) of hot water into a deep roasting tin and put it on a rack just below the centre of the oven. Set the oven to 400°F (200°C, Gas Mark 6).

Peel the stems of the broccoli if necessary. Put the broccoli into a pan, stems downwards, and pour in the boiling stock. Put the pan on the heat and as soon as the stock returns to the boil cover the pan and reduce the heat to moderate. Cook the broccoli for about 10 minutes, or until tender.

Drain the broccoli in a strainer set over a bowl. Then pour the drained liquor into a measuring jug and add milk to make it up to ¼ pint (125 ml).

Put the cooked broccoli into the bowl and mash it with a fork. It does not matter if a few coarse pieces remain. Leave to cool.

Melt the butter in a medium-sized pan. Blend in the flour and stir over low heat for 1 minute. Gradually add the broccoli liquor, beating vigorously to prevent lumps forming, and stir over moderate heat until it starts to bubble thickly. Remove the pan from the heat. Beat in the egg yolks, lemon juice and crushed garlic. Season to taste with salt, pepper and nutmeg. Cool the mixture, then beat in the cheese and the mashed broccoli.

Whisk the egg whites until stiff but not dry. Stir a heaped tablespoonful into the broccoli mixture. Then, with a large metal spoon, lightly but thoroughly fold in the remainder.

Gently transfer the mixture to the prepared soufflé dish. Set the dish in the roasting tin of water and bake for 45 to 50 minutes, or until the soufflé is well risen but still slightly creamy in the centre. Serve immediately.

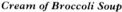

Cream of Broccoli Soup

When there is plenty of broccoli in the garden this is an excellent way to use it up. This soup is also delicious cold, with chopped chives sprinkled over each portion.

SERVES FOUR TO SIX
1 oz (30 g) butter
1 leek, white part only, thinly sliced
1 celery stalk, thinly sliced
1 lb (½ kg) broccoli

1 small potato, thickly sliced
1½ pints (750 ml) chicken stock
¼ pint (125 ml) single cream
Salt
Freshly ground black pepper
Lemon juice
Small croûtons, to garnish

Melt the butter in a large pan. Add the leek and celery, cover the pan and simmer until the vegetables are soft but not coloured. Add the broccoli and the potato. Pour in the chicken stock, cover the pan and simmer gently until the vegetables are soft.

Blend the contents of the pan to a purée in an electric blender, or rub through the fine plate of a vegetable mouli. Pour the purée back into the pan. Stir in the cream. Season to taste with salt and pepper, and intensify the flavour with a few drops of lemon juice.

Bring the soup to boiling point, but do not let it boil. Serve hot, garnished with tiny, crisp croûtons.

Broccoli alla Siciliana

Broccoli is a great Italian favourite. Serve this classic southern dish with roast chicken and such meats as beef, lamb or gammon.

SERVES SIX
2 tablespoons olive oil
1 Spanish onion, finely chopped
12 black olives, pitted and sliced
6 canned anchovy fillets, chopped,
  and the oil reserved
2 lb (1 kg) fresh broccoli
¼ pint (125 ml) chicken stock
¼ pint (125 ml) red wine
Freshly ground black pepper
1 teaspoon butter
1 teaspoon flour
Salt

Heat the olive oil in a large, flameproof casserole. Stir in the onion, olives and anchovy fillets. Simmer gently, uncovered, for 5 minutes.

Add the broccoli, turning the pieces over to coat them with the oil. Add the stock and wine. Sprinkle with 1 tablespoon of oil drained from the can of anchovy fillets and season with a generous grinding of pepper. Cover the casserole and cook over moderate heat for 15 minutes. Stir occasionally, to prevent the mixture sticking to the pan.

When the broccoli is tender, uncover the pan and continue simmering for 3 minutes longer. Using a slotted spoon, transfer the broccoli to a heated serving dish and keep hot.

Thicken the sauce in the pan with a *beurre manié* made by mashing the butter and flour to a smooth paste and stirring it in in small pieces. Add salt if necessary. Stir the sauce until it comes to the boil. Pour it over the broccoli and serve.

Brussels Sprouts

When Brussels sprouts are at their peak they need not be cooked at all. Shredded raw, they make a deliciously crisp and nutty-flavoured addition to a salad.

Sprouts should be picked while they are still very small, plumply rounded and hard between the fingers. Strip off any damaged, wilted or worm-eaten outer leaves and trim the stems. Then—this is important—nick a small cross in the stem to help the sprout to cook evenly. Wash the sprouts quickly in cold water and drain them thoroughly. Speed is the secret of cooking sprouts. Bring a large pan of salted water to a fast boil. Drop in the sprouts and cook them at a rolling boil until their stems can easily be pierced with a skewer. Boil them for no longer than 10 minutes or 6 to 7 minutes if they are to be cooked further with other ingredients.

Poached sprouts are best served with a knob of fresh butter, or tossed with buttered breadcrumbs or a slice or two of crumbled, crisply fried bacon.

Brussels Sprouts with Chestnuts

This dish is a traditional accompaniment for the Christmas turkey. If fresh chestnuts are not in season, canned ones make a perfectly good substitute.

SERVES FOUR
1 lb (½ kg) Brussels sprouts
Salt
1 oz (30 g) butter
¼ lb (120 g) fat bacon, diced
½ lb (¼ kg) peeled, cooked chestnuts
4 tablespoons poultry stock or water
Buttered breadcrumbs, to garnish (optional)

Poach the sprouts in salted water for 6 to 7 minutes. They should remain crisp. Drain well and keep hot.

Melt the butter in a deep frying-pan. Add the bacon and sauté until the fat runs. Add the chestnuts and toss over fairly high heat until they are thoroughly hot and lightly coloured.

Gently mix in the Brussels sprouts and moisten with stock or water. Cook gently, stirring frequently, until the liquid has evaporated.

Garnish if desired with buttered breadcrumbs and serve.

Brussels Sprouts with Mushrooms

Brussels sprouts cooked in this way make a good dish to serve with meat and poultry.

SERVES FOUR
1 lb (½ kg) Brussels sprouts
Salt
2 oz (60 g) butter
2 shallots, finely chopped
¼ lb (120 g) button mushrooms, thickly sliced
Lemon juice
Freshly ground black pepper

Poach the sprouts in salted water for 6 to 7 minutes. They should remain slightly crisp.

While the sprouts are cooking, melt the butter in a wide pan. Add the shallots and cook gently until they are soft and richly coloured. Add the mushrooms, tossing them to coat them with the buttery juices. Squeeze a few drops of lemon juice over them to help preserve their colour and cook gently until the mushrooms have softened and the excess moisture has evaporated, leaving the butter clear again.

Drain the sprouts thoroughly. Mix them gently with the mushrooms and shallots and season generously with salt and freshly ground pepper. Cook for 2 to 3 minutes longer, stirring frequently. Serve immediately.

Brussels Sprouts Baked in Cream

This dish is well worth the effort of preparation.

SERVES FOUR
1 lb (½ kg) Brussels sprouts
Salt
2 oz (60 g) lean ham, in one piece
1 oz (30 g) butter
Freshly ground black pepper
1 tablespoon flour
8 tablespoons double cream
1 oz (30 g) grated Gruyère cheese

Preheat the oven to 375°F (190°C, Gas Mark 5).

Poach the sprouts in salted water for 5 minutes. Drain them and toss them in the pan over low heat to dry them. Cut the ham into tiny dice and toss it with the hot sprouts.

Melt the butter in a baking dish that will hold the sprouts in a single layer. Turn the sprouts and ham into the dish. Season to taste with salt and pepper. Cover the dish with a lid or aluminium foil and bake for 10 minutes.

In a small bowl, blend the flour smoothly with the cream. Fold the mixture gently into the hot sprouts. Sprinkle with the grated cheese and continue to bake, uncovered, for 15 to 20 minutes, or until the sauce is bubbling and golden brown on top. Serve from the baking dish.

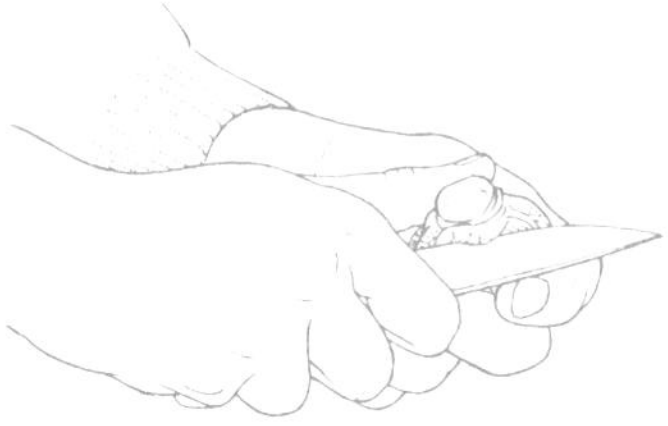

To prepare Brussels sprouts, use a sharp knife to slice off the stem of each sprout.

Puréed Brussels Sprouts

This is one of the nicest ways to serve Brussels sprouts. The purée has a lovely green colour and an excellent flavour. It can also be used as a base for making a soufflé—1 pound (½ kg) of purée will require 3 egg yolks and 4 egg whites.

SERVES FOUR TO SIX
1½ lb (¾ kg) Brussels sprouts
¼ pint (125 ml) single cream
½ lb (¼ kg) puréed potatoes
2 oz (60 g) butter, melted
Salt
Freshly ground black pepper
Nutmeg

Poach the sprouts in salted water for 5 minutes. Drain them well.

Purée the sprouts with the cream in an electric blender. Pour the purée into a large bowl. Add the puréed potato and the butter and beat well until the mixture is light and fluffy. Season to taste with salt, pepper and a grating of nutmeg.

Return the purée to the pan and reheat gently, adding more cream if necessary.

Serve hot.

Remove the outer leaves and wash the sprouts thoroughly or soak them for 10 minutes in salted water.

Drain well, then cut a cross in the base of each sprout so that they will cook more quickly.

Spinach & Other Leaves

Even the simplest dish of spinach cooked for 3 to 4 minutes, drained, seasoned with salt, pepper, a touch of nutmeg, or perhaps a squeeze of lemon or a pinch of rosemary or basil, and topped with a generous pat of butter is delicious, particularly when it is served with such meats as roast lamb, veal or grilled chicken.

Spinach has travelled a long way to reach our tables. Some say it came from Persia, others that it originated in the Far East. And as it travelled, it was welcomed by every cuisine along the way, adopting a variety of guises, in salads and soups, pastries and pies of all kinds, soufflés, omelettes and creams, proving its versatility in all but the sweet course.

True spinach is more delicate than any of the other leafy vegetables that are used as spinach substitutes. Spinach beet, or perpetual spinach, can be coarser in texture, but its abundance in all but the coldest weather and its reliability in conditions in which its namesake might fail, more than make up for this. Seakale beet, a cousin of spinach beet (its other name is Swiss chard), was known to the botanists of the classical world. Its stems are firmer than those of spinach beet, particularly those of the red chard, which are rather sweet and also attractive enough to plant in the flower garden.

New Zealand spinach and the splendidly named British native Good King Henry, which still grows wild in parts of the country, are other useful leaves that come into this culinary category. They can all be cooked in any of the ways recommended for spinach.

Like all low-growing leaves, spinach must be washed with great care; the slightest suspicion of grit in the finished dish will ruin it. The old custom of washing spinach in seven waters may be taking things too far, but two or three changes of water are necessary. There is less danger of leaving specks of grit among the leaves if they are lifted individually out of the rinsing water, rather than drained in a colander, which allows any remaining grit to seep back in.

Very young spinach leaves make an interesting salad, washed, dried and chilled, then tossed with a sherry dressing—for $\frac{1}{2}$ pound ($\frac{1}{4}$ kg) of spinach leaves mix 4 to 6 tablespoons of dry sherry, a tablespoon or two of light wine vinegar, 4 tablespoons of olive oil, salt, pepper, a pinch of sugar and a little chopped fresh basil or marjoram. Or shred the leaves, dress them with lemon mayonnaise and serve the salad garnished with chopped hard-boiled eggs.

To cook spinach, drop the leaves into a pan of salted boiling water—add a pinch of sugar for flavour—and simmer, uncovered, for 10 to 15 minutes, or until tender. Drain in a colander and refresh the leaves under cold running water. Gently squeeze the leaves as dry as possible and either reheat them in butter, or chop or mince them, as your recipe demands. This method of cooking spinach makes it more digestible and ensures that it never has an unpleasant, metallic aftertaste.

Another way to cook spinach is to put it in a pan over high heat without adding water—the water trapped in the leaves is sufficient to cook them. Cover the pan and cook the spinach for 7 to 10 minutes, or until the leaves are tender.

Spinach may also be pan-fried in oil or in a mixture of oil and butter. For 1 to $1\frac{1}{2}$ pounds ($\frac{1}{2}$ to $\frac{3}{4}$ kg) of spinach, 3 tablespoons of oil or 2 tablespoons of oil and 1 tablespoon of butter will be sufficient. Add any flavouring, such as onion, garlic or root ginger. Fry the spinach in a large, deep frying-pan for 7 to 10 minutes and serve immediately.

Because spinach can be frozen successfully it is well worth freezing a part of the crop. For however efficiently you manage your patch there will be times when there are no fresh spinach or beet leaves in the garden ready to be harvested. When using frozen spinach allow just over half the weight specified in recipes for fresh spinach. Frozen spinach may be thawed in a pan over low heat. Then stir it over high heat for a minute or two to evaporate excess moisture.

Spinach

Summer Spinach Soup

This is a light soup subtly flavoured with fresh dill. If fresh dill is not available, substitute half the quantity of the dried herb.

SERVES SIX

1 lb (½ kg) fresh spinach, cooked and finely chopped
2½ pints (1½ litres) chicken or light meat stock
¼ pint (125 ml) puréed tomatoes
2 medium-sized carrots, diced
1 large potato, peeled and diced
1 tablespoon chopped fresh dill
Lemon juice
Sugar
Salt
Freshly ground black pepper
Finely chopped hard-boiled eggs or thick soured cream, to garnish

In a large pan, combine the spinach with the stock, puréed tomatoes, carrots, potato and dill. Bring the soup to simmering point and cook gently, uncovered, for 25 to 30 minutes, or until the carrots and potato are soft.

Flavour the soup to taste with lemon juice and sugar and season with salt and pepper.

Serve each portion garnished with a sprinkling of chopped hard-boiled egg or a spoonful of soured cream.

Spinach and Cheese Quiche

Serve wedges of hot or warm quiche with drinks or as a first course.

SERVES SIX TO EIGHT

Rich shortcrust pastry made with ½ lb (¼ kg) flour
1 oz (30 g) butter
2 lb (1 kg) fresh spinach, cooked and finely chopped
¼ lb (120 g) curd cheese
2 oz (60 g) freshly grated Gruyère cheese
1 oz (30 g) freshly grated Parmesan cheese
¼ pint (125 ml) double cream
3 eggs, beaten
Salt
Freshly ground black pepper
Freshly grated nutmeg

Preheat the oven to 425°F (220°C, Gas Mark 7). Line a 9-inch (22 cm) tart tin with a removable base with the pastry. Line the pastry case with greaseproof paper or foil and fill it with dried beans. Bake the case "blind" for 15 minutes. Remove the paper and beans, and let the base dry out in the oven for a further 5 minutes.

Reduce the oven temperature to 350°F (180°C, Gas Mark 4). Melt the butter in a saucepan. Add the spinach and, stirring, heat it through. Remove the pan from the heat and beat in the cheeses, cream and eggs. Season to taste with salt, pepper and nutmeg.

Spoon the spinach mixture into the hot pastry case and bake it for 30 to 40 minutes, or until the filling is set and is lightly coloured on top.

Spinach Börek

The filling used in making the quiche can also be used for making little Middle Eastern pastries called börek. Börek are made with filo, a fine, strudel-like pastry, which can be bought in Greek grocery shops. One pound (½ kg) of filo will be required for one recipe of spinach filling.

Working with one sheet of filo at a time (they dry out rapidly when exposed to the air and should be kept wrapped in a damp cloth to prevent them becoming brittle), cut it lengthwise into 3-inch (8 cm) strips. Brush a strip with melted butter. Put a rounded teaspoonful of filling about 1 inch (2 cm) in from one of the shorter ends. Fold the end over the filling, then fold the strip over and over to make a fat little triangular packet.

Butter baking sheets and arrange the pastries on them. Brush the tops of the pastries with more melted butter.

Bake the pastries in a moderately hot oven, 400°F (200°C, Gas Mark 6), for 20 to 30 minutes, until they are puffed and a crisp golden brown. Serve them hot from the oven.

Spinach Cutlets

Served with chips or boiled new potatoes and a fresh green salad, spinach cutlets make a satisfying meal.

SERVES FOUR

1 oz (30 g) butter
1 medium-sized onion, finely chopped
2 lb (1 kg) fresh spinach, cooked and finely chopped or minced
1 large egg
Fine dry breadcrumbs
Salt
Freshly grated nutmeg
Freshly ground black pepper
Oil or bacon fat, for frying

Melt the butter in a large pan. Add the onion and cook gently until it is soft and lightly coloured. Remove the pan from the heat and add the spinach, egg and 2 ounces (60 g) breadcrumbs. Mix the ingredients together with a wooden spoon until smoothly blended. Season to taste with salt, nutmeg and pepper.

Shape the mixture into eight flat, oval cakes and coat them with dry breadcrumbs. In a large frying-pan heat the oil or bacon fat. Add the cakes and fry them on both sides until the crumbs are golden and the cutlets are heated through.

Creamed Spinach, Polish Style

Variations of this dish appear in almost all European cuisines. In Poland it is served as a main course topped with a lightly poached egg and garnished with bacon and croûtons fried in a mixture of butter and bacon fat. It can also be served Mediterranean style with veal escalopes.

SERVES FOUR

2 oz (60 g) butter
1 large Spanish onion, finely chopped
2 tablespoons flour
3 lb (1½ kg) fresh spinach, cooked and chopped
½ pint (250 ml) creamy milk
1 tablespoon tomato concentrate (optional)
Sugar
Salt
Freshly ground black pepper
Freshly grated nutmeg
Lemon juice
4 eggs, poached
GARNISH
4 rashers bacon, fried
Triangular croûtons

Melt the butter in a large pan. Add the onion and cook, stirring, until it is soft and golden. Add the flour and stir over low heat for 2 to 3 minutes to make a golden roux. Blend in the spinach. Gradually stir in the milk. Beat in the tomato concentrate, if used, and add a generous pinch of sugar to taste.

Bring the mixture to simmering point, stirring constantly. Partly cover the pan and continue to cook over low heat for about 20 minutes, stirring frequently.

Season with salt, pepper, nutmeg and lemon juice to taste. Continue to simmer gently for a further 10 minutes. Serve topped with the poached eggs and garnished with the bacon and croûtons.

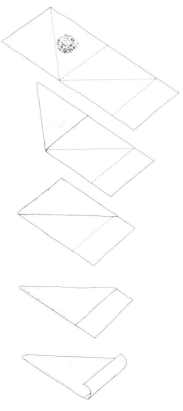

Cut a sheet of filo pastry into strips 3 inches (8 cm) wide. Brush a strip with melted butter. Place a rounded teaspoonful of filling at one of the shorter ends. Fold one corner of the pastry diagonally over the filling to form a triangle. Continue folding the triangle over and over until the strip of pastry is completely used up. Brush the triangular packet with more melted butter.

Stalks & Shoots

Stalks and shoots are a mixed bouquet—asparagus, artichokes and cardoons, celery and Florence fennel, seakale and rhubarb. To all appearances they have little in common except, perhaps, that most of them have enjoyed, at one stage or another in their history, a reputation as aphrodisiacs.

Some stalks and shoots are a luxury in the garden in terms of time, space and effort, but once in the kitchen patience and effort are rewarded. The unmistakable aroma of asparagus steaming on the stove is like a breath of summer—although Louis XIV, a great vegetable enthusiast, bullied his gardeners into providing him with asparagus in January.

The artichoke, once a strong contender in the aphrodisiac stakes, is a culinary enthusiasm that not all gourmets share; for some people, all those leaves represent a lot of work for little return. To them it is small consolation to be told that in southern countries, where artichokes flourish, the leaves are thrown away together with the chokes and only the delectable hearts are eaten. In Turkey, the hearts are quickly dropped into a bowl of acidulated water to preserve their colour. Then they are usually simmered in oil with a handful of baby broad beans, two or three sour green plums and a touch of chopped dill for flavouring. Sometimes they are coated with batter and deep-fried in olive oil.

When globe artichoke plants are about to be replaced they can be made to produce their last crop—of chards. These tender, blanched stalks may be cooked and served like cardoons.

Cardoons grow wild in Turkey, free for the picking, and children chew the stalks raw. But in England cardoons are regarded as vegetable curiosities. In spite of their resemblance to the artichoke (they are called "prickly artichokes" and are closely related) cardoons are grown not for the flower but for the leaf-stem. Its flavour is a cross between artichoke and celery. To prepare cardoons, discard the tough outer stalks. Remove the "strings" of the remaining stalks and cut into 5-inch (13 cm) or 2-inch (5 cm) lengths, depending on the recipe. Boil the stalks in salted water with a little lemon juice, to preserve their colour, for 20 minutes, or until just tender. Then drain the cardoons and either serve them cold with a *vinaigrette* dressing, hot with melted butter or in a light cream sauce.

Raw or boiled cardoon stalks are also delicious served with a *bagna cauda*, hot garlic and anchovy dip. To make the dip, melt ¼ pound (120 g) of butter in 8 tablespoons of olive oil in a heavy saucepan. Stir in 6 crushed garlic cloves and 8 anchovy fillets which have been drained, rinsed and finely chopped.

The root of the cardoon is also eaten. It is boiled until tender, sliced and served cold with a *vinaigrette* dressing.

Unlike cardoons, asparagus and artichokes, celery is an everyday vegetable. It would be sorely missed in the kitchen if the cook were deprived of it, be it in the form of stalks, seeds or salt. Celery can be used not only as a flavouring or garnish, or as part of a *bouquet garni*, but as a vegetable in its own right.

The blanched, bulbous stems of Florence fennel, sweet cousin of the seeds and green fronds of the pungent herb fennel, are rather similar to celery in texture, but very different in flavour. Because fennel has a pungent aniseed taste it is important that it be handled with discretion. Raw or parboiled, it can be grated into a salad, or it can be braised Italian style and served with butter. Fennel can also be baked with tomatoes and grated Parmesan, or frittered, and served with a wedge of lemon to squeeze over the top.

In contrast to fennel, which is notoriously difficult to grow in cool climates, seakale flourishes wild on the windswept coasts of Britain. The leaves are delicious when cooked like spinach or served raw in a salad. The leaves, washed and dried, are torn into pieces, dressed with a *vinaigrette* sauce and garnished with a sprinkling of finely chopped spring onions. The stalks, when blanched like celery and chicory and forced like rhubarb, are a welcome winter vegetable. Many people, however, prefer the flavour of seakale which is not forced and is cropped in late spring.

Seakale stalks may be steamed—they take about 25 minutes; be careful as overcooking toughens them—or simmered gently in stock. Serve the steamed stalks with melted butter or *hollandaise* sauce or cover them with a good cheese sauce and bake in a 375°F (190°C, Gas Mark 5) oven for 40 minutes, or until bubbling and golden brown on top.

Forcing plants is the gardener's way of extending their season, particularly through the winter months, when the garden has comparatively little to offer. When forced rhubarb comes on the scene, sour and sharp, it is a refreshing change from the winter's apples and pears, and from imported citrus fruits. Once a weed in Asia, rhubarb is today a very English vegetable. Its crisp, pink stalks are used to make compotes, pies and fools, chutneys and jams. The unforced, deeper-hued rhubarb of summer is often combined with other fruits to make more economical but delicious jams.

Rhubarb

Although rhubarb is botanically classed as a vegetable, it is usually thought of as a fruit for stewing, making pies, preserving and making wine. But it can also be substituted for gooseberries to make a mock gooseberry sauce for such oily fish as mackerel, or used to make a sweet soup, a favourite in northeastern Europe.

Make the most of rhubarb, especially in the early days. First to arrive towards the end of winter are the thin, pink stalks of forced rhubarb, to be followed by the thicker outdoor rhubarb, dark red and juicy. More sugar will be needed to sweeten the rhubarb as the season progresses. Some of its acidity can be toned down by blanching the stalks before cooking them with sugar. To blanch rhubarb, pour boiling water over the cut stalks in a pan. Bring the water to the boil again and immediately drain the stalks. Rhubarb cooks quickly and is liable to disintegrate if it is overcooked by even a minute.

The simplest sweet of all is a rhubarb compote, 1-inch (2 cm) chunks quickly and gently poached in an orange- or spice-flavoured syrup. An unusual and delicious touch can be added by stirring a tablespoonful or two of gin into the ice-cold compote just before serving.

Transform a classic English summer pudding into spring pudding by substituting stewed, sweetened rhubarb for the soft red fruits of summer.

Rhubarb will make a particularly delicious crumble. Use 2 ounces (60 g) of butter rubbed into 6 ounces (180 g) of self-raising flour and mix with about ¼ pound (120 g) of granulated sugar. Mix 2 or 3 tablespoonfuls in with the rhubarb chunks. Heap the rest lightly on top. Bake in a moderate oven for about 1 hour. Or make rhubarb ketchup or jam for the store cupboard. And remember that rhubarb's greatest allies are orange, lemon, preserved or ground ginger and cinnamon.

Rhubarb Fool

A taste of spring for a late-winter dinner party. Some people like the taste of ginger in rhubarb fool. To try this, add 1 ounce (30 g) of chopped preserved ginger to the fruit while it is cooking and leave out the orange liqueur.

The same mixture can also be frozen (stir it once or twice as it freezes) to make an unusual ice-cream.

Rhubarb fool is delicious served with sponge fingers.

SERVES SIX
1 lb (½ kg) rhubarb
¼ lb (120 g) Demerara sugar
1 oz (30 g) butter
Grated rind of ½ large orange
½ pint (250 ml) double cream
2 tablespoons orange liqueur (optional)

Cut the rhubarb into chunks. Put them in a heavy, enamelled pan with the sugar, butter and grated orange rind. Cover the pan tightly and cook over the lowest possible heat for 7 to 10 minutes, or until the rhubarb disintegrates. Mash the rhubarb with the back of a wooden spoon, mixing it with the buttery juices. Set aside to cool.

In a bowl, whisk the cream lightly with the orange liqueur, if used. Fold in the crushed rhubarb, and more sugar if necessary, although the flavour should be rather sharp.

Spoon the fool into small individual glasses and chill thoroughly before serving.

Rhubarb Kisiel

This is a simple, refreshing sweet, delicious served with a vanilla custard sauce or single cream.

SERVES FOUR
1 lb (½ kg) rhubarb
6 oz (180 g) sugar
Juice of 1 large orange
4 tablespoons cornflour

Cut the rhubarb into chunks and put in an enamelled pan. Add the sugar and the orange juice made up to ½ pint (250 ml) with water. Cover tightly and cook over low heat for 10 minutes, or until the rhubarb has disintegrated. Mash the rhubarb with a wooden spoon and mix it with the juices.

Blend the cornflour to a smooth paste with 6 tablespoons of cold water. Stir it into the hot rhubarb purée. Bring to the boil and cook over low heat, stirring constantly, for 4 minutes, or until the mixture is thick and has lost its floury opaqueness.

Divide between four dishes or pour into a decorative mould rinsed out with cold water. (The pudding will be firm enough to turn out.) Serve very cold.

Rhubarb Pie

Rhubarb varies in the amount of sugar that it needs. Forced pink rhubarb, for example, usually requires less sugar than mature stalks. The ½ pound (¼ kg) suggested here is an approximation and may need to be adjusted.

SERVES SIX
1 lb (½ kg) rhubarb
13 oz (390 g) frozen puff pastry
1 egg plus 1 egg yolk
½ lb (¼ kg) sugar
Grated rind of ½ orange
2 tablespoons flour
Salt
1 tablespoon softened butter
Castor sugar

Put a baking sheet on the middle shelf of the oven and set the oven to 450°F (230°C, Gas Mark 8).

Chop the rhubarb stalks into 1-inch (2 cm) lengths, shorter if they are thick.

Roll half of the pastry out to make a lid for the pie, and the other half to line the bottom and sides of a 2-pint (1 litre) pie dish. Capacity is as important as diameter, but the dish should measure 8 or 9 inches (20 or 23 cm) across.

In a bowl, beat the egg and egg yolk with the sugar and grated orange rind until fluffy. Sift in the flour and a generous pinch of salt. Beat until smoothly blended. Fold in the prepared rhubarb.

Spread the mixture in the pastry-lined pie dish and dot with the butter. Brush the rim with water. Place the lid in position and seal the edges, crimping them attractively. Cut slits in the lid to allow steam to escape and brush the top with water.

Put the pie dish on the heated baking sheet and bake the pie for 15 to 20 minutes. Turn the heat down to 350°F (180°C, Gas Mark 4) and continue to bake it for a further 30 minutes, or until the pastry is puffed and golden brown and the rhubarb feels soft when pierced (through one of the slits) with a skewer.

Serve the pie lukewarm dusted with castor sugar, with cream or a custard sauce.

Asparagus

Many people would insist that there is only one way to eat fresh asparagus—steamed or boiled and served with melted butter. Those lucky enough to have a superabundance of asparagus, however, may want to try other ways of cooking and serving it.

Fresh young asparagus is tender for most of its length, especially if the stem has been carefully peeled. Bend each stem until it snaps—the break will come at the point where the stem starts to become woody or fibrous. Rinse the stalk carefully, especially around the tight little green buds, which can harbour soil or grit, and nick off any stray buds or leaf points farther down the stem. Then, using a knife or a potato peeler, shave the stalk all the way down, starting below the buds and gradually digging deeper into the stalk as the knife progresses towards the butt. Drop the stalks into a bowl of cold water as you prepare them. Finally, grade the stalks according to thickness. Line up the tips and tie them into neat bundles in two places, under the tips and near the bottom. Trim all the butts to the same length. This will ensure that all the stalks in a bundle are ready at the same time. It is a good idea to leave one stalk loose so that it can be tested without disturbing the bundle.

To cook asparagus requires care. It should be steam boiled or steamed, but preferably not boiled. This is because the tips are tender but the stalks are less so. The Romans always cooked asparagus upright and this is still considered one of the best ways of cooking it. An asparagus pan, deep and narrow, fitted with a perforated basket, allows the tender tips to cook in steam while the stems boil gently in water. Another special asparagus pan is a steamer fitted with a liner on which the stalks lie flat. The liner can be lifted out easily when the asparagus is ready.

Failing a special steamer, you can improvise with a large saucepan. Stand the bundle of stalks upright in the pan with boiling, lightly salted water to come about three-quarters of the way up, supporting the tips with crumpled foil if necessary to keep them clear of the water. Use more foil to make a "cap" for the tips. Bring the water back to a gentle boil and keep it there for 10 to 15 minutes or until a stalk feels tender when pierced through the butt with the tip of a knife. A little flour worked to a smooth, thin paste with cold water and a tablespoon of white wine vinegar may be added to the cooking water to preserve the colour and enhance the delicate flavour.

When the asparagus is tender—and it cooks very quickly indeed (the Romans had a saying about doing something "as quickly as it takes to cook asparagus")—drain the stalks and serve them hot either with melted butter or a buttery sauce (see below). Alternatively, drain them dry on a clean napkin and chill them until required.

Properly cooked, asparagus should be neither crunchy nor so limp that their heads droop right over. Never throw out the cooking water or the trimmings. They make excellent soup.

How much asparagus you allow per portion will depend on the state of your asparagus bed, but $\frac{1}{2}$ pound ($\frac{1}{4}$ kg) for each person is a generous and satisfying amount.

Asparagus with Scrambled Eggs

A delicately flavoured first course or light supper dish. Serve on hot toast or in little pastry cases.

SERVES TWO TO THREE
6 eggs
2 tablespoons double cream
Salt
Freshly ground black pepper
1 oz (30 g) butter
12 asparagus spears, cooked and sliced
2 tablespoons grated Parmesan cheese

In a bowl, beat the eggs and the cream together with a fork until just mixed. Season to taste with the salt and pepper.

Melt the butter in a heavy saucepan. Add the asparagus and cook gently, stirring, for 1 minute. Pour in the egg mixture and, stirring constantly, cook over the lowest possible heat until the eggs begin to set in creamy curds. Stir in the cheese and, as soon as the eggs have set to the right consistency, remove the pan from the heat and serve.

Clear Asparagus Soup

Based on a Chinese recipe, this soup may be made more filling with the addition of rice or fine noodles. Make the stock from $1\frac{1}{2}$ pounds ($\frac{3}{4}$ kg) of mixed vegetables—use cabbage stalks, carrots, runner beans, potato peel or any vegetables that are available and simmer for $1\frac{1}{2}$ to 2 hours.

SERVES FOUR
2 oz (60 g) Chinese dried mushrooms
2 lb (1 kg) asparagus, cut into 2-inch (5 cm) pieces
1½ pints (750 ml) clear, strong vegetable or chicken stock, strained
1 tablespoon butter
1 tablespoon light soy sauce
¼ teaspoon monosodium glutamate (optional)
Salt
Freshly ground pepper

Preheat the oven to 300°F (150°C, Gas Mark 2).

In a small bowl, soak the mushrooms in warm water for 30 minutes. Drain them and remove and discard the stems. Cut the mushrooms into quarters.

Put the tougher asparagus pieces and the mushrooms into a casserole. Bring the stock to the boil and pour it into the casserole. Put the casserole into the oven for 30 minutes.

Add the asparagus tips and butter. Stir in the soy sauce and monosodium glutamate, if used. Season to taste with salt, if needed, and pepper. Reduce the oven temperature to 275°F (140°C, Gas Mark 1) and continue to cook for a further 30 minutes.

Asparagus

Crème d'Asperges
Making soup is a good way of using asparagus which is no longer at its succulent best.

SERVES FOUR TO SIX
1 lb (½ kg) mature asparagus
Salt
1 potato, peeled and sliced
1 small, mild onion, coarsely chopped
1 oz (30 g) butter
1 tablespoon flour
1½ pints (750 ml) hot chicken stock
2 egg yolks
¼ pint (125 ml) single cream
White pepper

Wash and trim the asparagus and cut it into chunks. Snip off a handful of the best tips to use as a garnish. Put the pieces of asparagus in a pan. Pour in just enough lightly salted water to cover. Add the potato and onion and bring to the boil. Cover the pan, reduce the heat and cook gently for 15 to 20 minutes, or until the vegetables are very soft.

Steam the reserved asparagus tips separately and put them aside until they are needed.

In another pan melt the butter. Blend in the flour and stir over low heat for 1 minute to make a pale *roux*. Gradually add the chicken stock, stirring vigorously to prevent lumps from forming. Bring the mixture to the boil and pour it into the pan of undrained vegetables.

Purée the contents of the pan in an electric blender or put it through the fine plate of a vegetable mouli. If there are any woody fibres still in evidence, rub the purée through a fine sieve. Then pour the mixture back into the rinsed and dried pan.

Beat the egg yolks and cream together just enough to mix them. Stir them into the soup. Season with pepper and a little more salt if necessary. Add the reserved asparagus tips and reheat gently, stirring. Do not let the soup reach boiling point again, or the egg yolks may start to curdle.

If the soup is too thick, thin it down with more hot chicken stock or cream.

Serve immediately.

Asparagus with Hot Butter Sauce
This is a classic first course, the simplest and best way of serving the pick of the crop.

SERVES FOUR
2 lb (1 kg) asparagus, cooked and drained
½ lb (¼ kg) butter
Lemon juice
4 tablespoons finely chopped parsley
Coarse salt
Freshly ground black pepper

While the asparagus is cooking, melt the butter in a saucepan. Take great care not to let the butter sizzle or colour. If you cannot keep an eye on it all the time, put the pan of butter in a larger pan of simmering water until the butter has melted and is very hot. Add lemon juice to taste and stir in the parsley.

Serve the hot asparagus sprinkled with coarse salt and black pepper, and accompanied by individual dishes of butter sauce for dipping.

To prepare asparagus, use a knife to peel each stalk. Peel thickly at the butt end and thinly near the tip.

Asparagus Hollandaise
Sauce hollandaise is another fine accompaniment for asparagus. *Hollandaise* can be transformed into a *sauce mousseline* by folding 4 to 6 tablespoons of whipped cream, 1 tablespoon at a time, into the hot *hollandaise* just before serving. Alternatively, it may be turned into a delicious *sauce maltaise* by substituting the strained juice of 1 or 2 blood oranges for the water and lemon juice, and adding the blanched grated rind of 1 blood orange to enrich its flavour.

SERVES FOUR
2 lb (1 kg) asparagus, cooked and drained
SAUCE HOLLANDAISE
½ lb (¼ kg) butter
2 teaspoons lemon juice
Salt
White pepper
4 egg yolks

Let the butter stand at room temperature until it is soft but not oily. Divide it into four equal portions.

In the top of a double saucepan, dilute the lemon juice with 1 tablespoon of cold water. Add a pinch each of salt and pepper. Fit the top of the pan over hot but not boiling water. Add the egg yolks and a portion of butter. Stir vigorously with a wire whisk for 5 minutes, or until the ingredients are thoroughly blended and the sauce begins to thicken.

Continue adding the butter, a portion at a time, whisking constantly until it is completely incorporated. (Do not neglect the corners of the pan.) Then carry on whisking rapidly until the sauce is very thick.

Taste for seasoning, adding more salt, pepper or lemon juice as necessary, and serve with the hot asparagus.

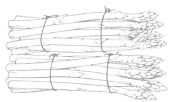

Using string, make bundles of about ten stalks. Line up the tips and cut off the ends of the stalks.

Baked Asparagus with Pasta
This is an economical way of making a little asparagus go a long way. Served as it is, this dish makes a good accompaniment for all white meats and poultry. It can also be turned into a main dish by the addition of some diced lean ham.

SERVES FOUR
½ lb (¼ kg) macaroni
Salt
½ lb (¼ kg) fresh or frozen asparagus
½ pint (250 ml) hot single cream
Freshly ground black pepper
2 eggs, beaten
5 tablespoons freshly grated Parmesan cheese
1 tablespoon butter

Boil the macaroni in a large pan of salted water, following the timing recommended on the packet.

Meanwhile, cut the asparagus into ¾-inch (2 cm) lengths and parboil them in just enough salted water to cover until half done—6 to 8 minutes in the case of fresh asparagus, only 4 minutes for frozen asparagus.

Preheat the oven to 400°F (200°C, Gas Mark 6).

Drain the asparagus in a strainer held over the pot of boiling macaroni. Then drop the asparagus into a pan containing the hot cream and simmer for 2 minutes. Season to taste with salt and pepper. Cover and put aside.

Drain the macaroni in a colander. Return it to the pan and stir with a wooden spoon over low heat for a minute or two to evaporate any remaining moisture. Cool slightly. Then carefully mix in the asparagus and cream, followed by the eggs and 3 tablespoons of grated Parmesan cheese. Correct seasoning.

Pour the mixture into a well-buttered baking dish. Sprinkle with the remaining Parmesan cheese and dot with butter.

Bake for 20 to 25 minutes, or until the mixture has set and the top is golden and bubbling. Serve hot.

If you do not have an asparagus pan, improvise with a glass jar. Stand the bundles in a glass jar almost filled with boiling water. Cover with perforated foil secured with a rubber band. Stand the jar in a pan half-filled with boiling water. After 30 minutes, lift the asparagus from the jar, drain and remove the strings.

Artichokes

With the arrival of spring, the vegetable markets of Rome are piled high with the most exquisite *primizie*, baby vegetables of all kinds, a glorious sight to gladden the heart of the artist as well as the cook. Among them are stacks of tiny globe artichokes so young that they have not yet had a chance to develop their fuzzy chokes. Consequently, they may be cooked and served whole, boiled, braised, deep-fried or baked.

When the choke has developed, true to its name it will be inedible and must be removed either before or after cooking. Before trimming an artichoke, prepare a bowl of water acidulated with lemon juice—1 tablespoon of lemon juice to 1 pint (500 ml) of water—so that the artichoke can be swished around in it each time any cuts are made. The cut surfaces rapidly turn brown if they are not treated in this way. When the artichoke has been prepared, drop the globe, head down, into the bowl of acidulated water and leave it to soak until needed.

The most delectable part of this extraordinary vegetable is the heart, also known as the *fond*, or bottom. Shaped like a little round saucer it is completely edible. Artichoke hearts discolour easily so rub them well all over with a cut lemon as they are trimmed and then drop them into a bowl of acidulated water until you are ready to cook them. Parboil artichoke hearts in lightly salted, acidulated water for 10 to 15 minutes (to set the colour). The hearts are now ready to be cooked further according to the recipe.

To cook the heads, select a pan large enough to allow them plenty of room. Fill the pan with lightly salted water and bring it to a rolling boil. Drop the artichokes into the water and boil them gently, uncovered, for 35 to 45 minutes, or until a leaf can be pulled out easily and the base feels tender when pierced with a skewer. Drain the artichokes thoroughly, heads down, in a colander.

Another way to cook artichokes is to steam them—either in a steamer or on a rack placed in a pan. If neither steamer nor rack are available, place the artichoke heads right way up in 1 to 2 inches (2 to 5 cm) of boiling acidulated water and cook, covered, for 40 to 45 minutes or until tender.

A tender globe artichoke makes a fine and simple first course served hot with melted butter or *hollandaise*, or cold with *vinaigrette* or a herb-flavoured mayonnaise.

To prepare artichoke hearts, break off the tough outer leaves of the artichoke.

With a sharp knife, slice off the artichoke stalk.

The remaining leaves should be cut off above the white base, or heart.

Rub lemon juice over the heart. Finally, slice off the green leaf bases.

Artichokes, Greek Style

These tiny artichokes, picked before the chokes have formed and cooked whole *à la grecque* may be served as an *hors d'oeuvre* or added to mixed salad.

SERVES FOUR
20 baby artichokes
Juice of 3 lemons
¼ pint (125 ml) olive oil
1 teaspoon fennel seeds
1 teaspoon chopped fresh dill
10 peppercorns
Bouquet garni, consisting of 1 celery stalk, 1 bay leaf, 1 thyme sprig
1 teaspoon salt

Parboil the artichokes for 5 minutes in enough acidulated water (using the juice of 1 lemon) to cover.

Drain the artichokes in a colander and rinse under cold running water. Drain and set aside.

Put the remaining ingredients in a saucepan and add 1 pint (500 ml) of water. Place the pan over high heat and bring to the boil. Add the artichokes. When the liquid returns to the boil, reduce the heat, cover the pan and simmer for 8 minutes, or until the artichokes are tender.

Remove the artichokes from the pan with a slotted spoon and put them in a bowl. Increase the heat to high and boil the liquid in the pan until it is reduced by half. Pour the liquid, through a strainer, over the artichokes. When the artichokes are cold, cover the bowl and put it in the refrigerator until required.

Artichoke Hearts
with Sherried Mushrooms

Artichoke hearts make a particularly luxurious appetizer. Whole artichokes, boiled until they are quite tender, make an equally delicious but less extravagant dish. Spoon the mushrooms and cream into the cavity left by the choke and serve hot. Serve with crusty French bread to mop up the sauce.

SERVES FOUR
8 large artichoke hearts, parboiled
¾ pint (375 ml) chicken stock
Lemon juice
½ lb (¼ kg) button mushrooms, trimmed
2 oz (60 g) butter
1 tablespoon cornflour
½ pint (250 ml) single cream
Salt
Freshly ground black pepper
4 tablespoons dry sherry

Drain the artichoke hearts. Rinse them in cold water and put them in a pan. Pour in the chicken stock and 1 tablespoon of lemon juice and bring to the boil. Cover the pan, reduce the heat and simmer gently for 30 minutes, or until the hearts are tender. Drain and keep hot. Reserve the stock.

If the mushrooms are very small leave them whole. Otherwise, halve or quarter them, or slice them thickly. Melt the butter in a heavy pan. Add the mushrooms and sauté for 2 to 3 minutes, or until lightly coloured.

In a small bowl, blend the cornflour smoothly with the cream and ¼ pint (125 ml) of the reserved stock. Season to taste with salt and pepper. Stir the mixture into the mushrooms. Bring the mixture to the boil and stir in the sherry. Simmer the sauce over low heat, stirring, for 5 minutes, or until it has thickened and is slightly reduced.

Fold in the artichoke hearts and serve as soon as they are thoroughly hot.

Artichokes

Casserole of Artichokes with Vegetables

This casserole includes a number of summer vegetables which enhance the flavour of the artichokes. Serve the casserole as a separate course or with a main dish of poultry or ham.

SERVES FOUR
8 small tender artichokes or 4 large
    artichokes
Salt
Lemon juice
¼ lb (120 g) butter
2 Spanish onions, thinly sliced
2 garlic cloves, crushed
8 baby carrots, scraped
4 new potatoes, scraped
2 baby turnips, peeled and quartered
6 celery stalks, cut into 1-inch lengths
Freshly ground black pepper
Bouquet garni, consisting of 2 parsley
    sprigs, 1 thyme sprig, 1 small bay leaf
3 tablespoons dry vermouth
¾ pint (375 ml) hot beef stock
2 oz (60 g) button mushrooms
2 oz (60 g) fresh green peas
3 tablespoons chopped parsley

If the artichokes are so young that they are still free of chokes, use them whole. Mature artichokes should be quartered lengthwise so that the chokes can be scooped out easily. Parboil the artichokes, whole or quartered, for 15 minutes in lightly salted, acidulated water. Drain them thoroughly in a colander.

In a heavy, heatproof casserole wide enough to take the artichokes in a single layer, melt 3 ounces (90 g) of the butter. Add the onions and garlic, and cook gently, stirring, until they are soft but not coloured.

Arrange the artichokes in the casserole together with the carrots, potatoes,

turnips and celery, turning them to coat them with the buttery juices. Season to taste with salt and pepper, and bury the *bouquet garni* in the centre. Cook gently for 10 minutes.

Add the vermouth and the stock and bring to the boil. Cover the pan, reduce the heat and simmer for 30 minutes, or until the vegetables are tender but still firm.

Meanwhile, in a small frying-pan heat the remaining butter. Add the mushrooms and cook, stirring, until golden. About 10 minutes before the end of cooking time, add them to the casserole together with the peas. Finish cooking uncovered. Sprinkle with chopped parsley and serve.

Cut off the top third of the artichoke. Rub lemon juice over the cut edges or dip into acidulated water.

Using scissors, snip off the tops of the remaining leaves. Rub the cut edges with lemon juice.

Baked Stuffed Artichokes

The stuffing for this recipe can be made in seconds in an electric blender. First drop in the bread, cubed. Then add the onion, cut into chunks, two or three sprigs of parsley, the anchovy fillets, capers and olive oil. Whirl for a few seconds and the stuffing is ready.

SERVES SIX
6 artichokes, chokes removed
Lemon juice
Salt
3 oz (90 g) fresh white breadcrumbs
1 medium-sized onion, finely chopped
6 anchovy fillets, finely chopped
3 tablespoons finely chopped parsley
2 tablespoons chopped capers
Olive oil
Freshly ground black pepper
¾ pint (375 ml) chicken stock

Leave the artichokes to soak in acidulated water for 30 minutes. Parboil them in salted water for 10 minutes and drain thoroughly.

Preheat the oven to 375°F (190°C, Gas Mark 5).

To make the stuffing, mix the breadcrumbs, onion, anchovies, parsley and capers together. Add 2 tablespoons of olive oil. Season generously with pepper (no salt because of the anchovies) and mix lightly with a fork.

Fill the centres of the artichokes with the stuffing. If there is any filling left stuff it between the leaves, using a spoon.

Select a deep baking dish just large enough to hold the artichokes side by side. Brush it with oil. Brush each artichoke with oil and sprinkle a little of it over the stuffing in the centre. Arrange the artichokes in the baking

dish. Add the stock and bake for 1 hour, or until a leaf from near the base can easily be pulled out. Baste regularly with the stock, which should almost all have been absorbed by the end of the cooking time. Serve hot.

Pull out the prickly leaves surrounding the choke.

Scoop out the hairy choke, using a teaspoon. Sprinkle lemon juice over the exposed heart.

Artichokes with Herb Mayonnaise

Herb mayonnaise is a delicious sauce to serve with any *hors d'oeuvre*, especially those made with fish or hard-boiled eggs. And just as *hollandaise* may be served with hot artichokes, spooned into the cavity left by the chokes, so mayonnaise, plain or lightly herbed, is a classic accompaniment for cold asparagus. (See pp. 144–9)

SERVES SIX
6 artichokes, boiled
HERB MAYONNAISE
1½ oz (45 g) fresh parsley
1½ oz (45 g) watercress
Salt
2 egg yolks
Juice of ½ lemon
½ teaspoon mild French mustard
Freshly ground black pepper
¾ pint (375 ml) olive oil
2 tablespoons finely chopped fresh
    chervil
1 tablespoon finely chopped fresh
    tarragon

Leave the cooked artichokes to drain and cool upside down in a colander. Then chill in a refrigerator.

Take 2 sprigs each of parsley and watercress. Discard the stalks and chop the herbs finely. Set aside.

Bring a small pan of salted water to the boil. Drop in the remaining parsley and watercress and boil rapidly for 3 to 4 minutes. Drain in a strainer. Spray the herbs with cold water and press them as dry as possible between the folds of a clean cloth or absorbent kitchen paper. Pound the cooked parsley and watercress in a mortar or purée them in an electric blender.

To make the mayonnaise use ingredients that are at room temperature. The oil should be clear. If it is cloudy, it is too cold.

Put the egg yolks, lemon juice and mustard in a bowl and mix gently with a generous pinch of salt and pepper. Pour the oil into a jug with a good pouring lip and start adding it to the egg yolks a drop at a time, beating vigorously

with a spoon, a hand whisk or an electric mixer. As the mayonnaise thickens add the oil in a thin stream. Should it become too thick before all the oil has been incorporated, thin it down with a little more lemon juice or cold water, as the flavour demands.

When the mayonnaise is thick enough to hold its shape on a spoon, whisk in the puréed herbs, followed by all the chopped herbs. Correct the seasoning with more salt, pepper or mustard. Chill the herb mayonnaise until ready to serve.

Serve the artichokes cold with the mayonnaise in a separate bowl.

Press the artichoke leaves together again and give the cut edges a final rub with a piece of lemon.

Celery

Celery is an essential flavouring, a crisp addition to salads and a fine cooked vegetable. Tender young celery is best eaten uncooked; a larger head may be braised or stewed but never boiled. In France, celery is usually blanched in boiling water for 10 minutes and then braised (in a slow oven) on a bed of bacon rinds, onions and carrots in a light veal, chicken or vegetable stock. The braised head is then drained, sliced in half lengthwise and served with a sauce such as *béchamel*.

In Britain, a head of celery is traditionally offered with the cheese board in a tall, clear glass with an inch of cold water in the bottom, a nice touch even if there is no great practical justification for the water.

Celery sticks also make a good alternative (economic on calories) to bread or pastry as a base for *hors d'oeuvre* or snacks. Slice the stalks into short pieces and stuff the channels with a savoury mixture—meat or fish pâté, a mixture of cream cheese, soured cream and red caviar, or a fine-flavoured blue cheese, Roquefort, Dolcelatte or Gorgonzola, pounded with a little softened butter and cream and sharpened with a touch of cayenne or paprika.

An attractive celery garnish can be made by slitting short lengths of celery at one end in several places and dropping them into a bowl of iced water. In a short time the slit strands will curl up like little tassels.

Never throw away the green leaves trimmed from the top of a head of celery. They are invaluable for flavouring meatballs, meat loaves, stocks and salads which do not call for the crunchiness of the stalk. They may also be deep-fried until crisp and used to garnish meat or fish dishes, just like parsley sprigs. Alternatively, if you have no immediate use for the trimmed tops, either collect them in a bag in the freezer, or spread them out on a baking sheet to dry—over the pilot light of a gas cooker or on a radiator. Then crumble the leaves between your hands and store them in a screw-top jar.

Celery Amandine

A distinctive yet subtle combination of flavours, this dish is excellent with roast poultry or fried fish.

SERVES FOUR

1½ lb (¾ kg) celery, trimmed
2 oz (60 g) butter
2 oz (60 g) almonds, blanched and slivered
2 shallots, finely chopped
Salt
Freshly ground black pepper
¼ pint (125 ml) single cream

Take the head of celery apart and cut the stalks into 1-inch (2 cm) pieces, splitting them lengthwise into two or three if they are very thick.

Heat the butter in a heavy pan. Add the almonds and sauté until crisp and a rich golden colour, taking care not to let them burn. Lift out the almonds with a slotted spoon and set them aside.

Add the celery and shallots to the pan, mix well with the hot butter and season generously with salt and pepper. Cover the pan tightly and cook over low heat for 15 minutes, stirring frequently.

Stir in the cream. Replace the lid and continue to cook gently for a further 20 minutes, or until the celery is tender and the cream reduced and thickened.

Mix in the sautéed almonds. Correct the seasoning and cook gently over low heat for 5 minutes before serving to allow the flavours to blend.

Celery with Tomatoes

A vegetable accompaniment that goes well with roasts and other rich meat dishes.

SERVES FOUR

1 medium-sized celery, trimmed
1 oz (30 g) butter
1 small onion, finely chopped
1 medium-sized carrot, coarsely grated
1 small can peeled tomatoes
4 tablespoons stock
Salt
Freshly ground black pepper

Take the head of celery apart and cut the stalks into bite-size pieces.

Melt the butter in a large pan. Add the onion and carrot and cook, stirring, until softened. Add the celery and stir over moderate heat for 2 to 3 minutes.

Add the tomatoes and the stock and season to taste with salt and pepper. Cover the pan and cook for 30 minutes, stirring occasionally. Then remove the lid and let the mixture bubble, uncovered, for 15 minutes longer, or until the celery is tender and the sauce rich and reduced.

Celery, Date and Apple Salad

Raw fruit and vegetables have long been appreciated for their health-giving qualities. Celery, apple and dates combine well with a yoghourt dressing to make a refreshing and attractive salad. It is best to use sour-sweet apples or add a little lemon juice to bring out the contrast of flavours of the main ingredients.

SERVES FOUR

½ pint (250 ml) yoghourt
2 tablespoons honey
1 tablespoon finely chopped fresh mint
1 medium-sized celery
12 dates, pitted
2 medium-sized apples
1 oz (30 g) walnut pieces

Blend the yoghourt, honey and mint in an electric blender or, in a small bowl, whisk the yoghourt, gradually add the honey and stir in the mint. Set aside.

Chop the celery into ½-inch (1 cm) pieces. Wash the dates in warm water. Dry thoroughly and cut into small pieces. Wash the apples, quarter them and remove the cores. Cut the apple into ½-inch (1 cm) cubes. Put the celery, dates and apple into a salad bowl. Pour in the yoghourt dressing and toss gently to mix. Scatter the walnut pieces over the top. Serve immediately or chill until required.

Celery

Baked Celery with Parmesan

With the addition of a little more meat—ham or bacon—this will make a filling main dish on its own.

SERVES FOUR TO SIX

1 large celery, about 2 lb (1 kg)
1 tablespoon olive oil
6 slices streaky bacon, chopped
1 Spanish onion, finely chopped
2 garlic cloves, crushed
4 medium-sized tomatoes,
    peeled and chopped
4 tablespoons stock or water
Salt
Freshly ground black pepper
3 oz (90 g) Parmesan cheese, freshly
    grated

Take the head of celery apart. Trim off the leaves and cut the stalks into 1-inch (2 cm) pieces. Slit the stalks in two or three lengthwise if they are very thick.

Heat the olive oil in a large pan. Add the bacon and sauté until the fat runs. Add the onion and garlic and cook, stirring, over moderate heat until soft and golden. Mix in the celery, the chopped tomatoes and the stock or water. Season to taste with salt and pepper. Cover the pan tightly and cook gently for 20 minutes, stirring occasionally.

Meanwhile, preheat the oven to 375°F (190°C, Gas Mark 5). With a slotted spoon transfer the celery, the bits of bacon and onion to a baking dish. Reduce the juices in the pan by fast boiling before spooning them over the celery. Sprinkle the cheese evenly over the top.

Bake the celery for 30 minutes, or until it is quite tender and the crust on top bubbling and a rich golden brown.

Celery in Madeira Cream

A light and pleasant accompaniment for such dishes as roast chicken and sautéed chicken livers with rice.

SERVES THREE TO FOUR

1 lb (½ kg) trimmed celery stalks
1 oz (30 g) butter
1 tablespoon olive oil
2 shallots, finely chopped
1 garlic clove, crushed
4 tablespoons chicken stock
Salt
Freshly ground black pepper
Sugar
1 tablespoon flour
4 tablespoons Madeira
1 egg yolk, lightly beaten

Cut the celery stalks into 1-inch (2 cm) pieces, halving them lengthwise if they are thick.

Heat the butter and the oil in a wide pan. Add the shallots and garlic and cook, stirring, until a light golden colour. Mix in the celery and moisten with chicken stock. Season generously with salt and pepper, and add a pinch of sugar. Cover the pan tightly and cook over very low heat for 15 to 20 minutes, or until the celery is soft but not mushy.

Mix the flour to a smooth paste with the Madeira and 4 tablespoons of water. Stir the paste into the pan and bring to the boil. Reduce the heat and simmer gently, stirring, for a minute or two. Then remove the pan from the heat and immediately mix in the egg yolk. When the sauce has thickened a little more, correct the seasoning and serve.

Cream of Celery Soup

Celery makes one of the best cream soups—delicately flavoured and smooth. The carrots in this recipe add a touch of colour to the creamy paleness.

SERVES FOUR TO SIX

1 large celery
2 carrots, thinly sliced
1 small parsnip, thinly sliced
1½ oz (45 g) butter
1½ pints (750 ml) chicken stock
About ½ pint (250 ml) creamy milk
Salt
Freshly ground black pepper

Take the head of celery apart, washing each piece carefully, and put aside about 3 ounces (90 g) of the delicate inner stalks. Slice the rest of the head into thin pieces. Put them in a pan together with the carrots, parsnip and 1 ounce (30 g) of the butter. As soon as the vegetables start to sizzle, cover the pan tightly and cook gently for about 10 minutes, or until they have softened slightly without colouring.

Pour in the stock and bring it to the boil. Cover the pan, reduce the heat and simmer for 30 minutes, or until the vegetables are very soft.

Meanwhile, slice the reserved celery stalks thinly to make a garnish for the soup. Melt the remaining butter in a small pan. Mix in the sliced celery, cover the pan and cook gently for 7 to 8 minutes, or until they are just tender. Set aside.

Blend the cooked diced vegetables and their stock to a smooth cream in an electric blender, or rub them through the finest plate of a vegetable mouli. Dilute the soup to the desired consistency with creamy milk. Remember that reheating the soup will also make it thinner. Pour the soup back into the pan. Stir in the celery garnish. Season to taste with salt and pepper, and reheat gently before serving.

Stir-fried Celery with Sesame Sauce

Stir-frying is a quick way of cooking vegetables and one which preserves their colour, taste and texture.

The Chinese ingredients in this recipe can be bought at most large supermarkets and at Chinese food shops. If sesame paste is not available substitute smooth peanut butter, either alone or mixed with sesame oil (2 tablespoons peanut butter, 1 tablespoon sesame oil).

SERVES FOUR

1 lb (½ kg) celery
3 tablespoons vegetable oil
1 small onion, finely chopped
2 garlic cloves, crushed
½-inch (1 cm) piece fresh root ginger,
    peeled and shredded
Salt
1 tablespoon dry sherry
1½ tablespoons soy sauce
1 teaspoon sugar
½ teaspoon monosodium glutamate
    (optional)
SESAME SAUCE
5 tablespoons sesame paste
3 tablespoons light stock
2 tablespoons soy sauce
2 tablespoons wine vinegar
2 teaspoons sugar
Chilli sauce
5 garlic cloves, crushed

First prepare the sesame sauce. In a saucepan combine the sesame paste with the stock, soy sauce and vinegar. Add the sugar and chilli sauce to taste. Cook over low heat, stirring constantly, for 3 minutes. Remove the pan from the heat and stir in the garlic. Set aside.

Cut the celery stalks diagonally in 2-inch (5 cm) pieces. Heat the oil in a large frying-pan over high heat. Add the onion, garlic and ginger and fry, stirring constantly, for 1 minute. Add the celery and salt to taste and reduce the heat to moderate. Turn the celery in the pan until it is well coated with the oil. Stir in the sherry, soy sauce, sugar and monosodium glutamate, if used. Continue to cook for 2 to 3 minutes.

Serve with the reheated sesame sauce in a separate bowl.

To make celery tassels, slice 2-in (5 cm) long pieces of celery into thin strips almost to the end. Place in a bowl of iced water. The ends will curl shortly.

Pods & Seeds

Peas, sweet corn and beans of various shapes and sizes—the long history of these pods and seeds embraces the world. Some of them, peas for example, have been in cultivation for so long that they cannot be found in a wild form. Others, such as the French or runner bean and sweet corn were only introduced into Europe and to the rest of the world after the opening up of the New World.

Broad beans are the only beans that the Old World can claim as its own. Their origins, too, are lost in the mists of prehistory. These are the *ful nabed* of the Pharaohs and the early Copts. The dishes that were made in ancient times are still prepared today—pastes, soups and the deep-fried spiced patties called *falafel*, now a national dish in Israel as well as in Egypt.

Dried seeds, such as broad beans and peas, were once a winter mainstay of the European peasants' diet. Some of the recipes have weathered the centuries well. Pease pudding, for example, which was served with the boiled salted meat that appeared so often on the medieval dining-table, was much enjoyed by King Edward VII as an accompaniment to pickled pork and is still a popular dish in Britain today. The broad beans and peas of bygone days, however, were hard, wrinkled and fit only for heavy simple soups and puddings. It took hundreds of years of developing civilization and prosperity for these vegetables to be grown and eaten young, tender and fresh.

It was probably the French, encouraged by the Italians, who first discovered the delights of eating young fresh peas, *petits pois*, lightly cooked or straight from the pod. In one of her letters, dated 1696, Madame de Maintenon describes how the ladies at the French court, "having supped with the King, and supped well", would then retire to the privacy of their chambers to feast in secret on dishes of *petits pois*. "*C'est une mode*," she concluded, "*une fureur*"—it is all the rage.

There is another type of pea—the edible-podded pea. It is harvested when the peas are immature and the whole vegetable—the pea and the pod—is eaten. In France it is known as *mangetout*, literally "eat-all"; in other parts of

the world it is known variously as snow pea, Chinese pea or sugar pea.

Asparagus peas, sometimes known as winged peas, do not have seeds. The pods, which like *mangetout* peapods may be eaten whole, have a flavour reminiscent of asparagus.

From China comes the most nutritious of all beans—the soya bean. Although in the West soy sauce is taken for granted, and Oriental food enthusiasts have long appreciated the importance of bean curd in the cuisines of China and Japan, only recently have soya beans themselves begun to come to the attention of Western cooks. Hailed as the great miracle protein, soya beans are gradually acquiring a gastronomic, as opposed to a purely nutritional, reputation.

Although the mung bean is probably native to India, it is from China that the West learned how to eat the newly sprouted bean. Easy to germinate, bean sprouts are a crisp and delicately flavoured vegetable and also provide a cheap and ready source of vitamins.

Of all the vegetables that came from the New World, the green bean and maize (the two major species are Indian corn and sweet corn) were the most important. The bean has a dual identity. When the pods are young and thin, they make a most delicate green vegetable. Left on the plant to swell to maturity, the beans are husked and dried for storage. Their culinary fortunes make curious reading—the dried beans were introduced to Europe and clever European cooks combined them with meat, turning them into rich casseroles. These dishes were then "re-exported" to America to become adapted to such famous dishes as Boston baked beans.

Maize (Indian corn and sweet corn), too, has an interesting history. Although southern Europe in particular was quick to recognize the potential of Indian corn as a cereal—it is difficult to believe that Italian *polenta* and Romanian *mamaliga* did not exist before the explorers returned from the New World—there was no great enthusiasm for the fresh cobs of sweet corn. They were, and are still, widely grown as cattle fodder. It was the Americans who taught the rest of the world how to prepare and appreciate fresh sweet corn.

Sweet Corn

According to an American saying, "you may walk to the garden to cut the corn, but you must run back to cook it". This may sound exaggerated, but the truth is that as soon as the cobs are cut, the natural sugar in the kernels begins to convert to starch. You can try to replace the lost sweetness by adding sugar to the cooking water, but leave out salt, which toughens the kernels.

Cook the cobs in a large saucepan. Strip off the husks and use some of them to line the bottom of the pan. Pull away the silks and lay the cobs on the husks. Pour over enough boiling water to cover the cobs and boil briskly, with the lid on, for 3 to 5 minutes, or until a kernel can be prised away from the cob easily. Serve with coarse salt and plenty of butter.

When a recipe calls for corn kernels, cook the cob first. Then scrape off the kernels with a sharp knife.

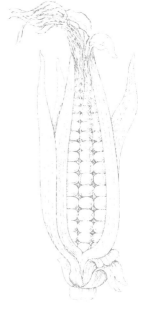

Corn Chowder

SERVES FOUR TO SIX

1 lb (½ kg) potatoes, peeled and diced
Salt
2 oz (60 g) fat salt pork or unsmoked fat bacon in one piece, diced
1 Spanish onion, coarsely chopped
1 tablespoon flour
½ pint (250 ml) milk
¾ pint (375 ml) chicken stock
¼ lb (¼ kg) sweet corn kernels
½ pint (250 ml) single cream
½ sweet green pepper, cored, seeded and finely chopped
Freshly ground black pepper
Paprika

Parboil the diced potatoes in salted water for 5 minutes. Drain them thoroughly in a colander and set aside.

In a large saucepan, fry the diced salt pork until the fat runs. Add the onion and continue to fry gently, stirring frequently, until it is soft and lightly coloured. Sprinkle with the flour and stir over low heat for 1 minute. Gradually add the milk, stirring to prevent the flour forming lumps. Then add the stock, the corn kernels and the diced potatoes and bring to the boil, stirring. Reduce the heat, cover the pan and simmer gently for 7 to 10 minutes, or until the corn and the potatoes are tender.

Stir in the cream and the chopped pepper. Season to taste with salt, pepper and a pinch of paprika. Bring the soup back to boiling point and serve.

Pan-fried Corn

This dish is especially good served with fried pork chops, lamb chops or fried chicken.

SERVES FOUR

2 oz (60 g) butter
1 Spanish onion, sliced paper thin
1 sweet green or red pepper, quartered, cored, seeded and sliced paper thin
1 lb (½ kg) sweet corn kernels
Salt
Freshly ground black pepper

Melt the butter in a wide, heavy pan. Add the onion and pepper and cook gently, stirring, until the pepper is limp and the onion is a pale golden colour. Add the corn. Season to taste with salt and pepper. Cook gently, stirring frequently, for 6 to 8 minutes.

If the dish is not to be served immediately, cover the pan and put it aside. Then reheat gently, stirring, just before serving. Serve hot.

Sweet Corn Fritters

Ideally served with maple syrup, these corn fritters make a delicious snack.

MAKES ABOUT TWELVE FRITTERS

¾ lb (360 g) cooked corn kernels
5 tablespoons double cream
4 tablespoons fine cornmeal (polenta)
2 teaspoons sugar
½ teaspoon baking powder
Pinch of salt
2 eggs, separated
Butter, for frying

Drain the corn kernels thoroughly. Purée all the ingredients except the egg whites and butter in an electric blender. In a small bowl, whisk the egg whites until stiff but not dry. Fold them gently but thoroughly into the corn mixture.

Heat plenty of butter in a frying-pan. Drop the batter into the pan in tablespoonfuls, well apart as they tend to spread, and fry the fritters until they are golden brown on both sides, turning them over once.

Serve straight from the frying-pan.

Corn Soufflé

This substantial soufflé is an ideal supper dish. Serve it with a crisp green salad.

SERVES FOUR

1 oz (30 g) butter
1 oz (30 g) flour
½ pint (250 ml) single cream
1 green pepper, cored, seeded and chopped
1 lb (½ kg) corn kernels
2 large eggs, separated
Salt
Freshly ground black pepper
¼ lb (120 g) bacon rashers, grilled crisply and crumbled

Preheat the oven to 400°F (200°C, Gas Mark 6). Grease a soufflé dish with butter and dust thoroughly with flour.

Melt the butter in a saucepan. Stir in the flour until it is well blended. Pour in the cream slowly, stirring constantly until the sauce is smooth. Stir in the green pepper and the corn and bring the mixture to the boil. Remove the pan from the heat.

In a small bowl beat the egg yolks lightly. Stir in some of the hot corn and cream mixture. Pour the egg mixture into the pan and return it to low heat. Cook gently, stirring constantly, for 5 minutes. Season to taste with the salt and pepper. Remove the pan from the heat and stir in the bacon. Cool the mixture slightly.

In a bowl, whip the egg whites until stiff but not dry and fold them carefully into the corn mixture. Pour the mixture into the soufflé dish and put it in the oven.

Reduce the heat to 350°F (180°C, Gas Mark 4) and bake for 30 minutes, or until the soufflé has risen and is golden brown on top and a knife or skewer plunged into the centre comes out clean. Serve immediately.

Using a sharp knife, slice the stalk off the corn. Reserve the husks to cook with the cobs.

Peas

Pisum sativum—this name covers a variety of plants each of which, in the eyes of the cook if not the botanist, provides a very different vegetable, ranging from green garden peas to *mangetout* peas—specially cultivated for their pods—and dried and split peas.

Mangetout peas are so delicate that care must be taken in their preparation. If they are very young and delectably tender, just top and tail the pods and serve them raw in salads. More mature pods require stringing. The best way to cook *mangetout* peas is to steam them with a little butter for 5 minutes. They may also be boiled in salted water for about 2 minutes, or until they are just tender. Drain well, season and toss in hot melted butter before serving. Alternatively, stir-fry them for 5 minutes in the Chinese style.

The stage at which green peas are picked is a matter of taste. The French and Italians like them very small and sweet. Anglo-American taste seems to favour rather larger, more mature peas. If they are very large and floury, however, no amount of sugar in the cooking water will disguise the fact that they are overgrown, and it is best to make them into a fresh pea soup or purée.

Do not throw pea pods away. They may be simmered in the stock that will provide the foundation for a pea soup. Or they may be cooked, puréed and used to thicken the soup, for when the pods are rubbed through a sieve or mouli their papery linings are left behind.

Asparagus peas are peas in name only. Harvest them when they are between 1 and 2 inches (2 and 5 cm) long and steam them whole for about 5 minutes, or until they are tender. Toss them in butter and season with a sprinkling of salt and freshly ground black pepper.

Fresh Pea Soup

Frozen peas or mature peas may be used for this soup. In summer, to serve the soup cold leave out the egg and instead dilute the soup with more cream. A few drops of lemon juice will also add a refreshing touch.

SERVES FOUR
1 lb (½ kg) green peas
1 medium-sized potato, peeled and thickly sliced
1 small, mild onion, thickly sliced
2 pints (1 litre) well-flavoured chicken stock
¼ pint (125 ml) single cream
1 egg yolk
Salt
Sugar (optional)
Tiny croûtons, to garnish

Boil the peas, potato and onion in the stock, covered, for 20 minutes, or until all the vegetables are very soft. Purée the contents of the pan in an electric blender or use a mouli.

Return the purée to the pan and bring it to the boil, stirring. Remove the pan from the heat.

Beat the cream and egg yolk together lightly and stir into the pan. Season with salt and a little sugar if necessary. Reheat the soup, but do not allow it to boil again as this will cause the egg yolk to curdle.

Garnish each portion with tiny croûtons and serve immediately.

Chinese Snow Peas

Use a mild-flavoured vegetable oil to stir-fry the peas, not olive oil, which has too strong a flavour of its own.

SERVES FOUR
1 lb (½ kg) mangetout peas
2 tablespoons vegetable oil
½ chicken stock cube
Salt
½ oz (15 g) lard

Wash the *mangetout* peas and drain in a colander. Top and tail them and string them as you would green beans, patting them dry with absorbent kitchen paper if there is any moisture left on them.

Heat the oil in a wide, heavy pan. Add the *mangetout* and stir them over low heat for ½ minute. Crumble the stock cube and sprinkle a little salt over the pods. Add 4 tablespoons of hot water and stir-fry for ½ minute longer.

Remove the pan from the heat. Stir and turn the pea pods carefully for 1 minute. Return the pan to moderate heat and cook the pods, stirring, until most of the liquid has evaporated.

Add the lard in small pieces and stir over low heat until it has melted and the pods glisten. Serve immediately.

Petits Pois à la Française

Buttered peas with lettuce is a classic dish from France, the country that taught the world how to eat fresh green peas.

SERVES THREE TO FOUR
3 oz (90 g) butter
2 lb (1 kg) small green peas
2 shallots, finely chopped
1 medium-sized, crisp cabbage lettuce heart, shredded
1 teaspoon sugar
Salt

In a pan with a tight-fitting lid melt the butter gently with 6 tablespoons of water. Mix in the peas, shallots and lettuce. Add the sugar and salt to taste. Cover tightly and cook gently, shaking the pan occasionally, for about 10 minutes, or until the peas are tender.

Remove the lid and cook for 1 or 2 minutes longer to evaporate any excess liquid.

Peas and Turnips

This delectable French dish, made with tender young vegetables, may be served either with cold meat or pâté, or alone after the main course.

SERVES FOUR
1 lb (½ kg) young turnips, peeled
8 fl oz (200 ml) water
2 oz (60 g) butter
2 savory sprigs
Salt
Freshly ground black pepper
Sugar
1½ lb (¾ kg) podded green peas
4 tablespoons lightly whipped cream

Cut the turnips into strips. Bring the water to the boil in a large saucepan. Add the turnips, half the butter, the savory and salt, pepper and sugar to taste.

Simmer the turnips, uncovered, for 5 minutes. Add the peas and the remaining butter and continue to cook, uncovered, until the vegetables are tender and almost all the liquid has evaporated.

Remove and discard the savory. Stir in the cream and adjust the seasoning.

> **"***The peascod greene oft with no little toyle***
> ***Hee'd seeke for in the fattest, fertil'st soile,***
> ***And rend it from the stalks to bring it to her***
> ***And in her bosome for acceptance woo her.***"**
>
> Britannia's Pastorals *by William Browne of Tavistock*

Delicate mangetout *peas may be lightly steamed, boiled or stir-fried in a frying-pan or wok—the round-bottomed metal pan traditionally used in China.*

"I eat my peas with honey,
I've done it all my life.
It makes the peas taste funny
But it keeps 'em on the knife!"

Anon.

Peas

Purée Clamart

The secret of a stiff but fluffy purée of fresh peas is to make it in an electric blender, not in a sieve, which traps the skins that give the purée its body. If, however, the purée does not thicken sufficiently, a little mashed potato may be added.

SERVES FOUR

1 lb (½ kg) green peas
3 shallots, finely chopped
2 oz (60 g) butter
4 tablespoons chicken stock
Salt
Freshly ground black pepper
Sugar (optional)
Finely chopped parsley or
  fresh chervil, to garnish

Put the peas, shallots, butter and chicken stock in a heavy pan. Season to taste with salt, pepper and a pinch of sugar if used. Bring to the boil, cover and cook gently until the peas are very soft and have absorbed most of the liquid.

Purée the contents of the pan in an electric blender. Test the purée. If it is too thin to hold its shape, blend in enough mashed potato to bring it to the right consistency.

Return the purée to the pan. Beating vigorously, cook the purée until it is hot.

Correct the seasoning and serve garnished with chopped parsley or chervil.

Eggs and Peas

SERVES FOUR

1 oz (30 g) butter
4 slices unsmoked bacon, finely diced
1 small mild onion, finely chopped
¾ lb (360 g) fresh green peas
Sugar (optional)
4 eggs
4 tablespoons double cream
2 oz (60 g) freshly grated Parmesan
  cheese
2 tablespoons finely chopped parsley
Salt
Freshly ground black pepper
8 triangular croûtons fried in butter

Melt the butter in a heavy saucepan. Add the bacon and onion and fry over low heat, stirring, until the onion is soft and golden but not brown. Stir in the peas and 4 tablespoons of water. If the peas are not very young, add a pinch of sugar. Cover the pan tightly and cook gently for about 8 minutes, or until the peas are just tender.

Meanwhile, in a bowl beat the eggs and cream together lightly. Mix in the Parmesan cheese, parsley and salt and pepper to taste.

When the peas are tender, pour in the egg mixture and continue to cook over the lowest possible heat, stirring constantly. The mixture will thicken into a rich creamy sauce, or it can be allowed to "curdle" into a version of scrambled eggs.

Serve each portion garnished with 2 croûtons.

Risi e Bisi

The Italians of the Veneto claim this dish as their own, regarding it as a very thick soup rather than a risotto—although it is eaten with a fork. To make this dish properly it is important to use tiny fresh peas and Italian rice. The quantity of stock required to cook the rice varies with the quality and variety of the rice.

To serve risi e bisi as a soup, thin the mixture down with more stock. Leave out the final ounce of butter and simply serve the thick soup garnished with Parmesan and parsley.

SERVES SIX TO EIGHT

2 tablespoons olive oil
3 oz (90 g) butter
4 thick slices fat unsmoked bacon or ham,
  finely diced
1 large, mild onion, finely chopped
¾ lb (360 g) Italian rice
2 to 3 pints (1 to 1½ litres) chicken
  stock, boiling
2 lb (1 kg) fresh green peas
2 oz (60 g) freshly grated Parmesan
  cheese
Salt
Freshly ground black pepper
2 tablespoons finely chopped parsley

Heat the oil and 2 ounces (60 g) of the butter in a large, heavy pan. Add the bacon or ham and onion and fry over low heat until the onion is soft and lightly coloured. Stir in the rice. Add ¾ pint (375 ml) of the boiling stock and simmer gently, uncovered, stirring frequently, until most of the stock has been absorbed.

Using a large fork, gently mix in the fresh peas. Pour in 1¼ pints (625 ml) of stock and continue to simmer over low heat for 15 minutes, or until both the peas and rice are tender and most of the stock has been absorbed.

Remove the pan from the heat. Add the remaining butter and 1 ounce (30 g) of the grated Parmesan cheese. Mix gently and season to taste with salt and pepper. Cover the pan and set aside for 5 to 10 minutes to allow the rice to absorb any excess stock. Serve sprinkled with the remaining Parmesan cheese mixed with the parsley.

Peas in Cream

Light and elegant, peas in cream may be served with almost any meat. This dish may also be flavoured with Madeira —leave out the mace and lemon juice and add 4 tablespoons of Madeira to the cream before it is stirred into the peas. Serve the peas with a garnish of buttery croûtons.

SERVES FOUR TO SIX

1 lb (½ kg) tender green peas
1 shallot, finely chopped
2 oz (60 g) butter
6 tablespoons stock
Sugar
Salt
Freshly ground black pepper
Mace or nutmeg
2 teaspoons flour
¼ pint (125 ml) single cream
Lemon juice (optional)

In a heavy pan, combine the peas, shallot, butter and stock. Add sugar, salt, pepper and mace or nutmeg to taste. Bring the mixture to simmering point over moderate heat. Cover the pan, reduce the heat and stew gently until the peas are barely tender.

Meanwhile, in a bowl blend the flour smoothly with the cream.

Drain the hot pea liquor into the cream mixture. Mix well, then stir it back into the hot peas. Bring to the boil over low heat, stirring gently. Simmer for 2 to 3 minutes, or until the sauce thickens. Correct the seasoning. A few drops of lemon juice may be added to sharpen the flavour.

Green Beans

When a recipe calls simply for "green beans" the cook is left to decide whether to use French beans (*haricots verts*) or runner beans. The choice is a matter of taste. When young, French beans are slender and stringless and have a more delicate flavour than the coarser, larger runner bean. The French bean is cooked and served whole, while the runner is either sliced diagonally or in long strips. Traditionally, the runner bean is more favoured in Britain. On the Continent, the French bean is preferred, although farther south, towards the eastern Mediterranean, the runner bean is considered superior.

Delicately flavoured, young French beans need the minimum of cooking. Runner beans, which are less fragile, can be submitted to prolonged simmering, in a casserole, for example, without loss of flavour or texture.

Both French and runner beans should be so fresh that they can be broken in half with a crisp snap. If they seem rather wilted, revitalize them by putting them in a plastic bag and chilling them in the vegetable compartment of the refrigerator.

Very young beans, in particular French beans, need only be topped and tailed before cooking.

More mature beans, especially the runners, can be stringy. Shave around the pods with a sharp knife or a vegetable peeler.

To avoid overcooking, French beans should be steamed, preferably, or boiled for about 5 minutes if very young, 12 to 15 minutes for older ones. Refresh the beans in a colander under running cold water, then reheat them gently in butter in a covered pan, shaking the pan frequently. They should remain *al dente*—slightly resistant to the bite.

The simplest, and many say the best, way of serving fresh beans is with salt, freshly ground black pepper and plenty of butter or buttered breadcrumbs spooned over the top. Another way to serve beans is with hot, crisp-fried bacon together with its fat in place of butter. Or toss the hot beans with sliced, white button mushrooms or a handful of blanched, slivered almonds which have been fried in butter to a rich golden colour.

Cold cooked beans are delicious when dressed with a *vinaigrette* and sprinkled with fresh herbs. Leftover green beans dressed in this way frequently appear on French tables as part of a mixed *hors d'oeuvre*.

Bean Soup
French beans and dried flageolet beans make an interesting combination and produce a soup of a delicate green colour. If flageolet beans are not available, dried haricot beans may be substituted.

SERVES FOUR TO SIX
2 oz (60 g) flageolet beans, soaked
1 celery stalk, chopped
1½ pints (750 ml) chicken stock
1 lb (½ kg) mature French beans
1 oz (30 g) butter
4 teaspoons flour
½ pint (250 ml) milk
Salt
Freshly ground black pepper
Lemon juice
Single cream or top of the milk
Freshly chopped parsley or chervil,
* to garnish*

Drain the soaked flageolet beans. Put them in a saucepan with the celery and 1 pint (500 ml) of chicken stock. Place the pan over high heat and bring to the boil. Cover the pan tightly, reduce the heat and simmer for 45 minutes, or until the beans are soft. Add the French beans and the remaining stock. Replace the lid and cook gently for 15 minutes.

Meanwhile, melt the butter in another pan. Blend in the flour smoothly and stir over low heat for 1 minute to make a pale *roux*. Gradually add the milk, stirring vigorously to prevent lumps forming. Continue to stir until the sauce comes to the boil and thickens slightly.

Add some of the bean liquor to the sauce. Then pour all of the sauce over the beans and bring to the boil. Cover the pan, reduce the heat and continue to cook gently until all the beans are soft enough to purée.

Purée the contents of the pan in an electric blender or in a mouli. If the green beans are at all stringy, rub the purée through a fine sieve as well.

Return the purée to the pan. Season to taste with salt, pepper and lemon juice. Dilute the soup to the desired consistency with cream or creamy milk. Correct the seasoning and garnish with finely chopped parsley or chervil before serving.

Haricots Verts à la Paysanne
A rather elaborate dish, but substantial and one which is well worth the trouble.

SERVES FOUR
1½ lb (¾ kg) young French beans
Salt
2 small potatoes, peeled and diced
¼ lb (120 g) fat salt pork or
* unsmoked bacon, in one piece*
2 oz (60 g) butter
2 medium-sized, mild onions, finely
* chopped*
8 young carrots, thickly sliced
2 teaspoons sugar
½ pint (250 ml) light chicken stock or
* water*
Freshly ground black pepper
2 tablespoons finely chopped parsley

Top and tail the beans and cut them at a slant into 2-inch (5 cm) lengths. Boil them in salted water for 12 minutes, or until tender but still very firm. Drain thoroughly.

Parboil the potatoes in salted water for 5 minutes. Drain well.

Meanwhile, cut the fat salt pork or bacon into short, thick strips. Put them in a small pan. Cover with cold water. Bring to the boil and parboil for 5 minutes. Drain thoroughly and dry on absorbent kitchen paper.

Melt the butter in a heavy pan. Add the pork or bacon strips and fry, stirring, until they are golden and the fat is transparent. Add the onions and carrots and fry gently until golden. Sprinkle with the sugar. Add half of the stock or water and cook gently until the liquid has evaporated and the vegetables are slightly caramelized.

Add the potatoes and the beans to the onion and carrot mixture. Mix well and pour in the remaining stock or water. Season to taste with salt and pepper. Cover the pan and cook until all the vegetables are soft but not mushy. Serve very hot, sprinkled with the chopped parsley.

Use a sharp knife to top and tail green beans.

Green Beans

Green Beans en Salade

This is the simplest bean salad of all. Add a crushed clove of garlic or a tablespoon of chopped fresh basil to the dressing, and wedges of tomato, a few black olives, chopped anchovy fillets and hard-boiled egg quarters to the beans and serve the salad as a light main course for a summer lunch.

SERVES THREE TO FOUR

1 lb (½ kg) young French beans
Salt
6 tablespoons olive oil
2 tablespoons mild wine vinegar, cider vinegar or lemon juice
Sugar
Freshly ground black pepper
1 small, mild onion, finely chopped
2 tablespoons finely chopped parsley

Cook the beans in a large pan of rapidly boiling salted water for about 10 minutes, or until they are just tender and still on the crunchy side. Drain thoroughly and set aside in a bowl.

Meanwhile, make the dressing. Mix the oil, vinegar or lemon juice, and the sugar, salt and pepper to taste. Stir in the onion and parsley.

Pour the dressing over the hot cooked beans and let them cool completely. Toss lightly just before serving.

Italian Beans with Tomato Sauce

The Italian name of this dish, *Fagiolini rifatti*, means "twice-cooked beans". If ripe, flavoursome tomatoes are not available, use instead 14 ounces (420 g) of canned Italian peeled tomatoes, together with the liquid.

SERVES SIX

2 lb (1 kg) young French beans
Salt
2 garlic cloves, lightly bruised
6 tablespoons olive oil
1 lb (½ kg) ripe tomatoes, peeled and chopped
1 tablespoon chopped fresh basil
Freshly ground black pepper

Cook the beans in a large pan of rapidly boiling salted water for about 10 minutes.

Meanwhile, in a large saucepan, sauté the garlic in the oil until golden. Remove and discard the garlic. Add the tomatoes and basil to the oil and cook over high heat for 10 minutes. Season to taste with salt and pepper.

Drain the beans thoroughly. Add them to the tomatoes and simmer for 15 minutes, or until the sauce is rich and reduced. Correct the seasoning and serve.

French Beans with Peppers and Parmesan Cheese

Serve this dish as an accompaniment to a strongly flavoured meat dish or a main-course quiche or tart.

SERVES FOUR

2 tablespoons vegetable oil
1 tablespoon butter
1 green pepper, cored, seeded and thinly sliced
1 shallot, finely chopped
1 garlic clove, crushed
1 lb (½ kg) young French beans
1 tablespoon chopped fresh basil or 2 teaspoons dried basil
Salt
Freshly ground black pepper
4 tablespoons freshly grated Parmesan cheese

Heat the oil and butter in a wide, heavy pan. Add the green pepper, shallot and garlic and fry until the pepper strips have wilted and the shallot is soft and golden.

Add the beans, turning them over to coat them with the buttery juices. Sprinkle with the basil and season to taste with salt and pepper. Pour in ¼ pint (125 ml) of boiling water. Cover the pan and cook over moderate heat for 10 minutes, or until the beans are tender but still firm. If at the end of the cooking time there is too much liquid left, raise the heat and cook briskly for a minute or two longer to evaporate the excess moisture. Remove the pan from the heat.

Gently mix in the cheese. Correct the seasoning and leave, covered, for a few minutes before serving.

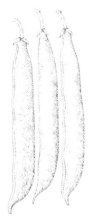

Runner Beans à la Grecque

A Mediterranean appetizer or main course to enjoy at an informal lunch, this dish can be served in the Greek style—lukewarm with crusty bread to soak up the sauce.

SERVES FOUR TO SIX

2 lb (1 kg) runner beans
Salt
1 large, mild onion, finely chopped
4 large, ripe tomatoes, blanched, peeled and chopped
6 tablespoons finely chopped parsley
6 tablespoons olive oil
2 teaspoons sugar
Freshly ground black pepper

String the beans and slice them lengthwise into thin strips. Put the beans in a colander. Sprinkle them generously with salt and rub the salt gently into the beans. Set aside for 1 hour to allow the beans to wilt and soften.

Rinse the beans thoroughly under cold running water, then shake off as much moisture as possible.

In a heavy pan, combine the beans with the onion, tomatoes, parsley and olive oil. Sprinkle with the sugar and add a generous grinding of pepper. Add just enough boiling water to cover. Bring to simmering point, partially cover the pan and cook gently for 30 minutes, or until the beans are tender and the sauce is thick. Remove the pan from the heat and set aside to cool.

Correct the seasoning with salt, more pepper or sugar and serve luke-warm in the Greek style, or cold.

French Beans in Mushroom Cream Sauce

If the mushrooms are very small and white, trim their stems and halve or quarter them. Otherwise, they should be thickly sliced.

SERVES FOUR

1 lb (½ kg) young French beans
Salt
2 oz (60 g) butter
1 small, mild onion, finely chopped
¼ lb (120 g) button mushrooms
Lemon juice
6 tablespoons single cream
Freshly ground black pepper

Drop the beans into a large pan of fast-boiling salted water and cook them briskly for 10 minutes, or until tender but still crisp.

Meanwhile, melt the butter in a large, wide pan and fry the onion gently until soft and golden. Add the mushrooms. Squeeze a little lemon juice over them to prevent them discolouring and cook gently for a further 3 to 5 minutes, or until they are golden and have softened slightly.

Drain the beans thoroughly and mix them with the onion and mushrooms. Add the cream and season to taste with salt and pepper. Cook over low heat, stirring gently, until the sauce comes to simmering point; then let it bubble for about 3 minutes until the sauce is reduced to a thick coating consistency. Serve immediately.

Broad Beans

A pocketful of boiled broad beans, still warm from the pot, was the favourite snack of small boys in eastern Europe. More elegant is the Roman custom of nibbling raw baby broad beans with pieces of Pecorino cheese and a glass of white wine.

When broad beans are very young, before most people would consider gathering them for shelling, they are delicious boiled and eaten in the pod. When the beans are very large and mature, their tough outer skins must be peeled off after the beans have been cooked.

Serve boiled broad beans with butter or parsley sauce; make a creamy white sauce well in advance of serving, crush a large bunch of parsley stalks lightly and stir them into the sauce. Just before serving, reheat the sauce, strain out the stalks and stir the finely chopped parsley tops and the freshly cooked hot beans into the steaming sauce.

Buttered Broad Beans
This is a way to serve broad beans in the pod. They must be very young, the pods thin and not more than 4 or 5 inches (10 or 13 cm) long.

SERVES FOUR
1 lb (½ kg) baby broad beans
Salt
2 oz (60 g) butter, softened
1 tablespoon chopped fresh chervil or
  2 teaspoons dried chervil
1 tablespoon finely chopped parsley
Lemon juice
Coarse salt
Freshly ground black pepper

Top and tail the broad beans and cut each one diagonally into three or four pieces. Drop them into a bowl of cold water and leave them to soak until needed.

Bring a large pan of salted water to the boil. Drain the beans in a colander and drop them into the boiling water. When the water returns to the boil, cook the beans briskly for 10 minutes, or until tender.

Meanwhile, cream the butter with the chopped herbs and a few drops of lemon juice. Divide the herb butter into 4 equal pats.

Drain the cooked beans thoroughly. Return them to the pan and toss over high heat for 1 to 2 minutes to evaporate the excess moisture. Season to taste with the coarse salt and a grinding of pepper.

Serve the beans very hot, each portion topped with a pat of herb butter.

Broad Beans with Bacon
A simple, easy way to prepare broad beans.

SERVES FOUR TO SIX
1 oz (30 g) butter
4 slices unsmoked bacon, diced
1 medium-sized onion, finely chopped
1 lb (½ kg) shelled broad beans
¼ pint (125 ml) stock or water
Salt
Freshly ground black pepper

Melt the butter in a heavy pan. Add the bacon and onion and fry until the onion is soft but not coloured. Stir in the beans. Add the stock or water and bring to the boil. Cover the pan tightly and cook over moderate heat until the beans are soft but not mushy.

If there is too much liquid left by the time the beans are ready, boil them briskly, uncovered, for 1 to 2 minutes to evaporate the excess moisture. Correct the seasoning with salt and pepper. Serve immediately.

Broad Beans in Cream Sauce
This elegant vegetable dish can be made in advance. When it is reheated, however, the sauce may have to be thinned down a little with more chicken stock, milk or cream.

SERVES FOUR TO SIX
2 oz (60 g) butter
¼ pint (125 ml) well-flavoured chicken
  stock
1½ lb (¾ kg) shelled broad beans
1 teaspoon celery seeds
½ teaspoon sugar
¼ pint (125 ml) double cream
Milk (optional)
Salt
Freshly ground black pepper

In a heavy, wide-based pan, melt the butter in the chicken stock. Add the beans. Sprinkle with the celery seeds and sugar. Cover tightly and cook over moderate heat until the beans are soft.

Drain off the bean liquor into an electric blender. Add about a quarter of the beans and blend them to a purée, gradually adding the cream, and a little milk if necessary, to make a rich, smooth sauce.

Stir the sauce into the beans. Season to taste with salt and pepper and reheat gently, stirring. Serve very hot.

Broad Beans au Gratin
A perfect supper dish. Serve it accompanied by a tomato and orange salad or with crisply grilled sausages.

SERVES FOUR TO SIX
2 oz (60 g) butter
¾ lb (360 g) mushrooms, thickly sliced
1½ oz (45 g) flour
½ pint (250 ml) light stock
½ pint (250 ml) single cream
4 tablespoons grated Parmesan cheese
Salt
Freshly ground black pepper
1½ lb (¾ kg) shelled broad beans
Dry breadcrumbs
Extra butter, for the topping

Melt ½ ounce (15 g) of the butter in a frying-pan. Add the mushrooms and fry, stirring, until they are just golden. Remove the pan from the heat and set aside.

Melt the remaining butter in a large saucepan. Stir in the flour and cook for 1 minute to make a pale *roux*. Remove the pan from the heat and gradually add the stock and cream, stirring constantly to prevent lumps from forming.

Return the pan to the heat and, stirring, bring the sauce to the boil. Stir in 2 tablespoons of the cheese and add salt and pepper to taste. Add the beans and the mushrooms, with their pan liquor, to the sauce and mix them in well.

Put the contents of the pan into a heatproof dish. Sprinkle the top with the remaining cheese and enough breadcrumbs to cover thinly. Dot with a little butter and place the dish under a hot grill until the top is bubbling and beginning to brown. Alternatively, if the beans, mushrooms and sauce are prepared in advance, reheat the dish on the top shelf of a 350°F (180°C, Gas Mark 4) oven for 25 to 30 minutes.

Ideally, haricot beans should be eaten when they are newly dried. They may be stored, of course, but they become tougher with keeping and the older the bean the longer it must be soaked before cooking. Young haricot beans should be covered with cold water, brought to the boil, boiled for 1 minute, then left to soak in the covered pan for 1 hour. Drain the beans thoroughly; cover them with fresh unsalted water and boil them for about 30 to 40 minutes, or until the skin of a bean bursts when you lift it out and blow on it gently.

Serve cooked haricot beans in the Mediterranean style as a cold appetizer, dressed with a well-flavoured *vinaigrette* and plenty of chopped fresh parsley. Haricot beans are used in many famous Tuscan dishes, such as *fagioli al tonno*, beans and tuna fish, and *ribollita*, a bean soup, or *fagioli nel fiasco*, beans cooked with garlic and olive oil in a Chianti bottle.

Fagioli al Tonno

One of the finest *antipasti* to come out of Italy, this is an earthy and deliciously satisfying dish. Its very simplicity makes it all the more important that its ingredients be of the best quality. Use good beans and Spanish or Italian tuna fish packed in olive oil.

SERVES FOUR TO SIX
½ lb (¼ kg) haricot beans, soaked
6 tablespoons olive oil
2 tablespoons mild wine vinegar
1 plump garlic clove, crushed
Salt
Freshly ground black pepper
½ lb (¼ kg) canned white tuna in olive oil
1 large, mild onion, thinly sliced
2 tablespoons finely chopped parsley

Drain the soaked beans. Cover them with fresh cold water and boil them until their skins burst when blown upon. Cooking time depends on the age of the beans. Begin testing the beans when they have cooked for 30 minutes.

Meanwhile, make a well-seasoned dressing. Beat the oil with the vinegar, garlic, salt and pepper. Empty the can of tuna into a bowl, together with its oil, and break it up roughly with a fork.

When the beans are tender, drain them thoroughly and put them in a serving dish. While the beans are still hot pour over the dressing, the tuna and its oil and the sliced onion. Mix gently but well.

Serve lukewarm or cold, garnished with parsley.

Baked Beans in White Wine

A variation on the familiar American dish of baked beans, which is a close relative of the French *cassoulet*. This is a spicy dish.

SERVES FOUR
1 lb (½ kg) haricot beans, soaked
2 Spanish onions
4 cloves
1 lb (½ kg) fat salt pork or
  unsmoked bacon, in one piece
1 oz (30 g) butter
4 tablespoons treacle
½ bottle (¼ litre) medium dry white wine
3 tablespoons dark rum
2 teaspoons dry mustard
¼ to ½ teaspoon crushed, dried red
  peppers
Salt

Drain the soaked beans. Put them in a large saucepan and cover them with fresh cold water. Add the whole onions, each one stuck with 2 cloves. Put the pan over moderate heat and bring to the boil slowly. Boil gently for 30 minutes, or until the bean skins burst when blown upon.

Meanwhile, cut the pork or bacon in half. Slash the rind and fat on top in several places. Put the pieces of pork or bacon in a bowl. Cover them with boiling water and leave them to soak for 30 minutes.

Preheat the oven to 275°F (140°C, Gas Mark 1).

Drain the beans, reserving their cooking liquor. Lift out the onions and as soon as they are cool enough to handle, discard the cloves and chop the onions coarsely.

Rinse and dry the pan. Melt the butter in it and fry the onions gently until they are ligntly coloured. Remove the pan from the heat. Stir in the treacle, wine, rum, mustard, red peppers and the cooked beans. Mix well and season lightly with salt. (Remember the saltiness of the pork or bacon with which they will cook.)

Drain the pork or bacon thoroughly. Lay one piece at the bottom of a heavy, ovenproof casserole with a tight-fitting lid. Pour the bean mixture over the top and bury the other piece of pork or bacon in the centre so that only the top is visible.

Bake, covered, for 3½ hours. Remove the lid and continue baking for another 30 minutes. If the beans dry out too quickly during cooking, moisten them with some of the reserved bean liquor. At the end of the cooking time the sauce should be rich and reduced.

Correct the seasoning with more salt if necessary. Serve from the casserole.

Haricot Beans with Roast Lamb

Try this dish when you are next roasting a leg or shoulder of lamb. It is extraordinarily good and a marvellous alternative to the usual dish of potatoes or rice. If you should find the lamb flavour too strong, increase the beans by 2 or 3 ounces (60 or 90 g) rather than disturb the balance of the sauce.

SERVES FOUR
½ lb (¼ kg) haricot beans, soaked
1 oz (30 g) butter
1 oz (30 g) lamb fat, finely chopped
1 medium-sized Spanish onion, finely
  chopped
2 garlic cloves, crushed
14 oz (420 g) canned Italian peeled
  tomatoes
6 tablespoons pan juices from the
  roasting lamb
Salt
Freshly ground black pepper
Finely chopped parsley, to garnish

Drain the soaked beans. Put them in a large pan, cover with plenty of fresh cold water and bring to the boil over high heat. Cover the pan, reduce the heat and simmer for 30 minutes or longer, depending on the age of the beans, or until they are barely tender and far from mushy.

Meanwhile, melt the butter in a heavy pan and fry the pieces of lamb fat (sliced from the joint before it was put into the oven) until the fat runs. Add the onion and garlic and fry until soft and golden. Add the tomatoes, with their juice, and cook gently, uncovered, for 15 minutes, or until they are reduced to a thick pulp. Cover the pan and set aside.

When the beans are done, drain them thoroughly. Mix them gently into the tomato sauce, together with the juices from the roasting lamb. Season to taste with salt and pepper. Cover the pan and continue to simmer gently for 30 minutes, stirring occasionally.

Sprinkle with parsley and serve.

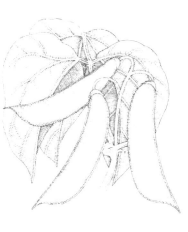

Soya Beans

Although soya beans have been cultivated in Asia for more than three thousand years, in the West, until recently, they were considered suitable only for animal fodder. Today, however, the great nutritional value of soya beans is widely recognized and their flavour and versatility are appreciated.

Young soya beans may be cooked in the pod and eaten, pod and all, with melted butter. Any but the youngest soya beans must, however, be shelled. They are difficult to shell unless they are first blanched. Drop the pods into boiling water for 5 minutes, drain them, then break each pod in half and squeeze out the beans. To cook the beans, boil them for 15 to 20 minutes or until they are tender.

Dried beans must be soaked overnight as they take a long time to soften. Then either pressure-cook them for 45 minutes at high pressure (15 lb) or simmer them for about 4 hours.

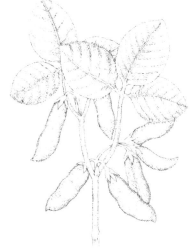

Soya Beans en Salade

By adding sliced or quartered hard-boiled eggs this salad can be turned into a satisfying and balanced main dish. Japanese soy sauce is best for the dressing, but if it is not available use good-quality Chinese soy sauce.

SERVES FOUR TO SIX

½ lb (¼ kg) dried soya beans, soaked overnight and cooked, or about 1½ lb (¾ kg) fresh soya beans, cooked
3 shallots, finely chopped
¼ lb (120 g) celery stalks, finely diced
4 tablespoons finely chopped parsley
DRESSING
4 tablespoons oil
1 tablespoon lemon juice
1 tablespoon Japanese soy sauce
½ teaspoon monosodium glutamate (optional)
Sugar
Sea salt
Freshly ground black pepper

Make a well-seasoned dressing with the oil, lemon juice, soy sauce, monosodium glutamate, if it is used, a pinch of sugar, sea salt and pepper.

Drain the beans thoroughly and, while they are still hot, mix them gently with the dressing. Let the salad cool to lukewarm, then mix in the shallots, celery and parsley. Correct the seasoning. Let the salad cool completely to allow the flavours to develop before serving it.

Soya Bean Cutlets

Served with a salad or a green vegetable, these cutlets will make as pleasant and satisfying a main course as any steak or chop.

SERVES FOUR

1 tablespoon rendered bacon fat
4 slices fat bacon, finely chopped
½ lb (¼ kg) dried soya beans, soaked overnight and cooked until soft, or 1¼ lb (600 g) fresh soya beans, cooked and drained
2 teaspoons chili powder compound
2 tablespoons finely chopped onion
4 tablespoons grated sharp Cheddar cheese
2 eggs
2 tablespoons finely chopped parsley
Salt
Fine dry breadcrumbs
Lard or oil, for frying

Heat the bacon fat in a large frying-pan. Add the bacon and fry until crisp. Add the beans and fry them steadily, stirring and crushing them with a potato masher or spoon. Remove the pan from the heat and stir in the chili powder, onion and cheese. When the mixture has cooled slightly, add the eggs and parsley. Mix well. Season to taste with salt and let the mixture cool completely.

Divide the mixture into 8 balls. Roll them in fine dry breadcrumbs and shape them into cutlets.

Fry the cutlets in hot lard or oil until they are hot and firm and the breadcrumbs are crisp and golden on both sides. Serve hot.

Soya Bean Casserole

Serve this casserole as a main dish accompanied by vegetables or salad as you would a meat casserole.

SERVES FOUR

1 oz (30 g) butter
1 large, mild onion, finely chopped
1 garlic clove, crushed
3 celery stalks, coarsely chopped
1 lb (½ kg) soya beans, cooked
4 tablespoons finely chopped parsley
2 tablespoons Japanese soy sauce
Salt
Freshly ground black pepper

Melt the butter in a saucepan or casserole. Add the onion and garlic and simmer, stirring, until the onion is soft and golden. Add the celery and stir over low heat until it is golden. Moisten with 1 tablespoon of water, cover the pan and cook gently until the celery is tender but still firm.

Stir in the soya beans and parsley. Flavour with soy sauce (use 1½ tablespoons if Chinese soy sauce is being substituted and add a pinch of sugar) and season to taste with salt and pepper. Cover the pan and cook gently for 10 minutes longer, or until the beans are hot.

Curried Soya Beans

This is a spicy curry. For a different flavour substitute two tablespoons of sweet mango or tomato chutney for the sugar.

SERVES FOUR TO SIX

2 tablespoons vegetable oil
1 medium-sized onion, finely chopped
2 garlic cloves, crushed
½-inch (1 cm) piece fresh root ginger, peeled and finely chopped
½ to 1 teaspoon cayenne pepper
2 teaspoons ground coriander
½ teaspoon turmeric
2 tablespoons brown sugar
1 lb (½ kg) dried or 1½ lb (¾ kg) fresh soya beans, cooked
14 oz (420 g) canned peeled tomatoes
Salt
Freshly ground black pepper

Heat the oil in a large saucepan. Add the onion, garlic and ginger and fry, stirring frequently, over moderate heat until the onions are soft and golden brown.

Stir in the cayenne, coriander, turmeric and brown sugar and fry, stirring, for 5 minutes. Stir in the beans and the tomatoes with their liquid. Season to taste with the salt and pepper. Bring the mixture to the boil. Cover the pan, reduce the heat to low and simmer for 1 hour.

Serve hot.

Bean Sprouts

Bean sprouts, a favourite vegetable of the Chinese, are the young shoots of beans, of the mung bean in particular. Lightly cooked or raw, bean sprouts are a valuable food—they have a high protein and vitamin content.

Raw bean sprouts added to a conventional salad provide a welcome crunchiness and a delicate, elusive flavour. Stir bean sprouts into clear soup and simmer for a few minutes just before serving. Or try a bean sprout salad dressed with a well-seasoned *vinaigrette*.

The Chinese stir-frying method is particularly suitable for cooking bean sprouts. They must be cooked quickly and eaten immediately or their precious crispness and delicate flavour will be destroyed.

There is no need to rinse home-grown bean sprouts, and resist the temptation to pick them over. Any stray little roots and hulls may look untidy, but they are full of vitamins and flavour.

Bean Sprouts with Green Peppers
An excellent dish to serve as part of a Chinese meal, or, European style, as a vegetable accompaniment to meat.

SERVES FOUR
4 tablespoons vegetable oil
1 lb (½ kg) bean sprouts
1 large green pepper, seeded, cored and finely chopped
2 tablespoons dry sherry
¼ teaspoon monosodium glutamate (optional)
Salt

Heat the oil in a large, heavy frying-pan. Add the bean sprouts and pepper and fry over high heat, stirring constantly, for 5 minutes. Add the sherry. Sprinkle with the monosodium glutamate, if it is used, and season to taste with salt. Stir-fry for 1 minute more. Serve immediately.

Bean Sprouts with Fresh Ginger
A simple, quickly made dish suitable for serving in the Eastern or Western manner.

SERVES FOUR
4 tablespoons vegetable oil
2 teaspoons finely slivered fresh root ginger
4 plump spring onions, thinly sliced
1 lb (½ kg) bean sprouts
1½ tablespoons Chinese soy sauce

Heat the oil in a large, heavy frying-pan. Add the ginger and the spring onions and fry over high heat, stirring, for 30 seconds. Add the bean sprouts and continue to stir-fry for 1 minute. Add the soy sauce. Lower the heat and continue to stir-fry for 4 minutes.

Bean Sprouts with Omelette Strips
A satisfying supper dish easy and quick to prepare; the bean sprouts with their unusual delicate flavour and crunchy texture make an excellent contrast to the eggs.

SERVES TWO
4 eggs
2 teaspoons Chinese soy sauce
3 tablespoons vegetable oil
½ lb (¼ kg) bean sprouts
1 tablespoon finely chopped parsley

Beat the eggs lightly with 1 teaspoon of soy sauce and 1 tablespoon of cold water. Heat 2 tablespoons of oil in a large frying-pan. Pour the egg mixture into the pan to make a thin, flat, pancake-like omelette. There is no need to turn it. Just brown lightly on the underside.

When the omelette is firmly set, cut it into thin strips. Cut the strips into two or three pieces. Set aside.

In the same pan, heat the remaining oil and stir-fry the bean sprouts for 3 minutes. Sprinkle with the remaining soy sauce. Add the omelette strips and parsley and stir-fry for 1 minute longer. Serve at once.

Noodle and Bean Sprout Soup
A light but delicious soup in the Chinese style. Vegetarians may use a strong, clear, vegetable stock and substitute finely slivered bamboo shoots for the shredded chicken.

SERVES FOUR TO SIX
1½ pints (750 ml) strong chicken stock
¼ lb (120 g) fine egg noodles
Salt
¼ teaspoon monosodium glutamate (optional)
2 teaspoons cornflour
¼ lb (120 g) shredded cooked chicken
6 tablespoons bean sprouts
6 watercress sprigs

In a large saucepan bring the stock to the boil. Drop in the noodles and boil for 2 minutes. Drain the noodles in a strainer over a bowl. Set the noodles aside.

Pour the stock back into the pan and return the pan to the heat. Add salt to taste and monosodium glutamate, if it is used.

In a cup, mix the cornflour with 3 tablespoons of cold water and pour it into the soup. Cook over moderate heat, stirring constantly, until the soup thickens slightly and becomes clear.

Stir in the shredded chicken, the bean sprouts and the noodles. Bring the soup to the boil. Reduce the heat and simmer for 2 minutes.

Ladle the soup into individual soup bowls. Add a sprig of watercress to each bowl and serve immediately.

Bean Sprouts and Prawns
This is a spicy dish. If a milder flavour is preferred, seed the chillies.

SERVES FOUR TO SIX
1 lb (½ kg) uncooked prawns
3 tablespoons vegetable oil
1-inch (2 cm) piece fresh root ginger, peeled and slivered
1 garlic clove, crushed
1 to 2 green chillies, finely chopped
6 spring onions, including the green part, sliced
1 tablespoon soy sauce
1 tablespoon dry sherry
1 teaspoon salt
1 teaspoon sugar
1 lb (½ kg) bean sprouts

Shell the prawns and remove the black, thread-like vein. Wash the prawns and dry them well with kitchen paper.

In a large frying-pan heat the oil over high heat. When the oil is very hot, reduce the heat to moderate. Add the ginger, garlic, green chilli and spring onions and fry, stirring, for 30 seconds. Add the prawns and fry, stirring, for 2 to 3 minutes, or until the prawns turn pink. Stir in the soy sauce, sherry, salt and sugar. Add the bean sprouts and fry, stirring, for 3 minutes.
Serve immediately.

Onions

The onion, with its myriad layered skins, was regarded by the ancients as a symbol of eternity, a sacred object, almost a divinity, to be invoked when swearing a solemn oath. Onions have also been regarded as a food and as a flavouring probably longer than any other cultivated vegetable. Indeed, the very thought of cooking without them is almost as absurd as trying to get by without seasoning.

The onion family can be divided into two categories, white and green. The most delicate of all the white onions is the shallot. French *haute cuisine* recognizes no substitute for it in classic marinades, butters and such sauces as *béarnaise* and *bordelaise*. Because shallots are expensive and sometimes almost impossible to buy, they are a very satisfying onion to grow. With proper storage in a cool, dry place, shallots from the garden will last for almost the whole year until the next crop is ready.

The "ordinary" onion, strong, direct and uncomplicated, is added without a second thought to the stockpot or roasting tin, or fried for stews and casseroles. But there is a difference between strong onions and the magnificent, large, mild onions—Spanish, Italian red or Breton—which are so sweet that whole slices can be eaten raw on buttered fresh bread, sprinkled with coarse salt.

For those who find even the mildest onions strong in flavour or indigestible, the answer is to blanch them. Pour boiling water over the onions after they have been sliced or chopped, and either leave them to stand for a little while or parboil them for 3 minutes. Drain them, pat them as dry as possible with paper towels and use them as you would raw onions.

Pickling onions, also called button onions, are the tiny, round bulblets, which should be picked before the onion has a chance to swell and grow. Besides being pickled they may be braised or sautéed. To peel pickling onions, first slice off the tops and tails. Put the onions in a bowl, pour over enough boiling water to cover and leave them to soak for 5 minutes. Then drain the onions and slip off the skins, which will come away very easily, particularly if the onions are still warm. After peeling, nick the root end with a small cross—this prevents the centres from popping out during cooking.

Garlic, a relative of the onion, is most often used as a herb, but it may also be used as a vegetable in its own right. It has a marvellously strange, Jekyll and Hyde character. Use one or two garlic cloves in a dish and the flavour is unmistakable. Take several heads of garlic, peel the cloves and pack them around a chicken or put them under a joint of lamb in a casserole, and somehow, after long, slow cooking, the pungency will have been transformed into a delicate sweetness.

The accepted procedure for crushing a garlic clove is to peel it, chop it into several pieces and then crush these to a paste with a sprinkling of salt, using the side of a broad-bladed knife. However, no matter how much the experts may demur, a garlic press is one of the most useful kitchen gadgets of all, not only for garlic but also for crushing small pieces of onion.

The green onions—chives, spring onions, Welsh onions, scallions—are usually eaten raw in salads or mashed into flavoured butters. Most delicate of all in appearance as well as in flavour are chives, those fine green spikes which, like a healthy lawn, grow all the better the more you cut them.

Chives are a summer herb, and in winter, spring onions, although rather more oniony, make a perfectly good substitute. Shallot and garlic tops may be snipped off here and there as they grow, too. Chopped into a dish, they lend a faint yet unmistakable taste of the parent.

Undeniably, the most majestic of the green onions is the leek. Unlike the other onions, the leek does not seem to have had difficulty in establishing its identity as a vegetable in its own right. Yet its reputation has had to withstand derogatory allusions over the centuries—something very insignificant was once considered "not worth a leek". Yet few vegetables can have been honoured like the leek, which was adopted by the Welsh as their national emblem. Apparently, the substitution of daffodils, although more picturesque, came about because it was thought that leeks and daffodils were one and the same—an error that the cook would certainly never make.

Welsh onions (true natives of Siberia not Wales) are small, leek-like bulbs with a delicate flavour. Cook them as you would very young leeks or use them to flavour stews. They may also be eaten raw in salads.

The tree onion, with its bulblets conveniently placed at the end of a stalk, may be used like an ordinary onion—pickled or cooked in stews or used to flavour stocks.

The potato onion is the sweetest, mildest and the most succulent of all the onions. Its pleasant chive-like flavour is delightful in salads and in cooked dishes.

Japanese bunching onions, so called because the bulbs grow in clusters, may be used as other onions in stews or casseroles. Their stalks and leaves make a tasty addition to salads.

Considering the extent to which onions are used in the kitchen, it is surprising how few people cook onions as a main dish or as a vegetable accompaniment. Yet, baked in their jackets, braised or steamed, stuffed or plain, glazed or frittered, onions make a most delicious dish.

When frying onions remember that only slow, careful cooking will bring out their flavour and sweetness. Raise the heat under the pan and, rather than speed up the process, you will only char the onions and make them bitter. The same is true of shallots and garlic.

A stew in which a large amount of onion is used will scarcely need any liquid. Use 1 pound ($\frac{1}{2}$ kg) of onions, raw or fried in butter or butter and oil, to 1 pound ($\frac{1}{2}$ kg) of meat. Provided the heat is kept very low, the onions will gradually dissolve into a purée, thick and rich enough to form the basis for the sauce.

To prevent streaming eyes when peeling and chopping onions, you can try paring them under running water—and using an auto-chopper—but usually the most effective solution is opening the window to ventilate the kitchen.

French Onion Soup
Once traditionally eaten in the early hours by the porters of the now defunct Paris vegetable market of Les Halles, this famous soup was also enjoyed by late-night revellers on their way home.

SERVES FOUR
$1\frac{1}{2}$ oz (45 g) butter
1 lb ($\frac{1}{2}$ kg) mild, sweet onions, thinly sliced
1 teaspoon sugar
$2\frac{1}{2}$ pints ($1\frac{1}{4}$ litres) well-flavoured beef stock
2 tablespoons brandy
Salt
Freshly ground black pepper
4 rounds French bread, 1 inch (2 cm) thick
3 tablespoons freshly grated Parmesan cheese
3 tablespoons freshly grated Gruyère cheese

Melt the butter in a large saucepan. Add the onions and the sugar and cook slowly, stirring frequently, for 20 minutes, or until the onions turn a rich golden colour.

Add the beef stock and bring it to the boil. Reduce the heat, partly cover the pan and simmer for 30 minutes. Add the brandy, season to taste with salt and pepper and simmer for 10 minutes longer.

Just before serving, preheat the oven to 450°F (230°C, Gas Mark 8). Toast the rounds of French bread on both sides. Pour the boiling soup into an ovenproof casserole or tureen. Float the pieces of toast on the surface and sprinkle with the grated cheeses. Bake for 10 to 15 minutes, or until the cheese is golden brown and bubbling.

Tarte à l'Oignon
An excellent *hors d'oeuvre*, this tart also makes a good main-course lunch or supper dish, served with a fresh green salad or grilled tomatoes.

SERVES SIX TO EIGHT
3 oz (90 g) butter
$1\frac{1}{2}$ lb ($\frac{3}{4}$ kg) large, mild onions, thinly sliced
2 tablespoons finely chopped parsley
2 teaspoons dried basil
Rich shortcrust pastry made with $\frac{1}{2}$ lb ($\frac{1}{4}$ kg) flour
$\frac{1}{2}$ pint (250 ml) single cream
3 large eggs
2 oz (60 g) Gruyère cheese, freshly grated
Salt
Freshly ground black pepper

TOPPING
1 oz (30 g) Gruyère cheese, freshly grated
4 tablespoons fresh white breadcrumbs

Melt the butter in a large saucepan. Add the onions and cook gently, tightly covered, for 15 minutes. Stir frequently. When the onions are limp, uncover the pan and continue to fry them gently, stirring frequently, for 15 to 20 minutes longer, or until they become very soft without colouring or losing their shape. Remove the pan from the heat and stir in the parsley and basil.

Preheat the oven to 425°F (220°C, Gas Mark 7).

Roll the pastry out and line a 10-inch (25 cm) tart tin with a removable base. Prick the pastry case with a fork and line

it with greaseproof paper or foil. Fill the case with dried beans and bake "blind" for 15 minutes. Remove the beans and paper and return the pastry case to the oven for 5 minutes longer to dry out the base. Remove the pastry case from the oven and set aside.

Reduce the oven temperature to 375°F (190°C, Gas Mark 5). Heat a baking sheet in the oven.

Beat the cream lightly with the eggs and cheese and mix it into the onion mixture. Season with salt and pepper.

Put the pastry case on the hot baking sheet and pour in the filling. Mix the grated Gruyère with the breadcrumbs and sprinkle over the top.

Bake the tart for 35 minutes, or until the filling is puffed and set and the crust is crisp and golden brown.

Pissaladière
The name of this onion pie from Provence, which is closely related to the pizzas of neighbouring Italy, comes from *pissalat*, a highly flavoured concoction of small sea fish.

SERVES SIX
4 tablespoons olive oil
$1\frac{1}{2}$ lb ($\frac{3}{4}$ kg) large, mild onions, finely chopped
1 large garlic clove, crushed
Thyme
Salt
Freshly ground black pepper
$\frac{3}{4}$ lb (360 g) once-risen bread dough

$\frac{1}{2}$ lb ($\frac{1}{4}$ kg) ripe tomatoes, peeled and sliced
2 oz (60 g) canned anchovy fillets, drained and halved lengthwise
16 large black olives, halved and pitted

Heat the olive oil in a heavy frying-pan. Add the onions, cover the pan tightly and fry them gently, stirring occasionally, for 15 minutes. Add the garlic and a pinch of thyme and cook, uncovered, for 15 minutes, or until the onions are reduced to a purée but are not coloured. Season to taste with salt and pepper. Set aside to cool.

Preheat the oven to 400°F (200°C, Gas Mark 6).

Roll the bread dough directly on the baking sheet into a circle about 10 inches (25 cm) in diameter. Spread the puréed onions evenly over the dough. Put the tomato slices on the onions and top with a decorative pattern of anchovy fillets and olives. Grind more pepper over the top.

Bake for 5 minutes. Reduce the oven temperature to 375°F (190°C, Gas Mark 5) and continue to bake for 30 minutes, or until the bread base is well risen and lightly browned underneath. Serve hot.

Glazed Button Onions in White Wine

Glazed onions are a traditional garnish for many classic French dishes. They are just as delicious mixed with an equal quantity of glazed oval-shaped carrots or button mushrooms.

SERVES FOUR TO SIX
2 lb (1 kg) button onions
2 tablespoons olive oil
2 oz (60 g) butter
½ pint (250 ml) chicken stock
1 bay leaf, torn in half
½ pint (250 ml) dry white wine
4 teaspoons sugar
Salt

Put the unpeeled button onions in a large bowl. Cover them with plenty of boiling water and let them stand for 5 minutes. Drain them in a colander. Peel the onions while they are still warm.

Heat the oil and butter in a pan wide enough to take the onions in not more than two layers. Add the onions and roll them about to coat each one in the fat.

Pour in the stock and add the bay leaf. Bring to the boil and cook briskly, shaking the pan frequently. When the stock has evaporated, add the wine. Sprinkle with the sugar and continue to cook until the wine has evaporated and the onions are soft and caramelized.

Discard the bay leaf and sprinkle the onions with salt. Serve immediately, or cover the pan and put it aside to be reheated when needed.

Mediterranean Onion and Pepper Appetizer

A summer appetizer that is typical of the south, this dish may be served either lukewarm or cold with good crusty bread. For a more substantial dish, criss-cross the top with anchovies and decorate with slices of hard-boiled egg. If any is left over it can be deep-frozen most successfully.

SERVES SIX
6 tablespoons olive oil
2 large, mild onions, thickly sliced
3 large green peppers
3 sprigs fresh basil, chopped, or
 2 teaspoons dried basil
Sugar
Salt
Freshly ground black pepper
14 oz (420 g) canned Italian peeled
 tomatoes
4 tablespoons finely chopped parsley
1 tablespoon capers
Black olives, to garnish

Heat the olive oil in a large, heavy pan. Add the onion, cover the pan tightly and cook over low heat for 10 minutes.

Meanwhile, quarter the peppers. Discard the cores and seeds, and cut crosswise into thick slices. Add the peppers to the onions. Sprinkle with the basil, 1 teaspoon of sugar and salt and pepper to taste. Continue cooking, stirring, for 2 minutes to wilt the peppers slightly. Stir in the tomatoes and the can juices and bring to the boil. Reduce the heat to low, cover the pan tightly and cook for 30 minutes. By this time the onions and peppers should be very soft but still keep their shape, and the tomatoes should be reduced to a thick sauce.

Remove the pan from the heat. Allow the mixture to cool to lukewarm and stir in the parsley and capers. Correct the seasoning, if necessary, with more salt, pepper and sugar. Serve garnished with black olives.

Onions in Madeira Cream

Marvellous with steak, liver or any grilled meat.

SERVES FOUR TO SIX
¼ lb (120 g) butter
4 large, mild onions, thickly sliced
¼ pint (125 ml) Madeira
Salt
Freshly ground black pepper
4 tablespoons double cream
4 tablespoons finely chopped parsley

Melt the butter in a wide, heavy pan. Add the onion slices and turn them thoroughly in the butter. Cover the pan and cook over very low heat for 10 minutes, shaking the pan occasionally.

Uncover the pan, increase the heat slightly and stir in the Madeira. Continue to cook, stirring frequently, until the Madeira has evaporated and the onions are soft and lightly caramelized.

Season to taste with salt and pepper. Stir in the cream and parsley and bring to the boil. Simmer for 1 minute. Serve hot.

Onions Agrodolce

This delicious regional Italian dish can be served either hot or cold, as part of a mixed *hors d'oeuvre* or as an accompaniment to roast meat or chicken.

SERVES FOUR
3 tablespoons olive oil
1½ lb (¾ kg) button onions, peeled
3 tablespoons white wine
3 tablespoons wine vinegar
2 tablespoons soft brown sugar
2 tablespoons pine nuts
2 tablespoons raisins
Salt
Freshly ground black pepper
Finely chopped parsley, to garnish

Heat the oil in a large, heavy frying-pan. Add the onions and cook over a moderate heat, shaking the pan occasionally, until the onions begin to brown. Add the wine, wine vinegar, sugar, pine nuts and raisins. Season with salt and pepper. Reduce the heat, cover the pan and simmer until the sauce has become syrupy and the onions are tender. Correct the seasoning and serve garnished with the chopped parsley.

Onions

Onion Dolma

A Middle Eastern favourite, these stuffed onions have now become popular all over the world. This dish may be eaten cold, as an appetizer, or as part of a mixed *hors d'oeuvre*, or hot as a main dish, accompanied by mixed vegetables or a green salad.

SERVES FOUR TO SIX

6 large onions, unpeeled
1 lb (½ kg) minced lamb
2 tomatoes, peeled and chopped
3 oz (90 g) long grain rice
Juice and finely grated rind of 1 lemon
1 small onion, finely chopped
1 tablespoon sugar
1 teaspoon turmeric
½ teaspoon basil
½ teaspoon oregano
Salt
Freshly ground black pepper
3 tablespoons olive oil, for cooking

Put the unpeeled onions in a large saucepan. Pour in plenty of boiling water. Boil for about 20 minutes, or until the onions are tender. Remove the onions from the pan, drain them and allow them to cool slightly.

In a bowl, thoroughly mix together all the remaining ingredients. Season to taste with salt and pepper. Set aside.

With a sharp knife, slit each onion down one side to the centre. Separate the layers, which will slip off quite easily. Discard the outer papery skins and the cores of the onions.

Take a small handful of the filling and work it into a sausage shape; squeeze out some, but not all, of the liquid. Reserve the excess liquid for use later. Lay the stuffing in one of the onion layers and fold it tightly around the mixture. Fill the remaining layers in this way. Do not overfill the layers as the rice must have room to expand.

Heat the oil in a pan large enough to take the stuffed onions in one layer. Add the stuffed onions, packing them in close together. Pour in any liquid remaining in the bowl. Reduce the heat, cover the pan and simmer gently for about 1 hour.

Half-way through the cooking time turn the stuffed onions over.

Carefully remove the dolma from the pan with a fish slice or spatula and serve immediately or set aside to cool.

Onion Pakoras

Pakoras—a variety of fritter—are among the commonest of Indian snacks. They can be made from almost any available vegetable, including spinach leaves, potatoes and aubergines. Usually fried in deep oil, they can also be shallow fried with equally good results. Serve pakoras with a tomato or coconut chutney.

SERVES FOUR

¼ lb (120 g) gram (chickpea) flour
1 teaspoon salt
½ teaspoon chilli powder
¼ teaspoon turmeric
½ teaspoon ground coriander
½-inch (1 cm) piece fresh root ginger, grated
Vegetable oil, for deep-frying
4 large onions, cut in rings or finely sliced

Sieve the flour and salt into a bowl. Beat in sufficient water (about ¾ pint, 375 ml) to make a thin, smooth batter. Mix in the chilli powder, turmeric, coriander and ginger and leave the batter

to stand for at least 30 minutes.

Heat the oil in a deep-frying pan until the temperature registers 375°F (190°C) on a cooking thermometer. If you do not have a thermometer drop a cube of stale bread in the oil; if it takes about 40 seconds to brown the temperature is correct. Coat the onion rings in the batter and add them, a few at a time, to the oil. Fry until golden brown, drain on kitchen paper and set aside in a warm serving dish. If you are using finely sliced onions, mix them in with the batter and then drop them by the spoonful into the hot oil. Repeat this process until all the onions are cooked. Serve immediately.

Stuffed Onions

For a more substantial main-course dish, stuff the onions with ½ lb (¼ kg) of sausage meat mixed with 4 tablespoons of fresh, white breadcrumbs, seasoned with salt and pepper. Sprinkle with more fresh, white breadcrumbs, dot with butter and bake for 40 minutes.

SERVES EIGHT

4 large, mild onions, peeled
Salt
24 button onions
2 oz (60 g) butter
2 oz (60 g) fresh white breadcrumbs
4 tablespoons freshly grated Parmesan cheese
8 tablespoons double cream

Put the large onions into boiling salted water and simmer them, uncovered, for 15 minutes. Drain them and set them aside to cool.

Put the button onions in a bowl. Cover them with boiling water and leave them for 5 minutes. Drain them in a colander, then peel and trim them. Set aside.

Preheat the oven to 375°F (190°C, Gas Mark 5).

Melt the butter in a small pan. Mix in the breadcrumbs and stir over a low heat for 1 to 2 minutes, or until they are just golden. Set aside.

When the large onions are cool enough to handle, cut them in half horizontally.

Scoop out and discard the centres. Arrange the onion "cups" side by side in a shallow baking dish and season lightly with salt.

Toss the button onions with the cheese and fill the onion halves with the mixture. Pour a tablespoon of cream over each half onion and spoon the buttered breadcrumbs over the top. Bake the onions for 25 minutes, or until both the large and small onions are tender when pierced with a thin skewer and the topping is crisp and golden. Serve hot.

Garlic Bread

Garlic bread is delicious. Serve it straight from the oven with soups or main-course dishes. It will also add a wonderfully appetizing and welcoming aroma to a cold buffet.

SERVES FOUR

1 long French loaf
¼ lb (120 g) butter, softened
2 plump garlic cloves, crushed
1 tablespoon finely chopped parsley
Sea salt
Freshly ground black pepper

Preheat the oven to 350°F (180°C, Gas Mark 4).

Slice the loaf diagonally at 1½-inch (4 cm) intervals to within a ¼ inch (½ cm) of the base.

Pound the butter with the garlic and parsley. Mix in salt and pepper to taste.

Carefully easing the slices of bread apart, spread each one with the garlic butter. Wrap the loaf tightly in foil and bake it for about 20 minutes, or until the butter has melted and the bread is hot and crusty.

Perhaps the leek would fare better in cookery books if it were not so familiar and easily come by. All too often it is only used as a flavouring for soups and stews when in fact it is a versatile and delicious vegetable which deserves a better fate.

Leeks may be served hot or cold, steamed or poached whole, or sliced and simmered in butter until reduced to a purée. A *bouquet garni* of fresh herbs and spices may be sandwiched neatly in a split leek, the halves tied together with string—just as efficient and much quicker to make than the traditional muslin bag.

Leeks require careful preparation, for every speck of grit must be washed out of them. To prepare leeks, first cut off the tops, leaving only about 2 inches (5 cm) of the green stem. The coarse green leaves are good only for the stock pot. Trim the roots. Slip off the outer skin of the leek, removing more than one layer if they have been damaged by the spade.

Rinse the leeks thoroughly under cold running water. If there is any doubt that the leeks are not completely clean, slit them down one side with the point of a sharp knife and let the water run through the layers.

There are a number of simple but tasty ways to cook and serve leeks. They make a delightful salad, steamed, then chilled and served cold with a *vinaigrette* dressing garnished with chopped hard-boiled egg and parsley. Or serve them hot covered with a *mornay* sauce. They may be parboiled for 8 minutes, drained and put in a baking dish with butter, sprinkled over with breadcrumbs and baked in a moderate oven for 25 minutes. Cook leeks *à la paysanne*—trim, slice and cook them gently in butter with diced bacon for 30 to 40 minutes. Or bake them in a pie—slice the leeks and put them in a lined pie dish. Season well and pour in some double or clotted cream. Cover with rich shortcrust pastry and bake in a moderate oven for 50 to 60 minutes.

Flamiche

The traditional recipe for this leek pie, which is a speciality both in Belgium and in northern France, calls for leeks, butter, cream and eggs. This version is slightly different in that sausages are included in the filling as well.

SERVES SIX

3 oz (90 g) butter
1½ lb (¾ kg) trimmed leeks, thinly sliced
8 thin sausages
Lard for frying
3 eggs
¼ pint (125 ml) double cream
Salt
Freshly ground black pepper
¾ lb (360 g) puff pastry
1 egg yolk, lightly beaten

Melt the butter in a large pan. Stir in the leeks, cover the pan tightly and cook over low heat, stirring occasionally, for 30 minutes, or until they are almost reduced to a purée. Uncover the pan, increase the heat to moderate and cook, stirring, for a few minutes longer to evaporate excess moisture.

While the leeks are cooking, prick the sausages with a fork (to prevent them bursting) and fry them in lard until they are well browned on all sides. Drain thoroughly on kitchen paper.

Preheat the oven to 425°F (220°C, Gas Mark 7).

Beat the eggs and cream together with a generous seasoning of salt and pepper. Remove the pan of leeks from the heat, mix in the cream and egg mixture and stir until it has thickened slightly. Correct the seasoning. Set aside to cool to lukewarm.

Divide the pastry in half and roll each piece into a circle 10 inches (25 cm) in diameter. Lay one pastry circle on a lightly dampened baking sheet.

Pile the leek mixture on to the pastry on the baking sheet, leaving a 1-inch (2 cm) border clear. Arrange the sausages in a star pattern on top of the leeks. Dampen the border of the pastry with cold water. Lay the other circle in position on top and carefully but thoroughly seal the edges of the pastry together. Flute or pinch the edges decoratively. Cut slits in the top to allow steam to escape and brush the whole pastry with the beaten egg yolk.

Bake for 10 minutes. Then reduce the heat to 350°F (180°C, Gas Mark 4) and continue to bake for 30 to 35 minutes longer, or until the pastry is puffed and golden brown. Serve hot.

Leek and Ham Rolls

A dish which requires no accompaniment except good crusty bread. These leek and ham rolls may be served as a first or main course.

SERVES FOUR AS A FIRST COURSE

8 thin leeks, trimmed
½ pint (250 ml) boiling chicken stock
4 large slices cooked ham
Butter
2 tablespoons flour
¼ pint (125 ml) double cream
4 tablespoons freshly grated Cheddar cheese
Salt
Freshly ground black pepper
3 tablespoons fresh white breadcrumbs

Arrange the leeks side by side in a wide pan. Pour in the boiling stock and bring it back to the boil. Reduce the heat, cover the pan tightly and simmer for 8 to 10 minutes, or until the leeks are just tender. Drain them, reserving the cooking liquid.

Preheat the oven to 400°F (200°C, Gas Mark 6).

Lay the ham slices flat on a board. Place 2 leeks in the middle of each slice and wrap the ham around the leeks. Put the rolls in a single layer in a buttered shallow baking dish.

Melt 1 ounce (30 g) of butter in a saucepan. Blend in the flour and stir over low heat for 1 minute to make a pale *roux*. Gradually add ¼ pint (125 ml) of the reserved leek liquid, stirring vigorously to prevent lumps forming. Stirring constantly, bring the sauce to

the boil. Stir in the cream and, as soon as the sauce comes to the boil again, remove the pan from the heat. Beat in 2 tablespoons of the cheese and season to taste with salt and pepper.

Pour the sauce over the rolled leeks. Mix the breadcrumbs and the remaining cheese together and sprinkle the mixture over the sauce. Dot with small pieces of butter.

Bake the leeks for 30 minutes, or until they are hot and the sauce is bubbling and golden brown on top. Allow the dish to rest and the sauce to stabilize for 10 minutes before serving.

Leeks

Creamed Leeks
A delicate vegetable accompaniment for grills, fried meats and roasts.

SERVES FOUR
2 lb (1 kg) trimmed leeks
Salt
½ pint (250 ml) double cream
2 tablespoons freshly grated Parmesan
 or sharp Cheddar cheese
Freshly ground black pepper
2 egg yolks, lightly beaten

Slice the leeks thickly. Put them in a saucepan. Sprinkle with salt and add just enough boiling water to cover. Bring the water back to the boil and cook the leeks, uncovered, for 6 to 8 minutes. Drain them thoroughly in a colander.

Pour the cream into the top of a double saucepan and place it over lightly simmering water. Stir in the leeks. Cover the pan and continue to cook gently for 20 to 30 minutes, or until the leeks are very tender but have not quite disintegrated.

Remove the top part of the double saucepan from the heat. Stir in the cheese and season to taste with salt and pepper. Stir in the egg yolks and put the pan back over simmering water. Stir gently until the sauce has thickened. Do not let it boil, or it will curdle.

Vichyssoise
It is a culinary irony that chilled Vichyssoise, one of the best of summer soups, should be made with what are essentially winter vegetables—leeks and floury potatoes. Serve Vichyssoise with hot garlic bread.

SERVES FOUR TO SIX
2 oz (60 g) butter
6 large leeks, white part only, thickly
 sliced
1½ lb (¾ kg) potatoes, peeled and thickly
 sliced
2 pints (generous 1 litre) chicken stock
Salt

Freshly ground black pepper
Freshly grated nutmeg
¾ pint (375 ml) single cream
Chopped fresh chives, to garnish

Melt the butter in a large saucepan. Add the leeks, cover the pan and simmer for 15 minutes. Shake the pan or turn the leeks over to make sure they soften without changing colour. Add the potatoes, pour in the stock and simmer gently, with the lid half on, for a further 15 to 20 minutes, or until the vegetables have begun to disintegrate.

Purée the soup in an electric blender or rub it through the finest plate of a vegetable mouli. Season with salt, pepper and a little nutmeg to taste.

If the soup is to be served cold, let it cool before diluting it with the cream. If it is to be served hot, add the cream and bring to boiling point. Garnish with chopped chives and serve.

To prepare leeks, cut away the coarse green leaves, leaving about 2 inches (5 cm) of green stem.

Leeks with Tomatoes and Olives
A traditional dish from Provence which may be served cold as an appetizer or salad, or hot as a vegetable accompaniment to meat or fish.

SERVES FOUR
2 lb (1 kg) trimmed leeks
3 tablespoons olive oil
4 large tomatoes, halved
2 oz (60 g) black olives, pitted
Juice of 1 lemon
Rind of ½ lemon, in one piece
Salt
Freshly ground black pepper

Cut the leeks into 1-inch (2 cm) lengths. Heat the oil in a large, deep frying-pan. Add the leeks, cover the pan and cook slowly for about 10 minutes, stirring occasionally.

Add the tomatoes, olives, half of the lemon juice, the lemon rind and salt and pepper to taste. Simmer, covered, for a further 10 minutes.

Remove and discard the lemon rind and add the remaining lemon juice. Adjust the seasoning. Serve hot or cold.

Trim the root end and remove the outer skin of the leeks and any brown or damaged layers.

Leeks in Soured Cream Sauce
A delightful dish to serve with hard-boiled eggs and cold meats. Home-made mayonnaise may be substituted for the soured cream.

SERVES FOUR
8 thin leeks
Salt
¼ pint (125 ml) thick soured cream
3 spring onions, finely chopped

2 tablespoons finely chopped parsley
1 small garlic clove, crushed
1 tablespoon horseradish sauce
1 tablespoon cider vinegar
Generous pinch sugar

Lay the leeks in a large saucepan. Pour in enough boiling water to cover and add salt. Cover the pan and cook over low heat for 8 to 10 minutes, or until the leeks are just tender.

Meanwhile, mix the remaining ingredients together and season generously with salt.

Drain the leeks in a colander. Let them cool to lukewarm; then arrange them side by side in a rectangular serving dish. Pour the dressing over and leave them to cool. Chill thoroughly before serving.

To ensure that the leeks are completely clean, slit them down one side with the point of a knife.

Leeks with Rice
This dish, originally from Greece, can be served as an accompaniment to sausages, hamburgers or grilled meat. As a variation, the leeks may be topped with grated cheese or accompanied by a rich tomato sauce.

SERVES FOUR
4 tablespoons olive oil
1 garlic clove, finely chopped
1 lb (½ kg) trimmed leeks, sliced
2 tablespoons tomato purée
1 teaspoon sugar
1 tablespoon lemon juice
1 teaspoon dried mixed herbs
Salt
Freshly ground black pepper
¾ pint (375 ml) water or chicken stock
½ lb (¼ kg) long grain rice, washed,
 soaked in cold water for 30 minutes
 and drained

Heat the olive oil in a large saucepan. Add the garlic and cook, stirring, over low heat for 1 minute. Add the leeks and cook, stirring, for 5 minutes. Stir in the tomato purée, sugar, lemon juice, herbs and salt and pepper to taste.

Pour in the water or stock and bring to the boil. Reduce the heat. Cover the pan and simmer for 10 minutes, or until the leeks are slightly tender.

Pour in the rice. Increase the heat to high and bring the mixture to the boil. Allow the rice to boil rapidly for 1 minute. Cover the pan, reduce the heat to very low and simmer for 15 to 20 minutes, or until the rice is cooked and all the liquid has been absorbed.

Correct the seasoning and serve.

Wash the leeks under cold running water until all traces of dirt have been removed.

Roots

In the past, the great advantage of root vegetables was that, with few exceptions, they could be pulled and stored in a cellar to tide the household over the winter months. But even today, with so many imported vegetables bringing variety to winter diets, root vegetables provide a cheap and nourishing staple.

The most important root vegetable—because of its nutritious properties and its culinary uses—is the carrot. Once considered a "bad weed" —its family connection with hemlock probably did not help—it is now a popular year-round vegetable and an essential ingredient in stocks, sauces and garnishes.

At the other end of the scale is the once-popular rampion, which has all but disappeared. Now known only in fairy tales, it was probably ousted from its commanding position by the arrival of the potato, and is now ripe for revival.

Parsnips, sweet, floury and filling, are an excellent vegetable. In the past, skirrets were confused with parsnips. Many chroniclers judged them to be the most delicious of all the roots, and Gerard pronounced them "sweet, white, good to be eaten and most pleasant in taste", which they are when scraped, parboiled then cooked in sizzling butter, or simmered to tenderness and dressed with butter or served in a creamy white sauce.

If the sweetness of parsnip and skirret is not to your taste, try the turnip-rooted chervil, also known as parsnip chervil. This vegetable deserves greater recognition. Chervil should be washed, never scraped. Steam or simmer the roots in salted water for about 30 minutes and serve them with butter or cream.

Everyone knows turnips, and their young, yellow-fleshed cousins, swedes, which Americans call rutabagas. But not everyone appreciates that the smaller they are the more delicate they will be. Swedes may be used in any of the recipes suitable for turnips or kohlrabi. Kohlrabi, which like the turnips and swedes belongs to the brassica family, is difficult to classify in culinary terms. It is definitely not like cabbage. Its flavour is, if anything, closer to that of turnip. Kohlrabi can swell to a great size. Resist the temptation to let them do so. Ideally, pull kohlrabi when they are about 2 inches (5 cm) in diameter. Strip off the leaves, wash the bulbs and steam them whole for about 20 minutes. Or peel and slice or quarter the bulbs and steam-boil them in a tightly covered pan for about 15 minutes. They are excellent served with butter, cream sauce or a *hollandaise*. You can also hollow them out, stuff them with meat, replace the tops and simmer them in a little water or stock until they are soft. Serve the stuffed kohlrabi with a savoury tomato or lemon

sauce diluted with the cooking stock or water.

Beetroots are an ancient vegetable, originally cultivated solely for their vivid young leaves. It was the Romans who finally discovered that their roots were equally delicious. Today, we happily eat both. And it is accepted that although the beetroot came originally from the regions around the Mediterranean and the Caspian, it thrives best in cooler climates, hence its prominence in the cuisines of northern Europe and North America.

Celeriac, a relative of the carrot, tastes and looks like a greatly magnified celery root. Although it is justly prized throughout Europe, it unfortunately receives less attention in Britain. Another knobbly root, Hamburg parsley, is also less well-known in the Anglo-Saxon world. On the Continent, it has been looked on with favour since ancient times, particularly in northern countries, where leaf parsley cannot survive the cold of winter in the open.

The strange, pale root, too long and thin and smooth to be mistaken for a parsnip, is salsify, also known as the vegetable oyster. How it got its nickname is a mystery, since it is impossible to find any resemblance to oysters either in its flavour or its texture. But it is very good indeed, and has a long and distinguished history. Scorzonera is similar to salsify, except for its rather dramatic black skin. Under this sombre exterior, however, the root is white and tastes as delicious as its cousin. Its name, which comes from the Catalan word for viper, is a reminder that scorzonera was once grown as an antidote for snake bites. Today, it is cooked in the same way as salsify. The third root in this group, scolymus, otherwise known as the Spanish oyster plant, is a member of the thistle family, with prickles to prove it. The roots are prepared like salsify, while the leaves may be cooked like cardoons. The salsify/scorzonera/scolymus tribe are grossly underrated, but as cooks become more inquisitive and gardeners more adventurous, they will regain their place in our kitchen gardens. Rampion's long fleshy roots may also be cooked in the same way as salsify.

Radish and horseradish stand apart from the rest of the roots, since both of them are considered condiments and "accessories" rather than vegetables in their own right. In the Orient, however, radishes occupy an important position in the cuisine. They may be red, white and even black, like the great Japanese *daikon*.

Although our gardens rarely provide more than a row of radishes at a time for the salad bowl or the drinks tray, radishes make an appealing snack served chilled with fresh butter and coarse salt or hollowed out and stuffed with a creamy cheese mixture.

Parsnips

Parsnips look like ghostly carrots, but there the similarity ends. If anything, they taste more like sweet potatoes with a touch of turnip.

The natural sweetness of parsnips makes a perfect marriage with butter and cream. But the simplest and one of the best ways to cook parsnips is to parboil them for 5 minutes, skin them, thickly slice or quarter them—if the parsnips are old remove the hard core—and then roast them. They may be put in the roasting tin with a joint to soak up the meaty flavour or brushed with fat and roasted in a shallow pan, which makes them crisper.

Young parsnips may also be steamed for about 35 minutes and then served with a cream sauce. Or they may be steamed, peeled, sliced, dipped in a fritter batter and fried. They may also be mashed with milk, flour and egg and dropped in spoonfuls into hot fat. Parsnips combine well with other root vegetables in a purée.

Parsnips in Cheese Sauce
In this dish the sweetness of the parsnips is counterbalanced by the sharpness of the creamy sauce.

SERVES FOUR
1 lb (½ kg) parsnips
Salt
1 oz (30 g) butter
2 tablespoons flour
¼ pint (125 ml) hot milk
¼ pint (125 ml) single cream
2 oz (60 g) Gruyère or sharp Cheddar cheese, freshly grated
Lemon juice

Scrub the parsnips and boil them in salted water for 12 to 15 minutes, or until just tender.

Meanwhile, melt the butter in a heavy pan. Blend in the flour and stir over a low heat for 1 minute to make a pale *roux*. Gradually add the hot milk, stirring vigorously to prevent lumps forming. Blend in the cream and bring to the boil, stirring, and simmer very gently for 4 minutes. Then beat in the cheese. When the cheese has melted, season to taste with salt and sharpen the flavour with a good squeeze of lemon juice.

Drain the cooked parsnips in a colander. As soon as they are cool enough to handle, peel them and slice them thickly, leaving the thin ends in one or two pieces.

Fold the parsnips into the sauce and reheat gently. Correct seasoning. Serve the parsnips as they are, or put them into a *gratin* dish, sprinkle with a little more cheese mixed with coarse, dry breadcrumbs, and brown the top under a hot grill.

Glazed Parsnips

SERVES FOUR
8 parsnips
Salt
2 oz (60 g) butter
2 tablespoons light-brown sugar
Juice of 1 large orange
2 tablespoons lemon juice
Generous pinch nutmeg or mace
Freshly ground black pepper

Scrub the parsnips with a stiff brush. Trim them top and bottom, and boil in salted water until barely tender—about 12 minutes. Drain the parsnips thoroughly and allow them to cool. Peel them and slice off the thin root ends, leaving them in one or two pieces. Slice the thicker ends in half lengthwise.

Put the butter, sugar, orange juice and lemon juice into a wide, heavy pan. Stir over low heat. When the butter has melted and the sugar has dissolved, stir in the nutmeg or mace.

Put the pieces of parsnip in the pan, turning them to coat them with the buttery juices. Season with salt and a grinding of pepper. Cook over low heat, partially covered, until the parsnips are glazed on all sides and have absorbed the juices. Serve hot.

Parsnip and Cheese Roast
This dish makes a substantial main course served with a fresh green salad. The bacon may be left out if desired.

SERVES FOUR TO SIX
2 lb (1 kg) parsnips
Salt
2 oz (60 g) butter
4 slices smoked streaky bacon, chopped
1 medium-sized onion, finely chopped
¼ lb (120 g) Cheddar cheese, grated
8 tablespoons double cream
Freshly ground black pepper
TO FINISH DISH
6 slices smoked streaky bacon, halved
2 oz (60 g) Cheddar cheese, grated
4 tablespoons porridge oats or coarse, fresh breadcrumbs

Scrub the parsnips and boil them in salted water for 15 minutes, or until they are tender.

Meanwhile, melt the butter in a frying-pan. Add the bacon and onion and fry until the onion is soft and transparent. Set aside.

Preheat the oven to 425°F (220°C, Gas Mark 7).

Drain the cooked parsnips in a colander. Rinse them with cold water and, as soon as they are cool enough to handle, trim them and rub off their skins with your fingers. Chop the parsnips and add them to the pan with the bacon and onions. Using a fork, mash the mixture to a purée. Then beat in the cheese, cream and salt and pepper to taste.

Turn the parsnip mixture into a buttered baking dish and with a spatula pat it into a smooth cake. Stick the halved slices of bacon around the sides of the cake and sprinkle the top thickly with a mixture of cheese and porridge oats or breadcrumbs.

Bake on the top shelf of the oven for 20 to 25 minutes, or until the topping is a bubbling golden crust. Serve hot.

Fried Parsnips and Potatoes with Eggs
An economical but unusual lunch or supper dish.

SERVES FOUR
1 lb (½ kg) parsnips, scraped
1 lb (½ kg) potatoes, peeled
Salt
6 slices fat bacon, chopped
1 oz (30 g) butter
4 eggs
Freshly ground black pepper

Cut the parsnips and potatoes into slices of the same thickness. Boil them in separate pans of salted water for 6 to 8 minutes, or until they are barely tender. Drain them in the same colander and leave to cool.

In a large, heavy frying-pan that has a cover, sauté the chopped bacon in butter until the fat is transparent. Add the parsnip and potato slices, and fry them steadily until they are a rich golden colour, turning them over and over with a spatula.

Spread the slices evenly in the pan. Make four hollows in the surface and carefully break the eggs into them. Season with salt and pepper. Cover the pan and continue to cook until the eggs are set to your taste. Serve straight from the frying-pan.

Carrots

Sweet young carrots, not more than two or three inches (5 or 8 cm) long and topped with green, feathery fronds, are a delicacy from the kitchen garden that those who have to rely on the supermarket can never know. Such young carrots are best steamed briefly and served with plenty of butter, chopped fresh herbs—parsley, chervil, mint, marjoram or dill, for example—and perhaps a squeeze of lemon and a pinch of sugar.

Because most of the vitamins in vegetables are only skin deep, carrots should never be peeled, even when mature. A good scrub with a stiff brush under running water is usually all that is necessary. If you must peel old carrots, however, rub the skin off after cooking.

Only when carrots are mature and ready to go into winter storage should they be used to make such dishes as soups, purées and soufflés. And this is when you will discover how magnificently their flavour is partnered by orange, spices and herbs, including caraway and dill seed.

Traditional recipes for Christmas pudding often wisely include grated raw carrot. Just 1 ounce (30 g) of grated carrot is enough to help keep a 2-pound (1 kg) pudding deliciously moist over a long period. Old cookery books included many recipes for sweet carrot puddings, pies and jams. Such imaginative use of carrots went out of culinary fashion until the Second World War, when housewives, deprived of sugar, turned to carrots to make a tart or cake for the rare family treat.

A little grated carrot mixed with the minced meat for hamburgers makes them lighter and juicier. And plain boiled rice looks unusually attractive if a little raw carrot is grated coarsely and forked into it shortly before serving.

Nothing could be simpler or more refreshing than a salad of coarsely grated carrots dressed with olive oil and lemon juice, salt and a pinch or two of sugar. Or try a carrot and red currant salad. Grate $\frac{1}{2}$ pound ($\frac{1}{4}$ kg) of carrots coarsely into a bowl. Add $\frac{1}{4}$ pound (120 g) of ripe red currants, stripped from their stalks and, only if necessary, washed and drained thoroughly on paper towels. Toss lightly. Sweeten to taste with sugar, dress with lemon juice and toss again. Serve chilled on a bed of lettuce leaves.

Carrots and apples are natural partners. Coarsely grate 1 pound ($\frac{1}{2}$ kg) of carrots and 3 ounces (90 g) of tart dessert apples into a bowl containing $\frac{1}{4}$ pint (125 ml) of soured cream or double cream. Mix in about 1 tablespoon of horseradish sauce, a generous pinch of sugar and salt to taste. Toss the salad lightly but thoroughly and serve garnished with sprigs of parsley, or fresh, crisp watercress.

Carrots Hollandaise

A luxurious but easy dish. The carrots may be cooked in advance, then reheated in the butter and mixed with the egg sauce just before serving.

If it is more convenient, put the sliced, cooked carrots with the butter and sugar in a shallow baking dish in a moderate oven to finish cooking. Then stir in the egg-and-cream mixture and return the dish to the oven for about 1 minute longer to allow the sauce to thicken without curdling.

SERVES FOUR
1 lb ($\frac{1}{2}$ kg) long, thin carrots
Salt
Chicken stock (optional)
2 oz (60 g) butter
2 teaspoons sugar
2 egg yolks
3 tablespoons double cream
2 tablespoons finely chopped parsley
Freshly ground black pepper

Scrub the carrots and steam them or simmer them in a very little salted water or stock for 10 to 12 minutes, or until they are barely tender. Put them in a colander and pour cold water over them until they are cool enough to handle. Trim the carrots and rub off the skins. Cut the carrots into 2-inch (5 cm) pieces and then slice them thinly lengthwise.

Melt the butter in a heavy pan. Carefully mix in the carrot slices, sprinkling them with the sugar as you do so. Cook over very low heat, shaking the pan occasionally, until the carrots are tender.

Before serving, beat the egg yolks with the cream. Mix in the parsley, salt and pepper to taste.

Remove the pan of carrots from the heat. Pour in the egg mixture and stir gently until it has thickened and amalgamated with the buttery juices to make a rich, creamy sauce. If necessary, return the pan to very low heat for 1 minute to allow the sauce to thicken without curdling. Alternatively, stand the pan in a larger one of barely simmering water to finish the sauce. Serve immediately.

Buttered Carrots and Mushrooms

A tasty accompaniment for poultry or roast lamb.

SERVES FOUR
1 lb ($\frac{1}{2}$ kg) carrots
Salt
1½ oz (45 g) butter
1 tablespoon oil
1 small onion, finely chopped
1 garlic clove, crushed
$\frac{1}{4}$ lb (120 g) button mushrooms, thickly sliced
1 whole cardamom pod, lightly crushed
Pinch of dried rosemary
Freshly ground black pepper

Scrub or scrape the carrots. Trim, and slice them at a slant. Steam the carrots or simmer in salted water for 5 minutes, or until the slices are barely tender. Drain well.

While the carrots are cooking, heat the butter and oil in another pan. Add the onion and garlic and fry, stirring constantly, until the onion is soft and lightly coloured. Add the mushrooms and, stirring to coat them with the butter, fry for 2 to 3 minutes longer until they are golden.

Mix in the carrots. Add the cardamom pod (crushed in a garlic press), the rosemary and salt and pepper to taste. Mix well. Cover the pan tightly and cook over very low heat for 15 minutes longer to develop and blend the flavours.

"The Yellow Carrot has a large long Root, great or thick, and yellow, big above and small pointed below, without any Fangs or Twines, of a pleasant sweet Taste, and therefore generally spent for Food."

The English Herbal *by William Salmon, M.D., 1710*

Nothing could be simpler or more refreshing than a salad of coarsely grated carrots dressed with olive oil and lemon juice, salt and a pinch or two of sugar.

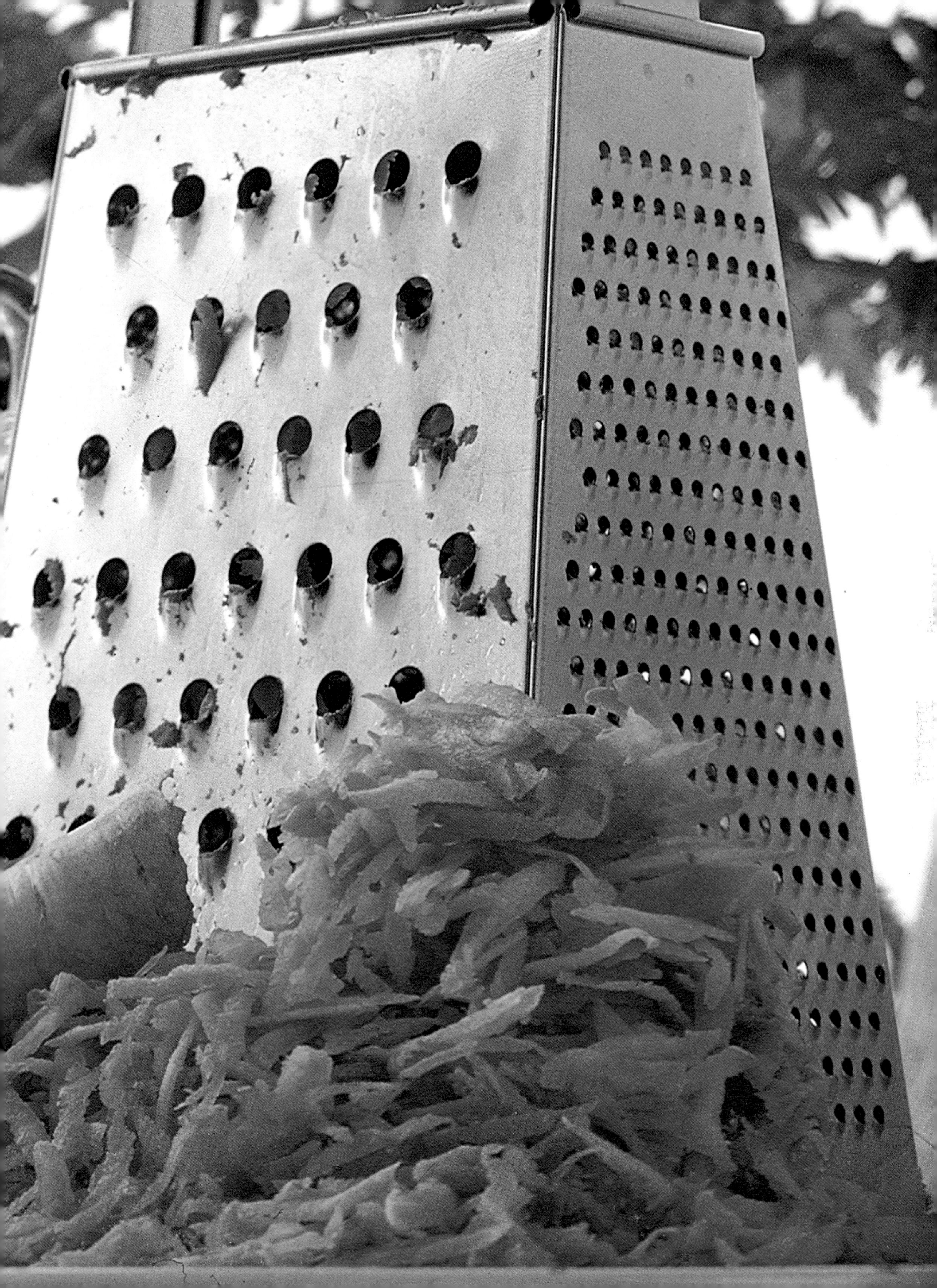

"Both seed and root are . . . good against the bitings of Venomous Beasts, Wind, and rising of the Mother."

The English Herbal *by William Salmon, M.D., 1710*

Marinated Herbed Carrots

This salad is made with cooked carrots. Since the dressing provides a rich flavour, more mature carrots may be used if they are not woody.

SERVES FOUR
½ lb (¼ kg) carrots
Sugar
Salt
1 tablespoon tarragon vinegar
¼ teaspoon Dijon mustard
4 tablespoons olive oil
1 small garlic clove, crushed
1 tablespoon finely chopped parsley
2 teaspoons finely chopped chives or spring onion tops
1 teaspoon chopped fresh thyme
Freshly ground black pepper
Lemon juice

Trim and scrub or scrape the carrots and cut them into 1½-inch (3 cm) long matchstick strips. Put them in a pan. Add 2 teaspoons of sugar, ½ teaspoon of salt and just enough water to cover. Bring to the boil and cook steadily, uncovered, for 5 minutes. The carrot strips should still retain their crispness. Set aside.

Prepare the dressing in a medium-sized bowl. Mix the vinegar and mustard together. Then beat in the olive oil, 1 tablespoon at a time, to make a creamy mixture. Stir in the garlic and herbs.

Drain the carrots thoroughly and while they are still hot mix them gently with the dressing. Season with salt and pepper, adding more sugar if wished. If necessary sharpen the flavour of the salad with about 1 tablespoon of lemon juice. Chill the salad for several hours before serving. The carrots will absorb most of the dressing.

Carrot Halva

This Indian sweet is traditionally decorated with edible silver leaf. Serve it at room temperature, accompanied by a jug of unsweetened double cream.

SERVES EIGHT
1 lb (½ kg) carrots, trimmed and scraped
3 pints (1½ litres) milk
¾ lb (360 g) sugar
2 tablespoons golden syrup
6 oz (180 g) unsalted butter
2 tablespoons blanched slivered almonds
Seeds of 12 cardamoms, coarsely crushed in a mortar

Grate the carrots into the milk in a heavy pan. Bring it to the boil over moderate heat. Lower the heat and cook steadily, stirring frequently, for 1½ to 2 hours, or until the mixture is very thick. Be careful not to let it burn.

Add the sugar, golden syrup and butter, and cook over low heat, stirring frequently, for 20 to 30 minutes, or until the mixture is thick and starts coming away from the sides of the pan.

Spread the *halva* evenly in a buttered, shallow dish. Sprinkle the top with the almonds and cardamoms.

Serve lukewarm.

Creamed Carrots with Peas

SERVES FOUR
1 lb (½ kg) young carrots
1 lb (½ kg) shelled peas
Pinch of sugar
½ pint (250 ml) chicken stock
2 tablespoons butter
2 tablespoons flour
3 tablespoons double cream (optional)
Salt
Freshly ground black pepper
CROUTONS
1 egg beaten with 2 tablespoons milk
Salt
Freshly ground black pepper
4 slices day-old French bread, ¾ inch (2 cm) thick
Fine, dry breadcrumbs
Butter and oil, for frying

Grate the carrots coarsely into a heavy pan. Add the peas and sprinkle with the sugar. Pour in the chicken stock and bring it to the boil. Reduce the heat, cover the pan tightly and simmer for 5 minutes.

Meanwhile, in another pan, melt the butter. Blend in the flour and stir over a low heat for 1 minute to make a pale *roux*.

Drain all the cooking liquid from the carrots and peas and add it gradually to the *roux*, stirring vigorously to prevent lumps forming. Gently mix the sauce with the carrots and peas. Cook over moderate heat, stirring constantly, until the sauce comes to the boil. Stir in the cream if used. Add salt and pepper to taste and more sugar if desired. Let the mixture bubble for 2 minutes longer.

Cover the pan and keep the vegetables hot while you prepare the croûtons.

Lightly season the beaten egg and milk with salt and pepper. Dip each side of the slices of bread into the mixture. Then coat each slice with dry breadcrumbs. Fry the bread slices in a mixture of butter and oil until they are crisp and a rich golden colour on both sides.

To serve, divide the carrots and peas between 4 heated plates and garnish each portion with a croûton. Serve immediately.

Carrot Cake

This is an unusual and delicious cake. No one will guess that it is carrot which contributes both the rich colour and the moistness. The cake is even better if left for a day or two before it is iced and eaten. A more luxurious Swiss carrot cake, made with ground almonds instead of flour, is traditionally decorated with tiny carrots made of marzipan. The cake may also be served without icing, in which case it should be baked in a loaf tin or an 8-inch (20 cm) cake tin for about 40 minutes.

ONE 8-INCH (20 CM) LAYER CAKE
6 oz (180 g) plain flour
2 teaspoons baking powder
1 teaspoon ground cinnamon
Mace
¼ teaspoon salt
¼ lb (120 g) grated carrots
Grated rind of ½ orange
2 tablespoons orange juice
¼ lb (120 g) softened butter
5 oz (150 g) castor sugar
2 eggs
2 oz (60 g) hazelnuts, toasted, skinned and coarsely chopped (optional)
Lemon-, orange- or caramel-flavoured icing, made with ¾ lb (360 g) sugar

Butter two 8-inch (20 cm) layer-cake tins and line the bottoms with discs of buttered greaseproof paper. Preheat the oven to 350°F (180°C, Gas Mark 4).

Sift the flour with the baking powder, cinnamon, a pinch of mace and salt. Mix the grated carrots with the orange rind and juice. Put aside until needed.

Cream the butter. Gradually beat in the sugar and continue beating until the mixture is white and fluffy. Beat in the eggs one at a time.

With a wooden spoon, beat in the carrot and orange mixture. Mix in the flour and spices, and the chopped hazelnuts if used.

Divide the mixture equally between the prepared cake tins, smoothing the batter evenly on top. Bake the layers for 30 minutes, or until they are well risen, firm to the touch and pulling away from the sides of the tins.

Cool the layers in the tins for at least 15 minutes. Turn them out on to wire racks and peel away the lining paper.

Sandwich the layers with half the icing. Then use the remainder to ice the top and sides of the cake.

Turnips

There are few vegetables for which thick peeling is to be encouraged. The turnip is one of the exceptions. Even young turnips seem to have a tough and fibrous protective outer layer. Once this has been removed, however, the vegetable which is left is marvellously delicate and juicy. If the turnip is young, steam it for 20 to 30 minutes. If the turnip is old, boil it in salted water for about 20 minutes if sliced or quartered and for 30 to 40 minutes if whole. Turnips take kindly to butter or a rich cream sauce flavoured with chives or spring-onion tops. Cut turnips into julienne strips, poach in light stock with an equal quantity of carrots, toss in melted butter and serve hot.

The flavour of turnip, light and subtle as it may seem, becomes surprisingly forceful when it is used in a bouquet of stock vegetables. Consequently it is best left out unless the turnips themselves are going to be served.

Spiced Turnips in Yoghourt

This unusually flavoured dish is a good accompaniment for grills and roasts.

SERVES SIX

2 lb (1 kg) young turnips, peeled
1½ oz (45 g) butter
Seeds of 6 cardamom pods, crushed
1 teaspoon turmeric
½ teaspoon ground coriander
1 garlic clove, crushed
6 tablespoons chicken stock
¼ pint (125 ml) yoghourt
Salt
Freshly ground black pepper
Lemon juice (optional)
Parsley, to garnish

Cut the turnips into quarters or sixths, depending upon their size. In a large, heavy pan, melt the butter and toss the turnip pieces in it to coat them well. Cook over moderate heat for about 5 minutes, or until the turnips are lightly coloured all over.

Stir in the spices and garlic. Add the chicken stock and all but 2 tablespoons of the yoghourt. Sprinkle lightly with salt and pepper and mix well. Put a piece of greaseproof paper down directly over the turnips, tucking it against the sides of the pan. Reduce the heat and simmer gently for 20 minutes, or until the turnips feel tender when pierced with a sharp fork or skewer.

Remove the greaseproof paper. Increase the heat to moderate and boil the turnips for about 5 minutes. By this time the liquid should have evaporated, leaving just enough to coat the turnips with a rich, savoury sauce.

Correct the seasoning. Stir in the remainder of the yoghourt and sprinkle with a squeeze of lemon juice if desired. Serve garnished with parsley.

Turnips in Cream

This is a most elegant dish, which may be served with roast turkey, capon or any of the meats. It is particularly delicious if the turnips used are young, small and sweet.

Unless the turnips are very small, about the size of golf balls, they should be quartered or cut into sixths.

SERVES SIX

2 lb (1 kg) young turnips, peeled
¼ pint (125 ml) double cream
5 tablespoons chicken stock
½ teaspoon dried basil
¼ teaspoon sugar
Salt
Freshly ground black pepper
1 teaspoon cornflour
2 tablespoons finely chopped parsley

Put the turnips in a large, heavy pan. Blend the cream with the chicken stock and pour the mixture over the turnips. Add the basil, sugar and salt and pepper to taste. Mix well and bring to simmering point over low heat. Cover the pan tightly and cook gently for 25 to 30 minutes, or until the turnips can be easily pierced with a sharp fork or skewer.

Remove the pan from the heat and, with a slotted spoon, transfer the turnips to a heated serving dish. Keep hot.

Blend the cornflour to a smooth paste with 3 tablespoons of cold water and stir it into the liquid in the pan. Return the pan to the heat and cook, stirring, until the sauce comes to simmering point and thickens slightly. Taste and correct the seasoning if necessary.

Pour the sauce over the turnips. Sprinkle with parsley and serve.

Mustard-glazed Turnips

A fine accompaniment for such meats as lamb, pork or ham, mustard-glazed turnips may also be served with vegetable pies, flans or cutlets. Depending on your partiality for strong flavours, increase the amount of mustard used, but never use English mustard.

SERVES SIX

2 oz (60 g) butter
2 lb (1 kg) young turnips, peeled
¼ pint (125 ml) chicken stock
1 teaspoon Demerara sugar
Salt
Freshly ground black pepper
2 teaspoons Dijon mustard
2 tablespoons finely chopped parsley

In a large, heavy pan melt the butter over low heat until it is frothy. Add the turnips, turning them to coat them well. Cook over moderate heat for about 10 minutes, shaking the pan frequently so that the turnips turn an even, deep-golden colour. Reduce the heat to low.

Pour in the stock and add the sugar, salt and pepper to taste. When the stock comes to simmering point, cover the pan tightly. Cook the turnips over low heat, shaking the pan occasionally, for 20 minutes, or until they feel tender when pierced with a sharp fork or skewer.

Using a slotted spoon, transfer the turnips to a plate. Stir the mustard into the pan juices and correct seasoning if necessary. Return the turnips to the pan and reheat them, swirling them around to coat them with the glaze. Sprinkle with parsley and serve.

Salsify, Scorzonera & Kohlrabi

Salsify, scorzonera and kohlrabi share a delicate, turnipy flavour. Salsify and scorzonera are best cooked as simply as possible—poached in salted water for about 15 minutes until barely tender, then well seasoned and finished in butter or folded into a well-flavoured *béchamel* sauce. Some people maintain that because so much flavour lies just under the skin, the roots should not be scraped or cut into chunks until they have been cooked, but in some cases it is more convenient to scrape and cut them before cooking. If the roots are scraped before cooking they should be put in acidulated water to prevent discoloration.

Kohlrabi, when young and small, can be eaten raw, peeled and coarsely grated into a mixed vegetable salad. To cook kohlrabi, either peel it thinly and steam or simmer it in water, or cook it first and then peel it. In either case the cooking time will be approximately 30 minutes.

Salsify Fritters

There is more than one way to make salsify fritters. Short lengths of boiled salsify can be dipped in batter and deep-fried in oil until crisp and golden. The method given here is more complicated, but worth the effort.

SERVES FOUR

1½ lb (¾ kg) salsify or scorzonera
Lemon juice
Salt
1 oz (30 g) butter
1 egg plus 1 egg yolk, lightly beaten
Freshly ground black pepper
Butter and oil, for frying

Quarter each salsify root crosswise. Scrape each piece, immediately dropping it into a bowl of water acidulated with lemon juice. Simmer the salsify in salted water for about 15 minutes, or until they are soft but not mushy when pierced with a fork.

Drain the salsify. Return the salsify pieces to the pan and shake it briefly over moderate heat to dry them out as much as possible. Then mash them to a purée, adding the butter. When the purée has cooled slightly, beat in the eggs. Season to taste with salt and pepper. Chill the mixture thoroughly; it will stiffen and become manageable.

Heat a mixture of butter and oil in a frying pan. Drop heaped tablespoonfuls of the salsify mixture into the hot fat, flattening them out into round little cakes. Fry them, turning them once, until they are crisp and golden on both sides.

Serve hot, sprinkled with lemon juice.

Stuffed Kohlrabi

When kohlrabi are out of season, young turnips may be substituted.

SERVES SIX

6 fist-sized kohlrabi
Salt
Butter
1 small onion, finely chopped
1 garlic clove, crushed
½ lb (¼ kg) lean pork, minced
1 egg, lightly beaten
1 teaspoon tomato concentrate
3 oz (90 g) trimmed brown bread,
    soaked in milk
Freshly ground black pepper
¾ pint (375 ml) chicken stock
1 oz (30 g) flour
Juice of ½ lemon
Finely chopped parsley, to garnish

Trim the kohlrabi, cutting off the stalks and shaving the bases so that each bulb will sit steadily. Peel the kohlrabi thinly. Cut a slice off the tops and scoop out the centres to make cups about ⅓ inch (1 cm) thick. Finely chop half of the scooped-out flesh and put it aside.

Place a steamer over a pan of simmering water. Arrange the kohlrabi cups upside down in the steamer. Sprinkle them with salt. Cover the pan and steam for 10 minutes.

Preheat the oven to 375°F (190°C, Gas Mark 5).

Prepare the stuffing. In a medium-sized saucepan, heat 1 ounce (30 g) of butter. Add the onion, garlic and chopped kohlrabi and fry, stirring occasionally, until they have softened and are lightly coloured. Remove the pan from the heat. Mix in the pork, egg and tomato concentrate. Squeeze the bread dry. Crumble it into the pan and mix it in well. Season to taste with salt and pepper.

Arrange the steamed kohlrabi cups side by side in a buttered baking dish. Put a flake of butter in the bottom of each cup and stuff them with the meat mixture. Pour ½ pint (250 ml) of the stock around the kohlrabi. Cover the dish loosely with foil and bake on the top shelf of the oven for 20 minutes. Uncover the dish, baste with the cooking juices and bake for a further 15 minutes until the kohlrabi are tender and the stuffing is cooked through.

With a slotted spoon, transfer the kohlrabi to a hot serving dish. Keep hot.

Melt 1 ounce (30 g) of butter in a small saucepan. Blend in the flour and stir over low heat for about 4 minutes to make a nutty brown *roux*. Gradually blend in the remaining stock, beating vigorously to prevent lumps forming. Add the juices left in the baking dish and a few drops of lemon juice to taste. Bring the sauce to the boil and simmer for 2 minutes. Correct the seasoning. Spoon the sauce over the kohlrabi, garnish with parsley and serve.

Salsify au Gratin

SERVES FOUR TO SIX

2½ lb (1¼ kg) salsify or scorzonera
Lemon juice
Salt
1 teaspoon sugar
1½ oz (45 g) butter
1 oz (30 g) flour
½ pint (250 ml) hot milk
¼ chicken stock cube
2 egg yolks
1 oz (30 g) Gruyère or Emmenthal
    cheese, freshly grated

Scrape the salsify and cut them into 2-inch (5 cm) lengths, quickly dropping them into water acidulated with lemon juice to prevent them discolouring. Fill a saucepan with water, add salt and the sugar and bring to the boil. Drop in the salsify and simmer for 15 to 20 minutes, or until the chunks are tender when pierced with a skewer. Drain well.

Preheat the oven to 350°F (180°C, Gas Mark 4).

Prepare the sauce. Melt the butter in a heavy saucepan. Blend in the flour and stir over low heat for 1 minute to make a pale *roux*. Gradually add the milk, beating vigorously to prevent lumps forming. Stir in the piece of stock cube. Bring the sauce to the boil and let it simmer gently, stirring occasionally, for 15 minutes. Remove the pan from the heat.

Beat the egg yolks lightly. Gradually beat a few tablespoons of the hot sauce into the yolks, then pour the mixture back into the pan. Flavour with a few drops of lemon juice and season to taste with salt.

Fold the salsify into the sauce. Pour the mixture into a *gratin* dish. Sprinkle with the cheese and bake for 15 minutes or until the salsify is heated through and the cheese on top has melted and begun to colour slightly.

Beetroots

When beetroots are very young, both the tops and the roots make good eating. The tops may be used for soup or they may also be cooked in the same way as spinach.

To prepare beetroots, first cut off the tops, leaving about 1 inch (2 cm) of stem. Wash them in cold water, taking care not to pierce the skin, or the beetroots will "bleed" as they cook. Drop the beetroots into boiling salted water and cook for 45 minutes to 1½ hours if the beetroots are small to medium in size, longer if they are large. Test to see if they are ready—carefully lift out a beetroot and press it gently with your fingers. If the skin slips off easily, the beetroot is cooked. Alternatively, the beetroots may be baked. Put them in a baking dish and bake in the oven at 325°F (160°C, Gas Mark 3). The timing is the same as for boiling. Cooked beetroots may be pickled in vinegar or sliced, flavoured with orange and served in a soured-cream sauce.

Harvard Beets

This is a classic American recipe. Harvard Beets, according to some American cook books, can be changed to Yale Beets by substituting fresh orange juice plus 1 tablespoon of lemon juice for the vinegar.

SERVES FOUR TO SIX
1½ lb (¾ kg) beetroot, cooked
2½ oz (75 g) sugar
1 tablespoon cornflour
6 tablespoons mild wine or cider
    vinegar
Salt
1 oz (30 g) butter

Trim the beetroots, rub off their skins and slice them thinly.

In the top of a double saucepan, blend the sugar and cornflour with the vinegar. Cook over low heat, stirring constantly, until the mixture comes to the boil and thickens.

Set the top part of the pan over simmering water. Carefully mix the prepared beetroots into the sauce. Season to taste with salt and cook gently, stirring occasionally, for 25 to 30 minutes, until the beetroots are hot and the sauce is a deep red.

Add the butter, stirring until it has melted. Serve immediately.

Christmas Beetroot Barszcz

There are numerous versions of barszcz, or borshch, most of them originating in eastern Europe. They range from light consommés, like this recipe, to thick vegetable soups reinforced with dried beans and chunks of meat. A Christmas barszcz is traditionally served in Poland on Christmas Eve, when meat is not allowed. It is garnished with tiny "ears", or dumplings, stuffed with a mixture of chopped dried mushrooms, onions and breadcrumbs. An Easter barszcz is, however, based on a light ham stock. All clear beetroot soups taste better garnished with a spoonful of thick soured cream.

SERVES SIX
6 beetroot, scrubbed, peeled and
    thickly sliced
2 large carrots, cut into large pieces
2 leeks, cut into pieces
1 small onion, quartered
1 slice celeriac
8 black peppercorns
3 allspice berries
1 bay leaf
2 dried mushroom caps
Salt
TO FINISH BARSZCZ
1 raw beetroot
Juice of ½ lemon
1 tablespoon sugar
2 teaspoons salt

Put all the vegetables, spices, bay leaf and mushroom caps in a large enamelled saucepan. Cover with 3 pints (1½ litres) of cold water. Sprinkle generously with salt. Bring to simmering point over moderate heat. Reduce the heat to low, cover the pan and simmer for 1 hour.

Meanwhile, scrub, peel and grate the raw beetroot coarsely into a bowl. Stir in the lemon juice, sugar and salt.

Strain the barszcz through a fine sieve. Pour a few ladlefuls of it over the grated beetroot mixture. Then pour it all back into the pan, together with the rest of the strained stock. Reheat gently, but do not allow the barszcz to come to the boil or its brilliant red colour may be destroyed.

Strain the grated beetroot out of the soup. Correct the seasoning with sugar, salt or lemon juice, if necessary. Reheat gently before serving.

Creamed Beetroot

This dish is traditionally served with such strong game as venison or hare, and with pot-roasted beef.

SERVES FOUR
1 lb (½ kg) cooked beetroot
1 medium-sized, tart dessert apple,
    peeled and cored (optional)
½ oz (15 g) butter
2 teaspoons flour
Single cream
Sugar
Salt
Wine vinegar or lemon juice

Trim the cooked beetroot, rub off the skins and grate coarsely into a bowl (or put through a meat mincer). Grate the apple, if used, into the same bowl.

Melt the butter in a heavy pan. Blend in the flour and stir over a low heat for 1 minute to make a pale roux. Remove the pan from the heat and gradually beat in 8 tablespoons of cream. Continue to beat until smoothly blended. Mix in the grated beetroot and apple. Add sugar and salt to taste and sharpen the flavour with vinegar or lemon juice.

Bring to simmering, stirring constantly. If the purée is too stiff, thin it with a little more cream. Simmer gently, uncovered, stirring occasionally, for a few minutes before serving.

Celeriac

Rough and knobbly as it may appear, celeriac is a marvellous vegetable for adding a fresh flavour to winter dishes. And it is very adaptable. Raw and coarsely grated, it may be added with advantage to many salads—for a more delicate flavour blanch the celeriac for 2 minutes in acidulated water. Cooked, it is not only a potent celery flavouring for stocks, sauces and stews, but it is also a fine vegetable in its own right.

Celeriac at its best should be the size of a large cooking apple, firm and unblemished. To prepare celeriac for cooking, trim and slice it, then peel it, dropping it immediately into acidulated water. If the celeriac is to be cooked whole, trim and scrub it and then cook it, peeling it later. Boil sliced or diced celeriac in salted, acidulated water for 25 to 30 minutes. Whole celeriac will take from 40 minutes to 1 hour to cook.

Celeriac may be served simply tossed in melted butter or dressed in a *mornay* sauce.

Celeriac and Ham Salad

The classic French version of this salad, *Céleri-rave à la Rémoulade*, simply combines coarsely grated raw celeriac with a mustard mayonnaise. This recipe makes a more substantial but equally piquant and delicious dish.

SERVES FOUR
¾ lb (360 g) celeriac root
Salt
1 egg yolk
2 teaspoons Dijon mustard
2 teaspoons tarragon vinegar
8 tablespoons olive oil

Freshly ground black pepper
¼ lb (120 g) lean cooked ham, cubed
2 medium-sized carrots, coarsely grated
2 tablespoons finely chopped parsley
Lettuce leaves, to garnish

Scrub the celeriac root thoroughly under cold running water. Drop it into a large pan of rapidly boiling salted water and boil for 30 minutes. The celeriac should still feel very firm when pierced with a skewer.

While the celeriac is cooking, put the egg yolk in a bowl. Blend in the mustard, vinegar and a pinch of salt. Beat in the olive oil, drop by drop at first, then in a thin stream as the mixture thickens. When all the oil has been incorporated, season to taste with salt and pepper. The mayonnaise should be highly flavoured.

Drain the cooked celeriac. As soon as it is cool enough to handle, peel it and cut it into neat cubes the same size as the ham.

Fold the warm celeriac, the ham, the carrots and parsley into the mayonnaise. Correct the seasoning if necessary. Serve very cold in a bowl lined with lettuce leaves.

Celeriac and Brussels Sprouts au Gratin

Celeriac and Brussels sprouts make a most attractive combination.

SERVES SIX
¾ lb (360 g) celeriac root
Salt
2½ oz (75 g) butter
1 onion, finely chopped
1 oz (30 g) flour
½ pint (250 ml) milk
¼ pint (125 ml) single cream
1 egg yolk
Freshly ground black pepper
Ground mace
1½ lb (¾ kg) Brussels sprouts, trimmed, cooked and halved lengthwise (see page 143)
2 tablespoons fresh white breadcrumbs

Scrub the celeriac under cold running water. Parboil it in salted water for 15 minutes. Drain it in a colander, then plunge it into cold water. As soon as the celeriac is cool enough to handle, peel it and cut it into ½-inch (1 cm) cubes.

Melt 2 ounces (60 g) of the butter in a saucepan. Add the celeriac cubes and onion and stir to mix. Cover the pan and cook over low heat for 15 minutes, shaking the pan or stirring occasionally to prevent the vegetables sticking to the bottom.

Sprinkle the vegetables with the flour and stir over low heat for 2 minutes to blend it with the buttery juices. Gradually stir in the milk. Bring to the boil and simmer for 2 minutes. Remove the pan from the heat.

Beat the cream and egg yolk together lightly. Blend them into the sauce. Season to taste with salt, pepper and a pinch of mace.

Preheat the oven to 350°F (180°C, Gas Mark 4).

Arrange half of the Brussels sprouts in a buttered baking dish. Pour over half of the celeriac and sauce. Cover with the remaining sprouts, followed by the remaining celeriac and sauce. Smooth the top with the back of a spoon. Sprinkle with the breadcrumbs and dot with the remaining butter.

Bake the dish in the top half of the oven for 25 minutes, or until the surface is golden and the vegetables are piping hot.

Celeriac Cups Stuffed with Mushrooms

An unusual dish which makes a delicious appetizer or an accompaniment for a meat dish, especially pork.

SERVES SIX
3 celeriac roots
1 lemon, halved
Salt
Melted butter
2 oz (60 g) butter
6 oz (180 g) button mushrooms, quartered or cut in eighths, depending on their size
3 spring onions, chopped
Freshly ground black pepper
2 tablespoons finely chopped parsley
2 tablespoons freshly grated Parmesan cheese
¼ pint (125 ml) thick soured cream
Paprika

Scrub, trim and peel the celeriac roots. Cut each root in half horizontally. Scoop out the flesh, reserving it, and leaving the cups ¼ inch (½ cm) thick. Rub the celeriac cups and the reserved flesh with a cut lemon half to prevent them discolouring.

Bring a large pan of salted water, acidulated with the juice of ½ lemon, to the boil. Put in the celeriac cups and simmer them gently, covered, for 10 minutes, or until they feel tender when tested with a skewer.

Drain them thoroughly. Brush them all over with melted butter and arrange them side by side in a baking dish.

Preheat the oven to 375°F (190°C, Gas Mark 5). Finely chop the reserved celeriac flesh. Melt the butter in a medium-sized saucepan. Stir in the celeriac, mushrooms and spring onions. Add the juice squeezed from the remaining half lemon. Mix well and season to taste with salt and pepper. Cover the pan and cook gently for 10 to 15 minutes, stirring occasionally. Remove the pan from the heat and stir in the parsley and cheese. Correct the seasoning.

Fill the celeriac cups with the mixture. Spoon soured cream over the top of each one and sprinkle with a pinch of paprika.

Bake the celeriac cups in the top half of the oven for 20 minutes. Serve hot.

Tubers

Tubers are a small but important group which includes the less well-known Jerusalem and Chinese artichokes as well as the potato, a giant among vegetables and a staple food in many countries.

The Jerusalem artichoke, a native of North America, is a knobbly, sweetish artichoke-flavoured tuber which adds variety to the winter diet. The Chinese or Japanese artichoke has a similar but more delicate flavour than the Jerusalem artichoke.

Surprisingly, the potato was not immediately accepted as a palatable vegetable. Although known in Europe by the sixteenth century, it was persistently treated as a curiosity.

The real hero of the potato saga is an eighteenth-century Frenchman, Antoine-Augustin Parmentier, who had a curious obsession for potatoes from early childhood. His missionary zeal was rewarded when Louis XVI appeared on the eve of the Feast of St Louis with potato flowers in his buttonhole. From then on, potatoes had arrived, at least as far as Louis's courtiers were concerned.

By the middle of the nineteenth century, cookery writers were taking the potato seriously too, and today it is calculated that there are nearly 500 different ways of serving potatoes.

Unfortunately, familiarity has bred contempt for the poor potato, and the everyday ways of serving them are not always as good as they might be. To cook potatoes well, however, depends primarily on the variety of potato. By and large, the guiding principle is that waxy potatoes are good for frying and floury potatoes are best for boiling.

Boiled potatoes, still called *pommes à l'anglaise* in menu French, rarely get the attention they deserve. To get the most flavour and nutrition from a potato, cook it in its jacket. If it must be peeled, then peel it very thinly, because most of the food value lies just under the skin. Boiling peeled potatoes in a large pot of water washes out even more goodness, so if possible steam them instead.

Once potatoes have been cooked and drained, dry them out by shaking them in a hot pan over low heat to steam off any remaining moisture.

The secret of really good puréed potatoes is freshness—they should be served as soon as they are ready. Cook, drain, dry out and peel the potatoes. Mash them smoothly, gradually beating in some nearly boiling milk and some butter —2 pounds (1 kg) of floury potatoes will take about ¼ pint (125 ml) of milk and 2 ounces (60 g) of butter. Beat the purée briskly over low heat until it is hot and fluffy. Season with salt, plenty of pepper and a light grating of nutmeg.

For baked potatoes, medium or large, floury white "old" potatoes are best. Scrub them clean, dry them and prick them with a fork in several places. Then rub them all over with a piece of buttered paper or, for an even crisper skin, use oil. Bake them at 350° to 375°F (180° to 190°C, Gas Mark 4 to 5) for at least an hour, or until they feel soft when pressed gently. Serve the baked potatoes immediately with plenty of butter and coarse salt—or with herb butter, or cream cheese mashed with garlic or herbs and a few tablespoons of cream.

The best way to roast potatoes is to have the fat (beef dripping or butter and oil) almost smoking hot before adding the potatoes, which have been peeled, cut into chunks and dried. Turn them over in the hot fat, sprinkle them with salt and roast them in a 400°F (200°C, Gas Mark 6) oven for 45 minutes, or until they are soft when pierced with a skewer, turning them regularly to build up an even, rich crust. For even more crust, parboil the potatoes for 5 minutes, dry them and score them with a sharp fork before adding them to the pan.

Deep-fried potatoes come in a variety of forms, from chips to *pommes allumettes* and *pommes pailles*, straw potatoes, and crisps or game chips, cut paper-thin on a mandoline cutter.

Use a proper deep-frying pan fitted with a basket. For safety's sake, never have the fat higher than 2 inches (5 cm) from the top. Beef dripping, lard, vegetable and olive oil each has something different to offer to the flavour of the potato. As a rough guide, you will need 3 pints (1½ litres) of oil or fat to fry about 2 pounds (1 kg) of chips. Finely cut potatoes (straws and crisps) should be fried in handfuls to give them enough room to float free.

Temperature is probably the one most important factor in deep-frying of any kind. For perfect chips, heat the fat to 350°F (180°C). The potatoes should be peeled, cut, rinsed and carefully dried. Put the potatoes into a frying basket, lower them into the fat carefully and deep-fry until they are soft and a pale golden colour—about 5 minutes. Drain them on kitchen paper and if they are not to be served immediately, wrap them in greaseproof paper. Then, shortly before serving, heat the fat to 425°F (220°C) and fry the potatoes for another 2 to 3 minutes, or until they are crisp, golden brown and dry. Drain again, sprinkle with salt and serve at once.

Thin-cut straw potatoes and crisps are fried once only, for about 3 minutes at 425°F (220°C).

Pommes Soufflés

These are the puff potatoes of classic French cuisine. They are rather tricky to make—and like so many of the best dishes they were discovered by accident. Apparently, the chef adding the final touches to a ceremonial dinner for the inauguration of the Paris–St Germain railway line in 1837 was suddenly told that the guests of honour, Louis-Philippe and his queen Marie-Amélie, would be late. The thinly sliced potato rectangles were already frying. He whipped them out, drained them and when the diners had assembled he plunged them back into even hotter fat. To the delight of all concerned, the shock of the contact with hot fat puffed the limp slices into crisp golden cushions.

If you wish to experiment with *pommes soufflés*, use good, old potatoes, preferably red-skinned ones. Cut them into paper-thin little oblongs, but do not rinse them. For the first frying, use oil at 275°F (140°C) and fry the potatoes briefly until they are soft but not coloured. For the second frying, heat the fat to 475°F (240°C). The potatoes should puff up and colour almost as soon as they touch the fat. But if all the slices do not puff up they can be served as crisps—even professional chefs admit to a high failure rate.

Potatoes Cooked with Yoghourt

This unusual and tasty Indian dish is a mixture of sweetness, sourness and spiciness.

SERVES FOUR TO SIX

3 tablespoons clarified butter or
   vegetable oil
1 medium-sized onion, finely chopped
1-inch (2 cm) piece fresh root ginger,
   peeled and finely chopped
1 tablespoon ground coriander
1 teaspoon turmeric
2 green chillies, finely chopped
3 medium-sized tomatoes, blanched,
   peeled and chopped
1 teaspoon salt
1 teaspoon sugar
½ pint (250 ml) yoghourt
¼ teaspoon ground mace
4 tablespoons raisins
1½ lb (¾ kg) small new potatoes, boiled
1 tablespoon chopped coriander leaves

Heat the butter or oil in a large frying-pan. Add the onion and ginger and fry, stirring, until golden. Add the coriander and turmeric and fry, stirring constantly, for 30 seconds. Stir in the chillies, tomatoes, salt, sugar and yoghourt. Simmer the sauce, uncovered, until it is thick.

Add the mace, raisins and potatoes and cook, stirring, for 5 minutes.

Turn the potatoes out on to a serving dish, sprinkle the coriander leaves on top and serve hot.

Buttered Potatoes and Mushrooms au Gratin

This is a very rich dish which goes particularly well with roast or grilled lamb or with scrambled eggs for supper.

SERVES FOUR TO SIX

2 lb (1 kg) potatoes
½ lb (¼ kg) small white mushrooms
1 tablespoon olive oil
¼ lb (120 g) butter
Salt
Freshly ground black pepper

Peel the potatoes and slice them very thinly. Spread the slices out on a cloth and pat them dry. Trim the mushroom stems. Wipe the mushrooms with a damp cloth and slice them thickly, stalks and all.

Preheat the oven to 375°F (190°C, Gas Mark 5).

Heat the oil and half the butter in a wide, shallow, flame-proof casserole. Add the mushrooms and toss them briefly over high heat so that they absorb most of the fat. Remove them to a bowl with a slotted spoon.

Melt 1 ounce (30 g) of the remaining butter in the hot casserole, swirling it around to coat the sides. Arrange an overlapping layer of the larger potato slices over the bottom of the casserole and a row of medium-sized slices around the sides. Replace the casserole over moderately low heat. Then alternate two layers of mushrooms and their juices with layers of potato, ending with a neat, overlapping layer of potato. Sprinkle each layer with salt and pepper. Dot the top with the remaining butter.

Bake the casserole for 40 minutes, or until the potatoes feel soft when pierced right through with the point of a sharp knife or skewer, and are crisp and golden on top.

Potato and Mussel Salad

A speciality of Boulogne, this tasty fish salad makes an elegant start to any meal.

SERVES SIX

3½ quarts (4 litres) mussels, scraped,
   washed and bearded
4 fl oz (100 ml) dry white wine
4 shallots, chopped
1 thyme sprig
6 parsley sprigs
Freshly ground black pepper
2 lb (1 kg) potatoes, boiled, peeled and
   thickly sliced
4 fl oz (100 ml) vinaigrette dressing
GARNISH
Finely chopped parsley
Finely chopped chives

In a large saucepan cook the mussels, wine, shallots, thyme, parsley and a generous amount of pepper over high heat for 8 minutes, or until the mussels open. Discard those that remain shut.

Lift the mussels out with a slotted spoon as they open, and remove them from the shells. Discard the shells and set the mussels aside.

Put the potatoes into a large bowl. Strain the liquid the mussels were cooked in and pour it over the potatoes. Set aside to cool.

When the potatoes are cold, drain them and arrange them on a serving dish. Put the mussels on top of the potatoes and pour over the *vinaigrette*. Sprinkle with the chopped parsley and chives. Chill thoroughly before serving.

Potatoes

Potato and Carrot Soup

This is the ideal soup for a cold winter night. Serve garnished with crisp, tiny croûtons fried in a mixture of butter and oil or in bacon fat.

SERVES SIX
3 large, floury potatoes
3 carrots
1 small parsnip (optional)
2½ pints (1½ litres) beef stock
1 oz (30 g) butter
1 large, mild onion, finely chopped
1 tablespoon flour
Marjoram
Milk or single cream
Salt
Freshly ground black pepper
Small croûtons, to garnish

Peel and slice the potatoes. Scrape the carrots and parsnip, if used, and slice them thickly. Put the sliced vegetables into a large pan. Pour in the stock and bring to the boil. Reduce the heat, half cover the pan and cook gently for about 45 minutes or until the vegetables are very soft.

While the vegetables are cooking, melt the butter in another large pan. Add the onion and fry gently, stirring frequently, taking care not to let it burn, until it is a rich golden colour. Sprinkle the flour over the onion and blend it smoothly into the fat. Stir over low heat for 2 minutes longer to make a golden *roux*. Stir in a pinch of marjoram.

Rub the vegetables and stock through a fine sieve or purée them in an electric blender. Add the puréed mixture, a little at a time, to the onion in the pan, stirring vigorously to prevent lumps forming. Bring the soup to the boil, stirring, and simmer for 5 minutes longer.

Thin the soup down as desired with milk or thin cream and season with salt and pepper. Bring to the boil again and serve accompanied by a bowl of croûtons to sprinkle over each portion.

Potato Salad au Vermouth

A summery salad, particularly good served with cold poached fish or shellfish mayonnaise, or with ham or hard-boiled eggs, sliced cucumbers and tomatoes dressed with *vinaigrette*.

The mayonnaise for this salad should be home-made, thick and richly flavoured with good wine vinegar and French mustard.

SERVES SIX
2 lb (1 kg) small new potatoes
Salt
¼ pint (125 ml) chicken stock
4 tablespoons dry white vermouth
8 tablespoons thick mayonnaise
3 tablespoons chopped chives, spring onions or shallots
2 tablespoons finely chopped parsley
Freshly ground black pepper

Wash the potatoes and boil them in salted water or steam them. Mix the chicken stock and vermouth in a jug.

Peel the hot potatoes and slice them thickly. Put them into a bowl, moistening each layer with stock and vermouth. Set aside until the potatoes are quite cold and have absorbed most of the dressing.

Carefully drain off the excess liquid —it may be used to fortify a soup. Fold the mayonnaise and herbs in carefully to avoid breaking the potato slices, and season to taste with salt and pepper.

Chill until ready to serve.

Potato Soup with Barley

A thick, satisfying soup that makes a fine main course for a family supper.

SERVES SIX
1 oz (30 g) butter
¼ lb (120 g) small white mushrooms, sliced
1 large mild onion, finely chopped
¼ lb (120 g) pearl barley, soaked overnight
2 carrots, scraped and diced
2½ pints (1½ litres) beef stock
2 large potatoes, peeled and diced
½ pint (250 ml) creamy milk
Salt
Freshly ground black pepper
Finely chopped fresh parsley or dill, to garnish

Melt the butter in the saucepan in which the soup will be cooked. Add the mushrooms and onion and fry gently, stirring occasionally, for 4 minutes, or until the onion is soft and golden, but not brown.

Drain the barley in a sieve and add it to the pan together with the diced carrots. Pour in the stock and bring to the boil. Reduce the heat and simmer for 20 minutes, or until the barley and carrots have softened.

Add the potatoes and continue to cook gently for 15 minutes longer until they, too, are soft but not mushy.

Add the milk. The soup should be rather thick. Season to taste with salt and pepper. Bring the soup to the boil, sprinkle with parsley or dill, and serve.

New Potatoes Baked in Foil

These fragrant new potatoes baked in a parcel of aluminium foil are even more deliciously flavoured than if the potatoes were simply boiled and tossed with herb butter.

SERVES FOUR TO SIX
1½ lb (¾ kg) small new potatoes
2 oz (60 g) butter
2 sprigs fresh mint or dill
Coarse salt
Freshly ground black pepper

Wash the potatoes under cold running water, rubbing off the skins with your fingers. Alternatively, the skins may be left on. Dry the potatoes well.

Preheat the oven to 400°F (200°C, Gas Mark 6).

Cut a double thickness of foil large enough to wrap the potatoes up in a parcel. Distribute a few small pieces of butter over the centre of the foil. Put the potatoes on top, burying the sprigs of herbs among them. Sprinkle the potatoes generously with salt and pepper, and dot the rest of the butter over them. Wrap the potatoes up, tightly sealing the edges of the foil. Put the parcel on a baking sheet.

Bake for 1 hour, or until the potatoes feel soft when squeezed gently through the foil. Protect your hand with a cloth.

Undo the parcel carefully. Transfer the potatoes to a heated serving dish. Discard the herbs and pour the buttery juices in the foil over the top.

Potatoes

Sautéed Potatoes with Garlic

Quick and easy to prepare, this recipe makes a rather elegant accompaniment for poultry and lamb. It is important not to pierce the garlic cloves when you peel them, and vital that they do not burn, otherwise they will impart a bitter taste instead of the subtle garlic flavour that goes so well with potatoes.

SERVES FOUR TO SIX

2 lb (1 kg) potatoes
3 tablespoons olive oil or 1 oz (30 g) lard and 1 tablespoon cooking oil
3 plump garlic cloves, peeled
Coarse salt
Finely chopped parsley, to garnish

Peel the potatoes and cut them up into cubes of about 1 inch (2 cm). Rinse the cubes in a colander and dry them thoroughly with kitchen paper.

In a large, deep frying-pan that has a lid and will take the potatoes in a single layer, heat the olive oil or the mixture of lard and oil. Fry the garlic cloves slowly until they are just golden. Add the potatoes and fry them, tossing them constantly, over moderate heat for 5 minutes, or until they have coloured on all sides.

Sprinkle the potatoes with salt. Cover the pan and fry the potatoes very slowly, shaking the pan and turning them occasionally, for about 15 minutes, or until they are crisp and golden brown on all sides and feel soft inside when pierced with a fork or skewer.

Lift the potato cubes out of the pan with a slotted spoon. Discard the garlic cloves. Drain the potatoes thoroughly and serve immediately, sprinkled with more salt and garnished with parsley.

To make chips, peel the potatoes as thinly as possible, using a potato peeler.

Gratin Dauphinois

Of the many fine French potato *gratins* this is without doubt the greatest and the best. It can partner any meat dish—roasts, grills, steaks and chops of all kinds.

SERVES SIX

1 tablespoon butter
2 lb (1 kg) potatoes
½ pint (250 ml) double cream
½ pint (250 ml) milk
1 garlic clove, crushed
Salt
Freshly ground black pepper
2 oz (60 g) Gruyère or Emmenthal cheese, freshly grated

Preheat the oven to 400°F (200°C, Gas Mark 6). Grease a large, shallow baking dish about 9 inches square (23 cm sq) with the butter.

Peel the potatoes and slice them about ⅛ inch (¼ cm) thick.

In a large saucepan, combine the potatoes with the cream, milk, garlic and salt and pepper to taste. Bring to the boil over moderate heat.

Pour the potato mixture into the prepared dish, spreading the slices out in an even layer. Sprinkle grated cheese over the entire surface.

Bake the *gratin* for 45 minutes, or until the surface is bubbling and golden brown, and the potatoes feel soft when tested with a skewer or the point of a knife.

Let the *gratin* rest on top of the stove for about 15 minutes before serving.

Slice the potatoes, then cut each slice into strips about ⅛ to ½ inch (1 cm) thick.

Jansson's Temptation

Traditionally one of a selection of dishes in a *smörgåsbord*, this famous Swedish potato and anchovy dish makes an excellent main dish for lunch or supper.

SERVES TWO AS A MAIN DISH, FOUR AS AN APPETIZER

4 medium-sized potatoes
Butter
1 large Spanish onion, shredded
¼ pint (125 ml) single cream
¼ pint (125 ml) milk
Salt
Freshly ground black pepper
2 oz (60 g) flat anchovy fillets, drained
4 tablespoons coarse white breadcrumbs

Peel the potatoes and cut them into matchstick-sized strips.

Heat 1½ ounces (45 g) of butter in a deep frying-pan. Add the onions and fry them gently until they are soft and transparent, but not coloured. Mix in the potato sticks and fry them gently for 3 minutes, turning them to coat them with the butter. Stir in the cream and milk. Season to taste with salt and pepper (but bear in mind the saltiness of the anchovies to come) and simmer very gently for a few minutes longer so that the potatoes just begin to soften.

Preheat the oven to 400°F (200°C, Gas Mark 6).

Spread half of the potato and onion mixture over the bottom of a shallow baking dish. Arrange the anchovy fillets evenly over the top and cover with the remaining potatoes, onions and cream. Sprinkle with the breadcrumbs and dot with a few pieces of butter.

Bake the dish for 30 minutes, or until the potatoes feel tender when pierced with a skewer and the top is golden and bubbling.

Using a clean tea towel, dry the chips carefully.

Potato Salad with Bacon Dressing

This rather strongly flavoured potato salad is an excellent accompaniment to cold meats, ham or poultry. Drain off any excess dressing before serving. It may be saved and used to dress a fresh green lettuce salad.

SERVES SIX TO EIGHT

2 lb (1 kg) new potatoes
Salt
6 slices bacon
1 large, mild onion, very finely chopped
8 tablespoons olive oil
4 tablespoons cider vinegar
2 teaspoons soft brown sugar
½ teaspoon coarse French mustard

Worcestershire sauce or Chinese soy sauce
Freshly ground black pepper
4 tablespoons finely chopped parsley

Wash the potatoes and rub the skins off under cold running water. Boil or steam the potatoes in salted water until they are tender but not mushy. Meanwhile, fry the bacon slices until crisp. Drain off excess fat and crumble the bacon.

When the potatoes are done, drain them and either slice them thickly or, if they are very small, quarter them or cut them into sixths. Put the potatoes into a bowl and lightly mix in the crumbled bacon.

In a small pan, mix the onion with the olive oil, vinegar, brown sugar, mustard, a few drops of Worcestershire sauce or Chinese soy sauce, a pinch of salt to taste and a grinding of black pepper. Over very low heat, bring this mixture very slowly to the boil, stirring constantly. When it comes to the boil, immediately pour the mixture over the potatoes and bacon. Add the parsley and mix gently but thoroughly. Taste for seasoning. Allow the salad to cool and serve slightly chilled.

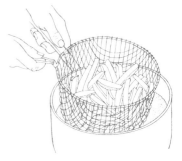

In a deep-frying pan, heat the fat to 350°F (180°C). Put the chips in the frying basket, carefully lower it into the fat and fry for 5 minutes. Drain the chips on kitchen paper and serve them immediately.

Potatoes

Rösti

This Swiss dish is traditionally served as an accompaniment for *émincé de veau*, veal in cream sauce, but it is equally delicious with any meat. It can also be served with fried eggs or an omelette. The Swiss make a special grater with larger-than-average holes for *rösti*, but an ordinary coarse grater will do very well.

SERVES FOUR
2 lb (1 kg) even-sized floury potatoes
Salt
2½ oz (75 g) butter
4 slices streaky bacon, finely chopped
1 small, mild onion, very finely chopped
Freshly ground black pepper

Scrub the potatoes with a stiff brush. Boil them in salted water until they are just tender. Drain them in a colander.

When the potatoes are quite cold, peel them and grate them coarsely into a bowl.

Heat ½ ounce (15 g) of the butter in a large, heavy frying-pan. Add the bacon and fry, stirring occasionally, until the fat is transparent. Add the potatoes, onion and a seasoning of salt and pepper. Fry the potatoes over moderate heat, turning them over and over with a spatula until they are flecked with brown. Make sure, however, that the bottom of the pan stays clean.

Using the spatula, pat the potatoes into a neat cake. Add the remaining butter, distributing it evenly around the sides of the potato cake. Cover the pan and fry gently, shaking the pan occasionally so that the *rösti* cake does not stick, for about 15 minutes longer, or until the underside of the cake is a crusty golden brown.

To serve, invert the cake on to a flat, heated dish and cut it into wedges.

Polish Potato Pancakes

These pancakes should be very thin, but quite moist in the centre with a crisp brown fringe. Serve them as a separate dish with a savoury anchovy or salt herring butter, or as an accompaniment for meat, particularly beef pot roast. They are also delicious eaten with a sprinkling of sugar or spread with jam or apple sauce and topped with soured cream.

MAKES TWELVE LARGE PANCAKES
3 lb (1½ kg) floury potatoes
1 small onion or 2 shallots
2 eggs, lightly beaten
2 tablespoons flour
Salt
Lard or oil, for frying

Peel the potatoes and grate them finely into a colander lined with a double thickness of muslin and set over a bowl. Draw up the sides of the muslin and squeeze out as much moisture as possible into the bowl below. Let the liquid stand until the starch has settled to the bottom. Then carefully pour off the liquid into a jug. Mix the grated potatoes with the starch.

Grate the onion finely into the po-

tatoes. Add the eggs, flour and salt to taste, and beat with a wooden spoon until smoothly blended. The mixture should have a soft, dropping consistency. If necessary, beat some of the reserved potato water back into the mixture.

Heat lard or oil in a large frying-pan. When it is very hot, drop in heaped spoonfuls of the potato mixture, well spaced apart, and spread them out thinly with a broad spatula. When the pancakes are brown on one side, turn them over to brown on the other side.

These pancakes are best served straight from the pan, but they may be kept hot for a short time in a warm oven, provided they are put on baking sheets in a single or a double layer.

Deep-fried Potato Balls

SERVES FOUR TO SIX
2 lb (1 kg) floury potatoes
Salt
¼ lb (120 g) butter
3 large eggs, separated
Marjoram
Fine dry breadcrumbs
Flour (optional)
Oil for deep-frying

Scrub the potatoes and boil them in salted water until they are just tender. Drain the potatoes thoroughly and peel them as soon as they are cool enough to handle. Mash them smoothly, adding the butter, egg yolks, a pinch of marjoram and a generous seasoning of salt. Cover the bowl and chill the potato mixture for 2 hours, or until the purée is firm.

Beat the egg whites lightly. Have the breadcrumbs ready in a large, flat dish. Taking a spoonful of the potato mix-

ture at a time, coat it with the egg white and roll it in the breadcrumbs. If the potato mixture sticks to your fingers, roll the balls in flour before coating them with the egg white and breadcrumbs.

Heat a pan of oil to 350°F (180°C). Deep-fry the potato balls, a few at a time, for about 4 minutes, or until they are crisp and golden on the outside. Lift them out carefully with a slotted spoon, drain them on kitchen paper and serve very hot.

Gnocchi di Patate

There are countless ways of serving *gnocchi*—with a rich tomato and meat sauce, or folded into a creamy cheese sauce, sprinkled with more cheese and breadcrumbs, and *gratinéed* under a hot grill or in the oven. Crisp buttered breadcrumbs or chopped onion fried in butter may be poured over the top, which gives the dish more of a central European accent.

SERVES THREE TO FOUR
1½ lb (¾ kg) floury potatoes
Salt
1 oz (30 g) butter
1 egg, lightly beaten
½ teaspoon baking powder
6 oz (180 g) plain flour
6½ tablespoons melted butter
6 tablespoons freshly grated Parmesan
    cheese
1 tablespoon fine dry breadcrumbs

Scrub the potatoes and boil them in salted water until just tender. Drain thoroughly, peel and mash the potatoes to a purée with the butter in a bowl. Beat in the egg, the baking powder and a generous seasoning of salt.

Put the flour into another bowl. Start adding it to the potato purée a handful at a time, working it in smoothly with your fingers. As the purée stiffens, turn it out on to a board dusted with more of the flour. Continue kneading in as much of the remaining flour as is needed to make a manageable dough. It may not be necessary to use all 6 ounces (180 g). Divide the dough into four portions and let them "rest" for 10 minutes.

Meanwhile, put a large pan of salted water on to boil. Have a kettle of water simmering in readiness and the grill hot, with a baking dish heating beneath it.

Shape a portion of the dough into a cylinder ½ to ¾ inch (1 to 2 cm) in

diameter. Cut it into 1-inch (2 cm) lengths. Drop the *gnocchi* into the pan of boiling water. They will first sink to the bottom and then float to the surface. Once they have done so, simmer them for 3 minutes. With a slotted spoon, transfer the *gnocchi* to a colander. Rinse them with boiling water and drain well.

Pour a tablespoon of butter into the hot baking dish. Put the *gnocchi* in it and sprinkle with another tablespoon of butter and 1½ tablespoons of grated Parmesan cheese. Put the dish back under the grill to colour the *gnocchi* while you cook the next batch. Repeat the process with the remaining three batches of dough, sprinkling each layer with 1½ tablespoons each of the melted butter and cheese. Top the final layer with a mixture of 1 tablespoon of breadcrumbs and 1½ tablespoons of cheese. Brown the top crisply under the grill. Serve hot.

Jerusalem artichokes are only very distantly related to the globe artichoke—through the vast daisy family—and have certainly no historical connection with the ancient city of Jerusalem. The word is said to be a misinterpretation of the Italian name for the sunflower, *girasole*, a much closer relative.

Use Jerusalem artichokes as soon as possible after they have been dug up because they quickly lose their creamy colour and begin to wrinkle and soften. Scrub them under cold running water. Scrape or peel away any discoloured patches and any excessive knobbles. Drop them into water acidulated with lemon juice (see page 150), since the cut surfaces will quickly discolour. Towards the end of the season, the skins will toughen and will have to be peeled away completely, a job easily done after cooking.

Jerusalem artichokes may be steamed, boiled or poached in milk for 15 to 20 minutes, or until just tender. Then they may be sliced and pan-fried in butter, or mashed with butter and a little cream or an egg yolk and garnished with crumbled bacon.

The Chinese artichoke is best eaten newly taken from the ground and should be cooked simply. Wash the artichokes carefully and poach them in chicken stock for 5 to 7 minutes, until they are tender but still crisp. Drain and finish the artichokes in butter in a covered pan, tossing them frequently. They will be ready in about 5 minutes.

Artichoke Fritters

SERVES FOUR

1 lb (½ kg) Chinese artichokes
1 pint (½ litre) chicken stock
2 eggs
Salt
Freshly ground black pepper
Fine dry breadcrumbs
Oil for deep-frying

Parboil the artichokes in the chicken stock for 5 to 7 minutes, or until they are tender but still crisp. Drain them thoroughly. Beat the eggs with salt and pepper to taste in a wide, shallow bowl. When ready to serve, drop the artichokes into the beaten egg. Coat them well, then lift them out on to a flat dish on which you have scattered a thick layer of breadcrumbs. Use two forks to separate the tubers and coat them individually if they are large, in bundles of twos or threes if they are small.

Heat the oil in a deep-frying pan to 375°F (190°C). Put in the coated artichokes a batch at a time and fry for 3 to 4 minutes, or until they are crisp and golden. Drain them on kitchen paper and serve immediately, sprinkled with more salt.

Jerusalem Artichokes au Gratin

A most elegant dish to accompany veal escalopes, roast chicken or ham. Garnished with crisp bacon curls, it can also be served as an informal main course.

SERVES FOUR

2 lb (1 kg) Jerusalem artichokes
¾ pint (375 ml) milk
¼ pint (125 ml) chicken stock
Salt
1½ oz (45 g) butter
2 tablespoons flour
2 oz (60 g) Gruyère and 1 oz (30 g) Parmesan cheese, freshly grated and mixed
¼ pint (125 ml) double cream, lightly whipped
Freshly ground black pepper

Scrub the artichokes and scrape them if necessary. Put them into a wide pan in one layer if possible. Pour over the milk and chicken stock. Season lightly with salt and bring to the boil. Reduce the heat, partially cover the pan and simmer for 15 to 20 minutes, or until the artichokes are just tender. Drain the artichokes in a colander over a bowl. Measure the liquid and if necessary return it to the pan and reduce it to a scant ¾ pint (375 ml) by fast boiling.

Melt 1 ounce (30 g) of the butter in another pan. Blend in the flour and stir over low heat for 1 minute to make a pale *roux*. Gradually add the hot artichoke liquid, beating vigorously to prevent lumps forming. Bring the sauce to simmering point and cook gently, stirring frequently, for 6 to 8 minutes, or until it has thickened and reduced slightly.

Meanwhile, cut the artichokes into thick slices. (If they need to be peeled completely, this is the point at which it should be done. It is probably easier to cut off any small knobbles than try to peel them.)

Remove the sauce from the heat and beat in two-thirds of the cheese. Let the sauce cool slightly. Gently mix in the whipped cream. Season to taste with pepper and more salt, if necessary.

Preheat the oven to 400°F (200°C, Gas Mark 6).

Fold the sliced artichokes gently into the sauce and pour into a shallow baking dish. Sprinkle with the remaining cheese. Dot the remaining butter over the top and bake on the top shelf of the oven for 20 minutes, or until the sauce is bubbling and the surface golden brown. Let the dish rest for a few minutes before serving.

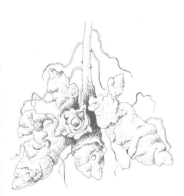

Jerusalem artichoke tubers on the root stem.

Cream of Artichoke Soup

This soup is also called Palestine soup —a name which perpetuates the myth of the tuber's connection with Jerusalem.

SERVES SIX

2 lb (1 kg) Jerusalem artichokes
Lemon juice
2 medium-sized, mild onions
2 oz (60 g) butter
2 pints (1 litre) chicken stock
½ pint (250 ml) single cream
Salt
Freshly ground black pepper
1 tablespoon finely chopped parsley
Freshly grated Parmesan cheese

Scrub the artichokes thoroughly with a stiff brush. Scrape them or peel them if necessary, quickly dropping them into a bowl of water acidulated with lemon juice to prevent discoloration.

Peel the onions and slice them thickly. Melt the butter in a large, heavy saucepan over low heat without letting it colour. Add the onions and fry gently, stirring with a wooden spoon to coat the slices thoroughly.

Lift the artichokes out of the water one at a time and slice them. Put the slices into the pan, turning them in the butter to coat them on all sides. Keep the heat low so that the vegetables do not colour. Cover and simmer gently for 5 minutes, shaking the pan frequently to prevent the artichokes from sticking to the bottom and burning.

When the artichoke slices have softened slightly, add the chicken stock. Increase the heat and bring the stock to the boil. Partly cover the pan, reduce the heat and simmer for 15 to 20 minutes, or until the artichokes are almost disintegrating.

Put the contents of the pan through the finest plate of a vegetable mouli, or purée in an electric blender. Return the purée to the saucepan. Stir in the cream and season to taste with salt and pepper. Bring the soup to just under boiling point, stirring. Garnish with parsley and serve with grated Parmesan to sprinkle over each portion.

To prepare Jerusalem artichokes, scrub them under cold running water, then peel or scrape away any discoloured patches or excessive knobbles.

To prevent the cut surfaces from discolouring, drop the peeled, sliced artichokes into acidulated water.

Vegetable Fruits

Tomatoes, cucumbers, pumpkins, marrows, courgettes, aubergines and capsicums are all fruits which are almost always prepared and served as vegetables. They all originated in distant, sunny lands and were brought by travellers and explorers to Europe, where they became an integral part of many cuisines. Today it is almost impossible to imagine what Italian cooks would do without the tomato, and the dishes of southern France and Spain would be far less interesting and colourful if the capsicums had never travelled abroad.

The cucumber is an excellent example of a vegetable fruit that is used in different ways in different countries. It can evoke a scene of afternoon tea with paper-thin sandwiches (such as those immortalized by Oscar Wilde in *The Importance of Being Earnest*), or lunching alfresco on pink salmon trout covered with a net of transparent cartwheels of pastel green. The scent and crunch of a cucumber can bring to mind any number of pictures, depending on your heritage—a garnish of crisp matchsticks in a creamy white casserole, a mixed, fresh salad chopped with Mediterranean abandon, in fact, anything from a fat dill pickle to the geometric poetry of a Japanese fish, its snow-white purity accented with lightly steamed cucumber lozenges.

Courgettes are fast becoming as familiar as cucumbers in British kitchens, and they can be substituted for each other in a number of dishes. Courgettes can be cooked whole or sliced. If you leave them whole, you can get an attractive green-and-white striped effect by peeling away thin strips of skin lengthwise all round each courgette before cooking it.

Vegetable marrows are basically mature courgettes, and they should not be grown to enormous, garden-show proportions. Pick them in good time and it will not be necessary to cook them to a fibrous pulp for them to become eatable.

The pumpkin is a vegetable fruit which has a good but limited repertoire in most of the countries where it is grown. In Europe its use is usually limited to soups, although the resourceful cooks of southwestern France use pumpkin purée with maize flour to make many other dishes.

Most pumpkin dishes are made by mixing pumpkin purée with other ingredients. Pumpkin purée is, however, delicious on its own, served hot as a dessert, with butter, cream and a sprinkling of ginger. It can also be served as a vegetable. Heat the purée, add a lump of butter, season with salt and pepper and garnish with parsley. When preparing pumpkin dishes, do not throw away the seeds. They are highly nutritious, and roasted and salted make a delicious snack.

Aubergines, peppers and tomatoes are the true exotics of the kitchen garden. With their rich colouring and sleek, generously rounded shapes, there is no mistaking their sun-soaked ancestry. And it was mainly because of their flamboyant appearance that they were, for years, regarded with deep suspicion in Britain. In the last few decades, however, the spirit of adventure has spread to the smallest towns and villages. Thanks to foreign travel and the persuasive arguments of cookery writers, these vegetable fruits, which were once considered to be outrageously daring and even dangerous, have become as acceptable as Brussels sprouts.

When cooking these vegetable fruits in the style of their countries of origin, strong flavours and fruity oils take the place of creams, butters and stocks. The smoky flavours of the south can be recreated by turning tomatoes or peppers over charcoal until their skins have cracked and blistered off. The tomatoes and peppers are then bathed in a mixture of olive oil, wine vinegar, garlic and such herbs as basil, oregano, rosemary, coriander and tarragon.

Wherever they grow in abundance, aubergines are made into tasty, filling dishes all remarkably similar, although they may originate in such dissimilar places as France and Egypt. One of the most popular dishes prepared throughout the Mediterranean and in the Middle East is "poor man's caviar", or, to give it its more sophisticated name *caviar d'aubergines*. To make this delightful *hors d'oeuvre* for four, bake 2 large aubergines on the top shelf of a moderate oven for 20 to 30 minutes, or until they feel soft and pulpy. When they are cool, peel them and chop the flesh finely.

Meanwhile, fry 1 large finely chopped onion and 2 finely chopped garlic cloves in 6 tablespoons of olive oil until soft and golden. Stir in 1 pound ($\frac{1}{2}$ kg) of peeled, chopped tomatoes, 2 teaspoons of finely chopped parsley, a generous pinch of sugar and salt and pepper to taste. Cook, stirring, until the tomatoes have disintegrated and the sauce is thick.

Add the aubergine pulp and continue cooking and stirring until the ingredients have blended into a thick purée. Cool and then chill the purée. Garnish with chopped parsley and black olives before serving with hot Greek *pitta* bread.

The tomato is the most versatile of all the vegetable fruits. Superb served raw in a salad flavoured with a handful of fresh basil leaves, it is also invaluable as a flavouring in dozens of cooked dishes. In addition, tomatoes can be made into tomato juice, tomato concentrate and tomato chutney.

Italy may have been the inspiration of modern Western gastronomy, but it is hard to imagine how the Italians earned their early culinary reputation without the tomato. For it was the tomato, more than any other vegetable except, perhaps, the potato, which changed the eating and cooking habits of the Old World.

The genius of the Mediterranean cooks lay in the ease with which they put this marvellous vegetable fruit to work. But for many years on both sides of the Atlantic, in northern Europe as well as in America, people were afraid to eat the tomato and little attention was paid to what the Italians were doing with it. Today, however, things are very different. The tomato is so popular in the West that, fresh or concentrated, it is an essential ingredient in hundreds of well-known dishes.

There are few dishes which cannot be enhanced by the flavour of the tomato. The Americans have even succeeded in using it to make a cake. This does seem a waste of effort, however, when a platter of sliced fresh tomatoes, seasoned with salt, freshly ground black pepper, a touch of sugar and a thick dusting of basil or other chopped herbs, is so easy to prepare and so good to eat.

To peel tomatoes, either spear them on a fork and turn them slowly over a hot flame until the skin shrivels and chars and can be rubbed off or blanch them in a bowl of boiling water for one minute, then dip them briefly in cold water and then peel off the skin.

Stuffed tomatoes, raw or cooked, served hot or cold, can be made with many different fillings. Left-over fish, meat, poultry or vegetables can be used, bound with cream or mayonnaise. Or there are the stuffings made with herbed or spiced meat and rice that are an outstanding feature of the Mediterranean kitchen.

To make stuffed tomatoes successfully, large, firm, fleshy tomatoes must be used. Drain the tomato by slicing off the stem end, give it a gentle squeeze to loosen the ball of seeds inside and leave it inverted, the cut surface rubbed with salt, on a rack or over a sheet of kitchen paper to absorb the juice. After this preliminary salting and draining the seeds and pulp can then be scooped out neatly and easily with a spoon without damaging the shell.

If the stuffed tomatoes are to be subjected to prolonged cooking, slice off the cap from the smooth end. The tomatoes then rest on the tougher stem ends as they cook.

Home-made concentrated tomato paste is superior to the commercial variety, which has a cruder flavour. Tomato concentrate is easy to make. Simply peel, seed and drain ripe tomatoes. Purée them in a blender or vegetable mouli. Simmer the purée in a heavy pan over moderate heat until it has reduced and is smooth and thick. Store in the deep freeze.

As summer draws to a close, there will inevitably be trusses of small, hard, green tomatoes that have missed their chance to ripen. They are ideal for making chutneys, jams or pickles.

Surprise Grilled Tomatoes

This is a fine variation on plain grilled tomatoes. The herbs you use will depend on the rest of the menu. Basil, oregano, marjoram, dill or just parsley—all complement the tomato flavour.

SERVES FOUR
4 firm tomatoes
4 tablespoons fine, dry breadcrumbs
1 small garlic clove, crushed (optional)
2 tablespoons finely chopped parsley
1 tablespoon chopped herbs
Olive oil or melted butter
Salt
Freshly ground black pepper
Sugar

Slice a cap from the stem end of each tomato and scoop out the centres. Leave the tomatoes to drain upside down until needed.

Dice the scooped-out pulp and mix it with the breadcrumbs, garlic, if used, and herbs. Moisten with 1 tablespoon of oil or melted butter and season to taste with salt, pepper and a pinch of sugar.

Fill the tomatoes. Brush them lightly with more oil or butter and put them under a moderate grill for about 10 minutes, or until they are heated through and have softened slightly.

Chilled Cream of Tomato Soup

With a basket of ripe tomatoes from the garden and an electric blender or an efficient vegetable mouli at your disposal, this excellent soup can be made in a matter of minutes, then left to chill in the refrigerator.

SERVES FOUR TO SIX
2½ lb (1¼ kg) ripe tomatoes
1 small shallot, roughly chopped
1 small garlic clove, finely chopped
¼ pint (125 ml) thick soured cream
3 oz (90 g) lean ham, diced
2 oz (60 g) cucumber, peeled and diced
2 oz (60 g) diced green pepper
Salt
Freshly ground black pepper
Sugar
Lemon juice
Double cream, to garnish (optional)

Rinse the tomatoes and chop them roughly. Purée the tomatoes, shallot and garlic in an electric blender or put them through a vegetable mouli. If using a mouli, first crush the pieces of shallot and garlic in a garlic press or pound them to a paste in a mortar.

Rub the purée through a fine sieve. Then beat in enough soured cream to make a smooth, thick soup.

Stir in the ham, cucumber and green pepper. Season the tomato cream with salt and pepper. Then taste again and, if necessary, add about 1 teaspoon of sugar and a few drops of lemon juice.

Chill until ready to serve. You may even find that it needs a few tablespoons of sweet cream to mellow the flavour.

Tomato Rice

This spicy, well-flavoured rice dish from India is the perfect accompaniment for vegetable cutlets or lamb kebabs.

SERVES FOUR TO SIX
2 oz (60 g) butter
1 lb (½ kg) ripe tomatoes, blanched, peeled and finely chopped
¼ teaspoon cayenne pepper
½ teaspoon sugar
Salt
1 large onion, sliced
½-inch (1 cm) piece fresh root ginger, peeled and finely chopped
1 garlic clove, crushed
¾ lb (360 g) long grain rice, washed, soaked in cold water for 30 minutes and drained

GARNISH
Chopped parsley
1 tablespoon chopped peanuts
2 hard-boiled eggs, quartered

Melt half the butter in a saucepan. Add the tomatoes, cayenne pepper, sugar and a little salt. Cook, stirring occasionally, for 10 minutes. Set aside.

Melt the remaining butter in a large saucepan. Add the onion, ginger and garlic and fry, stirring occasionally, over low heat until the onion is soft and golden.

Add the rice, increase the heat and fry, stirring, for 5 minutes. Pour in the tomatoes, season with more salt and add enough boiling water so that the liquid in the pan covers the rice by a

½ inch (1 cm). When the liquid boils rapidly, cover the pan, reduce the heat to very low and simmer for 20 minutes, or until the rice is cooked and all the liquid has been absorbed.

Spoon the rice into a heated serving bowl. Sprinkle the parsley and nuts on top and arrange the eggs decoratively around the sides. Serve immediately.

Basic Tomato Sauce

This is a simple, fragrant and versatile tomato sauce, ideal to have on hand. It will keep in the refrigerator for well over a week in a sealed container, provided its surface is kept covered with a thin film of olive oil. It may also be deep-frozen. Use a few tablespoonfuls to finish a dish of meat, poultry or fish, to simmer meatballs or vegetables, or to reheat left-overs for a risotto.

It makes a good pasta sauce. Allow a generous ½ pint (250 ml) per ½ pound (¼ kg) of pasta.

MAKES 1½ TO 2 PINTS (¾ TO 1 LITRE)
3 lb (1½ kg) ripe, fresh tomatoes, peeled, or 1½ pints (750 ml) deep-frozen tomato concentrate (see introduction)
5 tablespoons olive oil
2 medium-sized, mild onions, finely chopped
4 plump garlic cloves, peeled
½ large green pepper, cored, seeded and finely diced
1 large celery stalk, finely diced
1 bay leaf
2 teaspoons dried oregano or marjoram
1 teaspoon dried basil
Salt
Freshly ground black pepper
Sugar

If using fresh tomatoes, chop them up coarsely. Frozen tomato concentrate should be defrosted before use.

Heat the oil in a large pan. Add the onions and fry gently, until they are soft and golden. Add the whole garlic cloves, and as soon as they are lightly coloured mix in the pepper and celery. Fry gently, stirring occasionally, until the vegetables have softened.

Add the tomatoes, herbs and a light seasoning of salt and pepper. Bring the sauce slowly to simmering point, cover the pan and cook gently, stirring occasionally and mashing the fresh tomatoes with the back of a spoon, for 45 minutes to 1 hour, or until the sauce is thick and richly flavoured.

Adjust the seasoning, adding 1 teaspoon of sugar if necessary.

Remove and discard the garlic cloves before serving.

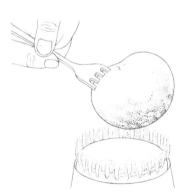

To peel a tomato, spear it on a fork and turn it slowly over heat.

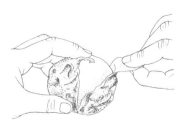

When the skin is shrivelled and charred it can be removed easily.

Ratatouille

Ratatouille is the classic summer vegetable casserole, one of the great dishes in the southern European tradition, varied and embellished by each local cuisine along the Mediterranean coast. Although ratatouille is not exclusively a tomato recipe, tomatoes are the one unvarying ingredient.

Ratatouille freezes well and is a useful stand-by either to serve on its own as a first course or as a vegetable accompaniment. With the addition of lamb, ratatouille makes a truly gourmet dish. To serve four, use half the ratatouille recipe and 1½ pounds (¾ kg) of lamb. Cut the lamb into pieces, brown it in oil and then cook until tender. Stir in the ratatouille and serve immediately with rice or crusty bread.

SERVES SIX TO EIGHT
1 lb (½ kg) aubergines
Sea salt
2 large, mild onions
½ lb (¼ kg) green peppers
1½ lb (¾ kg) large, firm, ripe tomatoes
1 lb (½ kg) courgettes
8 tablespoons olive oil
3 large garlic cloves, peeled and halved lengthwise
2 teaspoons sugar
Freshly ground black pepper
GARNISH
Finely chopped parsley
Black olives

Trim off the stem ends of the aubergines and cut into 1-inch (2 cm) cubes. Toss them in salt and leave them in a colander to drain.

Peel and slice the onions thickly. Remove all the white pith and seeds from the peppers, and cut the flesh into 1-inch (2 cm) squares. Peel the tomatoes, cut into chunks and scoop out the pulp and seeds into a strainer set over a measuring jug. Trim the courgette stems and cut into 1-inch (2 cm) slices. Finally, rinse the aubergines and gently squeeze them dry.

Heat the oil in a wide, heavy casserole. Add the onions and simmer, stirring frequently, for 10 minutes, or until they are a pale, transparent golden colour.

Lift the onions out of the oil with a slotted spoon and set aside. In the same oil, soften the peppers over low heat for 5 minutes and put them with the onions. Raise the heat to moderate and fry the courgettes until golden. Put them with the other fried vegetables. Then fry the aubergines in the same way. Return all the vegetables to the casserole, together with the chopped tomatoes and the garlic.

Rub the drained tomato pulp through the strainer and make up to ¼ pint (125 ml) with water or tomato juice if necessary. Stir in the sugar, 1 tablespoon of salt and a generous grinding of black pepper. Pour the mixture over the vegetables.

Carefully mix the contents of the casserole. Cover and cook over very low heat for 30 minutes. Turn the vegetables over from top to bottom and cook, covered, for a further 15 minutes, followed by a final 15 to 20 minutes uncovered to evaporate excess moisture. The vegetables should be soft but not disintegrating.

Allow the ratatouille to cool slightly before correcting the seasoning. Serve lukewarm or lightly chilled, garnished with finely chopped parsley and black olives.

Home-made Tomato Juice

When there is a glut of tomatoes count yourself lucky, for it gives you the perfect opportunity to lay up a supply of the most delicious, fresh, concentrated juice for the winter. Cocktails, clear consommés, soups and sauces can be made at a moment's notice. Just be sure to store the bottles in a dark cupboard, since strong light tends to fade the brilliant colour of the juice.

Rinse the tomatoes. Chop them up if they are large and pack them into a heavy saucepan. Add a sprinkling of salt and sugar, but no water. Put the pan over the lowest possible heat and cook very slowly, uncovered, stirring and mashing occasionally with a wooden spoon or pestle. When the liquid comes to simmering point, continue to cook gently until the tomatoes are quite soft. Continue simmering until some of the excess water has evaporated.

Purée the tomatoes and the juice through a vegetable mouli, discarding the seeds and skins. If the tomatoes are a very "seedy" variety, it is wise to push them through a coarse sieve first; too many seeds puréed into the juice can give it a bitter flavour. For the same reason, a blender should not be used without this preliminary sieving since it tends to do too efficient a job on skins and seeds.

Pour the juice back into the pan and let it simmer, uncovered, stirring occasionally, until it has thickened to a rich, creamy consistency.

Meanwhile, prepare screwtop bottles (tonic bottles are ideal) for the juice. Wash them, rinse them out with boiling water and leave them to drain upside down on a rack.

Season the concentrated tomato juice to taste with more salt, sugar and freshly ground black pepper. A leaf or two of fresh basil pushed into some of the bottles will make a delightful variation.

Prepare a double thickness of corrugated cardboard, or use a thick cloth, to line the bottom of a pan large enough to take the bottles closely side by side. Funnel the hot juice into the bottles and put on the tops, but do not screw them down tightly. Arrange the bottles in the pan. Pour boiling water to come two-thirds of the way up the sides of the bottles. Then slowly let the water come back to the boil and simmer for 30 minutes to sterilize the juice.

As soon as the bottles can be handled, lift them out of the pan. Put the bottles aside to rest for 2 to 3 minutes before screwing down the tops as tightly as possible.

Tomato Tart

Fresh sun-ripened tomatoes put this delicate tart into a class of its own. It can be served as a first course or as a main course for lunch or supper; all that it needs as an accompaniment is a crisp green salad.

SERVES FOUR TO SIX

1½ lb (¾ kg) ripe, firm tomatoes, peeled
6 oz (180 g) puff pastry, made-up weight
3 oz (90 g) Gruyère or mild Cheddar cheese, grated
1 oz (30 g) softened butter
4 tablespoons double cream
2 eggs, lightly beaten
Salt
Freshly ground black pepper

Preheat the oven to 450°F (230°C, Gas Mark 8). Put a heavy baking sheet in the oven to heat.

Cut each tomato into quarters. Squeeze the quarters gently over a colander to rid them of excess moisture. Chop the tomatoes and leave them to drain in the colander.

Roll the pastry out thinly and line a 9-inch (23 cm) fluted tart tin with a removable base. Sprinkle the pastry evenly with 1 ounce (30 g) of the grated cheese.

Work the remaining cheese to a fluffy paste with the butter and cream. Then beat in the eggs and season lightly with salt and pepper.

Season the chopped tomatoes and spread them evenly over the base of the pastry-lined tin. Spoon the egg and cheese mixture over the tomatoes.

Put the tart on the hot baking sheet in the oven. After the first 5 minutes, reduce the temperature to 400°F (200°C, Gas Mark 6); after another 5 minutes turn it down to 350°F (180°C, Gas Mark 4). Continue to bake the tart for 30 minutes longer, or until the filling is puffed and richly coloured and the pastry crisp and cooked through. Should the pastry brown too much around the sides before the tart is done, cover the top with a sheet of foil to protect it.

Stuffed Tomatoes à la Provençale

Serve these stuffed tomatoes as a first course or, using smaller tomatoes, as an accompaniment to grilled steak.

SERVES FOUR

4 large, firm tomatoes
4 tablespoons olive oil
1 small, mild onion, very finely chopped
1 garlic clove, crushed
4 anchovy fillets, chopped
8 tablespoons coarse fresh breadcrumbs
2 tablespoons finely chopped parsley
Salt
Freshly ground black pepper

Slice the tomatoes in half horizontally. Scoop out the pulp and seeds and rub the pulp through a sieve. Set the purée aside. Turn the tomato cases upside down to drain until needed.

Heat the oil in a frying-pan. Add the onion and garlic and fry, stirring occasionally, until the onion is soft and very lightly coloured. Mix in the anchovy fillets and continue to cook very gently, stirring occasionally, until they have practically dissolved. Add the breadcrumbs and fry gently, tossing with a fork, for 2 to 3 minutes longer to crisp them slightly.

Lightly mix in about 4 tablespoons of the puréed tomato pulp and the parsley. Season the stuffing with salt and pepper.

Preheat the oven to 375°F (190°C, Gas Mark 5).

Arrange the tomato cases side by side in an oiled baking dish. Divide the stuffing between them. Brush the cases with oil and bake for 20 minutes, or until the stuffing has become slightly crisp on top and the tomato cases have softened but are not too mushy to lift out of the dish. Serve hot or cold.

Another way to peel a tomato is to dip it in a bowl of boiling water for 1 minute.

Baked Eggs in Herbed Tomato Cups

A festive dish, baked eggs in herbed tomato cups makes a Sunday breakfast with a difference. You can vary the dish by putting a little finely chopped ham under each egg, by garnishing each case with a few thin slices of sautéed mushroom or by serving the tomato cups on crisp, round croûtons.

SERVES FOUR

4 large, firm tomatoes
Salt
Freshly ground black pepper
Butter
2 tablespoons freshly grated Parmesan cheese
2 tablespoons single cream
Generous pinch of basil
4 eggs

Carefully slice a cap across the stem end of each tomato and scoop out the pulp. Season the cases with salt and pepper and pack them tightly side by side in a buttered baking dish.

Preheat the oven to 350°F (180°C, Gas Mark 4).

Mix the cheese with the cream, basil and salt and pepper to taste.

Put the dish of tomato cups into the oven for 5 minutes to heat through. Carefully break one egg at a time into a bowl then transfer it into a tomato cup and spoon some of the cream mixture evenly over the top.

Bake for 20 minutes, or until the eggs feel set, but not hard, to the touch.

Remove the tomato from the hot water, dip it in cold water and then peel off the skin.

Capsicums (Sweet Peppers)

All the brilliant colours which the pepper adopts as it ripens are of no practical significance to the cook. Even the greenest pepper will be sweet enough for any dish, and for stuffing it will hold its shape better than one which is red and riper.

To prepare peppers, unless they are to be served whole, cut them in half, rinse out the seeds and with a sharp knife pare away all the white pith, which tends to be bitter.

To prepare a whole pepper for stuffing, cut around the stem with a sharp knife, ease out the stem and put it aside to plug up the hole later. Then, using a spoon, scrape away all the pith. Rinse out the seeds under cold running water and shake the pepper dry.

To peel a pepper, either hold it over an open gas flame or place it under a hot grill until the skin chars and blisters. Then rub the skin off under cold running water.

Sautéed Peppers

A versatile basic dish of sautéed peppers may be served as an accompaniment to beef, chicken or roast pork.

SERVES FOUR
6 tablespoons olive oil
2 garlic cloves, sliced
3 green peppers, thinly sliced
3 red peppers, thinly sliced
1 tablespoon wine vinegar
2 tablespoons tomato concentrate
Paprika
Salt
2 tablespoons finely chopped parsley,
   to garnish

Heat the oil in a large, heavy frying-pan with a lid. Add the garlic and fry, stirring occasionally, until soft and golden.

Add the peppers and stir until the slices are well coated with oil. Cover the pan and cook for 10 to 15 minutes, or until the peppers are soft but still slightly crunchy.

Mix the vinegar and tomato concentrate together and stir it into the peppers. Increase the heat and fry, stirring, for a few minutes longer to evaporate the excess moisture.

Season to taste with paprika and salt and serve very hot, garnished with parsley.

Peppers en Salade

Superb as an appetizer, this delicious salad from Provence not only tastes good but looks good, too.

SERVES SIX
2 large green peppers
2 large red peppers
8 tablespoons olive oil
3 tablespoons tarragon vinegar
2 garlic cloves, finely chopped
Salt
Freshly ground black pepper
2 tablespoons finely chopped, mixed fresh
   herbs, such as parsley, thyme and
   chervil
6 tomatoes, peeled and thickly sliced
6 hard-boiled eggs, thickly sliced

GARNISH
24 black olives, pitted
24 anchovy fillets

Wipe the peppers with a damp cloth and dry them thoroughly. Put them under a hot grill, turning frequently, until the skins blacken and blister. Rub off the skins under cold running water. Halve the peppers, remove the cores, wash out the seeds and cut each half lengthwise into 3 or 4 strips. Pat the pepper strips dry with kitchen paper.

Prepare the dressing with the oil, vinegar, garlic, salt and pepper—take care not to add too much salt because the anchovies for the garnish are themselves very salty. Stir in the herbs.

Layer the peppers, tomatoes and eggs in a salad bowl, sprinkling each layer with the herb dressing. Arrange the anchovies and olives in an attractive lattice-work pattern on the top. Leave the salad to marinate for at least 30 minutes.

Serve chilled.

Biber Dolma

Every restaurant in Istanbul has a tray of these peppers waiting to tempt the lunch-time customers. The stuffing for this delicious appetizer is a classic one and is also traditionally used to stuff vine leaves.

SERVES SIX
½ lb (¼ kg) short grain rice
6 large green peppers
8 tablespoons olive oil
2 large, mild onions, finely chopped
3 oz (90 g) currants, washed
1 oz (30 g) pine nuts
Salt
Freshly ground black pepper
Sugar
6 tablespoons finely chopped parsley

Put the rice in a sieve and rinse it thoroughly under cold running water. Pour a kettleful of boiling water over the rice and leave it to drain in the sieve for 1 hour.

Carefully cut out the stems of the peppers with the point of a sharp knife. Put them aside. Scrape out the pith and cores, taking care not to pierce the skins. Rinse the peppers under cold running water and leave them to drain, upside down, while the filling is prepared.

Heat the oil in a large frying-pan. Add the onions and fry, stirring, until they are transparent and a light golden colour. Stir in the rice, currants and pine nuts. Season to taste with salt, pepper and sugar. Continue to fry over moderate heat, stirring constantly, until

the rice is golden. Stir in the parsley.

Fill the peppers with the rice mixture, leaving room for the rice to expand. Place the reserved stems on top.

Put the upright peppers close together in a heavy saucepan large enough to take them in one layer. Carefully pour in enough boiling water to come halfway up the sides of the peppers. Put the pan on the heat and bring the water back to simmering point. Cover the pan, reduce the heat and cook the peppers very gently for 45 minutes to 1 hour, or until the rice is tender. If necessary add more water as the peppers are cooking.

Allow the peppers to cool in the pan before removing them to a serving dish. Serve chilled.

To prepare a whole pepper for stuffing, use a sharp knife to cut around the stem. Ease out the stem. Put it aside and use it later to plug the stuffed pepper.

"Cucumber . . . taken in meats, is good for the stomack and other parts troubled with heat. It yeeldeth not any nourishment that is good, insomuch as the unmeasurable use thereof filleth the veines with naughty cold humours."

John Gerard's Herball, *1633 edition*

The scent and crunch of cucumbers evoke memories of cool, green summer salads and afternoon teas with paper-thin sandwiches.

"Cucumbers grow in gardens when the moon is full, and their growth is as visible as that of sea-urchins."

The Sophists at Dinner *by Athenaeus*

Aubergines are very juicy, but sometimes the juice can be bitter and will make a dish taste unpleasantly metallic. The solution is to drain off as much of the juice as possible. Slice the aubergines, rub all the cut surfaces with salt and leave the slices to drain in a colander for at least 30 minutes. To drain them more thoroughly, particularly before frying, cover the salted aubergines with a plate and put a heavy weight on top. Then rinse the aubergine slices, squeeze them gently and press them dry with kitchen paper.

When frying aubergines, first dry the slices well and then seal them with a light dusting of flour.

Aubergine slices may also be grilled or baked. Brush them well with olive oil. Then either put them under a hot grill or on a baking sheet on the top shelf of a hot oven. Turn the slices over when browned, and brush with more oil.

Parmigiana di Melanzane

On the menu in every little restaurant in southern Italy there is a dish of *parmigiana di melanzane*, baked aubergines with cheese, which is served as a first or a main course. It is equally delicious hot, warm or cold.

SERVES FOUR

3 lb (1½ kg) round aubergines
Salt
Olive oil
1 medium-sized onion, finely chopped
2 lb (1 kg) ripe tomatoes, peeled, seeded and chopped
3 sprigs fresh basil, chopped, or 2 teaspoons dried basil
Freshly ground black pepper
Flour
5 oz (150 g) Parmesan cheese, freshly grated
½ lb (¼ kg) Mozzarella cheese, thinly sliced
2 hard-boiled eggs, thinly sliced

Trim the stems from the aubergines. Cut the aubergines lengthwise into thick slices. Sprinkle each slice with salt. Put the slices in a colander and cover with a plate. Weight the plate down and leave the aubergines to drain for 30 minutes.

Heat 4 tablespoons of olive oil in a heavy pan. Add the onion and fry, stirring, until golden. Add the tomatoes and basil, mix well and simmer gently, uncovered, until the tomatoes are reduced to a thick sauce. Season to taste with salt and pepper.

Preheat the oven to 400°F (200°C, Gas Mark 6). Oil a large, shallow, ovenproof dish.

Rinse the aubergine slices in cold water. Pat them dry and dust them with flour. Fry them in hot olive oil until soft and golden brown on both sides. Drain them on kitchen paper.

Cover the bottom of the baking dish with a layer of aubergines. Sprinkle with Parmesan cheese and cover with slices of Mozzarella cheese and a few slices of hard-boiled egg. Spoon some of the tomato sauce over the top. Repeat these layers until the ingredients are used up, ending with tomato sauce. Bake for 30 minutes.

Moussaka

Moussaka probably came from Turkey. It was adopted by the Greeks and is now the best known of all Greek dishes. A true *moussaka* is made with aubergines, but many variations have evolved, some using sliced or mashed potatoes instead of aubergines, others using courgettes as well as, or instead of them. Whichever version is preferred, this rich and substantial dish needs no accompaniment except, perhaps, a green salad and a bowl of yoghourt.

SERVES FOUR TO SIX

3 large aubergines
Salt
Olive oil
2 large, mild onions, thinly sliced
1½ lb (¾ kg) lean lamb or beef, minced
1 teaspoon ground cinnamon
Freshly ground black pepper
1 large, ripe tomato, peeled and chopped
2 tablespoons tomato concentrate
2 tablespoons finely chopped parsley
1 oz (30 g) butter
Flour
½ pint (250 ml) hot milk
1 egg yolk, beaten
¼ lb (120 g) freshly grated Kephalotiri cheese or a mixture of Gruyère and Parmesan cheese
Nutmeg

Wipe the aubergines and cut them crosswise into slices about ⅛ inch (¼ cm) thick. Put them in a colander, sprinkling each layer with salt. Weight with a plate and leave to drain for at least 30 minutes.

Heat 2 tablespoons of oil in a large, deep frying-pan. Add the onions and fry, stirring, until they are soft and golden. Add the minced meat and cinnamon and season to taste with salt and pepper. Fry steadily, stirring frequently, until the meat has browned. Mix in the tomato, tomato concentrate and parsley and continue to simmer for 20 minutes longer.

Meanwhile, prepare the sauce. Melt the butter in a saucepan. Blend in 1 ounce (30 g) of flour and stir over a low heat for 1 minute to make a pale *roux*. Gradually add the milk, stirring vigorously to prevent lumps forming. Bring the sauce to the boil and simmer for about 5 minutes, stirring constantly, until the sauce is thick and smooth.

Remove the pan from the heat and allow the sauce to cool slightly. Beat in the egg yolk and the cheese and season to taste with salt, pepper and a pinch of nutmeg.

Preheat the oven to 375°F (190°C, Gas Mark 5).

Wash the aubergine slices and dry them between the folds of a cloth or with kitchen paper. Coat the aubergines with flour and fry them in oil until golden brown on both sides. Drain well.

Line the base and sides of a deep, round casserole or baking dish with aubergine slices. Layer the meat mixture and the remaining aubergine slices in the dish, ending with a layer of aubergines. Pour the sauce over the top.

Bake the *moussaka* for about 40 minutes, or until the top is bubbling with a rich, golden crust.

Courgettes & Marrows

Courgettes are at the peak of culinary perfection when they are between 4 and 6 inches (10 and 15 cm) long and no thicker than a fat cigar, their skins like raw silk to the touch and the flesh inside crisp and creamy white.

When they are this size they may be cooked whole. Simply top and tail them, and either steam them with a sprinkling of salt or poach them for no more than 5 minutes. They should remain crisp. Finish them in a tightly covered pan with butter, coarse salt, freshly ground pepper and a dusting of chopped, fresh herbs. Crisp, cooked courgettes, served cold with *vinaigrette*, make an excellent first or salad course.

Sliced, raw courgettes may be cooked entirely in butter. Or first salted to draw out some of their moisture, patted dry, dusted with flour or dipped in a light batter and deep-fried in olive oil to make crisp little fritters. These are delicious served with yoghourt.

Stuffed courgettes are a classic Mediterranean dish. Scoop the pulp out from the stem end with a narrow corer or slim spoon, taking care not to damage the shells. Pack them with a savoury concoction of rice, meat and tomatoes, with cheese, anchovies or herbs for seasoning. Do not waste the pulp. Use it to make a variation of poor man's caviare. Cook onion with the pulp and tomato in olive oil. Season, add chopped parsley and cook until the mixture is thick. Serve lukewarm or cold.

Tender young marrows no more than 12 inches (30 cm) long also make excellent eating, when they are enriched with onions, tomatoes and cheese and are baked and served as a vegetable accompaniment.

Sometimes, inadvertently, you find yourself with large marrows on the vine and they must be prepared and cooked in a different way. The skin is tough and must be peeled away completely. Then cut the marrow across in half or in thick slices and carefully scrape out all the seeds and woolly fibres inside. Rub the shells all over with salt and leave them to drain for at least 30 minutes, the halves inverted on a rack, the slices in a colander, to allow the salt to draw out as much water as possible. Then steam or simmer in butter until tender and serve with a cream sauce or with herb butter.

To prepare courgettes for stuffing, carefully scoop out the pulp, using a narrow corer or slim spoon.

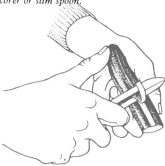

Courgettes look particularly attractive if, before cooking, thin strips of the skin are removed with a peeler to give a striped effect.

Baked Courgettes with Eggs and Cheese

This is a delightful dish to serve for brunch or supper. For hearty appetites, grilled sausage or bacon may be served as an accompaniment.

SERVES FOUR
6 tablespoons olive oil
2 garlic cloves, crushed
1½ lb (¾ kg) courgettes, sliced
1 large, mild onion, thinly sliced
2 tablespoons fresh chopped parsley
1 teaspoon fresh chopped marjoram
1 teaspoon fresh chopped basil
Salt
Freshly ground black pepper
6 eggs
4 tablespoons single cream
3 oz (90 g) grated Gruyère cheese
1 oz (30 g) grated Parmesan cheese
1 tablespoon butter

Preheat the oven to 350°F (180°C, Gas Mark 4).

Heat the oil in a large, deep frying-pan. Add the garlic and fry, stirring gently, for 1 minute without letting it brown. Add the courgettes, increase the heat and fry, stirring frequently, until they are lightly browned. Stir in the onion and the herbs. Season to taste with salt and pepper. Reduce the heat and continue to cook, stirring occasionally, until the onions are soft. Tip the contents of the pan into a baking dish.

In a bowl, beat the eggs lightly with the cream, mix in the cheeses and pour it over the courgettes. Dot with the butter and bake for 20 to 30 minutes, or until the eggs have set and the top is golden.

Deep-fried Courgettes

This dish makes an excellent accompaniment for lamb. If frying large quantities, keep the fried courgettes hot in the oven, set at 225°F (120°C, Gas Mark ¼), on a baking sheet lined with kitchen paper.

SERVES FOUR TO SIX
¼ lb (120 g) plain flour
¼ teaspoon salt
1 tablespoon olive oil
¼ pint (125 ml) lukewarm water
1½ lb (¾ kg) courgettes
Oil for deep-frying
1 egg white

Sift the flour and salt into a bowl. Make a well in the centre and add the oil and a little water. Using a wooden spoon, begin stirring the liquid, slowly incorporating the flour. Add the remaining water a little at a time. When the batter is smooth and it is thick enough to coat the back of the spoon, cover the bowl and set it aside for 30 minutes.

Meanwhile, trim the courgettes and slice them thickly.

Heat the oil in a deep-frying pan to 375°F (190°C) or until a cube of stale bread dropped into the oil turns brown in 60 seconds.

Just before frying, whip the egg white until it is stiff and fold it into the batter.

Put the courgette slices into the batter. Remove them with a skewer and drop them into the hot oil. Turn them once. Using a slotted spoon, lift out the courgette slices when they are golden brown. Drain well on kitchen paper and keep hot until all the courgette slices have been fried. Serve hot.

Marrow and Tomato Casserole

For a more substantial dish add a thick, creamy cheese sauce before baking.

SERVES FOUR

1 lb ($\frac{1}{2}$ kg) young marrows
Salt
1 lb ($\frac{1}{2}$ kg) tomatoes
$\frac{1}{2}$ lb ($\frac{1}{4}$ kg) onions
2 oz (60 g) butter
Fresh basil, chopped
Freshly ground black pepper

Cut the marrows into $\frac{1}{2}$-inch (1 cm) slices. Peel them and remove the seeds and woolly fibres if necessary. Put the marrow slices in a colander, sprinkle them with salt and leave them to stand for 30 minutes. Rinse the marrow.

Preheat the oven to 400°F (200°C, Gas Mark 6). Butter a deep casserole.

Slice the tomatoes and onions thickly. Put a layer of marrow in the bottom of the casserole. Cover this with a layer of tomato followed by a layer of onion. Dot each layer with a small amount of butter and sprinkle with a little salt, basil and a grinding of pepper. Continue in this way until all the vegetables are used up, finishing with a layer of marrow.

Flake any remaining butter over the top of the casserole. Cover and bake for 1 hour.

Cream of Marrow Soup

Marrows, when they are young and still tender, need not be peeled. Otherwise, peel and slice the marrows and remove the seeds, if necessary, before cooking. If you prefer a coarse soup, with bits of marrow still discernible in it, do not put the soup through a sieve.

SERVES SIX

2 lb (1 kg) marrows, thickly sliced
Salt
1 oz (30 g) butter
1 mild, medium-sized onion, chopped
1 small garlic clove, crushed
$\frac{3}{4}$ pint (375 ml) milk
$\frac{3}{4}$ pint (375 ml) single cream
Freshly ground black pepper
1 teaspoon sugar
2 tablespoons soured cream or whipped cream, to garnish

Stew the marrows, covered, in a little salted water until just tender. Drain them and mash them coarsely.

Melt the butter in a large, heavy pan. Add the onion and garlic and fry, stirring, over low heat until the onion is soft and golden, but not brown. Stir in the marrow, milk and cream. Season to taste with salt and pepper. Increase the heat and bring the soup to just under boiling point. Do not let it boil. Put the mixture through a fine sieve and return it to the pan. Stir in the sugar and correct the seasoning. Serve immediately, garnished with soured or whipped cream.

Marrow au Gratin

This dish makes an excellent accompaniment to roast or grilled meat, particularly lamb.

SERVES FOUR TO SIX

3 lb ($1\frac{1}{2}$ kg) marrow
Salt
2 tablespoons olive oil
2 oz (60 g) butter
1 large onion, coarsely chopped
2 large tomatoes, peeled and chopped
$\frac{1}{4}$ lb (120 g) mature Cheddar cheese, grated
Freshly ground black pepper

Cut the marrow into 1-inch (2 cm) slices. Peel the slices and remove the pith and seeds from the centre. Cut the marrow slices into 1-inch (2 cm) pieces. Put them in a colander, sprinkle with salt, toss well and leave to drain for 1 hour.

Preheat the oven to 375°F (190°C, Gas Mark 5).

Heat the oil and half of the butter in a large saucepan. Add the onion and fry, stirring occasionally, until it is soft and transparent. Add the tomatoes and simmer until they are reduced to a purée. Rinse the marrow chunks and add them to the pan. Stir to mix. Cover the pan and simmer over low heat for 7 to 8 minutes. Stir in 1 ounce (30 g) of the grated cheese and season to taste with salt and pepper. Transfer the contents of the pan to a shallow baking dish. Sprinkle the remaining cheese on top and dot with the remaining butter. Bake for 30 minutes, or until the marrow is tender and the topping is golden brown.

Stuffed Marrows

This is a spicy variation of a traditional English dish. If desired, mashed, cooked aubergines may be substituted for the meat.

SERVES FOUR TO SIX

3 lb ($1\frac{1}{2}$ kg) medium-sized marrows
Salt
$\frac{1}{4}$ lb (120g) short grain rice
1 tablespoon olive oil
$2\frac{1}{2}$ oz (75 g) butter
1 large onion, finely chopped
2 garlic cloves, crushed
$\frac{1}{4}$-inch ($\frac{1}{2}$ cm) piece of fresh root ginger, peeled and finely chopped
1 green chilli, seeded and finely chopped
1 teaspoon turmeric
1 teaspoon ground coriander
$\frac{1}{4}$ teaspoon cayenne pepper
1 lb ($\frac{1}{2}$ kg) lean lamb, minced
2 large, ripe tomatoes, peeled and chopped
1 tablespoon tomato concentrate
2 tablespoons chopped fresh coriander leaves or parsley
3 tablespoons raisins

Peel the marrows thinly and halve them horizontally. Scoop out the seeds and woolly fibres. Rub the marrows, inside and out, with salt and leave them to drain, upside down, for about 1 hour.

Parboil the rice in salted water for 3 minutes. Drain thoroughly. Heat the oil and $\frac{1}{2}$ ounce (15 g) of the butter in a saucepan. Add the onion and fry, stirring occasionally, until it is tender and golden. Add the garlic, ginger and chilli and fry, stirring, for 2 minutes. Add the turmeric, coriander and cayenne pepper and fry, stirring, over low heat for 5 minutes. If the mixture gets dry and begins to stick to the pan, stir in 1 tablespoonful of water.

Add the meat, increase the heat slightly and fry, stirring and mashing the meat down with a wooden spoon, until it is well browned. Stir in the rice, tomatoes, tomato concentrate, the chopped coriander leaves or parsley and the raisins. Season to taste with salt. Mix the ingredients well together. Remove the pan from the heat.

Rinse the marrow shells in cold water and wipe them dry with kitchen paper. Stuff the marrows with the mixture. Melt the remaining butter in a wide, flame-proof dish. Arrange the stuffed marrows in the dish and cook for 2 minutes. Cover the pan, reduce the heat and simmer gently for 1 hour.

Serve hot.

Pumpkins

In Britain, pumpkins are associated more with Hallowe'en and Cinderella than with the kitchen. Even in America, home of the pumpkin, cook books contain only a handful of pumpkin recipes—apart from pumpkin pie.

It was in fact the cooks of eastern Europe who devised what is probably the most satisfying culinary solution for this beautiful vegetable fruit—a spiced preserve.

Pumpkins also make delicious vegetable dishes, fine soups and good puddings. Most pumpkin recipes require pumpkin purée. To prepare the purée, cut the pumpkin in half horizontally and remove the seeds and strings. Peel the pumpkin and cut it into pieces. Cook the pumpkin in simmering water for 20 to 30 minutes. Drain and purée. Pumpkin may also be baked in a moderate oven and then puréed; cut it in half and scrape out the seeds and strings, but do not peel or cut it into pieces.

Pumpkin Soup

This warming winter soup can be made richer by adding $\frac{1}{4}$ pint (125 ml) of double cream just before serving.

SERVES FOUR
$1\frac{1}{2}$ lb ($\frac{3}{4}$ kg) pumpkin
$1\frac{1}{2}$ pints (750 ml) milk
1 tablespoon butter
1 teaspoon basil
Salt
Freshly ground black pepper
Sugar
2 tablespoons beurre manié (1 tablespoon flour and 1 tablespoon butter mashed together)

Remove the seeds and pith and peel the pumpkin. Cut the flesh into cubes. Cook the pumpkin in simmering water for 20 minutes, or until it is tender. Drain well. Purée the pumpkin in a vegetable mouli.

Return the purée to the pan. Stir in the milk and butter. Add the basil and season to taste with salt, pepper and sugar.

Bring the soup to the boil. If it is not thick enough, add the beurre manié a little at a time, stirring constantly, until the soup is the right consistency.

Adjust the seasoning and serve.

Spiced Pumpkin Preserve

Use a good wine vinegar for this preserve. A French vinegar marked at 6° or 7° is best—mild, mature but strong enough to pickle the pumpkin well.

MAKES ABOUT THREE POUNDS
$2\frac{1}{2}$ lb ($1\frac{1}{4}$ kg) firm, ripe pumpkin
Salt
$\frac{1}{2}$ lb ($\frac{1}{4}$ kg) sugar
1 pint (500 ml) wine vinegar
6 cloves
2 small sticks cinnamon

Peel the pumpkin, scrape it clean of seeds and pith and cut it into 1-inch (2 cm) cubes. Drop the pumpkin cubes into an enamelled saucepan of lightly salted boiling water. Parboil them for 1 minute and drain thoroughly.

In the same pan, over low heat, slowly dissolve the sugar in 4 tablespoons of water. Stir in the vinegar, cloves and cinnamon, raise the heat and bring to the boil. Return the pumpkin cubes to the pan and bring to boiling point. Remove the pan from the heat, cover it and put it in a cool place for 24 hours.

The next day, drain off the syrup into another enamelled pan and bring it to the boil. Pour the boiling syrup back over the pumpkin. Cover the pan and set it aside once again for 24 hours.

On the third day, slowly bring the pumpkin to simmering point in the vinegary syrup. Test the cubes with a skewer and if they have not softened sufficiently, continue to cook them gently for a few minutes longer. Set aside until quite cold, then seal the preserve in clean, dry, glass jars. Store in a cool, dry, dark place.

Soured Cream Pumpkin Pie

A variation on the traditional American Thanksgiving dessert, this pumpkin pie should be served with whipped cream.

SERVES SIX
Shortcrust pastry made with 6 oz (180 g) flour
1 lb ($\frac{1}{2}$ kg) pumpkin purée
$\frac{1}{2}$ pint (250 ml) soured cream
3 eggs, separated
$\frac{1}{4}$ teaspoon salt
1 teaspoon ground cinnamon
$\frac{1}{2}$ teaspoon ground ginger
$\frac{1}{4}$ teaspoon grated nutmeg
6 oz (180 g) castor sugar

Preheat the oven to 425°F (220°C, Gas Mark 7).

Roll out the pastry and line a 9-inch (23 cm) tart tin. Prick the pastry all over with a fork. Line the pastry with greaseproof paper and fill with dried beans. Bake the pastry shell for 10 minutes. Remove the paper and beans and reset the oven to 350°F (180°C, Gas Mark 4). Return the pastry case to the oven for 10 to 15 minutes to dry out the base.

In the top of a double saucepan, combine the pumpkin with the soured cream and the lightly beaten egg yolks. Mix in the salt, spices and half the sugar.

Place the saucepan over gently simmering water. Cook the pumpkin mixture, stirring constantly, until it thickens.

Whip the egg whites in a bowl until they form soft peaks. Gradually beat in the remaining sugar. Fold the meringue into the pumpkin mixture.

Spoon the pumpkin mixture into the pastry shell. Bake the pie for 45 minutes, or until the top is golden.

Savoury Pumpkin Mould

This attractive and unusual vegetable dish can be baked in a ring mould, turned out on to a plate and served with the centre filled with buttered peas or creamed mushrooms.

SERVES SIX
3 eggs
$1\frac{1}{2}$ fl oz (38 ml) milk
$1\frac{1}{2}$ lb ($\frac{3}{4}$ kg) pumpkin purée
$1\frac{1}{2}$ oz (45 g) butter, melted
1 oz (30 g) fresh breadcrumbs
1 small onion, coarsely grated
1 garlic clove, crushed
$\frac{1}{2}$ teaspoon chopped fresh parsley
$\frac{1}{2}$ teaspoon chopped fresh thyme
Salt
Freshly ground black pepper

Preheat the oven to 350°F (180°C, Gas Mark 4).

In a large bowl, beat the eggs with the milk. Mix in the pumpkin purée, butter, breadcrumbs, onion and garlic. Add the herbs and mix thoroughly. Season to taste with salt and pepper.

Pour the mixture into a buttered oven-proof dish and bake for 45 minutes, or until the mixture has set.

Cucumbers

In Britain, cucumbers are usually served raw and sliced. To prevent the juice from emerging and diluting other flavours, the cucumber slices may be salted, drained in a sieve or colander for 30 minutes, then rinsed and pressed dry between the palms of your hands. Never salt cucumber slices when they are being used as decoration.

Cooked cucumbers make a delicious vegetable and lose none of their vitality by being steamed or poached. Peel them, cut them in half length-wise and remove the seeds. Then cook the cucumbers for a few minutes. Serve dressed with melted butter, lemon juice and herbs.

Sautéed cucumbers are excellent with fish. Cut them into thick slices. Do not peel them unless the skins are tough. Soak the slices in iced water for 1 hour, then dry them, dust them with flour and sauté in butter and oil until golden. Dress them with butter, lemon and herbs or serve with a *hollandaise* sauce.

Cucumber Soup

A good soup to serve on a hot summer's day, this cucumber soup should be well chilled and liberally garnished with chopped chives and soured cream.

SERVES SIX
3 cucumbers, peeled
2 pints (1 litre) good chicken stock
1 oz (30 g) butter
1 medium-sized, mild onion, finely chopped
1 garlic clove, crushed
½ pint (250 ml) single cream
¼ lb (120 g) mushrooms, sliced
Salt
Freshly ground black pepper
GARNISH
Chopped chives
Soured cream

Reserving half of one cucumber, put the remaining cucumbers through the finest plate of a vegetable mouli.

In a large saucepan, bring the chicken stock to the boil. Add the puréed cucumber and simmer for 10 minutes. Heat half the butter in a frying-pan. Add the onion and garlic and fry, stirring occasionally, until they are soft and translucent. Add the onion and garlic to the soup and stir in the cream.

Heat the remaining butter in the same frying-pan. Add the mushrooms and fry, stirring, for 1 minute. Add the mushrooms to the soup and season to taste with salt and pepper. Simmer gently for 10 minutes.

Dice the remaining half cucumber and stir it into the soup. Remove the pan from the heat and set aside to cool.

Chill the soup thoroughly and garnish each serving with the chopped chives and soured cream.

Cucumbers in Soured Cream Dressing

The cucumbers should be sliced paper-thin for this delicious summer salad. Fresh double cream mixed with lemon juice may be used as a substitute for commercial soured cream. Leave the skin on the cucumber.

SERVES FOUR
1 large cucumber
Salt
¼ pint (125 ml) soured cream
3 tablespoons chopped fresh chives or dill
1 tablespoon chopped fresh parsley
Freshly ground black pepper
Sugar

Cut the cucumber, unpeeled, into very thin slices. Put them in a large colander, sprinkling each layer with salt. Leave the slices to drain for at least 30 minutes, then rinse them and squeeze out the excess moisture firmly but gently.

In a bowl, mix the soured cream with the chives or dill and the parsley. Gently stir in the cucumber slices and season to taste with salt, pepper and sugar. Serve immediately.

Tuna-stuffed Cucumber

This dish may be served alone as an appetizer or as part of a selection of mixed *hors d'oeuvre*. The herbs should be used according to taste and availability—a good mixture is thyme, oregano, tarragon and chives.

SERVES FOUR
1 large cucumber
Salt
7 oz (210 g) canned tuna fish, drained
1 oz (30 g) butter
1 oz (30 g) cream cheese
1 tablespoon chopped parsley
1 tablespoon chopped mixed fresh herbs
Freshly ground black pepper
1 lemon, thinly sliced, to garnish

Peel the cucumber and cut it crosswise into 2-inch (5 cm) pieces. Drop the pieces into boiling salted water and cook gently for 8 minutes. Drain and refresh the cucumber pieces in cold water until they are firm again and cold. Scoop out and discard the seeds and pulp from the centre of each piece. Dry the pieces on kitchen paper. Mash the tuna fish with the butter and cream cheese to make a smooth paste. Blend in the herbs and season to taste with salt and pepper.

Stuff the cucumber pieces with this mixture and chill until firm. Cut each piece across into ½-inch (1 cm) slices and serve immediately.

Mushrooms

Mushrooms are essential to fine cooking—their flavour is incomparably subtle and their texture both crisp and fleshy.

The commonest mushroom, and one of the best, is the field mushroom. It grows wild in open pastures free for the picking. It is the same type of mushroom as the kind grown commercially and those grown by amateur gardeners in their tool sheds and cellars.

When the mushroom first pushes its delicate white cap through the soil it is known as a button mushroom. As it grows, opening out like a parasol, it displays pinkish-beige gills beneath the cap. It can grow, if it is permitted, to almost 5 inches (13 cm) in diameter.

The button mushroom is delightful eaten raw, especially when it is perfectly fresh. To make a marinated mushroom salad, slice the mushrooms thinly, toss them thoroughly with light olive oil and lemon juice, using 2 tablespoons of oil and the juice of 1 lemon for ½ lb (¼ kg) of mushrooms, season and chill in the refrigerator for at least 2 hours. Before serving, garnish the mushrooms with chopped parsley, a little dill or a sprinkling of chives.

When cooking mushrooms, the golden rule is never to wash or peel them unless it is absolutely necessary. Clean mushrooms will at most need to be wiped with a damp cloth, or rinsed quickly in a sieve. Much of the flavour is in the peel and in the stalks, so just trim the stalks, do not discard them. If a recipe calls for only mushroom caps, keep the stalks in the refrigerator and use them to flavour a soup, or sauce or to make *duxelles*.

Having gone to the trouble of growing snow-white mushrooms, it is not difficult to preserve their perfection right up to the moment they arrive on the table, whether it be in the form of a garnish or as a dish in their own right.

The simplest way to prepare mushrooms for a garnish is to poach them in barely enough lightly salted water to cover, with a squeeze of lemon juice to keep them white. If the pan is tightly covered they will in effect steam, rather than poach, in a matter of minutes. The mushrooms can then be put aside until needed without loss of colour or texture.

Sautéed mushrooms—the kind that add a final touch to all sorts of dishes, from creamy *blanquettes* of poultry or veal to such rich casseroles as *boeuf bourguignon* and *coq au vin*—are cooked in fat rather than in water, but the general principles remain the same. Protect the colour with lemon juice and do not overcook them. Use butter, melted in a little oil to ensure that the butter does not brown. When the butter is foaming, add the mushrooms. Squeeze some lemon juice over the mushrooms and sauté

them over moderate heat, keeping the mushrooms constantly on the move so that they colour evenly. Initially, they will release an alarming amount of water, but this will rapidly evaporate. As soon as the butter is clear again, the mushrooms are ready to use.

There are many ways to use mushrooms, both buttons and the full-blown open caps, which are the ones to use for stuffing and for grilling and which some people prefer for their undeniably stronger taste.

The French have a marvellously practical and versatile way of using cultivated mushrooms—this is the *duxelles*, a concentrated paste or mince, often made from second-grade mushrooms. It is used for flavouring stuffings, soups, stews and sauces. To make a *duxelles*, first chop a couple of shallots or a small, mild onion as finely as possible. Melt 2 ounces (60 g) of butter in a wide, heavy pan and simmer the onion very gently until it has practically dissolved. Finely chop 1 pound (½ kg) of mushrooms—plus any stalks you have been saving in the refrigerator—and add them to the pan, together with another 3 ounces (90 g) of butter. Cook very gently, stirring frequently, for at least 1 hour, or until the mixture is thick and richly flavoured. Season at the very end.

Store the *duxelles* in a tightly covered jar in the refrigerator, ready to be dipped into whenever a sauce, a soup, a casserole—or even a plain omelette—calls for a boost. It will keep in the refrigerator for several weeks, but any surplus can be deep-frozen in convenient-sized cubes for future use.

Dried mushrooms retain such potency that just a few slivers will make their mark on a dish. If you are growing your own mushrooms and have some to spare, this is an excellent way to use them. Invest (and they *are* expensive) in 2 ounces (60 g) of best-quality dried mushrooms and put them away in an airtight container. These will be wild mushrooms, which have a stronger flavour and which you will later mix with your own dried mushrooms. Put your mushrooms out on a baking sheet lined with several thicknesses of kitchen paper. Cut the mushrooms in half vertically, stems and all, or leave them whole—they will shrink dramatically as they dry. Over the next few days, have the baking sheet ready to take advantage of any mild, *dry* heat—a switched-off oven, a cooling radiator or just a warm, well-ventilated kitchen. When the mushrooms have given up all their moisture and are as dry as leather, mix them with the bought mushrooms. Leave them for several weeks to allow the flavours to mix, and then you will have created a precious new flavouring ingredient to store and use when needed.

Mushrooms

Mushroom Pie

An ideal lunch dish, mushroom pie can be served with a mixed salad or with green vegetables. If desired, 2 ounces (60 g) of bacon may be fried with the onions.

SERVES FOUR TO SIX

1½ oz (45 g) butter
¼ lb (120 g) button onions, peeled
1 lb (½ kg) button mushrooms, cleaned
1 tablespoon finely chopped parsley
Salt
Freshly ground black pepper
2 tablespoons sherry or Madeira
8 fl oz (200 ml) double cream
2 egg yolks, lightly beaten
¼ teaspoon freshly grated nutmeg
¼ teaspoon paprika
Rough puff pastry, made with 6 oz (180 g) flour
Egg white, for glazing

Preheat the oven to 400°F (200°C, Gas Mark 6).

Melt the butter in a large frying-pan. Add the onions and fry, shaking the pan occasionally, over low heat for 5 minutes.

Add the mushrooms, turning them gently in the pan so that they are well coated with the butter. Stir in the parsley, season with salt and pepper to taste and cook for 2 minutes.

Using a slotted spoon, transfer the onions and mushrooms to a deep pie dish.

Increase the heat, pour the sherry or Madeira into the pan and stir well to mix. Remove the pan from the heat and pour the contents over the mushrooms and onions.

In a small bowl, combine the cream and egg yolks. Season with nutmeg, paprika and a little salt. Pour the mixture into the pie dish.

Roll out the pastry and cover the pie dish with it. Brush the pastry with egg white and bake for 30 minutes, or until it has risen and is golden brown. Serve immediately.

Mushroom Soup

A delicious and easy-to-make soup. Use a strong, well-flavoured stock.

SERVES SIX

3 oz (90 g) butter
4 shallots, finely chopped
1 lb (½ kg) button mushrooms, thinly sliced
Juice of ½ small lemon
2 tablespoons flour
1½ pints (750 ml) chicken or vegetable stock
6 tablespoons dry sherry
½ pint (250 ml) single cream
Salt
Freshly ground black pepper
2 tablespoons finely chopped parsley, to garnish
Paprika or cayenne pepper

Heat the butter in a large saucepan. Add the shallots and fry, stirring, until they are golden but not brown. Stir in the mushrooms. Squeeze the lemon juice over them (this helps to preserve the colour of the mushrooms) and cook over moderate heat for 2 to 3 minutes until the mushrooms have softened slightly.

Sprinkle the flour over the mushrooms and blend it into the butter. Stir for 1 minute longer over low heat. Stir in the stock and bring it to the boil. Reduce the heat and simmer the soup for 15 minutes. Stir in the sherry and the cream. Season to taste with salt and pepper and bring the soup to just below boiling point.

Stir in the parsley. Sprinkle each portion with a dash of paprika or cayenne before serving.

Mushrooms en Brioche

The addition of Madeira to the classic cream and egg sauce makes this a rich and delicious dish. It is an ideal first course for a dinner party. *Vol-au-vent* cases or soft round rolls may be substituted for the *brioches*.

SERVES SIX

6 day-old brioches
2 oz (60 g) butter
2 tablespoons olive oil
1 lb (½ kg) tiny button mushrooms, trimmed
1 shallot, finely chopped
Salt
Freshly ground black pepper
4 tablespoons Madeira
3 egg yolks, lightly beaten
½ pint (250 ml) double cream
1 garlic clove, halved
Melted butter

Cut off the tops of the *brioches* and scoop out the insides, making sure the shells remain undamaged.

Preheat the oven to 375°F (190°C, Gas Mark 5).

Heat the butter and oil in a large, wide pan. Add the mushrooms and shallot and fry gently, stirring, for 2 minutes. Season to taste with salt and pepper. Add the Madeira, mix it well in and cook gently for a minute or so longer. Remove the pan from the heat.

Mix the egg yolks and the cream together and stir them into the mushrooms. Return the pan to very low heat and stir for 10 to 15 minutes or until the sauce has thickened. The sauce must not boil or the egg yolks will curdle.

Alternatively, cook the sauce and mushrooms in the top of a double saucepan over simmering water, stirring occasionally, for 15 to 20 minutes.

Meanwhile, rub the insides of the *brioches* with the garlic and brush them with melted butter. Place them on a baking sheet in the oven for 15 to 20 minutes.

Divide the mushrooms and sauce between the hot, crisp *brioche* cases and serve immediately.

Mushroom and Barley Casserole

This may be served either as an accompaniment for lamb, beef or such game as venison, or as a substantial vegetarian main course.

SERVES THREE TO FOUR

Salt
1½ oz (45 g) butter
¼ lb (120 g) pearl barley, well rinsed
1 medium-sized onion, finely chopped
½ lb (¼ kg) button mushrooms, sliced
¼ pint (125 ml) single cream
Freshly ground black pepper
Milk
1 egg
2 tablespoons grated Cheddar cheese

In a saucepan, bring ½ pint (250 ml) salted water to the boil with ½ ounce (15 g) of the butter. Stir in the barley. Cover the pan tightly and simmer for 30 minutes, or until the barley is soft and has absorbed all the water.

Meanwhile, melt the remaining butter in another pan. Add the onion and fry, stirring, until it is soft and lightly coloured. Add the mushrooms and stir to coat them with the buttery juices. Fry gently for 2 to 3 minutes longer. Moisten with 4 tablespoons of the cream and season to taste with salt and pepper. Cover the pan and simmer very gently for 10 to 15 minutes longer.

Meanwhile, preheat the oven to 375°F (190°C, Gas Mark 5). Make up the cream to ¼ pint (125 ml) with milk and beat it lightly with the egg.

Spread half of the cooked barley over the bottom of a baking dish. Cover with the mushrooms and cream and top with the remaining barley, smoothing it out with the back of a spoon. Pour the cream and egg mixture over the top and sprinkle the surface with the grated cheese.

Bake the casserole for 20 to 30 minutes, or until it is set and golden on top, but still slightly creamy inside.

Fruit

It is curious how fruits seem to be endowed with the character of their season. The season of soft fruits is as short as an English summer, while the season of the orchard fruits is longer, without the urgency to make the most of only a few weeks' bounty. In the same way, soft fruits will take very little of the cook's time, while the apples and pears of autumn give the opportunity to make pies and puddings and all sorts of tarts which are certainly not quick to prepare.

The typical fruits of the kitchen garden are brambles, berries and currants and, possibly, one or two apple and pear cordons. The outsider is the vine, included for the sheer joy of growing grapes.

The most modest suburban kitchen garden is capable of supplying the kitchen with fruit throughout the year, even without the help of a freezer. And when you run out of one fruit for a favourite recipe there always seems to be another ready to take its place. A summer pudding becomes an early autumn pudding as the blackberries ripen. Then, later, you can make a winter pudding. Line a bowl with sponge fingers and fill it with an apple or pear mousse lightly set with gelatine. And when the first rhubarb comes in, you can make a spring pudding. Simply cut the rhubarb into short lengths, cook it slowly, until it has nearly disintegrated, with sugar and a little lemon juice in a tightly covered pan over low heat. Stir in a little butter, let it cool and pour it into a bread-lined bowl. Cover with more bread and leave overnight in the refrigerator until it is firm. Serve with cream or *crème anglaise*, the real egg custard sauce, for a refreshing sweet suitable for any occasion.

There are recipes galore for soft fruits. Blackberries are traditionally cooked with apples in pies, but they may also be made into pancakes. To make blackberry pancakes, mix 1½ cups of blackberries into a batter made from 6 ounces (180 g) of flour, 1 large egg, ½ pint (250 ml) of milk, 1 tablespoon of butter and a little sugar.

Loganberries, a dull red, acid fruit, may be cooked in much the same way as blackberries, but require more sweetening. They also make excellent jam.

Fresh summer fruits offer the opportunity to make magnificent fruit ice-creams, fresh creams and yoghourts based on uncooked purées and crushed fruits.

Red currants are the best of the currants to eat raw with a little sugar. They also make the best jelly. No oversweetened, commercial preserve can compare with fine-flavoured, sour-sweet, home-made jelly. And it is so easy to make because the red currant is endowed with more than its fair share of pectin.

White currants are red currants without any colour. Like red currants they look so pretty that they make lovely garnishes for cakes and tarts. To give them a sparkle, dip small bunches in lightly beaten egg white, then sprinkle with sugar. Leave the bunches to dry for 15 minutes and use immediately.

Gooseberries are related to currants and they have in common fine, translucent skins and acid, juicy flesh. The gooseberry leads a double life in the kitchen. The small, green gooseberries, picked when they are hard and unripe, are ideal for making compotes, pies, tarts and fools.

There is some difference of opinion concerning the origin of the word "fool". Some people say that it comes from the French verb *fouler*, to crush, and others that it is a humorous name such as trifle or whim wham. There are also two ways of making fool. In the first method the gooseberries are cooked with a little butter and sugar until the gooseberries are soft enough to crush with a fork. When the gooseberries are quite cold, an equal amount of whipped cream or *crème anglaise* is folded in, and more castor sugar is added if necessary. According to the second method, the cooked gooseberries are sieved or blended before the cream is folded in.

Green gooseberries may also be made into green gooseberry sauce, which is traditionally served with fried or grilled mackerel to counteract its oiliness.

Dessert varieties of gooseberries are left on the bushes to ripen and are delicious eaten raw, plain or with whipped *sabayon*-style sauces and wafer-thin biscuits.

Cooking and dessert gooseberries are both rich in pectin and acid and make good jam and jelly.

With autumn fruits the challenge is not what to do with them, but how, for example, to make an apple pie or crumble that does justice to the quality of the fruit that your garden has produced.

Grapes are not really a kitchen fruit. They are rarely cooked, but make excellent additions to both vegetable and fruit salads. And young, tender vine leaves are used in making *dolmas*, stuffed vine leaves, which are served as an *hors d'oeuvre* or main course, either hot or cold.

Many fruits have an affinity with cheese: soft fruit with lightly sweetened cream cheese, apples with cheddar and pears with any cheese from a well-matured, creamy Brie to a vintage Parmesan.

Fruits should never be considered simply as potential sweets. Roast guinea-fowl, partridge or even chicken, surrounded by a garnish of lightly poached apples stuffed with both fresh and frozen raspberries, sums up not only the principles of cooking with fruit, but also the whole philosophy of cooking—simplicity, elegance and sophistication without pretentiousness and with, above all, respect for the natural qualities of the ingredients.

"Comfort me with apples"—the cry echoes down through the centuries. The sighs of Solomon mingle with proverbs, maxims and nursery rhymes to make the apple the most written and talked about of fruit. It is so much a part of Western man's myths and legends, that it has come to symbolize perfection in shape, colour and taste.

Although it caused the fall of man—and woman—the apple has managed to retain its premier position, in spite of the modern market gardener. Unfortunately, too often the most expert and well-meaning research into yield and disease-resistance has resulted in apples which are totally without scent or flavour.

The best thing about growing your own apples is that you can choose the variety of apple you like and grow it for its taste and texture —sweet or sharp, juicy-crisp or mealy, good for eating, cooking with or storing.

English apples are among the best in the world. Even the most chauvinistic of the world's *grandes cuisines* are compelled to acknowledge the quality of British-grown apples as well as English apple pie, which, at its traditional best, served with cream or good Cheddar cheese, must surely rank among the world's top desserts.

Apples eaten raw are perhaps the best, but stewed, puréed, baked or cooked in pies, charlottes, puddings and flans they make some of the most universally popular desserts. To savoury dishes they add a refreshing tartness that no other ingredient can match.

When using apples in cooking there are a few points worth noting. Peeled apples left for any length of time will discolour if not treated with a brushing of lemon juice or acidulated water. Poached apples are less likely to disintegrate if they are simmered for two to three minutes in the prepared syrup, then tightly covered, the heat turned off and the cooking finished in the syrup as it cools. To prevent a baked apple bursting, score a very fine equatorial line around the skin before putting it into the oven.

To make apple sauce, purée apples in their own juice in a covered pan. A lump of butter at the bottom of the pan is usually enough to keep the apples moist for the few minutes it takes them to release their own juice. Even when cooking a very large pot of apples filled to the brim, keep the water to just a bare ripple at the bottom of the pan.

Experiment with dessert apples as well as cooking apples. "Start" them with a finely chopped onion or shallot and bacon softened in butter. In fact, apple sauce can be flavoured with anything that seems complementary to the dish it is intended to accompany, from the usual cinnamon-orange-lemon variations, fortified wine or a drop of fruit liqueur, right through to horseradish. There is no reason for apple sauce to always be smooth, either. Vary the texture by frying apple cubes lightly in butter and finishing them with a little dry vermouth and cream, or by adding another texture altogether—nuts or a crisp vegetable such as celery.

Apple Charlotte à la Polonaise

There are dozens of versions of charlotte, some simple, some very complicated. This one is easy to make and suitable for any occasion. If possible use vanilla sugar in preference to sugar and vanilla essence. It does make a difference.

SERVES SIX
APPLES
3 lb (1½ kg) cooking or well-flavoured, firm dessert apples, at room temperature
Vanilla sugar, to taste
2 teaspoons ground cinnamon
Finely grated rind of 1 orange (optional)
6 oz (180 g) sultanas
Lemon juice
1 tablespoon butter
PASTRY
1 lb (½ kg) self-raising flour
1 teaspoon baking powder
5 oz (150 g) butter, chilled
2 oz (60 g) pure lard or white vegetable fat, chilled
2 eggs
¼ lb (120 g) castor sugar
TO SERVE
Sifted icing sugar
Unsweetened lightly whipped cream

Peel, quarter and core the apples and cut them into small pieces. Toss them with vanilla sugar, cinnamon, orange rind, if used, and the sultanas. Sharpen the flavour if necessary with a few drops of lemon juice.

To make the pastry, sift the flour and baking powder into a bowl. Cut the butter and lard or vegetable fat into small pieces. Rub the fat into the flour until the mixture resembles breadcrumbs. Make a well in the centre.

Beat the eggs and sugar together until fluffy and lemon coloured. Work them into the flour mixture by hand until they blend into a dough. Knead briefly, roll into a ball and seal in plastic wrap or foil. Chill for at least 1 hour, until very firm.

Preheat the oven to 400°F (200°C, Gas Mark 6).

To assemble the charlotte, use a baking tin 2 to 3 inches (5 to 8 cm) deep and measuring roughly 10 by 12 inches (25 by 30 cm). Line the base and at least 2 inches (5 cm) up the sides with two-thirds of the pastry, returning the remainder to the refrigerator.

Bake the pastry base for 30 minutes, or until it is golden. Remove the pastry

from the oven and let it settle for a few minutes. Fill the pastry case evenly with the apple mixture. Dot the surface with the butter. Take the remaining dough, which should be chilled very hard, and grate it coarsely and evenly over the entire surface.

Return the charlotte to the oven. Bake for 45 minutes to 1 hour, or until the charlotte is a rich golden colour, the apples are soft and a piece of topping picked off with a fork tastes cooked.

Serve warm or cold, cut into rectangles, dusted with sifted icing sugar and accompanied with whipped cream.

Apfelstrudel

Follow this recipe step by step and you will have a strudel to be proud of. Use a good-quality, high-gluten bread flour. It will markedly improve the elasticity of the dough. Filo pastry, available at Greek foodshops, may be used by those nervous about making the dough.

SERVES TEN TO TWELVE
DOUGH
¾ lb (360 g) plain flour
½ teaspoon salt
1 egg, well beaten
3 tablespoons flavourless oil
½ teaspoon white wine vinegar
FILLING
1 oz (30 g) fine toasted breadcrumbs
2 teaspoons ground cinnamon
1 tablespoon grated lemon rind
Juice of ½ lemon
5 oz (150 g) castor sugar
3 oz (90 g) blanched, toasted almonds, coarsely chopped
3 oz (90 g) ground almonds
5 oz (150 g) sultanas
3 lb (1½ kg) well-flavoured dessert apples, peeled, cored and finely chopped
TO SHAPE
Oil
Flour
About ½ lb (¼ kg) melted butter
TO SERVE
Sifted icing sugar
Lightly whipped cream

First make the dough. Sift the flour and salt into a large bowl. Make a well in the centre. Pour in the egg, oil and vinegar, and work the mixture lightly with your fingertips until it is crumbly. Gradually incorporate ¼ pint (125 ml) lukewarm water, working it in evenly, until the dough is soft and very sticky. Slightly more or less water may be needed, depending on the absorbency of the flour.

Continue to work and knead the dough until it is smooth. Stretch and throw the dough on to a pastry board until it becomes satin smooth and shiny, leaving the board and fingers absolutely clean.

Shape the dough into a smooth brick. Brush it all over with a generous coating of oil and leave it to rest on the pastry board, covered with a warm bowl, for at least 2 hours.

To make the filling, assemble all the ingredients together in a large bowl, adding them in the order given, and tossing with a large fork so that the ingredients retain a crumbly texture.

To shape the strudel, cover a large table, about 6 feet by 4 feet (180 by 120 cm) with a cloth—a clean cotton bed sheet is ideal. Dust the cloth lightly with flour.

Place the dough in the centre of the cloth and press it out as uniformly as possible with the palm of your hand, keeping it to its rectangular shape as far as you can. Do not use a rolling pin.

Work your hands, palms downwards, under one side of the dough and gradually but firmly stretch it out by lifting the backs of your hands and easing the dough gently towards you, working your way steadily around the table so that the dough stays uniformly thin all over.

Continue until it is paper-thin. (The Viennese say you should be able to read a love letter through it.) The dough should measure about 5 feet (152 cm) long by 3 feet (90 cm) wide. Take care not to tear the dough—it is very difficult to patch at this stage. In warm, dry weather, you will have to work quickly as the dough soon starts to dry out and become brittle.

Trim the edges of the dough with a pair of scissors. Shake melted butter generously over the entire surface with a pastry brush.

Preheat the oven to 425°F (220°C, Gas Mark 7). Butter a large baking sheet. Starting at one of the shorter ends spoon the filling in a long strip on to the dough, leaving a clear border of about 2 inches (5 cm) on the three sides. Fold the two longer sides of the dough over the filling and brush the folds with melted butter.

Lift up the cloth at the end covered with filling and flop the dough over the filling. Continue flopping the dough loosely until it is rolled up to the end and ending with the seam underneath.

Transfer the strudel to the baking sheet, carefully bending it into a horseshoe. Brush generously with melted butter and put it in the oven. Turn the heat down to 350°F (180°C, Gas Mark 4) and bake for about 45 minutes, or until the strudel is crisp and golden brown.

Serve the strudel warm or cold, dusted with icing sugar and accompanied by a bowl of lightly whipped cream.

Special Apple Fritters

These fritters taste special, even if the liqueur is left out. If it is included, use apricot brandy with the apricot jam syrup, and Grand Marnier, Curaçao or Cointreau with either apricot jam or good-quality, rich, dark orange marmalade.

SERVES SIX
FRITTER BATTER
5 oz (150 g) plain flour
Salt
1 tablespoon liqueur (optional)
2 tablespoons oil
2 whites from large eggs
APPLES
4 small cooking apples or crisp, tart dessert apples
½ teaspoon finely grated lemon rind
1 tablespoon lemon juice
1 tablespoon liqueur (optional)
4 tablespoons icing sugar
COATING SYRUP
1 tablespoon sugar
6 tablespoons sieved apricot jam or thick, dark orange marmalade
TO FINISH
¼ lb (120 g) sponge finger biscuits, very finely crushed
Oil for deep-frying
Sifted icing sugar
Chilled, lightly whipped cream, to serve

Start by making the fritter batter so that it has a chance to rest for at least 30 minutes, longer if possible, before it is used. Sift the flour into a bowl with a pinch of salt. Make a well in the centre and gradually blend in ¼ pint (125 ml) of lukewarm water, and the liqueur, if used, followed by the oil. Beat vigorously to a thick, glossy cream. Cover and set aside.

Peel and core the apples, and slice them into ¼-inch (½ cm) thick rings. Sprinkle with lemon rind, the lemon juice mixed with liqueur, if used, and sifted icing sugar. Turn the slices to coat them evenly.

In a heavy pan, dissolve the sugar and the jam over low heat, diluting the mixture with enough water to make a syrup of coating consistency. Simmer the syrup for 1 minute and keep it warm. Coat each apple ring with the syrup, allowing the excess to drain off. Put the sponge finger crumbs on a large plate. As each apple ring is coated with the syrup dip it into the crumbs. Pat them on lightly but firmly on both sides. The apple rings may be left to dry out until they are coated with batter and fried.

Beat the egg whites with a pinch of salt until soft peaks form. Mix them into the batter with a broad-bladed knife.

Heat the oil for deep-frying to 375°F (190°C). Use two long skewers, one for coating the apple rings with batter, the other for taking them in and out of the oil. Deep-fry the apple rings until they are crisp and puffed, flipping them over once or twice. Drain on absorbent paper. Dust with sifted icing sugar and serve immediately, with a bowl of lightly whipped, chilled cream.

French Cream and Apple Tart

Vary this delicious apple tart by using apricot or orange liqueur instead of the brandy, and brushing the base of the pastry shell with warmed, sieved apricot jam or puréed orange marmalade before filling it.

Serve the tart lukewarm, cold or chilled, on the day it is made.

SERVES SIX TO EIGHT
One 10-inch (25 cm) shortcrust pastry shell, prebaked
CUSTARD CREAM
6 tablespoons sugar
Pinch of salt
3 tablespoons cornflour
¼ pint (125 ml) milk
¼ pint (125 ml) single cream
3 egg yolks, lightly beaten
1 tablespoon brandy or 1 teaspoon good-quality vanilla essence
¼ pint (125 ml) double or whipping cream
APPLES
1 tablespoon brandy
1 teaspoon lemon juice
4 large, fragrant dessert apples
2 tablespoons melted butter
2 tablespoons castor sugar, sifted

In a heavy pan, mix the sugar, salt and cornflour together and blend in the milk and cream. Bring the mixture to the boil, stirring, and continue to simmer for 3 to 4 minutes. Remove the pan from the heat and cool the mixture slightly, stirring. Then gradually beat in the egg yolks.

Return the pan to a very low heat and cook, stirring constantly, for 3 to 4 minutes or until the custard is very thick and smooth. Do not let the custard bubble. Stir in the brandy or vanilla. Cool, beating occasionally to prevent a skin forming on top. Set the custard aside in a covered bowl until you are ready to use it.

Prepare the apples. Mix the brandy and lemon juice with 2 tablespoons of cold water in a large bowl. Peel, quarter, core and slice the apples very thinly into the bowl, turning them in the brandy mixture to coat them.

Whisk the double or whipping cream stiffly and fold it into the custard. Spread the custard cream over the base of the pastry shell. Arrange the apple slices in overlapping concentric circles over the top, shaking them free of excess moisture as you lift them out of the bowl. Brush the apples with melted butter and dust with castor sugar.

Place the tart under a moderate grill and grill steadily for 15 to 20 minutes, or until the surface is golden and lightly caramelized. Regulate the heat of the grill so that the sides of the shell do not get too brown before the top is caramelized, or shield the pastry with a little crumpled foil.

German Apple Pancakes

The flavour of these pancakes depends entirely on the apples. Use well-flavoured dessert or cooking apples, using additional sugar if they are tart. Otherwise they need nothing at all. It is an excellent dish for supper or Sunday brunch.

SERVES FOUR
4 large apples
4½ oz (135 g) plain flour
1 teaspoon baking powder
Icing sugar
Salt
4 eggs, separated
½ pint (250 ml) milk
¼ pint (125 ml) double cream
1 teaspoon good-quality vanilla essence
Butter

Peel, core and slice the apples into thin rings.

Sift the flour, baking powder, 1 tablespoon of icing sugar and salt into a bowl. Make a well in the centre and work in the egg yolks, followed by the milk, cream and vanilla, beating vigorously to make a smooth batter.

Make the pancakes in an 8- or 9-inch (20 or 23 cm) frying-pan. Melt enough butter to swirl around the bottom of the pan. Pour in a thin layer of batter to coat the entire surface. As the underside starts to set, gently push a few slices of apple into the surface. Let the pancake brown on the underside and begin to turn firm on top. Then invert it on to a large, lightly buttered plate. Slide the pancake back into the pan to brown the other side. Serve apple-side up, dusted with icing sugar.

Chinese Caramelized Apples

These apples are a favourite dessert in Chinese restaurants in the West. Any other firm fruit can be used instead of apples.

SERVES FOUR
4 tart, firm cooking or eating apples
Lemon juice (optional)
Peanut oil for frying
Ice cubes
10 oz (300 g) sugar
Sesame seeds
BATTER
4 tablespoons cornflour
3 tablespoons plain flour
4 egg whites

Quarter, core and peel the apples, and cut each quarter in half. If they are not to be used immediately, toss them (and any other fruit that might discolour) with a little lemon juice.

With a wire whisk, mix the batter ingredients together thoroughly to make a smooth, coating paste. Fold in the prepared fruit, making sure each piece is individually coated.

Pour enough peanut oil into a wide, deep pan so that the cubes will float comfortably free of the bottom. Deep-fry them in batches to a light golden colour, making sure the oil does not get too hot. Remove the fritters with a slotted spoon and drain them on kitchen paper. Do not worry if they go limp at this stage.

Just before serving, pour 8 tablespoons of the peanut oil into another pan that will take a large batch of the fried fruit at one time. Have ready a large bowl of iced water.

Add the sugar to the oil and swirl the pan gently over a low heat until the sugar has melted and turned a light golden colour—the syrup and the oil will not amalgamate.

As soon as the caramel is ready, drop in a batch of fritters, turn them around with two forks so that they are all individually coated and sticking together in clusters. Still using the forks, lift the clusters from the hot caramel. Shake sesame seeds all over them and drop them into the bowl of iced water.

The syrup will instantly turn into a glassy caramel. Shake the chunks free of water and serve immediately.

Most dessert pears cook well, but the best and juiciest should be eaten uncooked. The rest may be poached, stuffed and baked, cooked in a tart or cooked in spiced and sweetened vinegar and served with meat. To poach pears, first dissolve 4 to 5 ounces (120 to 150 g) of sugar in $1\frac{1}{4}$ pints (625 ml) of water. Add a vanilla pod, a twist of lemon peel or a cinnamon stick to the liquid and simmer it down to 1 pint (500 ml). Peel, halve and core the pears, immediately brushing the exposed surfaces with lemon juice to prevent them turning brown. Drop them into the simmering syrup—1 pint (500 ml) will usually be enough for 6 medium-sized pears. Push a sheet of greaseproof paper right down over the surface and cook gently until the pears are tender. Cool in the syrup.

The simple, classic, ways of serving poached pears are still among the best—such as Cardinale (coated with a Kirsch-flavoured raspberry purée and sprinkled with flaked almonds) or Belle Hélène (two pear halves sandwiched together with vanilla ice-cream and served with hot chocolate sauce).

Pears in Red Wine

Any firm pears can be used for this dish, even those hard, thin pears which obstinately refuse to surrender to any other method of cooking.

There are many delicious variations on this basic recipe: having reduced the syrup to coating consistency, stir in 4 to 6 tablespoons of Cassis, black currant liqueur. For a luxury touch, poach the pears in port or sherry instead of red wine, adjusting the amount of sugar to take into account the sweetness of the wine.

SERVES SIX
6 firm pears
Lemon juice
$\frac{1}{2}$ lb ($\frac{1}{4}$ kg) sugar
2-inch (5 cm) cinnamon stick
2 cloves
2 strips orange peel
2 strips lemon peel
$\frac{1}{2}$ bottle red wine
Red food colouring (optional)
Double cream, lightly whipped

Peel the pears, leaving their stalks on. Drop them into acidulated water as you prepare them.

Dissolve the sugar in $\frac{1}{4}$ pint (125 ml) of water. Add the cinnamon, cloves, orange and lemon peel. Pour in the wine and bring to the boil. Reduce the heat and simmer for 10 minutes.

Arrange the pears side by side, upright in a wide pan or ovenproof casserole large enough to hold them comfortably without letting them tip over. Pour in the boiling wine syrup. Cover the pan tightly and either cook over the lowest possible heat or bake the pears in a 325°F (160°C, Gas Mark 3) oven, basting occasionally with the syrup. It will take from about 30 minutes to $1\frac{1}{2}$ hours for the pears to soften.

With a slotted spoon, transfer the pears to a wide, shallow serving dish. Boil the syrup down to a medium-light coating consistency. Test it by cooling the syrup a little and spooning it over the side of a pear. It should leave a definite gleam. If the colour is not bright enough, intensify it with a few drops of red food colouring.

Spoon the hot syrup over the pears and continue to baste them regularly until they are quite cold. Serve with lightly whipped, chilled, unsweetened cream.

Poires en Chemise

Solid, well-rounded, fragrant pears should be used for this dish. Serve hot, lukewarm or cold—the pastry will even hold well until the following day—with lightly sweetened whipped cream or a fluffy sauce such as a *sabayon*.

SERVES FOUR
4 pears, about $1\frac{1}{2}$ lb ($\frac{3}{4}$ kg)
Lemon juice
Castor sugar
1 egg white, lightly beaten
PASTRY
6 oz (180 g) plain flour
2 tablespoons icing sugar
Pinch of salt
$3\frac{1}{2}$ oz (105 g) chilled butter
1 egg, lightly mixed
ALMOND FILLING
2 oz (60 g) ground almonds
2 tablespoons icing sugar
1 tablespoon softened butter
1 egg yolk, lightly mixed
1 teaspoon lemon juice
Pure almond essence (optional)

First make the pastry. Sift the flour, icing sugar and salt into a bowl. Cut in the chilled butter with a knife, then rub it in lightly with your fingertips until the mixture resembles coarse breadcrumbs. Stir in the egg with a knife. Gently press the crumbs together with cupped hands until they hold together in a ball. Knead lightly until no buttery streaks remain. Divide the pastry in half, seal each ball in plastic wrap or foil and chill for 1 hour.

To make the almond filling, work the ground almonds, sugar and butter together with enough egg yolk to make a smooth, malleable paste. Flavour with lemon juice and 1 or 2 drops of almond essence, if it is being used.

Peel the pears thinly, leaving the stalks on, and carefully core them from the base. Drop each pear into a bowl of acidulated water as soon as it is prepared.

Preheat the oven to 375°F (190°C, Gas Mark 5).

Drain and dry the pears thoroughly with kitchen paper inside and out and stuff them with the almond filling.

Take one ball of pastry from the refrigerator at a time and divide it in two. Roll each piece out into a 6- or 7-inch (15 or 18 cm) circle and cut out a wedge of about one-third. Bring the cut edges together to make a "cup" for a pear. With a 2-inch (5 cm) pastry cutter, cut out 2 rounds from the leftover wedge of pastry—rolling out a little if necessary. Press one round gently into the base of the "cup" to reinforce it.

Put a pear in the cup and gently mould the pastry case around it, working it right up towards the stem with cupped hands, and making sure there is no air trapped between the pastry and the pear. Push the other little round of pastry over the stalk and press it down gently over the top of the pear. Dust the pastry very lightly with sifted castor sugar. Use the remaining scraps of pastry to decorate the pears, fixing the decorations on with a little egg white.

Arrange the pears on a lightly buttered baking sheet and bake for 30 minutes, or until the pastry is golden and the pears inside feel tender when pierced with a thin skewer. Brush the pears with lightly mixed egg white after the first 15 minutes.

Pears

Pear Bread

This is a sweet milk bread to serve with tea or coffee. If fresh yeast is not available use dry yeast. Reconstitute the dry yeast according to the instructions on the packet.

ONE LOAF
½ oz (15 g) fresh yeast
2 tablespoons sugar
2 tablespoons honey
2 oz (60 g) butter
4 fl oz (100 ml) milk
¾ lb (360 g) flour
Salt
1 egg, lightly beaten
¾ lb (360 g) dried pears, chopped
¼ lb (120 g) sultanas
Grated rind and juice of ½ lemon
1 teaspoon ground cinnamon
Port wine
2 oz (60 g) walnuts or pecans, chopped
Sweetened milk, to glaze

In a small bowl, mash the yeast, ½ teaspoon of sugar and 2 tablespoons of lukewarm water. Set the bowl aside in a warm place for 15 minutes, or until the yeast is puffed up and frothy.

Meanwhile, melt the honey and butter in the milk. The mixture should be no hotter than lukewarm. Sift the flour and salt into a large warmed bowl. Make a well in the centre and pour in the frothy yeast, the milk mixture and the egg. Using your fingers, mix the flour and liquid together to make a soft dough. Add more liquid if the dough is too dry or more flour if it is too sticky.

Pat the dough into a ball and turn it out on to a floured surface. Knead well for 10 minutes. Make a ball of the dough and put it into a lightly greased bowl. Cover with a greased polythene bag and set aside in a warm place for 1 hour, or until the dough doubles in bulk.

Meanwhile, put the pears, sultanas, the remaining sugar, lemon rind and juice and the cinnamon in a saucepan. Add ¼ pint (125 ml) of port wine and simmer the mixture, stirring frequently, for 20 minutes, or until the fruit is a soft mush. Add more wine, if necessary, to keep the fruit cooking without sticking to the bottom of the pan. The mixture should be very thick and moist. Stir in the nuts and set aside to cool.

Grease a baking sheet.

Punch down the dough and turn it out on to a floured surface. Knead it for 2 minutes. Roll the dough into a rectangle ¼-inch (½ cm) thick. Spread the filling over the dough leaving a 1-inch (2 cm) border all round. Fold the longer sides of the rectangle over the filling and roll from the shorter side to make a Swiss roll.

Transfer the roll to the baking sheet and set it aside in a warm place for 1 hour.

Preheat the oven to 400°F (200°C, Gas Mark 6).

Brush the top of the roll with the sweetened milk and bake for 10 minutes. Reset the oven to 350°F (180°C, Gas Mark 4) and bake for a further 50 minutes.

Let the bread cool completely before serving.

Pear Salad

Pears make marvellous salads. A ripe, well-flavoured dessert pear is delicious peeled, sliced and dressed with a lemon-based *vinaigrette* and served on a bed of lettuce leaves.

Pears diced and mixed with equal quantities of cucumber and pineapple, cucumber and grapes or cucumber and melon and dressed with a *vinaigrette* make a refreshing first course.

Pears have an affinity with cheese, particularly a mild blue cheese such as *Roquefort*, a creamy *Brie* or *Fromage de Monsieur Fromage*, the crumbly English cheeses Cheshire and Lancashire, and cream cheese.

Peel, halve and core the pears, stuff them with a mixture of cheese and cream and serve with a creamy dressing on a crisp lettuce leaf or mash the cheese into a *vinaigrette* and pour it over sliced pears.

Serve this salad with cold meat or poultry.

SERVES FOUR TO SIX
4 large, firm, ripe dessert pears, lightly chilled
Lemon juice
Lettuce leaves
Walnuts or pecan nuts, to garnish
DRESSING
2 oz (60 g) Roquefort cheese, crumbled
¼ pint (125 ml) home-made, thick, lemon mayonnaise
2 tablespoons double cream, lightly whipped
Salt (optional)

Peel, halve, core and slice the pears thinly lengthwise. Sprinkle the slices with lemon juice and arrange them on the lettuce leaves on a serving dish.

To make the dressing, beat the Roquefort into the mayonnaise. Fold in the cream. Taste the dressing and, if necessary, add more seasoning.

Spoon the dressing over the pears. Garnish with the walnuts or pecans and serve.

Pear and Ginger Tart

Serve this tart warm. The custard should be creamy and not set hard.

SERVES SIX
One 9-inch (23 cm) tart tin lined with rich shortcrust pastry
3 tablespoons sugar
1 tablespoon preserved ginger syrup
1½ lb (¾ kg) pears
2 egg yolks
2 teaspoons cornflour
½ pint (250 ml) single cream, hot
½ teaspoon vanilla essence
2 oz (60 g) preserved ginger, drained and chopped

Preheat the oven to 400°F (200°C, Gas Mark 6).

Line the pastry shell with foil. Weigh the foil down with dried beans and bake for 10 minutes. Remove the tin from the oven and set aside.

Reset the oven to 325°F (160°C, Gas Mark 3).

In a large saucepan, dissolve 1 tablespoon of the sugar in ½ pint (250 ml) of water. Stir in the ginger syrup. Peel, quarter and core the pears. Put them in the syrup and poach gently for 15 minutes. Remove the pears from the syrup and set aside to cool.

In a small bowl, beat the egg yolks with the remaining sugar and cornflour. Stir in the hot cream and the vanilla.

Arrange the pears in the pastry case. Scatter the chopped ginger over the pears. Pour the custard over the top. Bake for 45 minutes, or until the custard is set.

Serve warm.

Strawberries

If one had to choose just a single fruit to symbolize perfection in an English summer garden, it could only be the strawberry, jewel-red against its bright green cap. It should be treated with the care it deserves.

Unless strawberries are very dirty avoid washing them. If it is necessary, however, put them in a colander, one layer at a time, spray them with water and shake them dry. If they are not very dirty, dampen a clean kitchen cloth and roll the strawberries up in it carefully to avoid bruising them. Any grit will adhere to the cloth.

If strawberries have to be stored for any length of time, put them at the bottom of the refrigerator, then let them come back to room temperature before serving.

When serving strawberries, do not be inhibited by the purists, for whom it is cream or nothing. Eat them with orange juice or lemon juice, covered in raspberry purée, dipped in soured cream and brown sugar, or in sweet white wine, in red wine—even in champagne.

Strawberry Babas

This sweet takes something from two very different strawberry classics—the French *coeur à la crème* and the American strawberry shortcake. If French *Petit Suisse* is not available, curd cheese can be substituted. Before weighing the curd cheese, squeeze it dry in a piece of muslin. Curd cheese can be blander than *Petit Suisse*, so add a tiny pinch of salt and a drop or two of lemon juice to flavour it if necessary.

SERVES SIX
1 lb (½ kg) medium-sized ripe strawberries, hulled
3 oz (90 g) castor sugar
4 tablespoons orange liqueur or Kirsch
6 oz (180 g) Petit Suisse cheese or about ½ lb (¼ kg) curd cheese
3 oz (90 g) vanilla icing sugar, sifted
Lemon juice (optional)
¼ pint (125 ml) whipping cream
6 individual babas
Orange juice

Toss the strawberries with the castor sugar and the liqueur and set aside for at least 1 hour to draw out the juices.

Beat the cheese and icing sugar together until fluffy, adding a few drops of lemon juice if you are using curd cheese. Whisk the cream until soft peaks form and mix it lightly but thoroughly into the cheese mixture. Chill until required.

Carefully scoop out the insides of the babas to leave firm cases about ⅓ inch (1 cm) thick.

Drain the strawberries thoroughly. Measure the juice and if necessary make it up to ½ pint (250 ml) with fresh orange juice.

Shortly before serving, saturate the soft interiors of the baba cases with the juice. Reserve some of the cheese mixture for decoration and use the remainder to coat the insides of the cases. Divide the strawberries between them, piling them up attractively. Sprinkle any remaining juice over the strawberries.

Finish each baba with a swirl of the reserved cheese cream and either serve immediately or chill briefly—but no longer than it would take to reach the sweet course from the start of the meal.

Strawberry Shortcake

A traditional American dessert and a delicious way to serve strawberries and cream.

MAKES ONE 8-INCH (20 CM) CAKE
½ lb (¼ kg) plain flour
3 teaspoons baking powder
1 tablespoon castor sugar
½ teaspoon salt
2 oz (60 g) butter, cut into small pieces
6 fl oz (150 ml) milk
FILLING
1 lb (½ kg) strawberries, hulled
2 tablespoons castor sugar
½ pint (250 ml) double cream

Preheat the oven to 450°F (230°C, Gas Mark 8). Lightly butter two 8-inch (20 cm) cake tins.

Sift the flour, baking powder, sugar and salt into a mixing bowl. Add the butter and mix it in, using your fingers, until the mixture resembles coarse breadcrumbs.

Make a well in the centre and pour in the milk. Using your fingers, incorporate the dry ingredients into the milk until the mixture forms a dough. Knead the dough lightly on a floured board.

Divide the dough in half. Pat each half into the buttered cake tins and bake for 10 minutes, or until golden.

Turn out the shortcakes on to a rack and set aside to cool.

Slice half the strawberries into a bowl and sprinkle them with half the sugar. Whip the cream until it is very thick but not stiff.

To assemble the cake, spread half the cream on one of the shortcakes and arrange the sliced strawberries on top. Cover with the other shortcake. Swirl the remaining cream on top and decorate with the remaining whole strawberries. Sprinkle the remaining sugar on top.

Strawberry Meringue

A glorious concoction of strawberries, cream and crushed meringues. It can be flavoured with an orange liqueur, Kirsch, Framboise or brandy, or simply use vanilla sugar.

SERVES SIX TO EIGHT
2 lb (1 kg) strawberries, hulled
8 tablespoons icing sugar
6 tablespoons liqueur—see above
½ pint (250 ml) double cream, chilled
¼ pint (125 ml) single cream, chilled
Meringues, made with 2 egg whites

Chop the strawberries up roughly or leave small ones whole. Put a dozen of the most perfect aside for decoration.

Sift the icing sugar over the strawberries and sprinkle them with the liqueur. Mix lightly and chill for 1 hour.

Whisk the creams together until they hold their shape in firm peaks. Gently fold in the strawberries and their juices. Crush the meringues into pieces and fold into the cream and strawberry mixture. Taste and add more sugar if necessary. Pile into a serving bowl. Dot with reserved whole strawberries and serve immediately.

After strawberries, raspberries are the most popular of the berries. For the cook, however, raspberries are more versatile and useful. Unlike the strawberry, the raspberry freezes well, which is important when there is an abundance of soft fruit in the summer.

Raspberries are comparative newcomers in the kitchen. Few early nineteenth-century cookery books mention them except occasionally in recipes for vinegars, cordials and sometimes for jams and tarts.

Washing is disastrous for fresh raspberries. Just be sure they do not have the stray little worm or bad spot, and serve them as they are with a little sugar and cream. If you are tempted to flavour the cream with anything but sugar, do be discreet—a drop of lemon or lime juice, a little sherry, sweet port or Kirsch, or the raspberries' own liqueur, Framboise.

Raspberries can also be made into compotes, jam and ice-cream—raspberry water ice is particularly delectable and refreshing.

Raspberry Cream ice

The flavour of this cream ice can be changed by mixing three tablespoons of such liqueurs as Framboise or Kirsch into the purée, or by substituting a handful of red currants for some of the raspberries before puréeing. For either of these variations the lemon juice should be left out.

SERVES FOUR
½ pint (250 ml) raspberry purée made with about ¾ lb (360 g) raspberries
8 tablespoons castor sugar
Juice of 1 small lemon
2 egg whites
Salt
¼ pint (125 ml) whipping cream, chilled

Put the raspberry purée into a bowl. Add 5 tablespoons of the sugar and the lemon juice and stir until the sugar has completely dissolved.

Whisk the egg whites with a pinch of salt, and, as soft peaks begin to form, gradually whisk in the remaining sugar, a tablespoon at a time. Continue whisking vigorously until the mixture is stiff and glossy.

Whisk the cream to soft peak stage. With a large metal spoon or spatula, fold the cream into the meringue, then gently fold in the raspberry purée.

Freeze the mixture in a shallow dish until hard, folding the mixture over from sides to centre after the first hour, or when the edges have begun to harden. Then return to a refrigerator at normal setting for at least 1 hour before serving.

Raspberry Mousse

Use fresh or frozen raspberries for this delightful dessert. Serve the mousse decorated with whole raspberries and whipped cream.

SERVES SIX
½ oz (15 g) gelatine
1 lb (½ kg) fresh raspberries or 1½ lb (¾ kg) frozen raspberries
½ pint (250 ml) double cream
4 tablespoons castor sugar
4 eggs, separated
¼ lb (120 g) macaroons

Dissolve the gelatine in 2 tablespoons of water in a cup placed in a pan of hot water.

Put the raspberries in a blender and purée at high speed. Line a strainer with cheesecloth or muslin and strain the purée through it into a bowl. Set aside.

In the top of a double saucepan, whisk the cream, sugar and egg yolks together. Put the pan over barely simmering water and cook, whisking, until the custard is thick and smooth. Stir in the dissolved gelatine and the raspberry purée and set aside to cool, stirring occasionally.

Whip the egg whites until they are stiff and fold them gently but thoroughly into the raspberry cream mixture. Put the mixture into a serving bowl. Cover it and put it in the refrigerator until the mousse is nearly set.

Meanwhile, crush the macaroons into coarse crumbs with a rolling pin.

Remove the mousse from the refrigerator and fold in the macaroon crumbs. Cover the bowl and return it to the refrigerator and chill for 4 hours, or until the mousse is completely set.

Raspberry Bavarian Cream

A Bavarian cream should be creamy in texture, yet firm enough to turn out of a decorative mould. Raspberries picked from the garden on a dry day will purée to a slightly thicker consistency than those which have been frozen. If frozen raspberries are being used, either drain off the juice as they defrost—in which case it will take about ¼ pound (120 g) more to make up the ¾ pint (375 ml) of purée—or blend 2 teaspoons of cornflour with the sugar before beating it with the egg yolks to make the custard.

SERVES SIX TO EIGHT
About 1 lb (½ kg) raspberries—see above
½ oz (15 g) powdered gelatine
¾ pint (375 ml) milk
5 egg yolks
¼ lb (120 g) sugar
4 egg whites
Salt
2 oz (60 g) castor sugar
Lemon juice (optional)
¼ pint (125 ml) whipping cream, chilled

Prepare the raspberry purée and chill it in the refrigerator until required. Sprinkle the gelatine over 3 tablespoons of cold water in a cup and leave it to soften.

Prepare an egg custard. Scald the milk in a saucepan by heating it gently until the surface just begins to tremble slightly. Meanwhile, in the top of a double saucepan or a bowl, beat the egg yolks with the sugar until fluffy. Gradually beat in the scalded milk.

Fit the pan over the base of simmering water. The bottom of the top container should not be in contact with the water. Stir the custard steadily over simmering water until it is so thick that when you draw a finger down the back of the spoon you leave a distinct trail. Do not let the custard boil or it will curdle.

Put the cup of softened gelatine in a pan of hot water and stir until it is clear.

Pour the custard into a bowl. Stir in the dissolved gelatine and set aside until cool, but not yet beginning to set.

Whisk the egg whites with a pinch of salt. As peaks start to form, gradually whisk in 2 tablespoons of castor sugar. Continue to whisk until the whites form soft peaks. Whisk the cream to the same consistency in another bowl. Stir the remaining sugar into the chilled raspberry purée. Taste it—it should be very sharp and may need a tablespoon of lemon juice.

With a large metal spoon, fold the egg whites into the cream. Stir about two-thirds of the raspberry purée into the bowl of custard. Fold the rest of the raspberry purée into the cream mixture, then combine the two, folding the custard into the cream mixture.

Pour the mixture into a 3-pint (2 litre) mould rinsed out with cold water. Refrigerate for 6 hours, or until completely set.

To unmould, dip the mould in and out of a bowl of very hot water. Run a knife around the edge. Place a serving dish on top and reverse the mould on to it, shaking gently to ease it out. Refrigerate the Bavarian cream until it is served.

Herbs

Used imaginatively and with finesse, herbs add an exciting new dimension to cooking. The culinary role of herbs, from the simplest parsley sauce to the most sophisticated *paté aux fines herbes*, is essentially that of giving a dish character. Stuff a chicken with tarragon, for example, roast it and you have a classic French *poulet à l'estragon*. Substitute dill for the tarragon and the dish is unmistakably central European. Stuff the chicken with sage and onion and you have a dish as British as steamed pudding.

Some herbs taste best fresh, others contribute more flavour when they are dried. Some should be added in the early stages of cooking a dish. Others are so volatile that their flavour would be destroyed by prolonged cooking. And there are herbs—sorrel, chervil and parsley for example—which can be the dominating ingredient in a dish.

Herb sugars, made like vanilla sugar, are as delightful as herb-flavoured honey and as interesting as herb salts. Herb sugars can be used to flavour cakes, sweet breads and drinks.

Herbs may also be drunk in *tisanes*. A sage infusion was a popular drink in England until it was ousted by tea, and mint tea is still Morocco's national beverage.

Preserving Herbs

Herbs which are to be preserved should be picked at the height of their season, just before they flower. They should be cut in the morning on a fine day. Cut long stems and tie them loosely in slim bunches. Then leave them in a cool, dark place to dry naturally—avoid artificial heat if possible. An airing cupboard may be used, but only to finish off the drying process. Keep different herbs separate or the flavours will blend.

If you are drying for seed, cut the stems with the seed heads as soon as they are ripe. Dry the whole stalks, then thresh them out over a sheet of clean paper. Give the seeds a few hours further drying in the sun or in a warm, dry place. The airing cupboard is ideal.

Hang dried herbs in bunches in a dry place or rub the brittle leaves off the stalks between your palms and store them in tightly stoppered, dark glass jars. (A faded appearance is one of the sure signs of staleness.)

The flavour of dried herbs is much stronger than that of fresh herbs. One teaspoon of dried herbs equals approximately three teaspoons of chopped fresh herbs.

Freezing Herbs

Deep-freezing is the most successful method of preserving the natural flavour of herbs. To prepare herbs for freezing, cut them with their stems. Dip them carefully in boiling water to set the colour, pat them dry and deep-freeze, spread out loosely in well-sealed plastic envelopes. Another method is to chop the herbs finely, pack them tightly into individual ice-cube trays, cover with water and freeze. Put the frozen cubes in a plastic bag for storage in the freezer.

The herbs may also be chopped, mixed with butter to make a paste and deep-frozen in small, sealed boxes. Use herb butter to flavour and enrich delicate cream or buttery dishes. If the preparation of the dish involves frying, add the butter after this has been done.

Herbed Oils and Vinegars

A small bunch of fresh herbs—three or four sprigs—put into a bottle of olive oil or wine vinegar, will give it an exquisite fragrance. Add a pinch of sea salt and, if it is a strong herb like rosemary, a peppercorn or two. Give the oil or vinegar a few weeks to absorb the flavour of the herb (or herbs—you can make an oil or vinegar *aux fines herbes*) before using them.

Salted Herbs

Chop the herbs finely. Make $\frac{1}{4}$-inch ($\frac{1}{2}$ cm) layers, sprinkled generously in between with salt, in a glass jar. Use a dark jar or cover an ordinary jar with foil to exclude the light. Salted herbs will keep for several months.

A sharp knife and a flexible wrist is all you need for chopping herbs. For a large quantity of herbs, however, a mezzaluna is quicker and more efficient.

Basil

With its sunny-sweet, light yet spicy fragrance, basil is the ideal partner for vegetable fruits, above all the tomato. Try slices of tomato covered with a thick layer of chopped basil, parsley and shallot and dressed with oil and vinegar.

The Genoese use basil to make *pesto*, their superb classic sauce. A large bunch of basil leaves is pounded to a paste with 1 or 2 garlic cloves and 1 tablespoon of toasted pine nuts. Two or three ounces (60 to 90 g) of Parmesan cheese or a mixture of Parmesan and Pecorino cheese are gradually incorporated, and the paste is diluted with olive oil to make a thick sauce. *Pesto* is used to dress Italian noodles, or as a last minute flavouring for minestrone.

Bay

This is one of the few herbs which is better dried than fresh. The flavour of a dried bay leaf is not only more concentrated, but somehow richer, particularly if it is torn or crushed.

Bay, automatically included in the standard *bouquet garni*, improves the flavour of many different meat and fish dishes including *carbonades à la Flamande*, the famous Belgian beef stew made with beer, chicken fricassée and fish chowder. Use bay, too, when you are making soups, marinades and stock. It may even be added to rice pudding.

Remember, however, that you can spoil a dish if you use too much of this herb; an excess of bay is definitely unpleasant.

Chervil

Chervil and parsley are practically interchangeable—to the extent that chervil is often referred to as "flat-leaf parsley". The flavour of chervil, although stronger, is sweeter and more subtle than that of parsley.

Chervil plays a vital part in the classic *fines herbes*, and it may be added to *bouquets garnis* together with, or instead of, parsley. Sprinkle chervil over raw or cooked salads and delicate-flavoured soups.

Use chervil with other herbs, too. For example, a little chervil complements tarragon beautifully in chicken dishes, and it does the same for thyme.

The flavour of chervil is best preserved by freezing or salting.

Dill

Although a southern European herb by origin, dill is a northerner by adoption. Even its name is Norse. Dill is used extensively in Scandinavian and central European cooking and is commonly used to flavour pickled cucumbers.

Dill is at its best uncooked. Chop it into soured cream for a central European-style dressing for green salads or sliced cucumbers. Use it with mayonnaise for a Scandinavian fish salad, or with butter for young vegetables, in particular new potatoes, and sprinkle it over fresh vegetable soups.

Dill seed is less pungent than caraway. If you prefer the milder flavour, use dill seed instead of caraway to sprinkle over bread rolls and to flavour coleslaw.

Dill seeds dry well. Home-dried dill leaves are not usually a great success; the commercial manufacturers do it better. Dill leaves are, however, ideal for salting. Dill vinegar will be very useful, the oil less so.

Fennel

Fennel has the sweet, forceful flavour of anise. Its great role in cooking is for flavouring fish, particularly fish which is oily.

Otherwise, use fennel leaves and seeds as you would dill. A pinch of fennel seeds adds an unusual but pleasant flavour to a traditional apple pie.

Be sure that fennel seeds are perfectly dry before storing them in a jar, as they are prone to black mould.

Fennel oil and vinegar are invaluable for brushing over baked fish of all kinds and may also be used to make salad dressings and mayonnaise.

Horseradish

Grating the roots of fresh horseradish is more trying on the eyes than peeling the strongest onion. If possible, use an electric mincer—a hand grater should only be used as a last resort.

Grated horseradish may be folded into whipped cream to serve with roast beef, or mixed into a mayonnaise.

Boiled beef is superb with a rich cream sauce based on the cooking stock and flavoured with grated horseradish.

To preserve horseradish, grate it and cover with vinegar in a screw-top jar. Use it either just as it is, or mixed with grated cooked beetroot.

Marjoram

Sweet Marjoram, cousin to the wild oregano of the south, is almost as versatile as parsley. Its sweet, lightly spicy flavour will give a lift to soups. Rub marjoram into roasts, add it to casseroles and sprinkle it over such vegetables as baby carrots and turnips. And do not forget it when you are preparing a stuffing for chicken or lamb. Fish also benefits from a touch of marjoram.

Marjoram should be dried carefully and slowly. Use sprigs collected when the plant is flowering and store it either in bunches or crumbled.

Marjoram vinegar and oil are useful.

Mints

Probably the most useful varieties of mint are spearmint and the strongish Bowles mint. Both are good for making mint sauce. Use peppermint and apple mint for sweet dishes.

The flavour of mint enhances young vegetables and salads, and fruit salads benefit from just a touch of its flavour. Use a mint leaf to garnish raspberry ice-cream or half a grapefruit.

Preserve and store mint in the usual way or make a mint sugar using 1 sprig of mint to flavour 2 ounces (60 g) of sugar, to sprinkle over buns and cakes.

Parsley

Parsley, the most commonly used of all the herbs, boasts a staggering list of vitamins, headed by Vitamin C.

Parsley is the most versatile of culinary herbs. It may be used simply as a garnish or made into parsley sauce or soup. The French use parsley as one of the main ingredients of *persillade de jambon*, in which pink chunks of ham are set in a jelly coloured bright green with finely chopped parsley.

Parsley need not be dried, it survives the winter quite happily. Deep-freeze left-over parsley in cubes for economy rather than convenience—there is no point in letting it go to waste.

Rosemary

Mediterranean cuisines use a great deal of rosemary in all kinds of dishes. Its pungent fragrance, slightly reminiscent of a pine forest, flavours such delicate meats as veal, baby lamb and poultry, as well as beef casseroles enriched with wine. It is also used with vegetables and in summer fruit salads and drinks.

Although rosemary is an evergreen, it is sometimes convenient to have a store of dried sprigs. It is a wonderful flavouring for oil and vinegar as well as for sugar—use a large sprig of rosemary and the dried grated rind of a small orange to ¼ pound (120 g) of sugar.

Sage

If any herb, apart from parsley, could be said to characterize English cooking, it would be sage, as represented in sage and onion stuffing. But this is not to say that sage is exclusively British. Its warm, slightly camphor-like fragrance is familiar in many cuisines.

Sage complements the fatty flavour of rich meats, which is why it has been used traditionally to flavour stuffings for pork, duck and goose—remember the Cratchit family's lunch in *A Christmas Carol*?

Sage is also good for flavouring bland, soft cheeses and delicate meat dishes. Fresh sage leaves are used in the famous Roman dish *saltimbocca*, (literally "jump in the mouth").

Dried, rubbed sage is easier to use than fresh sage. Dry it very slowly to preserve the maximum flavour and colour. Crumble the leaves and store in an air-tight jar.

Sage vinegar and oil are worth making. A few mustard seeds added with the sage gives the oil a pleasant flavour.

Savory

Strong, spicy, bordering on the peppery, savory is such a natural flavouring for beans that the Germans call it *Bohnenkraut*, the bean herb.

Summer savory is milder than winter savory, but both should be used sparingly with all peas and beans, with cucumber and in salads. Cook heavy meats, like pork, with a touch of savory. Savory is also a classic fish herb, traditionally used to flavour trout.

Sorrel

It is difficult to deal with sorrel without mentioning spinach—the two are treated so similarly in the kitchen. Sorrel soup, for example, is made in the same way as the spinach soup on page 145, except that the dill is left out. For a more muted flavour, use a mixture of sorrel and fresh spinach.

Sorrel is also good in green salads, and it may be chopped into omelettes or puréed to a sauce for fish.

Sorrel can be dried, but it is better fresh.

Tarragon (French)

Tarragon, one of the greatest herbs of all, transforms any ingredient with which it comes in contact. Try wrapping a fresh egg in tarragon leaves. Seal the egg in foil or plastic wrap, leave it in the refrigerator for at least 24 hours, then soft-boil it. It will be an egg such as you have never tasted, for the flavour of the herb will have penetrated the porous shell.

Use tarragon with respect, however mild it may taste when picked, for no herb is more deceptive. A chicken stuffed with a few sprigs of tarragon and a lump of seasoned butter, will come out of the oven vibrating with flavour. When making dishes which need long cooking, tarragon should be added towards the end, not at the beginning.

Tarragon comes into its own in *sauce béarnaise*, the herbed version of *hollandaise*. This sauce makes a wonderful accompaniment for steaks, grilled chicken, fish, shellfish and various vegetables including artichokes.

French tarragon will not survive the winter in Britain. You may dry or freeze the leaves but do not salt them. Flavour oil and vinegar with the herb: use the oil to make dressings and to brush over roasts, barbecues and grills and the vinegar for dressings and sauces.

Thyme

Thyme has been valued for centuries, not only for its wonderful, pungent aroma, which enhances meats, soups, poultry stuffings, herb vinegars and such vegetable fruits as aubergines and courgettes, but also for its antiseptic and disinfectant thymol content.

The refreshing flavour of lemon thyme is used in herb butters, custards and in fruit salads. Thyme is best when fresh but is sometimes useful dried.

To dry garden thyme, pick the branches before flowering, then hang them in a cool, dry place for a few weeks. Rub the leaves off the stems and store in a tightly stoppered jar.

Parsley, bay leaves and thyme are the herbs most commonly used together to make a traditional bouquet garni.

Tie a bouquet of herbs in a split leek to make a convenient flavouring for stocks and stews.

A bouquet of dried herbs and flavourings can be tied in a small piece of muslin or cheesecloth.

Freezing

For the cook with a kitchen garden the freezer is a great ally. It safely stores all those vegetables and fruits that would otherwise go to waste, for there are few gardens that do not have a glut at one time or another.

Freezing preserves the texture, flavour and nutritional value of garden produce better than any other method of preserving. It is simple and efficient and, if the rules are observed and the food used intelligently, it is difficult to distinguish the frozen from the fresh.

Quality should be of prime importance. Only the youngest, freshest and best vegetables and fruit should be frozen. Once cropped they should go into the freezer as quickly as possible. Delay should not extend beyond a few hours, and during that time the vegetables and fruit should be kept cool to prevent deterioration and wilting. Correct processing and, later, thawing (when necessary) and cooking will all help to keep flavour and food value intact.

The techniques of preparing and packing food for freezing are easy to master and the equipment required is minimal and inexpensive. The storage life of most vegetables and fruit in the freezer will usually extend from one growing season to the next.

However large your freezer, every inch of space is precious and it is wise to work out a plan for how best to utilize it. Decide how much of the total freezer space you can devote to the vegetables and fruit you expect to come from the garden. Then divide it in three to take into account dishes that have been precooked, vegetables or fruit that are being frozen in portions (to serve a given number) and the produce that you intend to freeze in large bags, for drawing on as necessary.

Any precooked dish of fruit or vegetables will freeze admirably, except for those containing large amounts of such emulsified sauces or dressings as mayonnaise, *hollandaise* and *béarnaise*, which tend to separate when defrosted.

Blanching

According to many experts, almost every vegetable should be blanched before it is frozen. There are others, however, who think differently. They suggest that in some cases, provided the produce is garden-fresh and processed on the day it has been picked, blanching is quite unnecessary. If you have reservations, try both methods and compare the results. (See individual entries, which follow.)

When blanching is necessary, it should be done systematically, particularly for a large crop. Have ready a large, deep, wide pot of boiling water (at least 6 pints [3 litres] of water is needed for 1 pound [½ kg] of vegetables) and a blanching basket. A blanching basket is the only specialized piece of equipment you will need and you can substitute a large, wide sieve or a salad shaker, provided the mesh is fine

enough not to let through small pieces of vegetables. Next, put one colander in the sink under the cold tap and have another close at hand on the draining board.

Put a layer of vegetables, no more than 1 pound (½ kg) at a time, in the blanching basket. Submerge it in the pot of boiling water. The water must return to the boil over high heat before you start to time the blanching. As soon as the specified time is up, transfer the contents of the basket to the colander under the cold tap. Let cold water spray over the vegetables for the same length of time as the blanching took. (The water must be very cold. If necessary use ice to chill the water in a large pan or bowl and submerge the basket in it.) Finally, tip the vegetables into the other colander and let them drain while you blanch the next batch.

Packing

To avoid the danger of all the vegetables sticking together, unless you can be sure that the blanched or unblanched vegetables are quite dry, it is best to freeze them in a single layer on a tray before packing them in boxes or polythene bags.

It is also important to remember that liquids will expand as they freeze. Therefore space must be left to allow for this—½ inch (1 cm) will usually be sufficient. Boxes and bags should be tightly sealed so that air cannot circulate around the food itself while it is in the freezer. In the case of boxes, special self-sealing ones are available. Unless the food is particularly fragile and vulnerable—like asparagus spears, which have to stay in a rigid box to avoid the danger of snapping into pieces—the most economical way to use boxes is to freeze the vegetables or fruit in boxes and then to transfer the frozen blocks to polythene bags. Square or rectangular boxes are best since they will stack well. Round containers are difficult to fit in among the square ones and result in a great waste of freezer space.

If you are freezing directly in polythene bags, you must extract as much air as possible before sealing the bag. Fill the bag with the vegetables or fruit, gather the top together in one hand and insert a straw in the opening with the other. Then, holding the sides of the bag as tightly as possible around the straw, suck out the air inside until the polythene clings to the food inside like a second skin.

Always label and date the contents of bags and boxes. Be sure that any labels stuck on to the containers will not come adrift in the freezer. Tie-on tags or those that come already attached to a coated wire are the best for bags, and there are labels and sticker tapes treated with special adhesive available from stores specializing in freezer accessories. Use a ball point pen or special freezer pen for writing the labels. Ordinary felt pen or ink will smudge and become illegible.

To blanch vegetables, put them in a blanching basket and lower it into boiling water. When the water returns to the boil begin timing the blanching.

Transfer the blanching basket with the vegetables to a bowl filled with iced water and cool for the same length of time as for blanching.

Vegetable preparation and blanching chart		
Vegetable	**Preparation**	**Blanching time after water reboils, in minutes**
Asparagus	Wash. Trim tough stems and buds. Grade the stalks. Cut into even lengths to fit rigid containers. Or freeze cooked.	2 (thin) 3 (medium) 4 (thick)
Beans, broad (unblanched) Beans, broad Beans, French Beans, runner	Shell and freeze in bags or peel off outer skin, freeze in trays then put in bags. Shell, freeze in bags. Wash, string if necessary, top and tail. Keep whole or slice, freeze in bags or boxes. Wash, string, if necessary, top and tail. Slice diagonally in ½-inch (1 cm) slices. Freeze in bags.	1½ 3 (whole) 2 (sliced) 2
Broccoli	Trim off woody stems and stray leaves. Wash in salted water. Freeze on trays before packing in bags or boxes.	3
Brussels sprouts	Trim off outer leaves. Cut stems. Grade by size. Freeze in boxes or bags.	3 (small) 4 (medium)
Capsicums (sweet peppers)	Seed and core. Halve or cut in strips or rings. Freeze in boxes or bags.	1½
Carrots (young) Carrots (old)	Wipe clean. Leave whole. Freeze in bags. Scrape, slice or dice. Freeze in bags.	2 3
Cauliflower	Separate into large flowerets. Wash in acidulated water. Freeze on trays before packing in bags or boxes.	2
Chicory	Trim and wash. Blanch in acidulated water. Squeeze out moisture. Freeze on trays before packing in bags or boxes.	2
Courgettes	Wash, trim and dry. Cut into thick slices. Blanch in salted water. Freeze in bags or boxes. Or freeze cooked.	2 to 3
Globe artichokes Globe artichoke hearts	Slice leaves low and scoop out chokes. Cool in iced water. Freeze in boxes. Prepare and blanch. Cool in iced water. Pat dry and freeze on trays before packing in bags or boxes.	6 (small) 7 (medium) 8 (large) 4 (small) 5 (medium)
Leeks	Trim, wash and blanch. Freeze whole or sliced. Or freeze cooked.	1 to 2
Mushrooms	Whole or sliced. Cook in butter, flavoured with a squeeze of lemon juice. Freeze in bags or boxes.	
Parsnips (young)	Trim and brush clean, or peel thinly. Quarter or dice. Freeze in bags.	2
Peas (unblanched) Peas *Petit pois* (unblanched)	Pod and freeze in bags or boxes. Pod and freeze in bags or boxes. Pod and freeze.	1
Potatoes (new) Potatoes (chips)	Clean with damp cloth. Freeze in a large bag. Peel and slice. Deep-fry for 5 minutes. Drain on kitchen paper. When cold, freeze in a large bag. Or blanch and freeze. Potatoes for roasting may be treated in the same way.	3 (small) 4 (medium) 3
Salsify and Scorzonera	Trim. Scrape the scorzonera. Blanch whole or sliced. Freeze in bags.	2
Spinach	Wash carefully, leaf by leaf. Only blanch a little at a time. Squeeze out moisture. Leave whole or chop and freeze in boxes or bags.	2
Sweet corn Corn on the cob (unblanched) Corn on the cob Corn kernels	Strip off husks and silks. Do not wash. Freeze on trays. Wrap individually in freezer paper or self-sealing plastic wrap before packing in bags. Prepare as above but blanch before freezing. Blanch the cobs first as above. Scrape off the kernels. Dry on a cloth. Freeze in bags.	3 (small) 5 to 6 (medium) 7 to 8 (large)
Tomatoes	Freeze only as pulp, juice or in cooked dishes.	

Prepare a fruit pie in a foil pie dish as for baking, but brush the pastry shell and top with vegetable fat. Add 1½ times the usual amount of cornflour to the fruit. Place the pie in a polythene bag. Remove air and seal before freezing.

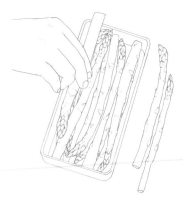

Pack asparagus head to tail in rigid containers to protect the fragile spears.

Freezing vegetables

Most vegetables freeze reasonably well, but there are some which, because of their high water content, are not suitable for freezing except in cooked dishes. These include most green salad plants, cabbage, celery, Jerusalem and Chinese artichokes, cucumbers, tomatoes (except as pulp), aubergines, marrows, pumpkins and mushrooms. Some vegetables, including soy beans, onions, mushrooms, cucumbers, beetroot and many other roots, are better stored or preserved in some other way.

Thawing vegetables

Vegetables, with the exception of corn on the cob, should not be thawed before cooking. Put the unthawed vegetables in a very little, salted, boiling water. When the water has returned to the boil, cover the pan and simmer until the vegetables are tender. If the vegetables were blanched before freezing, they will take about one-third to one-half the time it takes to cook fresh vegetables, a little longer if they were not blanched.

Asparagus

Speed is essential when freezing asparagus. Ideally it should go straight from the asparagus bed via the kitchen into the freezer. Trim off woody stems and stray buds and divide into bundles of stalks of equal thickness. Blanch for 2, 3 or 4 minutes, depending on thickness, and cool. Either pack the asparagus head to tail in rigid containers, or cook until tender, cool, arrange in boxes and cover with melted butter, lightly seasoned and flavoured with lemon juice. To use, put the frozen asparagus into the top pan of a double saucepan and heat over simmering water.

Beans, broad

There is no need to blanch broad beans. Shell them and either freeze them in bags or peel off the outer skins and freeze the beans on trays. (Once skinned, the surfaces tend to be moist, with the result that freezing them packed tends to make them stick together.)

If you wish to freeze the broad beans in the conventional way, the shelled, unskinned beans may be blanched for 1½ minutes, cooled, packed and frozen.

Beans, French

Top and tail. Blanch whole beans for 3 minutes, sliced beans for 2 minutes. Cool and pack in bags or boxes.

Beans, runner

If the beans are very young and have not yet developed strings, treat them like French beans. But if you prefer to let them grow to maturity, string them and slice them rather more thickly than usual. Blanch for 2 minutes, cool and pack in bags. Runner beans are also excellent in made-up, deep-frozen dishes, particularly Greek-style bean and lamb casseroles.

Broccoli, green/purple

Trim off woody stems and stray leaves and wash the sprigs carefully in salted

Use a straw to suck out as much air as possible from a polythene bag before sealing it.

water. Blanch the sprigs for 3 to 4 minutes, depending on the thickness of the stalks. Cool and drain thoroughly. Freeze on trays before packing in bags or boxes.

Brussels sprouts

Prepare the sprouts as for immediate use. Blanch for 3 to 5 minutes, depending on size. Cool and freeze, graded by size, in boxes or bags.

Carrots

Perfect, sweet young carrots should be frozen as soon as possible after they are pulled. Cut off the feathery tops. Wipe the carrots clean with a damp cloth. Blanch them for 2 minutes. Cool and pat dry; pack and freeze.

Mature carrots should be scraped, sliced or cut into cubes and blanched for 3 minutes before freezing.

Cauliflower

Separate the heads into large flowerets; trim them and wash them in acidulated water. Blanch the flowerets for 2 minutes. Drain very thoroughly and freeze on trays before packing in bags or boxes.

Chicory

Trim and prepare as if you were cooking the chicory immediately. Blanch for 2 minutes in acidulated water. Cool and drain thoroughly, squeezing out as much moisture as possible, taking care not to spoil their shape. Freeze on trays before storing in boxes or bags.

Courgettes

The only way whole courgettes can be frozen is to cook them through, cool, arrange in boxes and cover with melted butter, lightly seasoned and flavoured with lemon juice. To use, put the frozen courgettes into the top pan of a double saucepan and heat through over simmering water. To freeze sliced, uncooked courgettes, first cut them thickly then blanch them in salted water for 2 to 3 minutes. Drain, pat dry and freeze in boxes or bags.

Globe artichokes

Prepare the artichokes as you would for immediate use, slicing the leaves low and scooping out the chokes. Blanch two or three artichokes at a time for 6 to 8 minutes, depending on their size. Cool by plunging into a large bowl of iced water. You can also freeze artichoke hearts. Blanch them for 4 to 5 minutes, according to size. Cool as above; pat dry and freeze on trays. Store whole artichokes in boxes and hearts in boxes or bags.

Leeks

Wash leeks carefully and trim them. Blanch them for 1 to 2 minutes, depending on thickness. Cool and drain thoroughly. Freeze them whole, cut into chunks or shredded. However, you may prefer to precook the leeks, pack them in boxes, cover them either in seasoned butter flavoured with lemon juice or in a white sauce. To use, heat through in the top pan of a double saucepan over simmering water.

Parsnips

Scrub if very young or peel thinly. Quarter or slice, blanch for 2 to 3 minutes before freezing in bags.

Peas

Young, perfect peas should be shelled and frozen without blanching. If you prefer the conventional method, however, they need only 1 minute's blanching.

Even if you have decided to blanch everything else, on no account blanch *petit pois*. Blanching added to the inevitable cooking they will undergo before serving will destroy their flavour.

Floury mature peas that you would hesitate to serve as a fresh vegetable should be frozen, unblanched, in large bags for use in soups and casseroles of meat or poultry.

Potatoes

Potatoes can be frozen very successfully. New potatoes should be rubbed clean of soil with a damp cloth and blanched unpeeled for 3 to 4 minutes, depending on size. Cool, drain and pat dry. Freeze them in a large plastic bag.

Older potatoes should be peeled, imperfections cut out and the potatoes cut to a standard size for chips and/or roasting. They may also be kept whole, blanched for 5 minutes, cooled, drained, dried and frozen. Or—and this is the ideal solution for potatoes which are going to be roasted—dry the prepared potatoes thoroughly and deep-fry them for 5 minutes. Drain on kitchen paper. When they are quite cold, freeze them in a large plastic bag. When you need roast potatoes, take them straight from the freezer and put them around the roast—they will be ready in half the time it takes to roast raw or parboiled potatoes. Chips may be fried and frozen in the same way.

Salsify and scorzonera

Trim and wipe salsify clean with a damp cloth. Scrape scorzonera. Blanch for 2 minutes. Cool and pat dry. Pack and freeze.

Spinach

Spinach and other leaf vegetables are all dealt with in the same way. Wash carefully leaf by leaf under cold running water. Blanch for 2 minutes, a small portion at a time, shaking the basket gently so that the leaves do not stick together in a clump. Cool. Squeeze out excess moisture gently but firmly with the back of a wooden spoon. Then either leave the spinach whole or chop it finely before packing it in boxes or bags.

Sweet corn

Corn on the cob will freeze beautifully if it is handled properly. The speed at which the cobs travel from the garden to the freezer is important. Strip off husks and silks, but do not wash or blanch the cobs. They must be perfectly dry when they go into the freezer, since any drops of moisture, which would be left trapped between the kernels, would expand as they turned into ice, causing damage.

If you prefer the conventional method, blanch small cobs for 3 minutes, medium-sized ones for 5 to 6 minutes, large ones for 7 to 8 minutes. Freeze the cobs individually, either on trays or individually wrapped in freezer paper or self-sealing plastic wrap. When the cobs are frozen transfer them to a large plastic bag so that you can take as many as you need when you need them.

For frozen corn kernels, use up all the misshapen cobs first. Blanch the kernels on the cob before scraping them off. Dry them by spreading them out on a clean cloth. Transfer to bags and freeze.

Varieties for freezing
Asparagus: Connover's Colossal
Beans, broad: The Sutton; Imperial Green Windsor; Imperial White Windsor.
Beans, French: The Prince; Masterpiece; Tendergreen; Cordon.
Beans, runner: Achievement; Prize-winner; Streamline; Fry; Kelvedon Marvel; Hammond's Dwarf White.
Brussels sprouts: Peer Gynt; Prince Askold; Roodnerf Stiekema Early; Roodnerf Seven Hills.
Calabrese: Express Corona (F_1); Green Comet (F_1); Italian Sprouting.
Carrots: Amstel (Amsterdam Forcing).
Cauliflowers: All the Year Round; Snowball; South Pacific; English Winter St George.
Peas: Little Marvel; Early Onward; Kelvedon Wonder; Onward.
Seakale Beet: Silver Beet.
Spinach: Long-standing Round; New Zealand Spinach.
Sweet Corn: John Innes (F_1); Earliking (F_1); Kelvedon Glory (F_1); North Star (F_1); Early Xtra Sweet (F_1).

Freezing fruit
With the exception of strawberries, which present problems if you wish to serve them straight from the freezer (see below), and pears, some of which are not only too juicy but are also too delicately flavoured to withstand the freezer, the fruits of the kitchen garden are ideal for freezing, either in their natural, raw state (with or without sugar), transformed into purées, sauces and juices—or made into such dishes as tarts, pies, puddings and home-made, fresh fruit ice-creams and sorbets.

If you have been too busy to make all the jam you will need until the following season, simply freeze the raw fruit in a large bag, and use it when you have time, in midwinter if necessary. However, a certain amount of pectin is lost when fruit is frozen, so it may be necessary to make the jam—particularly strawberry jam—with commercial pectin or with another pectin-rich fruit.

The fruit should be of the best quality and frozen as soon after picking as possible. If the fruit requires washing, wash it in ice-cold water and dry thoroughly but gently with kitchen paper.

Fruit—particularly soft fruit—is often frozen with sugar. Place the hulled fruit on a tray, sift fine granulated or castor sugar over the fruit and mix it very gently. As soon as the fruit is well coated in the sugar, pack it in boxes, leaving room for expansion—$\frac{1}{2}$ inch (1 cm) for every 1 pound ($\frac{1}{2}$ kg) box or pack. The amount of sugar needed varies according to the fruit. The berries require $\frac{1}{4}$ pound (120 g) of sugar to 1 pound ($\frac{1}{2}$ kg) of fruit. Strawberries must first be pricked with a fork to release excess air before combining with the sugar. For 1 pound ($\frac{1}{2}$ kg) of currants use 5 ounces (150 g) of sugar, green gooseberries require 6 ounces (180 g) and rhubarb 4 to 6 ounces (120 to 180 g).

Thawing frozen fruit
Proper thawing lessens the tendency to mushiness in most frozen fruit. They must be thawed slowly in unopened containers. For the best results, thaw fruit for 6 to 8 hours in the refrigerator. If you are in a hurry, thaw at room temperature, which will take half the time. Dessert fruits (particularly berries) should be served just before they have completely thawed. Fruit which is to be baked in a pie or tart must be completely thawed first or the pastry will get soggy. Unsweetened fruit which is to be stewed may be added unthawed to the hot syrup.

To prevent any deterioration of quality and loss of nutritional value in the fruit, it must be used or served as soon as possible after thawing is completed.

Apples
Apples do well in the freezer, and you should never be without a supply of purée for sauces, charlottes and pies. If you have several varieties in your garden, start with the surplus of those that will not winter well in storage. For a supply of frozen apple rings, or quarters, prepare them as though you were going to use them fresh; dip them in water acidulated with lemon juice, then pat them dry and store them in large plastic bags—perfectionists might like to take the precaution of freezing them on trays, but this is not really necessary—or toss them quickly in butter over a low heat as though making a chunky apple sauce, cool and freeze in bags or boxes.

Black, red and white currants
Strip the currants from their stems, rinse, dry and pack them in boxes or bags and freeze. Or put them in boxes, cover with sugar, mix gently to coat well, cover and freeze.

Gooseberries
There are two stages at which gooseberries may be frozen—when they are ripe or when they are hard and green for use in pies and fools. Top and tail them, wash them if necessary, dry them and pack in bags. The only disadvantage—and it does not affect their flavour —is that even hard, green gooseberries become soft when they are defrosted.

Raspberries, loganberries, blackberries
No fruits come out of the freezer as little affected as these berries, except perhaps currants. On a dry day, the best way to pick them is to take a large basket filled with freezer cartons; transfer the fruit to them straight from the canes, then put the boxes in the freezer. If, however, the fruit is not quite perfect, freeze on trays so that any juice which escapes will not make them stick together when frozen. If you intend to make ice-creams and cream moulds out of season, you will find it more economical of space to store the fruit in blocks of sieved purée, sweetened or not as you prefer, frozen in boxes, and the frozen blocks then turned out into plastic bags. But make a point of measuring the purée and labelling it before freezing.

Rhubarb
Rhubarb is delicate and blanching often results in its disintegration when it is thawed and cooked. The early pink rhubarb should be washed, cut into short lengths, dried on a clean cloth, then packed in boxes or plastic bags as it is or coated in sugar. Mature rhubarb may be cooked to a purée, then frozen in blocks.

Strawberries
Whether or not you like defrosted strawberries is a matter of taste. Unless they are served chilled to the point of being frosty (and not everyone likes this), strawberries alter in colour and become limp when completely thawed. There is no way around this, but it is better to use small, rather than large, berries for freezing. Then instead of freezing them as they are, mix them into a very thick raspberry purée, which will not only provide an interesting and delicate summer-in-winter sweet, but also has a practical advantage, in that the juice released by the strawberries automatically blends with the raspberry purée.

To freeze finely chopped herbs, pack them tightly into individual ice-cube trays.

Pour enough water to fill the trays and freeze. Transfer the frozen cubes to a plastic bag and store in the freezer.

To use, thaw the frozen cube in a strainer. The water runs off, leaving the chopped herbs ready for use.

Bottling

Bottling is a convenient way of preserving fruit in sterilized conditions so that it can be stored for about one year. (The maximum storage period should be two to three years.)

Bottling vegetables, other than such vegetable fruits as tomatoes, is not recommended. It is more difficult and requires more elaborate sterilizing equipment.

It is important to follow the times and temperatures given in the chart.

Equipment needed for bottling fruit

Jars. Bottling jars vary in capacity from 1 pound to 8 pounds ($\frac{1}{2}$ kg to 4 kg). The timings given on the chart are for 1 pound and 2 pound ($\frac{1}{2}$ kg and 1 kg) jars. Beneath the chart, timings are given for large jars.

There are two types of jar available—screwband jars and clip-top jars.

Screw bands. Metal screw bands are put over metal lids fitted with rubber gaskets, or glass lids fitted with separate rubber rings. Screwed on loosely during processing, the bands allow air and steam to escape. Immediately afterwards they must be tightened so that a vacuum is created and air cannot enter the bottles.

Clip-tops. Flexible clips fit over metal rings, which are separated from the top of the bottle by a rubber ring. When the contents of the bottle become hot, the clip expands to let air and steam escape. During cooling, the clips hold the lid firmly in place.

Thermometer. If fruit is bottled by the slow-heating method a thermometer is essential.

Bottling pans. Use a special bottling pan or, if you are preserving only a small amount of fruit, use a fish kettle or a large, deep saucepan. The pan must be fitted with a false bottom to prevent the jars from touching its base. Use a rack, or make a false bottom out of pieces of wood, a cloth or folded newspaper.

Bottling may also be done in a pressure cooker, provided it is deep enough to hold the jars when the lid is in place. It must also be able to maintain 5 pounds of pressure (low setting).

Testing the equipment. Before bottling, examine each jar and lid for chips or cracks which will prevent the seal from being air-tight.

Rubber rings which have been exposed to heat or light may have lost their elasticity. After being stretched they should return to their original shape. Never use the rings more than once.

Preparing the equipment. Wash, rinse and drain the jars, but do not dry them, as fruit slips more easily into wet jars.

Soak the rubber rings for about 10 minutes in cold water. Dip them in boiling water just before you fit them on to the bottles.

Preparation of fruit. Wash and, if necessary, hull the fruit, which should be perfect, then follow the instructions on the chart.

Syrup. Fruit bottled in syrup has a better flavour than fruit bottled in water. Make syrup by dissolving granulated or loaf sugar in water. (See chart for quantities.) Bring the syrup to the boil and boil for 1 minute. If the syrup is to be used cold, make it with half the amount of water, then dilute it to the correct strength by adding the remaining amount of water, chilled. If the syrup is to be kept hot for a time, cover it to prevent evaporation.

Packing the jars. Pack the fruit into the jars tightly. Add the liquid, then tap the jars on a thickly folded cloth to dislodge any air bubbles. Put on the lids, the rubber rings, if separate, and the screw bands or clips.

Bottling tomatoes. Whole, small tomatoes, peeled if desired, are bottled in a brine of $\frac{1}{2}$ ounce (15 g) of salt to 2 pints (1 litre) of water. Larger tomatoes should be peeled, halved or quartered and packed into jars so tightly that no liquid is needed. Season with 1 teaspoon of salt and $\frac{1}{2}$ teaspoon of sugar for each 1 pound ($\frac{1}{2}$ kg) of tomatoes.

Five methods of bottling fruit

There are five methods of bottling fruit. Slow heating in water and quick heating in water are recommended both for economy of fuel and the appearance of the fruit. Bottling in a pressure cooker is quick and economical, but the fruit may not look as good. Bottling by the slow or moderate oven methods is uneconomical, less reliable (temperatures vary from oven to oven) and is not recommended for tall jars.

Slow heating in water. Fill the jars with fruit, then pour cold syrup almost to the top of each jar to cover the fruit. Put on the lids, rubber rings, screw bands or clips. Screw bands should be put on loosely.

Stand the jars in a large, deep pan which has been fitted with a false bottom. Use newspaper to prevent them touching each other or the pan sides. Cover the jars with cold water. Put a lid on the pan or cover with a board.

Heat the water very slowly, using a thermometer to keep a check on the temperature—after 1 hour it should be 130°F (54°C). After a further 30 minutes the water should reach the temperature on the chart. Maintain the temperature for the time specified, then remove the jars from the pan. Use wooden bottle tongs or ladle out the water until the jars can be gripped with oven gloves. Lift the jars out, one at a time, and put them on a wooden surface. Tighten the screw bands immediately.

After 24 hours, remove the screw bands or clips. Test the seal by lifting each jar by the lid. If the lid remains firm, a vacuum has been created. Label the jars with the name of the fruit, the type of liquid used (syrup or water) and the date. Store in a cool, dry place.

If the lid comes off when tested, the fruit must be reprocessed or served as stewed fruit within one or two days. Re-examine the jars, the lids and rubber rings for flaws.

To bottle small tomatoes, peel them, if desired, leave them whole and pack them tightly into jars.

Pour hot or cold brine over the tomatoes and cover them completely.

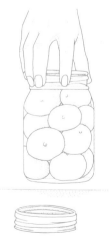

After processing, remove the screw bands or clips from the jars. Lift each jar by the lid to test the seal.

Quick heating in water. Although the temperatures are given, this method can be used even if a thermometer is not available. It differs from the slow-heating method in several ways. First, the bottles should be warmed before they are filled. Instead of using cold syrup, use hot syrup or water (140°F, 60°C). Put the filled and covered jars into the pan, which should be fitted with a rack or false bottom. Fill the pan with warm water (100°F, 38°C) and heat to simmering (190°F, 95°C) in 25 to 30 minutes. Keep simmering for the time given on the chart. Finish as for the slow-heating method.

Using a pressure cooker. Pour water into the pressure cooker to a depth of 1 inch (2 cm). Put in the rack and bring the water to the boil. Pack the fruit into warm jars, fill with boiling syrup or water, put on the lids, rubber rings, screw bands or clips and place on the rack. Loosen the screw bands by a quarter of a turn. Put on the lid of the pressure cooker, with the vent open, and heat until steam escapes. Close the vent, bring the pressure to 5 pounds and maintain the pressure for the time specified on the chart.

Then remove the pressure cooker from the heat and leave for 10 minutes before opening. Leave for 24 hours. Test and label.

Bottling in a slow oven. Preheat the oven to 250°F (130°C, Gas Mark ½). Line a baking tray with four thicknesses of newspaper and put it on a shelf below the centre of the oven. Pack the jars with fruit and place them, uncovered, on the tray in the oven. Leave space between the jars for the air to circulate. Heat for the length of time specified on the chart, then remove the jars from the oven, one at a time, and fill each one to the top with boiling syrup or water. Cover each jar with a warmed lid, a rubber ring, if necessary, and a screw band or clip. Leave for 24 hours. Test for leaks and label.

Bottling in a moderate oven. Preheat the oven to 300°F (150°C, Gas Mark 2). Pack the fruit into jars and fill with boiling syrup or water. Put on the lids and rubber rings. Place the jars in the oven and process for the length of time specified on the chart. Remove the jars from the oven and fit immediately with screw bands or clips. Leave for 24 hours, test and label.

There are two types of bottling jars: screw-band jars (above) and clip-top jars (below).

Fruit Preparation and Processing Chart

FRUIT	SUGAR to 1 pint (500 ml) of water	PREPARATION	METHOD 1 Temp F (C)	METHOD 1 *Time maintained in min.	METHOD 2 Temp F (C)	METHOD 2 *Time maintained in min.	METHOD 3 Time maintained at 5 lb (low) pressure in min.	METHOD 4 Time 1–4 lb (½–2 kg) min.	METHOD 4 Time 5–10 lb (2½–5 kg) min.	METHOD 5 Time 1–4 lb (½–2 kg) min.	METHOD 5 Time 5–10 lb (2½–5 kg) min.
Raspberries	1 lb (½ kg)	Discard stalks. Inspect for maggots.	165 (74)	10	190 (88)	2	1	45–55	60–75	30–40	45–60
Loganberries	1 lb (½ kg)	Same as raspberries.	165	10	190	2	1	45–55	60–75	30–40	45–60
Blackberries	½ lb (¼ kg)	Discard stalks and damaged fruit.	165	10	190	2	1	45–55	60–75	30–40	45–60
Strawberries	1 lb (½ kg)	Hull and rinse in cold water. Strawberries lose colour when bottled and are better made into jam.	165	10	190	2	Not recommended	Not recommended		30–40	45–60
Currants (red, black or white)		Discard stems and calyx.	180 (82)	15	190	10	1	55–70	75–90	40–50	55–70
Gooseberries (for pies) (for dessert)	½ lb (¼ kg) ½ lb (¼ kg)	Top and tail. If they are being bottled in syrup, prick the skins to prevent shrivelling.	165 180	10 15	190 190	2 10	1 1	45–55 55–70	60–75 75–90	30–40 40–50	45–60 55–70
Apples (in syrup)	4–6 oz (120–180 g)	Peel, core and slice. Immerse in salted water—½ oz (15 g) salt to 1 quart (1 litre) of water. Rinse before bottling.	165	10	190	2	1	Not recommended		30–40	45–60
Apples (solid pack)	8–12 oz (240–360 g)	After preparing, as above, blanch in boiling water for a few minutes or steam until just tender.	180	15	190	20	3–4	Not recommended		30–40	65–80
Pears	4–6 oz (120–180 g)	Peel, halve and core. Immerse in salted water, as for apples. Stew cooking pears until tender.	190	30	190	40	5	Not recommended		60–70	75–90
Rhubarb (for pies) (for dessert)	½ lb (¼ kg)	Remove leaves and trim base. Wipe stalks and cut into even lengths.	165 180	10 15	190 190	2 10	1 1	45–55 55–70	60–75 75–90	30–40 40–50	45–60 55–70
Tomatoes (whole)		Remove calyx. Peel if desired.	190	30	190	40	5	80–100	105–125	60–70	75–90
Tomatoes (solid pack)		Peel, halve or quarter. Pack into jars. Add 1 teaspoon of salt and ½ teaspoon of sugar to each jar.	190	40	190	50	15	Not recommended		70–80	85–100

*Increase processing time for large jars (methods 1 and 2):
3 and 4 lb (1½ and 2 kg) size by 5 min. all packs except tomatoes solid pack 10 min.
5 and 6 lb (2½ and 3 kg) size by 10 min. all packs except tomatoes solid pack 20 min.
7 and 8 lb (3½ and 4 kg) size by 15 min. all packs except tomatoes solid pack 30 min.

Jams & Jellies

Home-made jams and jellies should have a good, bright colour, a fresh, fruity flavour and should set well and keep well. Basically all jams and jellies are made by boiling fruit or fruit juice with sugar until the mixture sets lightly when cold.

The Fruit. Use dry, slightly under-ripe fruit as soon as possible after picking. Remove the stalks and leaves, and stones if desired. Wash the fruit just before using.

Pectin is a substance present in most fruit—without it jams and jellies will not set. Acid, too, is important as it helps to release the pectin. Fruits rich in pectin and acid include cooking apples, black and red currants and gooseberries. Blackberries, loganberries and raspberries contain a little less pectin, while pears and some varieties of strawberries have so little that they are difficult to make into preserves with a good set. When using fruits which contain little pectin, commercially made pectin or the juice of a pectin-rich fruit may be added. Acid deficiency may be corrected with 2 tablespoons of lemon juice to 4 pounds (2 kg) of fruit.

Pans. Pans should be large and heavy, made preferably of stainless steel or aluminium. If enamel pans are used they must not be chipped, because the exposed iron will spoil the colour of the preserve. To help prevent the preserves from burning and to reduce scum, rub the bottom of the pan with butter or glycerine.

Sugar. Use preserving, lump or granulated sugar. To help the sugar dissolve more rapidly, warm it in a slow oven before adding it to the fruit. For fruit rich in pectin and acid, you will require $1\frac{1}{4}$ to $1\frac{1}{2}$ pounds (600 to 720 g) of sugar to each pound ($\frac{1}{2}$ kg) of fruit. For fruit which have a moderate amount of pectin and acid, 1 pound ($\frac{1}{2}$ kg) of sugar will be sufficient for 1 pound ($\frac{1}{2}$ kg) of fruit.

Testing for Pectin. Test for pectin just before you add the sugar. Put 1 teaspoon of the juice of the simmered fruit into a warm glass. When the juice is cool, add 3 teaspoons of methylated spirit. Shake gently and leave for 1 minute. The pectin will concentrate into a jelly-like clot. If there is one fair-sized clot it indicates that there is adequate pectin. If the clot is broken into 2 or 3 pieces, the pectin is present in moderate quantity, but if it appears in many small pieces the pectin is inadequate.

Water. Usually only enough water to prevent the fruit from burning is required. Raspberries and other such soft fruits require no water. They are heated gently until their juices flow.

Testing for a set. Put a little of the liquid from the cooking jam or jelly on to a saucer and let it cool. If it wrinkles when pushed with a finger it is ready. While testing, take the pan off the heat.

A quicker and more reliable method is to use a thermometer. Keep the thermometer in hot water in between testing. Stir the jam and insert the thermometer into the centre without touching the bottom of the pan. The temperature needed is 220°F (104°C), but sometimes 221° or 222°F (about 105°C) may give better results.

Jam. Prepare and wash the fruit and put it in a large pan. Add water, if necessary, and simmer gently to soften the skins and release the pectin in the fruit. If extra acid is required add it at this stage. Test for pectin.

When the fruit is soft, and not before, add the warmed sugar—the pan should not be more than half full after sugar has been added—and stir until it is completely dissolved. Then increase the heat and boil rapidly, stirring occasionally. Cook the jam for as short a time as possible after the sugar is added. Cooking time varies from 5 to 35 minutes depending on the fruit. Test for setting.

When the jam is ready, remove the scum. Pour the jam into clean, dry, warm jars. Whole fruit jams should first be allowed to cool until a skin forms, then stirred and poured. This gives the jam time to thicken and to suspend the fruit evenly. Wipe the neck of the jars. Cover first with waxed discs, wax side down, and then with transparent cellulose covers. Secure with rubber bands. Label, date and store in a cool, dark, ventilated cupboard.

Whole-fruit Jam. Using 1 pound ($\frac{1}{2}$ kg) of sugar to each pound ($\frac{1}{2}$ kg) of fruit, layer the fruit and sugar in a bowl. Cover the bowl and leave in a cool place for 24 hours.

Pour the fruit and sugar into a pan, add acid, if necessary, and stir well. Bring slowly to the boil, stirring carefully to keep the fruit whole. Then boil rapidly—testing for setting—until the jam sets. Remove the scum. Let the jam cool until a skin forms and bottle.

Low sugar jam. Jam can be made with only $\frac{3}{4}$ pound (360 g) of sugar to 1 pound ($\frac{1}{2}$ kg) of a good setting fruit. Test for setting by the saucer test only. The jam will not have a firm set and will keep for only a few weeks. It will, however, have a very fine fruity flavour.

Jelly Making. Because the fruit pulp is discarded, you will get less jelly than jam from the same amount of fruit. Fruits with a rich flavour are best for jelly. Cooking apples can be added to improve the set. It is not possible to give exact yields in jelly recipes, but on average you can expect 10 pounds (5 kg) of jelly for every 6 pounds (3 kg) of sugar used.

Wash the fruit and discard any unsound parts. Cut large fruit into pieces. Put the fruit into a pan with water—$\frac{1}{4}$ to $\frac{3}{4}$ pint (125 to 375 ml) to 1 pound ($\frac{1}{2}$ kg) of fruit. Hard or firm fruit require the larger amount of water. Simmer slowly until the fruit is soft. Test for pectin.

Meanwhile, scald a jelly or muslin bag and hang it over a large bowl. Pour the softened fruit into the bag. Leave it, without stirring or squeezing, until the dripping ceases.

Measure the juice and pour it into a large pan. Bring to the boil and stir in $\frac{3}{4}$ to $1\frac{1}{4}$ pounds (360 to 600 g) of sugar to 1 pint (500 ml) of juice. Use the larger amount of sugar for fruit which gives one firm pectin clot when tested. Finish making the jelly as you would jam.

Apple Jelly

Although cooking apples and crab-apples do not have much flavour, they have good setting properties. Other fruits and flavourings can be added to make really excellent jellies.

To make a herb jelly, replace the spices in this recipe with a few sprigs of any one of the following herbs: chervil, mint, sage, marjoram, thyme, basil or tarragon. Ten minutes before the sugar is added, stir in 2 tablespoons of red or white wine vinegar. Remove the herb sprigs before potting.

If you are preparing large quantities of apples for chutney, bottling or freezing, the skins and cores can be used to make apple jelly.

4 lb (2 kg) cooking, crab or windfall apples
2½ pints (1½ litres) water
2 teaspoons ground ginger, cloves or cinnamon—or bruised root ginger or lemon rind in a muslin bag
Sugar

Wash the apples and cut them up roughly, discarding any bad portions. Put them in a large pan with the water. Add the spices and simmer for about 1 hour, or until the fruit is soft. Follow the instructions for making jelly adding 1 pound (½ kg) of sugar to each pint (500 ml) of juice.

If you do not have a jelly bag, improvise by tying a cloth to the legs of an inverted stool.

Blackberry Jam

Blackberries contain a moderate amount of pectin and apple is often added to improve the set and to stretch the fruit. If desired the fruit may be sieved to remove the seeds and then the pulp weighed and 1 pound (½ kg) of sugar added for each 1 pound (½ kg) of pulp.

MAKES ABOUT SEVEN POUNDS (3½ kg)
4 lb (2 kg) blackberries
¼ pint (125 ml) water
2 tablespoons lemon juice
4 lb (2 kg) sugar

Pick over the blackberries and wash them. Put them into a pan with the water and lemon juice. Simmer gently until the fruit is soft. Test for pectin. Add the sugar and stir to dissolve. Increase the heat and boil rapidly until setting point is reached. Remove the scum, pour into jars, cover and label.

Black Currant Jam

Black currants are rich in pectin and acid and make excellent jams and jellies. The first cooking should be gentle or the skins may be made tough.

MAKES ABOUT TEN POUNDS (5 kg)
4 lb (2 kg) black currants
3 pints (1½ litres) water
6 lb (3 kg) sugar

Follow the general instructions for making jam.

Mint Gooseberry Jelly

Gooseberries are rich in pectin and acid and both the cooking and dessert varieties can be used to make jams and jellies. If the mixture is cooked for any length of time after the sugar is added the jam will turn red.

A delicate muscatel flavour can be given to gooseberry jam if 12 elderflower heads, in a muslin bag, are boiled with the fruit for 30 minutes.

Dessert gooseberries make a red jam

and the colour and flavour can be improved by adding ½ pound (¼ kg) of raspberries to every 3 pounds (1½ kg) of red gooseberries.

The following jelly recipe uses fresh mint as a flavouring.

3 lb (1½ kg) gooseberries
Water to cover
1 tablespoon white wine vinegar
Sugar
Fresh mint

Wash the gooseberries and put them in a pan. Add the water and vinegar and simmer until the fruit is very soft. Strain the fruit and test for pectin. Add 1 pound (½ kg) of sugar to each pint (500 ml) of juice, and suspend a bunch of washed mint in the pan. Stir until the sugar has dissolved. Increase the heat and boil until setting point is reached, tasting from time to time and removing the mint when the flavour is strong enough.

Uncooked Raspberry Jam

For a traditional raspberry jam, follow the general directions for jam making. The fruit may be sieved before the sugar is added, to remove the pips. Uncooked

raspberry jam is not traditional, but is much more delicious.

Put equal weights of fruit and sugar in separate bowls in a 350°F (180°C, Gas Mark 4) oven for 20 to 25 minutes,

or until they are really hot. Add the sugar to the raspberries and beat them together until the sugar has dissolved. Pour the jam into jars and cover.

Make small quantities of this jam as it does not store well.

Stawberry Jam

Usually, small strawberries are used in jam making so that they can be left whole. This means they are not cooked to the stage when the pectin is completely extracted from the pulp and so commercial pectin or red currant or gooseberry juice is usually added. If red currant or gooseberry juice is used, add ¾ pint (375 ml) of juice to 6 pounds (3 kg) of strawberries.

Put equal quantities of hulled strawberries and sugar in a large saucepan and heat slowly, stirring carefully, until the sugar is dissolved. Add pectin (following the directions on the pack) and boil rapidly to setting point. Remove the pan from the heat and cool until a skin forms on top of the jam. Stir the jam and pour it into jars.

Rhubarb Jam

This is a fine jam to make in the spring. To vary the flavour, replace the lemon rind and ginger with any one of the following: 1½ pounds (¾ kg) of chopped, pitted dates, 1 pound (½ kg) of chopped, dried figs, the grated rind and juice of 2 medium-sized oranges, 1 pound (½ kg) of dried apricots, soaked for 24 hours and chopped, or chopped crystallized ginger.

MAKES ABOUT FIVE POUNDS (2½ kg)
3 lb (1½ kg) rhubarb
3 lb (1½ kg) sugar
Rind and juice of 1 lemon
About 2 oz (60 g) root ginger, bruised

Cut the rhubarb into chunks. Put it into a bowl with alternate layers of sugar and leave it for 24 hours.

Put the fruit and sugar into a pan with the lemon juice and lemon rind. Put the ginger in a muslin bag and add it to the pan. Follow the directions for whole fruit jam, removing the ginger before pouring into pots.

Pickles & Chutneys

The making of pickles and chutneys and, indeed, of jams and jellies, satisfies one of the most primitive human instincts—to store food for future use. Although the need to do so no longer exists, the pleasure of making preserves for the store cupboard remains.

Pickles are vegetables or fruits or both, preserved in vinegar or salt. Sugar, spices and herbs are sometimes added for additional flavour and can be adjusted to suit individual tastes. Try adding an extra bay leaf, a sprig of mint or peppercorns. Dried or fresh chillies, cayenne pepper and fresh root ginger will add extra pungency.

Vinegars. Distilled white vinegar, malt, cider and wine vinegars are all suitable for making pickles, but use bottled rather than draught vinegar as it is usually stronger and so ensures that the pickles keep better.

Spiced vinegar is used for some pickles and chutneys and is easy to make. Use whole spices as ground spices make the vinegar cloudy. To make spiced vinegar, tie 2 ounces (60 g) of mixed pickling spice or ½ ounce (15 g) each of stick cinnamon, cloves, mace and allspice and a few peppercorns in a muslin bag. Put the bag in a large pan with 4 pints (2 litres) of vinegar and 1 tablespoon of kitchen salt and bring to the boil. Cover the pan and boil for 5 minutes. Strain and use the spiced vinegar immediately or pour it into a jug to get cold before removing the spices. The cooled vinegar can now be used or bottled and stored. Use cold vinegar to make crisp pickles or hot for such soft pickles as plum and walnut.

Salt. Salt is used to draw out water from vegetables and to toughen them a little. If this is not done the vinegar will be diluted by the water in the vegetables and its preserving properties will be reduced.

Brine—a solution of salt and water—is sometimes used instead of salt; its action is more gentle. But for vegetables with a high water content salt is preferable. When vegetables are immersed in brine, weigh them down with a plate so that they remain below the surface. To make brine, dissolve ½ pound (¼ kg) of kitchen salt in 4 pints (2 litres) of water.

Pans. Use aluminium, stainless steel or unchipped enamel pans. Iron, brass and copper must *never* be used as the reaction of vinegar to the metal gives the pickles an unpleasant taste.

Jars. Any type of jar is suitable, providing it can be fitted with a suitable lid or cover. A vacuum-sealed lid is best as this prevents the vinegar evaporating. Metal lids must not be used unless they have a coating of plastic. Paper and cellulose covers are not recommended as they allow evaporation, which exposes the vegetables, causing them to discolour.

Making Pickles

Always use fresh, young vegetables. Trim the vegetables and, if necessary, peel and cut them into even-sized pieces. At this stage some vegetables are blanched. The vegetables are first put into boiling water for 1 to 5 minutes, depending on their size, and then in cold water for the same length of time.

Immerse the vegetables in brine or put them on a flat dish and sprinkle liberally with kitchen salt. Leave for 12 to 48 hours, depending on the vegetable, then rinse in cold water and drain.

Pack the vegetables into clean jars to within 1 inch (2 cm) of the top. Fill the jars with vinegar, covering the vegetables by at least ½ inch (1 cm). Fix the covers and store the jars in a cool, dry place.

Making Sweet Pickles

Sweet pickles are made from fruits and such vegetable fruits as tomatoes and cucumbers. They are stewed in sweetened, spiced vinegar to which thinly peeled lemon rind and bay leaves are added—use the rind of 1 lemon and 2 bay leaves to every 4 pints (2 litres) of spiced vinegar. If whole fruit is used, prick them with a needle or a fine skewer to prevent the fruit from shrivelling.

To make a sweet pickle, dissolve the sugar in the spiced vinegar. Add the fruit and simmer in a covered pan until it is just tender—be careful not to overcook the fruit. Lift out the fruit and pack into jars. Boil the vinegar rapidly until it forms a thin syrup and there is enough to cover the fruit. Pour the vinegar syrup into the jars. Cover the jars and leave the pickle for at least 4 to 6 weeks before eating it.

Making Chutneys

Chutney can be made from a variety of fruits and vegetables combined with vinegar, spices and sugar. The ingredients are usually chopped or minced. Long, slow cooking helps to blend the flavours, which improve if the chutney is left to mature and mellow after bottling. Chutneys should not be opened for two to three months and will keep for about three years. Uncooked chutneys, however, should be eaten within two to three weeks. If kept longer they discolour.

For a light-coloured chutney, add the sugar towards the end of the cooking time. For a dark chutney, add the sugar at the beginning. Brown sugar also gives chutney a rich, dark colour.

Use ground spices when making chutney. If whole spices are used, double the quantity specified in the recipe. Bruise the spices and tie them in a muslin bag. Remove the bag before bottling.

Dried fruit is often an ingredient in chutneys. If it is omitted, slightly increase the amount of sugar used.

Pans and jars used for chutneys are the same as for pickles.

Pickled Beetroot

Boil whole beetroot until tender. When cool, peel and cut the beets into $\frac{1}{4}$-inch ($\frac{1}{2}$ cm) thick slices or cubes and pack them into jars. Cover with cold spiced vinegar or, if the pickle is to be stored for some time, use boiling spiced vinegar.

Pickled Cauliflower

Separate the cauliflowers into small flowerets and soak them in brine for 24 hours. Remove the flowerets, rinse, drain and pack them into jars. Cover with cold spiced vinegar.

Pickled Gooseberries

1½ lb ($\frac{3}{4}$ kg) white sugar
1 pint (500 ml) spiced vinegar
2½ lb (1¼ kg) gooseberries

Follow the instructions for making sweet pickles, taking care that the gooseberries are very slightly undercooked.

Dill Pickles

This pickle is made in a slightly different way and will not keep as well as the other pickles.

4 lb (2 kg) small ridge cucumbers
Brine
Fresh dill sprigs
Peppercorns
Dill seeds
1¼ pints (625 ml) white vinegar
1¼ pints (625 ml) water
4 tablespoons kitchen salt

Wash the cucumbers, prick them all over with a fork and soak them in brine for 24 hours. Rinse the cucumbers, drain them well and pack them into jars. To each jar add a sprig of dill, 4 peppercorns and 1 tablespoon of dill seed.

Put the vinegar, water and salt into a pan and bring to the boil. Boil for 1 minute and pour into the jars to within $\frac{1}{2}$ inch (1 cm) of the top. Seal the jars. Leave for 4 days before eating.

Pickled Pears

2 lb (1 kg) cooking pears
1 lb ($\frac{1}{2}$ kg) white or brown sugar
1 pint (500 ml) spiced vinegar

Peel the pears. Cut the larger ones into halves or quarters and remove the cores. Leave small pears whole.

Follow the instructions for making sweet pickles.

Piccalilli

This is sometimes called mustard pickle, and is a little different from the other pickles as the vegetables are cooked in a sauce. It is a flexible recipe and the balance of flavours can be altered to suit personal taste. For a less pungent flavour omit the chillies and cloves and increase the turmeric and mustard. For a thicker sauce mix a little flour with the mustard. The vegetables may include cauliflowers, marrows, cucumbers, onions, French beans, green tomatoes; hard, sour apples may also be used.

6 lb (3 kg) mixed vegetables
$\frac{3}{4}$ lb (360 g) kitchen salt

SAUCE
3 pints (1½ litres) white vinegar
6 dried chillies
6 cloves
1½ oz (45 g) root ginger, bruised
$\frac{1}{2}$ lb ($\frac{1}{4}$ kg) granulated or loaf sugar
1½ oz (45 g) dry mustard
$\frac{3}{4}$ oz (25 g) turmeric

Prepare the vegetables and cut them into even-sized pieces. Put them in a large dish, sprinkle with salt and leave for 24 hours. Rinse and drain.

To make the sauce, pour all but 2 cupfuls of the vinegar into a large saucepan. Tie the chillies, cloves and ginger in a muslin bag and add them to the pan. Bring the vinegar to the boil and simmer for 20 minutes.

Add the sugar and stir until it has dissolved. Add the vegetables and simmer for a further 20 minutes.

Meanwhile, mix the mustard and turmeric with the remaining vinegar. Stir the mixture into the simmering vegetables and continue cooking for 10 minutes. Bottle, seal and store in a cool, dry cupboard.

Salted Beans

You will need 1 pound ($\frac{1}{2}$ kg) of kitchen salt (never use table salt) to every 3 pounds (1½ kg) of beans. These proportions are important. Use too little salt and the beans will not keep, use too much and the flavour will be spoiled. Wash tender, fresh young beans and string them, if necessary. Slice runner beans; leave French beans whole. In a glass jar or earthenware crock, layer the salt and beans, beginning and ending with the salt. Press the beans down well. This is important for if they are not pressed down hard enough the beans will not keep. Cover the jars with waxed paper or polythene sheeting and leave for four days. As the beans shrink the jars should be filled with more beans and salt. Repeat this until there is finally no more room in the jar. As the moisture is drawn from the beans a strong brine is formed which preserves them.

Cover the jar with polythene sheeting or waxed paper tightly tied. The beans can be stored in this way for a year or more.

To cook the beans: remove as many as are required and wash them several times in cold water. Soak the beans in warm water for no longer than 2 hours. Drain, rinse and simmer in unsalted water until tender.

Green Tomato Chutney

3 lb (1½ kg) green tomatoes
$\frac{1}{2}$ lb ($\frac{1}{4}$ kg) cooking apples
$\frac{1}{2}$ lb ($\frac{1}{4}$ kg) onions
$\frac{1}{2}$ lb ($\frac{1}{4}$ kg) raisins
$\frac{1}{4}$ lb (120 g) crystallized ginger, chopped
1 pint (500 ml) vinegar
$\frac{1}{2}$ lb ($\frac{1}{4}$ kg) brown sugar
2 teaspoons salt

Peel the tomatoes. Chop them finely with the apples and onions and put them into a large pan. Add the raisins, ginger and half the vinegar and bring to the boil. Reduce the heat and simmer, uncovered, until the mixture thickens.

Meanwhile, dissolve the sugar in the remaining vinegar and add it with the salt to the chutney. Continue cooking until the chutney is thick. Pour the chutney into jars and cover.

Uncooked Fruit Chutney

This chutney cannot be stored. Use it within two to three weeks.

1 lb ($\frac{1}{2}$ kg) cooking apples
$\frac{1}{2}$ lb ($\frac{1}{4}$ kg) onions
6 oz (180 g) red or green pepper
2 oz (60 g) pitted dates
$\frac{1}{4}$ lb (120 g) sultanas
1 oz (30 g) crystallized ginger
2 tablespoons white wine vinegar
1 teaspoon salt
1 teaspoon granulated sugar

Mince the apples, onions, pepper, dates, sultanas and crystallized ginger together. Stir the vinegar, salt and sugar together until the sugar dissolves and mix it into the minced fruit. Spoon the chutney into jars and cover.

Wine Making

Wine is basically easy to make, but it requires care, patience and time to produce good, consistent results. And it is not exclusively a country craft—virtually every early cookery book included a section on winemaking. However, to quote from P. P. Carnell's *Treatise on Family Winemaking*, published in 1814, "The causes that produce the effects of vinous fermentation are imperfectly known." Today we know exactly how fermentation works and, consequently, the home winemaker can produce wines that are made to suit his or her own particular palate.

Quite simply, wine is made by adding yeast to a liquid that contains sugar. The yeast converts the sugar into carbon dioxide and alcohol, in roughly equal proportions. If the sugar content is high to begin with, the amount of alcohol produced will kill the yeast before all the sugar is converted and the result will be a sweet wine. If the sugar content is low, the yeast will convert all the sugar and a dry wine will result.

Equipment and ingredients
The illustration opposite shows all the equipment required. If you use full-length wine corks, you should buy a corking tool. But you could use flanged corks, which can be inserted by hand.

Most serious winemakers use a hydrometer to assess the amount of sugar in the wine; but you can use your sense of taste instead—at least at first.

You will also require certain essential ingredients, in addition to the main fruit or vegetable, to help produce your wine.

Yeast. Wine yeast is best. There are many types. Start with an "All Purpose" yeast. Bakers' yeast will do if necessary, but never use brewers' yeast, except for making beer. If you use wine yeast the amount needed will be given on the label. If you use bakers' yeast, 1 level teaspoon will be enough for the recipes in this book.

Citric acid. Not always essential, but necessary to produce a "balanced" wine when the main ingredient is deficient in acid.

Sugar. Ordinary white sugar. Brown sugar has too much flavour for most wines.

Yeast nutrient. This helps the yeast to work better. Half a level teaspoon will be the amount needed for the recipes in this book. Yeast nutrient is sold at winemaking shops.

Campden tablets. Used for sterilizing the "must" or ingredients.

Pectic enzyme. Ingredients containing pectin will create a "pectin haze" if this enzyme is not added at an early stage.

Tannin. To introduce "bite" when the main ingredient is lacking in tannin.

Making wine
There are several different methods of making wine, but they are all variations on a basic procedure.

First, pour the main ingredients, and the sugar, into a plastic pail. Bring the water to the boil and pour it over the ingredients. You now have what is called the "must". Cover with a close weave cloth or plastic sheet.

When the must has cooled, add the Campden tablet or pectic enzyme if required. If either ingredient is added, wait 24 hours before the next stage.

Add yeast, yeast nutrient and acid. In a few days, when fermentation starts, everything will rise to the surface, forming a "cap".

Stir every day, breaking the cap thoroughly. Keep the must covered except when stirring. Continue this procedure for the length of time specified in the recipe.

Strain the must into a fermentation jar through a nylon strainer and funnel. Fit the fermentation lock and pour a little water into the S-bend of the lock. The bubbles popping round the S-bend tell you that fermentation is in progress. At first the bubbles will pass through every few seconds, but after a few days they will slow down considerably.

The completion time for fermentation is variable and depends on many things, the most important being temperature. In a warm place, fermentation might be complete in several weeks, in a colder place it might take several months. If the temperature rises above 90°F (32°C) the yeast will die. If the temperature drops below 50°F (10°C) fermentation will slow down or stop, but it will resume when the temperature is increased.

When there has been no movement in the fermentation lock for two days, taste the wine. If it is too dry, add some sugar and ferment on.

If the wine is ready, wait until all trace of cloudiness has gone and rack the wine off the sediment. To do this, place the full jar on a table and an empty jar on the floor. Dip one end of a siphon into the wine in the top jar, until it is 2 inches (5 cm) clear of the sediment. Drop the other end to a point lower than the sediment and place it in your mouth. Suck gently and the wine will flow smoothly down the tube. As soon as the wine trickles through, place this end of the tube into the neck of the lower, empty jar. Hold the tube in position while the wine transfers to the lower jar, but ensure that no sediment is dragged through. If this happens repeat the procedure when the wine has settled again.

It might take several rackings to clear the wine thoroughly. If it has not cleared after this, seriously consider buying one of the filter devices on the market. These ensure bright, clear wine every time.

Bottling
If your wine now tastes just right, there is no problem—just drink it. However, it is usually at least three to six months before the wine will be drinkable. So you will have to bottle it.

Fill the thoroughly clean bottles by racking. While you are doing this, place the corks in a saucepan of boiling water, taking each cork out of the water as required.

1 Plastic pail
2 Glass fermentation jar
3 Bottles
4 Large saucepan
5 Nylon sieve
6 Funnel
7 Corking tool
8 Siphon tube
9 Full-length wine corks
  and flanged corks
10 Fermentation lock and bung

Wine Making

Apple Wine

Apples produce a superb medium wine, provided enough fruit is used. At least 10 pounds (5 kg) are required if the wine is to have sufficient body. Cooking apples are ideal and require no additional acid, but if you have to use dessert apples, add ¼ ounce (7 g) of citric acid.

MAKES ABOUT SIX BOTTLES
11 lb (5½ kg) cooking apples
1 gal (4½ litres) water
Yeast and nutrient
½ teaspoon tannin
3½ lb (1¾ kg) sugar

Chop the apples very finely and put them in a plastic pail. Bring the water to the boil and pour it over the apples. When cool, add the yeast, nutrient and tannin. Stir in the sugar. When fermentation starts, allow it to continue for five days. Strain the must into a fermentation jar, fit the fermentation lock and ferment on.

Artichoke Wine

This wine is made from Jerusalem not globe artichokes. It makes an excellent dry wine. The recipe includes raisins, which give the wine extra body. If you would like to try a pure artichoke wine, add 1½ pounds (¾ kg) of artichokes and ¼ pound (120 g) of sugar to the recipe and omit the raisins.

Scrub the tubers well before slicing them. This is a time-consuming job because of the number of folds in the tubers, but if any soil is present it will spoil the taste of the wine.

MAKES ABOUT SIX BOTTLES
5 lb (2½ kg) Jerusalem artichokes, finely chopped
2 lb (1 kg) sugar
1 gal (4½ litres) water
Yeast and nutrient
½ lb (¼ kg) raisins, minced
½ teaspoon tannin
½ oz (15 g) citric acid

Place the tubers and sugar in a large saucepan, add the water and bring to the boil. Remove the pan from the heat. When cool pour into a plastic pail and add the yeast, nutrient, raisins, tannin and acid. Allow the mixture to ferment for 4 days. Strain into a fermentation jar, fit the fermentation lock and ferment on.

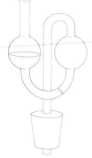

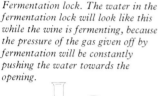

Fermentation lock. The water in the fermentation lock will look like this while the wine is fermenting, because the pressure of the gas given off by fermentation will be constantly pushing the water towards the opening.

Broad Bean Wine

One of the hardiest of vegetables, the broad bean often produces a glut of seed. When it does the kitchen gardener can utilize them to make an excellent dry white wine. It can be made as a sweet wine, but this produces a particular flavour that can only be described as an acquired taste.

MAKES ABOUT SIX BOTTLES
4 lb (2 kg) shelled broad beans
1 gal (4½ litres) water
2 lb (1 kg) sugar
¾ lb (360 g) sultanas, minced
Yeast and nutrient
½ oz (15 g) citric acid
¼ teaspoon tannin

Ensure that there are no beans that have been broken or split. Throughout the procedure do not stir or disturb the beans; if the skins break the wine will become cloudy and almost impossible to clear.

Put the beans in the water and bring to the boil. Turn the heat off as soon as the water boils. Leave to cool, then carefully strain off the liquid and add to it the sugar, sultanas, yeast, nutrient, acid and tannin. Pour into a fermentation jar, fit the fermentation lock and ferment on.

When fermentation has ceased, the water in the fermentation lock will level off at both sides, as shown. Ensure that the level has remained like this for at least two or three days before you start racking.

Carrot Wine

Carrots are one of the best vegetables for making excellent dry or sweet wine. Carrot wine has plenty of body and a good flavour. It is essential to scrub the carrots clean, because any soil left on will spoil the wine. If you want a dry wine, omit the currants and reduce the sugar to 2½ pounds (1¼ kg).

MAKES ABOUT SIX BOTTLES
9 lb (4½ kg) carrots
1 gal (4½ litres) water
4 lb (2 kg) sugar
½ lb (¼ kg) currants, minced
½ oz (15 g) citric acid
Yeast and nutrient
Pinch of tannin

Scrub (never peel) and grate the carrots. Put them in the water and bring to the boil, stirring the sugar in at the same time. Remove the pan from the heat and when the mixture is cool, pour into a plastic pail. Add the currants, acid, yeast, nutrient and tannin. When fermentation starts, allow it to continue for two days. Strain the must into a fermentation jar, fit the fermentation lock and ferment on.

Gooseberry Wine

Gooseberries are one of the best fruits for making a fine medium wine. With care, they can be made into a wine that your friends will not be able to distinguish from hock, Moselle or Chablis. But to do this you must use the wine yeast for those particular wines. Many home winemakers add raisins or other ingredients, but before you do that, try gooseberry wine just as it is.

MAKES ABOUT SIX BOTTLES
6 lb (3 kg) ripe gooseberries, crushed
3½ lb (1¾ kg) sugar
1 gal (4½ litres) water
½ oz (15 g) pectic enzyme
Yeast and nutrient
½ teaspoon tannin

Put the gooseberries and sugar in a plastic pail. Bring the water to the boil and pour it over the fruit and sugar, stirring. Allow the mixture to cool. Add the pectic enzyme and set aside for 24 hours. Add the yeast, nutrient and tannin. After fermentation has started, leave it to continue for 4 days, stirring daily. Strain the must into a fermentation jar. Fit the fermentation lock and ferment on.

Grape Wine

To make true grape wine you will require the juice from about 15 pounds (7½ kg) of grapes for only a few bottles of wine. This recipe, however, is more economical. It uses dessert grapes to make a medium wine. Because dessert grapes are deficient in acid, this has been added. A true wine grape is much more sour and does not require the addition of acid.

MAKES ABOUT SIX BOTTLES
9 lb (4½ kg) dessert grapes, crushed
1 lb (½ kg) sugar
¼ oz (7 g) citric acid
6 pints (3½ litres) water
1 Campden tablet
Yeast and nutrient

Put the grapes, sugar, acid and cold water in a pail. Crush and stir in the Campden tablet and set aside for 24 hours. Add the yeast and nutrient. After fermentation has started, allow it to continue for 6 days. Strain the must into a fermentation jar, fit the fermentation lock and ferment on.

Lemon Thyme Wine

This is one of the better herbs for wine-making. It makes a medium wine that is delicately scented with lemon. To measure the amount of thyme leaves required for this recipe fill a 1 pint (500 ml) mug to the brim with leaves (no stalks), pressing down lightly.

MAKES ABOUT SIX BOTTLES

1 pint (500 ml) lemon thyme leaves
2½ lb (1¼ kg) sugar
1 gal (4½ litres) water
1 lb (½ kg) sultanas
¼ oz (7 g) citric acid
Pinch of tannin
Yeast and nutrient

Put the thyme leaves and sugar in a plastic pail, add the cold water and stir well. When the sugar is completely dissolved, add the sultanas, acid, tannin, yeast and nutrient. When fermentation starts, allow it to continue for 3 days, stirring daily, then strain the must into a fermentation jar. Fit the fermentation lock and ferment on.

Marrow Wine

Plain marrow wine is rather insipid, but if raisins are added and brown sugar is used, it can be made into an excellent rich, sweet wine. If you really want to put some zip into the wine, add 1 ounce (30 g) of root ginger powder 24 hours before you strain the must into the fermentation jar.

MAKES ABOUT SIX BOTTLES

6 lb (3 kg) finely chopped marrow
¾ lb (360 g) raisins, minced
3½ lb (1¾ kg) demerara sugar
1 gal (4½ litres) water
½ oz (15 g) pectic enzyme
Yeast and nutrient
½ oz (15 g) citric acid

Make sure that the marrow is ripe—unripe marrow makes the wine taste woody. Place the marrow, raisins and sugar in a pail. Bring the water to the boil and pour it over the ingredients. When cool, add the pectic enzyme and set aside.

Leave for 24 hours. Add the yeast, nutrient and acid. When fermentation starts, leave it for 3 days, stirring daily. Strain the must into a fermentation jar, fit the fermentation lock and ferment on.

Parsnip Wine

Parsnip is one of the most popular vegetable wines, but it is rather insipid and requires the addition of other ingredients—in this case sultanas—to make a really pleasant, medium wine. On the credit side, its lack of strong flavour makes parsnip wine a good mixer, and it can be used safely with most other ingredients.

MAKES ABOUT SIX BOTTLES

4 lb (2 kg) parsnips, scrubbed and grated
2½ lb (1¼ kg) sugar
1 gal (4½ litres) water
Yeast and nutrient
1 lb (½ kg) sultanas, minced
¼ oz (7 g) citric acid

Put the parsnips, sugar and water in a large saucepan and bring to the boil. Remove the pan from the heat. When the mixture is cool, pour into a plastic pail and add yeast, nutrient, sultanas and acid. When fermentation has started, allow it to continue for 3 days. Strain the must into a fermentation jar, fit the fermentation lock and ferment on.

Pea Pod Wine

If peas are grown, the gardening cook will have plenty of pods left over after shelling. These are usually put on the compost heap, but save some and try pea pod wine. This recipe is for a dry wine, but if you have a sweet tooth, replace the raisins with currants and add 1½ pounds (¾ kg) of sugar.

MAKES ABOUT SIX BOTTLES

6 lb (3 kg) pea pods, finely chopped
2 lb (1 kg) sugar
1 gal (4½ litres) water
½ lb (¼ kg) raisins, minced
¼ oz (7 g) citric acid
½ teaspoon tannin
Yeast and nutrient

Put the pea pods, sugar and water in a large saucepan and bring to the boil. Remove the pan from the heat. When the mixture is cool, pour it into a plastic pail and add the raisins, acid, tannin, yeast and nutrient. When fermentation has started, allow it to continue for 4 days then strain the must into a fermentation jar, fit the fermentation lock and ferment on.

Pear Wine

Pears produce a wine that is too light for most people, so it is more usual to find pears in combination with other ingredients. Sultanas are added to the pears in this recipe to make a medium wine. If you want to try something a little different omit the sultanas and add the flesh of three ripe bananas. The wine can be made sweet or dry by adding or subtracting 1 pound (½ kg) of sugar.

MAKES ABOUT SIX BOTTLES

1 gal (4½ litres) water
3 lb (1½ kg) sugar
9 lb (4½ kg) pears, minced
½ lb (¼ kg) sultanas, minced
¼ oz (7 g) citric acid
Yeast and nutrient

Bring the water to the boil and stir in the sugar. Remove the pan from the heat and set aside to cool. Put the pears, sultanas, acid, yeast and nutrient in a plastic pail and pour in the sugared water. When fermentation starts, allow it to continue for 4 days then strain the must into a fermentation jar, fit the fermentation lock and ferment on.

Strawberry Wine

One characteristic of wine is that the final flavour rarely resembles the parent ingredient—orange wine does not taste of oranges and grape wine does not taste of grapes. One of the exceptions is strawberry wine, which has the aroma and the taste of the fruit. The most popular type of strawberry wine is sweet, and that is the recipe given here, but dry strawberry wine is superb also. To make the dry wine just reduce the sugar to 2½ pounds (1¼ kg).

MAKES ABOUT SIX BOTTLES

4 lb (2 kg) strawberries, crushed
1 gal (4½ litres) water
½ oz (15 g) pectic enzyme
4 lb (2 kg) sugar
Yeast and nutrient

If possible, use a Sauternes yeast. Put the strawberries and cold water in a plastic pail. Add the pectic enzyme and leave for 4 days, stirring daily. Then add the sugar, yeast and nutrient, and stir well. Strain into a fermentation jar, fit the fermentation lock and wait for fermentation to start. Leave to ferment on.

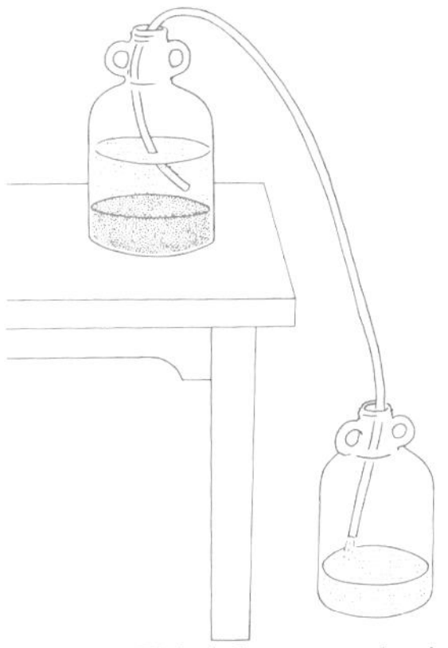

Racking. This is how to rack wine off the sediment and into another jar. Make sure that the top end of the siphon tube stays well clear of the sediment, otherwise it will drag some up. If this does happen, the wine can be re-racked after it has settled.

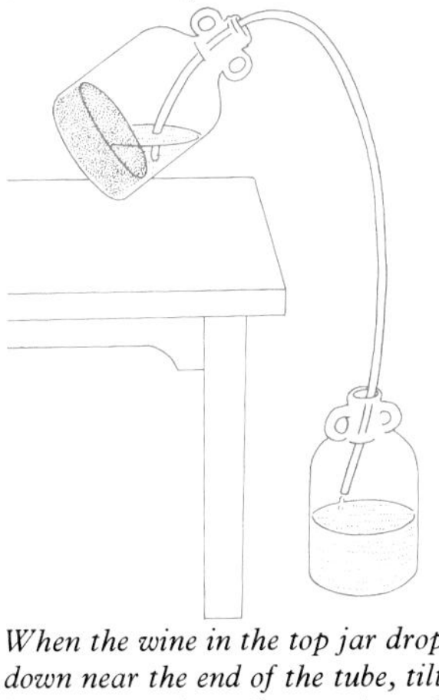

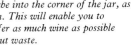

When the wine in the top jar drops down near the end of the tube, tilt the jar very gently *and move the end of the tube into the corner of the jar, as shown. This will enable you to transfer as much wine as possible without waste.*

Glossary/gardening

Acid soil. Soil lacking in lime.

Aggregate. A material—coarse sand, gravel, small pebbles or vermiculite—which is used to grow plants hydroponically.

Alkaline soil. Soil in which there is enough lime to counteract all acidity.

Aphis, aphids. Plant-lice (greenfly, blackfly).

Blanching. The process of excluding light to whiten such stalks and leaves as celery and endive, and make them less bitter.

Bolting. The premature flowering of a plant, which makes it "run to seed".

Brassicas. Wide range of vegetables, including cabbages, cauliflowers, Brussels sprouts and kales, which belong to the *Cruciferae* family.

Catch crop. Quick-maturing crop grown in ground in which another crop is to be raised later.

Chard. The young stems of salsify, Swiss chard and globe artichokes.

Cloche. Small portable glass or plastic structure under which plants are grown to protect them from the weather.

Compost. Confusingly, compost is both manure made largely from vegetable matter by bacterial action and a growing medium for seeds and plants, based on soil, peat and sand, or peat and sand, with added fertilizers.

Cordon. A fruit tree trained, usually, as a single stem. There are also double and triple cordons, which have two and three stems.

Crown. That part of the plant where root and stem meet.

Cultivar. The word is a contraction of "cultivated variety". It is the sub-division of a species which has acquired, in cultivation, certain characteristics distinguishing it from other forms of the species. Compare, for example, the huge Webbs Wonderful lettuce and the tiny Tom Thumb lettuce.

Diploid. Most plants have cells which contain two sets of matching chromosomes (the diploid number).

Drill. Shallow trench in the soil in which seeds are sown. It is usually made with a draw hoe, and is therefore V-shaped.

Dutch light. A light, wooden frame grooved to hold a single pane of glass measuring 56 × 28¾ inches (140 cm × 72 cm).

Earthing up. Drawing soil around the stems of plants for the purpose of blanching them, for example, celery, or to prevent the tubers of potatoes from being exposed to the light and turning green and poisonous.

F₁ hybrid. The result of crossing two true parent strains of plants—a vigorous hybrid with such characteristics as hardiness, early maturity, disease resistance and flavour. Because F₁ seed is pollinated by hand, it is more expensive than seed of ordinary varieties. Seed saved from F₁ hybrids does not breed true.

Fillis. Soft but tough string for tying up plants, particularly tomatoes.

Foliar spray. A solution of plant nutrients sprayed on the leaves and quickly absorbed by the plant.

Force. To hasten growth by providing warmth. Some vegetables, for example rhubarb and chicory, are forced in the dark.

Frame. A low structure of brick, wood, or metal and glass, in which plants can be given protection from the weather.

Fungicide. Fungi-killing chemical.

Germination. Sprouting of seeds.

Green manuring. Digging a growing crop, such as mustard or lupins, into the soil to enrich it.

Hardening off. Gradual process of acclimatizing plants grown under glass to colder conditions outside. It is usually done in a frame to which more air is admitted each day.

Haulm. Stem and leaves of some vegetables, for example peas and potatoes.

Heel. The base of a cutting taken from a plant that includes a little of the harder growth of the stem from which the cutting was taken. The heel aids propagation.

Herbicide. Weed-killing chemical.

Humus. Black, amorphous substance in fertile soil, derived from organic matter through the action of bacteria.

Hybrid. A plant produced as a result of crossing different species.

Hydroponics. Method of growing plants without the use of soil. The plants are fed with mineral nutrients in solution.

Inorganic fertilizers. Chemical compounds, which, when added to the soil, provide the plants with vital elements.

Insecticide. Insect-killing chemical.

Intercrop. A crop grown between rows of another crop.

John Innes composts. Seed and potting composts evolved at the John Innes Horticultural Institute.

Lateral. Side shoot growing from the leading shoot of a plant.

Leader. The leading shoot of a plant.

Legumes. Members of the *Leguminosae* family, such as peas and beans.

Loam. Well-balanced soil composed of sand and clay particles and humus.

Maiden. Fruit tree—usually one straight stem—in its first year after being grafted.

Main crop. The vegetable crop which is allowed to develop to maturity. The term is usually applied to winter roots which are to be stored.

Mulch. A covering, usually made of compost, peat or straw, which is spread over the surface of the soil to suppress weeds and conserve moisture.

Neutral soil. Soil with a pH rating between 6·5 and 7·5, which is neither too acid nor too alkaline. (See pH factor.)

Nymph. An immature insect resembling the adult, but without fully developed wings and reproductive organs.

Offsets. Bulbs growing from the parent bulb as one way of reproduction (for example, shallots).

Organic fertilizers. Matter such as farmyard manure, compost and fish meal which, when added to the soil, feeds it and improves its texture.

pH factor. Indicates the degree of acidity or alkalinity in the soil. Below pH 7 the soil is increasingly acid; above pH 7 the soil is increasingly alkaline.

Peat bags. Plastic bags filled with peat compost in which such vegetables as tomatoes and cucumbers can be grown.

Peat blocks. Blocks of compressed peat compost in which seeds are sown.

Pelleted seeds. Small seeds coated with soil-clay to make them larger and therefore easier to handle.

Perennial. A plant that lives for more than two years.

Planting-out. Transplanting a plant from a box or pot to the open ground.

Potting-off. Transplanting a young plant from a box to a pot.

Potting-on. Transplanting a plant from one pot to a larger one.

Pricking-out. Transplanting a seedling from the seed tray to another tray or pot soon after germination.

Propagator. Basically a heated box in which seeds are germinated and cuttings are rooted.

Remontant. A plant that blooms and fruits more than once in a season.

Ring culture. Method of growing plants, especially tomatoes, in bottomless pots called rings. The roots absorb nutrients via the compost in the ring and take up water from the aggregate (for example coarse sand, gravel or pebbles) on which the ring stands.

Rootstock. Plant on to which a scion, or young shoot, of a fruit tree is grafted.

Runners. Long shoots sent out by strawberries by which they propagate themselves. The runners root when they come into contact with moist soil and a new plant begins to grow.

Scion. Young shoot of a fruit tree grafted on to a different rootstock.

Seed leaves. The first two leaves that appear after germination. Some plants have only one seed leaf.

Seedling. Very young plant raised from seed.

Setting. The start of growth of fruits or seeds after pollination.

Spit. The depth of a spade when it is dug into the ground.

Spur. On most varieties of apple trees, the short branch growing close to the branches which carry the fruit.

Station. The position at which seeds are sown in ones, twos or threes, at intervals along a row.

Succession crop. Crop which follows another crop.

Thinning. Pulling up some growing seedlings to allow the rest adequate space to grow.

Thongs. Cuttings from the roots of seakale, from which the next year's crop is grown.

Tilth. Soil broken down into fine crumbs.

Transplanting. Removing a plant from one place and planting it somewhere else.

Triploid. Plants which have three sets of chromosomes in the cell nucleus.

True leaves. Leaves typical of the plant. They grow after the seed leaves have appeared.

Truss. Collective name for a group of flowers, such as those of tomatoes and apples, which will develop into fruit.

Tuber. Natural swelling of an underground stem. This is the edible part of a potato or Jerusalem artichoke plant.

Variety. The widely used term for a cultivar.

Virus. Invisible organism living in the soil and in plants. Viruses are the cause of some of the worst and, so far, incurable vegetable diseases.

Acidulated water. Water to which lemon juice or vinegar has been added. Cut fruit and vegetables are dipped in acidulated water to prevent them discolouring. Add 2 teaspoons to 1 tablespoon of lemon juice or vinegar to 1 pint (500 ml) of water.

Al dente. An Italian culinary term used to describe food which is cooked but remains resistant to the bite.

Antipasti. The Italian name for *hors d'oeuvre*.

Auto-chopper. A gadget for chopping vegetables, fruit, nuts and herbs. It is an enclosed zigzag blade attached to a spring which, when tapped, chops the food.

Bagna cauda. Hot oil and butter sauce flavoured with garlic and anchovies and served with raw vegetables. It is a speciality of the Piedmont region of Italy.

Bain-marie. A large pan of hot water in which smaller pans can be placed so that the water comes no higher than half-way up. Custards and sauces that are too delicate to be placed over direct heat are cooked slowly or kept warm in a bain-marie.

Bean curd. A cream coloured, custard-like, slightly spongy substance prepared from soya beans and used extensively in Chinese and Japanese cooking.

Béarnaise. Rich, delicate, classic sauce composed of butter and eggs, acidulated with reduced, herb-flavoured, white wine vinegar.

Béchamel. Basic white sauce made with a *roux* and milk flavoured with onions, carrots, herbs and seasoning.

Boeuf Bourguignon. Beef cooked in the Burgundian style, that is with red wine, usually burgundy.

Beurre manié. A paste made from equal quantities of flour and butter kneaded together. It is used to thicken soups, sauces and stews.

Blanch. Culinary term meaning to plunge fruits, vegetables or nuts briefly into boiling water to loosen skin prior to peeling; to reduce strong flavours or bitterness; or to set the colour and prepare food for freezing.

Bleed. A culinary term used to describe the loss of colour from some vegetables when their skin is broken during cooking or the loss of nutrients from sliced vegetables.

Bordelaise. Basic, rich sauce made with red wine, beef marrow, shallots and various herbs. It is usually served with roast beef, steak and game.

Bouquet garni. A faggot of various herbs, including parsley, bay and thyme, sometimes contained in a muslin bag. It is used to flavour many dishes including soups, sauces and stews.

Breadcrumbs, fresh. Breadcrumbs made from day-old bread. The crust is cut off then the bread is rubbed through a sieve or grated by hand or in a blender.

Breadcrumbs, dry white. Fresh breadcrumbs dried slowly in a very low oven or warm dry place.

Breadcrumbs, dry brown. These may be made from bread crusts dried in an oven and crushed with a rolling-pin or in a blender.

Brioche. Sweet bread made from a rich yeast dough.

Bruised. A term used to describe an ingredient which has been lightly crushed in order to release its flavour, as with garlic.

Caramelized. Culinary term used to describe sugar which has been cooked until it is a rich brown colour, and a process by which food is cooked with a little sugar and butter until it is coated with a rich golden syrup.

Cassoulet. French stew made with haricot beans, pieces of goose or mutton (or both) and various other ingredients.

Chili powder compound. Commercially prepared ground spice mixture.

Clarified butter. Melted, purified butter. The butter is melted and then cooked very gently without being allowed to colour. The scum is skimmed off and the butter poured through a strainer. It is then left to stand, and when the sediment has settled the clarified butter is poured carefully into another container.

Compote. Fresh or dried fruit cooked in syrup and served cold.

Daikon. Large Japanese radish, which can be eaten raw or cooked.

Duxelles. Primarily the name given to a paste made from minced mushrooms and/or mushroom stalks. It is used to flavour soups, stews and various other dishes.

Emincé de veau. Traditional Swiss dish of thinly sliced strips of veal served in a rich, creamy sauce.

Fool. Traditional English sweet dish of puréed fruit, which is stewed and usually mixed with whipped cream and served cold.

Glaze. Culinary term denoting a glassy finish given to food by coating it with egg, water, syrup or puréed jam after cooking.

Gnocchi. Small dumplings made of semolina, *choux* paste or potatoes. They are poached, drained and often mixed with butter, covered with cheese and baked or grilled.

Gram flour. Flour made from dried chick peas.

Gratin. Culinary term used to describe a dish which has been covered with a sauce, sprinkled with breadcrumbs and/or grated cheese and baked or grilled.

Herb butter. Butter which has been blended with various finely chopped herbs. It is used as a garnish or added to soups and sauces.

Herb salt and herb sugar. Salt or sugar which has been mixed with herbs and stored until matured. They are used to flavour savoury or sweet dishes.

Hollandaise. Rich egg and butter sauce acidulated with vinegar and sometimes with lemon juice. It is served with fish, eggs and vegetables.

Julienne. The name given to vegetables cut into small, narrow strips. It is also used to describe a clear soup to which narrow strips of various cooked vegetables have been added.

Mamaliga. In most East European countries *mamaliga* is the name for a type of corn meal porridge. It is a staple food in Romania.

Mandoline. Utensil used to slice vegetables. It is a blade set in a piece of wood. The blade, wavy or flat, can be adjusted to cut in various thicknesses.

Monosodium glutamate. The chemical name for a salty white powder that is used extensively in Chinese cooking to bring out the flavour of many foods. Also called gourmet powder, monosodium glutamate is sold under such names as Vetsin and Ac'cent.

Mornay. Béchamel sauce to which grated cheese, usually Gruyère or Parmesan, has been added. It is served with fish, egg and vegetable dishes.

Pan-fry. Culinary term used to describe the process of cooking food with a small amount of fat in a shallow pan.

Pecorino. Hard Italian cheese, similar to Parmesan, made from ewe's milk.

Pissalat. The Provençal name of a highly flavoured dish of small sea fish.

Polenta. Finely ground corn meal used in Italy to make a type of porridge.

Render. Culinary term used to describe the process of melting down fat into dripping.

Roux. A base for sauces composed of flour gently cooked in fat. According to the length of time it is cooked, the *roux* will be white (*blanc*), pale golden (*blond*) or a deep biscuit colour (*brun*).

Sauce Maltaise. *Hollandaise* sauce flavoured with the juice of blood oranges.

Sauce Mousseline. *Hollandaise* sauce with whipped cream folded into it. It is served with asparagus, seakale, grilled sole and other dishes.

Sauté. Method of cooking ingredients in very hot fat, shaking the pan to make them "jump".

Coating consistency. Sauce has reached a coating consistency when you can draw your finger down the back of the wooden spoon you have been using, and the edges of the trail this makes stay perfectly sharp and clear.

Tomato concentrate. A concentrated paste made from tomatoes.

Vegetable mouli (Mouli-legumes). A vegetable mill which has plates, with perforations of varying sizes, which fit into a metal base. A disc with a handle is rotated to push the food through the perforations to make a purée.

Vinaigrette. French dressing, made with oil, vinegar and various seasonings.

Metric Conversions

All metric equivalents in this book are approximate.

Weight: 1 ounce = 28·35 grams. For convenience it has been rounded up to 30 grams.

Volume: 1 pint = 568 millilitres. For convenience it has been rounded down to 500 millilitres.

Temperature: 32°F = 0°C. To convert Fahrenheit into centigrade: subtract 32, multiply by 5, divide by 9. The conversions used in this book are made to the nearest round figure. Oven temperature conversions are those recommended by the Association of Manufacturers of Domestic Electrical Appliances and the Metrication Board.

Tablespoons and teaspoons are standard British measures. Amounts given are for level spoonfuls.

Length: 1 inch = 2·54 centimetres. For convenience it has been rounded down to 2 centimetres and 2 inches to 5 centimetres.

Index/recipes

Index/general

Acknowledgements

A. E. Bicknell
Ray Desmond, The Garden History Society
Mike Janulewicz
The National Society of Leisure Gardeners Limited
Royal Botanic Gardens, Kew
The Royal Horticultural Society
Carol Todd

Artists:
Norman Barber
Helen Cowcher
Ian Garrard
Peter Morter
Jim Robins
Rodney Shackell
Kathleen Smith
Michael Woods
Sidney Woods

Indexer:
Brenda Hall, M.A., Registered indexer of the Society of Indexers

Photographers:
Rex Bamber
Chris Barker
Michael Boys
David Meldrum
Roger Phillips

Picture libraries:
Mansell Collection, pages 6, 13
Marshall Cavendish Picture Library (Rex Bamber, David Meldrum and Roger Phillips), cover
Ronan Picture Library, page 12
Radio Times Hulton, pages 13, 14, 15

Studio services:
A. C. Cooper
Face Photosetting
Roy Flooks
Mitchell Beazley Studio
Summit Art

THE ULTIMATE ENCYCLOPEDIA OF

eXtreme sports

Joe Tomlinson

CARLTON

THIS IS A CARLTON BOOK

Text and design © 1996 Carlton Books Limited

The GX trademark depicted on the cover is owned by Vision Marketing, Inc., The GX Team,
Inc., Newport, Rhode Island, USA, and is licensed by United Media, 200 Madison Avenue,
4th Floor, New York, NY 10016, USA.

Every effort has been taken to ensure the accuracy of the information given in this book.
No liability can be accepted by the author or the publisher for any loss, damage or injury
caused by errors in, or omissions from the information given.

ISBN 1.85868.192.8

Printed in Italy

EDITOR: Julian Flanders
PICTURE EDITOR: Sharon Hutton
PRODUCTION: Garry Lewis

ABOUT THE AUTHOR

Joe Tomlinson is the President and founder of The GX Team, an extreme sports marketing and
management company based in Newport, Rhode Island. The GX Team consults with advertisers
and marketing companies, working with them and providing today's extreme sports stars for
their campaigns. The GX Team also creates events and merchandise focusing on extreme
sports and the lifestyles they signify.
Joe was the extreme sports consultant to the producers of the Closing Ceremonies of the
1996 Atlanta Summer Olympics.
Joe has many years experience of boardsailing, skiing, mountain biking, snowboarding and
sailing, and also enjoys an occasional bungee jump. He lives in Rhode Island on the east coast
of America, with his wife Amy, and their three children: J.J., Elodie and Summer.

PICTURE ACKNOWLEDGMENTS

The publishers would like to thank the following sources for their permission to reproduce the
images in this book: Agence DPPI/F Clement; Allsport/Luciano Bosari, Shaun Botterill, Simon
Bruty, Mike Cooper, Glenn Dubock, Tony Duffy, John Gichigi, Mike Hewitt, Bob Martin, Gary M
Prior, Pascal Rondeau, Anton Want; Allsport/Vandystadt/Kurt Amsler, Pat Boulland, B Buffet,
Marc Cazals, Gerard Ceccaldi, Sylvain Cazenave, Sylvie Chappaz,Bernard Desestres, Vania Fine,
Jean Paul Galtier, Didier Givois, Vincent Kalut, Stephane Kempenaire, Didier Klein, Bernard
Lambolez, Jean Paul Lenfant, Jean-Marc Loubat, Richard Martin, Thierry Martinez, Alain Marty,
Remy Michelin, Gerard Planchenault, Philip Plisson, Alain Revel, Francois Rickard, Pascal
Tournaire, Simon Ward, Laurent Zabulon, Zoom; Allsport USA/Nathan Bilow,Vince Cavatio,
David Leah,Mike Powell, W. Sallaz, Tina Schmidt, Stephen Wade; Bluewater Freedivers/Terry
Maas; Cannondale; Rick Doyle; ©Hobie Cat; James Hudson; Image Bank/Jon Love, Marc
Romanelli, William Sallaz; Jason Lee; Brad McDonald; Phorum/Mark D Phillips; ©Schwinn
1994; Rex Features/Laski; Brian W. Robb; Stockfile/Steve Behr, Malcolm Fearon, Steve
Thomas; Stock Newport/Bob Grieser, Daniel Forster; TSI/Adamski Peek.

With special thanks to Daffyd Bynon.

Introduction

I have to assume that if you're reading this, you're interested in extreme sports. In fact, you may actually participate in one or more of the sports described within this book. It doesn't really matter though, because extreme sports are exciting, and that's why everyone wants to know what they're all about.

WHAT ARE EXTREME SPORTS ALL ABOUT? What is it that gets athletes charged up enough to put their lives at risk? Is it all just a big adrenaline fixation? I don't think so.

Which is not to say that there isn't a quest for an adrenaline charge in extreme sports—there is. Most athletes, however, who consider themselves to be extreme are not lunatics seeking an adrenaline buzz no matter what the consequences.

They get their adrenal rush because their skills allow them to perform safely under conditions that are dangerous or even life threatening. They can successfully do things that could kill those unfamiliar with their particular sports because they have dedicated themselves to performing within their limits, even while they have consistently challenged themselves to redefine what those limits are.

Extreme sports are about individuality, higher and higher levels of achievement, redefining performance boundaries, and the personal satisfaction that comes from trying your best. Extreme sports deliver a sense of accomplishment, whether you establish a new level of ability or simply challenge yourself while having a great time.

Extreme sports do not generally prohibit you from having fun because of your physical size or build, but they do require for you to be in shape. You can enjoy your sports without the threat of a 300-pound adversary slamming you to the ground or a competing 8-foot giant keeping you from your goal. What you are pitting yourself against in extreme sports, however, is a much less forgiving opponent, the Earth and its elements—Air, Land, and Water. To challenge "mother nature" is far more formidable than competing with any massive individual.

There is a level of respect that should be afforded all extreme athletes, whether they are experts or beginners. As the saying goes, "you have to be a kook sometime"—translation, you have to start somewhere. None of the extreme sports are easy enough for a first time attempt to be done well, or safely in some cases, without assistance or supervision. Extreme sports are passed down and across from athlete to athlete, and there is a true sense of satisfaction to be gained from introducing a newcomer to your extreme sport of choice.

The extreme sports movement has been quick to embrace the idea of the "crossover" athlete. Moving over from one extreme sport to another is encouraged. An expert snowboarder may find that mountain biking really turns them on, so they begin to develop their skills on a bike. That same snowboarder may also find that boardsailing is a thrill, and so begins the process of learning to boardsail. The snowboarding, mountain biking, boardsailing athlete may then decide to try hang gliding, climbing, kayaking, or any other number of extreme sports. As they build their repertoire of sports, they become better "crossover"

athletes, and each extreme sport adds a little to their skills in other extreme sports by broadening their ideas on how things can be done.

How extreme sports have impacted on each other is really the story of the evolution of extreme sports until today. Some of the sports are very old, like bungee jumping. Some of the sports are very new, like mountainboarding. Both have elements that can be found in other extreme sports.

The thrill of freefall was first bound in bungee, but it can be found in windsurfing, snowboarding, skiing, B.A.S.E jumping, etc. The joy of carving a turn on a mountain board is new, but it has its roots in surfing, skateboarding, wakeboarding, snowboarding, etc.

Extreme sports are about gravity, ingenuity, and technology. Gravity is the force that pulls climbers off rock faces, skiers down slopes and off cliffs, hang gliders toward the ground, and water downstream. Gravity makes warm air rise above cold, drives water to settle at the lowest available spot to create lakes and seas, creates the swirling mass of atmosphere that drives the winds. Gravity shaped our planet.

Ingenuity and technology are responsible for the multitude of ways we have discovered to use the forces of nature to enjoy nature. The evolution of extreme sports is a story of pushing available technologies and designs in order to improve performance. From high-tech fabrics to composite construction methods to innovations in design, extreme sports have evolved through the years thanks to the energies of many pioneers.

Extreme sports are exciting because they are full of energy and spirit. Of course, they are visually exciting, as the pictures throughout this book amply confirm. Most importantly, extreme sports have a life-affirming quality that stretches from the story of their evolution to the sheer pleasure they offer to those who participate at any level.

The world is a big place, with elements that offer plenty of challenges. Enjoy the planet and embrace the sports that celebrate being a part of it—extreme sports!

If you want to take your interest in any of these sports further, I have included information about books, magazines, associations and clubs that you would do well to contact. Do it—you'll thank me later.

Air
Sports

It's fair to say that sports performed in the air are extreme. It is also fair to say that taking part in these sports can be extremely life threatening.

9

FURTHER INFORMATION

BIBLIOGRAPHY
● *Bungee Jumping For Fun And Profit,*
Nancy Frase, ICS Books, Inc., Merrillville,
Indiana 1992
● *Skydiving,* Christopher Meeks,
Capstone Press, Inc., Mankato,
Minnesota, 1991
● *The Encyclopaedia of Dangerous Sports,*
Missy Allen and Michel Peissel, Chelsea
House Publishers, New York,
Philadelphia, 1995

ASSOCIATIONS & CLUBS

B.A.S.E. JUMPING
■ U.S. Base Association
12619 Manor Dr.
Hawthorne, CA 90250-4313
Jean Boenish, Dir.
Tel (001)213 678-0163

BALLOONING
■ Balloon Federation of America
PO Box 400
Indianola, IA 50125
J. Michael Wallace, Pres.
Tel (001) 515 961-8809
Fax (001) 515 961-3537
■ Sport Balloon Society of the USA
Menlo Oaks Balloon Field
PO Box 2247
Menlo Park, CA 94026-2247
Peke Sonnichsen, CEO & Pres.
Tel (001) 415 323-2757
■ Bill Harrop's "Original"
Balloon Safaris cc.
Email travela@aztec.co.za
PO Box 67
Randburg, 2125
South Africa
Tel (001) 011-705-3201/2
Fax (001) 011-705-3203
■ Dansk Ballonunion
Thorsager 12 k
Reerslev
DK-2640 Hedehusene, Denmark
Contact, Benny Clausen
■ UK Hot Air Balloon Passenger Rides
http://www.ftech.co.uk/balloons/
index.hts
■ *Balloon Life Magazine*
info@aero.com
Fax (001) 408 978 1201
■ Balloon Life Magazine Inc.
2145 Dale Ave.
Sacramento, CA 95815
■ Aerostar Balloons (retailer)
http://www.aerostar.com/

BUNGEE JUMPING
■ North American Bungee Association
2210 Samuel Coolcourt
Park City, UT 84060
Thomas Woodard, Exec. Officer
Tel (001) 801 649-2599
Fax (001) 801 359-4418
■ European Bungee Clubs
http://www.tardis.ed.ac.uk/
ark/bungee/europe.html
■ UK Bungee Club
http://www.ftech.co.uk/ go/ukbc/
Chelsea Bridge Tower
Queenstown Rd,
London, SW8 4NP
Tel (44) 0171 720-9496
■ List of Worldwide Bungee Jumping Sites
http://users.aol.com/bungeepage/

HANG GLIDING
■ U.S. Hang Gliding Association
559 E. Pikes Peaks, Ste. 101
PO Box 8300
Colorado Springs, CO 80933-8300
Jerry Bruning, Exec. Dir.
Tel (001) 719 632-8300
Fax (001) 719 632-6417
■ Skywings (e-zine, UK)
Office@bbpa.deman.co.uk
■ British Hang Gliding and Paragliding
Association
http://test.ebrd.com/SkyWings/
clubs.html
The Old Schoolroom
Loughborough Rd.
Leicester, LE4 5PJ
Tel (44) 0116 2611322
Fax (44) 0116 2611323

10

IMAGINE THE CONSEQUENCES of a parachute that doesn't deploy or deploys only half way, a balloon that suddenly deflates, a glider caught in a violent downdraft, or a sky surfer spinning out of control. Air offers little resistance, so it can't keep the forces of gravity from drawing our bodies to the earth's surface. Only the drag created as objects pass through the air limits the speeds at which they travel down to earth. Another useful fact about the air that covers our planet is that it varies in temperature. Warm air rises until it cools in the upper atmosphere, and then it travels downward once again to the earth's surface. Here, it is warmed again, and the cycle is complete. The air is much like an ocean, with its ever flowing tides and currents. Because the elements that make up the air are lighter than the ocean and the land, the air knows no borders. When it pushes up against land or sea, it simply follows the path of least resistance and moves on to pursue its intended direction. Understanding how air travels as it crosses the planet is of paramount importance to the creation and growth of extreme air sports.

TO FLY LIKE A BIRD

We have discovered a number of ways to defy gravity in the air. First we used vines and cords. Then we made balloons, parachutes, and wings, and using these to channel the air to create lift or sufficient drag to control the speed at which we fall to earth, we created sports that our ancestors could only dream about. Legendary Icarus was said to be the first to test the limits of flight only to perish in his famous tumble to earth after flying too close to the sun. Leonardo Da Vinci drafted many sketches after envisioning craft capable of flight, from the balloon to the helicopter. A

few short decades ago, many of the techniques currently used to test the air could have only been imagined in the pages of Flash Gordon or a Jules Verne novel .

The thrill of flying like a bird, hurtling to earth at high speed only to float to a stop, is what has drawn athletes to push the limits of what is possible in the air. One can only imagine that early balloonists would have considered it insanity if anyone had suggested jumping from their craft attached to an elastic cord or a parachute. Of course, these pioneers of aviation were then considered to be the crazy risk takers for pursuing flight. They were the early extreme air sports enthusiasts. In time, they were forced to create vehicles, namely parachutes, that could allow them to escape their balloons with their lives if the worst were to occur. Soon items of necessity became ones of play, and the limits of air were again redefined.

DEFINING THE POSSIBLE

Now athletes are surfing, flipping, gliding, and bouncing through the air in defiance of gravity. The opportunity to jump from aircraft is less than a century old. The first bungee jumpers used vines to break their fall to earth. There was a day when a high wire walk was a circus trick. It is safe to assume that during the course of the next century, athletes will continue to redefine what can and can't be done in the air until what is cutting edge today becomes commonplace.

Right now we can feel satisfied that all of the currently defined limits are newly defined. In the years ahead new boundaries will be established and what is in these pages may become arcane. Either way, there is no question that the core emotion and andrenaline rush that comes from pushing the limits of what can be done in the air will remain, and athletes will continue probing and testing the boundaries of aerial extreme sports.

B.A.S.E. Jumping

12

If any of the extreme sports can be considered truly high risk, then B.A.S.E. Jumping is that sport. For those readers who are unfamiliar with the term "B.A.S.E.", it is an acronym for Buildings, Antenna Tower, Span, Earth. B.A.S.E. jumpers are athletes who leap from objects which fall under the categories B.A.S.E. represents. Generally these objects are not very high off the ground, and so the jumper must deploy his parachute very quickly or risk impacting the ground at deadly speed.

ACCORDING TO *The Skydiver's Handbook*, evidence exists that suggests B.A.S.E. jumping can be traced back as far as 900 years. Whether or not these jumpers survived to leap again is unknown. Modern B.A.S.E. jumping is believed to have started in 1978, where daring parachutists first began jumping off of El Capitan, a 3,000 foot (915m) cliff high above Yosemite National Park. This site has remained a hotbed for U.S. B.A.S.E. jumpers.

The term B.A.S.E. was coined by B.A.S.E. pioneers Phil Smith and Jean Boenish. By January of 1981, the first four B.A.S.E. jumpers had completed jumps in all four B.A.S.E. categories, giving birth to the U.S. B.A.S.E. Association. As jumpers successfully complete all four categories, they receive their official B.A.S.E. number. Phil Smith of Houston, Texas is B.A.S.E. #1. As of April 1995, there were 450 registered B.A.S.E. jumpers worldwide. Today, there are 4,000 participants in the U.S. alone.

B.A.S.E. has an outlaw reputation in the U.S., and is illegal. There are several countries worldwide where B.A.S.E. is legal. Some of the more well known legal sites are in France, Norway, and Brazil. One of the most daring and highly publicized illegal jumps in the U.S. was made by John Vincent of New Orleans, Louisiana. John climbed to the top of the Saint Louis Arch using suction cups as handholds, and jumped. John was later arrested by the FBI for jumping from a national monument, and spent 90 days in a federal prison. Jumps in the U.S. are now punishable by up to one year in jail and $5,000 (£7,500) fine.

Redeployment point

Anyone considering becoming a B.A.S.E. jumper or doing any type of B.A.S.E. jump should have completed at least 100 skydives. B.A.S.E. jumpers must be extremely familiar and comfortable with their gear. The jumper must have particularly strong freefall skills, as the ability to maintain correct body attitude during freefall is key to a safe deployment and landing. The need for excellent canopy skills should not be underestimated. Obviously, a jumper whose

Sometimes illegal and always
dangerous, B.A.S.E. jumping
is a truly high-risk extreme
sport. But what a view...

Putting things in perspective. The appeal of B.A.S.E. jumping is not obvious to everyone, but this jumper's intentions are clear.

chute doesn't open properly or immediately, must possess the skills necessary to open or redeploy the chute, or that jump could well be their last.

The fundamental equipment used in B.A.S.E. jumping is the same as that used in parachuting. However, because B.A.S.E. jumping requires a much faster deployment, some of the traditional equipment must be modified. An example is the pilot chute, which is used to deploy the main parachute. Pilot chutes are always deployed by hand in a B.A.S.E. jump. Depending on the distance of the freefall, the jumper may elect to hold the pilot chute in their hand or stow it in an easily accessible pocket on their pack. The

jumper may also elect to use a small or large pilot chute depending on how quickly the main chute must be deployed. Some freefalls can be as small as 250 feet (76m), with only a few seconds separating the jump and any potential impact. Jumpers tend to use the hand deployment technique in short freefalls to reduce the potential for a missed pilot chute deployment and the resultant impact. Freefalls of 3,000 feet (915m), such as Angel Falls in Venezuela, can generally be done with the pilot chute stowed for deployment.

No time to think

Different jumps require different types of main parachutes, otherwise referred to as the

"canopy." The selection of the correct canopy is critical to insuring a consistent and timely deployment. Most B.A.S.E. jumpers prefer wing-like "ram air" canopies. Ram air chutes deploy very rapidly and afford the jumper more control and steering precision than the traditional round canopies. Quick deployment and steerability are particularly important when jumping from objects like antennas, which are secured by high-tension wires, or cliffs, which may have sizeable outcroppings which must be avoided. Ram air canopies provide the jumper with a directional deployment, whereby the jumper can be sure of continuing their predeployed direction on deployment. Additionally useful is the ability to steer the canopy away from objects on the ground, such as a river...or waiting police. Therefore it is easy to understand how jumping off the Empire State Building can pose an entirely different set of challenges than jumping from a 1,000 foot (300m) waterfall.

Part of the ritual of B.A.S.E. jumping is the climb to the "exit point." The process of climbing to the exit point is as much a part of B.A.S.E. jumping as the jump itself. It is during the ascent to the exit point that the jumper must carefully consider all of the aspects of the jump they are about to make. Visualizing the jump before it takes place during the climb allows the jumper to establish a mental image of what they are about to do, step by step. This is especially important since there simply is not enough time to think about it on the way down.

Each B.A.S.E. jump is unique. The jumper must consider all aspects of the jump prior to making it, or risk discovering an overlooked item during freefall. Only by fully considering each fall can the jumper make the most critical decision in every B.A.S.E. jump— whether or not to jump. The ability to differentiate between a jump that can be made, and one that can but shouldn't, is probably the most important skill any B.A.S.E. jumper can possess. This is the ability to preserve one's existence based on a calculated judgment, not a simple roll of the dice, and this is what makes B.A.S.E. a sport.

Even though B.A.S.E. jumpers are extremely safety conscious, there is still a statistically high incidence of fatality. In the U.S. during the past two decades, over 20 people have died while B.A.S.E. jumping. These numbers only reflect those who have been killed, the number of those severely injured by non-deployment or partial deployment may be substantially higher. I once met a B.A.S.E. jumper named Rick Harrison while with Phil Smith. Rick jumped from a building, had a partial deployment, and crushed both legs on impact. He proudly showed off his scars, and still jumps today. Given the meteoric rise in the popularity of B.A.S.E. jumping, it is fair to assume that the numbers of fatalities and injuries will increase.

For those of you who feel that B.A.S.E. jumping may be for you, be sure to find an experienced B.A.S.E. jumper or organization in your area before attempting any jumping. It is not the opinion of the author that B.A.S.E. jumping is safe, and only those with the required experience, and who are exercising good and sober judgment, can decide if they should attempt B.A.S.E. jumping at all. For those that do, I wish you good luck.

(Left) B.A.S.E #1 Phil Smith does the unthinkable and leaps off a span (bridge) in pursuit of his #1 sport.

(Below) This antenna tower jump requires all the skills of the world's top B.A.S.E. jumpers.

Ballooning

Floating about the clouds without a care is a feeling that many would like to be able to enjoy. In fact, of all the extreme sports, this may be the one that has the most universal appeal, in its less extreme forms of course. By that I mean ballooning for relaxation, and not the limit-testing stuff like altitude record setting or distance record setting. Recreational Ballooning is an easy sport to try out, as most regions of the world have commercial operations of some sort.

WHAT HAS BEEN REFERRED to as "The Holy Grail" of ballooning is the around the world attempt. As yet never successfully accomplished, the logistics required are enough to end most attempts, if the weather doesn't. Only a brief weather window exists each year when a trans-global balloon trip is even remotely possible, between mid-November and mid-February. During this time, global jetstreams capable of driving a balloon fast enough to make an attempt feasible are typical, but

A propane burner keeps the balloon air warm and creates buoyancy as it is cooled by the surrounding air.

often erratic. As recently as late 1995 trans-global attempts have been readied, most notably by Richard Branson of the Virgin Group. His attempt in a massive 900,000 cu ft (2,743 cu m) balloon proved that no amount of money or preparation can make the weather co-operate. Of the two other attempts that year, only one got off the ground, and that only briefly. Trans-Atlantic and trans-Pacific flights are more likely to succeed, and have several times. The most difficult and lengthy is the trans-Pacific.

Not anyone can fly a balloon, it requires a license. However, the examination process is not nearly as difficult as what is required of an airplane pilot—generally ten hours of lessons and one hour of soloing. A written test is required in most countries, consisting of ballooning rules and meteorology knowledge.

Almost all modern recreational balloons use air heated by a propane burner shot into the bag (or envelope) to create buoyancy. The burner is used constantly to keep the air inside the envelope warm enough that it maintains or gains altitude, as it is constantly cooled by the surrounding air temperatures. To descend, the pilot allows the air within the envelope to cool enough that the balloon loses altitude. If a rapid descent is necessary, a vent on top of the envelope is opened.

A basket, or gondola, is attached to carry passengers. Balloons are not steerable, so the pilot is at the mercy of the wind. Therefore, each balloon flight requires a ground crew who can follow the craft and meet it on landing. Flights in wind speeds exceeding 10 mph (16kph) are not recommended, and altitudes of 2,000 feet (600m) are roughly all that is sought unless there are mountains to cross. Top pilots can steer the balloon if they are aware of the wind direction at each altitude level. Since the wind directions vary with altitude, a good pilot can raise and lower their balloon to get close to where they want to go.

Ballooning is one of the oldest extreme pursuits in recorded history. Flight using a

Relaxation, ballooning style, over the Tunisian desert.

balloon was first successfully accomplished in late August of 1783—a busy year—when the Charles Balloon was launched at Champ de Mars, France by Ann-Jean and MN Robert. One month later, Etienne Montgolfier successfully launched the first passenger-carrying balloon under a waterproof envelope made of linen. The "passengers" were a sheep, a rooster, and a duck. Only the sheep was at risk.

First air accident

Next, Montgolfier joined with army officer Pilâtre de Rozier to build the first manned hot air balloon. On October 15, de Rozier rode the balloon up to 84 feet (26m), and stayed there for approximately 25 minutes. He reported after landing that there was "nothing up there to worry about," however he was said to be quite pale when making the statement.

De Rozier soon made an appeal to King Louis XVI to sponsor a manned hot air balloon flight, "for the honor of France." Benjamin Franklin was in France during 1783 and reported the balloon's weight to be 1,578 lbs (716.4kg), with a lifting force of 578 lbs (262.4kg). So began the race to define the possible in ballooning. In December Jacques Alexander César Charles invented and launched the first hydrogen balloon—the first

to possess a valve designed to release gas for quick descents. He also used sandbags to provide discardable ballast, and a barometer to measure altitude.

Opera singer Madame Thible broke the gender barrier by becoming the first female aeronaut during a flight from Lyon in June, 1784. The first recorded flight across a body of water was made by America's first aeronaut, Dr John Jeffries, a Boston medical student. Jeffries, with Jean-Pierre Blanchard, crossed the English Channel in January, 1785. Another limit of manned flight tested and broken. A less happy event took place in the same year, when pioneer aeronaut de Rozier became the first victim of an air crash. His revolutionary combined hot air and hydrogen-filled balloon burst into flames, and he fell to his death.

Strategists quickly noted that using a balloon allowed for a complete view of the opponents' layout and fortifications. In April of 1794, the first military ballooning school was began in Meudon, France. Luckily, ballooning's strategic importance was short lived with the appearance of the airplane, and so balloonists were once again left to their own devices where they could dream of testing the limits of balloon flight.

18

A festival of balloons in Metz, France, the home of the Montgolfières.

Bungee Jumping

The moment of truth: when the excitement overrides any physical discomfort.

The idea of experiencing a free fall only to be snatched from the jaws of death by a cord attached to the ankles is not new. Modern bungee jumpers can trace the roots of their sport back to an ancient legend told by the native tribe of Pentecost Island in the South Pacific.

VARIOUS VERSIONS of the legend exist, but the basic plot surrounds a woman who was fleeing an abusive husband. The woman climbed a tall tree and tied a vine to her ankles. Her husband followed her up and when he lunged to grab her she jumped out of the tree. He fell after her, dropping to his death while his wife was saved by the vine. Depending on who tells the story, the men of the island started to repeat her stunt either because they were impressed by her show of courage, or just in case their wives tried the same trick. Needless to say, only men are permitted to participate in these ceremonies.

The practice soon evolved into a harvest ritual. Each year the natives build a jumping tower on the side of a hill, clear all the rocks and sticks away, and pulverize the dirt to soften the impact of landing. The ritual was first seen by western man when a couple of *National Geographic* writers visited the island in 1955 and reported on the practice of "land diving." It wasn't until 1970 that another *National Geographic* reporter named Kal Muller became "the first outsider known to attempt the heart-stopping plunge."

"With incredible precision (the cord) snapped taught," reported Muller. "My head barely touched dirt as I rebounded, finally coming to rest upside down...I felt oddly unshaken. The excitement had overridden any physical discomfort."

Muller's jump led to other stories about the ritual and in 1979 Oxford University's Dangerous Sportsman's Club got a hold of the

This jumper, in Queenstown, New Zealand, gets an instant cooldown from a dip into the water at the bottom of her jump.

idea and jumped from the 245-foot (75m) Clifton Suspension Bridge in Bristol, England. Then they brought the idea across the Atlantic, jumping from the Golden Gate Bridge in San Francisco and from a bridge spanning Colorado's Royal Gorge. With that the bungee movement in the U.S. was born.

The early U.S. bungee jumpers were based mainly in California and spent a lot of time jumping off bridges in the Sierras. In 1987 New Zealander AJ Hackett brought a lot of attention to the sport with a jump off of the Eiffel Tower. Also in 1987 the first commercial operations were started by Hackett in New Zealand and Peter and John Kockleman in the U.S.., each using very different systems.

Two systems

The New Zealand System uses a single, all-rubber cord that is shortened or lengthened depending on the weight of the jumper. A towel is wrapped around the ankles and the cord is attached with nylon mesh webbing. At Hackett's commercial operation, the jumper is also attached to a static safety line.

The U.S. system utilizes military-spec nylon-wrapped shock cord and the connection is made with rock climbing harnesses and locking carabiners. Instead of lengthening or shortening the cord to accommodate weight, U.S. jumpers add or subtract shock cords. The basic formula is one cord for each 50 lbs (23kg), and each cord has a static breaking strength of 1,500 lbs (680kg), making each cord the weakest link in the system. U.S. jumpers also use two harnesses (either waist and shoulder, or custom ankle) and two anchor points for added security.

Each system has its own feel. The U.S. system is more expensive and technical. Its 2:1 stretch ratio means more free fall and greater deceleration as the cord "catches" and begins to slow the fall. The New Zealand system has a 4:1 stretch ratio, which means that the cord is shorter and catches sooner, especially for heavier jumpers, an arrangement that is generally regarded as more comfortable.

In both systems, the energy from the jump is stored in the cords while they stretch until the fall is stopped. The stored energy then propels the jumper back upward for an additional sensation and a few subsequent free falls before the jumper comes to rest.

...to the bottom.

Bungee jumping is considered one of the most dangerous extreme sports. In fact, it may be the safest. Whatever your point of view, a bungee jump is pure adrenaline, from the top...

Bungee jumpers soon tired of simple jumps from structures and bridges and started jumping backward, by hanging from their hands or feet, or holding various positions. Others began adding novelty to bungee by jumping off in kayaks, garbage cans, riding unicycles, and other somewhat silly things.

Jumping together

Hardcore bungee jumpers soon began "sandbagging" to increase the intensity and height of rebound they received from the cords. Jumpers sandbag by holding onto added weight until they reach the bottommost point of the fall, where they release the weight. This method allows a 150 lb (68kg) jumper to be propelled upward with the stored energy of a 200 lb (91kg) jumper by releasing 50 lbs (23kg) at the bottom of the fall.

Springing back this way resulted in a whole new set of problems, since it was now possible to be propelled higher than the point from which the jumper sprang. Jumpers took care of this by using a pendulum approach that ensured they are propelled up and away from their point of take-off. With the pendulum system, the cords are secured on the opposite side of the bridge from the jumping side. This causes the jumper to arch down into the free fall and arch up and away from the bridge on the other side.

As if sandbagging wasn't dangerous enough, jumpers soon began sandbagging using other jumpers as weight. The result of "the human sandbag" was a rebound that could send the jumper well above the launch point. More than a couple jumpers have been killed or seriously injured when their partners let go too early (sometimes hundreds of feet from the ground) due to the severe forces from the initial deceleration. Others have been lucky enough to survive falls as high as 150 feet (45m).

Jumpers have plunged from balloons and helicopters, seeking to add to the distance of the free fall. A handful of bungee jumpers are said to have free-fallen in excess of 1,500 feet (457m).

In an effort to increase the level of skill required to bungee jump, new competitive approaches to bungee are being tested. Competitions that require accuracy by grasping specific targets on the ground or in the water have added a new and exciting dimension to the sport. Other more acrobatic requirements are also being integrated into bungee.

Bungee is very safe for beginners. Bungee is often considered one of the most dangerous extreme sports, when in fact it may be the safest. There have been reports of injuries to jumpers' limbs and eyes from the shock of the deceleration, however, such reports have been grossly exaggerated. In fact, statistically, it is far safer to bungee than to drive a car, and of those who have been killed or injured while bungee jumping, all events were the result of human error.

As long as the jumpers have a complete understanding of the stretch of the cords, the distance of the fall, and the weight of the jumper, the jump should be uneventful. The fact is that if all of the safety considerations are met, the cord will stop the fall just as well as brakes stop a car when traveling downhill at speed to a stop sign on a cliff.

The new extremes of bungee jumping include leaping from helicopters and balloons, in a quest to add to the distance of the free fall.

24

This jumper adds to the thrill by going backwards.

Hang gliding is unquestionably the closest a human being can get to flying like a bird. Hang gliding is the essence of non-motorized, unassisted flight many of us have all dreamed of from time to time.

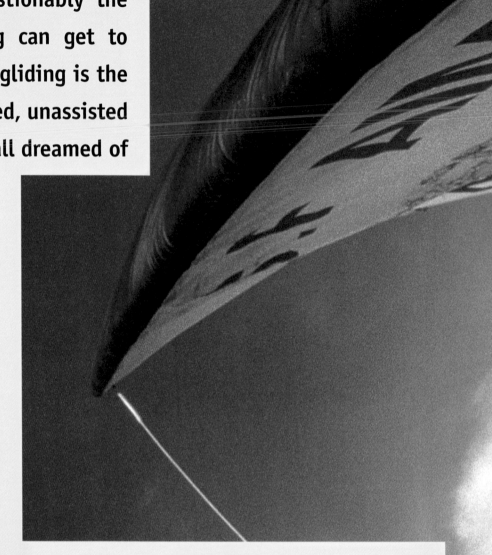

THE SPORT OF HANG GLIDING continues to progress today, as new technology allows the use of lighter and stronger materials. Extreme hang gliding is found only at the top expert level, where pilots can do virtually every trick imaginable, from full barrel rolls to inverted maneuvers. Stunt flying is a rapidly growing, and dangerous facet of hang gliding.

Records in hang gliding deal with extreme distance and altitude. Distances of more than 200 miles (320km) and altitudes above 10,000 feet (3,000m) are not uncommon. Larry Tudor currently holds the records for both distance and altitude. In 1985, Larry set the height record of 14,250.69 feet (4,343.61m) above Horseshoe Meadows, California. In 1990, Larry set the distance record of 303.35 miles (488.1km) in Hobbs, New Mexico, a longtime favorite spot for hang gliding.

Leonardo Da Vinci too dreamt of flight, and drew many flying machines during his life. A few are remarkably similar to today's hang gliders. The first manned hang glider flown was designed built and flown by German inventor Otto Lilienthal in 1893.

Hang Gliding

The closest a human being can get to flying like a bird.

The Wright brothers are said to owe much of their success at piloting their first motorized flight to their experience piloting hang gliders. However, with the emergence of power aircraft, hang gliding all but faded away into obscurity.

Looking for thermals

In the early 1960s, NASA began searching for a way to safely return the Gemini two-man orbital spacecraft to Earth. Scientists Francis and Gertrude Rogallo, in answer to NASA's request, invented a flexible wing that would allow the spacecraft to maneuver and land without the need for a parachute. This triangular wing design, known as the Rogallo Wing, is what lead to the design of the first sport hang gliders. The Rogallo design created a foil that was far easier to fly and control, and thereby opened the sport of hang gliding up to a whole new group of enthusiasts.

Pilots launch their hang gliders from hills or cliffs from a running start to generate the initial lift necessary for flight. Once airborne, the pilot must seek rising zones of warm air called "thermals." The pilot then circles within the thermal and they are lifted up as if they were in an elevator. Strong thermals can easily lift a hang glider 3,000 feet (915m). The pilot can then seek out additional thermals for added lift, or fly around until they require a further thermal to once again get to higher altitude.

Improvements to the design of hang gliders stemming from the Rogallo Wing and other technological advances, have spawned a tremendous rise in the popularity of hang gliding. Basically, these improvements have created hang gliders that are easier to fly, more comfortable, and much harder to crash.

Before some of the modern teaching techniques were developed, students had to struggle through a trial and error learning process and were forced to attempt new maneuvers cold. Flying a hang glider requires familiarizing oneself with the feel of each maneuver, which can often prove to be a long, difficult, and sometimes painful process. It is

Launch is from a running start, generating the initial lift needed for flight.

this factor that used to discourage many from pursuing the sport.

Learning to hang glide has become far easier with the introduction of tandem training techniques. Tandem training allows a qualified instructor to fly with their trainee and demonstrate new maneuvers in real-time, allowing students to get the "feel" of a move without having to master it first. It is estimated that this technique can shorten the learning curve for hang gliders by as much as 30 per cent. One of the principal reasons for the shortened curve is that tandem instruction allows beginners to experience and get the feel of even the most intricate maneuvers without the need to master hang gliding first.

Once a beginner has learned to hang glide solo, they start out flying beginner "ships" that are much less streamlined than performance versions. These beginner models are far more forgiving, allowing for some pilot error while skills are developed. Once they've learned the nuances of hang gliding flight, they are no longer considered to be a "wuffo," which in hang gliding circles means a bad pilot or someone who knows nothing about the sport.

28

Hang gliders are deceptively strong. They are built of aircraft quality aluminum and stainless steel with a sail (the wing) generally made of dacron. The structure is held together by a series of wires that create an amazingly stable geometry. A typical hang glider is capable of handling a load of over one ton without breaking. Today's hang glider technology allows them to be outfitted with full instrumentation, radios, and even rocket deployed emergency parachutes.

For those readers who wish to try their hand at hang gliding, look to your local organizations who can provide you with training manuals, videos, and where to get proper instruction. I have always dreamt of hang gliding, and hope to soon get out and do it.

Is it a bird, is it a human being?

Once airborne, the pilot looks to find 'thermals' - rising zones of warm air - on which to gain altitude.

High Wire

(This page and right) The amazing Jay Cochrane takes the high wire record for height and distance by crossing the Qutang Gorge in China. Millions of Chinese people watched his feat on TV. The 2,098 foot (640m) long wire was strung 1,350 feet (412m) over the distant Yangtze River.

For many centuries, tightrope walkers have captured the imagination of circus crowds. Often the daredevil performers would walk without the aid of a net to catch them should they misstep and fall. The famous Flying Walenda family of tightrope performers have achieved countless amazing high wire walks, including one which was captured live on television. Millions watched in shock as the senior Walenda fell to his death from a high wire walk between high-rise buildings, several floors above the ground.

31

THERE ARE VERY FEW high wire performers in the world. Of the few who practice high wire, Jay Cochrane, a 51-year-old Canadian, is the most extreme by far. Jay holds the Guinness certified world record for the longest and highest high wire walk. He also holds the world record for time spent balancing on a high wire—21 days and nights spent performing six shows a day to the crowds in San Juan, Puerto Rico.

He set the record for height and distance when he traveled to China and crossed the Qutang Gorge on a 11/8 in. (23mm) diameter zinc-coated steel wire. The wire was strung a distance of 2,098 feet (640m) across the gorge. The distance from the wire to the Yangtze River which formed the gorge, an incredible 1,350 feet (412m). The Chinese government estimated that 100,000 Chinese watched in person while hundreds of millions tuned in on state-run television to witness Cochrane's feat

Life and death

Jay performs all of his high wire stunts without the aid of a net. His only equipment is a 40 foot long (12m), 60 lb (27kg) titanium balancing pole, which he uses to stabilize himself as he walks.

It is unlikely that this extreme sport will gain an enormous following of aspiring high wire record setters, or high wire walkers for that matter. This is a sport which requires split-second reflexes, and a willingness to play a life and death game with each record attempt. For those, like Jay Cochrane, it is the ultimate test, for which they are willing to pay the ultimate price.

Ski Jumping & Ski Flying

Pointing your skis downhill as fast as you can is something that millions of us do every year when taking in any one of several ski resorts or cross country touring centers around the globe. Each skier has sought out a bump or jump from time to time, and all can appreciate the rush that even a small launch into the air can provide. That thrill has driven skiers to seek jumps for as long as there have been skis.

The "V" style, currently the state-of-the-art of ski jumping.

IN THE SMALL TOWN of Telemark, Norway, Sondre Norheim revolutionized skiing when he developed the loose heel binding system for nordic (cross country) skiers in 1861. The "telemark" turn and style of nordic skiing was born from the techniques Sondre developed, and soon accomplished nordic skiers began building small jumps to test their skills.

The first nordic skiing and jumping contests are believed to have been held in 1892.

The first dedicated jumping hill was built in Oslo in that same year. That location is still host to the annual Holmenkollen Ski Festival.

As Norwegians began emigrating to other countries, most notably the U.S. and Canada, they brought their nordic skills with them, and nordic skiing and jumping competitions gained a new base of enthusiasts. In 1924, Ski Jumping was included in the first Winter Olympics. The "Nordic Combined" Olympic medals are awarded to athletes competing for best in the world honors for combined cross country racing and ski jumping ability to this day.

As ski jumping matured, many techniques were created in an effort to travel the

At take off point the hill is not flat, but sloped downwards at 11 degrees.

maximum distance possible. A scoring system for jumps was created that considered not only distance but also style for each jumper. Over time, jumping styles included "windmilling" their arms while in flight, stretching their arms forward until landing, leaning over their skis in a jack-knife position, and finally the modern "V" style. Each style was considered state of the art for its time.

As ski jumping styles changed, so did the skis themselves, gradually becoming longer and wider. Modern jumping skis average 8ft 2in–8ft 10in (2.50-2.65m) in length and are roughly twice the width of traditional nordic skis. As the skis got longer and wider, they added lift to the skier, thus making for longer and longer jumps.

Finding the lift

Olympic Ski Jumping hills have traditionally measured 90 and 120 meters (300 and 395 feet). The rating is based on the distance from the jump to the "K-Point" on the hill. The K-Point is the point at which the hill begins its transition to a flat surface. To illustrate this measurement, a 90-meter jump has a K-Point that is 90 meters from the jump, a 120-meter jump has a K-Point that is 120 meters... and so on. As ski jumping equipment enabled jumpers to clear the K-Point by greater and greater distances, a new K-Point was needed.

The new K-Point was established at 140 meters (460 feet), and the sport of ski jumping became the sport of ski flying. The basic techniques are the same for ski flying as ski jumping. Today, the most frequently used technique is the "V" style in which the skier points their skis so that the tails are nearly touching, and the tips are wide apart, creating a V shape. With the "V" style, skiers are able to use the additional lift the position offers, and fly a trajectory that keeps them only 10 feet (3m) above the slope below them, versus older techniques that could have the skier hovering 20 or more feet above the slope.

Flying the jump

To jump, the skier starts down the hill to the jump site from a seated position high above the take off point. Skiers crouch down to optimize their aerodynamic form and minimize wind resistance. In this position, they accelerate to speeds exceeding 60 mph (96kph) before reaching their take off point. At the take-off point, the skiers lunge

Such a spectacular view is the province of only the top class ski jumpers in the world.

34

forward toward the tips of their skis, adding the final lift-generating form, their body. The take off point is not flat, but sloped downward at 11 degrees.

On landing, the skier uses a traditional telemark-style position, with one foot in front of the other. In that position, the front foot is flat with the knee bent, and the back heel is slightly elevated with the knee low and bent. This is the correct landing position for both ski jumping and ski flying.

Each jump is scored based on the style of the jump from take-off to the landing, and the distance traveled relative to the K-Point. Style points are awarded by a panel of five judges. Each can award up to 20 points for style. The highest and lowest scores are discarded, and the sum of the remaining scores is the skier's style total. Therefore, the maximum style points available to a jumper is 60.

Distance points based on the K-Point are added or subtracted based on a predetermined scale and are given in meter and half-meter increments. Skiers reaching the K-Point are automatically awarded 60 points. Distances beyond or short of the K-Point add or subtract from the overall distance score. Distance points are added to style points, and a winner is chosen. The current distance world record is held by Norwegian Espen Bredsen, who flew 209 meters (686ft).

The thrill of off-piste ski jumping has inspired the sports of Ski Jumping and Ski Flying.

Galondee Jumping

One of the less structured extreme ski jumping styles is referred to as galondee. In galondee jumping, skiers jump for distance using traditional alpine skiing equipment. Alpine skis use a fixed heel and toe binding system with rigid boots. Alpine skiing is the style generally practiced at ski resorts using lift-served terrain.

Galondee jumps are not nearly as long distance as ski jumping or flying using nordic equipment, since the fixed heel limits the skier's ability to generate lift. While galondee jumping can be done on ski jumping hills, it is often done in natural settings using steep hills with bumps and drop offs that are available. Galondee jumping competitions do exist, however, the spirit of most events is less structured than galondee jumping's Olympic counterparts.

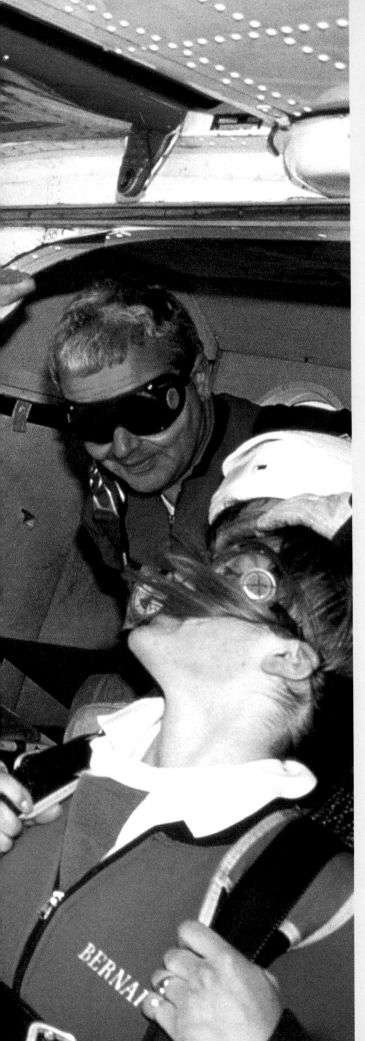

Sky Diving

Free-falling from an aircraft is one of the extreme sports that millions around the world take part in every year. The excitement of plummeting to earth with the time to think and enjoy the view is what attracts so many to jump from what most would consider a perfectly good airplane. Over the years, sky diving has evolved from what was once a necessary skill of self preservation to the source of inspiration for other sports like sky surfing and B.A.S.E. jumping.

Stacked canopy formation sky diving is a popular aspect of the sport today.

Having progressed through the learning stages (generally 15-plus jumps), new sky divers are ready to try more difficult maneuvers and tests of skill. With practice, they can soon participate in the sport of sky diving, including events like accuracy contests, formation free fall, canopy stacking, canopy relative work, freestyle, and perhaps even sky surfing and

38

OVER THE YEARS, the high standards developed for both jump schools and jumping operations have made sky diving a relatively safe sport. According to the United States Parachuting Association, during the last five years, only one jump in 80,000 has resulted in death, suggesting that sky diving may well be safer than driving a car in many places.

Traditionally, sky diving students have been taught by the "static line" method which automatically deploys the jumper's chute once clear of the aircraft. This method allows for no free fall time, so most schools are moving to the tandem and Accelerated Free Fall methods of instruction. In a tandem jump, the student can experience the thrill of free fall while safely connected to a certified instructor. The AFF method then allows the student to jump solo and free fall in the company of instructors, who free fall with the student until they successfully deploy their chute.

Another benefit of the evolution of sky diving is the development of the square "Ram Air"-style parachute which allows jumpers to steer their chutes and provides additional lift compared to the older round chutes. The additional lift makes for a softer landing, too.

B.A.S.E. jumping if they're so inclined.

Shortly before WWI, the idea of parachuting for sport was born when bi-plane tours became a popular attraction at fairs. In 1930, the first known parachuting contest was held in Russia. Contestants were scored on their ability to hit a ground target. Target accuracy is an aspect of parachuting competition that is still practiced today. Present day targets are merely 20 inches (0.5m) in diameter. The current record for accuracy is held by Russian sky diver Linger Abdurakhmanov, who landed on the target disk an incredible 50 consecutive times.

Formation free fall events take place when several sky divers free fall together, then move into positions enabling them to hold on to one and other in formation. The danger of formation free fall stems from the possibility of a high-speed collision mid-air, causing one or more jumpers to lose consciousness. The use of an Automatic Deployment Device (ADD) is one way to ensure that unconsciousness does not lead to a non-deployment. The current World Record for Free

Canopy Relative Work events consist of 2 or more people making geometric shapes in their jumps, here 80 women try for the world record in France, 1990.

"Ram-Air" parachutes allow sky divers additional lift and flexibility in their descent.

AFF jumping allows students and instructors to dive together.

Fall Formation is held by 200 sky divers who managed to link up over Myrtle Beach, South Carolina in 1992.

Another style of formation jumping occurs after deployment. In stacked canopy formation sky diving, the jumpers deploy their chutes and then physically hook their legs into the lines of the open canopy of a jumper below. Another series of jumpers then stack themselves on the canopies of the linked jumpers, until the final formation is completed.

The biggest risk in this form of formation sky diving is that the jumpers can get entangled in the canopies of other jumpers with deadly results. Jumpers all carry secondary canopies in case they must cut themselves free of entanglement. The current World Record was set in 1994 when 46

The organization required for CPW events is only possible because there are dive centers located in every major region in the world.

jumpers fell into a stacked canopy formation over Davis, California. The canopy relative work (CPW) event consists of two or more sky divers working together to form geometric formations. Geometric forms are created through aerial maneuvers that are judged.

Dancing in the sky

Freestyle sky diving is an aerial ballet that is captured on camera for judging. The freestyle sky diver performs an assortment of airborne gymnastic maneuvers prior to deploying their chute, and is judged on the style and artistic elements of the jump.

The sport of sky diving has an interesting history. There are reports of parachute-like devices being used in 12th century China as well as 16th century Venice. The first documented use of a parachute was in 1783, the same year balloons were first being experimented with. A large audience in Paris watched as stunt performer Andre Germain jumped with a parachute in 1797. In 1808, Jodaki Kuparento bailed out of a burning balloon several thousand feet above Warsaw in the first documented emergency use of a parachute. He survived.

Of course, most of the styles of sky diving would not be possible had Frenchman Leo Valentin not developed a technique for stabilized free fall in 1948. The fact that sky divers could free fall for prolonged periods under control is what led to the establishment of much of the modern sky diving elements. The first Parachuting World Championships were held shortly thereafter in 1951 in the former Yugoslavia.

The sport of sky diving is one of the easiest of the extreme sports to learn, and dive centers are located in every major region of the world. Anyone considering learning should seek out a center with new equipment and a history of quality instruction.

Sky surfer and camera-flyer - travelling at speeds of up to 120 mph (197kph) - are involved in a high-speed synchronized free fall ballet.

Sky Surfing

Parachutists have long experimented with different ways of using their bodies to steer them through the air during free fall. By stretching out in a horizontal fashion, sky divers found they could zoom about in different directions at remarkable speeds with quite a bit of directional control. It was, of course, simply a matter of time until someone tried free falling using a flat surface that could add to their speed, control, and push the limits of what had been done.

FIRST, AS EARLY AS 1980, a few skydivers in California started testing free fall while lying on top of boogie boards. These pioneers found that the boards added some speed and directional control but, most importantly, proved that jumping with boards could be done.

Next, Frenchman Joel Cruciani jumped while standing on a small surfboard which had been modified by mounting snowboard bindings to it. Joel strapped in and became the first skysurfer, a stunt that was featured in the film *Hibernator*. This board was reportedly unstable and difficult to surf on due to the size of the surface he needed to control in flight.

In 1988, another French sky diver, by the name of Laurent Bouquet, began experimenting with boards for free fall. His design used a skateboard-sized board that strapped to his feet. It was obviously much smaller than Cruciani's, and very easily controlled.

In 1989, yet another Frenchman, expert B.A.S.E. jumper and extreme parachutist Patrick de Gayardon, designed and perfected a binding cut-away system that allowed a sky surfer to release the board should he lose control in free fall. The addition of this binding system provided the opportunity for sky surfers to experiment with a number of shapes and sizes, evolving to the snowboard shape that is the favorite of most sky surfers. Later that year, de Gayardon portrayed the "Silver Surfer" for film-maker Thierry Donard's *Pushing the Limits 2*.

By 1990, the Silver Surfer inspired other European jumpers to try sky surfing. Soon news spread throughout the sky diving world of this new and exciting sport, and the stage was set for its exponential growth over the next six years. Many new tricks evolved as the sky surfers pushed the limits of their sport.

The flying eye

In the fall of 1990. the World Freestyle Federation (WFF) staged the first World Freestyle Championships in Texas, and introduced sky surfing as a featured demonstration. The 1990 World Freestyle Championships marked the first time that the "team video concept" was used. WFF founder Pete Mckeeman was the first to envision using a "camera-flyer" to capture a sky surfer's performance for judging purposes. Sky surfing instantly became a made-for-TV sport, accelerating the already rapid growth.

The introduction of a free-falling, cameraman partner into sky surfing created an entirely new series of complications. The highly maneuverable sky surfer is capable of traveling at speeds that can exceed 120 mph (193kph) in many directions during free fall. The cameraman also travels downward at similar speeds. Should the two collide the result can be unconsciousness or worse. Therefore, sky surfers and their cameraman partners use an AAD, or Auto Activation Device. The auto-deployment takes place at a predetermined altitude or time to prevent non-deployment in the case of injury or loss of consciousness. Sky surfers also run the risk of spinning out of control, in which case the AAD also proves invaluable.

In competition, a sky surfer and cameramen are scored as a team. With team video scoring it is the overall presentation that is judged. How the camera-flyer positions himself during free fall, how he frames his shots, and how in-synch he can stay with the sky surfer all factor into the score.

The resulting footage and the sport itself have evolved into a highly synchronized free fall ballet—with the sky surfer and camera-flyer executing simultaneous rolls, flips, and spins while hurtling toward the ground at around 120 mph. Winning teams display a coherence and consistency of movement between the sky surfer and the cameraman that is uncanny. At larger competitions, a direct feed from the camera-flyer's camera to a "jumbotron" monitor on the ground allows spectators to see the performance in real-time.

Sky surfing is very exciting to watch. For those wishing to try their hand at it, this is a sport to be left to only the very best and most experienced sky divers. For example, two time Sky Surfing World Champion Joe Jennings was killed in 1996 while sky surfing for a commercial in California, reportedly victim to a partial deployment.

43

Soaring

Soaring is a rush that can be realized by just about anyone. If the thought of quietly flying through the clouds with the agility of a bird is appealing, it can be done easily and inexpensively. There is no need to bruise yourself learning, for it's as easy as finding a soaring center where you can rent a ride.

BY DEFINITION, soaring and gliding are different, although they are commonly used terms to describe the sport of soaring. Soaring is defined as flying without engine power and without loss of altitude. Gliding on the other hand, is defined as flying without engine power, and a glider is a aircraft without a power source.

Gliders are towed from airfields by towplanes using tow ropes of between 150–200 feet (45–60m) in length. The tow ropes are light, stretchy, abrasion-resistant lines with high strength-to-weight ratios. Tow ropes are designed to be dropped by the glider once the desired altitude has been achieved. The glider is then left to the task of finding ways in which to increase its altitude without assistance.

Gliders all have a "Glide Ratio" which refers to how many feet the craft can glide compared to the altitude that it loses in flight. So, a glide ratio of 22:1 would signify that the glider is capable of traveling 22 feet for every 1 foot it loses in altitude.

A glide ratio of 22:1 is normal for many of today's gliders, such as the Schweizer 2-33, one of the most popular training gliders in the world. Gliders like the Schweizer have maximum speeds of around 100mph (160kph). There are many high performance gliders with ratios in excess of 50:1 that are capable of speeds exceeding 110 mph (176kph).

Of course once you have defined the glide ratio, you know how far your glider can fly before it reaches the ground. The object of soaring is to use rising warm air currents, or "thermals", to lift the glider at rates equal to or in excess of their glide ratio. Each time the pilot catches a thermal and rides it upward, they extend both the distance they can travel and the duration of their flight.

Understanding and being able to read the air currents in a search for thermals is where the art of soaring begins. It is also where the sport of soaring is derived. Much of soaring hinges on the pilot's ability to travel specific

With the tow rope dropped, the glider and its pilot are left alone and in silence to face the challenge of staying aloft using only the natural forces of the wind and sun.

distances, reach predetermined locations, or pass through specific zones, maximize or minimize total time spent aloft, and a mixture of these tasks. The trick to winning is utilizing the thermals to reach your performance goals.

Reading thermals is no easy task. They are invisible, yet they can be found by reading the horizon and cloud patterns for clues to their existence. Top pilots are also sound meteorologists, who understand the meaning of cloud formations and the effects of solar radiant heating as the day progresses.

In 1964, Al Parker became the first glider pilot to fly 1,000 kilometers (621 miles) non-stop. In 1977, Karl Striedieck completed the first 1,000-mile (1,600-kilometer) non-stop glider flight. Today, pilots continue to push the performance envelopes of their gliders. What seems to be the only barrier to the next record is technological advances in materials that can make the gliders lighter and faster with increased glide ratios.

Reaching for the sky

If you're wondering who started it all, you can thank Sir George Cayley, who flew the first manned glider in 1853. Since that day, soaring and glider technology have come a long way. Eventually the gliders were modified to be airplanes, which were modified to be towplanes, which gliders still use today to take off and gain their initial altitude.

After WWI, the first modern soaring competition was held in Wasserkuppe, Germany in 1920. In 1921, the first soaring flight using thermals to ascend was made by Wolfgang Klemperer. The Germans went on to perfect virtually all of the important soaring equipment and techniques used today.

Soaring is certainly an exciting and challenging sport that can be enjoyed by virtually anyone seeking the thrill of powerless flight and the challenge of staying aloft using the natural forces of the wind and sun.

Land
Sports

There are many natural elements we refer to as land that can be extreme and particularly challenging for survival, nevermind the pursuit of sport.

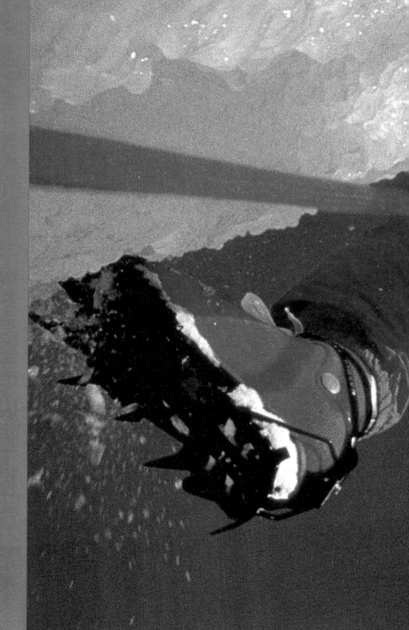

BIBLIOGRAPHY

● *Land Sailing*, Scott Robert Hays, Capstone Press, Mankato, Minnesota, 1992
● *Olympic Nordic Skiing*, By the Staff of the Ice Skating Institute of America in cooperation with the U.S. Olympic Committee, Children's Press, Chicago, Illinois, 1979
● *The Triathlon Training and Racing Book*, Sally Edwards, Contemporary Books, Inc., Chicago, Illinois, 1985
● *Rock & Mountain Climbing*, Ruth and John Mendenhall, Stackpole Books, Harrisburg, PA, 1983
● *Mock Rock The Guide To Indoor Climbing*, Sharon Colette Urquhart, Paper Chase Press, New Orleans, Louisiana, 1995
● *The Handbook of Motocross*, Jerry Murray, G. P. Putnam's Sons, New York, 1978

ASSOCIATIONS & CLUBS

AGGRESSIVE INLINE SKATING
■ Aggressive Skaters Association
171 Pier Avenue, Suite 247
Santa Monica, CA 90405
■ International Inline Skating Association
PO Box 15482
Atlanta, GA 30333
Tel: (001) 404-634-9032
■ US Amateur Confederation of
Roller Skates (inline)
4730 South St.
PO Box 6579 Lincoln, NE 68506
Tel: (001) 402-483-7551

BMX
■ American Bicycle Association
9831 S. 51st St., Suite D135
Phoenix, AZ 85044, also
PO Box 718
Chandler, AZ 85244
Tel: (001) 602 961 1903
Fax: (001) 602 961 1842
■ International Amateur Cycling Federation
Via Cassia 490I-00189, Rome, Italy
Tel: (0039) 6 331 2419
Fax: (0039) 6 331 0079

CAVING
■ International Subterranean
http://www.microsearch.be/isha/start.html
secretariat de j'AIPS, 94 Rue de la Culée
B-6927 Resteigne, Belgium
Tel: (32) 84 38 82 26
Fax: (32) 84 38 82 32
isha@microresearch.be
■ Caving WWWSites
http://cschp2.anu.edu:8080/cave/cave
link.html
■ National Caving Association (UK)
Monomark House, 27 Old Gloucester St.,
London WC1N 3XX, UK
■ National Speleological Society (U.S.)
2813 Cave Ave
Huntsville, Alabama 35810-4413
email: joshua@caves.org

CLIMBING (INDOOR)
■ Australian Indoor Climbing Index
http://www.ozemail.com.au/
~jayhawk/acga.html
■ Dutch Climbing Home Page
http://viper.es.ele.tue.tue.nl/esac/
dutch_climbing/
■ U.S. Climbing Gym List
http://www.dtek.chalmer.se/climbing/
commercial/gymsus.html

CLIMBING (OUTDOOR)
■ American Alpine Club
710 10th Street, Suite 100
Golden, CO 80401
Tel: (001) 303-384-0110
Fax: (001)303-384-0111
■ American Sport Climbers Federation
125 W. 96th St., #1D
New York, New York 10025
Tel: (001) 212-865-4383
Fax: (001) 212-865-4383
■ *Climbing* (magazine)
1101 Village Rd, Suite LL-1-B
Carbondak, CO 81623
Tel: (001) 970-963-9449
■ *Rock and Ice* (magazine)
http://www.rscomm.com/actsports/
rock/ind.ex.html

CONSIDER THE DESERTS, mountains, and glaciers that cover much of our planet. These landscapes have secured borders and civilizations over the centuries. A would-be conqueror whose forces lacked desert survival or mountaineering skills would be ill advised to try to beat the elements and his enemy at the same time. Recent history in Afghanistan shows that an understanding of survival skills and terrain can resist even a high-tech invader.

We are fortunate that extreme sports are not about conquering others, only the limitations of the athlete's mind, body, and equipment. Most land-based extreme sports take place in areas that would have hardly been considered hospitable a century ago. Thanks to technology, we can now travel to, and play in, these places in relative comfort. However, technology has not changed the landscape of the harshest elements, or the skill sets necessary to survive in them.

Technology and change have created some new landscapes. The urban elements are the endless miles of pavement, the stairs made from cement and stone and the railings affixed to them. As with the natural elements, the urban elements bring with them a new set of challenges and opportunities for sport. The urbanscape is also more accessible than natural elements. As a result, urban extreme sports are the ones most likely to satisfy athletes who can't play in the natural elements due to either time or money.

PUSHING THE LIMITS

It was the existence of each of these elements that spawned each extreme sport, not the harshness of the landscapes or the number of

man-made obstacles that have been created. It was, to paraphrase legendary explorer and mountaineer Sir Edmund Hillary, "because they were there." This was more than just a witty statement. In this phrase is the soul and the spirit of extreme pursuit. Hillary did not ascend Mount Everest because he needed to for survival. He did so to push his limits physically and mentally.

Extreme athletes look at the landscape differently than "normal" people. Climbers traveling through mountainous regions look at the series of potential routes on each face as they pass by. "Normal" folk simply see nice mountains. Skateboarders and inline skaters walk through a city park and see the flora and fauna, but tend to focus on the curbs, stairs, and railings as personal challenges to their technical abilities. "Normal" folks walk through parks and see only the birds and squirrels.

Land-based extreme sports have the greatest diversity of terrain. Each sport requires the athlete be able to ascend, descend, jump, and coast through any number of circumstances and unexpected obstacles. Quick reflexes and absolute focus quickly separate the best from the simply good.

TESTING OURSELVES

It is difficult to envision what the next extreme sport to be born will be as we redraw our urban landscapes and develop new materials that will allow us to redefine performance and perhaps better survive the harsher elements. As man and technology change and improve, our ability to test ourselves within our natural and urban environments will change. Extreme athletes seeking to push their limits will adapt new technology and thinking, creating new opportunities for future extreme athletes to redefine how to have fun on the planet.

49

ACW Climbing

A new sport that has emerged from the creation of indoor climbing facilities is that of climbing an Artificial Climbing Wall. ACWs were first constructed as a method of training and teaching without the concern of falling rocks and other natural hazards, weather, or long hikes to good routes. Because of their easy access in urban areas, ACWs have become a major draw at gyms.

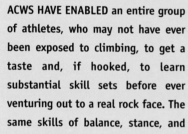

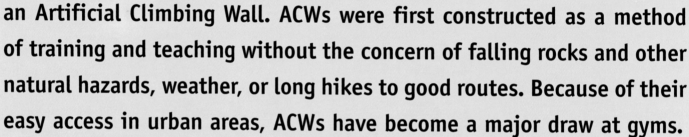

ACWS HAVE ENABLED an entire group of athletes, who may not have ever been exposed to climbing, to get a taste and, if hooked, to learn substantial skill sets before ever venturing out to a real rock face. The same skills of balance, stance, and movement needed on rock and ice (crampon and ice axe use excluded) are required to climb walls, and with the many new materials and modular construction techniques, ACWs can recreate any level of climb desired, except for constraints on the height of the climb that natural settings don't have. ACWs aid both experienced climbers and those new to the sport to achieve the flexibility, finesse, and strength required as well as allowing them to maintain the commitment to the sport that top climbers must have to be successful.

Climbing competitions are judged on the basis of a climber's ability to get through difficult routes without falling, and the speed at which the climber is able to ascend the wall. There are categories for both speed and difficulty in most competitions. International climbing competitions on ACWs have been organized since 1987 when the former Soviet Union began holding speed climbing events. The first World Championships were held in 1991 in Frankfurt, Germany, allowing the International Olympic Committee to offer the sport Olympic status that same year.

The difficulty of competitions is judged by determining the highest point on the route each competitor reaches within a set period of time. Each climber must climb the route "on-sight," without seeing the route before their climb, and without witnessing others attempting it.

Speed events are held on easier routes and are normally held in a double-elimination-style format, with two climbers racing simultaneously. The first to complete the route wins that heat. Losing two heats eliminates a climber from the event.

The wall at the World Speed Climbing Championships in Birmingham, England.

Substantial climbing skills can be learned on ACWs - balance, stance and movement on both rock and ice - the same skills required in the real world outside.

Karen Smyers of the U.S.A. in winning action in the Ironman, Kona, Hawaii, 1995.

Adventure Racing

Mark Allen, looks cool during the Ironman marathon, 1995.

Teamwork is essential for success in the Raid Gauloises, Argentina 1995.

I doubt many people would argue that triathlons are not grueling tests of an athlete's physical conditioning and mental toughness. For the unfamiliar, triathlons are events where competitors face off in a combination of swimming, biking, and a running race. Triathlons vary considerably from venue to venue. The original triathlon and the triathlon most deserving of the word extreme is the Ironman, an event that draws the world's top triathletes from 75 countries to Hawaii each year in October.

Whitewater action, Raid Gauloises, Borneo, 1994

WHAT MAKES THE IRONMAN the most extreme triathlon is not its distance—many world class triathlons have similar distances—it is the weather. Temperatures, with highs averaging 88°F (31°C) and humidity levels between 40–85 per cent, are sometimes accompanied by 60 mph (97 kph) winds. Athletes can expect to endure conditions that make this one event more torturous than most.

The Ironman got its start in 1978, when Navy Commander John Collins created a race based on three existing races: The Waikiki Rough Water Swim of 2.4 miles (3.9km), the Around Oahu Bike Race of 112 miles (180 km), and the Honolulu Marathon of 26.2 miles (42.2km). The first Ironman took place on Kialua, but was moved after three years to Kona to avoid the traffic around Honolulu.

At the back of beyond

Another race that can hardly be deemed anything less than extreme is the Raid Gauloises, an event that got its start as a ten-day, 400-mile (644 km) stage race conceived

The unexpected is always expected in the Raid, Borneo 1994.

by French journalist Gérard Fusil. The race takes place in a different area of extreme outback each year, such as Madagascar, Borneo, and Patagonia.

The Raid Gauloises participants are five-person teams from various countries sponsored by a variety of corporations. The teams race up and down 14,000-foot (4,267m) mountains, through swamps and down rivers, taking a massive toll on the team members, both physically and mentally. Each team member must complete the race for their team to be scored as finished. The Raid is a survivalist's dream race, arguably calling on more mental toughness than any other race in the world. This is clearly not a weekend warriors endeavor.

To find a new threat

The Raid Gauloises has given birth to a new adventure racing trend, with several aspiring adventure races establishing themselves, including the Eco-Challenge Series promoted by Englishman Mark Burnett, a former Raid participant. The Eco-Challenge has met several obstacles along the way to establishing itself, not the least of which are charges of onsite

and financial mismanagement. The basic theme of the race, however, will surely live on even if the organizing body itself changes.

Adventure racing in many ways appears to be a response to life in a world largely protected from threats to survival and the necessity of pioneering new frontiers. It is

The physical and mental toll on team members in the Raid separates the winners from the losers, Borneo 1994.

easy to draw parallels between what these teams are doing for sport and what mankind has done for centuries as we have redefined our borders. The major difference today is that should we run into a life-threatening problem during one of these events, a heli-lift to safety is not far off.

Best all-arounder

In fact, most adventure races now employ the use of hand-held GPS (Global Positioning Satellite) systems that not only enable the competitors to establish where they are within a few meters, but also enable rescuers to find them quickly if need be. There are devices called sextants, once used to navigate the seas and land by reading the stars, but they can be rendered useless by clouds, and can only be read by those holding them, and not those seeking to offer rescue.

Adventure racing draws from many different extreme sports: climbing, whitewater, and mountain biking for example. Surely event organizers and creators will find ways of including more and more extreme sports in their events until a decathlon style event is created which will act to find the best all-around extreme sports athlete in the world.

55

Aggressive Inline Skating

The ground broken by skateboarders over the past three decades has been invaded by a new group of urban athletes. Aggressive inline skaters have co-opted much of the style and culture of skateboarding into their sport. Aggressive skaters have taken what were initially just fitness and training devices and transformed them into urban assault vehicles that have been embraced by pop culture.

INLINE SKATES CAN TRACE their roots back to the Chicago Skate Company, and perhaps further, as evidence of wheeled boots dates back to the early days of bicycling. But it wasn't until brothers Scott and Brennan Olsen created the first Rollerblades in their Minneapolis basement in 1979, that the sport took off. The brothers stumbled on a pair of Chicago Skate Company's inline skates in the bargain bin of a used equipment store while looking for a way to train for hockey in the off season. The skates offered minimal support and awful wheels. The Olsens added greater support and urethane wheels, and the rest is history.

Scott Olsen bought the patent for inline skates from the Chicago Skate Company and began the Rollerblade Company. The first Rollerblades were nothing more than hockey boots with an inline chassis. By 1983, Scott Olsen sold Rollerblade to local businessman Robert Nagle, Jr. With new capital resources, new and improved Rollerblades were developed, and the beginning of a growth curve unparalleled in the sporting goods industry had begun.

At first, the Rollerblade inline skates were designed to provide cross-training for hockey skaters. Then skiers discovered that Rollerblades offered the ability to get a

The tools of the trade. Over 10 million pairs of inline skates are sold annually in the U.S. alone.

Inline skates are often used by sportsmen and women for cross-training when conditions are not right for their chosen sport.

carved-turn sensation on pavement, and became the second major group to used inline skates for cross-training. Inline skates soon became a heavily promoted and endorsed method for training in the off season within the ski industry.

The third and largest group to embrace the Rollerblade phenomenon was the Eighties' aerobic and fitness crowd. Fitness fanatics quickly recognized that skating was a great way to tone the legs and buttocks while increasing aerobic capacity with far lower impact than running. By 1989, over three million inline skates were being sold each year. By 1994, the U.S. National Sporting Goods Association estimated there were over twelve million inline skaters in the U.S. alone.

Prepared for anything

Soon the boom in inline skating reciprocated in reported injuries from falls. Most common were broken wrists, arms, and head injuries. This prompted an aggressive effort to teach skaters to protect themselves properly by wearing wrist, elbow, knee, and head protection when skating. Use of these items has greatly reduced the risks of injury in a fall. Smart skaters, whether skating for fitness or trick skating, have all found these items work well when needed.

Naturally, it was only a matter of time before the top inline skaters would seek to redefine their sport. No longer content to skate about town in a "civilized" manner, top skaters began to search for a new, less aerobic and fitness oriented identity. The new breed of aggressive skaters turned to the skateboard world for guidance, not only for cultural grounding but for a direction to push their sport forward. In turn, this gave way to "street style" and "vert" inline skating.

Street surfing

Like skateboarding, "street" inline skaters seek to jump over and grind across just about any obstacle imaginable. To do so requires special grind plates attached to the chassis of the skates, so that the wheels don't grab at inappropriate times, and the skate's chassis aren't destroyed by the moves. These needs wound up giving birth to

Inline vert skating borrows a number of its terms from skateboarding, as well as sharing many of its skate parks.

Like skateboarding, street inline skaters seek to jump and grind over anything they can find, however inappropriate it may look to other people.

an entire sub-industry created to serve the needs of aggressive skaters that the corporate manufactures are only now recognizing represent the future of inline skating. Open an aggressive inline magazine like *Box* or *Daily Bread* and you'll find everything from over-sized pads to T-shirts to Titanium skate chassis. Grind plates, custom chassis, and specialized wheels and many of the items that aggressive skaters used to fashion for themselves are now available via mail order.

Vert skating began when inliners first invaded the sacred territory of skateboarders, the half-pipe. At first, this invasion created tension at the skate parks, which in most places has died down as inliners have gotten better and now demand some respect for their abilities. Inline vert skating does differ in some ways from skateboarding vert, since the skater's feet are free to move independently. The skater who has had the most impact on technical independent foot moves presently is Australia's Tom Fry. His abilities are redefining vert skating, creating maneuvers that are truly the property of the aggressive inline movement.

Special terms

Aggressive inline skaters have created a number of terms to define the moves they make, both on the street and when skating vert. Many of the terms used come from the skateboarding industry, as well as many of

Aggressive inline is getting more popular these days. The increased media attention is not always to the liking of the skaters, but at least the sport is getting the recognition it deserves.

the maneuvers. The terms described in the skateboarding section of this book should provide the reader with a good start to understanding the language of inline skating, with the obvious difference that front and backhand placements to front and back feet are what determine which term is appropriate for which maneuver.

You should, however, bear in mind few terms which are unique to inline skating, and which refer mostly to the equipment that is also unique. ABEC is an acronym for Annular Bearing Engineering Council. ABEC ratings correspond to the speed and efficiency of the bearing sets which can be replaced, removed, cleaned, and reinserted into the wheel sets. The higher the rating (between 1–5) the faster the bearing will roll.

The durometer figure is how wheels are gauged for hardness. The higher the durometer number, the harder the wheel.

Rockering is the process of lowering or raising the middle two wheels or outside two wheels to create either a flat or curved skate contact with the surface being ridden. A curved rocker allows for quicker turning while a flatter rocker allows for greater stability, especially at speed.

Spacers are small round tubes that are used to separate the bearings in each wheel and create a protective barrier between the bearing and the axle. Chassis refers to the plastic, metal, or composite frame that is secured to the bottom of each boot and which holds the wheel sets. Designs can vary greatly. If you wear the best gear to look the part but can't skate to save your life, you'll be referred to as a "poser."

Cheese Grater Asphalt is poor or rough road conditions or surfaces. Bail-To Fall is an intentional fall to avoid a nastier wipe out, and Slam Tan refers to tan lines caused by wearing the protective elbow, wrist, and knee protection.

However, there will always be those who don't want to be organized, and just want to hang out and do stuff.

61

BMX

Just about every kid has attempted to jump their bike off something when they were growing up. Those that didn't certainly never became extreme sport athletes. The small and cruiser-style bikes of the Sixties and Seventies began a shift in how people viewed bicycle riding. Kids found that they were quite maneuverable, and the smaller wheels and fatter rubber tires made them more capable of enduring the thrashing a hard-riding kid could deliver. These new bikes redefined what could be done, and soon kids jumping things found they could jump bigger things, and could ride on softer surfaces, and the idea of dirt racing and jumping just kind of evolved naturally.

BICYCLE MOTOCROSS was born in Southern California in the Seventies, when organizers first began setting up weekend races on special dirt tracks resembling miniature motocross circuits. BMX dirt racing quickly grew into a national, and then international phenomenon. BMX racing went through a period when it was overlooked as the mountain bike craze hit, but it is now resurging, and many of today's mountain biking and motoX stars are former and current BMX racers.

BMX racing is organized to create ways for kids to compete safely and consistently. BMX now has local racing organizations in virtually every corner of the civilized world, and the impact on kids seeking a constructive outlet for their energy has been tremendous. Kids as young as five years old

In the Eighties vert riding in a half-pipe became the cutting edge of BMX. Today's top riders, like Matt Hoffman, have taken their tricks to new heights since then.

are encouraged to compete, and age categories ensure that kids compete against others of similar physical and skill levels. Pro BMX racing is not a kids' sport, however. The top pros are in their early- to late-twenties, paid well, and the business of BMX is to win.

Big and dirty air

By the Eighties, BMX had progressed beyond the limitations of the track. Riders seeking to push their limits and redefine what could be done on a 20-inch (51cm) bike pioneered trick riding, which included rolling tricks on a flat surface, called "flat land," and gravity-driven tricks in a half-pipe, called "vert" riding. Another outgrowth of BMX racing is the

Despite a dip in popularity when the mountain bike craze began, BMX races are still popular today.

"big air dirt" jumping, where riders go fast and high while pulling off mid-air stunts for style with friends, or points in competition.

Flatland riding resembles a kind of pavement ballet, where riders stand and step over and around their bike frames while the bike is moving. Foot pegs are added to the front and rear axles of the bikes to give riders additional places for their feet while doing moves. The addition of foot pegs allows riders to spin their bikes around beneath them and perform other balance tricks they could not do otherwise.

Here are some vert riding maneuvers:

- **540** – spinning 540 degrees while above the coping.
- **900** – spinning 900 degrees while above the coping — very few pros can do it.
- **TAIL WHIP** – holding the handlebars and spinning the bike 360 degrees beneath you while above the coping.
- **PEG GRIND** – sliding the bike on both grind pegs on the coping.
- **FEEBLE PEG GRIND** – sliding one peg while rolling the other wheel on the coping.
- **FAKIE GRIND** – peg grind on coping moving backward.
- **BACK FLIP** – doing a back flip above the coping and landing.
- **FAKIE BAR SPIN** – spinning the handlebars while above the coping.

- **NAC NAC** – kicking one leg over and across the top tube while above the coping.
- **SUPERMAN AIR** – letting both feet fly away with the body outstretched above the coping.
- **LEAN AIR** – getting the rider's bike and body horizontal above the coping.

Dirt jumping can be performed just about anywhere you can find dirt—and where you can't, look for other stuff to jump. Many riders look to vacant lots to build jumps, while others build "box" jumps and other ramps to get air. The object is to go big and do a stylish trick in the process. Many of the tricks, with the exception of coping moves, come straight out of vert riding (or is it the other way around?). Jumping stuff is one part of BMX that's been around as long as there have been bikes.

Flatland riding (top left) resembles a kind of pavement ballet and uses foot pegs added to the bike's axles. Dirt jumping (right), however, requires nothing more than some dirt, a bike, and if possible, some friends.

66

Vert riding also uses foot pegs, but here they are referred to as "grind" pegs, since they are used to do tricks on the half-pipe's coping, a 2.5-inch (63.5mm) diameter metal tube that sits on the top edge of every half-pipe. Vert riders perform most of their maneuvers well above the coping. Top pros are capable of launching their bikes upward of 10 feet (3m) above the coping, where they adjust the attitude of their bikes and reenter the half-pipe in the same way that a skateboarder or inline skater would.

All the moves

Vert riding has been impacted the most by Matt Hoffman, who at age 15 redefined what could be done in a half-pipe. Since then, "The Condor" has gone on to win the World Championships eight consecutive times. In addition to his wins, he also owns the World Record for a vertical jump, which he set by being towed behind a motorcycle into a 20-foot (6.09m) quarter-pipe (half of a half-pipe). He jumped an amazing 50 feet (15.24m) above the ground, and landed it. Matt burst his spleen from the g-forces at the bottom of the landing, and nearly died from massive blood loss, having not realized he'd injured himself until it was almost too late!

The top riders are highly-paid pros, usually in their early to late-twenties. The sport is most popular in the U.S. where it continues to expand its appeal.

Caving

Walking, scrambling on all fours, and crawling on your belly into the moist darkness of a cave is not everyone's idea of a good time, but it is certainly extreme. The labyrinth-like tunnels that can lead to huge sheer drop offs or expansive chasms are not for the faint of heart. Those prone to nightmares from watching too many reruns of Dracula also may not appreciate the propensity of caves to attract legions of bats.

APPROPRIATELY, those who do cave (serious cavers do not refer to their sport as spelunking or potholing) always travel to the inner depths of the earth in groups of two or more. Not surprisingly, cavers are subject to many dangers that one would expect could occur in a cave, such as death by starvation, falling, asphyxiation, drowning, and hypothermia from exposure.

Cavers navigate the subterranean routes with the use of lamps on their helmets. The lamps are either carbide-style, fueled by a jet of acetylene gas like in the old days of coal mining, or newer electric lighting systems using bulbs, batteries, and intermittent-pulsing lamp technologies. Having lights is so critical to a caver's survival that, as a rule, each caver should carry at least three independent sources of light with them

Cavers always travel to the inner depths of the earth in groups of two or more.

before entering any cave. Other equipment required for caving expeditions includes a helmet, kneepads, a small pack, good boots, gloves, and mental clarity, for a lack mental toughness can be as much to blame for caving accidents as fate.

Expert cavers can explore regions that require additional equipment such as wetsuits, rope, climbing gear for technical sections—such as chocks and harnesses for ascending and rapelling—cable ladders, and even scuba equipment.

Geological thrills

All cavers and aspiring cavers can reach the point at which they can explore truly extreme terrain, however, in order to get to that point, it is recommended that you join a grotto, which is a regional organization made up of cavers. Grottos are generally very helpful, and welcome new members and beginners as a way to grow their sport. Cavers are generally as interested in the historical and geological make up of the caves they trek as they are the thrill of traveling down into the damp darkness of the earth.

Once inside, caving requires most of the same technical skill that outdoor climbers use in the daylight. Some subterranean caverns are so extensive that they dwarf many frequently climbed outdoor climbing sites.

Caving is practiced globally, especially in regions that were once under water and so have the remains of aquatic creatures embedded in the earth which over geological time have turned to limestone. Most limestone is between 300 and 500 million years of age. In China, there are areas of limestone that can reach 2,000 feet (600m) in depth.

Caves offer tremendous historical evidence in some regions of the world. In France, for example, the famous Lascaux Caves have preserved drawings of prehistoric life, which now offer further insights into the origins of the human species. Similar evidence of man's history has been discovered in caves throughout the world.

Caving requires much of the same equipment needed for mountain climbing.

One of the main reasons caves offer so much evidence of history is that they provided shelter from enemies and storage for food and property that surface structures could not. Over the centuries, caves have also been useful places to stash loot and modern treasure hunters are still hard at work seeking to find the plunder.

Put it in, take it out

Caves, like the rest of the earth's treasures, are a limited and valuable resource, and a unique aspect of the global environment. There is a moral responsibility that all cavers

protect the caves they explore, minimizing the gradual deterioration that occurs once a cave is discovered.

One of caving's golden rules is that cavers take out of the cave everything that they bring in, since litter and pollution have already destroyed scientifically important caves across the globe. Even accidental damage can occur that prevents cave scientists from reconstructing evidence to get a better read on our history. As a result enthusiasts are now prohibited in many places from enjoying the natural beauty of the underground world.

It is essential that cavers take out everything they bring into the cave—this avoids destroying a unique and irreplaceable environment.

Extreme Motocross

As off-road motorcycle riders have become more skilled, and as the equipment available from manufacturers has become consistently lighter and more powerful with an ever-increasing range of suspension travel, the physical boundaries of what can and can't be done on a motocross (motoX) bike are expanding. In the early days of off-road motorcycling, the thought that riders would someday leap 40 or 50 feet (12–15m) in the air, regularly, would have seemed absurd. However that is precisely the state of extreme motoX today.

EXTREME RIDING is not as new as today's riders would make it seem, though. Hill climbs, trials riding (riders negotiate through a broad range of obstacles, requiring low speed, highly technical, balanced handling), and motoX racing have been part of motorcycle sport for years. In their day, many other riders pushed the limits of what had been done to that date. Daredevil rider Evel Knievel is a classic example of an early extreme pioneer, who also had a pretty good grasp of self-promotion.

The unique nature of the extreme sports movement today, is that extreme athletes have a multitude of other new sports and experiences to draw on. Extreme motoX is defined by more than just racing, although race series like the AMA Supercross Series have done much to showcase the talents of top extreme riders in the world. Extreme motoX riders push their machines in ways that are new and innovative and are drawing inspiration from other sports, such as skiing and snowboarding. Many of the top riders came from the ranks of BMX riders, and so a new freestyle orientation as to how a motoX bike is handled in the air is evident.

SuperX-over

AMA Supercross superstar Jeremy McGrath's rise through the motoX ranks is one example of taking BMX moves and bringing them to motoX. He is also a perfect example of what

Traditional motocross was simply off-road motorcycling, but the skills learned by the riders have had surprising results.

can be done when skill is coupled with newer technology and lighter motoX bikes. Along with others like Jeff Emig and Kevin Windham, he is redefining what can be done on a motoX bike. The Supercross riders are also impacting how the rest of the world views motoX. The brash and unique style of the AMA pros has been backed up by their ability to win races across the globe.

The best example of extreme motoX is the AMA Supercross Series. Here, the courses are designed to reward riders who can handle the most difficult of situations. The courses have many of the bumps and ruts of traditional motoX, but the obstacles and jumps are designed to maximize the height a rider can, and must, jump to win. Here is a brief description of a typical Supercross layout.

Supercross

The Start—as in traditional forms of motoX racing, the riders line up behind "the gate," a series of aluminum tubes that fall away from the riders when the start occurs. From here the riders go into Start Straight, where they tear out of the start and are forced into "the funnel," as the width of the straight decreases from 80 to 20 feet (24–6m) over the course of the 200–400-foot (60–120m)

section. This forces the riders to take a position in the "field" of riders before entering the first turn.

In Supercross, the First Turn is always a left—and it's crucial. As the riders leave the gate simultaneously, they are generally still positioning themselves as they come into the turn, so a few things happen. The front riders, especially the lead rider, have the advantage of getting through cleanly and extending their lead. But the First Turn forces riders in the main pack into one another, and a lot of crashes can occur. A rider can come through clean and get a shot at winning, or lose so much distance in a fall, that winning is virtually impossible.

The Obstacles—riders now weave their way through a series of turns that lead them over several obstacles (jumps), ranging from fairly easy to difficult and technically challenging. The jumps are designed to challenge a rider's ability to the fullest, create close racing, and maximize airtime. Jumps come in many sizes and are linked to create varying degrees of difficulty throughout he course. The jumps are categorized as:

● SINGLE JUMP – rider jumps 20–60 feet (6–18m) onto a flat landing
● DOUBLE JUMP – rider jumps off one obstacle and lands on the far side of the next, usually covering 20–70 feet of terrain

● TRIPLE JUMP – rider must get through three consecutive jumps and may choose to jump them as sets of two and one, or as a group of three (launching over an entire triple requires the rider to catch up to 25 feet (7.6m) of vertical air over a distance of 75 feet (23m) or more. Triples are real crowd pleasers)
● WHOOPS – a series of short and steep bumps across the entire width of the course that throw the rider about while crossing them.

The obstacles in Supercross give the riders enough time in the air to read *War And Peace*. Instead, they use the hang time to perform stylish trick maneuvers, many of which where created in BMX. Here are some of the most visually exciting:

● WHIP IT – moving the motorcycle from one side to the other in the air
● PANCAKE – pitching motorcycle and rider over to the side, as close to 90 degrees from vertical as possible
● CANCAN – taking one leg and bringing it across the motorcycle seat to the other side and back before landing
● NAC NAC – taking one leg off the back of the motorcycle and swinging backward to look at what's behind you while in the air. A move made famous by Jeremy McGrath

- **HELL CLICKER** – an insane move created by Kevin Windham where the rider lifts their feet and clicks their heels together in front of the motorcycle before landing
- **BAR HOP** – another insane move that's often practiced but unsuitable in a race where the rider takes their feet and places them on the handlebars before landing
- **SUPERMAN AIR** – another McGrath move where the rider holds on to the handlebars and lets the rest of their body to fly up away from the motorcycle while airborne.

The moves and obstacles in the Supercross Series are not natural, but many natural obstacles exist in areas that every rider can get to and play on. The machinery and technology of modern bikes has produced unprecedented opportunities to push the limits. Because the expanse of natural terrain is so broad, and so easily reached on a motoX bike, the only limitation of what can by ridden and how is defined by who's riding it.

One unfortunate aspect of motoX is that riders of all levels of ability and physical strength can get a motoX bike to go fast. As a result, every year riders are injured while performing stunts and tricks they are not prepared to handle, or over terrain they are unfamiliar with. The most important thing to remember for each motorcycle and motoX rider is that it's very easy to go fast and catch a lot of air, but it is not very easy to control and land the motorcycle. Take your time and learn at a reasonable pace, extreme riding requires years of practice, and excellent physical conditioning.

The Supercross series combines riding skills and balance with new technology and lighter bikes to produce spectacular riding action, both indoors and out.

Land & Ice Yachting

Land Sailing began hundreds of years ago in China when it was discovered that the power of the wind could be harnessed to make tasks like plowing and moving objects easier. Many historians believe the Chinese were the first to attempt to harness the wind for purposes of transportation, though there is reportedly evidence that the ancient Egyptians may have beaten them to it.

MODERN LAND YACHTS are capable of attaining speeds approaching 100 mph (160 kph)—the world record is 95.5 mph. Many modern land yachts are designed to swap out their wheels in the winter for ice blades. Ice yachts, with less friction to inhibit their speed, are now exceeding 150 mph (240 kph). Land and ice sailing designs are generally limited to modern three-wheel machines. There are some other approaches to land and ice sailing, such as skateboard-like systems employing either wheels or blades mounted to windsurfer rigs. These systems do not reach the velocities of their larger counterparts, but are none-the-less exciting and challenging to sail.

Land sailing on beaches is popular with enthusiasts, because wind blowing in off the sea, at right angles to the beach, is good for speed.

Finding the wind

Landsailing can be practiced on a broad range of surfaces. The dry lake beds of the U.S.A. are a favorite of landsailors globally.

Abandoned airfields are a great site for sailing, however they are more temperamental, since the asphalt direction and the wind direction don't always line up just right. Many land sailing enthusiasts enjoy sailing on beaches, which often offer a predictable breeze that is perpendicular to the required direction of travel, the preferred wind direction for beach sailing.

Ice yachts have a slightly easier time finding suitable ice to sail on. Their primary problem is finding lakes that are sizable enough to allow them to not only accelerate up to speed, but also to turn safely before coming ashore. There are techniques for spilling the air that allow the sailor to somewhat lower their terminal velocity, however, those techniques rely on the yacht

not changing direction away from the wind's quadrant because doing so will change their apparent wind and accelerate their yacht.

Both land and ice yachts must deal with the concept of apparent wind when negotiating the terrain's limitations. Perhaps the easiest way to explain apparent wind would be to park your car so that the wind is hitting it at 90 degrees to the driver's door. If you were to take a reading on the direction of a wind blowing at 20 mph (32 kph) as it hit the door, the apparent wind would equal 20 mph at 90 degrees. If you then accelerated away to 20 mph, your apparent wind would increase to reflect the speed you were traveling versus the 20 mph wind hitting the side of your car. The angle of the apparent wind also changes to roughly 45 degrees forward of the driver's side. If you were to turn your car, both the angle and the speed of the apparent wind would change with you.

If understanding apparent wind seems complicated, it is. To drive a land or ice yacht at high speeds of 100+ mph, requires total driver control. A poor driver is a risk to other sailors and to themselves. Striking another vehicle traveling at 100 mph when you are also traveling at 100 mph is certainly not something any sane person would want to do. Focus and lightning reflexes mean the difference between a good day and a ride to the hospital.

Reflexes are not always good enough. Imagine sailing an ice boat at 150 mph (240 kph) and hitting a raised crack in the ice. This does happen, and the results are

Ice yachts, with less friction to inhibit their speed, can now exceed speeds of 150 mph (240kph).

Driving land or ice yachts at high speed requires total driver control.

replacing these soft sails with hard adjustable wing designs that are lighter, more efficient, and allow for greater velocity. Wings are more easily "tuned" to either accelerate or decelerate the yachts, and the lift they generate to move the yacht can be positioned so as to effectively place the yacht into an "idle" mode.

The first recorded use of a land-sailing vehicle was around 1600 when Flemish Engineer Simon Stevin created a massive two-masted land yacht for beach travel. The yacht was capable of carrying a group of 28 passengers and could travel at speeds exceeding 20 mph.

Sailing the wild west

In the nineteenth century many attempts were made to create a sail-powered vehicle for transportation purposes. One of the more famous attempts was in the U.S., where the Baltimore and Ohio Railroad successfully used a special sailing railcar to transport, among others, the Russian Ambassador, who subsequently requested one for the Czar. Sailing railcars were most successful as workcars, and were reported to be capable of the speed of the fastest locomotives of the era. The sail railcars proved difficult to control and as unreliable as the wind, however, and soon vanished from the railroads.

Later around the time of the California Gold Rush in 1849, many settlers and prospectors heading across the plains attached sails to Contessa Wagons, enabling them to travel further and faster than without the aid of wind power. These wagons did, however, have some substantial handling problems, as their extinction would indicate.

One thing is for sure, even if land and ice yachts are now only reserved for extreme sports enthusiasts, the opportunity to harness the wind in order to travel will always exist, and the urge to push the limits of performance will continue to redefine these exciting and dangerous sports.

79

rarely painless. Many ice sailors have had severe leg injuries and been killed in such instances. Land sailors have similar concerns, especially that of "capsizing" (tipping over) their craft. Unlike ice boats, which can slide through such an occasion, land yachts that capsize crash hard. Land yachts also run the risk of hitting unseen, or unforeseen objects at high speed, especially on dry lake beds.

Sails and wings

Modern land and ice boaters are constantly seeking new technologies to make their yachts both faster and safer. The use of composite materials together with modular construction techniques have helped to make the yachts lighter and better able to withstand impacts due to either capsize or striking debris. However, it is questionable if a remedy can be created for high speed collisions.

One of the most exciting high-tech modifications is the removal of the old wire "stayed" mast systems for hoisting the sails that power these yachts. New technology is

Mountain Biking

Charging down a hill at warp speed on a bike is a rush that most of us have enjoyed at some time. As bikes developed they headed down the path of tradition, and for a while, all a bike buyer could find was a road-racing-style bike or a cruiser. Road bikes were fine for speed and offered a broad range of gears. But road bikes offered little comfort and didn't take very well to rough surfaces. Cruisers were very comfortable, but heavy and not geared very well. All that changed in the early Eighties when a Japanese bike company by the name of Specialized purchased a unique bike made in Marin County, California, and took it home for a closer look.

Mountain bikes have opened up extreme terrain even for recreational riders and family outings.

THE MOUNTAIN BIKE can trace its roots back to when a small and unknown group of riders in Marin County, California first began riding stripped down and beefed up Schwinns on mountain roads just prior to WWII. One can only assume that the natural propensity of extreme oriented riders continued to pursue downhill riding until a few notable pioneers of the modern mountain bike began simultaneously experimenting and redefining the equipment they were riding. According to one of those pioneers, Gary Fischer, the early Schwinn "Ballooner" Cruiser bikes everyone was riding were so heavy that they were pushed, not ridden, uphill. Fischer is reported to have been the first to equip a

Ballooner with multiple gears, an act that made it easier to pedal uphill, but also added 25 lbs (11.35 kg) to their weight.

Specialized bikes

Racing provided inspiration for many of the upgrades that are now taken for granted on modern mountain bikes. Not suprisingly, most of the advances in mountain biking took place after the first official mountain bike

Downhill racers travel at speeds of over 60 mph (97kph) requiring state-of-the-art equipment to help their aerodynamics.

Even the salt flats of Death Valley in Nevada prove little obstacle to today's high-tech mountain bikes.

race took place on 21 October, 1976. The racers on the 2.1 mile (3.4km) course down Mt. Tamalpais could not possibly have known the biking revolution they were starting that day. The race was dubbed the Repack since the brakes required repacking after each heat due to the extreme pitch. Repack organizer Charlie Kelly was reported to have considered the race so extreme that he couldn't imagine many riders would get into it for very long.

In 1977, pioneer racer and bike builder Joe Breeze became the first to build a mountain bike from the stiffer and lighter chrome-moly materials used in road-racing bikes. To that he added the most lightweight and rugged components, giving birth to the first modern mountain bike. Five years later in 1983, Specialized would release its StumpJumper, the first mass-produced mountain bike made commercially available.

The release and overwhelming success of the StumpJumper fueled an explosion of demand for the new-style mountain bikes. Recreational riders had long been turned off by the dropped-style handlebars on all standard road bikes. The mountain bikes were so rugged and versatile that they could be ridden anywhere. Amazingly, sales of mountain bikes grew to surpass the sale of road bikes by 1986, and an entire global industry was born.

An early Schwinn "Ballooner" cruiser bike - arguably the first mountain bike.

84

The surge in sales demanded an entirely new set of accessories that were mountain bike specific. The balloon tires of the early Schwinns were replaced by "nobby, fat" tires that looked more like motocross tires than the skinny road tires on the bikes they quickly replaced. Road-style swept down handlebars were replaced by straight handlebars that were more comfortable. The saddles became more comfortable, too. A broader seating surface and padding, versus traditional road bike hard saddles, made the comfort package complete. The sum of fatter tires, straight handlebars, and softer saddles made converts out of riders who couldn't have cared less that the bikes they were buying could climb steep hills and fly down at high speed with great control.

Space-age materials

More accessories were added and new approaches to old needs created. Riders soon discovered that the addition of bar ends could allow them to shift their weight forward and upward in climbing situations. Bar ends are short sections of tubing, either straight or curved, that attach to the end of the handlebars at an angle of roughly 90 degrees. They were soon a requirement for racing, and many mountain bikers who didn't race got them as well. New clip in peddle systems were created with mountain bikers in mind, replacing the strapped in toe clip-

Mountain biking organizations, like the IMBA and NORBA, are working hard at educating their members to preserve the environment of trails like this one in Colorado, U.S.A.

style retainers that didn't let a rider separate from their bike in a fall.

Innovation and competition continued to fuel the growth of mountain biking. Since Gary Fischer and Joe Breeze's first modifications in the Seventies, mountain bikes have been produced in a number of materials and frame styles, each focused on specific competitive needs. Materials now range from the chrome-moly in Joe Breeze's 1977 frame to aluminum, titanium, and space-age ceramic and composite materials.

The original one front sprocket (gear) and one rear sprocket single-gear set up gave way to three front and eight rear sprockets as gearing went from 1-speed to 3, to 10, to 15, to 18, to 21, to the highest currently available—24-speed gearing. Frame sets went from rigid to suspension forks with the introduction of the Rock Shock fork system. Soon, rear suspension was the rage, and full-suspension bikes continue to redefine performance on downhill and slalom courses. Now downhill racing bikes are created with full suspension in mind at the beginning of the design stage, not as an add-on feature. Suspension travel on some of the more radical designs exceeds 6 inches (15cm) in the front and 8 inches (23cm) in the rear, allowing for massive shock absorbtion at high speeds, increased tire contact at speed, and higher top end velocities. Downhill racers spent most of their time in "loose" tracking stances in early racing, with their rear tires drifting and their bikes constantly on the edge of control. Suspensions allow the riders to "carve" their turns now, using the suspension and their bodies to keep the tires locked into the terrain they are riding. New disciplines of mountain bike racing have evolved from mountain biking's popularity:

● CROSS COUNTRY RACING pits competitors against each other and the clock for best overall finish on a closed and gated course over grueling, technical terrain. Cross Country became an Olympic medal sport in 1996, replacing the dated and less popular road team time trial event.

● DOWNHILL RACING pits riders against the clock for best descent through a closed and gated course. The Eliminator race pits rider against rider for a best score of two runs. Speeds often exceed 60 mph (97 kph) and crashes are dramatic and painful.

● DUAL SLALOM RACING pits rider against rider on a closed gated course that requires the riders to execute a number of tight turns successfully on the way to the finish.

● OBSERVED TRIALS events require riders to complete a course consisting of obstacles and hazards. The riders must complete the course without "dabbing" (putting their feet down for balance). Riders are penalized by adding points for each dab. The rider with the least points wins.

● UPHILL RACING is a timed competition of sustained climbing where competitors finish at altitudes higher than where they started.

Take a hike

While all of these types of racing and styles of bikes have emerged during mountain biking's rapid evolution, the underlying allure of the kind of riding these bikes have allowed us to enjoy has not. The images and beauty of the outdoors are really why mountain biking has grown so rapidly. Mountain bikes have opened up an entire range of remote wilderness and landscapes that recreational trail hikers had never been able to get to so

Modern mountain bikes, like this Cannondale, utilize a whole range of innovations, like titanium, space-age ceramic and composite materials.

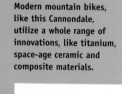

86

easily or quickly. Not suprisingly, many of the most popular mountain biking regions are established hiking areas.

With the emergence of bikes on hiking terrain came territorial issues of who should and shouldn't have access to the trails. Not surprisingly hikers complained that mountain bikers weren't environmentally friendly enough to the trails, and were leaving trash and erosion problems behind them as they rode. Many of these complaints were justified, and organizations like the International Mountain Biking Association (IMBA) and the National Off Road Bicycle Association (NORBA) in the U.S. have worked hard to educate their members in order to decrease the impact mountain biking can have on the environment and on trails. Mountain bikes quickly reshaped the inner city messenger business, too. Urban dwellers and travelers can't help notice the volumes of bike messengers in virtually every city in the world. Modern cities are filled with hundreds of riders constantly riding through traffic, over curbs and stairs, and through parks in a quest for timely delivery. Not surprisingly, many of these riders are competing or aspiring professional mountain bike racers.

Mountainboarding

Mountainboarding is a newcomer to the world of extreme sports, although it can track its lineage to a few other more "established" extreme sports like snowboarding and mountain biking.

ESSENTIALLY, THE MOUNTAINBOARD creators developed a hybrid skateboard/snowboard that allows aspects of each sport to be used on terrain where neither can be practiced. Which isn't to say that skateboarders have not tried using fat tires on their skateboards so that they can ride on loose sand and gravel—they have.

Snowboarders also discovered that their boards can be made to double as sand surfers. However, until the mountainboard the only way to travel downhill at speed on a mountain road, over rocks, or gravel was on a mountain bike.

The name Mountainboard is a registered trademark of the Mountainboard company in Colorado Springs, Colorado. The company is owned by creators Patrick McConnell and Jason Lee, two Vail snowboarders who developed the board as a way to ride Vail during the summer as a cross-training tool for winter riding. The two soon discovered that the design rode so well that friends were buying as many as they could make, and a business was born from the idea.

Freestyle dirt

Another athlete on another continent created a similar vehicle at just about the same time. Australian surfer John Miln developed a three-wheeled board (the Mountainboard uses four) using a different steering setup a short while before the Vail snowboarders began. The Outback Mountainboard design uses two wheels in front to steer the rig and one at the back, and includes a brake.

Both systems are steered just like a skateboard, by leaning the board's deck in the required direction. On dirt and loose surfaces, the boards respond much like a snowboard. Riders can drive the rear of the board hard into the turn, "scrubbing" (slowing) their speed by getting the rear of the board slightly loose in the turn. On hard surfaces like pavement, they roll faster with fully-inflated tires, and slower on soft tires. This means that the rider stops just like a skateboarder—by getting off. They are said to be highly stable and controllable with practice.

While only a single model of the Outback is available, the rival Mountainboards are available in a variety of lengths, just like a snowboard. Shorter versions are for freestyle riding, while the longer ones offer better directional stability and are better suited to speed riding. Both take a range of tires, from slick pavement tires to knobby dirt tires.

Only competitions will determine which board is the better. Generally the best handling and most controllable boards are the ones that win contests. These are just starting to be organized, so time will tell which design becomes popular.

Whichever wins consumers' hearts, there is no doubt that mountainboards are here to stay. Extreme athletes and enthusiasts will certainly take the opportunity to redefine what can be done on pavement or dirt, it only takes a few creative athletes to establish a new way to have fun doing it.

Mountainboards are a hybrid skateboard/snowboard that allows boarding on terrain which is not suitable for either.

88

Outdoor Climbing

Mountain climbing is as old as mankind. It has not always been a "sport," perhaps it was better classified as a survival skill. Now that we no longer require mountaineering skills to traverse the globe, those that still enjoy getting out into the mountains are clearly enthusiasts of the sport of mountain climbing. Furthermore, while mountain climbing is the act of ascending a mountain under your own power, extreme mountain climbing is hardly a leisure activity.

CLIMBING MOUNTAINS covers two basic categories, technical and non-technical. The latter requires little more than sheer energy and knowledge of one's own limitations. No special equipment, just a good rugged and supportive pair of hiking shoes. Technical climbing requires the use of ropes and other specialized equipment to ascend the terrain to be climbed. The equipment is used so that, in the event of a fall, the climber is both protected from injury and securely fastened to the rock or ice.

Technical climbing can be broken into two components, ice and rock. Rock climbing involves scaling cliffs and boulders in situations that could prove hazardous or dangerous.

The most extreme rock climbers can scale the rock without the use of equipment beyond their shoes and some chalk to aid them in gripping the rock. These climbers "solo" their way up the faces of cliffs that are a match for many expert climbers even when they are using ropes or gear to keep them attached to the mountain in the event

of a fall. Because extreme solo climbers ascend without these aids, solo climbers are either very good, or very dead.

Ice climbing entails scaling cliffs and boulders that are entirely covered with ice and snow. Climbing ice requires an additional level of specialized equipment such as "crampons," the metal spikes which ice climbers attach to the bottom of their climbing shoes. In ice climbing, even the most proficient extreme climbers require the aid of equipment that allows them to grip the ice and snow without slipping.

Part of a team

Extreme climbers must be familiar with all of the technical gear, and must spend substantial time "on the rock" to successfully undertake those difficult climbs requiring highly specialized technique. The most difficult terrain demands a level of physical conditioning and mental toughness that few sports require. An extreme climber who has command of their body, mind, and surroundings can be considered relatively

safe in conditions that "normal" people would consider perilous.

Serious climbers do not "solo" (or climb alone). Climbing requires teamwork and a focus on not just personal safety, but the safety of the other climbers. Because climbers constantly rely on others to ensure their safety, it is important that everyone is aware of not only their personal limitations, but of those they are with as well.

Extreme mountain climbing ascents like Mount Everest or K2 are world famous not only for the climbers who have successfully reached their peaks, but also for the many

Isabelle Patissier of France solos her way up a sheer rock face in California, using chalk, shoes and tremendous climbing skills.

Frenchman Patrick Edlinger soloing up the Sugar Loaf mountain in Brazil, a challenge for even the best-equipped climbers.

who have failed or died in the process of the climb. To successfully climb peaks of this level of difficulty requires months of planning and a team of tremendous talent. Top expert abilities in both ice and rock climbing are essential requirements for those considering attempting an extreme mountain ascent. Each team of climbers that reaches the top can point to their climbing team members as well as dozens of support people at different stages of the climb, without whom the climb would have failed.

Danger categories

A complete knowledge of lifesaving and first-aid skills are also much needed assets in each team member. With the extreme altitude of these climbs, abrupt weather changes can strand an injured climber on the mountain for days before rescue is possible. Without sufficient first aid, a climber can die before outside assistance is made available. Because temperatures can quickly drop off the scale, advanced life-saving protective gear is also required, and must be available during the entire ascent and descent.

Most climbing is not, however, done in remote areas on massive peaks. It takes place within hours of major urban areas and towns around the globe. The fact that many climbing areas are accessible does not make them any less extreme. A simple categorization system has been created in every country to classify the difficulty of a climb. In France the system uses a series of numbers and letters; in England ascents are graded on difficulty and danger; in the U.S. climbers use what is termed the "Yosemite

Despite appearances, most climbing takes place within hours of major urban areas and towns around the globe.

Ice climbing is arguably the most extreme sport of all. It requires meticulous planning, the use of specialized equipment and complete reliance on other members of a team in the most dangerous circumstances.

One of the most famous climbers today is France's Catherine Destivelle. Here she demonstrates the sort of equipment required for a serious climbing expedition.

scale" to help explain the various levels of difficulty climbers can attempt. The Yosemite grading system uses the following structure for each climb:

- CLASS I – Hiking, where most any footwear is considered adequate.
- CLASS II – Proper footwear is required for rough terrain and the use of handholds may be needed in some portions of the ascent.
- CLASS III – "Scrambling" on hands and feet when use of the hands is required frequently. Ropes should be carried and available if needed.
- CLASS IV – Ropes and belays (the system of using ropes between climbers) must be used continuously for safety. Belay anchors may be necessary in some situations. (Class IV Climbs differ from Class III in that the terrain immediately adjacent to the climb is treacherous and a fall in that direction can be deadly.)
- CLASS V – Leader protection (anchors placed into the rock and used to secure the rope) required above the belayer.
- CLASS VI – Direct Aids must be used.

Climbs at Class V use a decimal system to detail the difficulty of the climb. The current top, which is of course open to opinion, is somewhere around a V.15. Once climbers get into Class VI, a scale of A0–A6 is used to detail the difficulty of this level.

- A0 – Climb requires use of pre-existing aids (climber not required to place the assistance themselves).
- A1 – Climb requires use of "chocks" (cam devices that anchor into openings in the rock) that are easy to place.
- A2– Climb requires the use of chocks that are difficult to place.
- A3 – Climb requires the installation of a hook into the rock because chock placement is not possible.
- A4 – Very "sketchy," aids used where the likelihood of the aid holding in the event of a fall is not high, very risky climbing.
- A5 – Extremely sketchy.
- A6 – So sketchy, the likelihood of A6 levels being climbable is debatable

Even the most basic technical climbing requires a fairly high level of specialist equipment.

Other terms used in climbing:

- **PITON** – metal blades or angles with an open eye at the blunt end which are driven into cracks in the rock to secure belays and leader protection.
- **CARABINER** – snaplinks of varying sizes and shapes used for connecting climbing rope with a piton, sling, or chock. These are made with either a "non-locking" spring gate closure or "locking" screw lock mechanism.
- **ROUTE** – a path up the rock where the ascent is made.
- **FLASH** – successfully climbing a to the top of a route without falling.
- **ON-SIGHT** – attempting to climb a route without any previous information or guidance.
- **WHIP OR AIRTIME** – a long fall (all long falls stop suddenly whether the rope holds or not).
- **OVERHANG** – a portion of the rock which stretches upward past the vertical.
- **ROOF** – a severe overhang requiring upside down climbing.
- **BUCKET** – a very good hold.
- **SMEAR** – holding on to the rock using friction from the climbers rubber footwear.
- **LUNGE** – climber throws him or herself at an out of reach hold (missing the hold means a fall).
- **BARNDOOR**—an out of balance climber swinging away from the rock.
- **FLAG**—using a free leg as a counterbalance to maintain control during a barndoor.

Mountain climbing is as old as mankind. Ascending a mountain under your own power holds a fascination for people from all walks of life.

Skateboarding

Without question, skateboarding is the embodiment of the outlaw extreme image. Somehow, skateboarding's unique style and underground culture have been difficult for older generations to understand or appreciate. Skateboarding is a sport that continues to redefine itself, pushing the limits of what can and can't be done physically, mentally—and yes, culturally.

NO ONE IS CERTAIN of the origins of skateboarding. Some have suggested the first skateboard was crafted by a bored California surfer seeking to polish his skills on a waveless afternoon. Others deny its West Coast origins, and state that the first skateboard was a simplified version of a child's toy, the push-scooter. Push-scooters were popular toys in the Fifties, made from dismantled roller skates nailed to a board with a crate attached as a balance aid. Remove the crate, and you have a skateboard.

New technology brought better wheels and trucks. These advances made new tricks possible and learning easier, and in the Seventies skateboarding boomed. By the end of the decade there were hundreds of skate parks, millions of skaters, and an industry was born. Half-pipe and pool skateboarding were familiar images of early skateboarding. Names like Tony Alva, Jay Nelson, and Steve Caballero sprung up as heroes of this new sport.

Skateboarding's quick rise gave way to a decline in popularity due to inflated skate park admission fees and insurance issues. Many skate parks and manufacturers went bust. But hardcore skaters persevered, building backyard ramps and pushing streetstyle skating into the forefront of skateboarding's progression.

In action on the half-pipe, skateboarders are now part of the mainstream of today's youth culture.

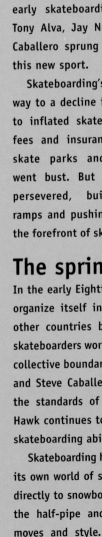

The springboard

In the early Eighties skateboarding began to organize itself in the U.S. Soon skaters in other countries began organizing too, and skateboarders worldwide began pushing their collective boundaries. Skaters like Tony Hawk and Steve Caballero pushed hard by setting the standards of achievement. Today, Tony Hawk continues to represent the pinnacle of skateboarding ability.

Skateboarding has impacted more than just its own world of sport. Skating can be linked directly to snowboarding, which has borrowed the half-pipe and many of skateboarding's moves and style. Skateboarding techniques

Street skating is the most technical style of skateboarding, and takes place anywhere using any available obstacles: benches (below) or bridges (right), hand rails, loading ramps and so on.

can be seen in modern surfing style with its jumps and re-entry moves. Skateboarding is especially evident in the progression of inline skating, which has taken much of the style and culture of skateboarding and sought to make it its own. Wakeboarding finds many of its roots in skateboarding. Street Luge is the most direct relative of skateboarding, and in fact got its start from folks lying down and going fast on skateboards before the term Street Luge was ever coined.

Street or vert?

Skateboarding is now growing internationally, and faster than ever. Skating is one of only a handful of sports that has been embraced by young people globally. The top athletes in skateboarding are renowned worldwide within skateboarding circles. The sport is quickly moving out of the underground and into the mainstream, just as it did before its last peak. Yet, it is fair to point out that there are forces in place now that should serve to keep skateboarding alive and well for quite some time. Consider the number of sports skateboarding has fostered. Certainly all of the participants in those sports can respect skateboarding for what it truly is, a very physically and mentally challenging sport. Those who participate in these sports will naturally look to skateboarding for cross-training, and will encourage kids to get into it instead of discouraging skateboarding at all. Once this is accepted and once it's embraced by the

mainstream, skaterphobics will be forced to relax their anti-skater rhetoric, back off, and let skaters do their thing.

Today's skateboarding can be categorized as either "street" or "vert." The object in both categories is for the skater to test the limits of his ability and skill by trying to successfully land a trick and continue skating.

Street skating is the more technical style of skating. If you have ever seen a group of skaters trying the same trick over and over, they are practicing streetstyle skating tricks. Street skating is extremely difficult to master. Most of the tricks and moves are difficult to appreciate unless you happen to be a street skater or have ever tried street skating. Street tricks are performed on any, and every, available obstacle that looks like it can be ridden over or jumped. Park benches, hand rails, loading ramps, garbage cans, and even monuments are fair game.

Vert skating takes place in a half-pipe. Pools and basins are also popular arenas for vert skating. The vert skating surface consists of two planes connected by a rounded transition. The name "vert" comes from the fact that the transition is from a horizontal plane to a vertical plane. Skaters drop down into the transition from the vertical plane, across the horizontal plane, back up the opposing transition to the opposing vertical plane. Or put quite simply, a half-pipe resembles a big "U" and the skaters go up and down inside of it.

Half-pipes are measured by overall width, the radius of the transition, the height of the vertical plane, or vert, and the length of the horizontal plane, or flat. A competition half-pipe is commonly around 32 feet wide (9.75m) with a 10 foot (3m) transition radius, 12–18 inches (30–46cm) of vert, and 16 feet (5m) of flat.

One component critical to making a half-pipe ridable is what is called the "coping." This is usually a 2.5 inch (6.35cm) diameter pipe that sits on the top of the vert plane. The coping sticks out beyond the edge around 0.25–0.375 inches (6–10mm) and acts as a physical and audible cue, telling the skater he's crossed the top of the half-pipe.

Steve Caballero performs a huge backside air.

Even the coping sometimes fails to help the skater keep control.

OKLAHOMA
SKATE SHOP

The coping also acts to deflect the skateboard back at the skater, allowing enhanced control of the board in the air. Too much coping makes the ramp unridable, too little, makes it extremely difficult to ride. Finally, the coping acts as the surface on which the skater can perform a number of tricks from a "grind" to a "blunt."

All skateboards are essentially the same and share the same basic components. Each skateboard has a deck which is the platform the skater stands on. Decks have been made of fiberglass and plastic, but are almost always made of wood these days.

Each board has a front, or "tip," and a back, or "tail." The length of the tip and tail is determined by the distance from the trucks to the end of the board. The sides of the deck are called rails. The front rail is on the toe side, while the back rail is on the heel side.

Stunt and cruiser

Mounted to every deck is a set of "trucks." Trucks are the steering and axle assemblies on which two wheels are mounted. Trucks are available in a variety of widths. Skateboards all have four wheels, two on the front trucks, two on the rear trucks. Wheels are available in a wide array of widths and diameters, and also in different compounds. Compounds vary by their hardness and traction. Generally, harder wheels offer less traction than softer wheels. Each skater has their own preference when it comes to wheel size and compound.

There are two basic types of skateboards: stunt boards and cruiser boards. Stunt boards are designed to be agile and easy to throw around when performing tricks. Stunt boards are either "old school" or "new school" designs and are used to skate street and vert. Old school boards are wide with longer, wider tails than tips. New school boards are narrower and with symmetrically shaped tips and tails, however their tips are longer than their tails. Old school boards generally use wider trucks than new school boards. Cruiser boards are a lot longer than stunt boards, and tend to use wide trucks for added stability and tracking at speed.

There are two ways to stand on a skateboard. A "regular foot" stance means that the skater places his left foot on the front end of the board. A "goofy foot" means that the skater places his right foot on the front end of the board.

Skateboarders have created a variety of names for the tricks they do. Many times skaters use a mixture of terms to name tricks. These are some of the more frequently used terms:

- FRONTSIDE TRICK – skater turns so that his heels are facing the inside of the turn
- BACKSIDE TRICK – skater turns so that his toes are facing the inside of the turn
- KICK FLIP – skater spins the board around the axis running from the tip to the tail of the board with his toe by kicking his front foot in a backward motion
- HEEL FLIP – skater spins the board around the axis running from the tip to the tail of the board with his heel by kicking his front foot in a forward motion
- FRONTSIDE AIR – skater jumps frontside and grabs the front rail with his back hand
- SLOB – skater jumps frontside and grabs the front rail with his front hand
- STALE FISH – skater jumps frontside and grabs the back rail with his back hand
- LEAN AIR – skater jumps frontside and grabs the back rail with his front hand

- BACKSIDE AIR – skater jumps backside and grabs the back rail with his front hand
- MUTE – skater jumps backside and grabs the front rail with his front hand
- INDY AIR – skater jumps backside and grabs the front rail with his back hand
- TAIL GRAB – skater jumps and grabs tail with front or back hand
- NOSE GRAB – skater jumps and grabs the tip with front or back hand
- INVERT – skater jumps and sets one hand down and balances while upside down holding the board with the other hand
- BLUNT – skater lands the tail on the coping or object in front of both trucks
- SHUVIT – skater jumps and spins the board in 180-degree increments without spinning his body
- SWITCH STANCE – skater lands on the board and rides in the opposite stance, ie. goofy to regular foot
- 540 – skater jumps and spins 540 degrees with the board
- MCTWIST – a 540 with an inverted twist
- CAB – named after Steve Caballero who invented it, skater spins 360 degrees without grabbing the board
- HALF CAB – skater spins 180 degrees without grabbing the board.

The coping on a half-pipe is crucial in letting the skateboarder keep in contact with the board.

Snowboarding

All forms of sport need an element of revitalization or they risk becoming commonplace. Skiing has been a part of life for anyone living near snow-covered or mountainous regions of the globe. With the advent of cheap international air travel, skiing as a sport for the masses progressed until it reached saturation point—interest and participation waned. And then the surfer-skateboarder axis saw snow glinting on distant hills...

IN 1965 a Michigan industrial gases engineer began toying with a design that would wind up saving the the entire ski industry some 25 years later. Sherman Poppen noticed his daughter attempting to stand up on her sled while sliding on the neighborhood hill. This inspired him to go to his garage, where he took a pair of children's skis and screwed them together with dowels, which he described as acting like "foot stops." His daughter Wendy took the "sled" to the hill and rode it. When the other kids saw what her dad had created, they all wanted him to build one for them, too. He did, and they were an instant hit.

Poppen's wife mixed the words surfer and snow together to coin the name "Snurfer," and a product was born. Poppen manufactured Snurfers and distributed them through sporting goods and toy stores, and over the next ten years sold millions. It was the Snurfer that would inspire snowboarding

Snowboarding has come a long way since the advent of the "Snurfer".

Without the culture associated with skiing, snowboarding is free to develop in its own sweet way.

Snowboarding in fresh deep snow delivers a sensation close to pure harmony.

The feeling of riding a snowboard is regarded by some as an almost spiritual experience.

pioneers like Jake Burton Carpenter to develop and manufacture designs that led to the modern snowboard in use by millions of riders today.

One board good...

Early converts to snowboard riding shared a passion that inspired others to give snowboarding a try. The feeling of riding a snowboard has been described many different ways, but perhaps the best term is "soulful." Just as skateboarding and surfing have a zen-like quality to them, snowboarding, especially in deep, fresh, powder, delivers a sensation that is about as close to pure harmony as any extreme sport offers. Anyone who has experienced snowboarding has a clear understanding of why so many young and older people are converting from skiing to snowboarding, and why so many swear they will never return to riding two boards.

Since its start, snowboarding has progressed from simple boards crudely constructed from wood with metal fins attached—meant as a steering aid—to many of the high-tech wood and foam-core construction methods that ski manufacturers have been refining for years. The result is that today's snowboards are so stable and controllable that many out-

Part of the appeal of snowboarding is its simplicity and its addictivness.

"Big air" competitions are part of the excitement at the annual Snowboarding World Championships.

perform skis in a variety of conditions, especially soft snow and "crude," when snow is chopped up and inconsistent in texture and density.

Early designs used clumsy footstraps that offered little control. Today, binding systems fall into two basic categories: hard boot and soft boot. Hard boot systems are the least popular, yet are necessary equipment for those racing gates. The hard boot eliminates the feel that riders seek, and dramatically alter the techniques needed for performance. Soft boot systems use rigid metal or composite frames mounted directly to the board, which utilize straps to retain the rider's boots in place. Soft boots deliver a truer sensation of what is going on under the board, but they are

more difficult to ride in hardpacked snow and ice—in loose snow and powder, there is nothing better.

The cultural revolution

Snowboarding was reviled for years by skiers and the ski industry. Until recently, most mountains would not allow snowboards on their lift systems or their slopes. Skiers, in particular, chose to see those riding snowboards as a hazard, often getting into shouting matches with riders for being on their snow. These confrontations were made worse by some riders whose style was to fight authority, enhancing skiers' perception that all snowboarders were bad news.

The unique culture of the young people who rode snowboards also fueled tensions.

Snowboarding's rising popularity has brought about a revolution in the type and design of clothing worn on snow covered slopes.

The growing popularity of the sport has forced people to sit up and take notice.

108

The baby boomer skiing culture did not understand the generation that rejected the sanctity of their sport and embraced snowboarding. Snowboards made a very different sound than skis, which frightened many skiers. Snowboarders wore apparel that was in a different universe than fashionable ski wear. These cultural boundaries are now breaking down, as skiers begin to appreciate two things: one, snowboarding is here to stay; and two, snowboarders have the same level of respect for the mountains and the same appreciation for riding the hill that skiers do. In fact, many non-skier snowboarders are trying out skiing, a shift that both the ski industry and skiers should be happy with.

Snowboarding has brought a new look to the hills, with its "fun park" concepts. These specially created areas have "hits" (jumps) and obstacles like rails, tables, and even buried cars and buses, that the riders enjoy jumping over and sliding across. Skiers have appreciated these additions because it meant snowboarders kept more to themselves and off the pistes. Snowboarders appreciate the parks because they offer a challenging alternative to some of the more mundane terrain that skiers covet.

Another major impact on snowboarding has been the creation of long half-pipes. Half-pipe riding is now a speciality of many top pro snowboarders, with many moves

directly adapted from skateboarding. The half-pipe gives snowboarders an opportunity to rhythmically link a number of airborne trick maneuvers as they descend the slope on which the half-pipe is constructed. They attract masses of riders to mountains that build them, and many riders prefer to climb up the side of the pipe for each ride rather than use the available chair lift system.

Find that "air"

Though discouraged by some snowboarding pioneers like Jake Burton Carpenter when

they were introduced at the first World Snowboarding Championships in 1983, half-pipe freestyle competitions are major events in most of today's top competitions.

Another fun and exciting snowboarding competition is called "boardercross," because the courses constructed for the races resemble motocross courses. There are a series of right- and left-hand turns on embankments called "burms" that let riders maximize their speed. Between the burms are jumps and bumps to keep the riders on the edge of control and add to the difficulty.

Boardercross offers a sharp contrast to skiing's traditional gate racing. The boardercross format pits as many six racers against one and other simultaneously, each fighting the other for position into the turns and, of course, at the finish line.

"Big air" contests make an exciting spectacle for spectators. The jumps are specially built and riders speed into them for style and dramatic air. Riders are scored on their performance by a panel of judges.

The most dangerous event is undoubtedly the steep "extreme" riding contests, generally

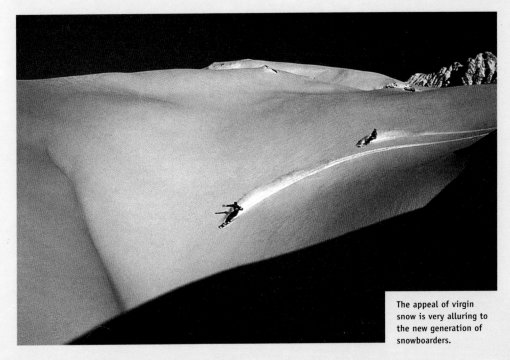

The appeal of virgin snow is very alluring to the new generation of snowboarders.

Snowboarders do have to be aware of obstacles hidden below the surface of the snow.

110

held on slopes exceeding 50 degrees in pitch. Falling almost certainly means losing the event, but it can also end in serious injury. Given the steepness of the angle, a rider may actually accelerate during a fall, tumbling uncontrollably past rock outcrops and possibly over large cliffs. The World Championships of Extreme Snowboarding, called "the King of The Hill" (the women's title goes to the "Queen") are held each year in Valdez, Alaska. Steep and extreme riding requires the highest levels of technical and physical skill to get top to bottom while seeking extra points for jumping over and off obstacles.

Not everyone enjoys communal activities on packed slopes. Many snowboarders prefer trekking into mountainous backcountry on snowshoes to find untouched powder. Climbing adds to the physical challenge of riding the backcountry, while pleasure and satisfaction may be gained from experiencing the mountain in the absence of other people. For those with the wherewithal and a preference for less initial effort, using a helicopter or snowcat and being dropped into the terrain to be ridden is an option. On clear days helicopters get you up fast and high, free to enjoy tens of thousands of vertical feet during the course of a day. Snowcats take

a bit longer, but have the advantage of being able to deliver in nearly all weathers. Remember, the powder is at its best when it's snowing hard.

Soon, the number of snowboards is expected to exceed that of skis. Younger and younger kids are drawn to snowboarding, so the growth should continue. The popularity of snowboarding lies in its alternative to skiing, and that it offers a winter crossover for surfers and skateboarders seeking fun in the snow. Snowboarding continues to attract new riders because the technology has made it easier to learn, and the feeling is addictive. Even if the terrain is not extreme, a snowboard is what it's best to be on.

Wind snowboarding

Once down at the bottom of the mountain, what do you do next? It wasn't long before boarders realized that adding a windsurfing-style sailing rig to their board would allow them to sail back up the slopes, without needing a lift or hike. All they needed was wind direction from the side or directly up the slope of the terrain. Directly uphill is preferable, as it has the added advantage of making it easy to sail down again, but a side wind is good for speed.

Snowboarders who are boardsailors and boardsailors who are snowboarders, can easily find enough stuff to put together a wind

snowboard. Any long snowboard will do the trick. Snowboard sailing doesn't require sails as large as boardsailing, because small sails and short booms are the most controllable, particularly on hard-packed snow.

The addition of foot straps adds to the stability of the rider, and a helmet is essential to avoid very painful contact with the snowy surface of the ground at high speed. Sailors also have to be aware of obstacles hidden beneath the surface of the snow.

The popularity of snowboarding lies mainly in its alternative to skiing. But many new fans are being attracted to the sport because it is easier to learn, and very addictive.

Though still in its infancy, wind snowboarding is a natural extension of boardsailing, that will grow modestly during the next few years. The main obstacle to its growth is that wind snowboard sailors need to be boardsailing experts before they start. It would be foolish to attempt to learn wind snowboard skills first, because mistakes are always painful and often dangerous, whereas it is still painful but less dangerous to be slammed in the water when learning.

The progress of the sport remains to be seen. Will boards be used to cover long distances? Will new designs be created especially for this new sport? Will drift jumping on wind snowboards become the new winter rage? Only time will tell. But if the history of extreme sports tells us anything, it tells us that these extreme athletes will push their boards and the technology to new lmits. The next decade of wind-powered snowboarding should prove to be quite interesting.

Snowshoeing appeals to many because it is an extreme sport that requires minimal equipment and, if administered responsibly, will not have a harmful effect on the environment.

Snowshoeing

Like some of the other extreme sports, snowshoeing got its start not as a sport but as a means of survival. Its roots go back some 6,000 years, when people who lived in predominantly snowbound regions needed to augment their footwear to get through untracked regions. In fact, snowshoes are directly linked to the spread of mankind into regions around the globe where heavy snowfall is a part of life.

AS LONG AS there have been snowshoes, snowshoeing has drawn users out for pleasure treks in addition to using them for survival. Therefore, it is difficult to pinpoint exactly when snowshoeing made the transition from survival skill to sport. Certainly, in the early twentieth century more and more people began getting outdoors for social trekking in the colder climate areas. Snowshoeing was widely used in both WWI and WWII as troops sought to secure regions in the Alps and other areas covered by snowfall. One of the more famous uses of snowshoes occurred when Admiral Byrd relied on them to get to the South Pole—certainly an extreme spot. Snowshoeing as sport has grown out of the outdoor, extreme sports movement. Snowshoes were long overlooked by other extreme athletes until it was realized that they are an effective method of transportation—now, snowshoes are required equipment in the snowy back country. In difficult and isolated terrain, snowshoes can deliver extreme skiers and snowboarders to locations that without the aid of helicopters or snowmobiles they would have otherwise only dreamt about. In fact, snowshoes help to keep the natural spirit of these sports from being overwhelmed by machines.

Breaking the trail

Snowshoe racing was an outgrowth of the Eighties fitness craze, and today hundreds of races are held around the globe each year. Racing has encouraged the participation of many who would have otherwise never snowshoed, and has broadened the appeal to include folks who would just like to get out and enjoy nature rather than being bound by the path of a snowplow.

Snowshoes are designed to be light and provide floatation in heavy and light snow. Getting out and traveling in fresh or untracked snow requires the lead snowshoer to "break trail." This is the most difficult aspect to snowshoeing, and can require as much as ten times the energy than "sucking trail," or following in someone else's snowsteps. This is because the person breaking trail must take strides that not only move them forward, but also pack and compress the snow beneath their shoes.

Getting cold-prepared

Snowshoes are also designed to ascend steep and icy terrain. They have "claws" on the bottom that stick down into the snow to provide additional bite for better traction. Ascending is when they are most frequently used by extreme mountaineers, skiers, and snowboarders.

Snowshoeing is growing rapidly because it involves getting away into remote, peaceful, and natural settings. The fact that the settings can produce fatigue, dehydration, and hypothermia should not be overlooked by anyone considering trying snowshoeing. However, with the right clothing and protective gear, snowshoeing is a great extreme sport that can be enjoyed by a wide range of enthusiasts.

Speed Biking

Traveling down a snow-covered 60-degree slope at an excess of 125 mph (200 kph) on a skis is without question extreme. In fact, the 150 mph (240 kph) record for speed skiing was recently established. Is there any doubt that riding a mountain bike down that very same slope and seeking to achieve that very same speed is extreme too?

OVER THE PAST FEW YEARS, downhill mountain bike racers have been pushing the limits of speed on specially outfitted mountain bikes, and have already broken the 125 mph threshold. The bikes are fitted with special aerodynamic fairings and tires modified with large spikes to grip the snow and ice-covered surface as they accelerate to maximum velocity before racing through a speed-trap zone (a timed distance that determines the official speed established by the rider).

Speed bikes are wind tunnel-tested to improve aerodynamics before racing. Both rider and bike are outfitted to slice through the wind, and the resulting forms are thin and offer little resistance. The bikes are both

Speed bikes are windtunnel tested to ensure that they slice through the wind with minimum resistance. Spiked tires allow the bike to grip the snow and ice surfaces on which they race.

suspended and unsuspended, and are raced in stock class and modified class. The suspension designs are stiffer than what you'd expect to get off the shelf and give the rider a margin of error at speed that a rigid frame cannot, allowing for higher terminal velocities.

The current world record for speed biking is held by Frenchman Eric Baron, who was

traveling at exactly 200 kph when he went through the speed trap. Considering the world record for speed skiing is now 60+ kph (150 mph) above that, we can expect to see far higher speeds as the technology of speed biking improves.

Speed biking is still relatively new as a sport, so it is safe to expect that the records established today will be broken and reestablished soon. Many world class mountain bike downhill racers and speed skiing racers crossing over to speed bikes will be working hard to determine the modifications needed for both equipment and training to make new records possible. The next few years should be very interesting.

Speed Skiing

Skiing in its own right is a pretty extreme sport, and has been for years. One skiing discipline that is as amazing as it is extreme is speed skiing. Imagine screaming down a mountain at 150 mph (240 kph) on skis. That is exactly what current World Record holder and 1992 Olympic Bronze medalist Jeff Hamilton of Truckee, California did in 1995 at Vars, France, becoming the first skier to break the 150 mph barrier, and the fastest non-motorized human on the planet.

Speed skiers' helmets give them the appearance of aliens from another planet.

CONSIDER THE FORCES at play when traveling at 150 mph. The skier is literally skiing faster than a sky diver in freefall. The skis are no longer even touching the ground at that speed. Instead they are riding on a cushion of air. Even the slightest error in judgment or form at that speed can be deadly.

What if a skier was to fall at speed? If they were fortunate enough not to break anything (legs, arms, etc.), it is unlikely they would avoid the residual burns that a high speed fall on snow leave behind. The suits the skiers wear, while great at reducing drag, are not good at preventing tremendous heat build up from the friction of the snow during a fall. The result is often severe burns that can take months to heal. Former World Champion Franz Weber was reported to have spent well over one year healing from burns suffered during a high speed fall.

Shaped like a plane

Clearly, if an athlete wishes to speed ski, they must be a top expert skier and in tremendous physical condition. The forces on the skier's body during acceleration and at terminal velocity are tremendous. Wind tunnel training is one key to finding a low-drag stance. It is expensive, but it allows top competitors to find a position through low-risk testing in a controlled environment. However, the fact remains that at some point, the skier will be asked to point their skis down a 2-mile (3.2km), 60-degree slope in an effort to establish a new record, or at least beat their competition. If that isn't enough, at the bottom of that run, when their muscles are at their most taxed, they will need to find the energy to stop.

Speed skiers employ many specialized pieces of equipment when performing their sport. First, their head protection is a strange looking helmet that is designed to fit flush with their upper body, minimizing any speed-robbing drag. Their poles are special aerodynamically-shaped units, complementing their low-drag theme. Even the boots are modified for reduced drag, and their lower legs are smoothed by the addition of wing-like pants to further eliminate drag. Of course, all of these aero-additions don't mean squat if the skier can't hold a decent position during their run. That is where physical conditioning and endurance, preparation and mental toughness differentiate first from last.

Speed skiing competitions are held throughout Europe, but mostly in France, where they are major events. In North America, there are no areas that are accessible for speed skiing, and insurance and tort law problems make attempting events difficult, so the sport is widely overlooked. Speed skiing is rapidly gaining exposure and popularity globally, as the demand for more and varied extreme sport competitions grows.

While popular in Europe and included in the Winter Olympics (as here in Lillehammer, Norway 1994), insurance and legal problems have kept the sport limited in North America.

117

Steep Skiing

For years skiing has symbolized the carefree pursuit of sport in paradise-like winter settings around the world. Since the first skier rode downhill somewhere in Scandinavia, skiing has drawn free-spirited athletes to the mountains. But enjoyment of the sport became for many only a lifestyle statement, and the thrill of challenging terrain and conditions seemed to dwindle. Now a new generation of extreme athletes are redefining the meaning of downhill skiing.

Ski boot and binding technology has improved dramatically over the last few years and added valuable control to the skiers armory of skills.

Backcountry skiing is ever more possible with the addition of snowcat and helicopter access.

Leading steep skiiers, like Scottie Ewing, always ski with snowshoes, climbing gear and avalanche safety equipment.

SKI RESORTS HAVE TAMED SKIING. Snowcats, towed terrain-grooming equipment, gentle pistes, vista spots, posh resort restaurants—not long ago skiing was a very different pursuit of sport and challenge, and the relaxation came from winning a personal test of ability. Early skis were more like coasting snowshoes, used for survival and hunting (and undoubtedly fun as well). Then some nordic skiers (on nordic skis only the toe of the skier's boot is attached to the ski), tiring of fighting their gear on difficult descents, started fixing their heels down to create what would become known as alpine skiing. That in turn led to the first ski lifts, since the whole idea of alpine skiing is to ride down, not up.

Opening up the slope

Steep descents in the early days of alpine skiing required many of the mountaineering skills that today's top extreme skiers continue to use. Snowshoes, climbing gear, and avalanche safety equipment remain standard gear, with the obvious addition of helicopter and snowcat access to remote regions. These new transportation options have expanded the amount of terrain available for skiing, as well as the difficulty of the terrain that can be skied. Slopes of 60 degrees or more are not uncommon for the very best to ski successfully.

Ski, boot, and binding technology has improved dramatically over the years, reducing the number of injuries and adding valuable control to skiers who seek out steep

Slopes of over 60 degrees are not uncommon for the world's top steep skiers.

terrain. Some resorts even invite skiers to sample lift-served steep skiing as the popularity of extreme skiing has grown.

Although alpine skis would seem the most appropriate, it's not necessarily so. Alpine touring binding lets skiers free their heels for limited movement, giving them a way to climb with their equipment. But nordic equipment has also been refined, and now gives free-heeled telemark skiers the kind of added control that was not available even in the early days of alpine technology. As a result, many different athletes ski extreme terrain on a broad range of skiing equipment.

Exotic locations

Extreme skiing has been widely popularized by film makers, like Warren Miller and Greg Stump, whose movies are favorites worldwide. As skiers became more familiar with the types of terrain that were skiable, extreme steep skiing grew among those who saw skiing as a personal challenge. With the glamorization of steep skiing and the top experts who are featured in these films, more and more skiers are pushing it to "go big."

Going big means skiing the steepest terrain, dropping off large cliffs, and flying through the air. With top skiers this usually means

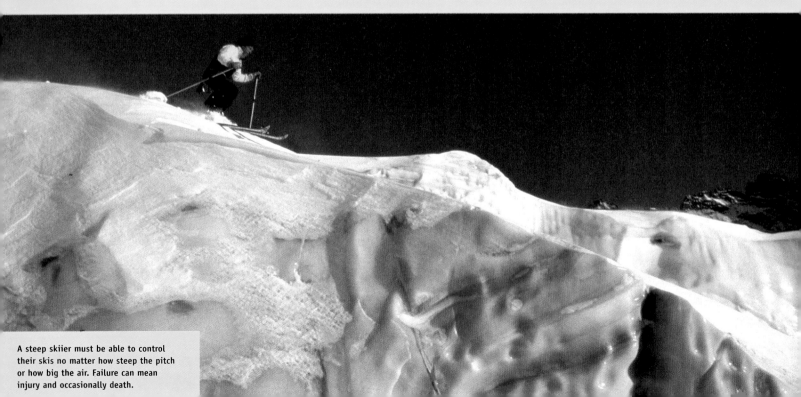

"Going big" on the Trash Chutes, Whitewater, British Columbia.

a controlled landing. With skiers who seek to emulate the top extreme skiers, but haven't yet developed the skills, this means pain. Every year, more and more extreme wannabees are getting themselves hurt, or even killed, attempting terrain and air that is too technical for their abilities. The lesson here is that to ski the most difficult terrain an athlete must be able to ski under control no matter how steep the pitch or how big the air. Even the best still get injured...and occasionally killed.

The European Alps, the North American Rockies, the South American Andes, and the Southern Alps of New Zealand all attract skiers from around the world for steep skiing adventures each year, and an entire industry has sprung up around providing access to

122

A steep skier must be able to control their skis no matter how steep the pitch or how big the air. Failure can mean injury and occasionally death.

There are few things in life that can match the feeling of charging down a steep powder run.

Steep skiing - the last frontier?

123

steep terrain. Each year thousands of skiers, and now snowboarders, travel to remote mountain peaks for a few thousand vertical feet of untracked terrain, an extreme skier's dream. There are very few things in life that can match the feeling of charging down a steep powder run.

The last frontier

A series of international events focusing on steep-terrain skiing have popped up over the past few years in each of these regions, with the World Championships held each year in Valdez, Alaska. These events are a fantastic showcase for not only the best extreme terrain skiers in the world, but also for some of the most beautiful places in the world. The interest in the events is exploding throughout the skiing world and beyond both because of the challenge and the scenery these events offer.

Extreme skiing is the last frontier of modern skiing, it fills the void for skiers who no longer find skiing in groomed terrain to be as exciting as it was. As skiing extreme regions becomes more and more popular, expect to find a lot more folks heading to the steeper challenges of technical terrain, and expect to see the future of skiing defined by extreme skiers.

Street Luge

The ice luge is an Olympic sport with which most of the world is familiar, and which few would deny is extreme. Enter the pavement version of the sport, street luge. While street lugers don't have specially-constructed tracks for their use, they do find steep and winding roads to roar down at speeds exceeding 70 mph (113 kph).

LIKE ICE LUGE, which can trace its roots to traditional sledding pushed to the limit, street luge is an extension of another form of downhill pavement travel...skateboarding. In fact, skateboarders have traveled downhill on their boards at speed, both lying down on their backs like a street luge, on their stomachs, and standing up.

The street luge is an evolution of the traditional skateboard design. The wheels and trucks (the combined axle and steering mechanism) used by skateboards and street luges are pretty much the same, though luges tend to have wider axles than skateboards. The decks used by skateboarders (the board part of a skateboard) are replaced by stiffer metal and composite-frame systems that allow the street luge to be made longer and track better than a skateboard.

Looking for velocity

Decks on street luges must be stiffer because as the speed of the boards increase, the stresses placed on the decks increase to the point that a deck that is not stiff enough will begin to move, allowing the wheels to wobble. The "high speed wobbles" are a big factor in limiting terminal velocity, not only in skateboards, but also inline skates, partly because the wheels do not have enough diameter or mass to stabilize themselves through centripetal force.

Once the luge deck is acceptable, the most important equipment to consider is, of course, the wheels themselves. At the speeds

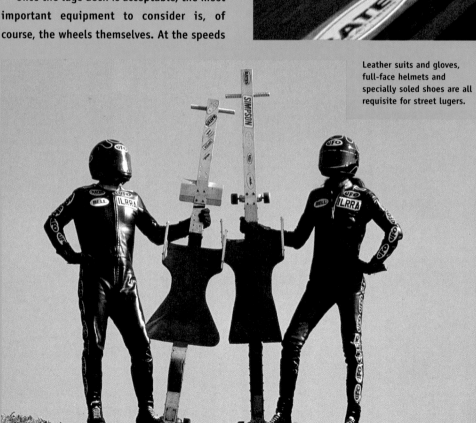

Leather suits and gloves, full-face helmets and specially soled shoes are all requisite for street lugers.

On the road in
Los Angeles,
California.

that street luges can travel, the bearings used to keep the wheels attached to the axles must work very hard, spinning almost as quickly as the wheels themselves. The slightest bit of friction within the bearing can "toast" a wheel, creating enough heat to melt the wheel where it contacts the bearing, and bringing a run to a quick stop. Therefore, street lugers pay particularly close attention to the details of cleaning and preparing their wheels before they start. Even so, dirt and dust particles can work their way into a bearing while the luger is moving, and the result can be the same.

Because lugers are traveling at high speeds on pavement, they must wear protective gear while riding. Most make use of the leathers worn by motorcycle riders and racers, which are generally expected to take all the abuse the luger's skin would suffer in the event of a fall. Leather gloves are also worn and a full-face helmet is necessary.

Pavement rockets

The final, and perhaps most important, piece of street luge equipment is the rider's footwear. The shoes are used as brakes, at which point they are exposed to the same kind of extreme heat as the wheels and bearings. Obviously, not just any shoe will work. Lugers use modified sneakers or boots to stop themselves. Typically, a section is

removed from an automobile tire and fixed to the shoes' soles, giving them grippy rubber capable of stopping a car without melting, never mind a luge.

Street luging got its unofficial start in the foothills of Southern California, where groups of riders first began flying down the steep, smooth, and winding roads for thrills. They soon began organizing races, and the sport was born. Street luging is still relatively new, and so we can expect a variety of improvements in the technology and speed of these pavement rockets as the sport develops. Who knows, someday maybe we'll even see specialty tracks like the ones used in ice luge.

Water
Sports

Water nourishes, and brings death. We are not naturally built to survive in it, but we are drawn to its many possibilities for extreme sports.

FURTHER INFORMATION

BIBLIOGRAPHY

● *Personal Watercraft*, Jack C. Harris, Edited by Michael E. Goodman, Crestwood House, Mankato, Minnesota, 1988
● *All Action Kayaking*, Alan Fox, Lerner Publications Company, Minneapolis, Minnesota, 1993
● *Performance Kayaking*, Stephen B. U'ren, Stackpole Books, 1990
● *A Trailside Series Guide: Kayaking*, Steven M. Krauzer, W. W. Norton & Co., New York, London, 1995
● *British Ocean Racing*, Douglas Phillips-Birt, Adlard Coles Ltd., 1960
● *Great Yacht Races*, Bob Fisher, Stewart, Tabori & Chang Publishers, New York, 1984
● *Surfing The Ultimate Pleasure*, Leonard Lueras, Workman Publishing, New York, 1984
● *Great Surfing*, Edited by John Severson, Doubleday & Co., Inc., Garden City, New York, 1967
● *The Complete Guide to Windsurfing*, Jeremy Evans, Facts on File Publications, New York, NY, 1983

ASSOCIATIONS & CLUBS

AIR CHAIR
■ Water Skier's Web - Air Chair
http://waterski.net/ac/index.html

BOARDSAILING
■ U.S. Windsurfing Association
PO Box 978, Hood River, OR 97031
Tel: (001) 503 386 8708
Fax: (001) 503 386 2108
uswa@aol.com
■ World Boardsailing Association
Feldafinger Platz 2,
München 71 D-8000
Germany
Tel: (0049) 89/781074
● *Body Boarding* (magazine)
PO Box 3010
San Clemente, CA 92672
Tel: (001) 714 492 7873
Fax: (001) 714 498 6485
■ *Windsurfing Magazine*
330 W. Canton
Winter Park, FL 32789
Tel: (001) 407 628 4802
Fax: (001) 407 628 7061
■ Windsurfing Glossary
http://allserv.rug.ac.be/
wdobbel/windserf/lexicom.html

JET SKIING
■ International Jet Ski Boating Association
1239 E, Warner Ave
Santa Ana, CA 92705
Tel: (001) 714 751 4277 or 714 751 8418

KAYAKING
■ Trade Association of Sea Kayaking
12455 N. Wauwatosa Rd.,
Mequon, WI 53097
Tel: (001) 414 242 5228
Fax: (001) 414 242 4428
■ American Canoe Association
7432 Alban Station Blvd, Suite B-226
Springfield, VA 22150
Tel: (001) 703 451 0141
Fax: (001) 703 451 2245
■ *Canoe and Kayak Magazine*
PO Box 3146,
Kirkland, WA 98083
Tel: (001) 206 827 6363
Fax: (001) 206 827 1893

LONG DISTANCE SWIMMING
■ Channel Swimming Association
Sunnybank
Alkham Valley Rd.,
Folkestone, Kent CT18 7EH, UK
Tel: (0044) 303 892229
Fax: (0044) 303 891033

SCUBA DIVING
■ SSI
2619 Canton Court,
Ft. Collons, CO 80525-4498
Tel: (001) 970 482 0883
Fax: (001) 970 482 6157
■ N. O. B. (Netherlands)
Nassaustraat 12, 3583 XG Utrecht,
Holland

WATER. NINETY PER CENT of our bodies are made of it. Two-thirds of the planet is covered by it. It is the most inhospitable of the the earth's elements for human survival, yet without it, life would cease. If indeed all life began in the water, as modern theories of evolution suggest, perhaps this explains why we are so attracted to it, and why being in or near it fosters a sense of synergy. It welcomes us through some ethereal sense of belonging, and we respond by seeking to find any way we can to have fun in and on it. For as long as there has been human life, there have been opportunities for sport in the water.

For centuries stories have been told about the terrible demise of sailors eaten by mammoth sea creatures. A legacy of artwork depicting scenes of horror, with monsters eating entire ships full of people, speaks volumes about how far from fearful superstition we have come. Many of the mysteries surrounding the depths of the oceans and lakes covering the planet have long been solved.

Sailboats are now built to be raced on courses that circumnavigate the globe. Consider that it was only 500 years ago that Columbus successfully crossed the Atlantic and found the New World, a trip that is now made daily in only hours by jet.

A DANGEROUS ELEMENT

Yet the oceans still have many dangers, both seen and unseen. Rocks or reefs clearly visible at a low tide might lie just beneath the water's surface at high tide. Being aware of them by seeing and understanding the clues they leave on the water's surface when they are submerged is a valuable skill, whether surfing or sailing. Being able to avoid them, especially at speed, can mean the difference between life and death.

Beneath the surface, the risks are far greater, ranging from being attacked by aggressive or hungry sea dwellers to falling prey to any one of several things that go wrong when using a

breathing apparatus. Human beings were not meant to survive under water, and by exploring its depths we leave ourselves exposed and vulnerable.

Rivers hold many of the same hidden dangers, yet they occur with such frequency that avoiding them is actually the sport. It is the rocks and boulders that give whitewater its name, not just the speed at which the water travels, and athletes wishing to test their abilities must be able to react quickly and decisively if they are to survive life-threatening situations.

When struck at speed, water takes on properties that are closer to cement than any liquid. The water's surface texture is ever-changing, creating opportunities for jumping, often at inappropriate times. Some sources for jumping are also sources of propulsion; such is the case with waves for boardsailors and surfers, who view surf very differently.

A VARIED CHALLENGE

How each athlete views water is as different as the sports they pursue. Large swells and waves make for great surfing, but without breeze, poor boardsailing. A strong breeze makes for great boardsailing, but strong winds can ruin an incredible surf day by changing the waves from clean and smooth to messy and chopped up.

What makes these water sports extreme is that each was created by redefining the limits of what was possible in terms of human and technological performance on and under the water. Anyone wishing to know how long a swimmer can stay submerged or how far a swimmer can travel under their own power can look to these sports for answers. That is because someone made it their task and their passion to find out for themselves what they were capable of doing in or on water.

■ ANU SCUBA Club (Australia)
Tel: (0061) 06 249 3490
■ Ontario Underwater Explorers (Canada)
contact Anthony Deboer
e-mail: (home) abd@herboid.reptiles.org
(work) abd@geac.com
Tel: (001) 905 508 4718
■ NYC Sea Gypsies (New York, U.S.)
e-mail: HarryW5594@aol.com
Tel: (001) 212 753 6603
■ Santa Clarita Dive Club
25335 Via Ramon,
Valencia, CA 91355
e-mail: xdcuste@dwp.la.ca.us
■ Dive Club 854 (Singapore)
Blk 510,
West Coast Drive, #09-319
Singapore, 0512
e-mail jgfsegny@technet.sg
(include phrase "To Tan Tsu Soo")
■ SCUBA Times (magazine)
14110 Peridido Key Dr., ste #16
Pensacola, FL 32507
Tel: (001) 904 492 7605
Fax: (001) 904 492 7607
■ SCUBA Diving (magazine)
http://www.scubadiving.com
6600 Abercorn St., Suite 208,
Savannah, GA 31405
Tel: (001) 912 351 08550
Fax: (001) 912 351 07550

SPEED SAILING
■ U.S. Sailing Association
PO Box 1260,
Portsmouth, RI 02871
Fax: (001) 401 683 0840
75530.502@compuserve.com
■ Yacht Racing Union International
60 Knightsbridge,
London SW1X 7JX, UK
Tel: (0044) 711235 9861

SURFING
■ International Surfing Association
5580 La Jolla Blvd, Suite 145,
La Jolla CA 92037
Tel: (001) 619 691 6893
Fax: (001) 619 691 0594
■ U.S. Surfing Federation
Kiernon and Angiulo
350 Jericho Turnpike,
Jericho, NY 11753
Tel: (001) 516 935 0400
Fax: (001) 516 942 4705
■ European Surfing Federation
45 Long Cram,
Haddington, Lothian EH41 4NS
Scotland
Tel: (0044) 62 0823973
Fax: (0044) 62 0823973
■ Surfing Magazine
33046 Calle Aviadar,
San Juan Capistrano, CA 92675
Tel: (001) 714 496 5922
Fax: (001) 714 496 7849
Subscription dept. Surfing Magazine
PO Box 54970
Boulder, CO 80322-4970
Tel: (001) 800 879 0484

WAKEBOARDING
■ Wakeboarding (magazine)
330 W Canton, Winter Park, FL 32789
Tel: (001) 407 628 4802
Fax: (001) 407 628 7061
http://www.rio.com/ wakezone/
■ Interactive Guide to Wakeboarding
(CD-ROM)
Tel: (001) 800 599 8856

WHITEWATER RAFTING
■ Nepal Association of Rafting Agents
PO Box 3586,
Kamaladi,
Kathmandu, Nepal
Tel: (00977) 220714
Fax: (00977) 226021
■ Wyoming River Raiders (retailers)
601 Wyoming River Blvd.
Casper, WY 82609
catalog: (001) 800 247 6068
■ The American Whitewater Affiliation
PO Box 636,
16 Bull Run Rd.
Margaretville, NY 12455
e-mail: 74663.2104@compuserve.com
Tel: (001) 914 586 2355
Fax: (001) 914 586 3050

Air Chair

The hydrofoil, a wing that creates lift in water, is not new, and hydrofoils are commonly used on powerboats today. They are even used on sailboats to minimize resistance and set speed records, which is itself an extreme endeavor. However, it wasn't until 1989 that a hydrofoil attached to a chair became commercially available for athletes seeking a new tow-behind water challenge.

THE AIR CHAIR, as it has become known, was designed by a couple of friends on the Colorado River, one of whom was the co-creator of the kneeboard (a waterski that the rider kneels on) and a hot dog waterski pioneer, Mike Murphy. Murphy's friend Bob Wooley became fascinated with the concept of riding a performance hydrofoil, and after several months of experimentation attached the foil to a "sit ski," a seated version of a waterski.

The seated foil rig was promising, and Wooley continued refining the design with Murphy. In 1989 they started the Air Chair company, and since then have sold thousands of Air Chairs. The device has proved popular for its radical spinning and flipping moves as well as the ease with which they can be learned. One of the sports pioneers and trick innovators is Tony Klarich, who has created a number of moves that are now considered standard.

Everyone's sport

The Air Chair is relatively easy to ride since once the foil is working the rig creates minimal drag. Jet-propelled personal watercraft and small boats with as little as 25 hp can tow the Air Chair. These advantages enable a broader spectrum of water sports enthusiasts to enjoy the device.

It is physically far easier to ride an Air Chair than it is to ski, kneeboard, or wakeboard. What makes the Air Chair extreme is that it uses technology to push the limits of performance. Reportedly the Air Chair is capable of attaining so much air in a jump that the only limitation on one's ability to achieve maximum air is mental. The foil breaks the shock of the landings, so impact is always pretty cushy and comfortable.

As a testament to how easy the device is to ride, Murphy's 77-year-old mother, Mary, rides an Air Chair. Whether or not she launches 20-foot (6m) jumps like Mike is another question. So while the Air Chair may not be the most physically challenging extreme sport, it is technologically cool enough to grab the attention of most extreme athletes.

131

The Air Chair is basically a sit ski (top), with the addition of a simple hydrofoil (left). This has created an incredibly mobile and enjoyable device which, despite appearances (below) is relatively easy to ride.

Barefoot Water Skiing

Sports are about competition, but also about contact. Sports which involve the thrill of speed invariably require specialized equipment to undertake them, but for the sportsman, the nearer to the elements you can get, the greater the sense of accomplishment. So for water skiers, what could make more sense than dispensing with the skis?

BAREFOOT WATER SKIING began in Winter Haven, Florida in 1947. Water skiing pioneer Chuck Sligh theorized that water skiing without skis might be possible if the ski boat went fast enough. A 17-year-old boy named AG Hancock proved him right, becoming the first water skier to drop a ski and continue barefoot successfully. Hancock left on a family vacation before he could show the trick to Cypress Garden's Dick Pope Sr.. A few days later, Pope's son Dick Jr. successfully dropped a ski and got all the glory— photographs, newspaper stories, newsreels, the works. Barefoot skiers soon adapted many of the freestyle moves of traditional waterskiers. Spins, backward maneuvers, body drags, and other tricks made barefooting an exciting new discipline. Due to the speeds required to barefoot, the tricks are especially difficult, and dangerous, since the water becomes very hard in a high-speed impact.

Barefoot water skiing quickly became a cult sport, especially in Australia. Barefoot clubs and competitions took place throughout the Sixties without too many people outside of the sport taking notice. Sometime around 1967 the Australians began experimenting with barefoot jumping. No one knows who the first barefoot jumper was, but he set in motion a chain of events that eventually brought his sport some long-overdue attention.

In 1973, the Australians introduced the Americans to barefoot jumping at the International Championships, held at Cypress Gardens. It wasn't until 1978 that jumping was included as an event at the first U.S. Barefoot Nationals. That same year Greg Rees of Australia set the first official world record at 44 feet (13.41m).

Bum jumpers

The techniques used at this time were foot-to-foot, where the jumper used his feet for both the take-off and the landing, and something called bum jumping. Bum jumpers went up and off the ramp on their buttocks and then tried to land on their feet, a technique that resulted in longer jumps, but was uncontrollable.

Even this spectacle wasn't enough to garner a lot of mainstream attention. That all changed in 1989 when U.S. jumper Mike Seipel accidentally invented the inverted style of jumping while training in Florida.

The first time it happened Seipel says the thought that occurred to him was "I'm going to kill myself," so he let go of the handle and splashed in. Then he realized that he had flown farther, so he tried it again, sticking the landing on his third try.

In the inverted style, the jumper pushes forward at the top of the ramp and lets the handle out. This puts the jumper horizontal to the water, flying most of the distance of the jump in that position, then swinging his body back down for a landing, hopefully on his feet and buttocks. The first time Seipel tried it in competition he broke the world record, flying 72.5 feet (22.10m).

The sport immediately exploded. Jumpers who were initially skeptical of the new technique quickly learned it, and average jumps went from 40–50 feet up to 60–70 feet. The current record of 90.88 feet (27.70m) is held by Australian Justin Sears, and the 100 foot mark is expected to fall soon.

(Left) Mike Seipel demonstrates his 'accidental' inverted style of jumping.
(This page) Marc Alexander of France shows what effect it had on him.

Boardsailing

Since it was first introduced to readers in a 1965 edition of *Popular Science* magazine, boardsailing has developed into one of the most visible and incredible of extreme sports. There is hardly a person alive who hasn't seen an athlete hurtling across the water or jumping into the sky on a wind-powered board.

THE SAILBOARD was invented by California surfer and businessman Hoyle Schweitzer and aeronautical engineer Jim Drake. Schweitzer reportedly conceived of the idea of putting a sail on a surfboard while Drake created the articulating sail rig that made the concept feasible. The two promptly applied for, and were granted, patents on their design and began the company that would be known worldwide as Windsurfer. For quite a while, the sport was known as "windsurfing," but because of trademark litigation, the growing industry renamed their sport "boardsailing." Either name is acceptable.

The original Windsurfer was a 12-foot (3.65m) long, heavy board made from pressure-molded ABS plastic. The boards were rough and their sail rigs were unrefined, using wooden booms (what the sailor holds onto) and inefficient sails. However, the sensation for early sailors was incredibly exciting and unlike what any other sailing vessel, including fast and exciting catamarans, could offer. Soon there were Windsurfers everywhere, and races began to be organized by enthusiasts. New equipment developed, including "harnesses" that allowed boardsailors to "hook in and hold on" for longer sessions with less fatigue.

Jean-Luc Vasse of France rides the big waves of Hookipa in Hawaii, widely regarded as the best wavesailing water in the world.

The exuberance of boardsailing is gaining the sport more and more popularity in all parts of the world.

Footstraps have ensured that being "slammed" is less likely for boardsailors.

The early harnesses had hooks on the chest that grabbed lines tied to the booms of the sail rig. Back fatigue and injuries resulted in a new "seat" harness designed to give better leverage and control over the rig, and decrease stresses placed on the sailor's back. But a problem the harness created was that a sailor hit by a large gust of wind, or off balance, could be catapulted forward and slammed into the water, or worse, into the board itself. Harnesses are now standard equipment for any boardsailor, however the opportunity to get slammed has not gone away.

Strapped for effect

The first groundbreaking modifications to Windsurfers were made by Hawaiian surfers. They started adding to their boards with footstraps and sails, and modern wavesailing was born. Early pioneers like Robby Naish are still leading athletes today. Windsurfer responded by creating their Rocket series of mass-production boards with footstraps and modified hulls. These boards were still heavy compared to the light fiberglass custom surfboard designs, but to the tens of thousands of people already boardsailing they delivered the thrill of sailing "strapped."

Ralf Bachschuster of Germany and Patrice Belbeoch of France demonstrate the relaxed attitude of today's top boardsailors to spectacular stunts, now part of their everyday repertoire.

Footstraps delivered a new dimension of control to boardsailing, allowing sailors to stay on their boards in winds that would have previously thrown them—being "slammed" became far less frequent. Being able to gain a more secure footing also let strong sailors break into new speed territory. Soon enough high-wind sailing made moderate winds look boring to extreme athletes, and the bigger heavy boards became the dinosaurs of boardsailing.

Riding a sinker

Custom and mass-produced performance boards became the "must have" equipment for expert boardsailors. As with many speed sports, lighter means faster, and stiffer means better control. Sailboarders seeking to sail in extreme conditions of high wind, or high wind and surf, found that once their boards were moving, they no longer required big boards. In fact, big hulls became unstable in high winds since the wind would constantly seek to rip the board away from the water and sailor. Smaller boards were easily made lighter, and those that could get started on them could do circles around other sailors. The smaller the boards became, the less buoyancy

they offered, to the point at which they no longer supported the sailor's weight unless they were moving and could ride on top of the water.

Riders wishing to sail these "sinkers" had to learn to do a "water start." In a water start, because the board cannot float with the sailor on it, the sailor lies in the water waiting for the sail to pick them up onto the board. As the sailor gets lifted up, the board begins moving, increasing its ability to support his weight. As the board accelerates, it planes (rides on top) on the water's surface, and is able to travel with little resistance. The sailor must keep the sail

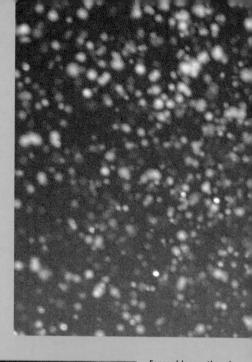

Forward loops, though still spectacular, are now standard fare for the world's top boardsailors.

properly trimmed (adjusted) to maximize the amount of force the available wind can give to move the board. Therefore, the better the sailor is at trimming the sail, the faster the board will travel.

Top experts can get their boards to travel at their maximum velocity for the wind and water conditions. The rest is a matter of strength and handling ability. An expert can steer the board with foot movement and weight transfer, using the board's rails (edges) to carve turns.

Board designs vary as to their maneuverability. Boards with straighter shapes and sharp (close to 90-degree angle) rails release the water from the bottom of the board better

138

Robby Naish demonstrates the ability that has kept him at the top level of boardsailing for many years.

and attain higher speeds, but are more difficult to turn, as they have a tendency to skip out of a hard turn. Boards with rounder shapes and loose (rounded) rails are highly maneuverable but don't go as fast.

Maintaining control

Boards also vary in rocker (the amount the bottom curves from the tip to tail of the board). Rocker placement varies from board to board, and on each board. Boards with more rocker in the tail will be slower but more maneuverable, while boards with less tail rocker will plane quicker and go faster. Each board designer places rocker in different places determined by the performance desired, and each boardsailor prefers a different feel and shape.

Early "short" board designs looked more like surfboards than today's top shapes. Board buoyancy is measured by volume, so less volume means less floatation. Designers shift the volume around in their boards, placing more or less in the tip or tail dramatically effects performance. Short boards started out with massive amounts of volume in the tail. One early design by top boardsailor Ken Winner actually had a hump though the middle of the rear deck of the board, and a pointy front. Designers gradually reduced the volume in the back of the boards, moving it forward under the mast base.

The volume-forward shapes were the predominant style of short boards until the early Nineties, when designers discovered they could reduce the length and increase board performance by centering the volume under the sailor, much like Winner's early design, but without the hump. The "no nose" designs have greatly reduced volume in the front, with much of the rail shape occurring farther back in the board. Essentially what they've done is to use a very short board and lengthen the tip to create a moderately short board. Either way, these boards are a vast improvement over designs only a few years old.

Getting up, of course, requires getting down, and top experts are in control during flight, using their sail as a wing to float down to the water. What boardsailors can do in the air has changed dramatically over the years as equipment has changed and sailors have redefined the limits of performance.

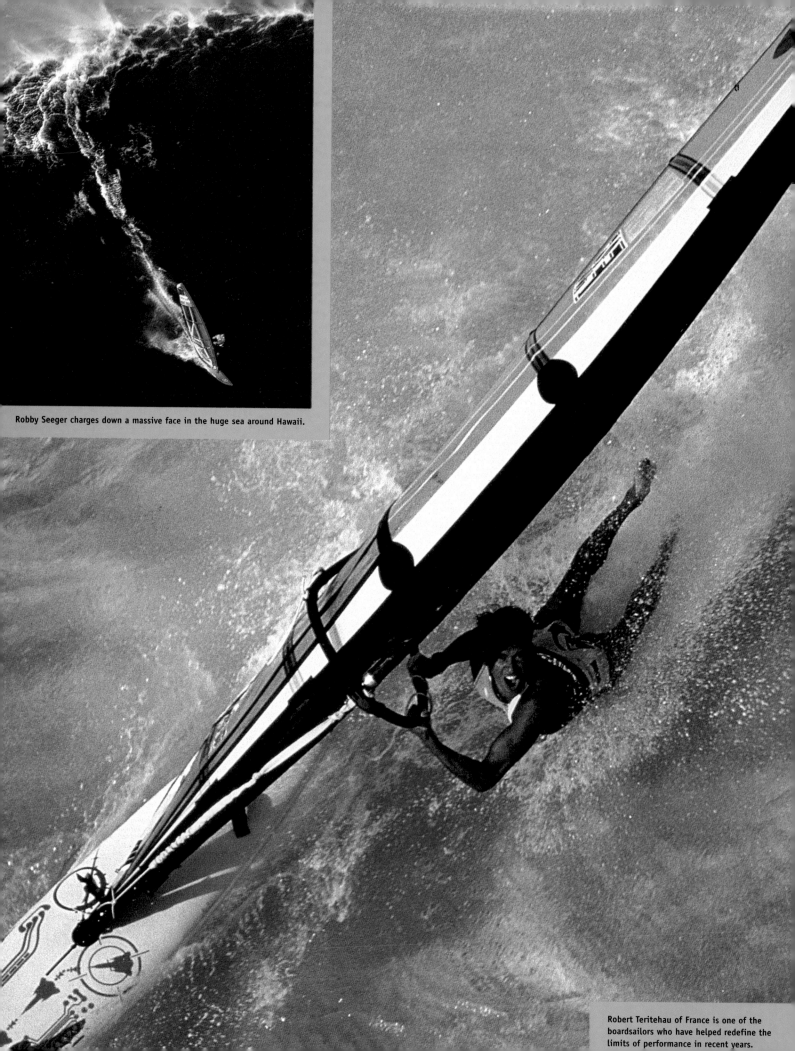

Robby Seeger charges down a massive face in the huge sea around Hawaii.

Robert Teritehau of France is one of the boardsailors who have helped redefine the limits of performance in recent years.

360 degree spins are also possible and visually stunning.

Tricks like "forward loops" (front flip) are now standard fare for top experts. In a forward loop, the sailor goes as fast as possible into a wave and, while airborne, pulls hard on the sail at the same time as leaping forward. This highly technical trick is amazing to watch—360-degree spins are also possible and exciting.

Rigged to wing it

One of the best technological advances in boardsailing was the introduction of the R.A.F. (Rotating Aerodynamic Foil) and Camber-Inducing batten systems. The R.A.F. system was the first to be introduced, and it allowed sails to take on more rigid, wing-like shapes when rigged. R.A.F. design made sails

far easier to handle in high and gusty wind conditions because they created smoother shapes with less drag. Drag pulls on a sail, sometimes violently, and decreases top end velocity. Camber Inducers were introduced when sailmakers added enough length to the sail's battens (fiberglass or composite sticks that add stability to the sail's shape) to connect them to the mast that supports the sail. Camber Inducers allowed sailmakers to design rigid shapes that are incredibly efficient and easy to handle. The softer R.A.F. designs are best used in the waves, while Camber sails are best used for speed, as they are more fragile and easily damaged in surf.

Owning the equipment is not cheap if bought new, however, good used stuff is out

there. When considering buying used gear keep in mind that the sail and rig are the "engine," and therefore the most important items. Even an old ugly board can out-perform a new one if the sails are better or equal. Look for signs of excessive wear on the cloth like abrasions, cuts, repairs, and stretched or threadbare seams. Any combination of these can point to a terrible sail. The only true way to tell if a sail is good is to rig it and look at the shape. Those who can't tell a good shape from a bad one should ask an experienced friend to help. The shape should look curved like an airplane wing.

The best sites

Sailing sites vary in their appeal. Some sites, like Hookipa on Maui, are world-renowned for their huge waves and high winds. Hookipa is widely regarded as the best wavesailing in the world, since it offers high winds running at 90 degrees to the large Hawaiian surf, allowing expert sailors to sail full speed into the huge faces and shoot as high as 30 feet (9m) in the air. Another great sailing site is the Columbia River Gorge in Oregon, where the wind roars at up to 60 mph (96kph) up the river against a current heading the other way. The strong current and wind work together to create huge rolling waves, which attract thousands of sailors in the late summer each year. Other heavily visited sites include the Canary Islands, Southern France, Southern Spain, and the Caribbean.

One of the great things about boardsailing is that all you need is water, wind, and a board. The fun is just part of the deal. Just about anyone who can swim can boardsail. Anyone brave enough to seek a little instruction will find it is remarkably easy to do if you know a few basics of how the set-up works. Once a new sailor has learned how to get up and ride a sailboard, the trip from big board to short board sailing isn't long. All that's needed is some time and patience, and a little perseverance.

141

Freediving

Swimming into the deepest reaches of the ocean is a feat that many divers have experienced to a degree. Some may go below 200 feet (60m), others deeper. All would be lost without the air they bring with them. There is a special breed of diver who can go deeper than most, without air tanks. These freedivers have pushed the limits of unassisted breathing dives to below 400 feet.

TO FREEDIVE TO DEPTHS of even 50 feet (15m) is an unsettling prospect for all but the strongest swimmers. To dive much deeper requires holding a breath for minutes. In fact, the world's best freedivers hold their breath for periods that rival many marine mammals.

There are three categories of freediving for depth. First there is "fixed weight" or "fixed volume" diving. Divers in this discipline swim down as deep as they can under their own power, and resurface the same way. This means using up valuable air in the descent, limiting the speed at which they can get deep, and the depths attainable. The current record is over 240 feet (73m), and was set by Frenchman Eric Charrier in 1995. Fixed weight divers use high-technology composite swim fins to aid them in going down and coming up.

Second is "variable weight" freediving, in which ballast is used to aid divers descend; up to one-third of body weight is considered legal. Variable weight divers can get down faster and with less effort than fixed weight divers, yet they must still swim back to the surface under their own power. Again the use of special fins is a requirement.

Third is called "absolute" diving, which allows unlimited ballast in the descent, with rates reaching between 12–15 feet per second (3.65–4.6m). To return to the surface, the diver grabs a lifting aid, such as an inflatable bag. Cuban diver Francisco "Pepin" Ferreras-Rodriguez holds the current record at 417 feet (127m), an amazing depth. Pepin boasts an extraordinary lung capacity, and has been freediving since age seven.

Advanced breathing

How divers like Pepin reach these depths is by learning to control their body's ability to sustain them between breaths. But regardless of how it is done, prolonged periods between breaths can result in latent hypoxia, or "shallow water blackout." Ironically, shallow water blackout occurs usually just below the surface and the diver can drown if unassisted. Many use advanced breathing methods, like the Tai'Chi yoga breathing technique. These methods aid the divers in controlling and even reducing the rate of their metabolism, thus decreasing the need for oxygen. Another—though less zen-related method—is to hyperventilate. This involves prolonged deep breathing before the dive, which increases the ratio of oxygen in the lungs and effectively "tricks" the body into lowering its need to breathe so frequently. This is not as effective as meditation.

Freedivers must economize their movement in order to maximize their time underwater. Each move requires oxygen, and there is clearly a limited supply. Good divers don't rush the process and, as a result, can remain underwater for longer periods.

Freediving embodies the extreme athlete's quest for inner control and improved performance in sports. Without question, a failed attempt can end in death and, as with so many other extreme sports, the athlete must be fully prepared both mentally and physically if they are to succeed.

Freediving is the province of the few. It embodies the athlete's quest for inner control and improved performance under the most difficult circumstances. Superb swimming skills, mental and physical preparation are essential for successful and safe freediving.

Jet Skiing

Motorcycles have always attracted people with a yearning for speed and an appetite for adrenaline. For years, the closest thing anyone could get to that sensation on the water was in a small boat with a big motor. These were fast, but could hardly be called maneuverable. Then in 1965 a Californian banker with a passion for motorcycles conceived of an aquatic version which would become known worldwide as the Jet Ski.

CLAYTON JACOBSON enjoyed building racing motorcycles in his spare time. He loved going fast on motorcycles—but crashing on hard pavement was not what he considered to be their appeal. The concept of the Jet Ski was born from Jacobson's theory that a motorcycle for the water would be just as fun to ride as the ones he enjoyed building, but without the pain of a hard landing if you fell off. Mr. Jacobson would be correct.

Jacobson built a few prototypes from his designs, and after being issued a patent in 1969, licensed his design to Ski-Doo manufacturer Bombardier. Bombardier ran into several problems and halted development a year later. Their license to use the design expired in 1971, and within months Jacobson signed a deal with Kawasaki to use his design. In 1973 Kawasaki introduced the Jet Ski, the first stand-up personal watercraft. Clayton Jacobson's concept soon became one of the most successful boat designs in history.

What made the Jet Ski possible was that Jacobson utilized a jet water-pump system rather then the Sixties state-of-the-art inboard or outboard motor propulsion systems. These motors utilize an external propeller to provide thrust. The Jet Ski design uses an internal water-jet motor for thrust. The motor draws water into itself and shoots a stream out again to generate thrust, without exposing potentially hazardous blades that can injure a rider. Current engines deliver in excess of 85

Jet skiing events are broken down into three classes. The first (above) is the Runabout, designed for craft that seat more than one person. The second (below) is the Sport Division with lighter, higher performance craft, and the third (right) is the Ski Division designed for one stand-up rider.

Freestyle jet skiing showcases the individual skills of each rider.

horsepower and can push the Jet Ski to speeds exceeding 50 mph (80kph).

The correct term for the jet-driven craft currently available is "personal watercraft." The term Jet Ski is a registered trademark of the Kawasaki Corporation. Kawasaki had exclusive domain over the jet-driven personal watercraft until 1987, when several would-be rivals entered the market with sit-down versions. Because the sit-down design is far less physically demanding than the stand-up Jet Ski, they have far broader consumer appeal, and now make up over 95 per cent of the personal watercraft market.

Both stand-up and sit-down designs offer a sense of freedom and performance that is unrivaled by other small motorized boats. They allow riders to use their bodies to enhance the watercraft's performance. Much like the motorcycles they were intended to replicate, personal watercraft give riders a wind-and-water-in-the-face sensation that is addictive to say the least.

Racing and freestyle

Competitive events are held internationally, and include closed-course racing and freestyle riding. The freestyle events are meant to showcase each rider's skills by requiring them to execute a series of difficult and creative maneuvers within a predetermined time period, generally two minutes. Each rider is scored by a panel of seven judges, issuing points from 1–10. The rider with the highest score wins. Riders execute a range of tricks, including submerging their watercraft and shooting it up out of the water, as well as jumps and spins requiring strength and agility.

The closed-course races require groups of riders to race each other around a set of buoys, with the winner determined at the finish line. The closed courses include a series of right- and left-hand turns, requiring riders to be strong all-around drivers. These races take place as a series of elimination heats. The top finishers advance to the next race until a group reaches the final heat. The finishing positions in the final heat determine the overall winners.

Events are broken down into three classes. First is the Runabout Division, consisting of sit-down personal watercraft designed to seat one or more. Second is the Sport Division, which uses lighter, higher-performance versions of sit-down watercraft. Third is the Ski Division, which comprises stand-up designs for one rider.

Safety first

In many ways personal watercraft have redefined water activities and their costs. These vehicles average around $8,550 (£5,700), bringing a new affordability to performance watercraft. This is especially inexpensive when you consider that many outboard motors of similar horsepower cost around the same price without the boat attached.

Because they were designed to be fallen from, each personal watercraft has at least one of two safety devices built in. First is an automatic steering mechanism to direct the watercraft in circles after a rider has fallen off. Second is a cord that is attached to the driver and the ignition system. If the rider falls off, the engine turns off and the watercraft awaits the swimming driver.

Even these safety devices cannot replace commonsense. All personal watercraft riders should wear floatation devices, and a helmet is a good idea too, when extreme riding. Many drivers like to spin their boats around and travel at high speed close to other riders, and often in opposing

One of the latest developments of the sport is indoor "Super Jet Ski" competitions like this one in Paris, France.

directions. Top experts may be capable of doing this with reasonable control, but novices should consider staying away from other watercraft, especially other novices, The craft are heavy, travel at deceptively high speeds, and collisions can have terrible consequences.

Jet-drive watercraft are used for a range of sports today, including waterskiing, wake-boarding, and—most dramatically—tow-in surfing, a sport that started in the massive waves off Maui, Hawaii, where personal watercraft drivers can quickly tow surfers on narrow high-performance surfboards out to big waves that would be unsurfable if the

surfers weren't moving before the wave caught them.

The popularity of personal watercraft is underscored by the frequency with which they are visible at beaches and on waterways around the world. There is not a beach resort anywhere that doesn't have at least one available for rent. The reason seems obvious, personal watercraft allow boaters and non-boaters the opportunity to get out on the water and experience a sense of freedom that was previously only reserved for motorcyclists.

147

Closed-course races run around a series of buoys, requiring the successful navigation of tight right- and left-hand turns.

Open Water Swimming

Swimming long distances for sport is a challenge that only the most fit and determined extreme athletes pursue. Its roots can be traced back to 1875 when Captain Matthew Webb became the first swimmer to cross the English Channel. Since then, crossing the channel has been one of the more defining feats of long distance, or open water, swimming. Open water is the appropriate term, since races and crossings are never held in a pool, that would be too easy and lacking danger.

OPEN WATER SWIMMING races are held globally, and were included in many of the early Olympic Games. Course lengths are usually 5, 10, 15, or 25 kilometers (3–15.5 miles) and require several hours to complete. The courses are set between two points on any large body of water. Some races require athletes to do several laps to complete a given distance, while others may consist of one very long lap.

Open water swimming may seem like an individual achievement, however open water swimmers always work with a coach, who travels nearby in a boat. The coach's job is to monitor the swimmer's performance, give feedback, and insure the swimmer doesn't get into danger while competing. The coach's boat also doubles as a rescue craft.

Although apparently a individual's sport, long distance swimmers cannot do without the support of a coach, who will offer encouragement, food and even the occasional drink.

Swimmers can come across several natural hazards during the course of an event, ranging from life-threatening sea creatures to debris and rough water. The coach endeavors to guide the swimmer around any hazards. A common hazard is jellyfish. The threat of being stung is ever present, and given that most stings occur directly on the face and neck, a most unpleasant event. Another is sharks.

When a shark is sighted, swimmers naturally react by swimming faster out of added adrenaline. Attacks, however, are not common, and it is the coach's duty to assess any shark presence for signs of aggressive behavior.

Swimmers are not allowed to wear any kind of wetsuit, so hypothermia (becoming super-cold) is a key concern during any event. Again, it is the duty of the coach to determine if the swimmer is becoming hypothermic, and if so to encourage them to work harder to boost their body temperature. If the swimmer is unable to combat hypothermia, it is the coach's job to get them out of the water and retire from the race, a task that is not always as easy as it sounds.

Physical demands

Open water swimmers must be in tremendous physical condition in order to deal with the demands these events put upon them. Athletes must train constantly, with little opportunity for diversity. The stamina and pain thresholds for each athlete must be at maximum for them to be competitive. Swimmers must maintain effort through rough and cold water, persevere in difficult currents, tidal surges, and wind-driven waves. Any one of these can cause the contestant to lose way, even lose some of the distance they've worked so hard to cover.

Open water swimming is an extreme endurance event in which only the most determined succeed.

Powerboat Racing

Creating vehicles capable of traveling at fantastic speeds has been one of the common goals of extreme sports for as long as the technology to do so has existed. Not very long ago, motorized boats capable of 30–40 mph (48–64kph) were considered fast. Now the technology of boat construction and the horsepower available to the engines has given us power boats able to exceed 140 mph (225kph).

THE DRIVING FORCE in the quest for powerboat speed has been racing. Since the first powerboat sped across the English Channel in 1903, the quest for speed has pushed powerboat technology forward tremendously. That sprint from Calais, France to Dover, England took place on a 39-foot (12m) hull powered by a 75 horse power Daimler engine. Pleasure boaters can use that kind of power plant on one of many small, light fiberglass boats commercially available without even blinking. Open-class racing boats today boast horse power ratings of over 1000.

Powerboats use two different types of engine. The first and original power plant is the "inboard" engine. Inboards are placed in the middle of the hull and turn a propeller via a driveshaft that passes through the hull toward the stern of the boat. Still widely used in racing, inboards offer a low center of gravity which improves the boat's stability.

Hulled for speed

Second is the "outboard." Outboards are essentially lightweight units clamped to the transom (the vertical plane at the stern). Outboards are commonly used to power smaller racing hulls and pleasure boats, and because they are compact and outside the hull, their use creates more room for gear and occupants. The drawback is the height of the weight placement of the motor, and the placement of the weight so far back in the hull. This makes outboard-powered hulls less

(Above) Outboard powerboat racing is popular as it is at the cheaper end of the powerboat spectrum. Unlike the modern racing "cats" (below) which have to exist in the corporate world of the sponsor.

stable than inboard-powered, especially when the motors are proportionately large compared to the boat.

Racing boats utilize three distinct hull designs. First is the "Deep V" originated by U.S. designer Dick Bertram. The hull has a V-shape running through the hull's center from the bow (front) to the stern (rear). The angle of the V is sharp at the bow and gradually tapers to a flatter angle at the stern. A series of "steps" runs the length of the hull, and provides lift and stability. Bertram's Deep V changed the powerboat world virtually overnight after winning the 1960 Miami Nassau Race in a record eight hours. The design, with its sharp angles forward and stepped hull, allowed his boat to travel faster in rougher conditions than the flatter, unstepped hulls of the period. Today, almost every modern V-hull utilizes Bertram's design.

Cats and foils

Second is a catamaran design consisting of two very sharp V-hulls mounted side by side. Modern racing "cats" are more efficient and therefore require less horsepower than the single V-hull design. Where races allow both V- and cat-hulls to compete, more powerful engines are usually allowed in the V-hull designs to offset the cats' advantage in efficiency.

Third is the hydrofoil design, which uses a wide, flat hull and two shallow asymmetrical cat-style hulls mounted forward and outside of the flat central hull. Used only in flat-water areas, these boats use tremendous horsepower to accelerate out of the turns in what are

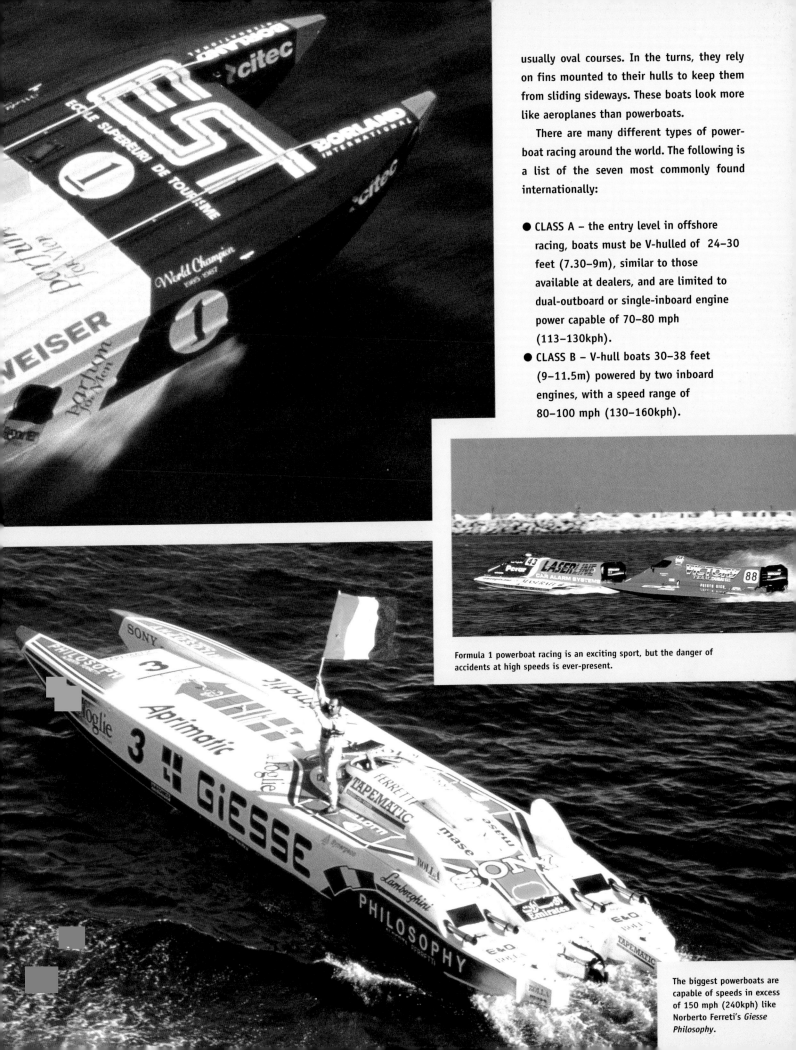

usually oval courses. In the turns, they rely on fins mounted to their hulls to keep them from sliding sideways. These boats look more like aeroplanes than powerboats.

There are many different types of powerboat racing around the world. The following is a list of the seven most commonly found internationally:

- CLASS A – the entry level in offshore racing, boats must be V-hulled of 24–30 feet (7.30–9m), similar to those available at dealers, and are limited to dual-outboard or single-inboard engine power capable of 70–80 mph (113–130kph).
- CLASS B – V-hull boats 30–38 feet (9–11.5m) powered by two inboard engines, with a speed range of 80–100 mph (130–160kph).

Formula 1 powerboat racing is an exciting sport, but the danger of accidents at high speeds is ever-present.

The biggest powerboats are capable of speeds in excess of 150 mph (240kph) like Norberto Ferreti's *Giesse Philosophy*.

154

- CLASS C – catamarans of 28–30 feet (8.5–9m) powered by two outboard engines capable of between 100–110 mph (160–177kph)—consistently one of the most evenly matched classes.
- CLASS P – "pro stock" racers, all cat designs of 30–38 feet (9–11.5m), with three outboard engines and top speeds averaging 100–115 mph.
- CLASS M – "Modified" class hulls can be either cat or V design. V hulls are allowed to carry more horsepower due to the efficiency advantage cat hulls have.
- OPEN CLASS – hulls generally in excess of 35 feet (11m), with engines of 1,000 horsepower and greater, capable of around 135 mph (217kph)—the premier class of offshore racing.
- UNLIMITED CLASS – unlimited hydrofoils—the fastest of powerboat racers, but their designs confine them to the calm waters of lakes and protected shore regions—are powered by inboards, outboards, and even jet engines capable of speeds exceeding 150 mph (240kph).

Powerboats are prone to violent crashes, mostly due to the unlevel surface of water. If hit at high speed, water behaves more like cement that you would imagine.

Offshore racing boats have a crew of two or three in order to effectively manage their hulls at speed. The driver must concentrate solely on steering and keeping the boat under control, while an additional crew member controls the throttle and navigates. A third may be onboard as navigator for the larger Open Class boats.

Powerboats are prone to violent crashes, largely thanks to inconsistent water surfaces. Even small waves hitting the hull in an odd or unexpected way are capable of sending boats flying out of the water where they become like uncontrollable aircraft. Sometimes landings can be smooth, but backward flips and hard impacts are more likely. And because of the excessive speeds, the results can be deadly—at 100+ mph, water behaves like cement.

Engine fires, fuel fires, and even explosions are other occurrences encountered. In fact modern racing boats are designed to self-destruct in the event of a crash in order to lessen the impact on the occupants, much like modern automotive designs. Impact zones and energy-absorbing construction techniques are doing much to reduce the frequency of serious driver injuries.

Prepared for disaster

Because the boats are prone to accidents, many occupants use a five-point harness system for protection. But some crews prefer not using safety harnesses in order to be thrown clear of the hull if they do crash—the greatest fear is being held underwater and drowned in the event of an accident.

Unlike most extreme sports, powerboat racing is expensive, and so crews rely on sponsors to buy signage on their hulls in order to offset the financial burden. Powerboats require a lot of time in testing designs and engines to insure competitiveness, further adding to the cost of racing. Many top teams spend well in excess of $1.5 million (£1 million) annually to be competitive and race.

The nature of powerboat racing requires participants to constantly test and reevaluate current technologies. As these technologies are advanced, it is conceivable that something will happen to enhance the safety of racing. However, it is unlikely that traveling at speed on the water will ever be considered a thrill that anyone but an extreme enthusiast will enjoy.

Cat hull-powerboats require much less horsepower than the single V-hull designs.

Round the World

The Trophée Jules Verne

When Jules Verne penned his classic novel *Around the World in 80 Days* in the late nineteenth century, he relied heavily on his imagination to propel hero Phileas Fogg and trusty servant Passepartout in their land, sea, and air circumnavigation of earth. Today, that imagination is embodied in the Trophée Jules Verne, a crewed non-stop race around the world. While Fogg and Passepartout traveled by ship for a fraction of their voyage, this race is entirely waterborne.

(Above and right) The *Commodore Explorer*, captained by Frenchman Bruno Peyron, in 1993 became the first sailing vessel to circumnavigate the globe by water in less than 80 days.

Yacht Racing

THE RACE BEGAN in the fall of 1993, when a French and a New Zealand entry passed an imaginary line stretching across the western approaches to the English Channel, which is also where they would be required to finish. The two multihulls streaked down the Atlantic Ocean until, somewhere south of Cape Town, South Africa, the New Zealand entry hit a submerged object. One of its hulls damaged, the crew were forced to life-saving measures to keep the catamaran afloat. They eventually made port under

their own power, to return a year later to play an important role in the development of this young race.

As the New Zealanders limped toward South Africa, the Frenchmen pressed on. A six-man crew led by world record-holder Bruno Peyron, and including American specialist Cam Lewis, were sailing a huge and powerful catamaran, *Commodore Explorer*. The craft measured 88 feet (27m).

Catamarans are among the fastest type of sailboat in the world. With their hulls spread

so far apart and the main power unit, the mast and mainsail, placed in between those hulls, catamarans can leverage the wind, sailing nearly twice as fast as the windspeed in a variety of wind and sea conditions.

Success

Harnessing and controlling speed, both windspeed and boatspeed, is a problem with multihulls, and is most problematic in the winds and waves of the Southern Ocean. With no land mass to slow the prevailing currents of

The *Commodore Explorer*'s arrival at the finishing line was greeted with a spectacular example of the effectiveness of flares at sea.

wind and water, the Southern Ocean, generally considered the body of water below latitude 50°S, is the most treacherous body of water on the planet. Wave heights topping 50 feet (15m) and windspeeds in excess of 75 mph (120 kph) can develop instantly, bringing with them hail, sleet, or blinding snowstorms.

With no visibility, radar is heavily relied on to see icebergs that could sink a boat with just a glancing blow. Most bergs are the size of a New York City street block, so the electronic seeing eye usually picks them up easily. Not so visible, however, are "growlers," large chunks of ice that break off the bergs. Growlers are typically half-submerged and commonly jut out underwater. They are so sharp that they can easily puncture the composite hulls of today's ocean racing sailboats.

The Frenchmen survived the trials and tribulations of a circumnavigation. They survived collisions with whales, they survived hurricanes, they survived hull damage, they survived hitting submerged logs, and they rewarded themselves by becoming the first sailing vessel to circumnavigate the globe by water in less than 80 days. They covered 27,372 miles (44,041 km) in 79 days, 6 hours, 15 minutes and 56 seconds, a total of 1,902 consecutive hours at sea.

Their record would stand for only a year, though. The New Zealanders returned, led by two of the more famous modern circum-navigators, and crushed *Commodore Explorer*'s record. Skippers Peter Blake, winner of the Whitbread Round the World Race, and Robin Knox-Johnston, the first man to single-handedly circumnavigate the globe non-stop, created a team full of experience and commonsense.

An extreme legend

They used the experience gained in their previous, aborted attempt to modify their catamaran. They increased its overall length to 92 feet (28m), modified the hull shape, and changed the rig configuration. The new and improved craft then took them and a crew of five around the world in a record time of 74 days, 22 hours, 17 minutes and 22 seconds, a record which still stands.

They sailed almost 1,000 miles less than the original record-setters because they went much deeper into the Southern Ocean, below latitude 60°S, taking advantage of the earth's natural curvature to sail less distance, and set 12 world records along the way. Their determination to risk their lives and their boat in order to establish a new level of global sailing performance is the stuff of extreme sailing legend, and a feat that will be difficult to better.

159

Peter Blake (left) and Robin Knox-Johnston (center) are congratulated by vanquished skipper Bruno Peyron, after they shattered his record in1994 by almost 5 days.

The Whitbread Race

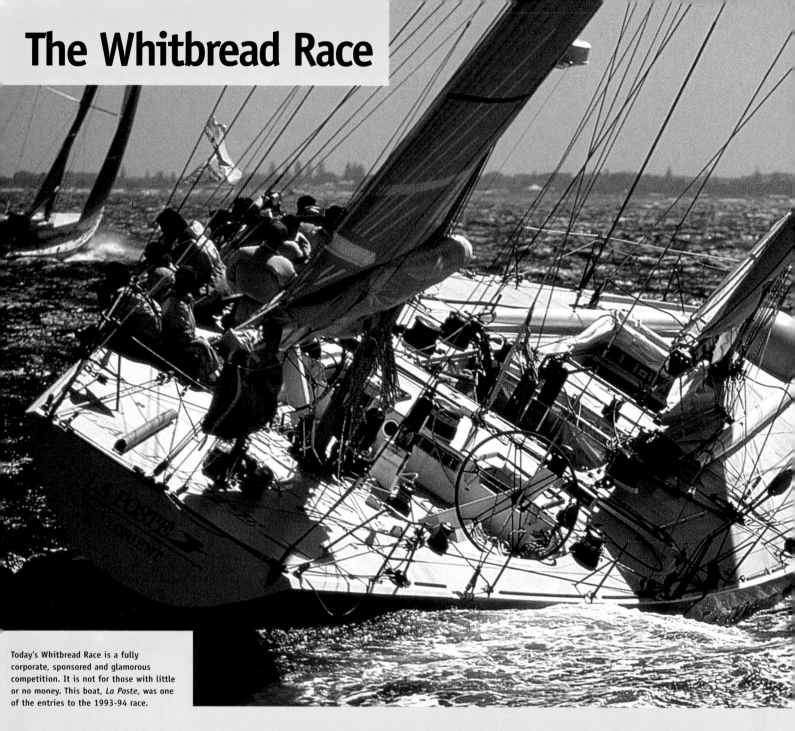

Today's Whitbread Race is a fully corporate, sponsored and glamorous competition. It is not for those with little or no money. This boat, *La Poste*, was one of the entries to the 1993-94 race.

Offshore sailboat racing has two distinct disciplines. At one end of the spectrum is singlehanded sailing, where a solitary skipper puts his sailing knowledge, navigational expertise, will—even his life—on the line. At the other is crewed sailing, where crews between 12–20 sailors, specializing in particular tasks, rely upon one another as a team in the quest for victory.

AMONG THE GREATEST RACES in the world in crewed racing is the Whitbread Round the World Race. Dubbed the "ultimate ocean race," it was the first of its kind, with origins dating back to 1973.

Four years earlier, in 1969, Englishman Robin Knox-Johnston had won the Golden Globe Race, and was the first to singlehandedly circumnavigate the globe non-stop. He was one of eight to start the challenge sponsored by London newspaper *The Sunday Times*, but the only sailor to finish. The event was considered more a challenge than a race because competitors were allowed to begin their voyage at any time between June and October of 1968.

Knox-Johnston's accomplishment started a frenzy of activity to organize the first official round the world race for fully-crewed sailboats. Watching with keen interest were the British navy and army, who were in the process of obtaining several 55-foot (17m) boats for adventure training. When rivals couldn't get a race organized by April 1972, the British navy forged ahead with the Whitbread, and in September 1973 a legend was born.

Lives lost

The first competition was historic for many reasons: it was the first, crewed, circum-navigational race of its kind; it was the first race of its kind to send crews into the treacherous waters known as the Roaring Forties and Screaming Fifties—the Southern Ocean; and it resulted in the fastest, crewed circumnavigation of its time.

The race—the Southern Ocean in particular—proved even more challenging than the competitors had imagined. Leg two of the four-legged course took the fleet of 17 entrants from Cape Town, South Africa, to Sydney, Australia; and leg three went from Sydney to Rio de Janeiro, Brazil. Not only were these extremely long distances to sail, but they covered the Southern Ocean, the great expanse of water separating the six inhabited continents from the seventh, Antarctica. Unimpeded by land, storm systems sweep across these deep southern latitudes, gaining so much force that they become life threatening.

Three lives were lost in the Southern Ocean, all the result of crew members falling overboard. One sailor was presumably unconscious when a sheet flung him over. Another was swept off the deck during a sail change, when a huge breaking wave hit the boat. The third man was lost as he went forward for a sail change, apparently lost his footing and fell overboard. Down below on the vessels, crews worked frantically to keep water out of the boats—an almost impossible task when you're sailing at latitude 60°S for two weeks at a time.

Today, the Whitbread Race is a fully corporate, sponsored, and highly glamorous competition. The event occurs every fourth year beginning in the fall, and finishes in the spring, some six months later. Whereas the first race in 1973/74 was largely a corinthian effort, today some skippers can earn as much as $150,000 (£100,000) to lead a corporation's entry. There are more legs for the next race than there were in the original, nine as opposed to four, and the boats are drastically different.

Mental peak

Unlike the crews of the original Whitbread, their counterparts today are as much concerned with how to get water into the boat as they are with keeping it out. The introduction of water-ballast systems (very common among the singlehanded spectrum) is a feature on the new Whitbread 60 class of boats, 60-footers (18m) capable of reaching speeds nearly three times as great in the Southern Ocean as the 1973-74 pioneers were able to.

The Whitbread incorporates a vast array of challenges ranging from surviving powerful storms, to exhaustion, and even continuing after crew deaths. The crews are aware that they too could be lost at sea, that their yachts may not return, and that—at the very least—they will be required to perform at their physical and mental peaks for months with only a few onshore breaks. This is team sailboat racing at its most extreme.

161

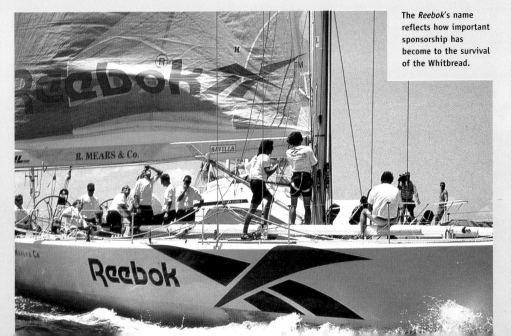

The *Reebok*'s name reflects how important sponsorship has become to the survival of the Whitbread.

The BOC Challenge and the Vendée Globe

Singlehanded racing is the aquatic version of marathon running, where the skipper has to draw from resources deep within himself for the endurance and stamina necessary to sail 30 days or more alone at sea. Unlike the marathon runner, whose most important equipment is his shoes, a singlehanded sailor's equipment is a sailboat often as large as 60 feet (18m) and its accompanying systems—and it all has to be maintained continuously.

(Above) Frenchman, Philippe Poupon in charge of his boat *Fleury Michon X* in the Vendée Globe race in 1989-90, and (below) taking a few moments to reflect on the task ahead of him.

JOSHUA SLOCUM is considered the grandfather of singlehanded sailors. Between 1895 and 1898, Slocum singlehandedly circumnavigated the globe in a wooden boat, making several stops along the way. Another 69 years elapsed before Francis Chichester completed a one-stop, singlehanded circumnavigation. Then, in 1969, Robin Knox-Johnston completed the first non-stop, singlehanded circumnavigation to win the Golden Globe Challenge.

Founded in 1982, the BOC Challenge is one of two singlehanded circumnavigation races. Its rival—and considered more difficult by some—is the Vendée Globe race. Instituted in 1989, the Vendée Globe is distinguished by its simpleness and extremeness; it is an all-out sprint departing and finishing in France whose basic requirements are leaving Antarctica to starboard and returning unassisted. With no stops or assistance allowed in the global race, sailors must learn to fix anything that breaks on their boat, or learn to live without

Full-rigged sailing boats in action, like the *Cacharel* pictured below, are an obvious reminder of why people love the challenge of the sea.

it. Their will must be strong enough to stitch themselves together after suffering a severe laceration in a knockdown, and then go on deck and stitch the sail together that ripped in the same accident.

Carbon fiber

The BOC has more stature worldwide because it led to a new generation of singlehanded sailors, as well as boats. Many speed-enhancing features now key to today's singlehanded sailor were developed and refined in the heat of BOC competition—water ballast systems, autopilots, twin rudders, and the use of carbon fiber as a construction material in the hull and masts.

Skipper preparation for either race is as important as boat preparation. Pre-race rest is crucial, since solo sailing skippers get very little sleep. A common routine sees many skippers catnap for 30 to 40 minutes when they become tired. But in a span of 24 hours, they are lucky if they get six such naps. Constant vigilance is the name of this game.

In terms of pushing the limits of individual performance, both mentally and physically, singlehanded around the world yacht racing is one of the most challenging sports in terms of danger and time spent at risk. Of course those that take part in the races will tell you it is for the love of being on the water that they do it.

Scuba Diving

The mysteries of the sea have driven many to brave the ocean depths to experience first-hand what it feels like to live beneath the water's surface. Those who pioneered modern scuba did so at great risk—our bodies were not meant to breathe under water, nor were they meant to breathe under the pressure of millions of pounds of liquid. As you go deeper into the sea, your body is no longer able to use the air you breathe as effectively as above the surface. As a result, hundreds of diving fatalities occur each year.

164

MAN'S SEARCH for a means to breathe underwater can be traced back to the ancient Romans, when early divers used a floatation device to support airhoses attached to leather helmets to provide oxygen.

It was not until 1819 that deep-sea diving became a practical reality, when German inventor Augustus Siebein developed the bulky brass dive helmet linked to an air compressor back on the ship.

Nearly 130 years later, famous marine biologist Jacques Cousteau invented the aqualung together with fellow pioneer Emil Gagnan. The aqualung finally released divers from the restraints of air hoses and compressors and allowed them to swim freely through the water. The aqualung is unquestionably the most important invention in modern diving.

Since the aqualung's introduction, scuba (self contained underwater breathing apparatus) has grown into an incredibly popular sport enjoyed by pleasure seekers, treasure hunters, researchers, and sportsmen globally. However, despite its popularity, scuba diving remains a dangerous sport that

Despite encounters like this one, with a white tip shark, human error is the most likely source of danger for the scuba diver.

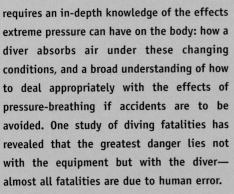

requires an in-depth knowledge of the effects extreme pressure can have on the body: how a diver absorbs air under these changing conditions, and a broad understanding of how to deal appropriately with the effects of pressure-breathing if accidents are to be avoided. One study of diving fatalities has revealed that the greatest danger lies not with the equipment but with the diver—almost all fatalities are due to human error.

Under pressure

There are other hazards. Hypothermia is a condition caused by the lowering of the body's core temperature, which can be fatal if prolonged. Sharp coral and rocks can cause injury, and strong underwater currents can separate dive partners (it's always advisable to dive in pairs at least) or, worse, sweep divers

Wreck diving, while dangerous, has always held a mysterious appeal for scuba divers.

Sharp coral and strong currents can cause serious injury to the inexperienced diver.

Technological developments, like this underwater scooter, have assisted divers in pushing the limits of their chosen extreme sport.

166

away from their support boat. Perhaps the most universally feared hazard is an encounter with a large shark or group of sharks. Smaller sharks can be docile if left alone, but they are never to be trusted. Larger sharks, such as tiger or great white sharks, are perpetually seeking food, and anything that swims is usually fair game.

Maladies associated with diving stem from how the body processes the air stored under pressure in the diver's tanks. As a diver swims deeper the body has to cope with increasing levels of pressure, measured in atmospheres. One "atmosphere" is the equivalent of the pressure exerted on the body at sea level, two atmospheres is double the pressure, and so on. As atmospheres increase, the pressure forces greater levels of breathed air into the bloodstream as gases. Under controlled conditions at relatively shallow depths, this is not a problem until the diver surfaces. As the diver ascends, these gases—most notably nitrogen—start escaping from the bloodstream. The ascent must be controlled and slow enough to allow the gases to be released through normal exhalation through the diver's lungs. If the diver ascends too quickly, the gases can bubble out into the body tissue, causing muscular pain and bodily damage. It's a bit like the effect you see when you open a can or bottle of pressurized carbonated soda.

The results can be deadly, causing the body to curl up and convulse spastically—hence the name of "bends" for the condition. Non-fatal repercussions of the bends include coma, neurological disorders, and intense abdominal pain. Nitrogen—the main component of divers' compressed air—can have other side effect. One of the most alarming is "nitrogen narcosis." It is more common on deeper dives, where the increased pressure forces more nitrogen into the bloodstream, and takes the form of drowsiness—potentially lethal under water.

Getting technical

A decompression chamber—a large tank that can compress the air inside to several atmospheres—is commonly found on vessels used as dive-support stations. Divers experiencing the bends are placed inside the decompression chamber and then quickly "returned" to the appropriate atmospheric pressure they were under in the water before the too-rapid ascent began. This allows the diver to complete the necessary decompression time and can halt the effects of the bends.

Diving using normal air mixtures—equivalent to the air we breathe every day—limits the depth and duration of dives. The deeper the dive, the less amount of time can be spent at the maximum depth. Knowing what the maximum lengths of time are for each depth is critical for diver safety.

Divers wanting to go deeper and stay down longer have to use different mixtures of air. Because of the extra requirements and the greater complexity of the process, deep dives are referred to as "technical" dives. Technical divers generally use enriched air such as "nitrox," a mixture with dramatically elevated amounts of oxygen. The use of enriched air mixtures is not recommended to any but the most experienced and well-trained of divers—Russian roulette is probably safer than technical diving without the required training and experience. A further system, called "rebreathing," utilizes a high-tech method of removing oxygen from exhaled air and recycling it for reuse.

Deep technical diving is the extreme end of scuba. Deep divers must have a rock solid understanding of the physiology and psychology of diving as well as strong stress-management skills. Planning each dive is imperative so that decompression occurs at the proper rate and accidents are avoided.

Get trained—and live

The current record for deep diving using a non-enriched mixture was unofficially established in 1994 by Dr. Dan Manion, who dived to 506 feet (290m) and lost consciousness during his ascent. The record for deep diving using a

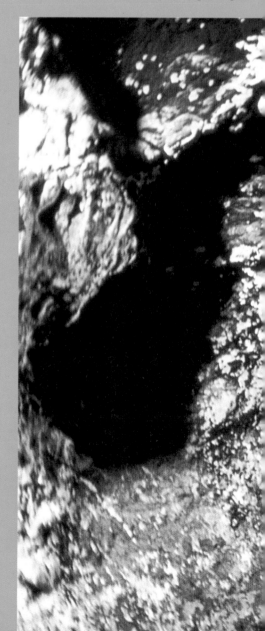

combination of rebreathing and mixed gases was made the same year by two technical divers in Zacaton, Mexico, the world's deepest underwater cave system. Jim Bowden and Sheck Exley attempted to descend to 1,000 feet (305m). Bowden reached 925 feet before returning to the surface. Exley disappeared at around 906 feet, and his fate is unknown.

Scuba is a dangerous sport, even for those seeking to dive for pleasure. Only those with enough training should dive. Even simple holiday excursions can result in tragedy. Extreme diving and depth record-setting is absolutely not recommended to anyone but the most expert divers, and even they are placing themselves at tremendous risk. Surely the depth record will be broken at some point, but almost as certain is that lives will be lost in the process.

Encounters with the inhabitants of the sea are not always as amicable as with these Bottlenose dolphins in the Caribbean Sea.

Exploring underwater cave systems, like the Devil's Eye off the coast of Florida is one of the more dangerous aspects of scuba diving.

Snorkeling

Snorkeling is a pleasureable way to swim gently along the beach or in clear waters where fish and reefs are in view. The detail from the surface, or up close in the shallow areas, is what most swimmers equate with snorkeling. However there is a darker, deeper, and extreme type of snorkeling that few would consider doing without a tank, if at all.

BLUE WATER HUNTERS are a combination of freediver and spearfisher, and swim down slowly into the water, careful not to disturb any of the larger, and tastier, inhabitants. The diver must maintain a state of calm and heightened awareness in order to get a glimpse of the big fish they seek to catch. Quiet, methodical movements are the only way extreme snorkelers will avoid scaring their prey.

Better divers release the seal around their snorkels and fill their mouths with water to prevent any air bubbles from alerting fish to their presence. They must constantly swivel around 180 degrees to

stay prepared for approaching fish, and the occasional shark. Incredible focus is required to notice oncoming fish and potentially unfriendly sealife in the distance before being seen, giving enough time to prepare for the shot. Divers keep a lookout for schools of bait fish that draw larger predators, and hope for "the big one" to show up.

Divers can effectively lure fish closer by staying horizontal and looking head on as they approach. If the fish feel the diver is as small as his profile, they may become curious and seek a closer look. Other methods of luring fish include making croaking noises and setting bait or artificial lures.

Divers typically rise to the surface for around 45 seconds before submerging again, and try to stay down as long as possible, usually 60 seconds or more. They try to position themselves for optimum shooting when a fish is in the area. The best angle for a shot is downward and around 10–15 feet (3–4.5m) away. Quiet divers can blend into their environment and get close enough to be in range.

Divers carry an assortment of gear on each trip out, including a wetsuit, snorkel and mask, fins, and a hand spear or spear gun. Additional equipment includes a weightbelt, dive knife, gear bag, and back-up items. A typical spear gun measures around 5–6 feet (1.5–1.8m) in length using 6-foot spears made from stainless steel. The butt end of the gun is weighted to afford the diver better balance and more control over the gun, as well as additional ballast to help them stay submerged. The ballast consists of lead shot which can be added or removed if needed.

Big catches

Extreme snorkelers do not generally seek out small prey, but are in search of larger stuff, in the 200–500 lb (90–270 kg) category. Blue- and yellow-fin tuna, black marlin, and other larger game fish separate this style of spear fishing from the tamer stuff. Many divers can tell stories of landing huge fish, only to be nearly drowned in the tow that ensued. It is therefore highly critical that the diver hit the target in the right spot and score a quick kill. Aside from the risk of a long battle while being towed, there is the very real risk of a physical confrontation with their catch, which can be a life or death struggle. Consider a 500 lb marlin coming full speed with its spear shaped nose pointed at you.

The sport is certainly not for the tame. It does, however, provide a new perspective on a sport that is relatively safe and rarely considered extreme.

(Left) A state of calm mixed with heightened awareness separates the good blue water hunter from the rest. (Below) This huge Spanish mackerel speaks volumes about this hunter's abilities.

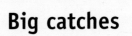

169

Speed Sailing

Speed has been a quest of sailing pioneers for as long as there have been sailing vessels. In early times, speed meant sailors could travel farther to catch bigger and better quantities of fish. Speed allowed explorers to gain access to new frontiers before supplies dwindled and starvation ensued. As warriors sought control of the seas, speed offered aggressors the opportunity of a swift attack, and gave those seeking escape the chance to elude their demise. Today, the quest for speed is all about establishing new levels of performance and securing a spot in the record books.

In the 1980s the Trifoiler smashed all previous speed sailing records. But its efficiency was limited by its design.

SPEED SAILING FOR SPORT has brought with it most of the current high-technology equipment and space-age materials now common in everyday sailing. Sailing faster requires lighter watercraft that hardly resemble the sailboats of even a decade ago— the vessel currently holding the speed sailing record cannot be turned, and can only sail in one direction! Speed sailing is a highly specialized sport requiring highly specialized designs. The only goal is to accelerate within a straight, closed course, and pass through a

The *Endeavour* crushed previous speed records because of a combination of the use of skis to keep it out of the water, and a large sail area. But how long will its reign last?

section of that course at maximum velocity in hope of recording a new speed record. To break the record in practice is only momentarily satisfying, as no speed is official without being recorded at a sanctioned event site, with official timekeepers present. So the object is to design a boat that can break records on any given day in any reasonable breeze—official events and perfect conditions do not always coincide.

For years the record books were filled with catamarans, and every successful attempt merely edged out the previous record. Catamarans are sailboats with two slender hulls that slice through the water, offering little resistance other than the inescapable surface tension between their hulls and the water. Going faster meant minimizing the amount of hull surface that contacted the water and maximizing the amount of horsepower the sails could generate. This meant huge rigs carrying tremendous sails on hulls that barely sustained the loads placed on them. This led to terribly overpowered sailboats that self-destructed under the forces they generated more often then they would set records.

Trifoils

In the Eighties, the records established by catamarans were suddenly destroyed by tiny, specially designed sailboards which were hardly in contact with the water at speed and required sails small enough that they could be supported by the sailor. Sailboards owned the world speed record for nearly a decade.

The Yellow Pages-sponsored craft *Endeavour* is a speed record-specific design. The crew sit in a tiny compartment at the end of one of its "wings".

Then in 1992 a new and radical sailing hydrofoil shattered the record by traveling at 50.02 knots on an official course at the French Trench outside of Calais, France. The Trifoiler designed by Californian Greg Ketterman was much smaller and lighter than previous record setters, with the obvious exception of sailboards. The Trench is famous for its strong sideways winds and narrow, protected waters that ensure a nearly perfect flat water surface. The Trifoiler reduced speed-limiting surface to a only a small fraction of what had been previously reached during years of effort.

This record-setting design did have a limiting factor, and that was the efficiency of the wing-like foils that lift the boat out of the water at speed. These create speed-limiting drag at top end of their performance,

making it impossible for them to travel faster. An Australian design dubbed "Yellow Pages," named after the craft's sponsor, used a design similar in appearance to Ketterman's Trifoiler, however rather than using hydrofoils Yellow Pages used small skis to ride on. This both greatly reduced the surface tension that earlier catamaran designs suffered and eliminated the top-end performance limits of the Trifoiler's.

Quest for speed

Yellow Pages was a speed-record-specific design incapable of turning or sailing in more than one direction. But it was fast enough to edge out the Trifoiler for top spot in the record books. Because it used skis to ride on, it was a step back in the direction of the

speed record-setting sailboards. But, because it used a large sail held up by stays (wires), it could carry far more sail area than any sailboard, and therefore had a tremendous horsepower advantage.

The quest for the World Speed Sailing record continues. Somewhere, now, there is a designer working hard to redefine the limits of wind-driven speed on water. Given that land-sailing vehicles are capable of exceeding 100 mph (160 kph), it is surely only a matter of time before sailboats will reach such speeds. When that occurs the way we travel over water will be forever changed. This is bound to expand the distances sailing vessels can cover, since unlike land sailcraft which are limited by the terrain available to cover, speed sailcraft will have an endless supply of water, and the distances traveled will be limited only by their design's ability to deal with a variety of surface conditions.

Surfing

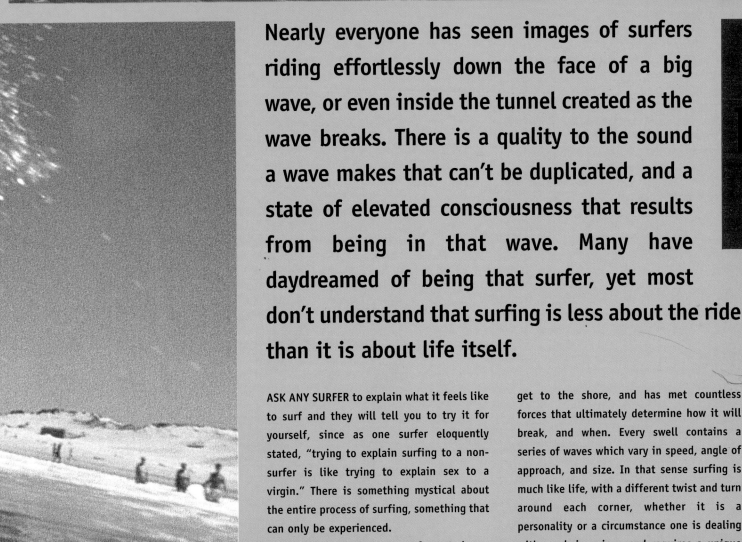

Nearly everyone has seen images of surfers riding effortlessly down the face of a big wave, or even inside the tunnel created as the wave breaks. There is a quality to the sound a wave makes that can't be duplicated, and a state of elevated consciousness that results from being in that wave. Many have daydreamed of being that surfer, yet most don't understand that surfing is less about the ride than it is about life itself.

ASK ANY SURFER to explain what it feels like to surf and they will tell you to try it for yourself, since as one surfer eloquently stated, "trying to explain surfing to a non-surfer is like trying to explain sex to a virgin." There is something mystical about the entire process of surfing, something that can only be experienced.

Each wave at every surf spot is as different from the last as one snowflake is from another. Consider that each wave has traveled hundreds or thousands of miles to get to the shore, and has met countless forces that ultimately determine how it will break, and when. Every swell contains a series of waves which vary in speed, angle of approach, and size. In that sense surfing is much like life, with a different twist and turn around each corner, whether it is a personality or a circumstance one is dealing with, each is unique and requires a unique response. As in surfing, the proper response means harmony, and the wrong response can be devastating.

Hawaiian, Laird Hamilton (right), leads American Pete Cabrina down this huge Hawaiian wave.

Hawaii is regarded as the home of surfing, the quality and size of the waves is unparalleled anywhere else in the world.

Surfing began centuries ago in the Pacific Island cultures where its roots can be traced to the beginnings of Polynesian society. By the seventeenth and eighteenth centuries, surfing was a widely accepted aspect of both the ruling and working classes in Hawaii. Surfing was to these people a part of their secular lives, replete with surfing gods, sacred rituals, and a strong set of social norms all linked to surfing.

Early Hawaiians took their surfing very seriously. Hawaiian chiefs could declare any of their favorite surfing spots "Kapu," meaning they were off limits to all but the

chief and his friends. Chiefs would direct their subjects to bring only the finest wood from the cold highland regions of the island. The best craftsmen would be entrusted with shaping the chief's board from the wood, often from the prized koa or the wiliwili tree. Commoners would ride boards of much less exotic wood. Yet regardless of the value of the surfboard, it was always treated with respect. A proper surfbuilding ritual was always performed out of respect for the surf gods so as to provide the owner with good waves and the safety of being protected from harm.

Surfer forefathers

Reports of surfing were first described to the civilized world by Lieutenant James King of the British Royal Navy in 1779. He remarked that he'd seen Hawaiians surfing massive "boomers" at Kealakekua Bay. In typical fashion of the self righteous explorers of the period, he described surfing as "most perilous and extraordinary, altogether astonishing and scarcely to be credited."

Surfing, of course, continued despite the lieutenant's comments and eventually over 150 years later, under the leadership of legendary Duke Kahanamoku, grew to become the international force in watersports it is today. Duke was the first recognized star of the surfing community. He was so famous that Hollywood stars flocked to Hawaii to meet and be photographed with him.

Duke is credited with being the founding father of modern surfing, and organized the first surf club in the world, the Hui Nalu. "Da Hui" still thrives today and is known throughout the world. Its membership consists of the biggest names in the surfing world, past and present, and loyalty among its members is extremely strong. Other notable surf clubs formed by influential Hawaiians include the Outrigger Club, and the Healani.

Surfing reached California in the Fifties where it spawned a cultural revolution, inspiring the popularity of the beach lifestyle that was reflected in the surf music of Dick Dale and the Beach Boys. Surf films glorifying the Hawaiian and Californian surf culture became wildly popular at the same time. Amazingly, though, some of the very first surf movies were produced by Thomas Edison, who filmed surfers at Honolulu's famed Waikiki Beach in 1898.

Big surf summer

Surf movies gained a wider audience with the work of pioneers like Bruce Brown, who captured the authentic surfing scene with his first feature film, *The Big Surf*, in 1943. His most notable film was *The Endless Summer*, which followed a few nomadic surfers on a quest for the perfect wave. Its sequel, *The Endless Summer II*, released in 1994, has inspired an international following similar to

Pete Cabrina is one of the leading toe-in surfers who has crossed from pro boardsailing.

that of his first film. Surf movies are available today by a host of film-makers, and are widely accessible on video.

Making big waves

Modern surfing has progressed tremendously since the days of massive wooden boards ridden by the pioneers of surfing in Hawaii and the Polynesian islands. Today's surfboards vary enormously in size and shape. Professional surfers own a "quiver" (collection) of different boards designed to perform in all ranges of surf conditions. Shorter boards in lengths of 5–7 feet (1.5–2m) are used primarily in smaller waves for maneuverability and work well with the shape of the faces on smaller waves.

Short boards have been credited for many of today's freestyle tricks. These moves are unlike any seen in the history of surfing, with many taking inspiration from what has been done in skateboarding. Riders are getting their boards out of the water like a skateboarder in a half-pipe, doing 360-degree spins, rail grabs, and other highly technical tricks that have come to redefine modern surfing. Freestyle surfing pioneers like Matt Archbold and Christian Fletcher have had a major impact on the freestyle movement as leaders of the new art.

Bruce Ellis of Australia, demonstrates the strength of the Hawaiian surf.

"Gun" surfboards of between 8–11 feet (2.4–3.4m) are used for speed and bigger waves. Their longer profiles give added edge holding in big surf where speeds are considerably greater than in lesser conditions. Big-wave surfing is also experiencing a renaissance, with new and hazardous spots like Mavericks in Northern California competing for attention with some of the more recognizable big-wave locations like Pipeline on the North Shore of Oahu. Mavericks gained international recognition for its extreme conditions when surf star Mark Foo lost his life after being

engulfed by one of Mavericks's moderate-sized waves. What makes Mavericks especially dangerous is the jagged rocks and caves beneath the surface that surfers get sucked into after wiping out.

Dinosaur returns

"Longboards" are now making a comeback in surfing after years of being thought second class to the newer short surfboards. For many years, longboards have been considered to be made for "old men" and "kooks" (surfer lingo for novices with no skills and even less

178

America's Ross Williams in classic surfing action.

intelligence). Now surfers are getting a new, almost nostalgic, respect for longboards and those who ride them, at least those who really know how to ride them.

The newest entrants to the surfboard world are the "tow-in" boards used to surf the biggest and scariest waves in the world. The sport was pioneered by Hawaiian surfing legend Gerry Lopez and a crew of surfers turned pro boardsailors, turned surfers, led by native Hawaiian Laird Hamilton. Hamilton

and other notables, including Dave Kalama, Mike Waltz, Peter Cabrina, Mark Angulo, and Rush Randall, all crossed over from surfing into the world of pro boardsailing where they learned the control advantages that footstraps offered.

Into deep water

This group began experimenting with short and narrow speed board designs that could be towed behind a Jet Ski, much like

waterskis. They found that by being towed, they could let go of the tow line while in large waves, and ride them even before they began to crest and break. This, they discovered, enabled them to get dropped into waves that could never have been ridden before, either because they were too long a paddle from shore, or because they were simply too dangerous to attempt to ride the old fashioned way. These surfers have ridden waves that without a doubt are

Laird Hamilton in action showing the control advantages that footstraps have given to the world's top surfers.

Laird Hamilton is continually on the quest for establishing new boundaries of performance for big wave surfers.

the largest ever successfully negotiated by any surfers in the world.

Ride the big wave

The most famous of the tow-in spots is a particularly dangerous reef, aptly named "Jaws." The mushroom-shaped reef, located "somewhere" in the Hawaiian Islands, creates a wave that jumps up and breaks in a crescent shape. The wave heights in a big swell easily exceed 50 feet (15m) and are certainly capable of killing anyone unfortunate enough to get caught in a bad wipeout. The waves are so powerful that it is not uncommon for them to hold a surfer down for 60 seconds or more in a wipeout. Surfers are reportedly experimenting with miniature tanks to provide much needed air in the event of a deadly hold down.

Big-wave and tow-in surfing appear to be the future of modern surfing. Both can certainly be considered extreme because they epitomize the common theme among extreme sports—the quest for establishing new boundaries of performance. It is hard to visualize what direction they will point surfing in, and even harder to imagine that surfing will continue to progress to riding bigger and bigger waves without losing a few top athletes to the forces of nature.

Trifoiling

The Trifoiler is an excellent example of how extreme sports and the yearning for technological advances to increase performance can change an entire category of sport.

JUST A FEW SHORT YEARS AGO the speed-sailing community was in awe of new speed records that were being set by specialized windsurfers breaking into the mid-40-knot (46 mph, 74 kph) speed range. Surely it would be these boards that would redefine speed sailing. However, a mechanical engineer named Greg Ketterman was at the time experimenting with the concept of a speed sailboat that progressed on hydrofoils, a concept that may well change the future of sailing.

Ketterman, widely known for his work on the Stars and Stripes Catamaran used in 1987 to beat New Zealand's enormous monohull and retain the America's Cup, first began playing with radio-controlled versions of a hydrofoiled sailboat around 1980. California speed sailor and yacht racer Russell Long commissioned Ketterman to build him a full size version of the hydrofoil design for a speed record attempt in 1989. He successfully set a new Class A speed record in 1992 at an amazing 50.08 knots at Saint Marie de la Mer, also known as "The French Trench." The site, widely recognized as the premier speed-sailing site in the world, is a long and narrow channel of water where prevailing winds are strong yet leave the water's surface almost unaffected.

The concept of creating a sailboat that could ride on a hydrofoil was not new. What was keeping designers from success was the nature of the hydrofoil wings. Hydrofoils are essentially like airplane wings that have been optimized to perform in water. Therefore, like an airplane wing, they generate lift, and must be controlled so that they do not seek to go straight upward. Airplanes use steering devices built into their wings which allow the pilot to determine the amount of lift they generate and to maintain a level path if desired.

Riding high

Airplanes have a distinct advantage over hydrofoils, because they need to travel through the same medium their wings do. The whole concept about hydrofoils is to get the boat out of the water, thereby nearly eliminating hydrodynamic resistance that the hulls create, and delivering virtually limitless speed potential. To be successful, a hydrofoil needs to ride high enough to get the boat out of the water and—since they only work in the water—low enough to stay submerged. Therefore, unlike airplanes, hydrofoil wings have a limited margin of error and must maintain a course that can only vary within inches to be effective.

Powerboat designers figured how to make hydrofoils work decades ago. The big problems occur with the addition of sails, because the force a sail generates is high above the boat, and constantly working to push the boat over onto its side. This

A trifoiler is a sailboat built for speed. By using a hydrofoil to raise the craft just above the surface of the water, but still keep it in contact, these craft are setting new speed records.

tendency for sailboats to tip is what held back designers for years.

Ketterman invented a new approach to keeping the foils in the water. He added a "sensor" to the foil design that could read the pitch of the foil (whether it was heading up, down, or level) and correct it to maintain a level track. The addition of the sensor was the breakthrough that made hydrofoil sailing a possibility. The sensor pushes the foil down if it's heading up, and pulls the foil up if it's heading down. The result is that the foil constantly corrects itself, keeping the hulls out of the water and the foils in.

The 20-foot (6m) Trifoiler design positions two J-shaped foils beneath its two sails in front of the boat's bobsled-like cockpit. The sails are positioned bi-plane style, maximizing the sail area and minimizing the sail's propensity to "heel" (tip) the boat out of its most efficient, flat stance. The Trifoiler is lifted from behind by a T-shaped foil on the bottom of the "rudder" (steering foil). The resulting triangular stance is highly stable and maneuverable. Because the foils are firmly "locked" into the water, the boat can turn quickly, pulling as much as 2 gees of lateral acceleration in a turn without sliding sideways, much like a toy slot-car on its track.

User friendly

Top speed on a Trifoiler is over 50 mph (80 kph), with only the efficiency of today's foil designs keeping it from going faster. In fact at top speed, the low pressure on the top of the foil resulting from the foil's lift, actually

boils the water, causing speed-limiting drag. Ketterman is working on new foil designs that will allow for higher speeds.

The Trifoiler design is so stable and user friendly that Ketterman's Trifoiler was recently purchased by Hobie Corporation (makers of the famous Hobie Catamarans) and is now available to anyone wishing to sail as fast as possible. The boats are easy enough to handle for even novice sailors to sail.

The Trifoiler design will certainly gain popularity over the next several years. Today, they simply can't make them fast enough. As the technology improves, larger and faster versions are sure to be developed. In the meantime, look for these extreme sailboats to show up soon wherever there is wind and water.

Wakeboarding

Wakeboarding is a relatively new extreme sport. Its heritage can be linked to waterskiing, surfing, windsurfing, skateboarding, and snowboarding, and it is quickly redefining how we look at boat-towed sports.

THE CONCEPT OF TOWING a surfboard behind either a boat in the water or a car on the beach on waveless days is as old as modern surfing. The need to ride on a board drives many "sideways" sports enthusiasts to try whatever they need to get out and ride on their boards. That's how skateboarding began, and later windsurfing and snowboarding. For decades, if there was no surf, surfers were known to grab a line and get pulled by a boat or even by a truck running onshore. This was no easy trick, since this was not the intended purpose of a surfboard. Strong surfers could pull it off and get some turns in on a flat day.

In 1985, San Diego surfer Tony Finn created and developed a waterski/surfboard he called the Skurfer. The Skurfer was narrower than a surfboard and riders could do snowboard-like turns behind their boats. Soon, with the addition of footstraps, skurfers were riding their boards and performing many of the same maneuvers that snowboarders were doing. That same year, Texas surfer Jimmy Redmond added footstraps to another early wakeboard design.

The early skurfers pushed hard and began getting big air and pulling off dynamic moves, however the appeal didn't grow far outside of the community of strong skiers because the Skurfer's narrow and highly buoyant design made it difficult to master. In 1990 waterski pioneer Hugh O'Brien gathered together many top surfers to create a board design that had many of the performance characteristics of a good surfboard.

The "Hyperlite" design that was created had neutral buoyancy, and was compression-molded like the waterskis O'Brien's H.O. Sports company was mass-producing. The neutral buoyancy design and thin profile rails (edges of the board) allowed the Hyperlite design to carve shorter, slalom-like turns than the Skurfer. The design also made getting up and mastering the board easier, growing the appeal of what would be called the wakeboard.

Doing the grind

Indents called "phasers" were added to help break up the water flow under the board, making the board feel "looser" (less stuck to the water) and making high-air landings softer on the rider. Phasers were borrowed from windsurfer and surfboard shapers seeking to create the same loose feel for their designs.

Wakeboarding soon exploded in popularity and continues to do so today. The sport is reported to have grown by as much as 400 per cent in recent years, adding a professional tour and a governing body to help it along the way. One of the reasons is that wakeboarding's top professionals are pushing their sport to new limits on a daily basis. The best have added new elements to wakeboarding that come straight out of skateboarding street style and snowboarding freestyle. These riders are doing grinds off obstacles like channel buoys and docks, and are even jumping on and over rock outcroppings where available.

Tight fit

Wakeboard binding systems have developed rapidly to deal with the added forces riders are putting on their equipment. Initially, the bindings used were simply upgraded or modified waterski-style. The new bindings offer tremendously more support and grip to hold riders on their boards. In fact, the new designs are so snug that liquid soap is generally a standard accessory to aid in getting into or out of the bindings. The reasoning is obvious: create new moves that your equipment can't deal with and you wipe out.

Wakeboarding parks are now being created where once waterskiing parks existed. Wakeboarders are discovering new uses for the overhead pull systems that resemble ski lifts, and now use the added lift to soar up and around the courses, doing spins and other moves never before seen at ski parks. Newer and younger riders are getting into the sport, and it is certain that they will bring with them even more innovative approaches to wakeboarding.

Wakeboarding is poised to do the same thing for waterskiing and tow-behind water sports that snowboarding did to revitalize the ski industry. It also provides a real indication of where board sports are headed... sideways.

Whitewater

Standing on the shore of a raging river is an explosion of visual and auditory sensations. There is a primordial feeling that rushing water sets off in us. To prove your mettle on a raft, canoe, boogieboard, or kayak against the most violent of nature's forces—the fury of moving water—is to participate in one of the most adrenaline-pumping of extreme sports.

THERE ARE VARYING DEGREES of difficulty to consider when choosing which watercraft best suits the needs of the rider. The first and least difficult method of getting down whitewater is via a raft, which can be easily found for hire near any thriving river community. Whitewater rafting is a big business, as it offers the opportunity to enjoy the rush of the ride without most of the risks associated.

Raft or canoe?

Which is not to say whitewater rafting is easy and lacking danger. Reputable tour operators offer quality guidance and top rate equipment, including two of the most important pieces of gear needed, a helmet and a life vest. Any time the river is entered on a watercraft, there are risks, and every year, people are seriously injured or killed on rivers all over the world while on rafts. Having said that, if whitewater is appealing, try a rafting expedition first to see how you like it.

Next in difficulty would be the canoe, which due to the open nature of the design, offers little protection from a capsize. Many canoeists are qualified to run rivers of sizeable power, however, canoes do not offer the "righting" performance (returning the boat to a rightside-up position) necessary in big rapids. Canoes are far less stable than rafts and require tremendous balance skills to ride through areas of whitewater.

The boogieboard, aka riverboard, a device first developed to ride beach surf while lying down, is a new entry into the whitewater-running category. Many whitewater enthusiasts, seeking to push the limits and try a new thrill began riding the foam boards in whitewater with success. One of the pioneers, Bob Carlson, now sells his Carlson Riverboards all over the world, many to top river runners. While certainly easier to stay on top of and right after rolling over, the riverboard is far more extreme than rafting or canoeing. On a riverboard the rider is completely exposed to the elements without

The thrills of whitewater rafting are amongst the most adrenaline-pumping of all extreme sports.

the protection of a boat's hull to ward off jagged rocks and absorb some of the shock the rapids can hand out.

The most extreme method of getting down a river, however, is on a kayak. Kayaks offer a completely enclosed hull design that allows the paddler to sit in the opening of the hull and seal themselves in using a neoprene skirt. Because the paddler is able to capsize and right the boat without filling the hull with water, they can handle practically any degree of whitewater. The act of righting a capsized kayak is called an "Eskimo roll," since it was created by the Eskimos. Because of the severely cold water, Eskimos have to stay dry and be able to right themselves without doing what is now called a "wet exit," meaning escaping the capsized boat.

For many reasons, doing a wet exit is the last thing a paddler wants to do unless they absolutely must. First, outside the kayak the paddler is immediately exposed to a multitude of dangers, from massive "hydrolics" (sections of the river where tons of water are being pushed downward), to sharp rocks, submerged logs, and other unknowns. Second, once outside the hull, the paddler's only floatation is their body and their life vest. The drop in floatation makes the possibility of the paddler being driven downward onto a hidden obstacle far greater. More than a few paddlers die each year from simply getting their foot stuck under a rock, and then being dragged under by the current. These two examples should be enough to illustrate why being able to do an Eskimo roll at will is essential to paddling heavy water.

Kayaks are incredibly maneuverable because of their low buoyancy and highly "rockered" shapes, which vary from design to design. Rocker refers to the curve in the hull from front (bow) to back (stern). The more rocker in the hull, the more maneuverable the kayak. Different designs accommodate different performance characteristics. One example is a slalom kayak. Designed to race through a series of gates, the hull is highly rockered, with sharp, angular projections along the top of the deck that serve to provide greater sideways stability, helping the paddler get across the current to the next gate more easily.

Taking a dive

Another is a low-buoyancy "rodeo"-style, or trick kayak, which is a minimally-buoyant design used in trick contests. The reduced-volume rodeo design allows the paddler to spin the kayak around on its ends effortlessly, as well as performing a number of other tricks. Low-buoyancy kayaks are also the preferred design for high waterfall drops that some of the more radical paddlers enjoy. Waterfall paddling is probably the most dangerous of all the whitewater activities, depending on the distance of the drop. Small waterfalls of 5–10 feet (1.5–3m) constitute normal conditions in extreme whitewater.

The larger waterfalls that the top extreme paddlers drop into can exceed 50 feet (15m). Clearly the opportunity for disaster exists at these heights, and the paddler must land the kayak end first, either bow or stern. Landing any other way results in "flatting out" (landing hard on the entire surface of the hull) which can severely injure a paddler. This is the kayaking equivalent of a belly flop. If the paddler lands on the end, the kayak dives down into the water with a relatively soft landing. Obviously these types of stunts are reserved for top experts only.

Regardless of the type of watercraft used, there is a system of classifying the level of difficulty for each section of a river. The level of difficulty varies from day to day as the amount of water traveling through a section can radically alter the whitewater characteristics. Rivers are measured in cubic feet, so a river traveling at 3,000 cfs (cubic feet per second) will behave quite differently on a day when it is traveling at 10,000 cfs. Snowmelt or torrential rains can dramatically change a river, and in the case of torrential rain it can

189

If whitewater is appealing, then rafting, though hard work, is the best way of enjoying the rush without most of the risks associated with the sport.

happen instantly. Therefore, it is important that river riders are aware of not only the weather immediately around them, but also the weather conditions upstream.

Learn rivercraft

Rivers are rated on a scale of 1–6. The higher the number, the greater the degree of difficulty. It is important to acknowledge that river sections can vary dramatically in difficulty, and it is not uncommon for a river to change from class 1 to class 6 within a matter of meters. Again, it is vital to get local information on the river before going downstream. The following outlines the classification system:

- CLASS I – easy, occasionally small rapids with few obstacles
- CLASS II – moderate, small rapids and waves which are easily navigated
- CLASS III – difficult, rapids, hazards, and irregular waves which should be scouted from shore ahead of time; complex maneuvers will be required
  CLASS IV—very difficult, long, large rapids and falls with dangerous hazards which must be scouted; precise moves will be required, including rolls; rescues will be difficult
- CLASS V – has extremely difficult, violent rapids and falls with narrow routes and many dangerous hazards; experts only!
- CLASS VI – nearly impossible, routes difficult to identify; only to be attempted by teams of top expert paddlers following all possible precautions.

It's useful to know a few of the terms commonly used in whitewater. *Beam* is the widest part of the boat. *Thwart* is a support which runs across the width of the boat. *Blade* is the thin cross-section, wide profile part of the paddle that passes through the water and provides thrust. *Shaft* is the "handle" of the paddle gripped by the paddler. *Draw* is a paddle stroke 90 degrees to the direction of travel to pull the boat sideways. *J-stroke* is a paddle

Whitewater raft races are becoming more popular with those addicted to the adrenaline.

190

stroke that ends in a steering maneuver. *River-left* refers the side of the river as it looks to the paddler, while *River-right* speaks for itself.

No one is certain as to exactly when the first boat resembling a canoe or kayak was built, but there is evidence that Polynesian and rain forest cultures used similar water craft. The Eskimos of north America and northeastern Asia are felt to have been the originators of the modern kayak.

Early Eskimo kayaks were built of lightweight wooden frames wrapped in seal or caribou skin. These kayaks held one or two paddlers, and were used primarily for fishing. Early canoes, such as those used by the north American Indians, and later adopted by settlers and trappers, were used for both transportation and hunting

Modern recreational canoeing and kayaking got their start after an English barrister named John MacGregor designed a boat he called the "Rob Roy." The boat was based on the Eskimo kayak, and he used the designs between 1845 and 1869 to explore many of the waterways of Europe. He wrote and lectured extensively regarding his explorations.

Purest form of play

MacGregor founded the Royal Canoe Club in 1866, with the Prince of Wales as Commodore, a post he retained until he was crowned king. The New York Canoe Club was founded in 1871 in response to the success of the Royal Canoe Club. These organizations were the first to actively recruit members, and provided a focused agenda for the growth of the sport.

Canoes are far less stable than rafts, and require tremendous balancing skills to ride through areas of whitewater.

Kayaking became an Olympic sport in 1936, and remains so today. Twelve of the 16 events are sprints held on flat water. Slalom kayaking is held in whitewater, and requires paddlers to traverse a series of gates, both upcurrent and downcurrent. This event is widely regarded as one of the most physically demanding paddling sports because it requires strength, lightning fast maneuverability skills, and a keen ability to read the currents.

Whitewater as a sport, whether Olympic or for fun, is one of the purest forms of play in a natural and changing environment. It is a great way to get out into the wilderness and enjoy an adrenaline-charged workout, and is one extreme sport that everyone can enjoy at some level.

Buckinghamshire College Group
Wycombe Campus